W9-BQW-626

BUDDHA

ALSO BY NIKOS KAZANTZAKIS

Fiction
Zorba the Greek (1953)
The Greek Passion (1954)
Freedom or Death (1956)
The Last Temptation of Christ (1960)
Saint Francis (1962)
The Rock Garden (1963)
Toda Raba (1964)
The Fraticides (1964)

Poetry
The Odyssey: A Modern Sequel (1958)

Philosophy
The Saviors of God – Spiritual Exercises (1960)

Nonfiction
Japan-China (1963)
Spain (1963)
Journey to the Morea (1965)
Report to Greco (1965)
England (1966)

BUDDHA

Nikos Kazantzakis

Translated from the Greek by
Kimon Friar and Athena Dallas-Damis

THE BRYANT LIBRARY
PAPER MILL ROAD
ROSLYN, N. Y. 11576

AVANT
BOOKS

Published in 1983 by Avant Books
3719 Sixth Avenue
San Diego, California 92103

Copyright© 1982 Helen Kazantzakis. All rights reserved under
International and Pan-American Copyright Conventions, including the
right to reproduce this book or portions thereof in any form whatsoever
except for use by a reviewer in connection with a review.

Library of Congress Catalog Card Number 81-71164.

Library of Congress Cataloging in Publication Data

Kazantzakis, Nikos, 1883-1957.
    Buddha.

    Translation of: Voudas.
    I. Title.
PA5610.K39V613 1983   889'.232   83-2642
ISBN 0-932238-18-1 (hardcover)
ISBN 0-932238-14-9 (paperback)

First Printing
Manufactured in the United States of America

CONTENTS

ABOUT THE TRANSLATORS

Kimon Friar was born of Greek parentage on an island on the Sea of Marmara, was brought to the United States at an early age, and returned to Greece in 1946. He has taught at the universities of Iowa, Adelphi, New York, Minnesota, Illinois, Indiana, California, and Amherst College.

His translations from the Greek include *The Odyssey: A Modern Sequel* (Simon & Shuster, 1958) and *The Saviors of God: Spiritual Exercises* (Simon & Shuster, 1961), both by Nikos Kazantzakis; *With Face to the Wall, Selected Poems of Miltos Sahtouris*, (Charioteer Press, Washington, D.C.); *Introduction to the Poetry of Odysseus Elytis* (Kedros, Athens, 1978); *The Sovereign Sun* (Temple University Press, 1974); *The Spiritual Odyssey of Nikos Kazantzakis: A Talk* (North Central Publishing Company, 1979); *The Stone Eyes of Medusa*, essays, (Kedros, Athens, 1981) in Greek.

Mr. Friar has directed The Poetry Center in New York for five years. His radio program on literature has been broadcast in New York, Chicago, and over The Voice of America in Greek. He is presently Greek Editor of *The Charioteer*, Greek associate of *Paideuma, A Journal of Ezra Pound Scholarship*, and Book Review Director of *The Athenian*.

For the quality of his translations and his contributions to modern Greek letters, Kimon Friar has received numerous honors and awards, among these the Greek World Award, 1978; a Ford Foundation Grant, 1975-77; and The Ingram Merrill Foundation Award, 1981-83.

Athena Dallas-Damis, is the translator of Nikos Kazantzakis' last novel *The Fratricides* (Simon and Shuster, 1964), his *Three Plays — Columbus, Kouros, Melissa* (Simon & Shuster, 1969), and R. Mouzaki's *Greek Dances for Americans* (Doubleday, 1981).

She has written two historic novels: *Island of the Winds* (Caratzas Signet, 1976-78), and its sequel *Windswept* (NAL/Signet, 1981), to be followed by the last of her Island Trilogy which deals with Greece during the 1800's.

Ms. Damis is also a recognized journalist and lecturer on the Greek experience. She is the recipient of many awards including the *Greek World Magazine Award*, the *Haleen Rasheed Award for Distinguished Achievement in the World of Letters*, and the *AHEPA Fifth District Nikos Kazantzakis Award*, and is listed in the Contemporary Authors Encyclopedia.

PREFACE
Michael Tobias

The many legends surrounding the life of Buddha all converge upon a river.
Having slipped from his native Nepalese village in darkness, he rode his horse
Kantaka up to a river's far bank, stepped down, and for the following six
years he struggled. Seated under the Bo-tree, steadfast to penance and
contemplation, he endeavored to acquit this world of suffering, warding off
the daily temptations of Mara, prince of evil. In deepest meditation, sustained
only by an offering of rice-milk brought to him by the woman Sujātā, he
strode bravely into a great and universal awareness, an electrical fence of
revelation. The Four Noble Truths and Eightfold Path comprise his principal
message, one that was variously interpreted throughout Asia. Whatever its
vagaries of style and emphasis — from Sri Lanka to Japan — Buddhism
proposed three compelling and homogeneous assertions: gentle self-denial,
compassion for all living things, and an approach to nirvana — the Absolute
Void — involving the human acceptance of contradiction throughout Nature.

China's magical Yangtze River contains all of the elements of Buddhism, in its
geography, associations, and manifest dualism. Plunging off the Golden Sands
(Kinsha) of Tibet into deep limestone gorges, it sweeps up Central Asia's
mineral into the richest wet rice plantations on earth. Dropping into Kiangsi
Province, heading Northwest, the river charges the land with wealth, becomes
myth, before emptying tranquilly into the sea near Shanghai. Saints, poets,
pandas, even the celebrated Yeti have mingled in caves and bamboo glens
along the river's shores. The founder of Sōtō Zen, Dōgen, worshipped such a
river as the very embodiment of perfect reality, the true dharma of
Buddhahood. Similarly, Genkū, twelfth century founder of Japanese Pure
Land Buddhism, saw the rivers and mountains as Buddha's one and only
paradise on earth. Such smooth-flowing contemplations have entered the very
pre-cognition of Oriental religion and nature worship. But if the river was a
heaven, it could also become a hell. Since ancient times the zealous farmer has
exhausted the soil underfoot, thereby prompting rampant erosion and
devastating floods. Hundreds-of-thousands of lives have been lost to the
confluence. No mere folklore, such yin/yang dialectics came to shape Chinese
agricultural civilization. The course of the river was, like Buddha himself, the
basis for Chinese cosmography.

Greek sensibility had its own access to cosmic antipodes. The most important
oracle of primordial Hellas was Delphi, where opposing personalities, Apollo

and Dionysus, were triumphantly merged. But the Greek mind stopped short of exhorting the Void. This life was just too luscious, nude, sensual and honey-washed to forsake so easily. The ascetic East and god-tanned West had never been so perfectly integrated in a drama before the work of Nikos Kazantzakis. His intoxication with nature was world-roving, at times severe and abstinent, at other times all-giving, indulgent. While he was attracted to monks and solitaires, to Spartan discipline and lofty ordeals, his sense of balance stayed ultimately clear of them. Only Kazantzakis' unique orientation to tragedy and spirituality, could have conceived and forged the striking juxtaposition which occurs in his play *Buddha*. The Yangtze River is not just a vital ecosystem, a religion of form and lavish beauty, a link between mankind and God. The river *is* Buddha, and the final flood is Buddha's deliverance. There in the river of dignity, where chaos usurps calm, and calm beckons after chaos, is the life of the farmer, the sage, the grandchild. All ancestors cavort and multiply in the haven of white water against which no bulwark, no sandbag is sufficient. The only salvation is to yield, to be ravished, carried in the wild spray, reborn.

INTRODUCTION
Peter Bien

"My method...does not involve a denial of
spirit and body, but rather aims at the conquest
of them through the prowess of spirit and body."
— Nikos Kazantzakis[1]

I

In the spring of 1941, Kazantzakis embarked on one of his most ambitious
works, the play *Yangtze*, now known under the title *Buddha*. If we consider
the seven months from Mussolini's invasion of Greece on October 28, 1940
until the capture of Crete by the Germans at the end of May 1941, we see in
condensed form the whole of human existence as Kazantzakis had conceived it
previously and had expressed it in earlier works. We see in the successful
Greek defense against Mussolini the noble and quixotic effort of a nation to do
the impossible, and then we see in the German victory the inexorable power of
an overwhelming fate nullifying all the effort that had preceded. Once more in
Buddha, as he had in the *Odyssey*, Kazantzakis set himself the task of
examining this totality of experience which seemed now to have been
confirmed in the political cataclysm he had just witnessed. The play is huge; it
presents not only the total situation but also various reactions to it, all of
which were facets of Kazantzakis's own conflicting reactions to the actual
events of 1940-1941. Specifically, it presents the reactions of a man torn
between the need to remain Buddhistically aloof from events and the opposite
need to participate in the world's ephemeral shadow-dance — to indulge in the
supreme folly of trying to act as though the phenomenal world were real. But
these contrary reactions are unified by the magic of the poetic imagination.
We may think back to a statement made by Kazantzakis in 1935:

> *I felt a great joy trying again to harmonize...fearful
> antitheses....Woe to him who sees only the mask! Woe to him
> who sees only what is hidden behind the mask! The perfect sight
> is to see simultaneously...the sweet mask and behind it the
> abominable face.*[2]

This statement provides as good a formulation as any of the essential material
of Kazantzakis's play, which shows imagination (perfect sight) comprehending
and reconciling the sweet mask of political action with the abominable face of
Buddhistic resignation.

Before examining *Yangtze* further, I would like to explore the problem of dating. We have four versions, three of which reached at least a completed draft. The first, written in Vienna in 1922, reflects Kazantzakis's extreme disillusion with politics as the result of the murder of Ion Dragoumis in 1920, the fall of Venizelos in the same year, and the abrupt end of Kazantzakis's own possibilities for action in Greece. The second, begun later in 1922, in Berlin, following the Asia Minor Disaster (September 1922) and Kazantzakis's meeting with a circle of communist Jewesses, reflects his growing ferocity, and his determination to act in some way, if not in Greece then in Russia. The third, planned during the period 1928-1932 but never executed, reflects Kazantzakis's disillusion with Soviet communism and with political activism. The fourth, which is the version we now possess, reflects, as I have suggested, the Albanian campaign against Mussolini and the subsequent defeat of Greece by Germany.

Let us survey the four versions in greater detail. The one begun in July 1922, in Vienna, was a tragedy in free verse. In *Report to Greco*, Kazantzakis describes his sojourn in Vienna at length, including how he contracted the hideous "ascetics' disease" as a result of his immersion in the Buddhistic vision. In a colloquy reported by a friend, he adds:

> I went to Vienna, where...I studied Buddhism with that chronic
> curiosity I had in my youth. I saw that there [in Buddhism] was to
> be found the vision of life toward which Nietzsche had been
> pushing me, and I became Buddha's disciple.

When Kazantzakis departed for Vienna three weeks after the elections that ended the Venizelist regime, he entered a lull between two periods of political activism: the Greek nationalism of 1919 and the communism that was to begin in Berlin in September 1922. Since he felt that the vanity of all effort had just been confirmed, he was ripe for a religious system which explained his sense of futility. At the same time, he was troubled by his continued attraction to literature. The relation of all this to the play is indicated in a letter:

> Whatever literature I write strikes me as an act of cowardice...,
> because I am afraid to confront the One: the only One who
> shouts inside me.... Individuality is worthless. But there used to
> be something else inside me, something higher than the wretched
> ego, something broader than myself....Alas, if only I could
> formulate these thoughts in "Buddha"! I'm telling myself that this
> work shall be art's last temptation for me....

Here, undisguised, is the agonizing so characteristic of Kazantzakis throughout his life. The attractions of beauty and metaphysics are clear from the passage, the attraction of politics just as clear from the context. His reaction here is also very characteristic: before giving himself over to political activity again, he must exorcise beauty and metaphysics by indulging them.

From the letter just cited, we might conclude that Kazantzakis was hoping simply to continue the free verse drama begun in Vienna. In the weeks that followed, however, he became more and more swept up in communist politics, and on October 15th he informed his wife Galatea, "I am rewriting *Buddha* in a new form—something fierce and bitter." Eventually, he reported that he had torn up the original version. The new effort was in highly stylized prose, presumably similar to that which he was to employ for the *Askitiki*[3] soon afterward. Subsequent passages in the letters confirm what we have already seen: his hope to exorcise the demon of art (beauty) and, through the play, to liberate himself for political action. When he finished the work he looked upon it as the beginning of a new phase in his development and said he wanted it "to become one of my major works."

We do not know how much of this second version survives in the final version. Probably very little. Near the end of his life, Kazantzakis told a friend that among the writings he had never published was one called *Buddha* in prose: "I tore it up."[4]

The third version occupied him off-and-on during the years 1930-1932, but never passed the planning stage. It is connected with his interest in the cinema, which he considered the perfect Buddhistic art form because of its "power to create people, ideas and passions out of light and shadow, and to annihilate them." "Oh, when will I begin *Buddha*, who is nothing but eye, who plays with the shadows, who knows that everything is an ephemeral creation of the ephemeral and complex human camera?" Obviously, we are moving in the direction of the play in its final form. This is seen even more clearly in a new prose work that Kazantzakis conceived in 1930. Provisionally named *En fumant*, this was meant to depict a period of reality encased between two dreams, the first involving art, the second metaphysics. He described it as "a work completely crazy, because I have in mind that it will never be printed. ...It will be the final form of *Buddha*." But external pressures never allowed him to go further with either project. Though he kept reading relevant books until 1932, he then began to speak of the work simply as "the future *Buddha*." Naturally, a theme that had meant so much to him over so long a period could not be forgotten. His chance came during the German occupation of Greece, which gave him an extended period of enforced solitude. In addition, the political events of 1940-1941 provided him with a renewed impetus to examine his conflicting needs (a) to remain aloof from events, and (b) to participate in the world's ephemeral shadow-dance. The subject of Buddha was a perfect one for a man who in the short span from October 28, 1940 to May 30, 1941 had seen enacted before his eyes the seemingly inevitable frustration of human hopes (the vanity of all desire central to Buddhistic teaching) and yet who, because of his renewed attachment to Greece, refused to accept the Buddhistic teaching easily and determined to indulge in the folly of trying to act as though the phenomenal world were real.

We know that *Yangtze* was begun during the terrible spring of 1941, with German planes flying overhead and strafing his neighbors. It was completed in first draft sometime before August 12th and then set aside while Kazantzakis turned his attention almost immediately to *Zorba the Greek* and afterwards to his translation of the *Iliad*. The second draft must have been composed between October 1942 and June 1943.

It is extremely important for anyone wishing to understand the final version to realize that it was written in this distressing period. On the other hand, it is equally important to remember that the call of Buddha to which Kazantzakis responded then (in the novel *Zorba* as well as in the play) is a call which he felt not only in 1941-1943, in a context of the Greek victory against Mussolini followed by defeat, but also in July 1922 in a context of disillusion with Greek nationalism, in October 1922 in a context of dedication to communist activism, and in 1928-1932 in a context of the extreme subjectivism that stemmed from his failure at direct action in the Soviet Union and manifested itself in his fascination with the cinema. At each stage we see a confirmation of Kazantzakis's ongoing need both to act in the world and to understand that such action is ultimately futile. In addition, in the third stage we encounter his discovery of a technique — reality encased in dream — by which he was finally able in the fourth and final stage of *Buddha* to create an appropriate form for this need of his to see simultaneously the sweet mask and behind it the abominable face.

II

We are now in a position to examine the play itself. The setting is China in the early twentieth century. As the curtain opens we view the central square of a village, with a huge statue of Buddha in the middle, the bamboo huts of the local whores on one side, the great gates of the palace on the other. The principal characters are Old Chiang, the war-lord; his son, Young Chiang; his daughter, Mei-Ling; and a Magician. Secondary characters are Young Chiang's wife, Li-Liang; the chief slave and his son; a Mandarin; Old Chiang's grandson; peasants, musicians, whores, and ancestors. Lastly, there are Buddha, his disciples, tempters, etc. The main plot is very simple. The Yangtze River is rising, threatening to flood the village and drown its inhabitants. The characters react to this threat in various ways that bring them into dramatic as well as philosophical conflict. As the curtain falls, the river is about to drown the entire cast (those who haven't already been killed or committed suicide) and presumably to wash away ancestors, bamboo huts, palace, and even Buddha. Except that the river *is* Buddha!

Added to this realistic part of the play, encasing it, is vision — art at the beginning, metaphysics at the end. In addition, the visionary element is inserted into each of the acts through the three pageants that are interwoven into the realistic action. These are the work of the Magician, who in turn is the functionary of the Poet who as Prologue makes us realize that everything we witness — Yangtze, suicides, passions, Buddha, heroism, resignation — is a plaything of the aesthetic imagination. All that we think is life, Kazantzakis is telling us, is a dream ending in nothing.

But the play's greatest surprise is that this seeming nihilism is not the last word. The last word is imagination, which explains why the author could insist in a gloss that his work, although it might seem pessimistic, is actually "a hymn to the pride and dignity of man." As for Kazantzakis's own career, this play is crucial because it is his first entirely open announcement of art as the ultimate salvation, subsuming activism (politics) and renunciation (Buddhism) without denigrating either. We remember Kazantzakis's yearning in 1922 to overcome his cowardice and to confront the One who was shouting inside him. Then, however, he still saw art as an impediment. Now, in the definitive version of the play, he speaks directly out of this Oneness in the person of the Poet who, by awakening imagination, makes possible the multiplicity that we call life. What Kazantzakis is attempting to say to us is that our normal concept of reality is outrageously incorrect, so incorrect that we come closer to truth with "play" than with seriousness. This is why he makes the Magician reject the commonsensical approach and instead play with the illusion of multiplicity, showing us the oneness behind youth, maturity and age, or behind life and death. He is the Artist and, as such, the source whence spring all the various characters, passions, births, deaths, hopes and fears of the deceptive multiplicity. This happens implicitly in every work of art, but Kazantzakis, by introducing the Magician and employing the frame technique, makes the artistic transformation explicit; although we react separately to the various actors and their problems, we also remain aware of the integral artistic energy behind them, an energy which stands as a positive value after everything else is annihilated.

When the Poet finishes his introduction and the "realistic" action finally begins (i.e. when the shadows commence to behave as though they were real), the subject matter is precisely the same as that already presented in the Poet's prologue and also in the Magician's preliminary instructions to a cast which projects the facets of his own oneness. This action is presented on two levels, on each of which we trace a kind of parabola meant to comprehend the totality of life and death. On the upper level, through the pageants, we see the life of Buddha. In the first pageant we have conjured up for us the attraction of women and earth, the temptations of activism, pride, anger, domestic concerns, patriotic duty — life's enticing multiplicity. In the second, we observe Buddha's spiritual exercises by which he overcomes the deceptive multiplicity of other egos and other civilizations, progressing toward the salvation of oneness. Finally, in the third pageant, Buddha debates with Wisdom and then with two ancient Greeks who speak movingly of "the power, the serenity, the nobility of the human species" and of mankind's willingness to fight for freedom. But for Buddha all this beauty and political struggle is a mask, a phantasmagoria of nothingness. Our salvation comes only after the cessation of desire and the welcoming of death as a release from life's torment. Thus at the end of the final pageant Buddha passes through the successive doorways of nonexistence until nothing remains except the song of the canary (imagination). In this, as in the previous two pageants, we are led from the unreal mask to the reality of nothingness as Buddha escapes the senses, conquers hope and fear, and finds in death the only consolation for pain, hate and blood. We mount the parabola of life and then descend again toward death. But Buddha is himself the sweet call of death; hence, paradoxically, Buddha is annihilated by Buddha. What we are meant to understand is that the two Buddhas, the one who strives and the one who negates, are the same.

The lower level is similar, except that lying in wait at the end of the parabolic journey is not Buddha this time but the Yangtze. Yet this difference is misleading. At the very end, as the river is about to wash away all the people, passions and buildings of the preceding "realistic" multiplicity, Old Chiang, guided by the Magician, realizes who the Yangtze really is. Crossing his arms and bowing to the rising river, he welcomes Buddha — and the lower level is united with the upper.

The journey from life to the acceptance of death, shown on the upper level through the history of Buddha, is shown on the lower through the minor characters and also through the two major ones. It is here, in this "realistic" part of the play, that Kazantzakis attempts to create the illusion that what the characters are struggling over is truly important. Said in another way, he attempts to convey the prowess of spirit and body that he had seen in real life ("real life"?) in 1940 and 1941 as he watched his nation confront first Mussolini and then Hitler. His challenge in this part is to keep Buddha from swallowing up life. Thus he gives us a "magic act" designed to cause us to mistake the puppets for living beings so that we, too, at least for a moment, may fall into the error of valuing the mask for its own sake. We should remember his admonition: "Woe to him who sees only what is hidden behind the mask..."

His technique on the lower level is to allow diverse personages to react in differing ways to the human condition. Let us consider the minor characters first. The whores persist in wanting flesh and kisses; they're not ready for salvation. The Mandarin places his hopes in history, thinking that he can anticipate disaster. But his "wisdom" is exposed as an inadequate defense against fate. Li-Liang, the wife of Young Chiang, has no independent being apart from her wifely role; therefore, when her husband falls victim to fate she commits suicide. The husband is very different. Europeanized, fiery, progressive, revolutionary and brutal, he is the antithesis of his father. He rebels against Buddha, ancestor worship and hashish smoking, replacing them with science, pragmatism and the cult of the future instead of the past. He wants to conquer slavery, injustice, hunger. He has the "divine sickness -- youth," which means that he wants to change the world overnight. His reaction to fate is a quixotic one: refusal to admit its existence. Yet, despite his youthful bravura, he is unable to make headway. His armies are defeated, his attempt at a palace coup fails, the dams he builds collapse and drown all the people he and his sister have indoctrinated in the new ways. In sum, he fails to conquer fate. Ironically, the great freedom-fighter ends as a kind of slave.

This is not true of the major characters, each of whom achieves freedom and salvation, but in a different manner. Mei-Ling, sister and accomplice of the revolutionary Young Chiang, is the opposite of the wifely Li-Liang; she is a "virgin lioness" who does not condescend to expend her energies upon husband, friend or son. Scorning small virtues, she knows that the ultimate virtue is to sacrifice herself futilely in a lost cause — futilely, that is, on the pragmatic level of results, tangible honor, and political efficacy. Though Mei-Ling throws herself into the river, no temple or plaque will be erected in her honor, the river will not be placated, the populace will not be saved — yet a "cry" will remain, affirming human solidarity and man's ability to confront fate with dignity. Like everyone else, Mei-Ling mounts one leg of the parabola of life and death and then descends the other. Europeanized and pragmatic like her brother, she ridicules the god Yangtze (here she embodies the scientific spirit ridiculing fate), calls for stones, cement and iron to subject death itself to man's service, indoctrinates the villagers, and tries to awaken her entire country to a spirit of self-improvement. But her brother is killed by their father, the dams break, the indoctrinated peasants are drowned. Mei-Ling is left with nothing except her individual dignity. All of her political endeavor has proved futile, and indeed she realizes the blindness and even cruelty that characterized her committed, political life. "Father," she cries, falling at Old Chiang's feet, "forgive me. Until this morning I was still very young, very cruel, deaf, blind, armed with hopes. But now at last I understand." She has finally surpassed hope, but she must also surpass despair, "conquering" fate by willing what it wills. This she does. But Mei-Ling's suicide is not just a personal exit, it is the definitive political act, a futile good deed that nevertheless affirms human solidarity because in giving herself she bequeaths a final hope to those unable to surpass hope and therefore unable to conquer fate in their own right. Thus her individual need for marriage with the abyss coincides with a wider social need: behind her affirmative suicide remains the double "cry" of individual dignity and communal solidarity.

Mei-Ling's complementary opposite, Old Chiang, reaches his salvation in an entirely different way — not through the quixotic activism of youth but through meditation and inner struggle. From the very start of the play, he has understood the vanity of all endeavor, though only theoretically, not experientially. His problem as the action unfolds and as the inhuman universe does its worse, is to struggle with the biological force which makes him naturally shrink from the metaphysical truths his mind has understood. Once again, we see the full parabola. Old Chiang is a complete man, his passivity and renunciation at the end acquiring validity because he has arrived at this Buddhistic acceptance of death by way of caring for life.

Though nominally the leader of a flock, he is treated in the play as the pure, unaccommodated, existential man: an isolated individual confronting the human condition. As the action progresses, he is stripped of everything that is meaningful to him in life until he is left completely alone with the Yangtze (Buddha). At first, his life has meaning because he is in a context extending backwards and forwards in time. He is the descendent of the all-powerful ancestors, the progenitor of the all-important progeny. He fears the former, places all his hopes in the latter, and lives in a seesaw world where the claims of one must be balanced against those of the other. At one point the ancestors weigh more heavily and at their behest he kills his son to appease the river, though he also takes steps to assure that his grandson will survive. From this point onward, Kazantzakis can take him up the various steps leading to salvation. He first learns to conquer his fear of the ancestors and, by extension, of the full domain of death represented by the Yangtze. Then he learns to conquer hope. In effect, he has no choice, for the plans laid for his grandson's escape go awry. Deprived of his cultural and human supports, without ancestors, son, daughter-in-law, grandson, daughter or kingdom, he remains in the pure existential situation, but this aloneness, together with his victory over fear and hope, opens the gate to salvation. How should he react at this point? What form of energy must be applied to the wheel of self to push it past this dead center? Kazantzakis's answer is clear. It is dignified acceptance. Whereas the common man screams, whimpers or runs imploringly to authority when he sees his death approaching, Chiang's response is lordly, displaying a quietude refined out of struggle. In him, spirit and body are not so much denied as conquered through the prowess of spirit and body. Because he has understood the self-deceiving nature of his efforts to achieve permanence, he is now — in a paradoxical way — above fate. Starting with an inherited, automatic philosophical position, he has transformed this theoretical position into an experiential one, earning the right to open his arms at the play's end and to welcome the flood (= Buddha). Now he truly knows that all of life's cares that we take so seriously are, beneath their deceptive multiplicity, a unified stream which is going where the waterfall is going: over the brink. This realization, this feat of human consciousness, gives him a pride and dignity that remain in the air as a cry after the universe has annihilated him. His Buddhism becomes strangely affirmative.

III

Though the play *Buddha* might strike some as nihilistic, it is not a pessimistic work, but rather a hymn to the pride and dignity not only of its characters but also of its author. What I claimed for Old Chiang can be claimed for Kazantzakis as well — namely, that his resignation becomes strangely affirmative because we feel that it has been earned. The play is not the expression of a man who was attempting to evade experience by passing it through the sieve of metaphysics, but of one who had been pushed by experience to question his assumptions all over again from the beginning and to emerge with a fresh consciousness of his relation to everything around him. In other words, it is the product of a man who had been pushed by experience to renewed and expanded self-consciousness. Kazantzakis would claim that human nobility lies precisely in this capacity for self-awareness and that self-awareness, furthermore, is the non-material goal of material evolution. The play gives artistic flesh and blood to these claims.

I have tried to show the comprehensiveness of *Buddha*, drawing attention to the Poet and Magician who serve as frame, to the action itself, with its upper and lower levels, and to how in each of these areas we are given the full parabola of life and death. I have also tried to indicate the experiences which lay in back of the play's prolonged gestation over several decades, culminating in Kazantzakis's exposure to his country's vicissitudes in 1940 and 1941. In writing the play, Kazantzakis attempted once more to synthesize the disparate aspects of himself, in particular his desire for political action versus his tendency toward philosophical resignation. He succeeded in this attempt by making activism the necessary precondition of a genuine futility. In other words: he justified activism in the short run because it places a crown of heroic dignity upon those who strive with open eyes, and in the long run because it leads to the non-material result of expanded self-consciousness.

Yet the ultimate solution presented by the play is the aesthetic one. All the foregoing is encased in art; imagination subsumes both politics and metaphysics. In this work, Kazantzakis does not trace the actual growth of the artistic position; he was to do this in his next book, *Zorba the Greek*, whose hero learns to deal with both activism and Buddhism by means of artistic creativity. In the play *Buddha* the artistic solution is already fully developed at the start — it is a given. By implication, however, we know that Kazantzakis felt that it, too, could be validated only after struggle, felt that active participation in life is the only path whereby imagination can earn the right to step back from life and treat it aesthetically with engaged aloofness. The artist accepts the unaesthetic as the necessary precondition of saving himself through the aesthetic.

These were the answers Kazantzakis arrived at in his renewed attempt, under the pressures of the events of 1940-1941, to reconcile the disparate aspects of himself (could we say "his deceptive multiplicity"?) and emerge with a coherent whole. The answers were not new; they are found in the *Odyssey* and other works. But of all of Kazantzakis's immense output, the play *Buddha* is the most straightforward in its exposition of his definitive position, because it so unapologetically presents the aesthetic as the primary way to salvation. A few months before he died, he told some Buddhist monks in China that of the three paths — meditation (metaphysics), good deeds (politics) and beauty (art) — he had followed the path of beauty. No wonder, then, that shortly before this he had declared: *"Buddha* is my swan song. It says everything. I'm glad that I have managed to utter...my final word in time, before I go."

[1]Letter to Elsa Lange, late August 1925, printed in Helen Kazantzakis, *Nikos Kazantzakis: A Biography* (New York, Simon and Shuster, 1968), pp. 125-6.

[2]Reprinted in *Japan China* (New York, Simon and Shuster, 1963), pp. 50-51. (George Pappageostes's translation, with some slight changes.)

[3]Translated into English by Kimon Friar as *The Saviors of God: Spiritual Exercises* (New York, Simon and Schuster, 1960).

[4]Mrs. Kazantzakis is certain that the only portion from an earlier version that survives in the final version is the episode of the two Greeks encountering Buddha. She also suspects that the second version, despite Kazantzakis's hopes for it, was destroyed or suppressed almost immediately — in any case before May 1924, when she and Kazantzakis first met. (Letter to Michael Tobias, March 16, 1982.)

CHARACTERS

The Poet

Buddha

Brahma

Siva

Vishnu

God of Wisdom

Temptation

Magician, (Hu-Ming) Buddha's disciple

Mogalana, Buddha's disciple

Saripoutta, Buddha's disciple

Hanna, Buddha's servant

Chiang, warlord

Old Man, Chiang's father

Li-Liang, Chiang's wife

Mei-Ling, Chiang's sister

Old Koag, the Old Man's head slave

Young Koag, monk, Old Koag's son

Mandarin, scribe

Markalo, Husband of Earth, an old man

Azure Butterfly, First Whore

Blossoming Cherry Tree, Second Whore

Fruit-Laden Lemon Tree, Third Whore

Moonglow, Fourth Whore

Li-Li-Foo, Fifth Whore

First Sentry

Second Sentry

Third Sentry

First Greek

Second Greek

Young Man

Moudita, his wife

Herald

First Musician, tambourine

Second Musician, drum

Third Musician, clarinet

First Soldier

Second Soldier

Third Soldier

The People

First Woman

Second Woman

Third Woman

First Man

Second Man

Third Man

First Old Man

Second Old Man

First Slave

Second Slave

First Disciple

Second Disciple

Third Disciple

Fourth Disciple

Peasant

Men and women both old and
    young, peasants, soldiers,
    servants, disciples

PROLOGUE

POET   Omnipotent Mind, merciless Father, you give birth to the sky,
land and sea, to the visible and invisible, to flesh and spirit;
You give them birth, love them and then blot them out —
Come, let us play.
My palms tingle; I long to grasp air, earth, water, fire — to
create. Heavy is my loneliness tonight;
Let me give life to the earth; let me open furrows that rivers
may run; let me build temples and palaces of air;
Let me adorn the wasteland with women, with peasants,
with gods, with monks, with noblemen.
I am tired; I am weary of loneliness; a sweet swoon saps my
strength this twilight.
I want to see and touch; I want to be seen and touched;
hands, eyes and mouths are what I long for,
And many shadows fighting, merging, parting, making
patterns in the wind.
O unborn spirits, be born! Spirits, take on flesh! Behold, I
stoop, take mud from the riverbank and knead.
The trough is good, the dough plenty and pliable, my palms
are deft, I pummel both men and gods.
Eh, Sun, stay and bake them!
(Bows to audience.)
My lords and ladies, welcome to my workshop this evening.
Open the eyes of your bodies and look; open the eyes of
your minds and see:
Behold, I tread on the land and level it out to create the
endless, tranquil land of China;
I cut the earth with my fingernail and open up a furrow for a
ribbon of water to enter and flow,
And it's the fearful, almighty river, the Yangtze. Bow down
and worship its grace.
I thrust a small stone into the clay and it becomes a majestic
tower with moats and bridges, battlements, stone gods and
many-colored, glowing lanterns.
I stoop and sift the lightest yellow porcelain clay, and blend it
with rosewater, nutmeg and cinnamon; I blow upon it and
shape lords and ladies, magicians, musicians and sages;
I take coarser clay, used for making jugs and pitchers, and

1

shape peasants and slaves, both male and female. At once
the shameless creatures move their hands, their feet, their
loins,
And long to couple.
Let them couple, we have plenty of earth and water; let's
shape guests as well; let a great festival burst across the
wasteland tonight
To while away the hours.
Men and gods, ethereal spring clouds, descend and take from
my hands the faces I give you;
Open your mouths; drink the holy communion of wine and
flame, the words I choose for you;
Don your festive nuptial garments; adjust your masks. The
Mind is to be married! Brightly adorn his bride, the Earth.
Let them come
Mounted on horses, waves, dreams, on great thoughts; let the
in-laws come,
Let bodies and spirits come!
Rise, O four winds, rise out of my temples; the sky overbrims
with stars; the earth overbrims with wheat.
Sift and winnow!
(The thick scrim lifts and the set appears: A Chinese village
with a square, a giant statue of Buddha in its center; on the
left, five bamboo huts; to the right, the great gate of the
Tower. In the rear, bowing in a row to the audience like
marionettes, are the principal players of the tragedy.)
Reverence and pity overwhelm me. What are these wisps of
smoke that have risen from the erect hairs of my head,
secured themselves to the air
And have become a village with statues and a tower?
What is this army of clay toys that has spilled out of my ten
fingers?
Open your hearts, your inner eyes, and look: They are not
clay toys, not wisps of smoke;
They are warm human beings, and each has a name, a bitter
history, an unbearable destiny.
They struggle like drowning mutes, opening and closing their
mouths in vain to cry: "Help! Help! Help!"
They are the ephemeral toys of the mind, azure wisps of
smoke above the wet plain.
O, mortals

2

I blow upon your earthen eyes to open them; I blow upon
    your earthen ears to open them; I blow upon your lips to
    warm them, to make them shout.
Lift up your heads, and look: Above the cobwebbed cellars
    of your existence rises the uppermost level of the world —
    weightless, full of light, thought, and smiles —
Buddha!
Listen! Behind the frenzied growl of the Yangtze, beyond the
    hoarse lament of drowning man
Buddha plays his flute sweetly, seductively, like a master-
    shepherd who at dusk invites the sheep into their pens.
The waters cry out in my entrails, the beasts speak, embassies
    of birds arrive in full dress; the gods descend with their
    begging bowls,
Buddha enters my head like a king entering his kingdom and
    the whole city creaks.
The unborn cling to the crags of my mind, burrowing into
    the subterranean passages of my heart; they don't want to
    leave.
Small children cry within me, women wail, beasts bellow,
    numberless birds cling to the tree of my entrails and warble:
"Father, give us a body, we are cold; give us a name, we are
    lost; give us a gender. We want to become male and
    female, to couple and give birth, so that we may not
    vanish.
Father, we yearn to suffer in earthen hands by loving, giving
    birth and dying.
Open the dark cage of your bowels; let us out!"
I stoop and press my ear to my breast; I hear humming within
    me, and I pity mankind.
I will unfurl a lightly-haunted tale, a yellow silken flag to
    declare war on suffering, ugliness and death.
Buddha! Buddha! Buddha!
I look to the North and South; I look to the East and West,
Buddha! Buddha! Buddha!
This world has no other consolation.
See how he stood and stretched out his hand quietly, without
    joy, without grief, then opened the door of nonexistence
And entered.
See how he turned his translucent head and bade the world
    farewell...how he spread his glance like a setting sun over

3

all people until, from head to toe,
They were dressed in saffron robes.
My children, a wind blows, ripening the buds on the trees,
and the world stirs. The secret Vine has risen out of my
bowels and entwines men, gods and ideas like shoots and
grapes.
The mountains glow like great thoughts; the starry sky
sways like a blossoming mandarin tree; the river Yangtze,
my broad royal vein, spills over my neck and refreshes me.
My children, shatter the iron bars of Necessity! Doff your
little earthen blouses; free the soul from the lime twigs of
the flesh,
For all is a dream; suffering, ugliness and death are illusions.
They do not exist.
Life is a game, death is a game — let's play awhile!
(Unhooks the gong.)
Let's play awhile! I unhook the gong from the abyss, strike it
three times to awaken the Imagination, that great bird
perched on the cliffs of my mind, and I cry.
(Strikes once and calls seductively. The curtain moves.)
Come!...Come!...Come!
*(Strikes the gong a second time. Distant footsteps are
heard.)*
He's coming...He's coming...He's coming...
*(Strikes the gong a third time, hangs it up again, then steps
back. The Magician appears.)*
Here he is!
(The Poet disappears.)

ACT I

(The Magician advances, dressed in the saffron robe of a Buddhist monk and wearing the mask of an old man. Two other masks hang from his neck.)

MAGICIAN
I've come. Three times I heard my name. Then a mysterious power — not at all mysterious, *my* power — stretched the wind taut, like a drum, from one end of the abyss to the other, then it sounded three times, and here I am.

Man must have need of me again. The fairy tale that conceals the truth must be torn and hanging like a rag again.

Man saw what was hiding behind it and became frightened. He cried out my name to the wind three times...

Help!...Help!...Help... Help is my name.

And here I am, with my unconquered army — the multi-colored, multi-winged, multi-eyed regiments of the imagination that fly over the dung heap called man's mind.

My army will destroy the breakwaters of the brain. It will disrupt and pillage all certainties.

I close the eyes of the body, I no longer see the ephemeral, I gaze on the eternal — a China reclining on clouds, made of water, sun and a gentle breeze.

She sails peacefully in the abyss with a prime wind, neither joyous nor sad, beyond time and place, beyond necessity.

I open the eyes of the body; instantly the eternal disappears, and I see before me a Chinese village beside the dreadful Blue River, the Yangtze,

Foul, muddy, filled with sweating men, pregnant women and swarms of children — it smells of human dung and of jasmine;

At the top of the village sits the Tower of the Master with its guffawing stone lions, foundations of seven times seven layers of bones, seven times seven layers of sighs from the slaves of the dreadful clan of Chiang.

At the foot of the Tower is a town square festively adorned with lanterns, myrtle and banners. In the center is a lightning-blasted, wild oak tree,

And the statue of Buddha with his four chins, four bellies, and four open doors leading to the fortress of his mind so the four winds might enter.

5

It's Buddha, Buddha; he looks at the people and bursts with
   laughter.
*(Young Koag, a slave, appears, dressed in a saffron robe. He
bows before the statue of Buddha, claps his hands, prays
softly, then hangs two silken lanterns to the right and left of
Buddha.)*

YOUNG KOAG   Buddha, Buddha, pity the people, pity the plants and animals,
   pity the stones, the waters and the soil.
   Blow upon the world, O Redeemer, and make it disappear.

MAGICIAN   *(Laughing softly.)*
   It's the beloved slave of the Master, Young Koag, with his
   doe-eyes and his long lashes.
   He's still too young to know how firm, sweet and full of
   essence the phantasmagoria of the world is.
   He hungers, thirsts and yearns, so he does not reach out his
   hand; he's ashamed and disgusted, yet he does not reach
   out his hand for food, wine, woman.
   This is not bread, he says; it is a chain that binds the soul
   with the body even more tightly, and God with filth. This
   is not wine, he says; it is the blood of Mara, of
   Temptation, that infects the blood of man with madness.
   This is not woman, he says; it is a building with cellars and
   sub-cellars, with open terraces over the precipice, with
   gardens and cesspools. It has an entrance, but no exit.
   Pity him, O souls who know the secret. His eyes, ears and
   mouth are still unopened buds. His life is still a heavy
   sleep in which he dreams of Buddha.
   But the hour has come. Tonight, woman will awaken him;
   his five senses will open and sprout leaves and flowers,
   and then bear round, downy, aromatic fruit —
   Death!
   Koag, eh Koag, our young monk!

YOUNG KOAG   *(Turns, murmuring with fear.)*
   The Magician!
   (Falls to his knees in reverence.)
   Command, O Lord!

MAGICIAN   What village is this, my young doe-eyed Koag?
YOUNG KOAG   O great Master of the rites of Buddha, you know. Why do
   you ask?

MAGICIAN   What holy day is this, doe-eyed Koag?

YOUNG KOAG   You know, Lord; why do you ask? You know all — past,
             present, future.
             You have three heads, Lord, and you see everything: what
             will be and what has been, the good, the evil, the visible
             and the invisible.
             You have three hearts, Lord; one pities, one mocks, and the
             third, the most compassionate, kills all things. You hold
             the strings Lord, and you control the Universe.

MAGICIAN   I do know all, Koag. Go, it's true, I have three hearts. The
             first pities and weeps; the second does not pity, it laughs;
             the third neither laughs nor weeps — it is silent.
             I hold three spools of string — white, red and black — and I
             control three paper kites with tassels and bells, with colored
             lanterns in the wind, the three great concepts —
             Life, Love, Death!
             I've brought all three spools with me tonight. A prime wind
             blows; I'll launch all three kites and entangle them in the
             murky air.

YOUNG KOAG   I kiss your feet, O great Master of the rites of Buddha. The
             moment has come; cut the strings that hold us to earth —
             the white, the red, the black,
             That we may be delivered.

MAGICIAN   (Laughing.)
             You are impatient, Doe-eyes, impatient...I like you...Go; I,
             too, am impatient.
             (Koag bows and turns to leave.)
             Koag!

YOUNG KOAG   Command me, Lord.

MAGICIAN   Are the players ready? Old Chiang? His son? His daughter?
             His daughter-in-law? The old Mandarin, the three
             musicians, the three sentries, the five whores?
             I need all these phantoms tonight, my young doe-eyed Koag.

YOUNG KOAG   All are ready, just as you commanded, Lord. They wait
             behind the curtains, costumed and painted, their hearts
             pounding and their ears cocked to hear your voice.
             When will you summon them, Lord?

7

MAGICIAN   When I wish. Go! And tell young Koag — my doe-eyed Koag
             — to be ready also. Do you hear? Ready, even to die.

YOUNG KOAG   I ask no other favor of you, Lord, but to die, to escape. I no
             longer want this world; pity me Lord, I no longer want it.
             I am like the butterfly that falls into the spider's web as
             that terrible weaver pounces upon it, swaddles its wings,
             wraps it round, and smothers it;
             So does the world entrap me...I am lost!
             Help me, Lord, to break my strings, to free my wings, to fly.

MAGICIAN   Patience, patience, my doe-eyed Koag; we shall soon reach
             salvation. Already I can feel the moist roots of the grass on
             your face.
             We are but a lightning's flash away, Koag, but do not fear,
             there is still time. I will thicken the spirit to make it flesh;
             I will thin the flesh to make it spirit. I will shatter the
             inner walls, confuse the elements, fit lion masks on rabbits.
             I will waken the people within God's bowels; I will play!
             I, too, have grown weary, Koag. The world moves too
             slowly, too sluggishly. We cannot wait for the seed to take
             root, to sprout leaves, buds, blossoms and fruit, and then
             to rot. We give the wheel and laggard time a push — seed
             and rot will become one.
             But you must help me, young monk of Buddha. Stretch out
             your hand and give the wheel a push; call the performers
             to assemble before me that I may give them my final
             instructions — how to speak, how to be silent, how to die...
             Do you hear, doe-eyed Koag?

YOUNG KOAG   I hear, Lord, and I obey.
             (Bows and exits.)

MAGICIAN   Wretched men...caught in the nets of flesh, they struggle to
             break free, to be saved...falling into even thicker nets, the
             nets of the Mind.
             And this they call Salvation!
             They merely exchange prisons — the walls are no longer of
             rocks, whitewash and iron bars, but of hopes and dreams.
             They exchange prisons,
             And they call this Freedom!
             (Laughs.)
             Let's change their prisons for them tonight!

8

(Looks around.)

Let's cast all cares aside! On this great festival tonight
the people will eat, drink and smoke hashish. The old
Master will descend from his Tower, the people will ascend
from the mud, and they'll all worship Buddha.

On a night like this, they say, Buddha untangled himself from
the nets of the flesh, slipped out of its five snares and found
invincible, immortal refuge —

He found Nothingness!

On a night like this, they say, Buddha left the world, escaped
from the conspiracy and ordered the five conspirators —
earth, water, fire, air and mind — to dissolve.

The humbly devout come tonight to see how the Chosen are
liberated, that they too, after thousands of incarnations,
after thousands of years, might one day find freedom.
What freedom?

Nothingness!

(Claps his hands and shouts.)

Eh! Eh! Eh!

*(The main characters enter and line up before him: Old
Chiang, Young Chiang, Mei-Ling, Li-Liang, the Mandarin, the
Three Musicians, the Three Sentries, the Five Whores. Behind
them, in a shapeless mass, is a crowd of people. Behind them,
the savage, muddy river, the Yangtze.)*

Welcome! Welcome! The moment has come, my children, for
you to show your skill before so many noblemen and ladies
this evening — don't disgrace me.

Art is a difficult task, a noble and dangerous balance over
the abyss; be careful.

Dance neither to the left, on the precipice of truth, nor to the
right, on the precipice of falsehood, but straight ahead,
across the abyss, upon the thin thread of freedom.

This dance is called Art.

Talk, laugh, cry, without the vulgar shouts and gestures of
foolish, living men. Subject the word, the smile, the tear,
to the stern, noble outline of human dignity.

Eh, old Chiang, do you understand? Come closer, don't be
afraid; you have much to wrestle with tonight — wrath,
love, pain — hang on tightly old Chiang, lest the Word
throw you.

You are the central pillar that supports the roof of my

9

imagination tonight — do not bend.

You are not the common people to whine and degrade
   yourself; you are not a god, a heart of stone, unable to
   feel pain, or love, or fear —

You are a nobleman, a lofty balance between the two
   precipices: the precipice of Man, and the precipice of God.
   You suffer, but you don't whine; you love and fear, but
   you don't degrade yourself. You look at the people and
   say, "I am to blame." You look at God and say, "No! I am
   not to blame; *You* are, but I assume the responsibility."

Eh, old Chiang, head-ram of my herd of shadows tonight,
   lead my fat ewes straight ahead toward the precipice;
   don't be frightened, do not change course.

This is the way, there is no other. Walk nobly to the end, for
   there lies salvation.

Rough, azure, full of flintstones is the path. And on the
   flintstones lie thick drops of blood.

It's not a precipice, old Chiang, it's not a precipice; it's
   salvation.

And you, young Chiang, condescend, take a step forward,
   come closer, irreverent soul of youth. You have no
   patience; you have no mercy. You hold the thunderbolt
   in your palm and you say:

"This is not a thunderbolt, it's a candle of peace; hang it in
   your homes to shine at night."

You are flesh of my flesh, you have no patience. You want
   to move the world in a day, to make it go further. I like
   you — strike!

O Mei-Ling, beloved, come forth; closer still, that I may
   touch you...what joy you gave me, joy and pride. I created
   you! Virgin lioness, you do not condescend to expend your
   strength on husband, friend or son; hold your head high
   my child, until the end.

It's a cruel fate to be pure, unsubduable, without faults; to
   scorn small joys, small virtues, small, sure truths.

To say: "I know a secret sweeter than life, more bitter than
   death. I know, but I tell no one, and I die for its sake."

Mei-Ling, you are a great, warm drop of my blood; my
   blessings upon you.

(Approaches, tenderly caresses Li-Liang.)

Li-Liang, wife of the fierce warlord Chiang, graceful and

soft-spoken, all passion, silence and nobility, companion of
    man,
I gaze upon you and my untamed heart grows tame; even at
    this late hour I can change the course of your destiny. I
    pity you, Li-Liang, I pity you, but I must not. Follow your
    fate, straight to the end, and let it take you where it may.
    This is the meaning of salvation.
Do not weep, unhappy girl; free yourself.
And you, musicians, sentries and whores; and you, old
    Mandarin with the gourd of wisdom on your shoulders;
    and you, workers, peasants and slaves, ballast of my ship;
And you, Blue River, blue-yellow, mud-covered mask that I
    will place tonight on the face of Destiny —
Take care! Are you ready?
I clap my hands, the performance begins!
(A canary sings. The Magician raises his head and listens
several minutes in ecstasy.)
Yes, yes, my canary, don't complain, I've not forgotten you,
    O pinnacle of freedom!
The omnipotent, mute powers are moving now to choke you.
    You still have a little time left, a little throat. Raise your
    head high and sing!
May the last voice heard above the waters that shall come to
    drown us be yours, O canary, O freedom! Sing!
And now, silence! Musicians, sit cross-legged in the corner,
    tune up your instruments, the tambourine, the drum, the
    clarinet; prepare yourselves.
Awaken the numberless, multi-colored birds that sleep in the
    dark throat of Nothingness.
Musicians, open the cage, the heart of man!
The wind is filled with sobbing, with erotic murmering, with
    laughter and signs of desperation: "Save our souls! Save
    our souls!" we shout. Onward, musicians, that we may
    finally hear our voices!
Good are the three keys you hold; the drum, the tambourine,
    the clarinet can open the abyss,
My heart has grown savage, I'm in a hurry! Leave, all of you!
    Let only these five whores remain.
(They leave. The three Musicians sit cross-legged in the
corner, at right. The five whores gaze in their little mirrors,
arranging their curls, painting their lips, as they walk toward

11

the Magician.)

Welcome! Welcome, deflated secrets, communal fountains at
the crossroads, O doors to Paradise open day and night,
wider even than the bowels of God,

Where ascetics and criminals enter — gay, young blades and
hunchbacks, beggars and kings —

Where all receive communion.

O five, welcoming sacred Doors: Azure Butterfly, Blossoming
Cherry-Tree, Fruit-Laden Lemon Tree, Moonglow, and
you, sweet-kissing Li-Li-Foo,

Come forward, the blessed hour is here; raise to your lips
the words I buried in your hearts; unwind all the deeds I
wound up for you.

O, five, great martyrs of love, cast a farewell glance in your
little mirrors, paint a final beauty mark on your small
cheeks, prepare yourselves. The performance begins. In the
name of God!

*(The five Whores run to their bamboo huts where they
hurriedly primp.)*

Oh! Oh! The little women of love come and go, shaking their
behinds like fatted ewes.

They've hurriedly unfolded their overworked beds and hung
their multi-colored lanterns, and now, here they are,

Dressing, adorning themselves, dousing themselves with
perfumes so they won't stink; and they stand like a ship's
figurehead freshly painted, their hands crossed beneath
their accommodating, hanging breasts, two communal
fountains,

Waiting for men.

It has snowed on the high mountains; it has rained, it has
rained forty days and forty nights on the plain. It has
rained, and the Blue River, the Yangtze, has swollen. It
leaps and rams its banks to knock them down, to drown
the world.

Let men open their ears. The soft hum of their laughter, their
quarrels, their crying children, and their boiling pots drown
out

The mighty roar of the Yangtze

But I hear one thing only, not women, or babies, or pots; I
hear one sound only:

The mighty Roar. I roar, too, like the Yangtze, and I descend!

I can hold back no longer; I will open the ears of my father,
my son and my friend to hear the Yangtze descending, to
hear a hoarse voice leaping out of the soil: "We are lost!
We are lost!"
Let them awaken!
(Whistles seductively and calls softly.)
Blossoming Cherry-Tree, enticing songstress, come closer,
begin, sing!
Passion has made you lean, my Blossoming Cherry-Tree, and
you sigh, because you have fallen into sin. What sin?
You have crammed the Creator into one creature, infinity
into one body;
You chose one among men, young Koag, doe-eyed Koag, and
you said:
"It's him I want, not the others. It's for him I dress and
undress, it's for him I sing."
What a shame; you stopped the masks that roll over the face
of Destiny, and you said: "Let all masks be gone; let only
this one remain."
Rise up now, and pay for your sin.
But first, before you are killed, sing.
I want to hear the song you dislike, the one I rubbed violently
on your lips, like honey.
Sing, Blossoming Cherry-Tree.
(Sings enticingly:)
"Dear God, put out the sun, or I'll be lost..."

BLOSSOMING CHERRY TREE	(Dressed in a kimono embroidered with a branch of a blossoming cherry tree, sunk in lethargy, she listens to the Magician. Gradually her face comes alive, she is carried away, claps her hands and begins to sing.) "Dear God, put out the sun, or I'll be lost..."
MAGICIAN	Sing louder; stop shaking your hips so shamelessly; you've entered the sacred forest of art; walk with reverence.
BLOSSOMING CHERRY TREE	Dear God, put out the sun, or I'll be lost; descend, O night, at length that I may rest and lie in bed alone; all day long in the streets I hawk my wares and to all, old and poor, I sell my bare young body, flesh and bone.

What may the eyes see when they open wide?
But when I close my lashes tight, inside
what happiness awakes,
for then a dream, a doe, leaps into sight
and fills my aching, empty arms with pride,
with downy, curly locks.

Dresses of rustling silk then shall I wear
and douse myself with perfumes, and with care
besprinkle my beloved beau,
as over us the cherry trees will bloom,
the black-eyed hours then will cease too soon,
and in our village — O,

dear God, let not one sound of crowing burst
in air, nor let the sun, may it be cursed,
rise with the cocks at dawn,
but let each lovely lass sleep, ring on ring,
a deathless, charming and enchanting spring,
with lads on every lawn.

(Turns uneasily toward the Magician.)

MAGICIAN   You sang well. Don't tremble, Blossoming Cherry-Tree; don't
tremble, or all your blossoms will fall to the ground.
And now, light your red lantern, it's dark; hang it by your
door,
My little firefly.
(Whistles invitingly.)
Eh, Fruit-Laden Lemon Tree, it's your turn! Come here, angry
girl, don't be afraid of me, scold me. I speak with your
lips; don't tremble. You are merely the reed
On which I blow and play whatever tune I please.
And you, beloved Li-Li-Foo, go inside, unfold your mattress,
douse your bedsheets with rosewater, open your kimono,
I'm coming!
(The whore leaps angrily towards the Magician, wearing a
kimono embroidered with fruit-laden lemon-tree branches,
shaking her hands menacingly.)
Splendid! Frown more with your eyebrows; place your hands
on your hips, scream! Do you remember the words, "Eh,
monk, for shame"? That's how you begin...

Courage, Fruit-Laden Lemon Tree, it's not you who speak, I
tell you; it's I who speak with your lips. Don't be afraid.

FRUIT-LADEN Eh, monk, for shame! Lift your eyes across to the holy
LEMON TREE mountain; cock your ears to the air;
Those flames are not fires lit by shepherd boys, those are not
sheepdogs barking, monk, it's your Monastery burning!
The monks are leaping in the flames; their saffron robes
have caught fire.
A demon, you know the one — his tongue is fire — has seized
your monastery in his claws and he's licking it!
Rise, monk, they say your power is great, that you hold
magic and thunderbolts in the palm of your hand. Rise
and fight!
Why do you stroll here and spin the air? Rise and fight!
You know it's not a demon; it's Chiang, Chiang, son of the
Tower Master, may he be cursed!

MAGICIAN It's not Chiang, it's not Chiang, it's hoarfrost. It's not a
monastery, it's hoarfrost.
Stop shouting, Fruit-Laden Lemon Tree, everything is
hoarfrost. Even Buddha himself is hoarfrost, but he knows
it —
That's why he's Buddha.
Don't frown. Everyone in this world performs his duty well,
very well. You comb your hair, shake your hips, simp
and smirk, glue a smile on your face, and then wait for men.
The Nobleman inside his tower eats, drinks, holds Injustice
on his knees, caresses her and rejoices —
He caresses Injustice and the world appears just to him, and
God a firm Tower — his tower.
And out there, as you say, the valiant fight for hoarfrosts
and phantoms; they fight and are killed — good for them!
And I sit here — good for me! — and spin the air.
All's well, Fruit-Laden Lemon Tree, all the actors are in their
places —
The Blue River, the Monastery, the Tower, the Master, the
People — and Death.
All the actors are in their places; the performance will go
well tonight. Light your lantern, too, Fruit-Laden Lemon
Tree; the words I placed on your lips have ended, go!
It's your turn, Azure Butterfly.

15

AZURE BUTTERFLY   *(Turns toward the statue of Buddha.)*
I raise my arms, I clap my hands, I cry out: "Buddha,
    Buddha,
(Pointing to the Magician.)
Blow upon this shameless structure of bones and flesh that
    it may rot!
He has no shame, no fear, he has gone beyond the boundaries
    of man. He's no longer man, but he's not yet a demon,
    he's somewhere in the middle. This is the moment, Buddha
    — kill him!"
(To the Magician.)
What performance, monk? For shame! Tonight you must
    conduct a great liturgy: the people and the nobles have
    trembled all year long, anxiously waiting for this night —
Bring God down from the heavens, raise the souls of the
    Ancestors from the earth, break our bodies, the thick-
    skinned husks of our souls;
Then all of us, slaves and masters, gods and men, the living
    and the dead, shall become one.
It's a terrible moment, thrice-blessed holy man; it's your duty,
    monk, to draw your mind away from food, drink and
    women, that you may fight
With that untamed element, the miracle.
But your lordship has come dressed in silk like a bridegroom.
    Instead of a sword, you hold a quill; instead of a shield,
    two masks hang from your neck; and you are not ashamed
    on such a night as this
To squander your strength on women.

MAGICIAN   How else, my Azure Butterfly, how else can I gain
    momentum? If I fall upon food, I become heavy, I cannot
    walk — and it's my great duty to dance.
If I fall upon great thoughts, I whirl like fire; I am hurled
    into the sky; I play tenpins with the clouds; and woe to
    the heart on whom the lightning bolt falls!
Woman sits in the middle between food and great thoughts.
    She sits with bared breasts and open knees,
And I touch her...I touch her,
And lo, what can it be, my Azure Butterfly, what can this
    mystery be, my Fruit-Laden Lemon Tree? The moment I
    touch her, then weight and whirlwind mingle divinely

16

within me,
And I dance!

MOONGLOW   *(Laughing.)*
Come then, my dancer — dance with me. Look, I have bathed,
combed my hair, bared my breasts.
I am a woman, and I, too, sit, as you say, between food and
great thoughts and open my knees — come here and refresh
your strength.

MAGICIAN   The smelt needs octopus as bait, the mullet needs cheese, the
male cuttlefish a female cuttlefish. Every form of life on
land and sea, as you know, has its own bait, and is caught.
By God's will, every man has his own woman as bait, and
he nibbles.
Forgive me, Moonglow, I will go to the hut of my old friend,
Li-Li-Foo
To nibble a little.
*(Walks slowly towards Li-Li-Foo's hut, then turns to the
Musicians.)*
Eh, Musicians, tambourine, drum, clarinet, why do you stand
there and gape at me? The performance has begun, let
your hearts go!
Words reach as far as the door of Paradise, but they can't
enter. The Mind pounds on the door of Paradise, shouts
that it's the great Nobleman, the Mind, but the door won't
open.
Yet when music comes, it filters in through the cracks.
Drum, tambourine, clarinet — say now what words have no
power to say. The time has come for my terrifying shout to
rise out of the earth.
Until then, I go to woman to refresh my strength.
*(Unloosens his belt, puts on the black-bearded mask that
hangs on his chest and enters the hut of Li-Li-Foo. The
Musicians play a savage, muffled tune for a long while.
Suddenly out of the bowels of the earth a serpent's strong
hissing and a harrowing cry are heard: "We are lost!" The
music stops abruptly. The Four Whores dash out of their
huts, frightened.)*

AZURE BUTTERFLY   Did you hear? Did you hear? Fs-s-s-s, like a serpent…We're
lost!

17

BLOSSOMING CHERRY TREE	Yes, yes, I heard…we're lost! *(Falls to the ground, covering her ears.)*
FRUIT-LADEN LEMON TREE	Why are you trembling, Blossoming Cherry-Tree, my little sister? *(Suddenly terrified.)* Do you think it was…?
BLOSSOMING CHERRY TREE	Yes, yes, it was, it was! I know their voices…I'm afraid.
MOONGLOW	The Ancestors?

BLOSSOMING
CHERRY TREE
	Yes, yes, the Ancestors…The Ancestors are calling from
	    under the earth.
	They've opened their earth-filled mouths and are crying out.
	What do they want now? Haven't the gluttons had enough?
	    Of all the bountiful blessings men bring us from God in
	    payment for a kiss, we, poor wretches,
	Who work all night, give them their share every morning —
	Rice, honey, wine.
	And what do *they* do, the parasites? Do they stand on their
	    doorsills calling out to customers like magpies, craw, craw,
	    craw?
	Do they kiss, lie awake and expend themselves all night long?
	    Do they brim with saliva, sweat, pinches, cigarette burns,
	    stench from wine-soaked breaths, from spit, from filth,
	Like garbage pails?
	No, no, the masters lie in the cool earth, open their
	    bottomless mouths two spans wide, and shout, "Hey, you
	    living, we want food! Hey, you living, we want wine!" And
	    we go, poor souls, filling their earthen pots as they eat and
	    stuff their bellies.
	Eh, enough! The dead eat too much; let them eat us too, and
	    so release us! Let's also become the dead — to eat up the
	    living!

BLOSSOMING CHERRY TREE	They're not hungry, they're not thirsty, Fruit-Laden Lemon Tree. Don't you hear them? They're afraid.

AZURE BUTTERFLY	Are they afraid of a night like this? Of Buddha's festival when
	    all the passions — hunger, thirst, fear — become light and
	    turn into air?

MOONGLOW	Oho, Chiang must have dug up the bones from the Monastery graves, Chiang, excommunicated Chiang,

And the souls have dispersed in the wind and now weep.

FRUIT-LADEN   *(Placing her ear to the ground.)*
LEMON TREE   Listen...Listen...Hoards of moles are running...and
              screeching...

AZURE BUTTERFLY   No...no...It's not moles you hear...It's not our Ancestors...
                      Oho, it's —
                  (Jumps up terrified.)
                  It's the waters running...waters, waters, waters under the
                      earth.

BLOSSOMING   The waters! Do you think it could be...We're lost!
CHERRY TREE

MOONGLOW   Oh! Oh! Could it be...?

FRUIT-LADEN   Who? Who?
LEMON TREE

ALL THE WHORES   The Yangtze?
                 *(Terrified, the four crumple to the floor. Music filled with
                 fear is heard. Three young monks wearing saffron robes
                 appear. They bow in reverence to the statue of Buddha and
                 decorate it with flowers, chanting softly.)*

THREE MONKS   Like a silkworm, Buddha has anchored
              on the boughs of unflowering silence;
              he's eaten all the leaves,
              he's eaten all the leaves of earth's mulberry tree,
              he's eaten all the leaves and turned them into silk!

BLOSSOMING   *(Bursting into tears.)*
CHERRY TREE   He's eaten all the leaves...He's eaten all the leaves...Oh, a
                  caterpillar is eating
              The leaves of my heart.
              Buddha, Buddha, I'm not ready yet; all my flesh has not
                  become spirit yet; I hunger, I hurt, I love, I still want to
                  kiss.
              You know my secret, Buddha,
              Take away the grace you've given me; I don't want it
                  anymore!
              Take it away! I don't want
              Salvation!

MOONGLOW	Let her cry, she'll feel better; what would we poor women do without tears? She's remembering her little Koag, doe-eyed Koag, and she's crying. *(Runs to the first hut and shouts:)* Li-Li-Foo! Li-Li-Foo!
AZURE BUTTERFLY	Moonglow, why are you calling her? Hush!
MOONGLOW	She knows many spells; let her cast her spells on the demons in the air so we'll find relief.
FRUIT-LADEN LEMON TREE	*(Scornfully.)* What spells? She knows only one, the one that enslaves men: "Command me!" Nothing more. She's sly, she won't say, "I want!" She's shameless, she won't say, "Come!" She's a wheedling whore, she won't say, "Give me!" She only says, "Command me!" and she enslaves men. *(Laughter is heard from the first hut.)*
BLOSSOMING CHERRY TREE	Who's with her? Who's she laughing with? Her hut is shaking ...Li-Li-Foo *(To Fruit-Laden Lemon Tree.)* Why are you laughing, Fruit-Laden Lemon Tree?
FRUIT-LADEN LEMON TREE	She's in all the nine heavens now; how can she hear you? If you open her door, you'll see on her mattress a strange beast with four feet, four hands, two heads and forty claws.
MOONGLOW	Is she with her lover, the Magician? Don't be sinful, hush! The Magician will conduct the liturgy tonight; he'll present the Holy Passions of Buddha in this very square. He must not touch food or wine or woman for three days and nights. He must keep his mind clear and light; he must rise above the clouds and look down from there upon the world crawling in the mud like a worm. He must see it, pity it, then fit it with wings that it may escape.
FRUIT-LADEN LEMON TREE	I saw him I tell you; I saw him with my own eyes. He's full of food and wine, and he smells like a he-goat... He carries a long blue feather like a shepherd's crook and

goads the spirits on.

AZURE BUTTERFLY How did you recognize him? He can become a youth, a
mature man, an old man, whatever he wants to be.
Around his neck he wears the three fundamental faces
and keeps interchanging them — and no one knows his real
face.
Eh, Musician, beat the drum louder! Louder! Louder, till it
breaks!
*(The door of the Tower opens abruptly. An old and a young
man rush out, holding whips. The music stops.)*
It's old Koag, the Master's head-slave,

MOONGLOW And his son, doe-eyed Koag.
(Holds on to Blossoming Cherry-Tree so as not to fall.)
Blossoming Cherry-Tree...

BLOSSOMING *(Looking with longing at young Koag.)*
CHERRY-TREE How pale he is...He's melting away...Buddha licks you like a
lion and eats your face away, my boy...
*(The young man bows, pays homage to Buddha, and prays
silently in deep meditation.)*
He's going to take him away from me...he, Buddha,
Buddha, let me, also, complete all my cycle. Let me kiss,
let me have my fill that I may be liberated...don't take him
from me.
*(Rushes toward the young man, but old Koag cracks his
whip in the air and she stops, terrified.)*

OLD KOAG The Master wants silence. Silence!
(Turns toward young Koag.)
He's kneeling before the Ancestors; he's praying.
He's bathed and adorned himself; he's put on his huge wings,
and he's talking now with the Ancestors.
Cross your hands, musicians; close your mouths, women;
silence!
Like a torrential rain, prayer erodes the soil, softens rocks,
opens furrows and descends into the deep graves;
The white skulls rise, ears grow back again and listen — be
quiet, so that they may hear the words of the Master.

YOUNG KOAG Patience, my sisters; salvation approaches...The sun is setting;
soon the full moon will rise over the fields. Masters and

21

people will merge,
And the liturgy will begin.

BLOSSOMING CHERRY TREE   My brother, doe-eyed Koag, turn your eyes and look at me; stretch out your hand and pity me. Pity me, my boy; give me your lips to quench my thirst.

If you allow me to lie under the earth with my thirst still unquenched, you'll carry a great sin on your head, doe-eyed Koag,

For I will be born again, and you'll be to blame; I'll wander from body to body — and you'll be to blame — that I may find you, kiss you, that I may be liberated. Don't you pity me?

Hasten my liberation!

YOUNG KOAG   My sister, Blossoming Cherry-Tree, lower your eyes, close your lips and listen: Sweet is the evening, compassionate, mute, like the last evening of the world —

Don't contaminate it.

BLOSSOMING CHERRY TREE   Doe-eyed Koag, if this is the last evening of the world, then throw away the whip you're holding. What do you need it for?

Sweeten your lips, perfume your hair, I've opened my arms for you, come!

YOUNG KOAG   O Buddha, stretch out your hand and heal this woman. She's sick, sick; she thinks of nothing else but kisses. Heal her!

(Stoops and chants softly.)

When will this sack, my body, become exhausted,
when will the tears that choke me flow away,
when will this earth sprout wings and be entrusted,
O Buddha, to fly away?

(Turns to Blossoming Cherry-Tree.)

When will you, too, Blossoming Cherry-Tree, sing those words of the holy prostitute Vimala, who donned the saffron robe?

BLOSSOMING CHERRY TREE   When I am old, when my teeth, my breasts and my hair have fallen. My body's still a beast that wants to eat. I stretch out my hand;

22

Have mercy on me, young Koag,

YOUNG KOAG I stretch out my hand, sister, have mercy on me! Yesterday I
cut my hair and laid it at the feet of Buddha; tomorrow I'll
go crawling into the Monastery like a worm, to knit my
cocoon, to work on my wings;
Don't obstruct my salvation.

OLD KOAG Silence! Silence! The Master wants silence. Eh, ladies with
the little white teeth, come near, here's a piece of mastic
to chew on so your mouth will smell sweetly,
So it won't cry out.
*(The two Koags enter the Tower. The four women sit cross-
legged in front of their huts.)*

AZURE BUTTERFLY Let's sit crosslegged on the ground; let's make our eyebrows a
little larger; let's make our curls fall over our ears.
Men grow crazy and scatter-brained when they see us, and
they open their hearts and their purses.

BLOSSOMING *(Passionately.)*
CHERRY-TREE I don't want to! I don't want to!
*(She dishevels her hair, breaks her combs, tears off the
flowers at her breast, takes dirt and smudges her face.)*
I don't want to!
*(Terrifying music suddenly bursts forth. A cry is heard
again, as though from the depths of the earth: "We are lost!")*

ALL THE WOMEN *(Stretching out their arms in fear to Buddha.)*
Help! Help, Buddha!
*(The Magician appears in Li-Li-Foo's doorway, girds himself
slowly, removes the manly mask and becomes an old man
again. He looks at the wailing women and laughs.)*

MAGICIAN *(Pointing to Buddha.)*
Are you asking him for help? Him? Never!

MOONGLOW Don't laugh, can't you hear the Ancestors calling? Don't you
hear them calling from under the earth?

MAGICIAN Close your shell-pearled ears, my ladies, so you won't hear
them. The Ancestors do not speak to women,
They speak to men.

23

BLOSSOMING CHERRY-TREE	But we hear their voices too.
MAGICIAN	Sing, laugh, jingle your bracelets so you won't hear their voices. Men hear and reply; mercy on the world if women begin to reply too. Your daily wage in the world is of another kind, it's sweeter.
	Li-Li-Foo! Laugh, my wagtails, laugh I say! Throw your arms around men, don't listen to the earth!
	Li-Li-Foo!
LI-LI-FOO	(*Appears, and bows.*)
	Command me!
MAGICIAN	Beloved Li-Li-Foo, wash my feet; they have a long way to go tonight. Bring me perfumes; I shall ascend and talk to the spirits. If I smell of human sweat, they'll not come near me.
	Bring me tea to drink, so my mind may waken from its numbness, and may spread out its net from the top of my head down to my heels. There are many fish it will catch tonight, goldfish and dogfish!
	(*Li-Li-Foo bows, enters the hut. She reappears shortly, bringing tea. Then she kneels and washes his feet.*)
	Li-Li-Foo, I like you. You speak only two words, the most feminine of all, the most powerful: "Command me!" Woman needs nothing more.
BLOSSOMING CHERRY-TREE	I bow, monk, and worship the shadow of your head; How do you know the secrets of women so well, monk?
MAGICIAN	In another life, I, too, was a compassionate working woman like you.
	I, too, lugged a mattress on my back from villages to cities, shouting, "Kisses, sweet kisses for sale! Eh, soldiers, merchants, sea captains, peasants, workers, craftsmen, apprentices, I sell kisses — first come, first served!"
	But enough, get ready, you too have much to do tonight, many bodies to drown in honey.
	(*The women scatter and light the lanterns, singing softly.*)
	Night has fallen, I'm hungry. Night has fallen and I'm off to the hunt. Like lions, like rhinoceri, like scorpions, the words of Buddha stalk the forest.
	(*He sniffs the air, holds his nose.*)

Mildew, mould, filth, and flesh that hasn't seen the sun. I sniff
    the air; Wisdom strides over the earth and approaches,
    that coarse nanny with her hanging dugs filled with ink...
A hundred-year-old baby with white eyebrows has clambered
    into her arms, and suckles.
It suckles from above, sucks red, black, blue and purple inks,
    then excretes them and befouls its diapers with letters...
Its nanny crows with pride, changes the baby's diapers. It
    befouls them once more.
It befouls them again and again, leaving behind it *The
Chronicles of Man.*
He's coming, he's coming...here's the old Mandarin, the aged
    baby of Wisdom.
*(The old Mandarin appears, out of breath, holding a huge
notebook under his arm.)*

MANDARIN   I've clambered up, panting, to the village square of insanity,
    for here tonight the impious Magician will break the laws;
    he'll get Necessity drunk, he'll topple the world into chaos
    again;
He'll prod that multi-colored army of insanity, the miracles.
He'll scatter in a moment all I've weighed, arranged and
    locked up in the chests of my mind these many years. All
    that in thousands of years the Ancestors have built with
    hammer, trowel and stone,
This man, with a long feather held aloft, will topple.
He builds the foundation of men's houses with clouds.
Instead of placing a brain in man's head to measure with, to
    weigh all things well, to write with, this elf-brained fool
    places a canary.
But tonight I can't bear it any longer. Here in this wide
    village square of insanity
I've brought with me, under my armpit, *The Chronicles of
Man.*
I shall fight!

MAGICIAN   Oh welcome to our wise Mandarin, the fearless skipper of
    our walnut shell!
Your fleet is a walnut shell and sails into open waters to
    attack.
Your God is a clown who holds paper and pen, sits on the
    pier, watches the ships coming and going, and writes:

"All are mine!"

He hears the cocks crowing, the goats and sheep scrambling
    downhill, the fortresses banging away, and he writes:

"All are mine!"

He's dying of hunger and thirst, so he sits and writes "Bread!"
    and his hunger is appeased. He writes "Wine!" and he
    becomes drunk. He writes "Woman!" and he fathers
    children.

A thousand welcomes to the wise Mandarin with the round,
    buzzing pumpkin on his shoulders! He's ill, poor soul, he's
    ill; he's come out with a large boil, look at it!

A large boil under his armpit!

MANDARIN   This isn't a boil, bird-brain; this is *The Chronicles of Man*.
        Don't laugh! I've lugged it here with me tonight to read it
        to the Master and the people,

To bring the people you want to lead astray back to the right
    path; to cut the wings you want to plant on them tonight;
    to open their eyes so they may see

How man has fought, worked and conquered on earth, how
    he has not walked with wings,

But with feet!

(Coughs, his knees give way and he sits down cross-legged.)

MAGICIAN   *(Helps him to lie on the ground, laughing.)*

His legs aren't strong, his loins are weak, his phallus has
    shrunk to a raisin...Eh, don't laugh, he's the God of
    Wisdom.

MANDARIN   Haven't you any respect for man's labors? Can't you face
        truth without bursting into laughter? You scramble up the
        heads of men

And crow like a rooster.

MAGICIAN   Hold your tongue, Wisdom, your nakedness is showing; the
        head has seven holes — close all of them.

Old man, we've come to the edge of the precipice — jump!

MANDARIN   You talk, you laugh, you hold a cup and drink tea, but your
        hand doesn't tremble, as though you haven't heard...

Haven't you heard? We're lost!

MAGICIAN   I know.

MANDARIN	It's Chiang, Chiang, the cursed general...
MAGICIAN	I know. I know. I know everything!
MANDARIN	Then how can you laugh? My God, where do you get the strength to play?
MAGICIAN	I pretend I don't know, you old codger. I live, eat, sleep, kiss, drink tea, as though I don't know. That is my strength. You see, I can't stop the river Yangtze from descending, I can't change the world I see – death, ugliness, shame, vulgarity, cowardice – I can't; but it's not even necessary. There's only one thing I can change, one thing only, but that is enough.
MANDARIN	What is that?
MAGICIAN	The eye that sees the world. I change the eye, and the world changes – this is the great secret, This is my magic.
MANDARIN	You're the cock of the earth with long feathers and – forgive me – little wisdom. Have you thought to ask me? I'm half blind from studying *The Chronicles of Man*. Here, here. *(Leafs through notebook.)* It's written here in large red letters: "Every time the Yangtze overflows and drowns the world, the Ancestors leap from their graves and shout: 'We are lost! We are lost!' and they weep." Don't laugh, gather your wits together and listen. *(Leafs through and reads:)* "To the glorious dynasty of Song, during the reign of..." The worm's eaten a word here "...of the king... The Yangtze overflowed, broke the dams, drowned four hundred villages and forty large..." The mice have eaten a word here – must be "cities" – "forty large cities. And when the waters receded, they left on the fields a sediment of sand and bones the height of three men..." Do you hear, cock of the earth? Sand and bones! This is what I read, and my heart breaks.
MAGICIAN	*(Laughing.)*

Aren't you ashamed, wise old man? Were you frightened? Haven't you yet learned man's long history? Hasn't your heart turned to stone by now?

MANDARIN   To stone?

MAGICIAN   No, not stone, it crumbles. Nor iron, it rusts, Air!

MANDARIN   Air?

MAGICIAN   *(Laughing.)*
Your heart is still an inkwell. Well then, carry your penknife about, whittle your reed pen, grind your black paint, prepare new ink, fill up your heart and write!
There's a great festival tonight; I'll launch a many-colored kite in the wind, with small bells, lanterns and a tassled tail — my mind!
Prick up your ears, old penpusher; listen to what I say and write, write,
Then take your writings, make them a paper boat and toss it into the river
(Sarcastically.)
To bring the news to future generations.
Ah, ah, if only the waterworms knew how to read, how they would laugh down in the mud, at the bottom of the river!
This is how airbrained man launches his soul; he shapes it into a paper boat, draws God on it as skipper — and then tosses it into the abyss.

MANDARIN   Laugh, laugh, airbrained bird of the wind! But I don't hold a feather, like you; I hold a scale and I weigh; I weigh, and I've found...

MAGICIAN   What have you found?

MANDARIN   That we're lost!

MAGICIAN   The little worm holds a scale and weighs the universe. But the true wise man, O penpusher, doesn't hold a scale; he doesn't hold notebooks; he holds a fan made of peacock feathers
And he fans the air! And then he thinks, without sweating under his armpits, that we're all lost!
Don't shout; look at Buddha and struggle to be like him. Do

28

you know why he laughs?

MANDARIN   No.

MAGICIAN   I know. If I tell you, you'll fall flat on your back with fear.
His laughter goes beyond wisdom, beyond insanity, beyond
boundaries, to the other shore.
Don't ask, you won't be able to bear it. Woe to the man who
wants to undress truth and see her nakedness! He is
blinded, not at all by her beauty, but
By fear!
(A distant roar is heard, as of waters rushing.)

MANDARIN   Listen, listen to the river! It has swelled, it's become angry, it
bellows like a beast. I must leave.

MAGICIAN   Where will you go? All roads are blocked. He's come, the
Uninvited Guest has come. Don't leave, don't degrade
yourself; dip your reed pen into your heart, and write.
What month is it?

MANDARIN   April.

MAGICIAN   What day?

MANDARIN   The 23rd of April.

MAGICIAN   Write! Not on the first pages, my old man; don't you
understand yet? Here, here on the last page, in the
epilogue. Write: "On the 23rd of April, at the festival of
Buddha, when old Chiang was Master, with the blue
dragon on his banner,
When the moon was full, when the heavens opened and
merged with the earth, when it rained and rained and
rained for forty days and forty nights —
It was then the world sank."
Courage old man, don't be afraid, it's nothing...
It's nothing; it's only Death.

MANDARIN   Gather your wings, accursed, rapacious vulture, shut your
mouth — the people are coming.
Pity them, don't pounce upon them!
*(The people arrive, the terrified old men in front. Behind are
the peasants with their tools; further back, the women. The
whores run to their doorsteps and call out to the old men.)*

FRUIT-LADEN LEMON TREE	Eh, old men, we have eternal water here. Look! *(Bares her breasts.)* Two refreshing springs; come and drink!
MOONGLOW	Come and drink, and your hair will turn black again, your mouths will fill with teeth again!
AZURE BUTTERFLY	They can't hear, they're old; they don't thirst, they're old. Their minds are on Buddha.
MAGICIAN	*(To the Mandarin.)* Write! *(Cross-legged, the Mandarin listens and writes. The old men have escaped the whores, encircled the statue of Buddha, and have raised their hands.)*
OLD MEN	*Buddha, with your large earrings, you who keep* *your watch on land and sea, devoid of hope,* *who cast the leaves of mulberry tree to cope* *with human worms that creep,* *Help us, O help! The dead stir in the earth,* *the ground has cracked, and in its deep ravines* *all human skulls have broken through and seem* *to clack their mouths in mirth.* *Buddha, you have a thousand, thousand hands* *of fierce revenge, of hunger, and of rage,* *of sweetness and hope, of silence that from its cage* *of stars falls on our lands,* *and of a great, wild scorn. Pity our nation,* *pity all men now on this holy night* *and over their hearts spread out from a great height* *the hand of your compassion.* *(The men arrive, angry. They carry weapons which they throw with rage to the ground.)*
FIRST MAN	Buddha, Buddha, listen to our sins, take them with you, throw them into oblivion! Look, I turn my heart upside-down at your feet, wash it, and rinse it in the river — and I reject Chiang! I throw down my weapons and reject the son of Chiang. I reject the gods he brought us

From the white demons.

SECOND MAN   I will tear down the factories he built, and the schools, and
              the baths; I will burn the railroads, the telephones, the
              telegraphs, the automobiles. I will fall again before the
              magicians, the exorcists, the astrologers,
              And beg them to sell me the wind, that I may travel; to
              advise me where to build my home so the spirits won't tear
              it down; where to dig my parents' grave so they won't
              come back to haunt me;
              And how to embrace my wife so the demons won't deform
              my seed inside her womb.

THIRD MAN   Buddha, Buddha, look, we throw Chiang's weapons at your
              feet; we don't want to fight and more; we shout:
              "Buddha, put out your hand, stop the Yangtze! Stop the
              Yangtze, Buddha, don't let it drown us!"

MAGICIAN   (Softly, to the Mandarin.)
              Don't write that down, old man; do me the favor and don't
              write it down. They're people, little people, let them shout.
              Don't write it down, don't give the dark powers the right to
              say: "Such souls are better off drowned; the world has been
              cleansed."

MANDARIN   (With fear.)
              Drowned? Drowned? Will we drown?
              (Jumps up.)
              My children!

MAGICIAN   (Pulls him down.)
              Don't shout; a wise man doesn't shout; he knows the loudest
              cry is silence, and he falls silent.

MANDARIN   I will shout! We must run to the hills, climb the trees, save
              ourselves!

MAGICIAN   (Laughs.)
              Save ourselves?
              (The Mandarin is about to reply but the Magician comes and
              puts his hand over his mouth.)
              Shut that mouth of yours, that large, shameless wound.

MANDARIN   May you be cursed! You tear down the boundaries that
              separate man from the demon; you break the sacred chain

31

that holds the brain inside the head of man.
Cut out his tongue Buddha, gouge out his eyes!

MAGICIAN   Don't worry, if Buddha could, he would have gouged out my
eyes long ago, for I have learned his secret. I saw! I saw! I
saw!
We both conquered hope, we conquered fear; I, too, am a
king, like Buddha, a king of Nothingness; and I wear a
royal crown
Of black air!

MEN   Be quiet! Be still! The women open their arms; be still, so
Buddha,
The Great Lover, may hear them.

FIRST WOMAN   Buddha, Buddha, I renounce Mei-Ling, the cursed sister of
Chiang. I renounce Mei-Ling.
I heard nothing; she told me nothing; I never spoke to her!

SECOND WOMAN   I, too, empty my heart before you, grandfather; I wash it
again and again. I will lock myself in my house. I will yoke
myself to the holy submission of daughter, wife and
mother.
A slave, a happy slave, with three sacred, beloved chains —
one is called Father, the other Husband, the third Son.
And I will again cram my foot inside the iron mold.

THIRD WOMAN   A curse on schools and letters; a curse on ships that go to
foreign shores!
A curse on eyes that gaze beyond China!

FIRST WOMAN   Buddha, look, we bring you a bowl of milk, so you may
remember your mother, the milk that suckled you, so you
may take pity on woman.

SECOND WOMAN   Look, we bring you blossoming branches; it's spring, the trees
are swollen, our breasts are swollen; give us time,
grandfather, to kiss, to give birth...

THIRD WOMAN   ...To make our little life immortal.

MAGICIAN   *(To the Mandarin.)*
The trees are swollen, the breasts are swollen, the waters are
swollen.
Poor little souls; they shout, and God is deaf; they cry out to

him, "Lean over and look," but God is blind. They plead, "Put out your hand, help us," but where will He find hands and feet and brains, where will He find a heart to pity mankind. He's
A River, and He descends!

FIRST MAN O Buddha, Buddha, give orders to your slave, Yangtze. He moves slowly; he's blind and deaf; he doesn't understand. Order him not to devour the just and the unjust alike — but only one.
Do you hear his name? Chiang! Chiang! Chiang! Do you hear? Chiang! Let him devour *him*, only *him!*

FIRST WOMAN And his sister, Mei-Ling! And his sister, the accursed Mei-Ling! Don't forget Mei-Ling, grandfather.
She's to blame for what I've done. She moved heaven and earth to take me from my home, from my cares, from my woman's heart!
Buddha, help me!

MAGICIAN (To the Mandarin.)
Wretched men, they don't know...they don't know the great secret...

MANDARIN What great secret?

MAGICIAN Lean over, they must not hear us...Buddha and Yangtze... Gather your little wits together, old man, or they'll escape you...

MANDARIN Buddha and Yangtze?

MAGICIAN Why are you trembling? Do you understand? Do you understand the great secret?
Buddha and the Yangtze are one!

FIRST OLD MAN Eh, Magician, eh, great exorcist! Why do you sit idly by and talk so sweetly during the greatest danger? All year we feed you, give you drink, clothe you, for this very moment.
Perform your magic, gather the wind, pound it with the hammer of your mind, mold it into a sword — and plunge it into Chiang's neck!

MAGICIAN (Weary, softly.)
Wretched little people, let's help them.

	(He rises, stretches out his hand and approaches Buddha. His lips move, as though murmuring an exorcism.)
FIRST OLD MAN	He's casting the great exorcisms, be quiet! He's calling the spirits, cluck, cluck, cluck — like baby chicks!
FIRST MAN	I hear voices, the clashing of arms, the honing of knives, and horses descending from the air. Horses pass through our brows — and our brows cast off sparks like stones.
SECOND OLD MAN	It's the spirits...the spirits! Be quiet!
MAGICIAN	*(Chants the exorcism and claps his hands as though in invitation, then turns toward the old men.)* Let the old men approach. Come close, don't be afraid. Who among you is the eldest? Which of you has seen the most light, the most darkness, has licked the most honey, drunk the most poison? Let him come forward!
FIRST OLD MAN	I'm the one! Today I'm a hundred years old. I was born on the same day, on the same hour as the rebel's father, the old Master. He, Lying on a velvet-strewn bed, on a downy mattress — and I on the manure in his courtyard. But both of us, praise God, were born naked, were born naked snails. We came naked and we'll leave naked; God is just.
MAGICIAN	Give me your knife. *(The old man takes the knife from his belt and gives it to him. The Magician turns to Buddha, mimics, in dance, the act of murder. Everyone watches silently. Suddenly Buddha slightly bows his head. The crowd falls to the ground in frenzy.)*
PEOPLE	A miracle! A miracle! Buddha moved his head! I saw him! I saw him! I heard him, he said "Yes!"
MAGICIAN	*(Sitting cross-legged, smiles.)* Poor, wretched little people...
MANDARIN	Is this your magic, you mocker of gods? I'll write it down,

I'll denounce you to future generations. I'll say: See with what lies the famous Magician Hu-Ming tricked the people...

MAGICIAN   *(Laughing)*
And the gods! The people and the gods! Mark the gods down too, penpusher; don't be afraid!

MANDARIN   Good! Good! Good!
(Writes with passion.)

MAGICIAN   Write, write, penpusher! You think a miracle is some rare bird that descends from the sky, a dragon that rises from Hell and upsets laws.
The true miracle, old man, is the heart of man.

MANDARIN   And Buddha, what of Buddha who moved his head?

MAGICIAN   Eh, what can the poor gods do? They've a secret machine inside them. After all, we put them together,
We put them together, I tell you.
You press a button and they obey. You press lightly, and they say no; you press harder, and they say yes.
The soul grows bitter; it grows bitter on pondering its secrets...
(Beats his chest.)
Smothering, dark, sly, full of paints and rags and gold paper is this workshop...

MUSICIAN   *(Beating the drum wildly.)*
Oh! Oh! Oh!
(Chiang's soldiers arrive panting, ragged, wounded.)

FIRST OLD MAN   Eh, eh, gallant lads, who's chasing you? Wait!

FIRST SOLDIER   Rejoice, brothers, we were conquered! The Ancestors have won, the immortal dead arose, shouted,
And Chiang's army was scattered!

PEOPLE   The miracle! The miracle! The beginning of salvation!

MANDARIN   Don't shout, your work is finished, but mine is just beginning. Come here, you with blood on your chin!
What's happened? How did it happen? When did it happen? Speak clearly, so I can write it down, that you, too, may be saved, you poor wretches.

FIRST SOLDIER	Buddha! It was Buddha! Brothers, listen; listen old man, and write. While we were digging the graves in the Monastery...
SECOND SOLDIER	...And laying bare the sacred bones of the Ancestors to burn them...may Chiang be cursed!
THIRD SOLDIER	...Buddha leaped out of the earth...Buddha, my brothers, and he roared.
PEOPLE	And Chiang? Was Chiang killed?
FIRST SOLDIER	Killed? Are demons ever killed? My tongue is dry, I can't... *(Turns to second soldier.)* Comrade, *you* speak!
SECOND SOLDIER	What can I say? We were killed or crippled; we left our noses, our hands, our ears on the fields.
THIRD SOLDIER	We're lost! We're lost! *(To the whores.)* Open your arms, women, comfort us.
WHORES	Come! Come! Come!
FIRST WOMAN	Where is my son? I don't see him.
SECOND SOLDIER	*(Pointing to the ground)* Down there.
SECOND WOMAN	And my husband? Has anyone seen him? Where can he be?
SECOND SOLDIER	*(Pointing to ground)* Down there.
THIRD WOMAN	My three brothers? My nephews?
THIRD SOLDIER	*(Pointing to ground)* Down there! Down there! Down there! Stop crying, women; this is war, it wants to eat; it's a tiger, it doesn't eat grass, It eats men! *(Forcefully opens the window of the Tower. The crowd huddles together, frightened.)*
PEOPLE	See how forcefully he's opened the tower window! Now the Old Man will appear.

	Quiet!
MANDARIN	Friends, who will bring him the good news, that his soul may sweeten? Tell him that his rebel son was defeated.
PEOPLE	You go... No, no...you! He'll pour boiling water on us again from the battlements.
MAGICIAN	Li-Li-Foo!
LI-LI-FOO	Command me.
MAGICIAN	Go, beloved, knock and shout: "Master, your son Chiang has been defeated!"
LI-LI-FOO	I'm going. *(The people step back, frightened, and watch Li-Li-Foo knocking on the Tower door.)* Master! Master!
MAGICIAN	Louder!
LI-LI-FOO	Master! *(The tower door opens. Li-Li-Foo bows in obeisance.)* Master, your son Chiang has been defeated!
OLD MAN	*(Joyous voice from within)* *Say it again!*
LI-LI-FOO	Master, your son Chiang has been defeated! *(Loud, strong laughter is heard from inside. The music rises joyously as the Old Man appears. He is holding his ivory staff of authority. Behind him Old Koag holds the Old Man's sword across his outstretched arms. As the Old Man crosses the threshold, the two lanterns, as huge as urns, light up on each side of the door. Behind the Old Man follows Young Chiang's wife. The people and the soldiers prostrate themselves.)*
MAGICIAN	*(To the Mandarin.)* Look at his right hand; it drips blood.
MANDARIN	Blood? Blood? I see nothing.
MAGICIAN	Tomorrow, you'll see.

37

(The Old Man remains silent, walking slowly among the prostrated crowd, toward Buddha.)

MANDARIN   *(To the Magician.)*
Li-Liang, the wife of Chiang! Look, her lips smile,
But her eyes are filled with tears.

MAGICIAN   The miracle! This is the miracle of woman. Patience, virtue, sweetness. Her heart breaks...but she smiles. She bows her head...but her body rises to twice its height.
She remains silent...but her silence rips mountains apart. She sees the man she loves dying...but she takes him quietly by the hand,
And leaves with him.

MANDARIN   *(With fear.)*
Who's dying? Who's leaving? What are you ranting about?

PEOPLE   Quiet! Be still! The Nobleman has spread out his arms and prays.

OLD MAN   The Nobleman carries cities and villages on his shoulders and reports to Buddha every night before sleeping.
The Nobleman thinks of farms — seeds, crops, sun, rain —
And the fields turn green...He thinks of sheep, oxen, mares — and fields and mountains bleat, moo and whinny.
He thinks of mankind — and cradles overflow with babies, fireplaces crackle...
All joys, all disasters are his; if the river swells, it's his fault; if the crops rot, it's the Nobleman's fault.
It's my fault that my son, that cursed rebel, raised a hand against you, O Buddha, but I refused to eat or drink or sleep for three days and nights. I cast spells against the dark, invisible forces — and see, I've struck him down!
(Strikes the ground with his staff.)
Ancestors, eh, Ancestors! The ground swells, the dead rise...
(Listens.)
What did you say, grandfather? I can't hear.
(To the people.)
Quiet! Be quiet! The Ancestors are speaking!
Yes, yes, his army has been conquered and scattered, the earth has finally returned to its eternal rounds. Rise out of the earth; the rain has stopped, twilight is falling, no one

38

will see you. Sit to my left and right, the festival is
    beginning. O, both dead and living, there's a great joy, a
    double joy to be celebrated tonight:
The rebel has been defeated, and Buddha has been set free
    into the air!
*(Li-Liang holds back her sobs with difficulty. The Old Man
turns and places his hand tenderly on her shoulder.)*
Li-Liang, beloved wife of my stubborn son...
(Strokes her hair, turns to the crowd.)
Every virtue has two heads: one is all light, the other all
    darkness. War, too, has two faces: the one is called Peace.
    Peace has two faces: the other is called War.
You can see only the one, but I see both, because I am your
    Nobleman. That is the meaning of Nobleman.
(Sighs.)
Life is heavy, the heart two-sided, and I don't know what I
    want...
(Raises his hands to Buddha.)
O Lord, dreadful spirit, dark mouth, you speak and I don't
    hear; my head is a deep cave filled with bears and haunted
    honeycombs.
Untamed powers, gentle powers, inhabit my breast and
    quarrel. Buddha, great thought, make them friends.
I bow, look rapaciously at earth and say: "It's mine!" But
    immediately I quiet down, the honeycomb melts and drips
    inside me — and I divide the earth among men.
I look at man and want to kill him. Why? I don't know. I
    want to. I look at woman, my eyes blur and I want to
    sleep with her. I look at my son,
The blood rises to my eyes, and I shout: "Cursed is the seed
    of man!"
My virtue is a pure-white lily that sprouts out of fertile layers
    of dishonor, then swiftly withers; to the right and left of
    me are the dark forces of madness, and my heart struggles
    to keep its balance as it labors to cross, with fear and
    trembling, the thin bridge of a hair.
Through how many thousands of years, through how many
    thousands of bodies must I still pass, O Lord, to throw off
    my burdens? That my flesh may become spirit — and the
    spirit, air?
O Buddha, you have cast off your burdens, you have emptied

and cleansed your heart, your loins, your liver, your
bladder, your phallus — you have escaped.
Help me to escape too!
That is why I restrain myself from killing. That is why I sit
quietly in my Tower and smoke hashish and sail like a
cloud in the wind...
And that is why each year, today, on your day of festival, I
celebrate your liberation — that you may remember me,
too, Buddha, and liberate me.
I light the huge lanterns, send invitations, slaughter oxen,
distribute wine and hashish generously, that the people
may be happy, and then bring the renowned Magician
from his Monastery
To place wings on Necessity that it may fly!

MAGICIAN   *(To the Mandarin.)*
Look, look at him — how green he's become, how swollen, like
a drum...he's floating on his back over his Tower...
And holding a baby in his arms.

MANDARIN   What did he do? What's happened to him? I can't hear...

MAGICIAN   He's been liberated!

OLD MAN   Raise your eyes and see, Buddha: It's for you I call the
renowned Magician to cast his spells, to turn the wheel, to
bring the future before us,
To give flesh, bones and a voice to man's hopes.
(Claps his hands.)
Eh, Hu-Ming!

MAGICIAN   *(Rises, approaches.)*
I stand before you, Noble One. Command me.

OLD MAN   Life's a heavy burden, Hu-Ming, lighten it; place wings on our
shoulders so we may escape. Take the screwdriver and
unscrew our temples so our minds may widen, so we may
see. Are you ready?

MAGICIAN   I was never more ready, O Noble One, than I am tonight.
Buddha never blew upon me so strongly, never has he been
so weighed down with heavy, intoxicating aromas as he is
tonight. Command me!

OLD MAN   Put us to sleep that we may dream; or if we are sleeping now perhaps, nudge us that we may waken.

Call the spirits, open the five doors of the senses, turn life into
a fairy tale.

(To the two slaves.)

Bring the large censors to dispel the stench of man, that the
spirits may come. And place stools to the right and left of
me for the Ancestors,

And you, beloved Li-Liang, come, sit beside me, to see the
truth and be unburdened. The world is a cloud, Li-Liang,
a little cloud;

Sit down and let's watch it scatter...Don't cry, please,
Li-Liang, mother of my one dear grandson, don't cry, for
if your milk turns sour and my grandson becomes ill, then

The world will end.

MAGICIAN   *(He prays first before Buddha, then before the Nobleman, and
finally before the People. With the long blue feather he holds,
he lightly traces a magic circle.)*

I bring down from the sky and carve on the earth the magic
circle with its twelve signs of the zodiac;

I open an arena where the great athletes, the characters of my
fantasy, may enter and fight.

No one must step inside the holy circle!

*(The people step back and sit down cross-legged. Slaves enter;
they light censors, and perfume the surroundings. The
Magician nails twelve multi-colored figures around the circle,
murmuring.)*

I nail on earth the twelve mystic beasts that the sun, the
Buddha of the sky, carries with him on his rounds: The
Cock, the Hare, the Tiger, the Ape, the Pig, the Snake,
the Ox, the Dragon, the Dog, the Sheep, the Rat, the
Horse.

*(Slaves bring two chairs on which the Old Man and Li-Liang
sit. Stools are placed to the right and left for the Ancestors.
The slaves light the Old Man's pipe. He smokes and closes
his eyes in bliss. A sweet seductive music begins. Slaves bring
the people narghiles, who smoke hashish and also close their
eyes in serenity. For a while nothing is heard but the music.
The Old Man opens his eyes.)*

OLD MAN   Eh, Hu-Ming, hurry, call out to the Hopes, those great nurses

of man. Call out to the Hopes to come, to give us their
breasts.
*(He closes his eyes again. The Magician puts on a round,
yellow mask. Music. Silently the set crumbles, as in a dream.
The scenery changes — the Yangtze encircles all like a ring.
In the center is an island, and in its center a huge, dried-out
tree. Underneath the tree, sitting cross-legged, is Buddha.)*

MAGICIAN   I place the yellow mask of the Spirit on my face. Descend,
horrid bird of prey, and eat.
O creations of earth, water and air, open your eyes, open
your ears — enter into your liberation.

PEOPLE   Oh I see a holy vision, I see old grandfather River descending
quietly, quietly, quietly.
I see an enormous tree rising without leaves or flowers or
fruit.
Brothers, we've anchored on a desert island. It has darkened
and an invisible lion roars in the darkness.
It must be the Spirit; it's not a lion, it must be the Spirit. Be
quiet!

MAGICIAN   Don't shout; Buddha stirs in the darkness; his beloved disciple
Mogalana has fallen at his feet — be quiet so we may hear
what they're saying.

BUDDHA   Mogalana!

MOGALANA   Here I am, Lord, command me!

BUDDHA   Mogalana!

MOGALANA   I'm at your feet, Father, lower your eyes to see me.
I heard your voice as I was descending the stairs of the
monastery, bathed and wrapped in my yellow robe,
holding the beggar-bowl in my hand. And like the eagle
that grabs a lamb and lifts it to the clouds, and then
suddenly plunges down and casts it into its nest,
So did your mind seize me and fling me at your feet, O Lord.
Command me!

BUDDHA   Mogalana, dextrous and compassionate disciple, cast your
eyes along the banks of the river; those are not ants you
see, they are not grasshoppers, they are not waterworms,
They are people! Do you pity them?

42

MOGALANA   Forgive me, Lord, I do pity them; I've not yet been able, with
            great thoughts and constant fasting, to transform my heart
            and turn it into spirit.
            A piece of flesh cries inside my breast, a piece of fat, a piece
            of man. A Cry. Forgive me, O king of air!
            I know well, O Merciless Thought, that all these, all souls
            and bodies, are but phantoms of the mind, of the invisible
            fakir who plays. I said:
            "I shall sit cross-legged and will not rise until I empty out my
            entrails." I said:
            "Reject your eyes, Mogalana, reject your ears, your nose,
            your tongue, your touch, even compassion; reject the
            creations you see; they do not exist. Reject the weeping
            you hear; it does not exist. Reject the perfumes and stench,
            reject water, milk and bread; stretch out your hand and
            choke your heart.
            Reject good and evil, freedom and force, gods and animals;
            they do not exist. Blow upon the lantern of the mind and
            put it out, that the world may be extinguished with it."
            I shouted, I shouted in the desert, but I could not tear down
            my chest, Father.
            And a little while ago as I was descending the stairs of the
            Monastery, I thought of mankind, and my eyes blurred.
            Forgive me, Father, I cannot as yet turn my heart into air.

BUDDHA   Mogalana, steady your flesh, descend, step on earth, appear
            before the people. Raise the Great Seed you hold,
            Mogalana, and cast it.

MOGALANA   What Seed, Father?

BUDDHA   The Buddha. Run, Mogalana, and toss it into the earthen
            furrows of their minds. Help it take root inside them, to
            blossom and bear fruit that their entrails may eat.
            With patience, with sweetness, Mogalana, unleash into their
            minds the final, triumphant march.
            The Liberator has risen, he has risen to help them, and like an
            elephant has turned his head slowly and bid the world
            farewell...
            Open, Mogalana, unleash your mind like the deep river, bring
            down mud, trees, scorpions, gods, ideas — drown the world
            with your brain, Mogalana.

43

Pity the world, Mogalana, uproot the houses of men, set
    them sailing upon the sea of imagination, crush them like
    boats, crush them that they may be saved!
Stretch out your hand to the wind, Mogalana, turn back the
    wheel of earth —
Let Buddha die again.

PEOPLE   It's Mogalana, brothers, the dreadful disciple of Buddha! He
    swings his right hand joyously in wide circles — as though
    he's sowing seed.
I'm afraid. He turns his face upon us slowly.
Like a moon eaten up by darkness, like a moon suddenly
    appearing from behind a mountain and hanging above the
    ravines — look, it's his head!
Open your mouth, Mogalana! I can see mountains in your
    eyes and a large flock of yellow birds,
And a large turtle dove in front with a huge neck leading the
    way.

MOGALANA   He's coming, he's coming; he's descending the mountains,
    passing over the waters as he shines in his saffron robe like
    the sun, and holding his beggar-bowl upside-down;
He doesn't want to eat anymore, he's had his fill of food and
    drink.
He's coming, he's coming; bare your shoulders and worship
    him, the fully Awakened One is coming!
As pure white as the light, he set out with his mind loaded
    with great ideas, his hands loaded with deeds; he crossed
    through forests and mountains, over gods and thoughts; he
    passed through the whole ravine of futility, bidding the
    world farewell slowly, lingeringly.
The Perfect One is looking on all things as though for the
    first time. The Perfect One is looking on all things as
    though for the last time; and see, soon he will arrive
    beneath this tree where he was born,
To lie down, blow on himself and vanish,
In a village, when sickness struck him severely, then Buddha,
    the Lord of life and death, swallowed a piece of meat, like
    a grain of wheat,
But his soul would not accept it, and Death appeared.
Death stood before him and uncovered his own shoulder with
    terror to worship him, but the great athlete raised his

impregnable head encircled with towers and airy
battle-ments, smiled and said to the Mind:
"Take up your sword, don't let anyone approach. Who is this
slave who stands before me and bares his shoulder to
worship me? Don't let him approach.
I want to reach the tree where I was born; with my knees
locked to my chin, holding the much-travelled soles of my
feet in my hands, and rolled up into a round ball the way
I was once crammed into a small womb, I want to return
to that large womb, the earth."
He spoke, and the Mind raised its sword, and Death stepped
back in seven large strides, like a slave, and waited for
Buddha to command.
The Master rose from the ground, and then, without haste,
holding out his empty and yet sated beggar's bowl, he
started out again.
The days and nights moved with him like white and black
birds — and he went on ahead, leading the way.
He bent over the rim of every well and blessed the waters;
and at once the waters relaxed and smiled serenely,
brightly, like the eye of Buddha.
He stood at every lookout and sang in a quiet, calm voice
as though casting magic spells on invisible forces, as
though he were a shepherd calling out to his sheep...
The great Traveler went on and on. Like a king after a great
war, he was returning to his capitol — to Death.
A few days ago, at noon, he stood beneath a silver-branched,
bare fig tree, touched a bough and shook it slowly,
cordially, like the hand of a friend. For a long while he
remained silent, and then, turning to Ananta, his beloved
disciple, he spoke softly and instructed him:
"Beneath this fig tree, Ananta, Temptation slid one noon and
found me. I was hungry, and he held a bowl of rice in his
hand; I was thirsty, and he held a jug of refreshing water
on his shoulder. I hadn't touched a woman in seven years,
and now a girl I had once longed for in dream, when my
soul was still asleep,
Slithered toward me full of desire, her breasts naked.
But I embraced the barren, bone-dry fig tree, and all at once,
Ananta, my hunger was filled, my thirst was quenched, as
though I had eaten a basket of cool, honeyed figs;

I became serene, as though I had embraced a woman, and
Temptation laughed and vanished.
Ananta, the holy fig tree is also laden with visions like
honeyed figs, is laden with deeds. This is my command:
Commemorate this tree.
It, too, stood by my side in battle."
He climbed, he climbed the rocky slopes, he climbed and his
memory increased — at times he thought of a green lizard
that once upon a time used to sit on this rock and sun
itself;
At times he thought of an apple that, once upon a time, hung
from a tall branch at noon and smelled sweetly;
And at times he thought of an idea which, as once he had
climbed up this high mountain peak, plunged down upon
him like an eagle and dug its nails into his head.
He went on and on...Behind him followed the days and the
nights, behind him his disciples, behind him the sky and
the stars — together they all followed the holy traces of his
feet.
And at night, when we had washed our earthen bowls, when
we had washed our hands and mouths, we sat cross-legged
around him — and then with upturned hands that glowed in
the moonlight the Teacher began to speak in the night —
And as he spoke, the honeysuckle blossomed above him, the
sky blossomed above him like a garden, and on earth
insects, dogs and foxes crawled on their bellies behind the
disciples and struck up a dance of their own,
All ears, silence and obedience.
The sweat ran from our armpits, our backs undulated like
waters when sharks glide beneath the surface, our minds
crossed the bridge of hair above the abyss of madness;
And there, with his towering, unsweating brow encircled by
night-butterflies, and glowing like phosphorus in the
darkness;
There, looking straight ahead, neither up at the sky nor down
at the earth but lightly, straight ahead at the height of man,
with slim, sharp fingers, signifying his thought,
There sat Buddha, smiling
But yesterday at dusk, before the stone hut of an old
shepherd, the pale Teacher stopped and said, "I'm tired."
Greatly agitated, the trembling disciples surrounded and

46

supported him...Ananta spread out the lion skin his father, the King, had given him to sleep on,

And Buddha sat on it cross-legged, holding his head high, bright and motionless — like a flame in a blue and windless night...

He turned his gaze to the North, toward the graves of the Ancestors — and there, from the sky's foundations a thick, blue-black cloud appeared, like a crow descending, widening, filling the sky, and approaching...

"It's Death! Death!" But the Master smiled,

Closed his eyes and slept, and seven stars above him like swords kept guard. And the disciples, like honey-bees that encircle the Queen Bee for fear of losing her, clung and clustered about him mournfully,

And I, lying low beside him, watched in the starlight two mystic wheels shining under the soles of his feet.

I watched the sky turning like a wheel, the stars marching all together toward the West, and the North Star, too,

— In which sea-warriors and mule-drivers trust as certain and unmoving —

I watched it also moving toward the West...

I jumped up. Compassion for mankind cut through me deeply as I strode over the sleeping swarm, made the rounds of the villages at midnight, beating on the doors and shouting:

"Come! Come! Come! The Liberator is striding over the earth, he's striding over life, desire and fear — and he's coming to lie down under the holy Tree where he was born, to gather his strength and scatter in the wind!"

Compassion cut through me for the animals also, for the birds and the worms: "Brother beasts, birds, worms," I shouted, "Come, Buddha, the Great Brother, is crossing the forests, the mountains and the waters on his way to die. Come, all of you,

Let's all plunge into his tranquil eye, before it closes!"

A groaning arose from the caves; the earth broke open as the worms appeared; the wind shone like the head of a great leader from the red, yellow and blue feathers descending...

I pitied the gods, too; I raised my arms to the sky and shouted: "Gods, O all-powerful phantoms of man's head, mount the clouds, roll down the rainbow, emerge from under the brainless minds of man, come, come!

Buddha has stretched out his hand, he's thrust back the bolt, he's opened the door of freedom! Latch onto his saffron robe, O gods,
And free yourselves with him!"

PEOPLE　Brothers, Mogalana has stopped speaking. He wipes away his sweat, he's smiling...
He smiles, and a fire licks his lips, rolls down his neck, his chest, his thighs, his feet — and spills over the earth.

BLOSSOMING　*(Bursts into wails.)*
CHERRY TREE　Ah, ah, I didn't know that Buddha lurks in ambush behind the kiss.
O flesh, we are lost! Koag, don't touch me!

YOUNG KOAG　O Blossoming Cherry Tree, I didn't know that the kiss lurks in ambush behind Buddha. Forgive me! Let me touch your lips for a lightning moment before they rot!
Quiet! Quiet! Mogalana is opening his mouth again!

MOGALANA　My brethren, join hands in a hopeless, happy dance around the Holy Tree!
I dance, I clap my hands, I raise my neck and shout. But I don't shout — I sing.
Sing, also, beloved shadows, sing with me.

ALL TOGETHER　*(Singing.)*

Like the gold silkworm, Buddha has moored
On the branch of flowerless silence.
He's eaten all the leaves,
He's eaten all the leaves of the mulberry tree,
He's eaten all the leaves
And turned them into silk.
He doesn't want to eat anymore, or smell, or touch...
His bowels have emptied, his heart has lightened,
He's become all mind and air in the wilderness,
He's become mind and air
And is lightly scattered.

(A heavy sigh is heard. Mogalana stops the song.)

MOGALANA　Who sighed? I feel a human breast resisting...Open up, make way...who sighed?

48

YOUNG MAN	A young man. A free spirit that rises above the abyss of liberation and speaks his mind...

YOUNG MAN A young man. A free spirit that rises above the abyss of
liberation and speaks his mind...
Mogalana, you've never
Loved woman, and life seems to you like smoke that weaves
and unweaves, becomes a city, a cloud, a woman, an idea,
and that climbs and disappears
Over the flaming desert of your mind...
With what right, Mogalana, do you speak and judge? What
can he know about the spirit who has not loved the flesh?
It's your life, Mogalana, that's but shadow and smoke,
because you've loved only ideas that play, intertwining in
air and disappearing — and they have no poisoning voice,
they have no lips for you to kiss,
They have no body for you to grasp tightly in the hour of
the great separation and to feel it in your arms, between
your legs, quivering and warm
As it escapes you.

MOGALANA O human breast, O warm, tortured flesh! This flesh suffers
so much, my brothers, that it turns into spirit...Be silent
that we may hear.

YOUNG MAN Ascetic Mogalana, the earth is real, the spirit is real, the body
of man is real, all flesh and tears, because one woman
became for me, as your own teacher says,
A murderess, a thief, a mother, a mistress, a sister, a wife
and a slave.
She killed me every midnight, Mogalana, when we lay down
together to sleep; she fought, pale and mute; froth rimmed
her clenched teeth as she hissed and entwined her body
around my thighs;
And she snatched whatever these worker's hands of mine
earned, Mogalana, and adorned her lovely head like a
gaudy ornament...
And at other times she took me to her breast and cradled
me and struggled to thrust me inside her flesh, bearing
me like a son...
And at other times again, at dawn, she laughed and shook
me by the shoulders. We'd wake in the high rosy
mountain air; we'd stride joyously, one beside the other,
beating our staffs and our thick wooden clogs on the
stones...

And when I became ill, she stayed awake all night by my
pillow, like a sister, and we talked about our lives as
children, about the rain, about the fields, about our parents.
And my chest breathed quietly, resting beside the small
breast of my sister.
And when, dressed in my rough working clothes I leaped up
and bounded across the threshold, as the dog went
ahead, barking, with raised tail, and the waddling cattle
straggled behind, then the two of us set out for the
fields with our work-tools over our shoulders, harnessed
to the holy day's work,
And I would turn to look at her, and as wheat bread
comforts our entrails, so was I comforted.
And when I returned, as the lanterns were lit, and sat in our
courtyard, Mogalana, she knelt like a slave and with
refreshing water soothed my flaming feet and my knees;
she lit the lamp, Mogalana, above the fireplace, she
moved inside the house like a pure spirit and spread our
humble meal in the yard under the grape arbor...
And I sat, Mogalana, motionless, with half-closed eyelids
and admired her — and I trembled lest it was a dream,
lest my beloved full-bodied woman disappear and scatter
in the wind...
And one morning, barefooted, sheathed in his saffron robe,
stretching out his beggar's bowl, Buddha came and leaned
against my door-post.
My wife went out to the courtyard and was terrified to see a
column of fire swirling at the threshold, passing beyond
the rooftop, setting fire to the neighborhood.
And as she screamed, the fire subsided, and a lion then
stood in my courtyard and looked at my home calmly,
innocently — like its landlord.
Then the beast faded in the glittery air, and my wife was
startled to see a lean figure, eaten away by fasting and
the rain, by the sun and the mind,
Standing silently at the threshold, smiling at her.
Thunderstruck by such magic, my wife fell at your
teacher's feet, weeping and shouting: 'Take me!
Take me, for my house can no longer hold me, words and
deeds can no longer contain me; I'm in despair, take me!
I shall stand by your side, Master, to cool you with a fan

of peacock feathers."

And when I returned at night, Mogalana, it was the first time
  I had not seen my wife running from the threshold to take
  the work-tools from my shoulder and to lighten my load —
  the door of my house was open, the bed empty, the
  hearth darkened...

Then the neighboring women came, told me everything, and
  I fell to the ground weeping, beating my head against
  the stones, cursing your Teacher...A curse,

A curse on the souls who never knew the bitterness, the
  sweetness, the warmth of a woman and yet judge the
  world! A curse on your Teacher!

MOGALANA   Blaspheme, my brother, blaspheme. Hatred, anger, evil
  words and blasphemy are all a sickness in us — spit them
  out, brother, spit them out and be cleansed.

You have reached the summit of pain; liberation begins
  from the summit of pain...My brother, what was your
  wife's name?

YOUNG MAN   Moudita.

MOGALANA   Moudita! My brother, like a wild palm tree in the scorching
  sun, with a long fan of peacock feathers, your wife
  stands erect by the side of the Liberator
And fans and cools Buddha.

YOUNG MAN   I'll grab her by the hair and bring her back home!

MOGALANA   What hair, my brother? You'll see but a phantom fanning
  Buddha...a phantom, and it wears a saffron robe, its hair
  is cut to the roots, its breasts have sagged, its ribs glow
  from holiness and fasting...

It's not a phantom, it's your wife; it's not a crazed bitch,
  it's not a dry bamboo reed, it's not a tumble-down shack
  — it's your wife.

Awaken, brother, awaken, brothers, toss your heads, free
  your bodies from the yoke of life, liberate yourselves from
  the threshing and winnowing, set your cattle free.

The fields of Buddha are made of green air, his yoke is a
  blue shadow, and his ox-goad
Is a tall, compassionate thought.

51

PEOPLE   Mogalana leans on the Holy Tree, and all the branches
          shake and intertwine like arms.
          A shrill cry, like that of a new born babe's rises from the
          roots...
          My knees buckle with fear, brothers. Over our heads,
          desperate, serene, pure saffron, like a tree in autumn,
          Rises the Spirit!

MOGALANA Brothers, don't shout; it's the Holy Tree under whose shade
          the Liberator was born, and the sweet cry of the babe
          you hear is his voice.
          One day at dawn, as the Liberator's mother, Maya, was
          strolling slowly by, pale and heavy with child, she spied
          this Tree in full bloom; and as she stood on tiptoe to cut
          a flowering branch,
          Her body creaked like a Palace that opens its golden doors
          for the King to pass. Then labor pains seized her, and
          before her maids could even support her,
          The infant dropped upon the blossoms like a burning coal.
          The earth glowed, and all the gods leaned from the heavens
          to see the small, plump soles of the baby's feet — and
          they were terrified, for on them, like two roses in full
          bloom, flashed
          The two wheels of the law.

PEOPLE   Ah, each leaf of the tree is a people crying out!
          And the ripe, honeyed fruit at the top is Buddha!
          The whole tree rejoices to its roots because it dreams it
          does not exist.

MUSICIANS *(Playing a wild, fast tune and shouting with terror.)*
          Oh! Oh! Oh!

PEOPLE   Who is this gnome of the forest, full of hair, leaves and soil?
          He holds a goad made of a bull's horn, as behind him,
          bleating, groaning, neighing, meowing, follow the tame
          animals, the wild beasts and the insects.
          Brothers, the air is polluted, it stinks like a he-goat in heat.
          What is this thing, my brothers?
          It's no longer a beast, it's not yet human — it must be one of
          the old, great Grandfathers. Be quiet!

MOGALANA Be quiet! It's the Husband of Earth, that greasy Grandfather
          with his exhausted loins, old man Markalo!

MARKALO   Eh, cunning ascetic with your saffron robe:
              Where are we going? Why are we shouting? Why are we
                  weeping? What is that yellow bird that disrupts the air?
              I feel my shoulders shaken by beasts, I see the hills staggering
                  under the feet of goats, sheep, bears and rabbits in a rush
                  downward —
              They climb up my shoulders and my neck; snails, crabs,
                  scorpions and lizards seek shelter on my huge head; turtles
                  boom on their hollow shells and run; birds begin to wail;
                  that deathbird, the owl, leads the way and all the feathered
                  retinue bursts into threnody and sets out.
              Why? Where? I stretch out my neck, I ask, I shout. "Why?
                  Why? Where are they going? Where?"

MOGALANA   Welcome to lascivious Markalo, welcome to that great, holy
                  martyr, the Scarab, welcome to the dark, heavy loins of
                  the Mind, that shameless He-goat,
              You adorn and arm yourself with feathers and horns, you
                  gasp, you stick out your gossiping tongue, you shout:
                  "Why? Why? Where are we going?"
              Fall down and worship the earth; wait and you shall hear.

PEOPLE   The air and earth have filled the night with horns and wings.
              A huge cicada has hooked on to the Holy Tree and is sawing
                  the wind.
              The great Ascetic has seized him, placed him on his palm and
                  welcomes him.

MOGALANA   Welcome cicada with your translucent steel wings, with three
                  drops of blood on your forehead, with your breast over-
                  brimming with song.
              Hook unto the Tree of Death, pierce it, that it may gush with
                  honey, that you may eat and become satiated. You're not
                  one to live on air and the sky's dew; your insides need
                  solid food
              To sing.
              Pierce the black bark of the Tree, pass through the shield of
                  earth, touch its warm, soft heart, like the heart of man.
              Sing! Hurry, brother, hurry, there's no time! The green
                  locust will arrive at midnight; it will come and we won't
                  know it, because it will resemble the spring leaves of trees;
                  it will come

53

And it will mow down our slim, singing throat, like grass.
If only we had time to sing but one song, one quick tune, to
utter one shrill cry, flying hurriedly from one branch to
another in the night.

PEOPLE   The cicada leaps, buries itself in Mogalana's hair, and begins
to sing.
The great Ascetic bends down and welcomes the animals, the
beasts, the insects.

MOGALANA   Welcome, welcome, welcome to all the Saints!
Under the stones and waters, under the green trees, some of
you hermits, others in couples, others in herds, pummel
The earth, the water, the wind. You eat the dead and the
living, until the mystic elaboration begins, the invisible
changes into the visible, the certain to the uncertain, the
fruit to seed, and you labor to dissolve the breast of earth
entirely
And turn it into Spirit.
Every small insect is a small intact Buddha — a small, intact
Buddha that thrusts into the earth and works at liberation
night and day.

MUSICIANS   (Playing softly, sweetly, joyfully.)
Oooh!...

PEOPLE   I hear voices, I see flames shooting from the sky to the earth.
It's the spirits!
The spirits, the spirits descending with their multi-colored
wings!
A red hawk has clutched the top of my head like a flame! I'm
on fire!

MOGALANA   The mustering of the Bodiless begins. Make room, men and
beasts, the spirits are forming and approaching in herds at
the edge of my eyes.
A thousand times welcome, spirits of the water, of silence, of
the wilderness.
The riverbanks have filled with wooden clogs, stones glitter
from snow-ankled feet, reeds shout like throats — the time
has come again for legends to walk the street like men.
Make way, step back; I've seen the holy birds of the mind,
the parrots, setting fire to the wind with their golden
plumes.

My brothers, I hear that Saripoutta, the greatest disciple of
   all, is plowing the earth with his holy ox-cart, sinking into
   the soil the four heavy, cypress-wood
Wheels of the law.
Saripoutta! Saripoutta! Great rivers separated us, mountains
   and years stood between us. He sowed the Word to the
   right, and I sowed it on the other bank, to the left. I went
   on
Alone and raging, shouting in the wilderness. He, I hear,
   roamed the inhabited world in an ox-cart with women,
   dancers, ascetics and monkeys. He entered large cities,
   pitched his tent at bazaars, and crowds gathered about
   him, laughed at him, goaded him, pelted him with stones.
And he, quiet, smiling and motionless, with the strength of
   his mind alone in the empty light, wound, rewound and
   wound again the youth, the flight, the passions and the
   liberation of Buddha.
At once the cities filled with saffron robes, hearts grew
   calm again, brains behind walled brows blossomed like
   jasmine and scented the air —
And Saripoutta yoked the ox-cart again, marshalled and
   gathered his holy army inside himself again, and all
   together, laughing, playing and whistling, they all set out
   to
sow liberation further still.
And as loyal shepherd boys rove around their flocks, going
   at times to the front with the shepherd like his foster sons,
   at times spreading out to the sides and the tail-end of the
   flock, to keep it together lest it scatter,
So, I hear, do parrots like dogs of the wind follow
   Saripoutta's divine flock, and at times sit on the oxen's
   horns and mock the people, at times sit on Saripoutta's
   right shoulder
And mock the mighty gods.
And as they approach the cities, these intelligent birds scatter,
   scamper up the eaves of the houses, hang from the
   windows, hold onto the women's skirts and shout like
   heralds
Of a caravan great in words, proverbs and fantasies: "Come!
   Come! Come!"

PEOPLE   Oh, red, yellow and green birds fill the air with their wings.

55

The herald has arrived, dressed in parrot feathers; he stands
under the Holy Tree and shouts.
What is he shouting? Quiet, so we can hear!

HERALD   (Dressed like a parrot.)
Come! Come! Come! Saripoutta has arrived in his ox-cart,
    Saripoutta is here with his miracle-working fakirs,
Saripoutta has arrived with his trained gods and monkeys,
    with a great variety of bodies and demons!
Wash your feet, rub your beards and your hair with heavy
    aromas, paint your fists and the soles of your feet, raise
    your hands high — the sun has set, the moon rises, the mind
    rises from skulls like the moon,
Saripoutta with his holy ox-cart stands before you.

PEOPLE   Oh, is this a spirit, a man, a bird, or a gigantic yellow
    feather that leaps from the steering wheel of the ox-cart and
    touches the ground?
It's not a bird, it's not a feather, it's not a spirit, it's not a
    man. It's Saripoutta,
Saripoutta, brothers, who treads on earth and opens his arms.
The two great disciples embrace. They touch cheek with
    cheek, motionless, speechless... They cry and laugh and
    caress each other, slowly, emotionally,
Like wild doves in a weed-grown monastery courtyard.
Quiet! The Two Great Masters are speaking!

MOGALANA   Brother, there's nothing left of you for me to clutch. See how
    the Great Thought has eaten up all your flesh! Only your
    throat remains to laugh with.
Only your brow stands like a tower over a vanished city.

SARIPOUTTA   You hold the Spirit firmly, brother, lest it eat you. I marvel
    at you, touch your shoulders, and my hands are contented
    as though I had lain them
On the shiny rumps of a bull.
I lean my head on your chest — and I hear a sea beating and
    laboring, I hear people shouting, rivers descending,
The Spirit blowing over cities like a great fire, like a great
    sickness, destroying streets. A thousand times welcome!

MOGALANA   My joy is so sweet and holy at seeing you, my brother, that I
    can't conquer it.

56

Ah, what is this earth, with what harmonious entanglement
   do shadows skillfully embrace and nestle in the heart of
   man
And no longer want to leave the body.
I hold you like a holy toy at dawn, filled with light and
   meaning.

PEOPLE   These two famous disciples seem to me like two great rivers
   that have watered villages and cities, that have raised
   numberless generations of men, numberless generations of
   fishes, numberless generations of reeds, and now suddenly,
   at the bend of an enormous mountain,
They merge, foam, dance and become one.

MOGALANA   Just as the beetle carries the yellow pollen of flowers on his
   feet and wings, on his horns and belly, and goes leaping
   across the gardens,
So do you, brother, pass by in your saffron robe, mounting
   the earth with your ox-cart.
You pity the people; they battle, but are unable to see great
   thoughts in the air — and you pity them and give a simple
   and gaudy form to the invisible. Your mind gives birth and
   then is dismembered and sits on the temples and breasts of
   men.
Animals talk, waters shout, fakirs scramble up the air on
   invisible ladders, ideas dance like women, gods climb down
   chewing like monkeys.
Men see, hear, smell, taste and touch the great theories.
Your holy ox-cart seems to me like an animal, brother, the
   way it groans and climbs the mountains at noonday;
And at night — the way it shines with multi-colored lighted
   lanterns surrounding it and walks slowly through the
   sleeping plain —
It seems to me like a bright constellation on the dark throat of
   night.

SARIPOUTTA   It's not an animal, my brother, it's not a constellation on the
   dark throat of night. It's Buddha, my brother Mogalana;
   this ox-cart is Buddha, armored well with cypress wood,
   irons and sheepskins.
And his head is filled with dancers, ascetics and monkeys.
It's Buddha, and he's coming — the young man with the black,

curly hair and the golden sandals.

It's Buddha, and he's coming — the man who has struggled
under the fruitless Tree and after seven years of agony and
struggle has grasped salvation in his fist like a rounded
fruit.

It's Buddha — the old man who has travelled forty years,
burning, enlightening, liberating the world.

It's Buddha, and he's coming like a black swan, serene and
silent, to watch with a lingering glance

His own image dying.

*(The sad song of Blossoming Cherry Tree is heard
softly.)*

BLOSSOMING   *When will this sack, my body, become exhausted,*
CHERRY TREE   *when will the tears that choke me flow away,*
    when will this earth sprout wings and be entrusted,
    o Buddha, to fly away?

*(Slowly the vision dims; the crowd sinks into ecstasy. All
that can be seen is a dark, unmoving lake with a drifting
black swan. Slowly, slowly, this, too, disappears. Music...
but it stops abruptly. Young Chiang appears, angry, dressed
in khaki and holding a whip. A blood-spattered herald
follows him. Chiang watches the people smoking hashish in a
narcotic haze, and he shouts.)*

CHIANG   O heart, disdainful lady, be silent! Be silent, don't become
angry.

How many times have I not taken you for a stroll and showed
you mankind? You followed me like a tiger and wanted to
pounce upon the passersby. "I don't want them, I don't
want them," you shouted, "I don't want them!"

Heart, don't shout; this is what people are, erect swine,
red-assed monkeys, premature babies, cowards, sickly
gods — pity them. Don't ask them for virtue, justice,
nobility — they have none.

It's better so, it's better! If they did, what need would the
world have of you, Chiang?

If they did, what reason would you have to squander your
life, Chiang, like a nobleman?

Don't ask for gods as co-workers, my heart; they don't exist.
It's better so! When they did exist, the gods never deigned

58

to take us as co-workers; they wanted us for slaves.
They thundered, flashed, flooded the rivers, scattered disease,
   killed masses of women and children just like that, without
   reason, to take the wind out of our sails.
Gods, farewell! Have a good trip! I, man, take on the
   responsibility of the world and sit on the emptied throne.
If I win? Then all the glory is mine. If I lose? Then all the
   blame is mine — that's what it means to be a nobleman.
I become disgusted, get angry, kill and hate because I love
   more deeply than others.
I sacrifice my joy, the sweet comforts of my home, my life,
   all for these blockheads. Why? Who has entrusted you, my
   heart, with the entire nation? Who gave you such pride or
   such humility?
Don't ask; forge on, but hold on tightly to the leveling
   instrument of holy mania.
Chiang, don't forget that you're a man — a man. That is the
   great title of your nobility.
I'm not God and thus unable to progress further on; I'm a
   man — and find myself on a journey.
The climb is steep, Chiang, it requires patience, care and
   stubbornness; it requires love.
Be angry, Chiang, but hold back your anger; be scornful
   Chiang, but hold back your scorn; love, Chiang, but let no
   one know it.
Don't forget, Chiang: a nobleman is not one who has
   conquered the great passions and extinguished them — that
   is a saint or a wise man. Nor is he one conquered by
   passions — that is but a brute. A nobleman is one who has
   many passions and can subdue them, and he who can
   subdue them for a great Purpose is a king.
The time has come for me to subdue my passions for the great
   Purpose. The time has come for me to take authority.
(To his escort.)
The conch!
(His escort blows on the conch. At once the whole vision
dissolves, the Magician removes his yellow mask, the first set
re-appears; the crowd, as though awakening from a deep
sleep, shake themselves and rub their eyes.)

PEOPLE   O Buddha, don't leave!

Buddha, take us with you, don't go!
He's gone!

MANDARIN *(Jumps up, frightened.)*
It's Chiang!

PEOPLE *(With fear.)*
It's Chiang! Chiang!
(Chiang approaches his old father.)

MANDARIN Now the two beasts — father and son — will come to blows. I'll
get closer to speak to him...I'm old, I know much, it's my
duty!

CHIANG *(To his escort who is blowing the conch.)*
Stop!

MANDARIN *(Falling at Chiang's feet.)*
Don't raise the whip, Chiang; these are your people! Don't
bite your lips in anger; it is your old father!
He once tore out a fistful of his body and molded you; he
took up the end of the chain, joined you to the Ancestors —
and made you immortal.
Bow and worship him, Chiang!

CHIANG *(Pushing back the Mandarin with disdain.)*
Go!

MANDARIN Respect the great Laws, Chiang, that keep the world from
falling into chaos!

CHIANG I respect the great Laws and trample on the small; I am thirty-
five years old, on the peak of my ascent! My turn has
come.

OLD MAN *(Still dazed from the vision.)*
Who is it? Throw him out! Who blew on the holy vision and
extinguished it?

CHIANG I did!

LI-LIANG Master, I bow and worship your power. Welcome.

CHIANG Mother of my son, stand up. Don't bow down before me;
you're not a slave, you're my wife. You bore a son, and
may raise your head before kings.

60

LI-LIANG   Your slave in life and death, my Lord; I want no other glory.

OLD MAN   Who is it? I hear a voice, I see no one; I see Buddha in the air
still, like golden flower-dust...
Who are you, great denier? Who let out a shrill cry and
shouted: "No!"?

CHIANG   *(Taking a step forward.)*
It's your son, father!

OLD MAN   I hear, I tell you, but I can't see; the eyes of my flesh have
been blinded, praise God! The eyes of my soul have
opened, praise God!
The entire air is a silken saffron flag on which Buddha is
embroidered.
Who are you?
(He rises, looks, then steps back in horror.)
You! You! Ah, the flag is torn, the stones have appeared
again, and the soil, and the filthy deeds of man!
O Ancestors,
(He looks at the empty stools at right and left.)
O Ancestors, alas, this is my son!

LI-LIANG   *(Opening her arms pleadingly to Chiang.)*
Master, husband, I beg of you, don't be angry; he's the last
god of your race, untouched, sacred, full of secret
powers —
He's your father.
One of his feet is still on earth, the other is already climbing
up the iconostasis where the Ancestors lie enthroned...Bow
down and worship him!

CHIANG   I know my duty to my parents; I know my duty to my
parents; I know how far reverence must go; don't be afraid,
Li-Liang, I beg of you, go suckle your son; that is your duty;
we must exchange manly words here.

MANDARIN   Oh, he's reaching out his hand for his father; the world is
crumbling!

OLD MAN   *(Stepping back angrily.)*
Why are you reaching out for me? What do you want of me?

CHIANG   The thing you hold — the staff of authority.

MUSICIANS   Ooh!
             (For a while, wild, muffled music.)

OLD MAN   *(Raising his staff high.)*
             I've not died yet.

CHIANG   You have died, father, you have died. Your eyes are still
                 open, your mouth still emits a sound, you tread stones and
                 the stones still move,
             But your soul has died, old Chiang, it has died!

OLD MAN   I have not died! I have not died! I live and I rule!

CHIANG   You're dead, father, you're dead, your day's work is done, it's
                 my turn now! Both your feet are already in the grave. I'm
                 still whole on the earth, my turn has come. Every
                 generation has its own duty — the one to leave, the other to
                 rule, the third to wait.
             It's my turn to rule.

OLD MAN   Put down your hands! I will not surrender; I call on the
                 Ancestors: Help!

CHIANG   I call on the Descendants: Drive him away!

OLD MAN   I will not leave!

CHIANG   I can't talk with old men; their veins are blocked and won't let
                 the blood pass through; the ditches of their brains are
                 blocked and won't let the soul pass through; life has turned
                 to gangrene in their thighs and their brains.
             Forgive me, old Chiang, I want power and power wants me;
                 don't stand in my way!
             *(Old Koag advances, bows, goes to give the sword to the Old
             Man. With a blow, Chiang throws him down, but
             immediately regrets it.)*
             I didn't mean to do that, old Koag, forgive me...
             (To his escort.)
             Take him away.

OLD MAN   Ancestors, help me!

CHIANG   *(Grabs the sword, breaks it, and holds out the sheath to the
             Old Man.)*
             Your soul has died, old Chiang, and the sheath is empty;

take it.

Go into the Tower, wash and comb your hair, perfume it, then call on the Ancestors. Open your ledgers and give an accounting; tomorrow at dawn, with the new sun, I shall seize power.

OLD MAN   *(Beating his staff on the ground.)*
Ancestors, help!

CHIANG   *(Laughing sarcastically.)*
Shout, shout, they can't hear! Just now at Buddha's Monastery I threw them out of their graves, I heaped their bones, set them on fire, and scattered their ashes over the earth — there is no better fertilizer for good crops.
In the same way — so be it! — may our worthy sons scatter us, when the hour comes.

MANDARIN   We're lost! Life no longer has a foundation. How can it survive? The world is falling apart!
(The Old Man raises his staff, froths at the mouth, and his words become confused.)

LI-LIANG   *(Falling at the feet of the Old Man.)*
Father, set aside your rage; you are a nobleman.

OLD MAN   Traitor! You've sold your soul to the White Demons; you've broken the holy chain of the Ancestors!
You dress, you eat, you laugh, you talk, you fight like the Westerners, rebel!
(Turns to Young Koag.)
The whip!
(To Buddha)
He's reached the summit of evil. Buddha, give him a push, crush him.
(To Young Koag.)
The whip!

MANDARIN   Master, give me permission to speak.
(Shows his book.)
It's written here: "When the people raise their heads, the world is lost." Harmony! Harmony!

MAGICIAN   Don't come between them, penpusher! Let the beasts fight; that's why God gave them claws, teeth, horns — to fight with.

Chiang, you're off, leaping toward the precipice — and there's nothing I can do for you. What help can one give a great soul? None! None!

It asks for the impossible, as it should. It leaps to its destruction, as it should — that is the meaning of a great soul, Chiang.

You've reached the edge of the precipice: Jump!

CHIANG   I overthrow old Chiang and seize power!

I abolish the worship of Ancestors and erect the worship of Descendants. We shall no longer look back, we shall look forward.

I sense one country within me, better than this country outside me, and I don't want to die before my eyes see people, plains, and rivers as I want them.

(He turns to the people.)

Brothers, brothers, come with me! Follow me, I bring you salvation.

PEOPLE   We don't want to be saved, we don't! Saved from what? From slavery, from injustice, from hunger? We're used to them now, we've adjusted, let us alone!

Let us alone! We were born to plow the earth, that noblemen might eat; to plow woman, that the Master's slaves might multiply.

Freedom? Salvation? Heroism? These are anxieties for noblemen. We're not noblemen, let us alone!

Let us alone! We bow and worship the great powers — the rain, the wind, the river, the caterpillar that eats our cabbage, the worm that eats our apples, the Master who eats them all. We want no more cares; let us alone!

Let us alone! Why do you want to disturb the order? Everything is fine; hunger, poverty, injustice, filth, and even the Master's whip, the shivering cold of winter and the heat of summer —

Everything's fine, everything, everything! Don't disturb the order; let us alone!

CHIANG   I will not let you alone!

(Slowly.)

My heart, do not forget, we've reached an agreement: you

64

              must not break!

MANDARIN   Eh, Chiang, listen to me, to this old man also. You'll be
           destroyed, Chiang, because you're concerned about saving
           others; such audacity belongs only to the gods...
           What are we? Men, little people, each man out for himself!

OLD MAN   *(Pacing back and forth in a fury, shouting.)*
           The whip! The whip!
           (Young Koag appears from the tower with a whip.)
           Bring it here!

LI-LIANG   *(Embracing the Old Man.)*
           Don't father! Think of Buddha! Here before us still, his holy
           cart shakes in the wind...Can't you see the black swan,
           father?

OLD MAN   I see nothing; don't hold me back. Buddha was an evening
           cloud filled with air. It has scattered! This one is flesh and
           bones; I will strike him!

LI-LIANG   You're a nobleman...

OLD MAN   I'm a nobleman; it's my duty to strike.

MAGICIAN   Strike!

OLD MAN   *(Raises his whip in fury.)*
           My curse upon you!
           *(Overcome with rage, he rushes toward Chiang, like a bull.
           Chiang draws back; the Old Man loses his balance, rolls on
           the ground, tears his clothing as foam rims his mouth.
           Frightened, the people surround him.)*

PEOPLE   The evil has hit him again!
           The great sickness of his clan has struck him.
           He's foaming at the mouth; his eyes have turned white!

CHIANG   Cover him!

LI-LIANG   *(Covers the Old Man with her shawl; turns to the crowd.)*
           For shame, don't look!
           (To the Magician.)
           Beloved and skillful exorcist, I beg of you: Drive off the evil
           spirits, that his soul may return to its familiar body.

MAGICIAN   My Noble Lady, bring him your son, I have no other spell;

bring him his only grandchild — he will look at it and his soul will return to entwine itself once more with its beloved flesh.

LI-LIANG   I shall go.
(Leaves hurriedly toward the Tower.)

MAGICIAN   The crowd is right in fearing for its salvation; the old man is right in resisting; you, too, are right to be in a hurry, Chiang; that is your duty.
The better you carry out your duty, the nearer you approach your destruction; that's the way it is. If you were not so great a soul, if you were a bit cowardly, if you forgot, or if you failed a little — what happiness!
But you do not condescend, great soul! I like you!

CHIANG   Sly monk, you too, are like your master, Buddha. You look at the world and burst into laughter.

PEOPLE   Silence...silence...Li-Liang is bringing her son.

CHIANG   Don't hurry, Li-Liang, my soul wants to leave, too — but this child holds it back. Wait a moment, I want to see his face...
(Looks at his son and his face lights up for a moment.)
Thank you, Li-Liang, go now...
(Pushes her toward the Old Man. To himself:)
This is my son; this is the world to come, the real, certain god of earth — I bow and worship his grace!

LI-LIANG   *(Kneeling.)*
Father...father...open your eyes, it's your grandson!

OLD MAN   *(Opens his eyes, lets out a happy cry.)*
Ah!

LI-LIANG   Take him in your arms, father...

OLD MAN   No, my breath can still poison; take him!
(Sits up and covers his face with his hands.)
O, Ancestors, forgive me; for a moment I lost the balance of nobility.
Hu-Ming, Buddha's words have gone for nothing...His cart has vanished, the great disciples have vanished, the black swan has flown away...To my shame, I could not rein in

66

my fury.

(To his son.)

Eh, Chiang, Chiang, help me put my heart in order, say a
good word to bring me peace.

Why do you look at me in silence? You betrayed the
Ancestors! You are no longer Chinese, you've not yet
become a Westerner; you're in the middle, like a mule!

Your panoply will not be hung,

No, it will not be hung beside the panoplies of the Ancestors.

I cursed you with every bone in my body, Chiang!

CHIANG   I accept it, old Chiang; may my son, one day, too, leave me
so far behind and frighten me so that I, too, may give him
my curse.

There is no better blessing for the young; thank you, father.

OLD MAN   Out of my sight! I cast you from our race; I cast you from
our graves, from my home's hearth, from my courtyard's
well, from the ancient threshold of our ancestors. Go!

CHIANG   I'm not a dog to be shouted at and slink away; I'm not a bird
to fly dangling in the air;

I'm a tree, and my roots plunge deep into the yellow mud of
China. I will not go!

OLD MAN   You made a son; I have my grandson; I don't need you.

(He holds his grandchild up to the full moon.)

O round moon, sweet sun of night, thrice-noble youth of the
sky,

Spread out your lily hands, caress my grandchild, fill his
palms with silver; his entrails are overflowing with milk.
This is my grandson!

I place the whole world on one side of the scale, the five seas,
the seven shores, the nine strata of the wind, and on the
other, this small piece of flesh.

I have no other hope in the world.

*(Wild, frightened music; the First Sentry enters, muddy from
head to toe.)*

PEOPLE   The First Sentry of the river! He must be bringing terrible
news. Look, he's all muddy!

His lips tremble, he cannot speak!

He speaks; be quiet!

FIRST SENTRY	Master, brothers...O my general, Chiang!
OLD MAN	Don't speak to him! My curse spilled over his body like leprosy; don't speak to him! *(Raises the staff of authority.)* I am the master and the father of my people. I will account to the Ancestors when I descend into the ground; I am the lips, the ears, the brain of the land. Speak to *me!* Raise your eyes Sentry, look at me; I grant you permission.
FIRST SENTRY	Master...Master...
OLD MAN	What are those agitated waters that rise and fall in your eyes?
FIRST SENTRY	It's the river Yangtze, the dreadful Blue River, Master.
OLD MAN	It's the mighty god of the land; I bow and worship to its grace. Speak!
FIRST SENTRY	I'm choking, I can't speak, I'm afraid. Swear that you'll not raise your whip, Master.
OLD MAN	Speak!
FIRST SENTRY	You will not swear?
OLD MAN	I will not swear; speak!
FIRST SENTRY	Three days and three nights, Master, I didn't close my eyes. Bent over my lookout, I gazed down Where the Westerners further on were completing the third, the final dam to hold back our river, our mighty god, the Yangtze. Their cursed machines glistened, groaned and filled the air with smoke. The Yangtze was silent; it flowed, peacefully, thickly, deeply, and it didn't speak. It's a god, you see, and it was patient. It restrained its strength and did not condescend to pay the slightest attention to men. But I, who understand its nature, looked at it and trembled... Don't drown us, my God, I murmured as I trembled, don't drown us, my God...
OLD MAN	You talk too much; lean against the wall or you'll fall; be brief.
FIRST SENTRY	Let me speak, Master, let me unburden myself...I'm afraid and I can't gather my wits together to know what I should say

and what I should not...

And suddenly there were songs and joyous rifle shots until the tents of the Westerners shook. I turned and looked. They had finished their task; they had harnessed the river with enormous breakwaters; they were laughing, dancing and making merry.

I leaned over and what did I see? The god shuddered, his back reddened, laughter broke out far and wide, and for thousands of yards, to the left and the right, the earth began to crack...I didn't think of anything dreadful...It must be playing, I said...

But the next day, at dawn, my lookout began to shake...I leaned down but saw darkness only. I could see nothing, but I heard a terrible roar; the waters were not laughing any longer; they were groaning, threatening, beating against the barriers, knocking down plane-trees, rising higher and higher...

And on the third day...the third day...

OLD MAN   Speak! Go on! I'm glad! Good health to you, Almighty Dragon with your blue fish-scales!

The Westerners thought they could harness you, and this one here brought them, with their impious, grimy machines that contaminate the pure air of China.

O Almighty Dragon with your blue fish-scales, your green eyes, your yellow teeth, Great Ancestor!

(To Chiang.)

Why are you laughing?

CHIANG   We chained your dragon, the Yangtze, with stones, cement and iron — three chains. It, too, will enter the service of man.

OLD MAN   *(Frightened at the blaspheming, he covers his ears.)*

I heard nothing! O Yangtze, you hear everything — and I surrender him to you!

PEOPLE   O Yangtze, long-bearded grandfather, you bring us life — rice, corn, watermelon, cotton, sugar cane; you bring us fishes, eels, barges and boats...

You bring us the great shadows — the sun, the moon, the birds, the clouds — and take them out to sea...

Enough! Enough! Don't bring us death, too!

OLD MAN
Don't start the dirges! God detests the man who weeps.
(To the Sentry.)
Speak! Your mouth is still full.

FIRST SENTRY
The third day, Master...on the third day the waters turned green, red, black; they knocked down the plane trees, they foamed and laughed, until my lookout became a boat floating on the waters...
Master, don't raise your whip; it's not my fault.

OLD MAN
Speak! Speak!

FIRST SENTRY
On the third day the Westerners laid out huge tables on the high terraces of the temple, slaughtered the sacred geese from the Yangtze Monastery, removed the taps from its wine-barrels — and began to eat and drink.
The Westerners ate and drank, vomited and ate again; they threw the bones, the peelings, the wine dregs into the river and laughed raucously. "Here, here," they shouted to the river: "eat!"
And the Old God accepted all and swallowed all; but suddenly, as the Westerners rose from their tables, unbuttoned, bare-headed and befuddled with drink,
The cataracts of the sky opened, Master, the cataclysm burst, Master, the waters swelled, rose and fell, and the peasants rushed between the river and the first barrier, loaded themselves with food, tools, clothing, babies — and ran off! They picked up their tubs, their cradles, their gods — and they ran off!
It's raining, it's raining on your villages, Master, and the people and the houses are dissolving, they're turning back into mud again...

OLD MAN
O Yangtze, do not drown my people. Stop to distinguish between them. The Westerners are the White Demons — drown *them!* These yellow bodies here are my people, Yangtze, they are your children, Yangtze, mud of your mud, have mercy!

FIRST SENTRY
Mothers gathered their babies to their breasts, girls opened their hope-chests and said goodbye to their dowries,

	And your daughter, Master, your daughter Mei-Ling...
OLD MAN	My daughter Mei-Ling? *(To Chiang.)* May you be cursed! You went to widen a woman's heart, but you broke it!
CHIANG	*(Grasps the Sentry's shoulder.)* Speak! My sister Mei-Ling? Come closer!
OLD MAN	Speak to *me!* My daughter Mei-Ling?
FIRST SENTRY	She won't eat, she won't drink, she won't sleep, Master...She runs from village to village ringing the bells, shouting...
OLD MAN	What is she shouting? Why did you stop? *(Laughs bitterly.)* You think I can't bear it? Speak, I can bear it! What is she shouting?
FIRST SENTRY	Just what her brother Chiang is shouting, Master..."Stones, cement and iron," she shouts, "don't be afraid! Stones, cement and iron" — and she mocks the almighty god, the Yangtze...
MUSICIANS	*(They play in fear, then as they see the peasants arriving, they shout:)* Oh! Oh! Oh! *(The peasants arrive soaked, drenched with mud, carrying bundles and babies. They wail as they look, terrified, behind them.)*
PEASANTS	It's coming! It's coming! It's coming!
PEOPLE	Who! Who!
PEASANTS	The Yangtze. It broke the first barrier and sank our villages... A curse on whoever's to blame! A curse on whoever's to blame! I dug, I planted, I watered; I waited. I waited for the sun, the rain, the weather — the three great noblemen. I waited, I trusted. I knew That this is the grindstone: plowing, planting, waiting...I said: the harvest will come. But the river came and swept everything away! A curse on whoever's to blame!

71

OLD MAN   Who's to blame? Raise your eyes, look at me!

PEASANTS   A curse on whoever's to blame!

MAGICIAN   Peasants, people, courage! You will see even more terrible
things; this is only the beginning; but later
You'll see killings, drownings, love-making, you will see gods
weeping — courage, my children!
You'll see the Yangtze itself opening this very door and entering.
Steel your hearts to bear it; say secretly to yourselves: "It's
only a game, my heart, only a game, don't be afraid."
Do you hear? That's what you must say, that's the secret of
enduring life; to face death, sickness, injustice, fear, and to
say: "It's a game, my heart, a game, don't be afraid."

MANDARIN   Accursed tongue, stop speaking! Chiang has grown pale, he's
pushing through the crowd, seeking his sister Mei-Ling.

CHIANG   *(Runs, opens his arms)*
Mei-Ling!
*(The sky becomes cloudy; the moon is hidden; thunder is
heard from afar; blue lightning tears through the air; the
storm approaches. Mei-Ling, drenched, gasping, falls into the
arms of her brother. Chiang caresses her tenderly.)*
Sister, comrade who stood beside me, Mei-Ling.
(Music, all passion and gentleness.)

MAGICIAN   *(Looking insatiably at Mei-Ling, to the Mandarin.)*
What are the white candles doing here? Why is she dressed
like a bride?

MANDARIN   You can't mingle with the spirits and go unpunished...You're
dreaming, or you're seeing things — what candles?

MAGICIAN   What are the white candles doing here? Don't you see them?
Why is she dressed like a bride?
*(Brother and sister gaze at and caress each other with
inexpressible love.)*

MEI-LING   Chiang, Chiang, my brother!

CHIANG   Hold your head high, Mei-Ling...

MEI-LING   Chiang, my brother, the first barrier has broken...
(Silence.)
They're gone, my brother, the villages that followed our

72

lead are drowned...They no longer drank or smoked
hashish, or gambled...
For years they struggled, brother, for years, and now...in
one night...

CHIANG   The people around us are watching; raise your head high, my
sister.

OLD MAN   Mei-Ling!

MEI-LING   The Old Man is calling me — I don't want to speak to him, I
don't!

CHIANG   Go to him, Mei-Ling, he's old, don't mind him; he's old, and
behind the times;
Speak softly to him as we speak to the dead.

OLD MAN   Mei-Ling!
(Mei-Ling approaches with restrained anger.)
I'm listening.

MEI-LING   I've nothing to say.

OLD MAN   *(Ironically.)*
You've nothing to say?

MEI-LING   I have. The Yangtze has broken the first dam, it's drowned
the villages, it's risen to a man's height above the
rooftops — you've got what you wanted.

OLD MAN   *(Turns to his daughter-in-law.)*
I'm falling apart inside, Li-Liang.

LI-LIANG   *(Holds him in her arms so he will not fall.)*
Father...

OLD MAN   Ah!...The God of China has stirred and crushed the
Westerners!
(To Mei-Ling.)
Yes, that's what I wanted, that! I cried out, and my God
heard me!

PEOPLE   Master, save us! You are our Nobleman; it's your duty. You
always had three bowls, three cups, three beds, but also
three swords — a triple portion of joy, but also a triple
portion of danger.
Nobleman, find out who's to blame and strike him; strike him

	and save your people.
OLD MAN	Don't shout — put your hands down!
PEASANTS	Strike him, whoever he is, and save your people; that is the meaning of Master!
	Listen, God thunders, he speaks; listen to him!
OLD MAN	My entrails are filled with drowning villages, and I am myself a sinking province.
	(Turns to a mother who opens her mouth to speak.)
	Silence, shut your mouth, that shameless wound! You speak your pain and are relieved, but I must take it all within me.
	You shed tears and empty your hearts, but I am a nobleman, and I can't weep...I mustn't! The tears accumulate inside me, they can't open a channel to escape — I'm drowning!
	(Paces back and forth groaning; muffled music is heard. Suddenly he leaps toward his son.)
	You're to blame! You! You! You! You brought these new shameful gods here, and our old gods have grown angry; they've armed themselves and are descending!
	(Raises his whip, strikes Chiang on the face furiously.)
	May you be cursed!
MAGICIAN	*(Joyfully.)*
	Ah! The wheel spins. Fate rolls up her sleeves to rush into the fray!
PEOPLE	*(With dread.)*
	He struck his son!
	He struck his son in the face with a whip!
	Blood spurted!
	Back! Back! Now the two beasts will come to grips!
	Make way for them!
	(Chiang starts, steps back, wipes the blood as it spreads over his face, then grasps the knife in his belt, holding the handle tightly, biting his lips. Abruptly he pushes back the Mandarin who has risen and is trying to block him and Li-Liang. He continues, slowly, craftily, toward the Old Man.)
MEI-LING	*(Crouched.)*
	Strike!
PEOPLE	Listen, the thunder approaches, the earth trembles...He's going

to kill the Old Man now!
Look how the knife throbs in Chiang's fist!

MEI-LING   Strike!
(Li-Liang touches Chiang's arm, pleadingly, but he twists away, pushing her back. Mei-Ling rushes to Li-Liang and pushes her aside. For a moment the two women glare at each other with hatred. Chiang fixes his eyes on the Old Man who stands erect and waits. Wild music. Old Koag runs and brings the Old Man a new sword, but with a violent movement the Old Man pushes him back.)

MEI-LING   Strike!
(Chiang has finally reached the Old Man but passes him by, barely touching him provokingly, then proceeds and reaches the closed door of the Tower. He stops, lets out a shrill cry like a vulture and then with sudden fury plunges the dagger into the Tower door and leaves it there, erect. The First Musician rises, bows to the audience, takes down the gong and strikes it hard, once. Curtain.)

(End of Act I)

ACT II

(Dawn. The large hall of the Tower. On the wall hang the Ancestors' seven panoplies, with death masks covering the faces, and black-handled daggers thrust in the belts. Beneath them is a narrow balcony along the length of the wall. From the center and back the area is raised in three steps; an open curtain divides the area in two. Far back is a huge statue of Buddha with three-fold bellies and overlapping chins, bursting with laughter. There are three doors: one behind Buddha, a large one to the left, and a low one to the right. Dim lights. The canary in the cage has awakened and is warbling. The three musicians are sitting cross-legged in their places, to the right, playing and creating the mood. The Old Man is sitting cross-legged on the balcony under the panoplies, smoking a long pipe. A seven-branched oil lamp glows weakly before him. To his right and left, relieved of their panoplies, the seven Ancestors sit. The Old Man watches them anxiously.)

OLD MAN   Has no one found him innocent? No one? O Terrible
      Ancestors, don't you pity him?
(Points to the low door at right.)
There, inside there, he sleeps in his ancestral home with the
      trust of a child...Listen to his breathing. It's soft and
      peaceful, like a baby's.
For months now he's been roaming the villages and fighting,
      he too, in his own way, to help the people.
He may be wrong, lawless, I know, but his heart is pure, O
      Ancestors, pure and clean, I swear!
Open his heart, open and look, what do you see?
Our China,
Our country with her fields and villages, with rivers, with
      gravestones...Happiness...Happiness...Our country is in his
      heart, as green as an emerald,
Wealthy villages, clean streets, harbors filled with ships,
      thresholds filled with children — and peaceful smoke rising
      from every hut.
Within his heart, O Ancestors, is the perfect China, the future
      China, strong and happy,
Drinking his blood and casting up its first sprouts.
Have mercy, Ancestors, pity him; he's tired and he's come at

night to lean against you, O immortal dead, to gather
strength, to go further on.

Lean over his bed, look at his face, lean a little more, look
into his heart.

You gaze upon him and say: "He's wild, cruel, he loves
bloodshed; but inside, his heart is tender, fresh, like the
heart of the sugar cane."

Here,

(Takes out a paper from inside his shirt.)

Here are a few of his rhymes, for he, too,

(Turns left.)

Like you, father, loves to weave songs, to ease his heart when
it overflows.

Listen to what I found on his table the other day...

(He reads.)

> *Fields, mountains, and serenity!*
> *It's raining, and the land*
> *Drinks sweetly and quiescently.*
> *Ah, I saw you stand*
> *Misted in your sunny rain,*
> *Your face wet in a strange blend,*
> *Weeping and laughing once again,*
> *O fatherland!*

(He watches the Ancestors anxiously. They remain unmoving,
silent. The soft sound of a knife being sharpened is heard.)

Eh, my tongue is sore from pleading and shouting all night;
I'm weary of it! It's not proper for me to speak and not be
answered.

I'm like you, too, Chiang; I, too, have my weapons, and
above the doorway of my tower, and on my silken banner
and gold seal is the same ancestral monogram as yours:

(Makes a forceful gesture in the air.)

A tiger!

Eh, Ancestors, I stamp my foot; give me a sure sign! Not
your slanted, customary chewed-up words, but speak
clearly so I will know what to do!

The spirits fly in a straight line; they speak to me honorably
and frankly, like men.

(Silence. The sound of a knife being sharpened grows louder.)

Oh, don't make me do something terrible, something I'll regret
later!

Eh, old men, be careful! I seem good, soft, I restrain my
hands, I don't kill — but don't awaken the beast in me...
(Beats his chest.)
In here sleeps a yellow tiger with black stripes — be careful!
(Turns to the right.)
Grandfather, you spent all your life fighting to free the
people...They were beasts, you wanted to make them men;
they were slaves, you wanted to make them free.
And the day your first son was born, my father, you gathered
seven thousand slaves from your fields, seven thousand
souls, and as one opens up a cage, you stretched out your
hand and freed them. Open your mouth now, grandfather,
and say a kind word.
(Points to the low door.)
And this great-grandson of yours follows in your footsteps;
he, too, struggles like you to do good to the numberless
swarm of China. He, too, fights like you — your great
breath churns within him. He wants to turn it into fruit
that you may be glad your seed was not scattered to the
winds.
Let him go, and we'll see; give him time, grandfather, he's
young, his blood is still boiling. Give him time to settle, to
find the right path — *your* path, O Ancestors!
(The sharpening of the knife now is heard more loudly.)
Eh, eh, stop sharpening the knife! Enough! Let him live, I say!
A great heart but unsubdued; a great virtue but without
discipline. He's young. That is the meaning of being young.
Give him time, grandfather, to mature, to recover from the
divine sickness — youth!
All of us, if you remember, were young once. We, too,
wanted to tear down the world and rebuild it; our blood
was like wine-must, it boiled. The time came, the boiling
stopped, the must cleared, it became wine. Keep your trust
in youth.
Ancestors, god-protectors of our lineage, I bow and worship
you. I've told you what I wanted; my heart has emptied,
my brain has emptied — judge now, decide!
Grandfather, speak first!
*(The Grandfather stretches out his hand, grasps the knife that
was being sharpened and wedges it into the hand of the Old
Man. The Old Man is startled, and the knife drops to the
ground. The canary, disquieted, begins to sing.)*

Oh!

(Turns to the Ancestor to his left and touches his knee.)

Father! You were good, sweet, you loved all living things, the
   birds, the flowers, the people. You took the quill and wrote
   songs on silk. And your closed heart opened as a garden
   opens, with blossoming tangerine trees, and you strolled
   through it.

And at other times you held in your arms this son of mine,
   Chiang, and danced him in your lap and said what I say
   now to my grandson: "I have no other hope in the world."

And here he is now; your grandson has grown big and strong,
   he's become a man — listen, lean over so I can tell you, that
   your heart may rejoice: he has the same voice as you, the
   same height, the same walk...

The old men look at him, open their eyes wide and say: "His
   grandfather has been resurrected! His grandfather has risen
   from the earth!" And now,

You've heard what I've prayed for all night, father...I spoke of
   him, your grandson: pity him. Open your mouth, say a
   kind word!

*(The father puts out his hand slowly, silently, grabs the knife
from the floor, thrusts it in the fist of the Old Man. The Old
Man lets out a cry, throws the knife away and rises,
staggering.)*

You, too? You, too? I have one thing more to say to you, O
   terrible Ancestors! One word, one last word...

*(But at that moment the roosters begin to crow, and the
Ancestors dissolve in air. The Old Man looks around him,
bewildered, throws his pipe away, and rubs his eyes.)*

Ooh! With whom was I talking? Who was I begging? Who
   placed this knife in my hand? Why do my lips drip poison?
   O dark powers, O voices of my heart!

(Looks at the panoplies.)

Listen to me, Ancestors, don't cloud my brain! Don't howl
   like jackals in the night! Speak clearly, like men. I'm not a
   slave to be afraid; I'm not a woman to be compassionate;
   I'm not one who wants to escape without paying his debt.

I'm a demon too, like all of you; I'm a Chiang, too,

I uproot my heart from my chest —

And I pay!

(The roar of the river is heard.)

Who roars?

(Jumps away from the window. The roar of the river is heard clearly, distant tolling bells, thunder. The Old Man listens.)

Hold on, old Chiang! Hold on, old Chiang! Don't be afraid. The river roars below, God roars above, and you stand between them. Roar, too!

Who placed this sharpened knife in my fist? Who took it from the Ancestors' panoplies?

(Raises the lantern and looks at the panoplies.)

Oh, it's gone from the savage grandfather's iron belt!

(Steps back, murmuring with horror.)

No! No! No!

(Approaches the low door, listens.)

He's sleeping...I hear his breathing like that of a small child's...It's peaceful, peaceful.

Beloved rebel, if you only knew! This whole night I've been fighting all the terrible shadows for you...

(Throws the knife on the balcony, opens his eyes wide, looks at it with terror, shouts.)

I won't! I won't!

(Abruptly the musicians begin to play. To the left, the large door opens, the First Sentry enters, mud-splattered. The Old Man recovers and raises his head calmly.)

I'm listening.

FIRST SENTRY Master...

OLD MAN Don't be afraid, speak. Look I've just risen from the earth; my mouth and throat and my entrails are filled with death, and I endure. Speak, then; don't be afraid!

Did you go to the villages I sent you? Did you see?

FIRST SENTRY I saw.

OLD MAN Well? I'm listening.

FIRST SENTRY Master, the world is turning to mud again...God regretted creating man, God regretted creating the animals and the trees, and it rains, it rains, it rains...

O God, you're turning the world back into mud again!

OLD MAN Leave God alone. If you have something to say, say it to me, and I'll tell God.

This is what order means! What did you see with your eyes,

80

	slave, that's what I ask you. Anything beyond that is not your concern.
FIRST SENTRY	Master, the river is angry, it swells and tears down the shore; the valley has become a lake, and drums, sheep, dogs and cows are floating in it.
OLD MAN	Not so loud, don't shout; there are women here, they might hear. Go on! Forget the sheep, the dogs, the cows; it's the people I pity, the souls. What happened to the people? Speak!
FIRST SENTRY	They're floating in the water, Master, on their backs, with their feet toward the sea...From yellow they've turned green, from green to black; crows swoop upon them and eat their eyes.
OLD MAN	Nothing else? Nothing else? There's still more poison on your lips; you've turned green.
FIRST SENTRY	I'm afraid...
OLD MAN	*(Frightened, grabs his arm.)* Did you see anything? A large phantom? Did he give you any orders for me? That's it, that's it! I see it in your eyes! What orders? *(To himself.)* Hold fast, my heart!
FIRST SENTRY	Master, just now, at dawn, I saw...
OLD MAN	Don't stammer. Close the door, close the window so I can hear.
FIRST SENTRY	I saw phantoms on the water, moaning...They were full of foam and seaweed...they rose and fell, with big mustaches stiff with anger. They roared, they threatened, they rushed toward your Tower, Master, I swear...And they wore...
OLD MAN	Why do you look at the wall with fear? Speak! They wore...
FIRST SENTRY	...These panoplies, Master...these exactly! And they roared and shouted, and I heard your name! Your name and the name of your son!
OLD MAN	Oh! Oh! Didn't they ask you to tell me something? To give

	me some order? Didn't they say: "Tell the Old Man..."
FIRST SENTRY	No, no! They didn't even turn to look at me. They passed in front of me, staggering and stumbling over one another. They thundered, they mounted the river and descended.
OLD MAN	Remember well. *(Grabs his shoulder.)* Tell the truth! They said nothing, nothing?
FIRST SENTRY	I swear, Master, nothing...
OLD MAN	*(Sighs in deep relief.)* Thank God!
FIRST SENTRY	They merely sighed, Master, and rumbled like buffaloes.
OLD MAN	And then? Then? Try to remember.
FIRST SENTRY	I don't know — the cocks crowed, they disappeared...
OLD MAN	Go!
FIRST SENTRY	Master, I have one more thing to say — give me permission to speak freely...
OLD MAN	Freely? Where did you learn that word? How did it pass the frontiers of China and enter here? I will raise breakwaters, I will build towers, I will open trenches to keep foreign demons from entering my fields. Lower your eyes — no one looks at a nobleman above the chest...Even lower. Speak now, what do you want? You have my permission.
FIRST SENTRY	Master, I'd like to speak of my pain...You said: "I've returned from the earth and carry death in my entrails." — I, too, have returned from the waters, Master, and I carry death in my entrails. If you would condescend to look into my eyes, You will see them filled with drowned people.
OLD MAN	Very well, very well, I see them! I've heard the message you bring me; it's entered my blood — leave us alone now, them and me, to fight! Why do you hesitate? Do you carry more poison?
FIRST SENTRY	Nobleman, the people cling to you. This is what everyone is

82

shouting, wherever I go. They look to you, Master, they expect much from you.

OLD MAN   Expect what?

FIRST SENTRY   Salvation...They say you are savage, but good and just. Dressed in silk, you eat and drink in peace under the green trees in summer, beside the hearth in winter, as your people work safely under your shadow.
Where there is danger, you are the first to enter.

OLD MAN   I know; raise your eyes, look!
(Opens his chest.)
My body is filled with wounds, from head to toe. I've done my duty.

FIRST SENTRY   *(Slowly, trembling.)*
It's not enough...

OLD MAN   *(Restraining his fury with difficulty.)*
What?

FIRST SENTRY   *(Trembling.)*
It's not enough.

OLD MAN   Not enough?

FIRST SENTRY   You're a great nobleman, Master, and you know the secret the smaller noblemen do not know...

OLD MAN   What secret?

FIRST SENTRY   That above manliness stands another, more brilliant virtue.

OLD MAN   You have something terrible on your mind, slave! Why do you choke on every word and swallow your tongue? What virtue?

FIRST SENTRY   *(Barely audible.)*
Sacrifice.

OLD MAN   *(Worried, agonizingly.)*
Sacrifice? What sacrifice?

FIRST SENTRY   Why do you ask? You know. You know very well who is to blame for infuriating the terrible god, the river.

OLD MAN   I don't know! Don't look at me; lower your eyes.

	(Silence.) Why do you shout?
FIRST SENTRY	I didn't shout, Master, I didn't speak.
OLD MAN	You shout from head to toe; go away so I won't hear you!
FIRST SENTRY	Master, it's not me you hear but the secret voice inside you... And you know well, you know very well what I mean.
OLD MAN	*(Raising his hands in despair.)* My God, don't give me all I can bear! *(To First Sentry.)* Go, I want to be alone with these. *(Points to the panoplies.)*
FIRST SENTRY	I'm leaving, but my voice will remain, Master, because it's not I who shout; it's you who are shouting, nobleman Chiang! Better for one person to be lost, Master, than thousands!
OLD MAN	*(Leaps with sudden fury and shakes the Sentry by the shoulders.)* Go! *(The Sentry leaves. The Old Man rushes toward the low door, raises his hands.)* My child! *(Slowly steps back, drags himself toward the knife, wipes the sweat from his brow, stares hypnotically at the knife on the balcony, puts out his hand but draws it back again. Shouts.)* Eh, eh, that's enough, you almighty dead, don't pull me — I'll go no further! *(The door at center depth opens. Quickly the Old Man leaps for the knife, hides it inside his clothing against his chest and holds it there tightly. Li-Liang steps out from behind the statue of Buddha, carrying a tray with the morning's tea, and stands on the first step, hesitating. The Old Man speaks, softly.)* Heart, old, ancient heart of Chiang, hold fast!
LI-LIANG	Father...
OLD MAN	Li-Liang...Go...Go...Pity me, Li-Liang-Go... *(Li-Liang watches the Old Man as tears fall silently down her cheeks. The Old Man shares her pain.)* Come!

(Softer.)
Come, unfortunate girl, come...
(Li-Liang descends the three steps, kneels, places the tray down and bows. The Old Man kicks the tray over, spilling the tea. Li-Liang kneels at the Old Man's feet.)

LI-LIANG   Father...

OLD MAN   Li-Liang, my child, forgive me, I'm in pain.

LI-LIANG   I know, father, all night I heard you sighing. You haven't slept all night, father.

OLD MAN   No, I was not sighing — I was talking.

LI-LIANG   You were talking, father?

OLD MAN   Get up, my dear, get up...
(Sighs.)
Man is a small island surrounded by waves, waves, waves of the dead. Another great storm is brewing tonight; they'll drown me, Li-Liang, the dead will drown me; help me!
No, no, don't stretch out your hand, don't open your mouth. I don't want help! You too, are a charming little island, the waves beat at you also, and there is no bridge...Why do you put out your hand? There is no bridge...
Don't cry; go, leave me alone. I'm talking with the Ancestors.

LI-LIANG   Let me stay in this corner, father; give me your permission. I'll sit in a little heap, I won't speak, I won't cry — let me; I won't look, I won't listen, let me...

OLD MAN   No, no, I'm talking with the male Ancestors. Women are not permitted here, Li-Liang;
We make decisions...
(Sighs deeply.)
We've found salvation.

LI-LIANG   What salvation, father?

OLD MAN   Be quiet!
(Looks worriedly toward the low door.)
Did he waken? Speak softly, my child.

LI-LIANG   What salvation, father?

OLD MAN   *(Worried.)*

Did he waken?

LI-LIANG Why are you frightened, father? He's sleeping. He won't waken, poor dear; he's tired, going from village to village, gathering an army. He's had many cares — didn't you see him? He's wasted away.
What salvation, father?

OLD MAN Listen how the river roars! It's angry, it has swollen, it will drown my people. Open the window, my child, so I can hear it and take courage.
(Li-Liang opens the window. The dreadful roar of the river is heard, the Old Man breathes deeply.)
Ah! Ah! Welcome! He's a dreadful god, he does not forgive; they say he favors no one; he eats people...What do you say, Li-Liang?

LI-LIANG There's only one thing I'm thinking of, father: what salvation?

OLD MAN Li-Liang...

LI-LIANG Command me!

OLD MAN Do me a big favor, my child...

LI-LIANG Command me, father.

OLD MAN Bring me my grandchild. This loneliness is unbearable, this hour is hard to endure — bring me my grandchild!

LI-LIANG He's sleeping. He, too, didn't rest all night, as though he were having an evil dream. He was babbling, shrieking like a bird,
Then at dawn sleep finally came. Shall I wake him, father?

OLD MAN Wake him; I want to see him, to touch him, to take courage ...Go on...
(Pushes her gently, persistently.)
Don't you pity me? Go on...

LI-LIANG *(Stands in agony.)*
Father, why do you send me away?
(Embraces him, feels the handle of the knife against his chest, and lets out a harrowing cry.)
Ah!
(Falls at his feet and embraces his knees. The Old Man throws

86

the knife on the balcony.)

OLD MAN   *(Caressing her hair.)*
Don't cry, don't cry, unfortunate child — there's no other
    salvation...All night we held court here; the Ancestors
    came, they stepped down from their panoplies; they sat
    here, look, here, to my right and left...
I talked and talked, I spoke till my tongue swelled from
    talking, my voice cracked from pleading and shouting...All
    night long, and now, see, just before the cocks crowed...

LI-LIANG   Just before the cocks crowed?

OLD MAN   The decision was reached. Quiet now, don't cry, pity me...

LI-LIANG   The decision was reached?
(Drags herself on her knees to the low door, stretches full-
length over the threshold, as though to block anyone from
passing through.)

OLD MAN   *(Raising his arms toward the panoplies.)*
O Ancestors, there's still time, give me a sign. Seize my hand,
    forbid me!
There, I will count to seven. O Ancestors, I give you time to
    give me a sign...To call me! No — don't! Rise! Come out of
    your graves, I'm counting!
(Counts slowly, hoarsely, his voice trembling more with each
word. The loud regular beat of a drum accompanies each
word. The Old Man looks at the seven Ancestors on the wall,
one by one.)
One — Two — Three — O Ancestors, O dreadful powers,
    mercy! Raise a shrill cry, let the doors creak, let Buddha
    shake his head, let a cry be heard in my skull. a No! I ask
    for a sign!
Four — Five — Nothing! Nothing!
Six...
(Approaches the window.)
It's raining, raining, the sky has exhausted itself, may it be
    cursed! Eh, Ancestors, are you deaf, are you mute? Give
    me a sign!
Ancestors, I've reached the edge of the precipice, I send you
    my last cry: Seven!
(Stands in agony watching the Ancestors. Savage music. The

canary is singing sweetly, joyfully. The Old Man bends and slyly walks toward the knife gleaming on the balcony. He looks at it with terror but an irresistible power pushes him. He groans, resists, but still advances, and then suddenly, driven almost insane, seizes the knife. With a powerful leap, wailing, he strides over Li-Liang, opens the door, enters and bolts it from inside. A few moments of silence. Li-Liang raises her head and listens. From inside comes the deep, heavy sigh of the Old Man, and then, suddenly, a harrowing scream.)

LI-LIANG *(Leaps up and claws at the door, shaking it.)*
Help! Help!

OLD MAN *(Opens the low door violently, rushes out in a daze, his hands dripping with blood, then leaps on the balcony and rubs the blood on the ancestral panoplies, groaning.)*
There, there, there! I rub your beards, your mouths, your
    nostrils, your neck; eat, eat and be satisfied!
O Almighty Gods, O voices out of the earth, I did what you
    wanted. I did what you wanted, alas for me!
(Crumbles to the ground, sighing.)
I did what you wanted; now keep your word too: Turn back
    the river so it won't drown my people!

LI-LIANG *(Crouching, crawls to the threshold, kisses it, then enters the room of the murdered man.)*
I'm coming...I'm coming...I'm coming.

OLD MAN *(Raises his head, listens. Silence for some time. The roar of the river is heard growing more savage.)*
No, no, it can't be, no! It's not the river! Didn't we agree?
    I've given it the guilty man! It ate, it's satisfied, it will calm
    down. I owed and I paid.
The Ancestors placed the knife in my hand, I thrust it into
    my heart! I did what they wanted, let them now do what
    I want!
(Listens again, then suddenly leaps up angrily.)
No, I tell you, it's not the river! O royal vein, be silent, that
    I may hear.
(Leans from the window, listens to the dreadful roar.)
It's the river, it's the Yangtze! Be patient a little longer, my
    heart, do not break. The Ancestors commanded, and they

do not lie; keep your trust!

(Suddenly a sarcastic laugh is heard behind him. He turns and looks at the statue of Buddha.)

Who laughed? You! You! O horrible, insatiable mouth of Nothingness, Buddha!

(Suddenly, as though a terrifying thought cuts through his mind, he claps his hands.)

Koag, old Koag!

O horrible insatiable mouth, that's why you laugh! You want to eat us all...all. You won't get away with it! Koag!

(Old Koag appears. The Old Man hides his bloodied hands behind him.)

My grandson, hurry!

(Koag moves toward the center door. The Old Man turns to Buddha.)

Not him! Him you won't eat! Koag!

(The slave returns.)

Softly, gently, Koag, don't wake him, he's sleeping. And wrap him well so he won't catch cold.

(The slave leaves. The Old Man to Buddha:)

No, no, don't laugh, you won't eat him!

Ah, ah, if only this were a dream and I would waken,

Oh, but I think — Buddha, help me! — I think this is real!

(Raises his hands, looks at the blood, tastes it with his tongue and lets out a cry.)

Oh, I see it's real! This isn't paint, it's my own salty, warm blood

(Koag returns holding the baby.)

Is he sleeping?

OLD KOAG He's sleeping, Master, he's sleeping —

OLD MAN (Leans over and admires his grandson.)
O miracle, O immortal miracle of ill-fated man. I have no other hope, Koag, my loyal slave, I have no other hope...

OLD KOAG I know, Master; command me.

OLD MAN Listen, Koag, bend over, listen to this secret: We're all lost here — the Yangtze will eat us all...Be quiet, I can't leave; I'm a Nobleman, I can't desert my people. But you, Koag, you are a slave; for you it's not disgraceful to run from danger,

Go! Take my grandson and go! There's still time.
Go far from the river, take our sturdiest cart,
Harness our strongest oxen, be off! Don't stop anywhere, go!
Hold him tightly in your arms, faithful slave; of all the
    dreadful clan of Chiang, he alone remains. The clan of
    Chiang has no other seed. If he's lost, we're all lost, and
    the Dead will die.
Who will give them immortal water to drink by bearing them
    a new grandchild? It will be gone, gone! The clan of
    Chiang will sink into deepest shame — into Oblivion.
Is it dawn, Old Koag? Has the Morning Star melted away?

OLD KOAG   The sky hasn't a single star, Master, it's raining...raining.

OLD MAN   Louder! This river has deafened me, I don't hear very well.
    (Points to Buddha.)
    Do you hear his laughter?

OLD KOAG   *(Loudly.)*
    Clouds! It's raining!

OLD MAN   Ah! Ah!
    (Groans, paces back and forth.)
    Shut the window so I won't hear it.
    (Old Koag shuts the window.)
    Come here, take the keys from my belt, Koag, open the
        large chest, take all the gold and go! Take the five noble
        treasures of the Chiangs,
    The castellated ruby, the red sword, the gold ring, the ivory
        staff of authority and the holy, yellow banner with the
        green dragon!
    Take them and go; they're his. Give them to him when he's
        grown up; they're his.
    Koag, eh Koag, raise him well, wild and proud; raise him not
        to hoard his riches but to scatter them; that's the meaning
        of nobility. Not to hoard one's youth but to scatter it;
        that's what youth means. To hope for nothing from the
        gods, do you hear? Nothing! Tell him that's what his
        grandfather orders: to hope for nothing from the gods.
    (Pauses a moment, hesitates, then makes a decision.)
    Nor from the Ancestors!
    (Old Koag steps back in fear.)
    Why do you tremble? You don't dare repeat the words

I've commanded?

OLD KOAG   Forgive me, I'm a slave, such words suit a nobleman, Master, not me.

I'm a slave, huddling under the feet of Buddha.

OLD MAN   I wasn't speaking to you, I was speaking to my grandson. Tell him to keep courage in his heart,

Nothing else exists in this world but the heart of man, neither gods nor demons. You hear, Koag?

Tell him he has my blessing, and to return to our soil, here, not elsewhere, to build our Tower again on the same foundations, to cast roots in our soil again,

To marry and bear sons. Wild and good and noble and honorable is the clan of Chiang; it must not vanish from the earth.

If it is lost, the world will be poorer, a brilliant beast will be missing from God's jungle — the tiger. Do you hear, Koag?

OLD KOAG   I hear, Master...

OLD MAN   Go now. In your hands, my faithful slave, I entrust these almighty few pounds of flesh.

Wait, don't rush; let me bid him farewell.

(He bends over, looks at the child, then draws back.)

No, no, I mustn't wake him. Wrap him tightly so he won't catch cold...Go, and tell your doe-eyed son to come. I want him.

(Sobs are heard behind him. Li-Liang had come from the murdered man's room and was listening. The Old Man turns to her.)

Li-Liang, my child, do you want to go with him?

(Staggering, Li-Liang approaches. She looks at the baby, kisses the sheet on which it is wrapped, and shakes her head.)

LI-LIANG   No, father —

OLD MAN   Go, Koag. Goodbye. Goodbye.

(Koag leaves. The Old Man turns to the panoplies.)

Ancestors, famished spirits, you saw, you heard, we have no other hope. Dismount from the river, surround his cart, push the wheels so they won't sink in the mud, goad the oxen so they will run.

Spread yourselves across my grandson so he won't get wet; wrap yourselves around him so he won't be cold! He's the last Chiang, there is no other. I did all I could to save him.

But I am human, my power reaches only to the tips of my fingers. O almighty dead, I surrender my grandson into your hands.

(Climbs the three steps, stands and looks at Buddha.)

Buddha, Buddha, I ask only one thing of you — don't extend a hand to strike him; let the Ancestors alone.

Yes, yes, everything's but wind and mist and a wink of the eye; everything, everything; only my grandson here is real flesh; don't touch him!

(Turns, looks at Li-Liang who is also kneeling before the statue of Buddha.)

Li-Liang, my child, life is poison, poison —

LI-LIANG   It doesn't matter, father, death is sweet.

OLD MAN   Do you know how great my pain is, my child?

LI-LIANG   Yes.

OLD MAN   And you would give me your hand?

(Li-Liang offers him her hand, weeping. The Old Man steps back.)

No, no, I can't touch it; look at my hands...Forgive me!

Don't! Be quiet! Don't say anything...to say No is a heavy burden, and to say Yes, also. Be quiet!

May life be cursed! I raise my two bloodied hands: may life be cursed!

YOUNG KOAG   *(Enters from the center door, bows.)*
Master, command me!

OLD MAN   Koag, go down to the courtyard, ring the large bell, call the people to the Tower. Today is a great day; I want to talk to them.

And take out the great uniform from the chest, the uniform I wore when my son was born, the one I shall wear on the day I die —

Take out the swords, the feathers, the rubies — and I shall come that you may dress me.

(Koag leaves.)

This is a difficult moment, hold fast, old Chiang!

(Leaves from the center door.)

LI-LIANG *(Kisses the earth.)*

Goodbye, my beloved, bloodied, tormented country, O
  China! Farewell...

(Picks up the bread that had fallen from the tray and kisses it.)

Goodbye, holy, salty bread of man; I bow and worship your
  power — farewell!

My child, my very being, my blood became milk to nourish
  you; I was born in this world for you, and now...farewell!

*(Looks around her, dazed; drags herself toward the threshold
of the murdered man's room.)*

Why this pain? Why this hatred? Why this bloodshed? How
  long? O terrible, inhuman laws! I struggle, I try hard, I
  can't understand them. They pass through my heart and
  crush it; they pass through my brain and shatter it; if I
  raise my eyes to see them, I am blinded.

I bow my head and obey. I obey, there's nothing more I
  can do. Our laws are beasts, hungry lions and tigers and
  wolves — who will save us Buddha, who?

(As though listening.)

Yes, yes — Death! Death! The cool door — you open it and
  leave.

(Bows before the low door.)

My husband, who will prepare tea for you below the earth?

I'm coming! I'm coming! Who will prepare hot water for you
  in winter, your clean, cool shirt in summer? I'm coming!
  I'm coming!

With you in life and in death; I place my hand in yours — let
  us go!

Ah, one moment, my beloved, while I comb my hair and
  adorn myself, while I perfume my breast. I'm coming.

*(Opens the chest, takes out her small mirror, her comb, her
perfume, her rouge. Softly sings a song much like a dirge.)*

"Three sentries did I post for you, my dear, for your sweet
  sake..."

*(Combs her hair swiftly, applies the cosmetics, singing softly
as the music accompanies her mournfully.)*

"I placed the sun among the mountains, the eagle in all
  valleys,

And the North wind, the cool North Wind, I placed in every

93

vessel..."
(Mei-Ling enters from the center door, hears the dirge and stops, startled. She motions the musicians to cease, and the music stops abruptly. Li-Liang sees Mei-Ling.)

MEI-LING   *(Sarcastically, with disdain.)*
Why are you wailing, sister?

LI-LIANG   *(Raising her head proudly.)*
I'm not wailing; I'm singing. I'm getting married tonight.

MEI-LING   *(Mockingly.)*
You're getting married tonight? Your eyes have grown wild;
what's wrong, Li-Liang?

LI-LIANG   I won! I won!

MEI-LING   What? Who?

LI-LIANG   I won! I won! Don't ask!
(The loud ringing of the tower bell is heard.)

MEI-LING   The danger bell! Who ordered it to be rung?

LI-LIANG   Father. He's calling the people and the guests to come; I'm
being married tonight.

MEI-LING   Come to your senses, Li-Liang, and listen to me, it's important:
I had a terrible dream...

LI-LIANG   *(Smiles bitterly.)*
A dream? Just a dream? I spread out my hand and it fills with
blood...

MEI-LING   Just now, at dawn...I don't believe in dreams, but this one
frightened me...

LI-LIANG   *(Tired, quietly.)*
What dream?

MEI-LING   *(Softly.)*
Is he sleeping?

LI-LIANG   Yes...Yes...

MEI-LING   It seems our old father was sitting under a blossoming plum
tree. He was holding a pipe, smoking, looking at the sky
and admiring a white dove flying...

94

Suddenly a scream was heard and a hawk pounced but missed and caught its beak in the earth.

In a frenzy it rushed at the dove again, but the dove hid against father's chest.

"Give me the dove!" the hawk shrieked, "It's mine!"

"Don't you pity it?" father asked, and held the white bird tightly in his arms.

"Why should I pity it?" replied the hawk angrily, "I do my duty; I eat flesh; I was born for this."

"You are a cruel, merciless creature," said the Old Man, "and God, one day..."

"What?" screamed the hawk, "What God? It's He who created me like this. If He wanted to, He would have created me to eat grass too, and I wouldn't be molesting living things. But He made me a hawk. Give me the dove!"

The Old Man bared his arm. "Here, eat of my flesh, gorge yourself, but let the dove be..."

The hawk swooped down, hooked itself onto the arm and began to eat. It ate the one arm, it ate the other, then jumped on the chest. "When you've had enough," the Old Man whispered now and then, "when you've had enough, stop."

But the hawk never had enough! It ate the chest, it ate the shoulders, it ate the legs, it ate and ate...

Finally, all that was left was the head. It grabbed this in its claws and flew away.

LI-LIANG   And the dove?

MEI-LING   It flew away — I don't know what happened to it.

LI-LIANG   I know, sister.

MEI-LING   Did you see the same dream, the same dream, Li-Liang?

LI-LIANG   I saw a white dove flying in my dream...and suddenly a hawk pounced upon it...It must have been the same hawk, Mei-Ling, the same, the same,
And it was not yet satiated.
(She paints her lips, her eyebrows, singing the dirge softly.)
"But O my darling, the sun has set, the eagle has fallen asleep,
And the North Wind, the cool North Wind, was taken by every vessel..."

MEI-LING   Your mind is elsewhere, Li-Liang, the world is falling apart,
             and you have enslaved your mind to the bedroom and
             the soles of your son's feet.

LI-LIANG   You, Mei-Ling, have no husband, no son, no roots; all you
             have are wings,
             Only the misfortune of wings and freedom.

MEI-LING   Don't shake your head. My road is long; it stretches
             thousands of miles, to the ends of China. And on that
             road only two walk, side by side, and they don't want a
             third —
             My brother and I!
             And now, we must go, there's much work ahead of us — to
             fetter the river. I've come to wake him; I've saddled the
             horses, we're off!

LI-LIANG   Won't you leave him with me for a few minutes, Mei-Ling?
             He's my husband, the father of my son.

MEI-LING   No!

LI-LIANG   *(Startled, shows her the low door.)*
             Go, take him!
             *(Mei-Ling slowly opens the low door, afraid of startling her
             brother, and enters. The bell is heard again.)*
             Ah, Ah, there's nothing sweeter than death...
             Thank you, my husband; you've taught me to love life and
             to love death!
             *(Suddenly a harrowing cry is heard. The low door opens,
             Mei-Ling rushes out and seizes Li-Liang.)*

MEI-LING   Who?...Who? The Old Man?
             (Li-Liang bows her head.)
             And you, why didn't you call for help?

LI-LIANG   From whom? Help from whom, Mei-Ling?

MEI-LING   *(Grabs the mirror, smashes it into a thousand pieces.)*
             May your face smash into a thousand pieces, too.
             (Breaks the comb and the perfumes.)
             Ah! So that's why you were dressing yourself like a bride;
             that's why your eyes shoot flames!
             (Points to Buddha.)

	You planned it with him; you took him from me!
LI-LIANG	Now he's mine, eternally! Why are you shouting? I'm his wife; I'm going with him. *I*, not you. I've won! *(Opens the chest as she speaks, selects a scarf, checks it to see if it's strong, wraps it around her neck, then turns to the canary that has begun to warble.)* Farewell, my canary! *(Bows to Mei-Ling.)* Farewell, my little sister...
MEI-LING	Where are you going?
LI-LIANG	I've saddled the horses, we're leaving! *(Climbs the three steps, closes the curtain. For some time a savage and mournful music plays. Mei-Ling bends down and grasps the bloodied knife. The curtain opens and we see Li-Liang fallen at Buddha's feet. The Old Man appears dressed in his official uniform. He does not see Li-Liang and he does not see Mei-Ling who has flattened herself up against the wall under the panoplies. He raises his fist angrily at Buddha.)*

OLD MAN	Shame, shame on you. It's I shouting, old man Chiang!
	What shame that God should condescend to play
	With man's dread and danger!
	You may be a lion, perhaps; but know this:
	I'm not a lamb to stretch out my neck for slaughter!
	You can do one thing only: you can kill me. Kill me, then!
	But before I die I will let out a cry, Buddha,
	I will let out a cry...
	*(Bursts into sobs, descends the three steps, and walks toward
	the outer door. Mei-Ling shows herself suddenly, hiding the
	knife behind her back. The Old Man pauses, then stretches
	out his hand.)*
	My child, forgive me, it had to be — it had to be done, to
	    save the people. Yes, ask the Ancestors, too! They thrust
	    the knife into my fist...
	*(Mei-Ling paces back and forth silently. The Old Man watches
	in agony.)*
	Ah, she's still young, she doesn't understand!
	I bend before you, Mei-Ling, forgive me — Do you hear? I, I
	    who stand erect when I speak with God and listen to His

words and answer back — I, whom no one ever saw with
bent head — not God nor man, nor beast of the forest,
I, I, Old Chiang, bend before you, O inexperienced, dream-
ridden woman, and I beg of you: Forgive me!
(Waits, then suddenly, with fury:)
No? No? Don't set my blood boiling! Don't open the trap
door inside me for the demons to fly out!
I will plunge the knife into your heart, too! Why don't you
speak? Why don't you scream out your blasphemies?
*(Mei-Ling paces back and forth, slowly smearing her brother's
blood on her face.)*
Mei-Ling, I can't endure your silence, speak!
No, no, I don't regret it; you'll not see me cry again; look
at me! He's a real man who steps into water and does not
get wet, into fire and does not get burned, into death and
does not cry.
(Touches his eyes with his finger, then takes them away.)
There, dry!
*(Mei-Ling clasps the knife tightly, raises it slowly and
approaches the Old Man. He bows his head quietly and
stretches out his neck. Savage music, then silence for some
time.)*
I'm waiting. Why are you taking so long? Strike!
*(Mei-Ling throws away the knife. The Old Man lifts his
head and sighs.)*
Gone...gone...Chiang's generation has become weakhearted.
Chiang's generation cannot kill anymore.
*(Young Koag opens the large door at left. The loud clamor of
the people is heard, shouts and weeping.)*
What are those voices? No one shouts before the Master's
Tower.

YOUNG KOAG   It's the people; you've invited them, Lord; they're coming.
The old men lead the way with their staffs; behind come
weeping women carrying honey wrapped in green leaves to
sweeten Buddha; and in the center are the men, shouting.

OLD MAN   Open the doors of the Tower, put the people in the courtyard
and bring the chiefs, the men and the women before me. I
have something of great importance to tell them, news of
dreadful import. Go!
(Young Koag leaves.)

98

Bloodthirsty, many-headed beast, now you will drink my
blood, you will eat my flesh, and be satisfied!
I sit on my ancestral throne, on my tiger skin, and I wait...
The people give their accounting to the nobles, the nobles
to God, and God to no one. This is what order means!
But now, alas,
God gives an accounting to the nobles, the nobles to the
people, and the people to no one!
These new demons that will devour the world were brought
by the Westerners, a curse on them!
*(The large door opens, the people enter shouting and weeping
—the old men ahead, the women behind.)*
Don't all shout at once, I can't hear! Put your complaints into
some order; speak one by one!
(To the Mandarin.)
Speak, wise old man. Come close, don't tremble, I won't eat
you. You're a scribe, you sit in the marketplace with your
paper and ink — and your ears are large, like Buddha's; they
cover the marketplace, the city, all of China; you hear
everything and you write it down, scratch, scratch,
scratching the soul of man.
Speak, what did you hear in the marketplace? Don't tremble
I say; speak, what do the people want?

MANDARIN   Master, if you cut up a difficult deed, you'll see that it is
made up of thousands of little ones; it's then easy to act.
If you cut up an easy thought, you'll see that it's made up of
thousands of difficult ones; it's difficult, Master, for a man
to think and to speak his thoughts.

OLD MAN   *(Angrily.)*
Is that the meaning of wisdom? Is wisdom then a cuttlefish
that squirts its ink and clouds the water? Why don't you
speak as honestly, as simply, as straightforwardly as one
tosses a spear?

MANDARIN   I'm afraid, Master, I'm afraid...What I have to say is difficult,
I can't find the words. And if I did find them, I don't
have the strength to reveal them to you, Master; and if I
did have the strength,
I don't want to, I don't want to, Master, because I pity you...

OLD MAN   You pity *me*? You? Pity *me*?

(Fearfully.)
So, I've been reduced to this!

MANDARIN Master, I don't want to remain silent; necessity prods me. I
don't want to speak; I'm afraid. What shall I do?

OLD MAN Don't speak, don't remain silent, you wretched man. Write!
That's your job, old penpusher — a sly, cowardly job for
slaves, for eunuchs and monks like you! Get out of my
sight!
(Turns to an old peasant.)
Speak, peasant! You're not a wise man; your mind is not a
ball of thin tangled threads;
It's an axe and it slashes! Slash, then!

PEASANT Nobleman, the old river has grown savage; it mounts the
villages, drags behind it a long trail of sheep, oxen, dogs,
people, carcasses. It eats, it eats, it eats, Master, but it is
never satiated...
We fall on our faces to the earth, and we hear it shout;
"I want! I want! I want!" It shouts, and keeps descending.

OLD MAN What does it want?
(To the Mandarin who is about to speak.)
You, be quiet!
(To the peasant.)
What does it want?

PEASANT *(Quietly, slowly.)*
Your son!
*(A clamor rises from the people as they all step back with
fear and stare at the Old Man. The Peasant remains alone in
front of the Old Man, motionless. The Old Man closes his
eyes and breathes deeply. Music is heard.)*

OLD MAN What did you say, old peasant?

PEASANT Your son, Nobleman. It's your son the River wants. Your
son!
*(The agitated people look toward the door, to leave. The Old
Man opens his eyes.)*

OLD MAN Silence! Silence!
(To Young Koag.)
It's getting dark; light the lanterns, Koag, open the window so

they can see me. This is a great moment, it needs light.
Don't shout; be quiet! Let the men stand to the right, the
women to the left,
(Points to Buddha.)
And God in the center. I will speak!
For a hundred years I ate, I drank, I dressed, I made merry, I
sat down at the sumptuous table of China —
And I paid nothing;
I was a nobleman, an idle drone, eating alone, drinking alone,
reveling alone. I made no honey — I ate honey, and I paid
nothing!
I've accumulated a large bill — one hundred years of
sumptuous living — but now I must pay. Look!
*(He raises his bloodied hands which were hidden inside his
wide sleeves.)*

PEOPLE   Blood! Blood!

OLD MAN   This morning at dawn, God brought me the bill and I paid! I
took out my heart, that great purse, and I paid!
Look, I did not wash my hands so you could see. Look!
(With a harrowing cry.)
My son's!

MANDARIN   *(Raises his hands in despair.)*
Your son's? In vain, in vain, you wretched man, in vain!

OLD MAN   What? What did you say? I can't hear.

MANDARIN   Nothing! What more can I say? Nothing!

OLD MAN   My son! I gave it my son! It ate, it ate, but it never had
enough. Peasants and horses were not enough to satisfy it.
So I cut out and gave it my entrails.
Is it satisfied? Is it not? Why is it still shouting? My mind
shakes.

MEN   Immortal is the Dynasty of Chiang, it comes out of the loins
of Buddha. During great joys, it's not sorry to take a
double portion; during great tragedies, it's not afraid to
take a double portion.
I bow in veneration, Master. You've taken all our suffering
upon yourself.
We've escaped! We're saved! Your son wanted to let loose the

101

terrible tiger, Freedom, into our homes and hearts, to eat us. We're saved!

The river will calm down again. God will go back into his sheath; our little life will turn green on the earth again.

OLD MAN *(Looking at his hands.)*

Only I and these hands of mine know that happiness does not exist...

(Suddenly grows fierce.)

Be quiet, leave me! I don't want to hear you any more! Alas, is it then for these mouths, these bellies, these feet and this mess of meat

That I've slaughtered a great soul?

(Rushes and grabs two or three peasants.)

Why are you living, you worm? And you, you frog? And you, you monkey? Ah, ah, to save thousands of rats I've killed a lion!

(Falls exhausted on his seat.)

Should I have done it or not? Ah, who's to tell me?

WOMEN Don't be angry, Master, don't be sorry...You'll see, all the fearsome powers will mellow. Here, we've gathered honey in these green leaves to spread on the lips of Buddha;

We women have no other answer for gods or for men!

OLD MAN Honey? Poor little people, he wants meat! Meat! Meat!

(Alights from his seat, climbs the three steps, opens the curtain.)

Buddha, Buddha, this wretched people say they're bringing you honey, do you hear? Honey to turn you sweet!

O dreadful lion...

(Stops suddenly, terrified, for behind Buddha he sees Li-Liang hanging by her scarf. He stumbles toward her. The people gather behind him. The Old Man falls and kisses Li-Liang's feet.)

Beloved Li-Liang, you're gone...gone...I bow and worship your feet. To our reunion, to our good reunion, my child...

(The people are agitated, shouting. The Old Man turns angrily.)

Quiet! Li-Liang, my child, give my regards to the Ancestors. Did I do my duty? Ask them, did I do my duty? I'm all confused now. Goodbye! Farewell!

(He falls to the ground. Music. The Old Man raises his head, listens to the music, becomes tranquil and calls softly.)
Hu-Ming! Hu-Ming!

MAGICIAN   Command me, old Chiang, I'm here beside you.

OLD MAN   I'm in pain, Hu-Ming. Ease my pain, don't leave me! Are
all these things I see and hear and touch real? I won't have
it, Hu-Ming, I'm choking with anger.
Who made the world so narrow, Hu-Ming, so evil, so inferior
to the heart of man? I don't want it any more!
Hu-Ming, take me, alive, to the land of Myth. You are a
great craftsman; throw a silken bridal veil over the abyss.
Stitch it with red, with green, with yellow embroideries;
scatter suns on it, birds, gods, paradises, and console me.
Tell me that all is a dream, all is a dream, my son is a spring
cloud, and death — death is a strong, sweet fragrance that
makes us dizzy.
(He is overcome with sobs, then shakes himself in shame.)
I think of the Ancestors, I think of the Descendants, I think
of my race and pity it.
Hu-Ming!

MAGICIAN   At your command, Nobleman.

OLD MAN   Are you ready?

MAGICIAN   Ready! All those hours you struggled, entangled in the webs
of Necessity, I, free of sons, nobilities and old debts, have
been working.
I was shaping the world as you had ordered, old Chiang, wide
and deep enough to hold the heart of man.
I fitted Necessity with wings and turned it into freedom.
I raised hot winds that caused buds to swell and stumps and
heads to blossom.
I'm ready. Order them to light the incense burners, to scatter
intoxicating aromas that man's brain may sprout wings to
follow me.
Master, you no longer need intoxication; you have the largest
wing of all — Pain!
With your permission I shall tear down the boundaries of the
visible and the invisible, I shall abolish the world, I shall
cover the abyss with a veil. I shall begin!

OLD MAN   Onward! Hu-Ming, do what God had not the courage to do!
                 Turn the wheel, put us in the unmoving center, in the axis,
                 that we may admire the world moving.
             Give the reel a kick, wind and unwind the fairy tale!
             Hu-Ming, the heart of man is a tangled ball of caterpillars;
                 blow on them and turn them into butterflies.

MAGICIAN   *(Traces a circle again, puts the twelve signs of the zodiac in
             their places again, murmuring the name of each.)*
             Cock – Hare – Tiger – Ape – Pig – Snake – Ox –
                 Dragon – Dog – Sheep – Rat – Horse!
             *(Slaves appear with censers and sprinkle the people with
             perfume. Music.)*
             Keep order! Don't mix the living with the dead, freemen with
                 the slaves, men with women, humans with animals.
             Vision is an army, it needs discipline.
             Here, in the first row, the spirits...Can't you see them? Good,
                 then! If you saw them they would disappear. Behind the
                 spirits, in the second row, the free peasants; further back
                 the slaves, and then the house dogs, the oxen, the
                 monkeys, the parrots...
             Where did we stop, my Nobleman, do you remember?

OLD MAN   I remember. Saripoutta's ox-cart had arrived filled with
                 dancers, ascetics, monkeys.
             He stooped, Buddha stooped, I remember, like a black swan,
                 he stooped over the waters and watched his image dying.
             And around him the visible and the invisible gathered, and
                 waited.

MAGICIAN   Alas for you, Old Man, Buddha has not yet freed your
                 memory, for you remember. Let me lean, then, a large
                 ladder against the air, Master, that you may climb to the
                 top level of truth where neither forgetfulness nor memory
                 exist.
             Blood does not exist, nor water, nor tears, nor sweat; nothing
                 exists! Nothing! I clap my hands and begin.
             *(The Magician puts on the yellow mask of the Spirit, and
             immediately the set changes. Sweet, unworldly music is
             heard.)*
             Take your places, animals, spirits, people! Make circles
                 around the Holy Tree, and let each one stand according to

his rank in nature.

Animals, dark, indestructible roots of mankind,

(Claps his hands.)

Come! Come! Spirits, descend from the trees, ascend from the
waters, no one is watching you, come forth! And you,
people, sacks filled with blood, tears, urine and sweat,
come to purge yourselves.

And you, fellow-athletes, dancers, ascetics and monkeys,
shake loose from Buddha's ox-cart, scatter across the
threshing floor and plant the imagination with both fists.

These are the people, lost in their passions, drowned in
tears, caught in the web of Necessity. Pity them! Their
heads, their breasts, their loins are overstuffed with straw;
set them on fire, that they may shine; throw Buddha upon
them like burning coals.

Brother, my eyes are dazzled. Just as a king, overcome with
wine, grabs a large golden tray overbrimming with
emeralds, sapphires, turquoises and rubies, and tosses them
into his marble courtyard,

So did this ox-cart overbrim and scatter itself over the earth.

Women leap from the cart as copper bracelets jingle on their
feet and arms; gold coins weigh down their high, warring
breasts — my brother, the whole world is a woman dancing.

MANDARIN   Toss your heads, chase away the nightmare, my children.
They're casting spells over you; resist them! Don't let your
brains become blurred!

PEOPLE   Don't listen to the old sage; he's turned senile; Look! Look!
The dancers have hung their ornaments like offerings, and
the entire Holy Tree has sprouted with silver belts and red
sandals.

Look, the black slaves have set up a royal tent of heavy silken
velvet, and puffing and panting, are carrying the holy
instruments of the liturgy.

The threshing floor has filled with wooden masks; it has taken
on a voice and soul; it laughs and mourns, like a man, like
a woman.

This is not an ox-cart; it's a head, my brothers, the head of
Buddha — and it has opened.

Women and men bend in rows over the river, and before the
liturgy begins they bathe and comb their hair, paint

themselves, pour perfumes over their hair, their ears, their
    armpits.
Saripoutta has freed himself at last from baths and perfumes;
    from head to toe he's become spirit. He is standing in the
    middle of the threshing floor and is offering a sacrifice.
He is offering for a sacrifice the shadow of a large yellow
    parrot, the shadow of a large yellow parrot!
(Music.)

MAGICIAN   All sit cross-legged on the ground; be quiet! Open your
    minds, people; shake the earth from your eyelashes, all of
    you! Look:
The spirits of the wilderness approach with reverence,
    trembling to hear the commands of the Mind.

PEOPLE   Brothers, the bones of my head are coming apart with great
    joy! I see stones, unburdened of their weight, slowly
    rising, uniting by themselves and fitting together like a
    great thought...A Royal Palace, like a multi-colored mist,
    rises noiselessly in the sun and shines at the river's edge.
Oh, in the large, marble courtyard the doors open wide and
    I see a prince entering, standing tall in a silver carriage
    drawn by four horses...
And in front, holding the red reins, a tall naked man towers
    like a bronze god with a wide, golden belt around his loins.
The slaves run, but slowly the prince moves his hand and
    turns his gaze upon us like a setting sun.
Ah! His eyes fill with tears as he looks at us.
Mogalana rises and stretches out his hands toward us.

MOGALANA   Be silent! Be silent! It's Buddha, my brothers, Buddha, in the
    flower of his age, with his black, curly hair, with his
    towering, impregnable brow.
Buddha speaks to Hanna, his slave.

BUDDHA   Hanna, faithful slave, a great cry split the air: "Buddha!"
    That's the terrible name I heard, Hanna.
I was frightened, I covered my ears, and the voice issued
    stronger and clearer from my entrails: "Buddha, rise, that
    the world may rise. Waken that the world may waken!
    Buddha, crop your curly hair, doff your royal, golden
    clothing, desert your wife and your son! Buddha,
Set out for the forest, alone, without fire, without water,

without woman, without hope. Pity the trees and the birds, pity the beasts and the gods, pity mankind."

HANNA   O Lord...

BUDDHA   Hanna, my loyal slave, saddle Kantaka, my beloved horse, wrap his hoofs with velvet so they won't clatter on the stones, and wait at the outer door of the Palace;
I go to see my son's face and to bid my wife farewell.
Quiet now, don't cry, don't fall at my feet, Hanna; help me to save myself, to save us.

PEOPLE   Ah, my entrails are tearing apart, brother, as I abandon my son, my wife...For deep within me I feel it is I in another body who mourns and struggles to free himself from the world's web
And to shout the great "Farewell."
The whole world has grown lighter and sails under the moon, like a green cloud...O Buddha, like a crowned athlete returning to his country as breakwaters crumble to welcome him, O Buddha, tear down the ramparts of the flesh also.
Brothers, be silent! Hanna is returning, weeping, and he's bringing with him a pure white, slender horse.
Hanna is embracing it now, he's talking to it, as though it's a man, and both of them have broken out in lamentation.
Buddha has stretched out his hand, quietly, sweetly, pleadingly, and he's caressing it.

BUDDHA   Kantaka beloved, remember how I fed you from my palms, remember how I loved you like a brother, and what talks we had, the two of us, on our long rides.
And now, my brother, I'm asking you for a favor: Help me! Sprout wings, pass through the castle gates, trick my father's sentries so they won't see you, won't hear you, and take the path of the wilderness
That we may be saved. Kantaka, don't neigh angrily, don't refuse me. I shall leave.

HANNA   Master, they say that a wife's tears melt even the hardest stone; they say that a son's tears cause even stones to blossom,
Master, did you bid farewell to your revered wife and your son?

BUDDHA   Hanna, my son was resting at his mother's side, cuddled
         against her breast as though he were still unborn...I bent
         down to see his face, to take it with me as a consolation.
    But his mother had thrown her arm around him like a lioness
         and guarded the precious newborn head — and I left softly,
         lest I wake them...
    Faithful slave, I touch your knees; if ever I have spoken
         harshly to you, forgive me...I believed I was immortal, a
         brilliant thought that leapt from the head of Brahma.
    I thought all other men were but dust scattered by the feet of
         God as he walked upon the earth.
    Now, brother, I recognize you in the lightning flash of death;
         forgive me.

HANNA   Gautama, my prince, may you live for many years. I kiss
         your shoulders, I kiss your hands, I kiss your knees; let
         me go with you.

BUDDHA   Forgive me, my brother, I cannot. Alone, without a
         companion, I shall thrust into the dark, cool heart of the
         forest; the wilderness does not hold two, my brother.
    I take back my heart, Hanna, I tear it away from my beloved
         ones; I take back my eyes, Hanna, I take back my mind, I
         take back my entrails, I unsheath myself from the world —
         farewell.
    And you, Kantaka, my brother, I will leave you at the
         entrance to the forest. Kantaka, your eyes have brimmed
         with tears, they fall warm and heavy on my palms. Ah,
         the glance of an animal and its mute pleading!

TEMPTATION   Gautama, I will come with you.

BUDDHA   Who are you?

TEMPTATION   Mara, the spirit of Temptation; I am an ascetic too, you see,
         and I enjoy the wilderness.

BUDDHA   Come.

MOGALANA   An earthquake is destroying the foundations of the earth;
         the Palace has sunk into the pit of our minds; only one
         road remains and it shines endlessly;
    And Buddha, grasping the mane of his horse tightly, throws
         off hills and plains behind him and rides on.

Bearded, vociferous gods rise from ravines, descend from
    mountain tops and, leaning on their knobby staffs, bend
    to catch a glimpse of the rider.
"Is it Brahma or Vishnou, or can it be Siva, the indestructible
    god who, without mercy, unites, gives birth and kills?
Who is it? Who is it?" the wild glens shout and echo.
A young man and a girl embracing under a tree break away
    frightened; an old elephant turns its furrowed head, and its
    face glitters like that of a man.
And the apelike god, Hanouman, finds his voice again in his
    turbid brain and from a tall date tree shrieks his advice:
    "Go straight ahead, Gautama, with my blessing!"
The savage mountain tops catch fire, the dawn is breaking,
    the Morning Star hangs like dew from Buddha's curly hair,
And behold, an enormous Tree appears before him, without
    leaves, without fruit, without shade;
And only at its peak, five long branches toss and beat in the
    windless air and struggle to conquer their fate — to turn
    into wings.
And now Buddha, Buddha — look at him, brothers — he
    stops, jumps down to earth, waves his hand, and cries:
    "Greetings, tall Tree of the struggle! Here where your deep
    roots strive to become wings and to fly away, I will sit
    cross-legged, and I swear:
I will not rise until Salvation is wedged here between my two
    hands.
My loyal Kantaka, it's time for us to part; you've performed
    your duty well, very well. If I am liberated, you will
    become a white, immortal flame shining inside my mind."

PEOPLE   Ah, the great-spirited horse neighs mournfully and leans its
    wet, steaming neck against Buddha's shoulder,
And then suddenly it falls lifeless to the ground.

MOGALANA   Buddha gently steps over the warm, beloved corpse, and
    without turning to look, moves toward the desolate Tree
    and sits cross-legged at its roots.
Silence! Silence! The great task of asceticism now begins;
    motionless, with trunk erect like a pillar of fire,
    Buddha glows under the tall fruitless and
    flowerless Tree.

PEOPLE	Oh, he has sunk into ecstasy! His eyes have turned inward; the top of his head has risen like bread. What are those black shadows, what are those blue flashes of light that pass over him?
MOGALANA	They are the days and nights; they are the suns and the moons; they are the years.
PEOPLE	An arena of light spreads around him, an arena of light, seven arm-lengths wide.
MOGALANA	It's not an arena; Buddha is passing through the first cycle of his asceticism; motionless, with his eyes turned inwards, he sees the whole forest. He struggles, the sweat runs from his armpits; Buddha trembles like a snake floundering in the sun, coiling around rocks and struggling to shed its skin.
PEOPLE	The bright arena around him opens and widens; he sees mountains, rivers, cities and people in the translucent air.
MOGALANA	Buddha's reason opens and widens...It passes beyond the forest, it conquers India...Buddha's head fills with mountains and cities; swarms of men ascend from the furrows of his brain; They work, weep, kiss and then return into the furrows of his brain. Buddha cocks his ears and listens: Like a vast silk factory his country sprawls everywhere, and like silkworms the people crawl, opening and shutting their mouths voraciously — And standing over them, feeding them, is Buddha. Only he, in all the world, remains standing; he distributes forage to the people and waits. "Let them eat, let them eat," he thinks, "to complete the full cycle of the worm, to sprout wings and fly away."
PEOPLE	Buddha grows pale, he dissolves; his strength spills out and flows over the ground.
MOGALANA	He holds the infants of all of India to his breast and suckles them; he is the Father, he is the Mother, he is the Son of India. Approach with reverence and listen: He weeps like a baby in

its cradle; he laughs and quivers like a groom with his bride; he sings like a woman in love at dusk behind a thick lattice.

Now he falls silent and shudders — an earthquake erupts! A city topples inside him, a wound opens and heals, everything is lost...

The sun ascends, doors open and swarms of people pour out over the soil; the sun descends, the black tide withdraws, doors shut again, and the people disappear.

Buddha's breast opens and closes as though it were the door of India.

PEOPLE   Brothers, Buddha is dancing! His numberless hands go up and down, his numberless feet go up and down. Buddha is a wheel of lightning flashes; I grow dizzy.

MOGALANA   Step back, people, or his wings will touch you! The ghosts have been let loose, the chains have broken, the doors have become unhinged, the land shakes to its foundations. Old Man Time has become bewildered, Wisdom has gone mad — Buddha is dancing!

The sun rushes headlong, dawn and dusk have merged, noonday has vanished. The moon flashes in the sky like a sickle; the eye has barely time to see it before it swells, becomes a breast full of milk, then pours out its milk, deflates, becomes a sickle again, becomes a silver thread and dissolves in the air.

Winter has fallen, the earth has grown barren; Buddha turns his eyes, and at once grass spreads over the spring plains, and the trees blossom; he turns his eyes again, and the leaves wither, the fruit rots, the snow falls.

The weather and the land get drunk; Mind, that hoarder, opens his chests and scatters gold coins and precious stones he has treasured with such miserliness as he dug and sifted the sky and the earth...Buddha opens and shuts his eyes and the universe lights up and darkens.

PEOPLE   Help, Mogalana! I see fiery horsemen rushing upon me! Help me!

MOGALANA   They're not horsemen, don't be afraid, brothers; they are the thoughts of Buddha.

111

PEOPLE	I see beggars now, Mogalana, with saffron robes, with begging bowls — and I, too, am happy to give a piece of bread as charity — my soul.
MOGALANA	They're not beggars in saffron robes; they are the thoughts of Buddha. He thinks: "I want to conquer the world!" He frowns and says: "I will unleash armies, I will burn cities, I will rush down like a horseman with his spear and slaughter the earth; I am War!" And then, immediately after, he thinks, serene in the coolness of his mind: "I will find a filling and simple word, and I will divide it among all begging bowls that the people may be satiated; I am not War, I am Buddha!"
PEOPLE	Oh! Oh! A gnome, a sly black boy leaps and crouches before him. I'm afraid!
MOGALANA	Don't be afraid, don't be afraid! It's his faithful companion, the brave upholder of the ascetic, the thrice-enchanting hermit, Temptation! He's arrived, brothers, Temptation, the black Buddha, the black touchstone of man's trial has arrived; he will rub himself now against yellow Buddha, To see, it's said, if Buddha is in truth pure gold.
TEMPTATION	Gautama, eh, Gautama! He does not hear...His head has stiffened; his unmoving eyes have thickened and glazed; his nostrils, his ears, his lips are blocked with soil — Gautama! Alas, the curly hair of your youth has fallen, your skin is flaking away and rotting; your breath stinks, your spine scatters like a broken rosary, And your holy royal head has shriveled like a gourd and hangs in the air, Gautama. The owls were fooled, they took you for a hollow tree and laid their babies in your belly; and the small sparrow, the skylark, the green linnet, the chaffinch, have uprooted your beard to build their nests... All winter, buried beneath the rotted weeds, you hissed and panted like a turtle; all summer you barked like a dog, howled like a wolf, slunk through graveyards like a jackal and dug up the dead. You dug up dead people, you dug up dead times and thoughts

112

and played with their bones;
Your brains preened with pride, you sat cross-legged in the
center of the earth, motionless, and the entire Universe —
stones, people, stars, ideas — whirled, whirled and whirled
around you.
But now, unplug your ears from the weeds and soil and
listen to the message I bring you: Gautama, the gods
promenade you through the sky and howl with laughter:
Listen to what I heard Siva shouting last night as he laughed:
"Gautama seems to me like a shameless over-trained monkey;
I will stretch out my hand, seize him by the throat and toss
him into my courtyard.
The little red-assed monkey who once played there has died;
its chain lies empty. I will tie up Gautama in its stead!"

BUDDHA   Who shouted this?

TEMPTATION   Siva.

BUDDHA   Who?

TEMPTATION   Siva!

BUDDHA   Mind, thrust these words of the god Siva deeply inside you
like a knife. Memory, famished hyena, rise, seize these
words of the god Siva like meat!
Who laughed? Why do you laugh?

TEMPTATION   Aha! Gautama has still not conquered anger and pride!
You have devastated your body in vain, your mind has
shaken the universe in vain; Gautama has still not
conquered Gautama!

PEOPLE   Buddha falls prone on the earth in shame!
The whole sky above him laughs and mocks!
Be quiet; Hanna, his faithful slave, appears again on horseback.
He dismounts, holds a long sword in his hand and hurriedly,
panting, approaches Buddha.
He bares his right shoulder, he opens his mouth.

HANNA   Gautama, my prince, may you live for many years. Get up!
Enemies have set foot on your parents' Palace; your old father
lies on the threshold, drowned in blood; your faithful
slaves are lying around him, their warm corpses are still
steaming and the flames are devouring your rich cellars.

113

Get up, Gautama, take up arms and let your horses' hoofs shoot sparks again on your country's stones.

Don't you recognize me, Lord? I am Hanna, Hanna, your faithful slave.

BUDDHA   I hear a beloved voice and weeping in the wind...Who calls me? I heard my name.

HANNA   Your son calls you, Lord, your son and your revered wife... There, look at them: their arms tied behind their backs, blood-spattered and half-naked, they are dragged off to slavery by their mocking conquerors.

Rise! I bring you your father's sword, Gautama, and your faithful horse, Kantaka...Ah, you've recognized him, Lord, you shake the earth from your body, and he paws the ground and neighs with joy.

BUDDHA   Faithful, beloved companion, my brother Kantaka, how glad I am to see you.

HANNA   Lord, my Lord, rise up! Do not seek liberation in the wilderness. Leave the shadows, seize flesh, and knead. The world is not made of thoughts, sighs and visions; it's made of stones and waters and people.

Rise up and take your post in the battle!

BUDDHA   Enough! Give me the sword; my heart leaps like a tiger.

HANNA   Take it!

BUDDHA   Aaah!

PEOPLE   The sword was made of air and it disappeared!

The faithful slave disappeared too, he became but swirling smoke in the air; and the horse was but white mist that scattered.

Buddha grovels on the earth and weeps.

Hunched and crouching like a dog that bit his master, Temptation lurks behind the tree and trembles.

Buddha rises and looks sadly around him.

BUDDHA   Mara...Mara...don't be afraid, come closer...I realized too late that you were Temptation; but your words, filled with bitterness and meaning, shook my heart...

Yes, yes, there still remains a lump of mud inside me, warm

114

and beloved mud that does not want to be freed, to become
spirit and to scatter...
And inside this lump of mud are three famished sprouts —
Father, Son, Country —
That have not yet understood the secret, and struggle to
blossom.
Love, duty, hope, I blow upon you, scatter!

PEOPLE   Ah, my eyes can no longer look upon his agony. Buddha has
drowned in the soil and the weeds, his flesh has thickened
and hardened like a turtle shell; smoke rises from his holy
head.
He's rolling now over a mountain of skulls, searching among
them, biting them, climbing up and down and growling
over the bones like a hungry dog.
He barks, laughs, wears the skulls, in a wild intoxication,
and each skull is different.
Look, like a bird now, he dances, bends and pecks the earth
with a beak as large as a pelican's as though searching for
worms to eat.
Now, like a rhineroceros, he tramples the earth and with
erect horn jabs at the skulls and tumbles them down.
Ah, there he is, changing masks again; he lifts himself up like
an ape and tries to stand on his hind legs, to see. To see
what? The man of the future!

MOGALANA   Silence, people! Lightning slashes his brain; Buddha struggles
to remember.
He's going through the darkest, most difficult struggle. His
mind has surpassed the boundaries of India; it has taken up
the whole earth — the whole sphere of the world has
become his head.
These are his skulls, these, that in numberless lives Buddha
filled with eyes, with teeth, with brains; he filled them with
trees, sky, women and ideas.
And now he struggles to remember the bodies he passed
through; what animal he was, what god he was before
he walked the earth wearing his final skull — the skull of
Gautama.
For thousands of years he has lived, barked, howled, neighed,
chirped; for thousands of years he has glittered like a god,
become a woman, become a man, killed, loved, sinned,

115

died, returned to earth again, loved more, sinned less, understood all, until he became Gautama.

And now, look at him with terror; he's struggling to stop at last the wheel of birth, to pour out his body and his soul into the earth, to empty himself of animal, god, and man — to become flame and to die out.

PEOPLE   The earth and sky seem an egg to me, and inside it like a yolk, is the sun, and in the sun there's a bird — Buddha!
And it pecks the shell with its beak to break it and leave.

MOGALANA   A Drone is Buddha, my brothers, a large Drone. In spring when the thyme blossoms on the mountains, and the Queen Bee sighs in her fragrant beehive, she begins to feel constrained, stretches her wings, tries them out, licks her belly and prepares herself.
A large Drone is Buddha as he shines in the sun and wears the great panoply of Eros.
His sight intensifies — his unmoving eye governs the entire dome of the sky, he holds the East and West, the North and South like four multi-colored kites;
His hearing intensifies — he hears the Queen adorning herself, he hears her lady friends, her bridal maids, buzzing around her, encouraging, advising and pushing the bride out of her waxen home;
His taste intensifies — he tastes all the wells and all the roots; he pillages souls as though they were honey-cakes; his tongue flicks between earth and sky like a knife harvesting honey, and eats;
His smell intensifies — he smells the fragrant bridal body in the wind, and secret messages descend into his loins;
His touch intensifies — beneath his joyous belly he feels the downy body of the Queen nestling and filling;
His mind intensifies — like a male octopus it spreads, slowly caresses and squeezes life, that female octopus, in its multi-mouthed tentacles.
Buddha has put on the great panoply of Eros and the whole earth has become a Bee-Mother.

PEOPLE   He doesn't bark any more, he doesn't laugh, he doesn't cry, he doesn't fast, he doesn't struggle. He has reached the peak of endeavor and entered the smooth road of

116

liberation.

Bathing is no longer a temptation, food now nourishes his soul only; sadness, joy, sleep, wakening, speech, silence, all serve their master.

And Mara too, has become a lance, a faithful lance that shines among the armies of Buddha's head.

Underneath the stars, throughout the whole earth I can distinguish only Buddha's head shining like a midnight sun.

Help, Mogalana! What is this miracle I see? The air has filled with wings.

MOGALANA   Open your eyes, brothers, close your mouths; the gods are descending.

How do scorpions leap and thrash and writhe on the lighted hearth? So do the gods — look at them! They leap, thrash and writhe inside the fiery head of Buddha.

PEOPLE   Buddha leans on the dry Tree and oh, miracle, the withered Tree fills with blossoms. They fall slowly, thickly, on his hair, his shoulder, his chest —

And they cover Buddha!

Ah, how slowly, how serenely does salvation fall, like flowers, like tufts of snow that cover the earth.

Salvation sits like a baby nine months old wrapped in Buddha's entrails, and all his veins, blood and thoughts bestir themselves to feed it.

Oh, Buddha is rising now, brothers, and the whole world with its mountains, waters and ideas rises with him.

Saripoutta has moved, he has spread out his right hand, drawn back the invisible reins and holds the bridle tightly...

The spirits have set out too eagerly and now he orders them to assemble, to turn back.

All faces have frozen, their eyes have clouded, their bodies have emptied, they tremble in the air and vanish.

Ah, Saripoutta gathers the whole wealthy procession again inside his high forehead.

Don't shout! Saripoutta has opened his arms and prays.

SARIPOUTTA   Thank you, Mind, great nobleman of the imagination, wealthy, dexterous and omnipotent Lord of Ceremonies. You marshaled them all so well in the air, filled with flesh

117

and light, legend and truth.

You leaped out of my forehead, you played like a child
    frisking on the foaming shore of the sea. You grasped the
    sand and said:

"This is flesh, man and woman." You blew upon it and
    immediately the flesh began to speak, to hurt, to want;

You blew again, and it ceased to exist.

You grasped a fistful of azure air and said: "This is Buddha"
    —and inside the darkened heads of men flashed the youth,
    the flight, the struggles and the liberation of Buddha. You
    blew again, and Buddha vanished.

Like an eagle that snatches its weak-winged children on its
    strong wings and sweeps them high to the wind's peak,

And with one forceful shake scatters them to the winds and
    lets them fly as best they can,

So did you snatch all men also, and winnow them in the air.
    Now set them down on earth again, cover their eyes with
    earth again, and cut away the wings from their temples;
    you've played well, but enough!

PEOPLE   How do the deceiving invisible powers play us on their
    fingertips!

Ah, how do thirsting brains open to receive the miracle and
    are still insatiable!

I see Mogalana and Saripoutta still embracing, cheek to cheek.

All during the time we tossed on the wind's peak, these two
    did not even move.

And the ox-cart still stands covered, motionless, and the
    buffaloes chew their food under the Holy Tree...

Only inside our temples did all this variegated fluttering
    of wings explode.

BLOSSOMING   Buddha, Buddha, O azure wind, take me!
CHERRY TREE

VOICE OF THE   We're lost!
FIRST SENTRY   *(The Old Man jolts upright, the people let out a cry, the
    vision disappears. Muffled, troubled music. The door at the
    left is forcefully opened, the Second Sentry enters panting,
    covered with mud.)*

SECOND SENTRY   Master, brothers, we are lost!

YOUNG KOAG	O Buddha, Buddha, do not pluck the red wings from my temples, do not take the wine from my lips, do not empty my arms.
BLOSSOMING CHERRY TREE	O miracle, O sweet caress of the wind, farewell!
MANDARIN	O Mind, I have sinned, forgive me; I did not know the imagination had so many secret joys and that, even above truth, the Myth shines As round and full of light as the full moon.
OLD MAN	*(To the Magician.)* Thank you Hu-Ming, you have filled my heart with cool shade; you took me to liberation by the quickest well-shaded path. *(To the Sentry.)* Why are you shouting? *(To the People.)* Don't listen to him, my children. He'll tell you that we enter a dark cave, stumble, slip and knock our heads on stalactites — but then suddenly an invisible hand thrusts a lighted torch in our fists and the whole cave is illuminated, our hearts grow steady again and we proceed in the glow without stumbling — The word of Buddha is like that lighted torch.
SECOND SENTRY	Master, I kiss your feet; bend your revered head, hear me.
OLD MAN	Who is this crude peasant who rips freedom's silken net? Rise, Buddha, Spider of the sky, and swaddle him That he may not stir, or shout, or resist; that this peasant, too, may enter into blessedness.
SECOND SENTRY	*(Touches the Old Man with fear, as though he wanted to wake him.)* Master...
OLD MAN	Who touched me? My eyes are blinded from too much light. Who are you?
SECOND SENTRY	Don't you recognize me, Master?
OLD MAN	How can I recognize you? All the boundaries have crumbled; I lay down to sleep, and dream I am a cloud; I wake, and

become a man.

Am I a cloud? Am I a man? What is sleep? What is awakening? I wonder, do I wake or am I being transformed? Or could both be true? Or both fantasy? Or nothing? The Nothing that fills the abyss?

O Buddha, Buddha, the mist unceasingly becomes a fortress and the fortress becomes mist. I look at it from the bottom level: it's a fortress; I look at it from the upper level: it's mist.

Ah, only now do I understand: the mist, only the mist is the impregnable fortress.

SECOND SENTRY   Don't rant, Master; wake up, listen to me, forget Buddha. Look at me!

OLD MAN   How can I forget him? He won't forget me; Buddha still hangs on my eyelids...Who are you?

SECOND SENTRY   The second river sentry, Master!

OLD MAN   What river?

SECOND SENTRY   What river! The Yangtze.

OLD MAN   Ah! The great mist thickens, it becomes solid, China is coming.

We enter the dream again, the other dream, the earthen one. See, there is our village, our fields, the road that ascends, the Tower.

Ah, welcome! Yes, yes, you are the second sentry; speak, I am ready.
(Points to the people.)
And all these with their saffron robes, they're ready, too... Well?

SECOND SENTRY   *(Shouting.)*
Master, the second dam has also fallen!

OLD MAN   *(Quietly.)*
Very well. The second dam has also fallen; is that all?
(Laughs mockingly.)
On a small star, on a narrow strip of land called China, on one footprint of earth, a water-worm swelled, a water-worm called Yangtze —
And it drowned a few miniscular ants called men that scurried back and forth in the mud.

120

	Is that all? Is that why the hairs on your head stand on end? Is that why you troubled to come, you thick-headed peasant, and have frightened away that great wing, the vision?
SECOND SENTRY	But Master, don't you understand the terrible news I bring? *(To the people.)* Brothers, the river broke the second dam, it's drowning the villages; corpses are descending to the sea layer on layer! Master...
OLD MAN	Very well, very well, why are you shouting? I'm not deaf.
SECOND SENTRY	Brothers, why are you waiting? Get up, let's leave! Grab your babies in your arms, make a bundle of your lives, load the old people on your backs and let's be off! At any moment now the river will break the third dam, the last one, and it will come here and drown us! *(Runs up and down through the people, shakes them as though to wake them.)*
PEOPLE	*(Frightened, they rub their eyes and yawn.)* I'm seeing a lovely dream, don't wake me! The Yangtze? What Yangtze?
SECOND SENTRY	Wake up, brothers, why do you look at me so foolishly? Blow that azure smoke, Buddha, from your brains! The Yangtze has broken the second barrier, too — we'll be lost! *(Pounds loudly on the low door at right.)* Chiang! Chiang! Chiang! *(The door opens, Mei-Ling comes out, pale, fierce, but restrained. Music.)* Mei-Ling, O fierce and stubborn lady, your brain has not clouded over; you see, you hear, you make decisions. The Yangtze has toppled the second barrier — save your people!
MEI-LING	*(To the Old Man, with hatred.)* Why don't you rise? Why don't you take command? Didn't you hear?
OLD MAN	I heard, Mei-Ling, I heard...The second barrier fell...more villages drowned...the Yangtze is coming. *(To the Sentry.)*

Isn't that what you said?

PEOPLE   *(Startled awake.)*
Master, Old Chiang, let's leave! The Yangtze is coming!

OLD MAN   Let no one move! I want no tears; my eyes are filled too —
    I don't want our tears to mingle.
(Points to the ancestral panoplies.)
It's with these I have to settle accounts. Give way, make
    room!
Eh, Ancestors, if you've tricked me, if blood has been spilled
    in vain, then watch out! I'll dig up your graves with my
    own nails, I'll toss your bones to the watermill, grind them
    into flour, I'll bake them into bread,
I'll cast them to the dogs!

MEI-LING   Let the Ancestors be, they're dead; look to the living,
    murderer Chiang,
There's still time!

OLD MAN   I did all I could, more than I could; don't shout!
I'm tired, I'm disgusted! Enough! I've made all the gestures of
    a man fighting...I've spoken all the brave, proud words a
    nobleman should say...I've pleaded, threatened, killed, like
    a nobleman.
I'm drained out, I'm drained out, Mei-Ling, and now I make
    the final, the wisest gesture of man: I cross my hands.
I cross my hands, Mei-Ling; I close my mouth; I hold my
    head high, and wait. What am I waiting for? I don't know.
    I wait.
(To the Mandarin.)
What are you muttering?
(To the People.)
And you, what are you shouting? Poor, wretched people!
    They still want to resist. So you still don't understand?
    Was it in vain then, withered leaves of the plane tree, was
    it in vain that the autumn wind of Buddha blew upon you?
(To the Mandarin.)
Are you still muttering, you old ruin? Haven't the words run
    dry in your throat yet, you old gossiper? If you have
    something to say, say it openly before my people.

MANDARIN   *(Slowly.)*

Master...Master...In vain, in vain, in vain you killed your
   son...In vain...
*(Mei-Ling comes closer to hear; the Old Man shakes with
fear.)*

OLD MAN   Are my ears buzzing? Stop, Earth, that I may hear. Come
            closer, you old ruin; what did you say? In vain?

MANDARIN   Master...

OLD MAN   Go on! Strike, then; don't be afraid!

MANDARIN   The river did not want your son...It was useless! Useless! You
            killed him for nothing, old Chiang!
            *(The Old Man clutches the wall, as though there is an
            earthquake, shouts to the Magician.)*

OLD MAN   Help, Hu-Ming, help! This one here is tossing me into a
            nightmare again — into China, into the Yangtze, into
            bloodshed! Awaken me!
            (To the Mandarin.)
            Come closer...I swear I will not kill you! I heard nothing but
            a roar, like the collapse of mountains — mountains or
            entrails!
            (To the people.)
            Silence, so I can hear! You hang little gold and clay people
            on Buddha as pledges — and you're appeased! I hang my
            entrails on him — and I'm not appeased!
            I beg you, old sage, dear friend, say it again.
            *(The Mandarin opens his mouth, but the Old Man rushes
            toward him and covers it.)*
            Help, Hu-Ming! Give me a lump of clay, give me a trowel
            and whitewash and stones so I can plug up his mouth!
            *(Silence. The Old Man looks dazed at the Mandarin, at his
            bloodied hands; suddenly a madness overwhelms him and he
            bursts out in wild, bitter laughter.)*
            In vain? In vain? In vain?
            *(The Second Musician rises, takes down the gong, strikes it
            twice. Curtain.)*

ACT III

(Dusk of the same day. The same hall of the Tower. The Old Man is sitting under the panoplies, listening to the canary singing. Now and then he sighs. Suddenly he leaps up and opens the window. The canary stops as the terrible roar of the river is heard.)

OLD MAN   Buddha, Buddha, I think, we're approaching liberation...The world is beginning to be liberated, to thin out, to become transparent. I can make out the river beyond the dark walls,
And beyond the river, the sea; and beyond the sea, old Chiang sailing like a light cloud over Nothingness, unraveling thread by thread and disappearing...
I don't hurt any more, Buddha, may you be well! I'm not afraid, I don't love, I want nothing...Night is falling.
Night is falling, and just as the rider pets his horse to relax it at the end of a journey, so does someone over me — it must be death — caress
My sweating ears, my frothing chest, my bloodied feet.
He frees me from my harness, takes away the bridle, speaks tender words I do not understand — yet I know, this is liberation.
Gratefully I smell its breath in the air.
The villages have drowned, the bells have fallen silent, people no longer raise their hands to cry for help; this, Buddha, must be liberation!
They've folded their hands, sealed their lips; they've understood; they've lain flat on their backs and have surrendered to the Yangtze with trust.
True, true, this is as it should be; our entrails are quiet now, they don't resist, they don't hope, they no longer call on Virtue, that unkissed poison-nosed old maid, to come and defend us.
She, too, lies drowned on her back, surrendered to the current — and there she goes towards the sea...Bless her voyage!
Nor do they even call to Justice or Love any more, to gods or demons...To nothing, to no one!
Poor, wretched man! He's finally realized it: he is alone!

124

Ah, my heart is a sunken city! I lean over, and underneath
the waters I see houses and towers and bones licked clean.
No, no, it's all lies! I see nothing — only a large carcass from
one end of the heart to the other —
A large carcass with glass eyes looking at me — my son!
Be quiet, my heart. Tears are a weakness, laughter is a
weakness, cries are shameful. To whom can we call? I
called to the Ancestors, I fell at their feet, and they gave
their word,
But they've tricked me!
Be quiet, old Chiang, be quiet, old Chiang, don't disgrace
yourself...Why should you lick the foot that kicks you? For
shame! You're not a dog, you're a man; you're not a man,
you're a nobleman;
Hold fast!
(Mei-Ling enters from the large door at left, exhausted, pale.
She looks around.)

MEI-LING   With whom were you talking?

OLD MAN   (Beating his chest.)
           With this one!

MEI-LING   You have a fever, your eyes are burning; you're ranting!

OLD MAN   That's how all of you, rotted by the Western World, adjust
           yourselves and explain everything. Are your eyes burning?
           Then you have a fever! Did you dream the Ancestors were
           rising from the earth, armed, and giving orders? It's
           nothing, you must have overeaten! Do your ears buzz, do
           you hear secret voices in the wind? You're suffering from
           blood congestion! Put on some ice packs!
           And the soul, what do you do with the soul, Mei-Ling?
           (Bends over Mei-Ling, his voice trembling.)
           Is it done?

MEI-LING   (Controlling her sobs with difficulty.)
           It's done; it's all over.

OLD MAN   Did you hang...

MEI-LING   Yes...yes...a large stone around his neck.

OLD MAN   And...

125

MEI-LING   Don't ask me!
           (Wails.)
           My brother! My brother!

OLD MAN   *(Tries to caress her hair.)*
           Beloved Mei-Ling!

MEI-LING   *(Drawing back.)*
           Don't touch me!

OLD MAN   You're right!
           (Looks at his hand.)
           Ah, an axe to cut it off! Sometimes I sit and think, Mei-Ling:
           what torture life would be if Death did not come to
           unyoke us.
           Very well, very well, don't frown, Mei-Ling; go on, I'm
           listening: Why did you come? Surely not to stand at my
           aged side this difficult hour.

MEI-LING   No.

OLD MAN   Well? Do you need anything more? Give away everything,
           squander everything, don't ask me!

MEI-LING   The waters are finally nearing the third barrier; the people
           have climbed the tallest trees and are shouting...I've yoked
           all our carts; I've sent boats out; I've saved as many souls
           as I could...

OLD MAN   You've done well!

MEI-LING   They were hungry; I slaughtered a flock of our sheep, and
           they ate.

OLD MAN   You've done well.

MEI-LING   They're cold; shall I order our large ancestral trees to be cut
           down?

OLD MAN   Let them be cut down! The trees long to be cut, to become
           wood; the wood to become fire; the fire to become ashes;
           that is the road,
           Let's follow it, Mei-Ling!

MEI-LING   That's your road: downhill. *I* will fight! I've sent engineers and
           workers, I've ordered them to put strengthening boulders and
           iron bars to reinforce the third barrier; that one will not fall!

126

OLD MAN   (Sarcastically.)
            Unfortunate little people!
            (As though delerious.)
            And our weathervane, our iron rooster on the rooftop, he
                too will be drowned.
            It's him I pity, him! Why are you staring? You think I don't
                know what I'm saying? I'm a hundred years old, and I've
                never spoken with such prudence...
            I pity that iron rooster...
            Once I talked like you, like prudent little people, and
                everyone admired me: Nobleman Chiang is prudent!
                Nobleman Chiang is wise, intelligent, sly! And I was
            But a liar, a light-headed sparrow. Now I'm an old eagle and
                sit on a desolate, hopeless rock and watch the world from
                on high.
            What are you saying? I can't hear; I see only your lips
                opening and closing...

MEI-LING   I'm not saying anything. I feel you are suffering deeply, and
            this is the only pleasure I have now.

OLD MAN   (Trying to laugh.)
            I, suffering? But you should know that I keep getting lighter
                and lighter. I'm not in pain; don't rejoice yet! I'm
                jettisoning the ballast, and I'm leaving. I'm jettisoning my
                son, the Ancestors, hopes, gods — and I'm so much lighter!
            I watch my daughter kicking and wanting to leave — and I
                rejoice...Solitude! Solitude!
            I'm jettisoning the world; goodbye little people, I'm leaving!
            Eh, Mei-Ling, when I was happy I trembled lest I lose
                happiness — now I'm relieved.

MEI-LING   There's not enough room here for both of us, old Chiang. The
            air grows heavy, I'm going.

OLD MAN   The air grows heavy; a daughter hates her old parent.

MEI-LING   Yes.
            (Silence. Suddenly the Old Man bursts into bitter laughter.)

OLD MAN   Thank you, Buddha, you destroy all the bridges around me;
                this is what you want. This is what I want, too. Solitude,
                solitude, wilderness! I admire you, Mei-Ling — you are on

                            127

one side, a young girl, a weak, slim reed, and on the other side, the terrible river Yangtze. And you're not shattered, you fight it...

(Silence.)

Mei-Ling, you remind me...

(Stops, moved.)

MEI-LING   What? Your eyes have filled with tears...

OLD MAN   Of the heart of man.

(Abruptly.)

Go! Go cut down the trees, that the people may keep warm...

(Laughs.)

That they may sink warm to the bottom of the river.

MEI-LING   My curse on you, old Chiang!

(Leaves.)

OLD MAN   May you be well, my child.

(To himself.)

The people are crying, "Mercy, mercy!" They're afraid, they're hungry, they're cold...But you, my heart, you scorn mercy now because you have climbed higher and govern the whole circle of futility.

You're serene, because all the agonies of earth have merged inside you and not one is missing. You're without hope and condescension, my heart, because you're proud, and you know.

You know! Why should you shout? To whom shall you speak your pain? You pass noiselessly, slowly over the waters like a mute eagle.

You look at the wheel of the sky turning and grinding the stars; you look at the mind tormented and tied to the wheel, shouting...

You leap, draw circles in the air, trace secrets in the light, signs without order, without meaning...

You play without any purpose, because you're strong; you play by yourself, alone, because you're without hope.

You build towers on the banks of time, you mold gods, sons, and grandsons with water and sand —

You open your eyes, and the creatures come alive; you close your eyes, and they disappear.

128

You dance, my heart, you dance in the wilderness. You love no
  one, you hate no one, you hope for nothing, you are free!
*(Pulls the curtain and gazes at the statue of Buddha that is
bursting with laughter.)*
Buddha, Buddha, you are laughing! I know the secret, too,
  I know it, but I cannot laugh.
That's our difference Buddha, no other; and that is why
  you're a god and I'm a worm.
(The slaves arrive carrying a khaki uniform.)
What do you want? What are you holding? Go away!

FIRST SLAVE   You ordered us, Master…It's the uniform of General Chiang…

SECOND SLAVE   Your son's, Master.

OLD MAN   Eh, eh, don't bend your knees; the time has come for all of
  us — masters and slaves — to become one *(Looks at the
  uniform.)* Whose did you say?

FIRST SLAVE   Your son's, Master, Chiang…General Chiang's…

OLD MAN   *(Searching through it.)*
It isn't yellow mist? It isn't twilight clouds? If I blow on it,
  won't it vanish? Eh, eh, come here; don't you, too, try to
  fool me. Is this all that remained? This? Nothing else?
And the flesh that was inside, the bones, the voice, the soul?
  What became of them? You're to bring them to me, do you
  hear? Those are what I want!
(Turns to Buddha.)
We're to blame, Buddha, you're right, we're to blame! If there
  were no parents, Death would die of hunger!
(To the slaves.)
Don't be afraid, I tell you; masters and slaves will all become
  one; the waters are coming to bring justice.

FIRST SLAVE   We kiss your feet, Master, command us. What shall we do
  with these clothes you ordered us to bring you?

OLD MAN   *(Lifting the uniform, looking at it.)*
Is this my son? This? These trousers, this jacket, these bronze
  buttons? Is this my son?
Thirty five years I raised him; he filled out with flesh and
  bones and ideas…And now?

SECOND SLAVE   What shall we do with the clothes, Master, command us.

129

OLD MAN	Stuff them with air, construct a savage mask of cloth and paint, tie everything to a rod, make a scarecrow and nail it on the riverbank.
	The river will see it; it will become frightened, they say, and turn back.
	(Gasps, tears his shirt open to catch his breath.)
	Ah, I'm smothering!
SLAVES	Master...Master
OLD MAN	*(Recovering.)*
	Ah, is it you, my faithful slaves? You've brought the uniform? Why haven't you spoken all this time?
	Fine! Fine! Climb up the wall and hang the uniform beside the Ancestors...I cursed you, my son, I cried: "Your panoply will not be hung beside the Ancestors' panoplies." I disowned you.
	But now, to spite them, stand at their side, my son Chiang.
	Don't growl at me, Ancestors; I've finally reached the edge of despair, the cliff of freedom — and I fear no one!
	Don't sharpen your knives again; you can't kill him now, he's become immortal, like you. Don't be afraid of them, my child, stand beside them.
	(To the slaves who have climbed the wall to hang up the uniform.)
	A little more to the right...No, no, that's where my own armament will hang; more to the right...there!
	(To himself.)
	You have a son, he walks and the earth creaks; and you take pride in him and say: "I'm not afraid of death any longer; I have a son!" And then you try to touch him,
	And only a uniform of war remains in your hands...
	(The slaves tumble down, terrified.)
FIRST AND SECOND SLAVES	Master...Master...
OLD MAN	What happened? Did you see something?
	(Points to the Ancestors.)
	Did they tell you anything? Speak!
FIRST SLAVE	There, where we climbed, Master, and were hanging...Ah, ah, I'm still trembling!

130

SECOND SLAVE	I saw...
FIRST SLAVE	*I* saw, *I*...you were leaning over, you didn't see...
SECOND SLAVE	I did, I swear it, Master...I saw, too; here, touch my hands, they're frozen...
OLD MAN	The whip! *(Searches for the whip.)*
FIRST SLAVE	Don't be angry, Master...Look, all the panoplies have moved and have drawn back!
SECOND SLAVE	As though they don't want to touch your son's clothes...
FIRST SLAVE	As though they were angry; their knives stirred in their belts.
OLD MAN	Go! *(Chases them away with the whip.)* Ancestors, eh, Ancestors, I've done what you wanted, enough now! You gave me a knife, and I returned it as you wanted it — red from tip to haft. Enough now! I, too, have the right to speak; in a few hours I'll descend into the earth; I, too, will become an Ancestor, a great nobleman of earth, like you. Don't be angry. You don't like his company? I like it; he's my son, your grandson, your great-grandson, your great-great-grandson; whether you like it or not, he'll stand beside us, too! *(The large door opens abruptly, Mei-Ling enters and stands at the threshold. She is pale. Silence. The Old Man walks towards her slowly.)*
OLD MAN	Did the third barrier fall?
MEI-LING	Yes.
OLD MAN	And the engineers, the iron rods, the cement, the White Demons? *(Mei-Ling bows her head; the Old Man raises his hands.)* Mei-Ling, my child, man has only one value; haven't you understood that yet? Only one... *(Mei-Ling raises her head as though to question him.)* To watch the Yangtze come, to watch it and not cry out. *(Noise outside. The river waters are heard roaring. The people*

fill the Tower courtyards and shout. The slaves run,
frightened, and watch the Old Man, not daring to cross the
threshold.)

OLD MAN   Open the doors!
          (The slaves hesitate.)
          Open the doors!
          (The slaves open the doors, the people rush forward,
          terrified.)
          Eh, eh, paint your faces, put rouge on your cheeks! What
              faces are these? What mud is this? I don't like it!

PEOPLE   We're lost! Our end has come; we will drown!

OLD MAN   Is this the first time you've thought of death? Is this the first
              time the Black Master-Shepherd has whistled to you in the
              darkness? Get out of my sight, cowards!

PEOPLE   Save us, it's your duty. We're not masters to disdain life; we're
              slaves — we want to eat, to give birth, to fertilize the earth.
          It is your duty to save us, old Chiang; save us!

OLD MAN   Don't shout; don't scream; you climb over each other and run
              like rats smelling an earthquake.
          (To the Five Whores.)
          Why have you brought these white candles? Is this a
              wedding?

PEOPLE   Master, the third dam has fallen!

OLD MAN   I know!
          (Beats his chest.)
          Now the fourth dam will fall, this one!
          (To the Musicians.)
          Eh, musicians, let's see what you can do! Play! A great
              Nobleman has reached the foot of our Tower. His Serene
              Highness has condescended to visit us; the great Nobleman
              has arrived with his escort —
          Cradles, window shutters, tubs, carcasses, camels and sheep
              and beasts and people — all drowned!
          His Serene Highness arrives with his wealthy attendants, layer
              over layer of crocodiles below, layer over layer of crows
              above — and in the middle, the great Nobleman, Yangtze.
          Play loudly! Not like that, not like that — joyously!

132

(Beating the drum himself.)
There, like that; as at a wedding, when the bridegroom is
    coming.

MANDARIN   Hold on to your wits, old Chiang, or they'll leave you. Don't
    forget you're a nobleman.

OLD MAN   Open the doors! Open both sides! Light the lanterns, all of
    them! Raise my flags, the green dragons!

PEOPLE   He's gone crazy with grief! Who can save us now? We're lost!

MANDARIN   Make room so I can sit down and listen. Fate has grown
    savage; each word now has taken on value, it drips with
    blood and tears; it's my duty to keep it from falling.
You all depend on me now to be saved or not in the
    chronicles of China. All of you here will die; I will die,
    too.
(Shows his notebook.)
Only this will remain immortal.
I see the Magician rising, moving his lips; he wants to speak.
    Make way, friends, that I may hear and write.
(Writes. Recites pompously.)
"Now at this solemn hour, the Magician of that time,
    Hu-Ming by name, rose, bowed before the Nobleman and
    said..."
(To the Mandarin.)
Speak, Hu-Ming, I'm writing.

MAGICIAN   *(Bowing before the Old Man.)*
Shall I begin? Shall I bring Buddha down again, to relieve
    your heart, my Nobleman?
You'll see, everything's but mist and clouds. The strong wind,
    the Spirit, will blow, and everything will scatter...
And your bloodied hands, old Chiang, will turn white, as
    white as the moon.
(Softer.)
Old Chiang, there is no other salvation.

OLD MAN   I know.

MAGICIAN   Shall I begin?

OLD MAN   Wait...wait...My heart still has room, it can contain
    everything shamelessly. Don't be in such a hurry...

(To the women who are holding the white candles.)
Why are you carrying these white candles?

MANDARIN   *(Approaches the Old Man, trembling.)*
It's an old custom, my nobleman, to save the people...

OLD MAN   You don't answer? Why do we need white candles?
(To the Mandarin.)
You, be quiet!

WOMEN   *(Falling at Mei-Ling's feet.)*
Oh, Mei-Ling, young noble lady...

MEI-LING   Why are you kissing my feet? Get up!

WOMEN   Pity us, noble lady, save us!

MEI-LING   I? I?

WOMEN   Only you can save us, my lady...

MEI-LING   Oh, if only I could save you! If only my soul might not
vanish but be built as a foundation in the mud...a
foundation for China...
(To the women.)
Why don't you speak? How can I save you? Why are you
crying?
(To the Mandarin.)
Old scribe, I caught sight of you talking with the women;
what do they want?

MANDARIN   It's an old custom, my lady, to save the people...to tame the
river...

WOMEN   Today, my lady, as you crossed the river, we saw...
The Old River's back was swelling, swelling like a tiger that
sees his female...
It's you it wants, my lady, it's you it's looking for, it's
aroused now and is descending to drown us...

MANDARIN   An old custom, my lady, to save the people...to tame the
river...
What are you thinking of, my lady?

MEI-LING   Nothing...nothing...
(Suddenly lets out a harrowing cry.)
My brother, I'm coming!

134

MANDARIN	I swear I heard the River murmuring and wailing like a human..."The noble lady, the noble lady..." it murmured and sighed, "the noble young lady..."
OLD MAN	(Who has been listening. Now he rushes savagely, stands in front of Mei-Ling and spreads out his arms.) No, no, enough! My son died in vain, only she is left me... Enough!
MEI-LING	Let me be, father...let me be...and let me vanish, for my only joy now is on that other shore.
OLD MAN	No, no, I won't let you! Enough now!
WOMEN	Mei-Ling, the great moment comes once in a lifetime, only once — to become or not to become immortal. The entire soul hangs, Mei-Ling, on the movement of a hand, on the rise and fall of an eyebrow, on one small word... Move your hand, Mei-Ling, let your eyebrows rise and fall, say "yes" Mei-Ling...
OLD MAN	No, no, I will not let her go — I have no one else! Ah, I thought my heart had become stone, that when struck, it shot sparks — but it's a sick, complaining monkey that weeps...No, no, I will not let her go!
MANDARIN	Master, do not trample the holy customs of the Ancestors. Rivers are great male beasts, Master...When they get angry, they want a woman to calm them...It's an old custom — the noble lady of the land is dressed and adorned like a bride, and then thrown into the river. The river's a man, you see, and he wants to embrace; he embraces and at once shrivels up, his strength softens, he looks at the world and pities it — he understands now the meaning of gentleness, of child, of the embrace — and he turns back. Listen, Master... (Opens the book, searches, reads.) "During the glorious kingdom of the Mings when the king was..."
OLD MAN	(Grabs the book and tramples on it with fury.) Shut your mouth!
MANDARIN	(Jumping back in terror.)

135

The Ancestors...the Ancestors are in there...Books are sacred, like cemeteries.

OLD MAN   (*Sarcastically.*)
The Ancestors! I'm not afraid of them any more; I'm free! He was right, this one!
(*Points to Chiang's uniform.*)
My son, Chiang!
I'm free of Ancestors, I'm free of graves!
(*Smiles bitterly.*)
Too late...too late...at this moment I'm entering the graveyard...

PEOPLE   We're lost! What blasphemies are these, Master? You're shaking the foundations of the world.

OLD MAN   Enough, I say! So I'm shaking the foundations of the world? Brainless cowards, but haven't you understood it yet? The foundations of the world are smoke and air!
Go back! I gave up my son for nothing! For nothing!
(*Points to the panoplies.*)
They fooled me! Good for them!
(*To the Magician.*)
I wish I knew, Hu-Ming, where all that lost pain of man goes and settles. Somewhere on the earth — not in the sky, nor in Hades — somewhere on the earth, our Mother, there must be the large reservoirs where the tears of men are gathered — and one day these will overflow.
This must be the terrible Yangtze of man. Yes, yes, it is! And then, joy to the living! The gods will sit on their stools, gods and men will open their large ledgers, they'll come to an accounting — this is what we gave, men will say, so many barrels of tears, so many cisterns of sweat, so many rivers of blood.
And what was our share? A poor uncultivated strip of field, all thorns and stones, a dark, ill-fated brain, a woman full of teeth and nails and cries — the final bill will be issued and the gods will pay.
All then, Hu-Ming, all will be paid, all of it!
(*To the People.*)
Why are you crowding around me? Go! I said I will not give her. Let the bridegroom himself come and take her.

PEOPLE   It will be on your conscience.

OLD MAN:	Let it be on my conscience; I will not give her!
MANDARIN	Say yes, Old Chiang, say yes, give her willingly, otherwise the sacrifice won't succeed.
PEOPLE	*(They surround the Old Man threateningly as the circle becomes narrower.)* Say yes, Old Man, to save us!
OLD MAN	*(Trying to break the circle smothering him.)* Do you want to choke me? Go away!
PEOPLE	Say yes...
OLD MAN	No!
MANDARIN	Think of your grandson!
OLD MAN	Don't try to frighten me, you penpusher! My grandson is far, far away, safe; I no longer fear anything! He will fill my fields with men again. No, the Dynasty of Chiang will not vanish! So long as my grandson lives, I am immortal. Yes, yes, I played the Yangtze's game, I've fooled it! *(Old Koag suddenly appears at the large door, wet, muddied, holding the grandson in his arms. The Old Man starts, cuts through the crowd, stands before Koag and shouts.)* No! No!
OLD KOAG	Master...
OLD MAN	No, no, it's not you!
OLD KOAG	Master, forgive me...
OLD MAN	No, no, I say! My eyes are on fire, my ears are buzzing... Mei-Ling, help! I see ghosts, I hear ghosts, help! Who is this before me?
MEI-LING	Koag, old Koag, our faithful slave.
OLD MAN	What is he holding in his arms? The truth! Speak the truth; don't pity me.
MEI-LING	Your grandson, father.
OLD MAN	Who?
OLD KOAG.	The river flooded the valley, Master...I rushed with the

oxcart, the oxen were drowned, the water rose to my neck;
I held your grandson over my head...
I took another road; I've been struggling since dawn —
I shouted, I pleaded, I fought — I could not get through,
forgive me.

PEOPLE   Master, you've played your game now with the Yangtze...

OLD MAN   May it be cursed! If only it had a body, if only it were a
man! But it's all slime and water and can't be grasped...
Oh, if I, old Chiang, were a river, too, I'd rush upon it and
fight it!
(As though seeing Koag for the first time.)
Koag, you here? You've returned?

OLD KOAG   Master, forgive me...

OLD MAN   A curse on hope! Wretched man forgets himself for a moment
and says: "Perhaps there's a door open...perhaps. Very
small, like the footstep of a baby..."
And he runs to slip through, to save himself — and becomes
degraded.
I've lost the game; I, too, raise my hands, Mei-Ling; I
surrender.
I cross my oars, I cross my hands, I cross my brain, I give
myself up to the torrent. I shout: "Eh, torrent, wherever
you're going, I too have been going. I'm glad you've come;
I leap and mount you bareback! Let's be off!"
Nothing bothers me now; I've reached the summit of pain;
from there on liberation begins!
(To his grandson.)
Come here, you!
(Grabs him in his arms, caresses him.)
Quiet, quiet, my child, we've lost the game...
Mei-Ling, good luck to you, go.
*(The Women run to Mei-Ling, throw a white veil over her
and place a wreath of flowers on her head. The white candles
lead the procession. The Old Man turns to Mei-Ling and
speaks calmly.)*
Mei-Ling, are you leaving?

MEI-LING   I'm leaving, father.

OLD MAN   In vain...all in vain...

MEI-LING   I know. Does it matter, father?

OLD MAN   No, it doesn't matter; go. If you see anyone down there, tell
           him I'm coming.

MEI-LING   (Smiling.)
           I'll see worms.

OLD MAN   Tell them I'm coming.
           (The Women light the white candles. Mei-Ling calmly falls on
           her knees and kisses the ground.)

MEI-LING   Sun, rain, plow, dung, beloved grass, O China, farewell.
           (Falls at the Old Man's feet.)
           Father, forgive me; until this morning I was still very young,
              very cruel, deaf, blind, armed with hopes...But now, at
              last, I understand.
           Father, place your bloodied hands on my head; give me your
              blessing; I'm leaving.

OLD MAN   (Places his hands on Mei-Ling's head.)
           My blessings on you, Mei-Ling.
           This, Buddha, is the most humiliating torture: to see your
              loved one leaving forever, forever, forever — and not feel
              sad.
           What is the soul, then? Mud? But even mud remembers your
              footprint when you step on it.
           (To Mei-Ling.)
           Farewell! Farewell! If I lived on, I'd build you a temple,
              Mei-Ling, small and charming, like your body, a temple on
              the banks of the Yangtze where you may be worshipped.
           And over the doorway I'd insert a bronze plaque, and on it I'd
              engrave with embellished and sacred letters:
           "Mei-Ling, nobleman Chiang's beautiful, young, virgin
              daughter, Mei-Ling, married the nobleman Yangtze to save
              her country. In vain! In vain! In vain! O passerby, toss a
              white wildflower on the river waters and cry three times:
              'In vain! In vain! In vain!'"

MEI-LING   (Smiling bitterly.)
           Yes, father.

OLD MAN   But I'm not going to live, I won't build a temple, I won't
              engrave a bronze plaque — does it matter, Mei-Ling?

MEI-LING   It doesn't matter, father. Farewell.

OLD MAN   Wait, don't leave yet, my child; do me this last favor: give me
           your blessing.

MEI-LING   I?

OLD MAN   Give me your blessing, my child.

MEI-LING   Beloved father, I remember the hawk I dreamt about, that
           ate all your flesh, strip by strip...
           I cannot speak any more, farewell.
           (To the Women.)
           Let us go.
           *(The Women take Mei-Ling, pass the threshold at right,
           descend the steps singing wedding songs softly. The Old Man
           runs to the window, tightens his arms around his grandchild
           and shouts.)*

OLD MAN   My child!
           (To Buddha.)
           Here I am, Buddha, just as you wanted me: they've plucked
           my two great wings, my son Chiang and my daughter,
           Mei-Ling — only the worm remains.
           Break, O my small heart; aren't you ashamed to endure?
           Break at last, to show your nobility.
           O Buddha, you kill all, without being bloodthirsty; you
           show compassion to everything, without being
           compassionate. Your laughter is a cataract made of all
           mankind's tears; and your own tears Buddha, are the pure,
           refined, and distilled quintessence of all the people's
           laughter.
           (To his grandson.)
           This is Buddha, your plaything, my child; do not be afraid.

PEOPLE   *(With agony.)*
           Has the river grown calm? It's still roaring...Help us!

MANDARIN   Don't be in such a hurry. God is in no hurry, and that's why
           he is God...When he's had enough, he'll remember the
           people and perform his miracle.

OLD MAN   Quiet; I can't bear you any longer! What will grow calm? The
           river? The river? My curses on virtue, sacrifice, nobility! I
           am caught, entangled in my own virtues, and that's why I

can never escape.
The free man has no friend; not even death.

MAGICIAN Old Chiang, my nobleman...

MANDARIN He doesn't hear; he's floating on deep waters...speak louder
to him.

MAGICIAN Old Chiang!

OLD MAN Ah! Is it you, Madam Imagination, you versatile whore?
Where were you when I lost my way? We haven't met for
years and years...

MAGICIAN Years, my Nobleman?

OLD MAN You see, Hu-Ming, each drop of time became heavy —
like a corpse with a rock hung around its neck and tossed
into the waves.
Where are you, Hu-Ming? Give me your hand.
Hu-Ming, resourceful thinker, forgive me, I take back my
harsh words; the free man has *one* friend: you.

MAGICIAN My Nobleman, the waters have risen up to here
(Indicates his neck.)
The mouth will remain free for a little while. It still has one
cry, one free cry inside it. Don't let it vanish, my
Nobleman, don't let it vanish in the grave.

OLD MAN The cry of freedom must not vanish, Hu-Ming, my beloved,
it must not vanish into the grave; you are right,
And when the whole world is drowned, that cry will still fly
over the waters and shout.

MAGICIAN Onward then, let's not waste time. I rally my brave
co-workers — the wings, the yellow mask, the twelve signs
of the zodiac, the multi-colored words, the difficult
rhymes, the gaudy metaphors, the eyes, the ears, the fiery
wind, the Dance, and Music, and the Word — the father,
the mother, and the son!
(To the Second Musician.)
Beat the drum; I'm ordering a mobilization!

OLD MAN My blessings on you, Hu-Ming. Get a good start, lift man
above man. But quickly, for I feel the water under

my chin.

MANDARIN   *(To the Magician.)*
            Aren't you ashamed! Have you no heart? Don't you see the
            people weeping? We're lost! We're lost, and you, you cheap
            actor, are you still playing?

MAGICIAN   Where did we stop, my Nobleman? Do you remember?

OLD MAN   Don't ask; at the edge of the precipice — give us another
            shove, push us over.

MAGICIAN   Farewell, people, farewell old Chiang. If I said anything that
            sets heavy on your heart, forgive me; if I said anything to
            lighten your heart, if I did you some good, forgive me. I
            bid you farewell, farewell, because I don't know if I'll come
            out of this performance alive...
            I'm afraid for you, too, old Chiang.

OLD MAN   Don't be afraid for me; my heart is a closed-in garden of
            rocks, no tree, no water, no grass, just stone.
            And the garden is filled with birds: with crows. Speak
            fearlessly.
            *(The Magician makes the circle, pins down the twelve signs of
            the zodiac, says an exorcism.)*

MAGICIAN   Are you ready, old Chiang?

OLD MAN   I'm ready.

MAGICIAN   Can you endure one more word, the last I have to tell you?

OLD MAN   Go on, I tell you, I can.

MAGICIAN   The One divided, old Chiang, and we are to blame; the One
            divided and became Life and Death.
            Before we were born, He was One; as soon as we die, He will
            become One again; it's we who get in the middle and
            thwart Him.
            Life is an eclipse of God; let's draw back, old Chiang, that His
            entire face may shine.

OLD MAN   Let's step back, Hu-Ming, that His entire face may shine.
            Buddha, stretch out your hand, bless these creatures who
            moan at your feet — stretch out your hand and drown
            them.

142

Help man, Lord, to leap across the terrible threshold, without
mind or memory, without fire, without water and earth
and wind — free at last!

MAGICIAN O Mind, who are all-powerful, help me!
*(Puts on the yellow mask and immediately the set changes; we
return to the vision.)*

PEOPLE What is that sound, that fluttering of wings, those flashes of
sparks on the stones? Clouds have gathered in the sky.
Don't shout! It's the disciples of Buddha — some mounted on
gigantic wings, some on the backs of lions, some riding on
white clouds...
Some come from the sky, others rip through the earth and
ascend; some have taken to the river, sit cross-legged on
water-lilies and sail with the tide...
One sings, another falls silent; one thinks, another cries.
Each with his own given aptitude rejoices in liberation.

YOUNG MAN And that woman, who is that woman, without hair,
without breasts, dressed in a saffron robe, holding a long
fan of peacock feathers and fanning Buddha...
The elephants have slowly turned their round, calm eyes
toward Buddha and their brows glow, as though it were
dawning;
And the little beasts, the weasels, the foxes, the squirrels, the
ferrets, rise on their hind legs, as though the moon had
suddenly appeared.
And with erect tails, satiated, without a care, they begin to
dance around Buddha.
Oh, the earth has filled with disciples in saffron robes. One
goes in front, fat and serene, riding a white-browed cow,
and advances, well-nourished, toward nonexistence.
And beside him a ferocious ascetic strides over the earth,
exhausted with holiness and hunger.
I see a huge-bodied disciple, bursting with strength and rage,
approaching, stomping like a gorilla. He is speaking with
invisible enemies, explaining the teachings as he raises his
fist and beats the air.
And behind him another disciple, bathed, painted, smiling,
with a heavy gold earring, with a valuable fan of white
ostrich feathers, follows the procession slowly, proudly.

Mogalana — look at him, brothers! — has rushed among the
disciples, embracing, kissing, greeting the comrades of the
struggle, and their bronze begging-bowls clang joyously,
like war shields;

And Saripoutta is standing quietly, silently, sunk in ecstasy,
rejoicing in nothing.

The dancing swells, the faces of the disciples glow, their songs
have caught fire! The smiling, newly-bathed disciple speaks
first, slowly, calmly, as though singing a lullaby to an
infant child, as though exorcising

The invisible spirits of virtue and of evil.

FIRST DISCIPLE   We waken, descend to the river, we wash, clean and polish
our swords — our bodies.

We ascend with the sun and go, glittering, serenely and
without hope, toward the city.

We stand erect beside the low doors of the people, and for
many hours wait for a crumb, with patience and
acquiescence.

And when the holy begging ends, we return, again with the
sun, and sink like gold worms in the forest. We gather
leaves, and then sit cross-legged with head erect, as the
circumference of our faces shines from unsleeping
contemplation.

Motionless and smiling, we release the power of our mercy to
go forward, to flood the North; to go back, to flood the
South; then to the right to reach the East, and then to the
left to reach the West.

And then to rush to the sky's zenith to abolish the good
powers, the gods; and to descend below, deep into Tartarus
to abolish the evil powers, the demons.

Almighty is our power; as quiet as sleep, as sweet as death;
it floods the world and tames the five great ghosts — wind,
earth, fire, water and the spirit.

PEOPLE   A slender, young disciple gets up to dance, but changes his
mind, then throws himself down and weeps.

The bountiful grace of Buddha must have fallen upon him and
he cannot bear it.

Ah, the savage disciple has taken the lead in the dance, his
brain has caught fire and he begins singing.

144

SECOND DISCIPLE   Buddha's word is a conflagration! We did not come to make
                  the homes of men secure. We did not come to plant, to
                  marry people or to bless phalluses and wombs.
                  We are quiet, simple, and wait with patience — but when the
                  thunderbolt is deserved, then even more unwaveringly than
                  the god Indra, we hurl it on earth!
                  Fire is our bread and wine, fire is our home and our wife. Fire
                  is our plow, and we came to plow, to open and cleanse the
                  earth, and to plant burning coals,
                  Our holy seed.

PEOPLE   A pale disciple is blushing, he can't restrain himself and begins
         a song, singing like a woman in love;
         His almond-shaped, downy eyes sparkle and play.

THIRD DISCIPLE   Lord, Lord, when I am far away from you and hear your
                 voice proclaiming liberation,
                 Then my breast melts, Lord, my knees tremble and I am lost.
                 A deep precipice opens between every other word you
                 speak, Lord, a deep precipice, and I fall into it.
                 But when I approach and see you, Lord, my heart grows
                 calm, my knees grow strong, and I walk firmly from one
                 word to the other — as when we jump from rock to rock
                 over the water in crossing a stream.
                 And when I sit at your feet and touch you, Lord, everything
                 disappears...There are no rocks, there are no waters, there
                 is no onward march; I was a lighted candle and I've melted
                 away.

PEOPLE   Oh, the hungry, flesh-eaten ascetic has taken up the song.
         The trees, the waters and the beasts have fallen silent to
         hear him.

FOURTH DISCIPLE   I sit, quietly blissful, my hands empty, my entrails empty, my
                  heart empty...I love no one, I hate no one, I want nothing.
                  I say: I am not perfect, I will be reborn; and I feel no
                  sadness. I say: I am perfect, I will not be reborn; and I feel
                  no joy.
                  I've escaped from my father and mother, I've deserted my
                  wife and my children, I have thrown off my burdens. I've
                  escaped from gods and demons, I've escaped from hope,
                  and my bones whistle and sing like the reeds of a
                  dilapidated hut.

I've escaped from the flesh and the spirit; I walk airily over
    heads, like a cloud, and the people in the fields rejoice and
    say: "It will rain, the earth will become cool again, the
    seedlings will ripen."
And I pass over them without rain, without coolness, without
    a wind. I am
A small, small, parched thought belonging to Buddha.

MOUDITA   *(To her husband, the young man.)*
Why are you staring at me? I'm not a bitch, I'm not a
    dilapidated hut, I'm not a ghost; I'm not your wife.
I am a reed on the riverbank of Buddha.

YOUNG MAN   A curse on God who leads man to such perfection!
Come back beloved Moudita, come back again to man's warm
    body and save yourself.

MOUDITA   I am a reed on the riverbank of Buddha; ah, when will I
    become the sound of a flute, to fade away?

PEOPLE   I'm afraid, brother. Buddha doesn't look, he doesn't speak or
    move...He sits cross-legged underneath the dry Tree and
    his head, his hands, his feet glitter.
The head of Buddha has grown large, it has flared up like the
    sun, whitened like fiery iron; no one can go near him.
Mogalana has bared his right shoulder, he has taken a step
    forward with much pain, he has taken another, but he's
    panting, he can't go on; the earth shook in seven different
    ways beneath his feet;
And Mogalana has turned back and clutches Saripoutta so as
    not to fall.

YOUNG MAN   Buddha, I gaze upon you and my skull empties, my brain
    spills out, my spine drips over the abyss,
Ah, in vain did I sink into the five pits of my body like a pig,
    to escape from you.

BLOSSOMING   Lord, pity the men!
CHERRY TREE   Cast all your rage mercilessly upon me, the woman, O
    Savior!
The man, Lord, is always ready for salvation, but I won't let
    him. The man sits at the river's edge, crosses his legs,
    crosses his heart and his mind, and swears:

"I will not eat, I will not drink, I will not sleep with woman;
I seek salvation."

But Lord, I pass by, my eye catches sight of him and I yearn
for his savagery, his strength and his ugliness; all at once a
fire leaps between my two breasts and I say: "I want to
sleep with him! I want to sleep with him!"

My breasts weigh me down Lord, they are heavy, full of
milk, I can't walk! I hurt; I want a son to clutch my
nipples, to drink all of me.

I wander through the mountains, walk through the cities,
enter temples, sit at windows — and call to men.

It's not I who call, Lord; it's my mother inside me who calls,
that hairy ancestor, an inconsolable female beast calls from
inside me — the entire Earth.

Put out this fire in my entrails, Lord, and save the world.

The abyss shrank, became body, became voice, bathed,
painted and adorned itself, sprouted breasts, became a
woman. Ah, I waste my strength in merging with the abyss.

The mind of Buddha turns, turns, ascends, descends, eats up
the earth.

His chins move and grind; the blood and brains of all men
flow from his lips.

Don't look to the right, don't look to the left, no one can
escape. Let's not resist, let's proceed with a quiet, firm
tread, freely toward that mouth.

I want to leave! I want to leave! I left my son in his cradle;
who will suckle him? I left my husband at the plow; who
will bring him food?

Buddha will suckle him, don't worry, my sister; and Buddha
will feed your husband with earth.

Buddha, Buddha, mercy! My heart is a piece of meat and
fat, Lord, and it believes in bread, in the child and in the
flesh; don't kill me!

Don't shout at it; it doesn't hear, it doesn't speak, it doesn't
move; don't degrade yourself. The world is a river, a river
that spills over

Into the pit of your eye.

I can see a dark well in the center of the earth and we all run
hurriedly, fighting, laughing, crying, and we all fall into
the well

With bloodied cotton wadding in our mouths.

This is not a well, brothers; this is the third, the secret eye of
  Buddha, that lies unmoving between his eyebrows and
  swallows us.

MANDARIN Don't be afraid my children. I'll rise and defend you. I'll call
  the three great gods, I'll cast exorcisms in the wind; I'll
  force the invisible powers to take on flesh and descend
  from the air;
Brahma, Siva, Vishnu, help me!
The air flashed, it moved! Brahma, that crimson lion, treads
  on the nine levels of the sky, step by step, and descends.
As blue-green as poison, Siva wraps a snake seven-fold
  around his loins and descends; and Vishnu, cross-legged
  upon a green leaf, serenely balancing his two arms to the
  right and left, slowly flutters to the ground.
Behind him numberless battalions descend from the nine skies
  ...The spirits sit cross-legged on multi-colored carpets
  where their kingdoms glow embroidered
With red, yellow, and green air.
Oh! Oh! Like the shed leaves of autumn the gods fall to the
  earth.
And Mogalana has bared his right shoulder with reverence,
  has taken two strides and stands like a nobleman of the
  earth, welcoming them.

MOGALANA I bow and greet the head of the world, the wind of life, the
  onrush of breath, Brahma.
I sit cross-legged in the silence of night, encircled by the
  dark powers; and Earth, that painted and primped whore,
  begins to dance in my mind;
And you rise, Brahma, you fix your eyes upon her — this
  Earth to you seems like a woman, the sea stretches across
  your temples like a wide bed, and all at once you leap from
  my head like sperm, and say:
"I want to fill her womb with children!"
And I let you escape from my mind, to merge, to spill into
  the imagination that generations may multiply, that flesh
  may be molded, that spirits may struggle, that elements
  may suffer and pass through every exploit, and I
  meditate:
This earth is a precious, multi-colored, nonexistent essence,
  and the husband of this essence, Brahma, is precious,

148

multi-colored and nonexistent; let's rejoice, serene and
unruffled, in the merging of this holy couple.

I bow and worship to your grace. May you be welcome, O
Brahma, O bridegroom. Approach with reverence and curl
up like a gold insect in Buddha's palm.

PEOPLE   Oh, oh, Brahma extends his begging-bowl to Buddha in
supplication.

BRAHMA   Lord, Lord, you built me tall, strong and righteous; you gave
me hands, feet, a heart, a head. I was hungry, and you
nurtured me with hymns. I was thirsty, and you gave me
your palms filled with the tears of men, and I drank and
was intoxicated.

You said: "Just as salt seasons the whole sea and no one can
separate the two, so does Brahma invisibly penetrate the
Universe." — I believed you, and rushed to give taste and
savor to the Universe.

Lord, I am tired, pity me! Open your mouth and give me the
signal for liberation. I'm tired now of standing upright; all
this turbulence of the elements is but a meaningless
absurdity, a heavy illness; life is a futile intoxication.

We suffer, we shout, we contaminate the air with our
breathing, we contaminate the waters with our tears, we
infect death with our bodies.

Lord, give me the supremest health, give me the clearest, most
sober meditation — complete obliteration. Think secretly in
the pit of your mind: "Brahma does not exist!" and I will
disappear. Look upon me with mercy Lord, that I may
vanish.

PEOPLE   Buddha reaches out his hand, places a small ball of earth
between Brahma's lips, and Brahma falls silent.

Siva rolls down before him like a wheel all arms and
legs...Look at him, look: he stops now and begins to
tremble.

MOGALANA I welcome Siva, the savage and gallant youth of the Unreal!

You shout: "Shatter, earth, that I may pass. Open, sky, that
I may enter. Break, heart, that I may nestle.

I don't want them, I hate the creations of Brahma! Who said
that flesh or the brain could contain me?

149

Mogalana, step back, I am Siva, I am the Great Fire, the
beginning and the end. Shatter into pieces, Mogalana, that
I may pass!"
You shout and shout, and I hold you in my palm, Siva, I
smile and say: "A small poisoned scorpion is Siva; let him
stand away in fear from Buddha's burning coals."

PEOPLE   Quiet, brothers; Siva extends his begging-bowl to Buddha in
supplication.

SIVA   Lord, I cannot make the people vanish. They're like ants
creeping out of the earth; I uproot a son —
And ten sons and daughters sprout in his place.
I ride on a black horse and unite the ends of the earth; I hang
clusters of slaughtered souls on my saddle like partridges;
doors shut, streets become deserted, people whirl, turn pale
and fall —
And suddenly, behind me, as I pass, under the trees, inside
caves, amidst ruins, I hear men and women embracing,
and flocks of little children chasing me...Wherever I pass
the earth cracks; I swallow villages, I dance on skulls and
shout: "The seed of man has been liquidated, it's been
wiped out, the earth has been disburdened!" But suddenly
from the ruins a girl fourteen years old appears, and from
the mountain top a chubby shepherd boy descends — and
they unite laughing and shrieking on the stones.
And then, in their happiness, they build a firm hearth, they
gather wood, light a fire, pound branches into the earth,
build a hut, eat, kiss, sleep, gather strength, waken.
The man goes to work, plows, sows, pens his sheep, milks
them, whistles at his dogs, goes hunting;
And the woman draws water from the well, sets the caldron
over the fire, prepares the food, sits at the threshold,
opens her breasts and suckles her son.
Ah Lord, man and woman kiss with such lavish sweetness
that life cannot be wiped out. Like wheat, a dead man is
thrust into the ground, but in nine months' time he sprouts
and rises, a wheat stalk armed with seeds, a grandson from
the soil.
I'm tired of fighting men; I raise my hands and surrender;
help me to die, Buddha.

PEOPLE   Buddha stretches out his hand, places a small lump of earth
             between Siva's lips and silences him.

MOGALANA   Quiet, brothers. The great god Vishnu is in a hurry to
             approach and speak of his pain, too.
             Vishnu, balanced reason, firm step among two frenzied
             dancers, Brahma and Siva,
             Welcome!
             You stand for a moment above chaos, unafraid, O skillful
             Tightrope Walker, and smiling gallantly, dance to the
             right, dance to the left, and greet everyone politely
             Before you fall into chaos.
             You hold a scale between your eyebrows, you weigh and
             mingle visible and invisible powers, tiptoeing on the high,
             taut rope, and you reflect:
             "The world is a delicate game of scales. I tremble over the
             abyss, I grow dizzy; fearful visions of gods, men, beasts
             and ideas rise in my head. I can't endure it any longer! Ah,
             when will I finally fall headlong and find relief!"
             Great Vishnu, my weary athlete, approach with trust, don't
             tremble; smile, bid the empty air farewell for the last time,
             and rest, O great martyr,
             Within the azure certainty of Buddha.

PEOPLE   Great, sacred moment! Vishnu, the mightiest god of all,
             extends his begging-bowl to Buddha in supplication.

VISHNU   Lord, Lord, you placed me in a cool darkness where I sit
             cross-legged; and my eyes shine like a well-fed lion's,
             rested, calm, without cunning. I cock my ears and hear the
             footsteps of the faithful gliding over the flagstones lightly,
             fearful
             Of waking me from my holy sleep.
             My fists overflow with fruits, flowers and warm offerings,
             with spices and honey...
             A maiden places a white rose in my open palm and secretly
             confesses: "The sun has darkened me, my Lord; make me
             white that I may be pleasing."
             And a poor field-worker unfolds his apron, heaps my fist with
             wheat and prays: "Father, rise, look out of your temple
             door — our fields are thirsty, the soil has hardened and
             holds the seed in idleness. Rain, Lord, that we may not die

of hunger."

And a mother behind him rushes out and places her dead boy on my knees. She screams, fixes her eyes upon me and commands: "Resurrect him!"

And I hold the terrible burden in my arms and weep secretly, sensing God's incurable misery.

Buddha, Buddha, I walk trembling on a taut hair stretched over two precipices, and I hold two red apples to balance myself — death in my right hand and life in my left.

I know, Lord, that a balanced mind is the greatest virtue and nobility of god and of man; I know, but I can endure no more. I'm tired, Lord, and I tremble over the abyss; pity me!

I can't keep my balance; I want to fall. Raise your hand, Buddha, and order the tightrope walking to end.

PEOPLE   Buddha stretches out his hand, places a small lump of earth between Vishnu's lips and silences him.

The Gods have been reduced to phantoms of the mind, to great ideas, to gaudy metaphors, and all of them carry bowls and beg for alms.

MOGALANA   The gods approached Buddha, turned into myths and fainted in the air.

As when we throw three water-lilies into the funnel of a great river to amuse ourselves, and they dance, shine, twist and turn for a moment like three heads and suddenly are swallowed up by the whirlpool,

So has Buddha swallowed the three great gods.

Don't shout, don't cry, don't be glad; Buddha but turned the wheel of earth a little faster and the Universe vanished.

MANDARIN   Oh Mind, last-born god, clear, faultless eye! The elements have rebelled again, they've broken their chains, they've leaped from chaos and torn down the boundaries of reason.

They're drunk, Lord; all certainties have gone astray, all numbers have adorned themselves with gaudy feathers, like parrots.

I shout, I command, but my voice boomerangs in chaos and strikes me like a stone. I hold the great keys of reason in my hands, and I lock, unlock and dislocate but air.

Come down, all-powerful Mind, and bring order to Chaos!

PEOPLE   The water-brained God of Wisdom is coming, he's stooping

152

down and rummaging through the earth, smelling and ransacking the graveyards.

He stops confused and looks around him; he's trapped, he wants to leave, but he cannot.

MOGALANA   Welcome, welcome newborn beast of human arrogance! Your legs buckle under, you are knock-kneed, you stagger and stumble, you can't lift your pumpkin head, as heavy as an elephant's.

Your loins, O wretched God of Wisdom, are drained; your phallus has shrivelled and hangs like a withered apple; your heart is a bag of questions: "Whence? And where? And why?"

Don't tremble; yes, yes, it's I, do you remember? It's Mogalana.

One day I entered your kingdom to converse with you; you went ahead proudly and showed me your Palace —

"These are my gardens, my peacocks, my fountains; these are my soft beds, my wives, my sons, my slaves...And these all round about are my overflowing cellars..."

And as you crowed, O royal rooster, I thought: "This god lives too brazenly." And as I was thinking this, O God of Wisdom, I summoned up an earthquake and your Palace toppled.

But now I see you've taken courage again and have come to this holy gathering. What do you want?

GOD OF WISDOM   To leave! To leave!

MOGALANA   Have you lost your wits?

GOD OF WISDOM   Yes, I've lost my wits. What kind of world is this? What rebellion! The laws have taken wing, they've gone! I pick up a pebble to measure it but I can't take its measurement, for as I touch it, it lengthens, widens, thins out and at times

Becomes a cloud, at times a turkey puffed up like a nobleman, and at other times a ship with full sails cruising on the ground.

I want to leave, to leave! I've lugged my tools here in vain — the measure, the compass, the level, the scale, my notebooks...Who calls me?

153

MANDARIN   I called you, Lord; I, your faithful servant, who holds *The Chronicles of Man.*

Lord, Lord, save the world! Look, Buddha, the proud rebel of Thought, sits under the Tree quietly, motionless, and winds the world around the reel of his power.

Raise your omnipotent voice, Lord, and exorcise him! Lord, don't you hold the bow of truth eternally taut? Shoot him with your deadly arrow!

GOD OF WISDOM   Don't shout, let me go! My arrows must find flesh in order to kill; otherwise they are useless.

How can I fight the air? How can I wound dreams?

MANDARIN   If you cannot wound dreams, we are lost, Lord!

MOGALANA   Ah, the wingless, four-cornered brain couldn't find firm ground here on which to walk; it has ascended to the upper level and grows dizzy!

You see, Buddha is not flesh to be eaten; he's not stone to be built; Buddha is a compassionate precipice beyond the brain, beyond your scales and your levels, miserly Hoarder of Wisdom!

O bubble, you've risen very high, you've reached the feet of Buddha where the air is thin and rare — and you will burst!

Aha! You've burst, you've deflated, you've become lighter! Your gigantic head was but a wind-bag!

PEOPLE   Gone, scattered are the notebooks, the scales, the levels of the God of Wisdom. They've become butterflies and flutter around Buddha's shoulders.

They've become cool, multi-colored fans to refresh him.

Quiet; two strangers have appeared dressed in short white tunics with wild olive wreaths crowning their curly hair. Handsome, sun-burned, happy.

They seem to be gods of a naive, newly-born people. Be quiet, old Mandarin, don't cry, so we may hear what they're saying.

FIRST GREEK   Beloved fellow-traveller, I believe we've reached the goal of our great journey. Motionless and pellucid in our minds now shine the mountains, the waters, the countless villages, all the barbaric riches our insatiable eyes have accepted and stored.

154

On this, our spiritual Asiatic expedition.
I never knew the world was so large, that one could travel
for years outside the bright boundaries of Greece, could
pass plains and mountains and waters as the foundations
of the sky opened unceasingly and the earth seemed to have
no end.

SECOND GREEK   And I never knew, beloved comrade, that beauty has so many
faces, that so many roads lead to the eternal good, and
that people with barbaric speech exist who love, hurt and
feel the way we Greeks do;
And that they, too, shape thoughts and statues with wood,
stone and the mind.
When I return to Greece, with the power of Hermes the
Traveller, and re-enter my sunlit workshop with its many
unfinished statues of gods,
I shall paint the lips of Athena crimson, I shall hang thick
curls on Apollo's brow, and over the robust body of Zeus,
I shall strew precious stones and gold and ivory.
My brain moves now like an oriental peacock in my hard,
Aeginan skull.

FIRST GREEK   Let's proceed, dear comrade, toward this gathering. I see
multi-colored tents, people shouting, crying and clapping
their hands in the air;
And a slim, naked ascetic sits cross-legged, with lowered
eyelids, under a dry tree, sunk in an ecstatic,
incomprehensible happiness.

SECOND GREEK   My heart cries out, comrade, that this is the sage we've been
seeking. See how his arms and legs glow, how his robe
shines like a gold cloud at dusk,
How his face moves, serene and suspended, like a spirit.
The small bronze statue of Athena we brought with us as a
holy gift from Greece leaps in my bosom, comrade, as
though it is frightened.

MOGALANA   Don't go any further, don't talk, don't disrupt the holy
gathering.

FIRST AND   We wish to speak with the Buddha.
SECOND GREEK

155

MOGALANA   O human images of distant lands, what country do you call
            your own?

FIRST GREEK   We are the children of a meager land with azure seashores;
                  we've been walking for months, like two pilgrims,
               Advancing always toward the rising sun.

MOGALANA   And what, I wonder, are you seeking, fellow-travellers,
               toward the rising sun?

FIRST GREEK   We've learned that a wise man was born past the Euphrates,
                  that he travels from city to city and puts the thoughts and
                  deeds of men in order,
               And we've come, that he may give us laws to take back to
                  our country.

MOGALANA   There is no country, there are no laws, there is no wise man,
               there are no Indies. Nothing exists.

FIRST GREEK   *(To the Second Greek.)*
               I think, beloved friend, that we've come to the land of the
                  Lotus-Eaters. This dream-taken nobleman has tasted the
                  sweet, poisoned fruit and remembers nothing now; his
                  memory has cleansed and emptied.
               He sits under a white cypress tree beside the well of
                  Forgetfulness, his whole body is a bottomless jug from
                  which the world pours.

SECOND GREEK   Comrade, let me speak to him, let me hold Greece up before
                  his clouded eyes, that he may be enlightened and his mind
                  awaken.
               (To Mogalana.)
               I saw a youth in Aegina, when he was returning in his curved
                  ship as a victor from Olympia. He jumped from the ship's
                  prow, rose from the waves, stepped on the hard, foaming
                  shore and walked ahead, gleaming in the sun like a bronze
                  god.
               The whole island came to the shore to greet him — they tore
                  down the walls of the city that he might pass through. And
                  I — do you hear, ascetic? — I approached him, touched him
                  with this hand, grasped his knees, his thighs, his back, his
                  firm neck, his curly, crowned head...
               I admired the power, the serenity, the nobility of the human
               species. I said: The species of man is more handsome

156

than the horse, more multi-faced than water, richer than
the richest imagination.
There is no greater joy than to have eyes and hands to see
and touch the body of man.

MOGALANA   Shadows! Shadows! Shadows!

FIRST GREEK O Naked Sophist, those barbarians who trampled Marathon
one morning were not shadows. Our women on the ships
tore their hair, the plain flooded with barbaric tents and
horses, and the sea was thick with red and yellow banners.
And when the triumphal hymn resounded: "Onward young
men of the Hellenes!" our bodies were not shadows, nor
our blood, nor our beating hearts.
That longed for freedom.

MOGALANA   You were fighting shadows with shadows.
Brothers, these are Hellenes, the eternal children of the
imagination, the mindless fish that frisk and play inside
the traps of fishermen, thinking
They are frisking and playing freely in the vast sea.
Their histories are but a dream made up of blue waves, of
meager farms, of ships and horses. With these nonexisting
elements they play, work and create wars, gods, laws and
cities in the drowsy air.
Unfortunate race! For years you fought in Troy for Helen,
and you never suspected you were fighting only for the
shadow of Helen.
You armed ships, you set out together with leaders, prophets,
horses; you travelled in your sleep; you spied a castle made
of clouds, and your blood caught fire; you shouted: "This
is Troy! This is Troy!"
You shaded your eyes with your hand, discerned black spots
moving on the walls, and you shouted, "These are our
enemies!" And the shadows merged, separated, merged
again on the ground
For ten years.
And all this, O unfortunate race, was a game of light and
darkness...The spirit of the Cunning One sat cross-legged
in the air and created the castle, the ships, the sea and
Achilles' wrath and Helen's beauty.

FIRST GREEK   And if Helen were a shadow, Naked Sophist, blessed be her
                shadow! For in fighting for that shadow we widened our
                minds, strengthened our bodies and returned to our
                country, our brains filled with wandering and manliness,
                our ships
                Filled with valor, embroidered garments and oriental women.
                For ten years we spilled our blood as Helen's shadow drank,
                and slowly, tenderly wrapped itself in human flesh. And
                after ten years of pleading and fighting, Helen stood before
                us, her pulsing body warm and firm, her wavy hair playing
                in the sea and wind till all the Greeks were blinded by the
                realization of this incomparable woman's beauty; and those
                ten years flared and vanished in our brains like a flash
                of lightning —
                And all the mountaintops of Greece glowed brightly in
                proclaiming the miracle.
                Generations passed and disappeared but immortal Helen lives
                on in song; she sits at the tables of noblemen and in the
                assemblies of the people. She climbs at night into the beds
                of newlyweds like a bride, and all the daughters of Greece
                resemble her; she is the wife of all the Greeks.

SECOND GREEK   Blessed be the gods! This is how we Greeks give flesh to
                shadows, this is how we work and carve the air — as
                though it were marble.
                All the Earth, O ascetic, imagines a Helen plunged in tears
                and tricks, newly-bathed, as her small, bloodied instep
                glows,
                Like the instep of Victory.

MOGALANA   O vain visions of the intoxicated head, O Ephemeral
                Creatures! How long will you flounder like male scorpions
                caught in the erotic deathly teeth of Life — the great female
                Scorpion?
                Wake up, uproot desire, rip out your entrails and shout:
                "I want no more!"
                Smother your hearts and your brains, that they may not
                babble and infect the immortal silence. Listen: the hills
                are shouting, the waters are shouting, tree leaves are
                moving like lips and shouting:
                "Come, come! You'll become one with the earth, with the
                kindly rain and the holy wind; you'll lie down at the

                                    158

roots of trees in the cool, underground darkness; you'll
pour out again into the earthen womb of the Mother.
Come! Come!"

FIRST GREEK   I will not come! I lean over my heart and hear the whole
Earth calling me: "I am the dark animal; rise, my son,
enlighten me! I am the moment that appears and vanishes;
rise, give me voice, give me body, kiss me, make me
immortal."

Air is good, good and real are water, bread and earth. I open
my eyes, my ears; I see, hear, smell and rejoice in the
upper world. And if this ship of Earth were to sink with all
its crew and cargo, with all its souls —

I, O ascetic, will resist and fight to the death to save it.

Like the brave sailor who works the pump night and day as
his ship takes in water, and the water constantly rises,
certain and unconquerable, one hair's breadth every hour,

While some on the ship cross their hands, others curse, and
others weep or raise their eyes to the heavens —

And only he, stubbornly, biting his lips, raises and lowers his
hands, working the pump incessantly, transforming futility
into bravery,

Thus do I try to work the ship of Earth we have boarded and
that is slowly filling with water.

This is what I like, this is what my heart wants. I listen: All
the mountains, the rivers, the trees, the sea, call to me:
"Give me a face that I may not vanish; look at me that I
may live!"

MOGALANA   Light-headed, Ephemeral Creatures! Never has the cunning
spirit of life cast its fishhook more skillfully.

Rise, throw off the blinders from your eyes and look beyond
at chaos! All things march on toward death; march on with
them. The free man is he who takes the inhuman law of
nature and — easily, willingly — turns it into his own law.

The earth spins for a moment in chaos, its crust opens, it
festers, it fills with plants, animals, people, it fills with
ideas and gods — like a wound filling with worms.

It was Buddha who first saw the onrush of the Universe, he
saw the eternal law and said:

"This onrush is ours; this is the law I enacted; I march on
toward death, a free man."

Unfortunate man! You sit at the crossroads of the Cunning
    One and the sweat runs from your armpits; women and
    men and cities detach themselves from your loins, ships
    set out from your sweating breasts and sink in the air...
Rebel! Don't cover the abyss with visions! Raise the gaudy
    curtain — the stars and the seas, men and gods; keep chaos
    open and look: nothing exists!

FIRST GREEK   Other gods rule us, O ascetic; their nostrils steam, their hearts
    beat, they sit at our tables, they snuggle at our hearths,
    they climb into our beds,
They couple with our wives, we couple with their goddesses,
    and our bloods intermingle. The swarming breed of
    mankind is refined, brightened, deified; the race of the gods
    is sweetened, warmed and pacified.
Before we came, the immortals shrieked like vultures; they
    ranted and could never fasten their minds on simple, sober
    words;
But we hunted words high above chaos, we brought them
    down to earth, cut their wings and fastened them over the
    abyss
Like Wingless Victories.
We raised cyclopean walls around the Mind and would not
    allow madness to enter.
Like a coral atoll embedded in the restless bowels of the
    Ocean, that with unending struggle works and transforms
    currents into stone,
Then opens, spreads, secures itself, heaps carcass upon
    carcass, transforming death's trophies into strata of life
    that slowly, slowly become an island,
Like such an island, O Lotus-Eater, do we also erect man's
    mind above chaos.
We conquered fear by erecting a small, peaceful, armored
    statue of Athena before the abyss.
We took a rock, carved a smile on it, and the whole rock of
    the world smiled.
And now, as an antidote for the poisoned lotus that crumbles
    the foundations of your holy Memory, we bring a gift from
    luminous Greece for your leader — this bronze, fully-armed
    small statue of Athena. Step back, ascetic, don't get in our
    way; we've come to speak with the Buddha.

MOGALANA O children of the imagination; don't go near the crystal-clear fountain of truth; you'll see your true faces and be frightened. Stand on the outside circle of the arena, with cardinals, hoopoes and peacocks,
Then fall to the earth, bow down and worship.

FIRST GREEK We do not bow down and worship. We will stand erect as we speak with him — that is the custom in Greece.
O great sage who bring, we hear, a new measurement to measure truth and falsehood, who bring new laws to separate the just from the unjust,
And proclaim new motives for love, listen to our voices.
We have come from the navel of earth to this edge of the world to hear your word, to select whatever suits us, to take it with us and to leave.
We have cities and laws, we have arenas, theatres, temples and oracles. We have ships and silver-leaved olive trees and grapes and figs; we have all the riches,
But we lack one: we lack concord. We fight, brother against brother, and our gods are divided too, and fight like humans. Dissension has risen and seized even the heavens.
O Serene Law-giver, all silence and all smiles, open your mouth, give us a new law of love.

PEOPLE Buddha turns and his almond eyes gaze upon the strangers.
He smiles with sweetness and tolerance...The smile of Buddha covers the two odd pilgrims like a setting sun.

FIRST GREEK O silent sage, you've heard the voice of Greece; why don't you answer?

SECOND GREEK Quiet, my brother; he has answered; don't you feel it? My heart has overbrimmed with his reply.
A deep, serene smile overbrims from the Buddha's brain; it spills over his lips, his chin, his neck...
It's not a smile, it's light and it licks the world.

FIRST GREEK Beloved friend, it seems to me you've tasted of that barbaric fruit, the lotus, and that it has unsettled your mind.

SECOND GREEK: Ah, if I could only snatch this smile and take it to our country! This, beloved friend, is the answer we have been seeking for years.

161

FIRST GREEK	Comrade, let us go! This air is heavy and filled with demons!
SECOND GREEK	Where can we go, dear friend? This is our country, this is our journey's goal, this holy rock, the Buddha,
	And above him I discern a huge temple made of wings and air.
FIRST GREEK	Rise comrade, don't fail your lofty lineage. These are the barbarians who trample once again on the steady light of Greece. Forward, O young men of Greece! Think of our triumphal hymn, think of the morning at Salamis!
SECOND GREEK	Ah, if I could preserve his face in Pentelic marble! I see all our twelve gods playing on the rippling flesh of his face.
	His whole face is a suspended drop of water, and inside it the sky lights up and darkens, the earth lights up and darkens, the universe tearfully laughs;
	I have never enjoyed such infinity with a Greek god.
FIRST GREEK	We must leave! See how his barbaric disciples leap, clap their hands and begin to dance. Some laugh, others cry, the women undress...
PEOPLE	My eyes have clouded. I see a flaming egg burning under the Holy Tree, and in its heart, inside the yellow yolk, a drop of light glows, like a seed. It's Buddha!
	I see a giant caterpillar eating the Tree of the world; it eats forests, descends into cities, crosses thresholds, and without anger, without hunger,
	It eats men and gods and stones drowsily.
MOGALANA	Brothers, bare your bodies, bare your souls, throw into Buddha's fire
	Your eyes, your ears, your tongues, your nostrils, your phalluses and your wombs!
	Shout: "I renounce the mind and the flesh; I renounce virtue and sin, joy and pain; I renounce the Yes, I renounce the No! I am free!"
FIRST GREEK	Why do they shout? What do they see? Why do these barbarians dance? They contaminate the modest face of the earth. Beloved friend, let us go!
SECOND GREEK	Don't resist, brother. Let's join the dance too.

Silently, without stirring, soberly, the Buddha, overbrimming
with immortal water, pours into these wine jugs of
humanity.

In the same way, comrade, does our own Dionysos, the
fountain of intoxication, stand soberly and pour out his
intoxication.

Give me your hand, comrade, I will let out a cry, that I may
not burst!

MOGALANA   Mercy, mercy, the moment has come, Buddha, speak! Pity the
earth and sky, say a good word.

Speak, Lord, that this world may be saved, may vanish, may
become spirit and no longer exist.

Be quiet, brothers, don't stamp your feet, don't beat your
breasts.

Take the animals and birds as examples, see how quietly and
trustingly

They turn their eyes toward Buddha.

PEOPLE   Saripoutta approaches, he kisses the two wheels of law on the
soles of Buddha's feet and spreads a lionskin for him under
the Holy Tree that he may lie down.

Mogalana now opens his arms toward Buddha and prays.

MOGALANA   Lord, Lord, thoughts sprout and branch out like twisted horns
between your eyebrows, above your forehead, back behind
your ears and the nape of your neck,

Your mind, Lord, is not like the stud ram who mounts
five or ten ewes, then crawls, shriveled up, into the shade,
his eyes and his saliva dripping as he coughs and creaks
like a cracked water-jug.

Instead, your mind is like the great River, Lord, that waters
villages as it descends, turns watermills, increases, swells,
widens,

And runs overjoyed to the sea.

One day I saw the baby river Yangtze gushing from under
huge mountains; I saw it leap from its crib and toddle on,
giggling playfully, like an infant child trampling the pebbles
lightly with its little, soft feet.

Then slowly it rushed out from the ravines, growing,
increasing, as rocks gave way that it might pass. It
descended, and as it rushed down, its disciples, its

163

tributaries, ran from all parts of the earth and poured into it. The rains fell from the sky and watered it, the snows on distant mountain-tops melted and fed it,

And down it came, no longer speaking, no longer laughing, operating noiselessly, accepting the earth and the sky, transporting the earth and sky forward without delay, unhurriedly toward the sea.

Thus does your mind work, Buddha!

OLD MAN   Buddha has opened his eyes. Buddha has opened his eyes and is looking at me!

Ah, suddenly my hair falls out; how did a begging-bowl get into my hands?

A WOMAN   Buddha looked at me, too. He nodded to me! My memory has emptied and cleansed! My heart has emptied and cleansed!

I raise the palm of my hand,

I see the bones, I see the marrow inside the bones, I see the worm eating the marrow, and I see Buddha inside the worm, sitting cross-legged,

Playing with my son between his fingers.

The Earth, the Great Monastery, has filled with yellow monks!

MOGALANA   O Lord, O fully awakened Ascetic, now that you are leaving, speak the richest, most secret, most powerful word of Liberation —

Buddha, from all your treasures, choose the Great Pearl!

PEOPLE   Buddha has fallen into silent thought; his eyebrows are moving, rising and falling like a balancing scale.

One by one he is weighing his treasures, and he chooses.

He has reached a decision, his lips move; he has weighed well, he has found the heaviest Pearl.

MOGALANA   O Master, trust us with the one great word of Liberation.

BUDDHA   Freedom!

FIRST AND SECOND GREEK   Freedom?

PEOPLE   Oh, the dry Tree has sprouted blossoms from its roots to its crown!

The pure, white flowers are falling, falling on the head, the shoulders, the feet of Buddha.

A deep, compassionate smile is licking his face; his arms and legs are glowing!

FIRST AND Freedom?
SECOND GREEK

SARIPOUTTA Hold your breath, brother shadows! Buddha is now passing through the first door of nonexistence; he glows from head to heel and all of him rejoices.

His body rejoices to descend and be consumed in earth; his mind rejoices to leap over his head; his mind rejoices because it is vanishing.

PEOPLE What do you see? My eyes have dimmed.

Ah, his feet hang over chaos! I bend and look into his eyes: We have all vanished, all drowned, brothers, in their still, black waters; the disciples have vanished, the animals have vanished, the birds and the gods;

The pupils of his eyes have emptied and cleansed.

MOGALANA O Lord, I cannot tame my heart; forgive me, I weep. Do not go, beloved one!

SARIPOUTTA Mogalana, he's gone, don't try to keep him by holding him; he's gone!

Now he's passing through the second door of nonexistence; his mind no longer rejoices in vanishing, his body no longer rejoices in returning to its country.

He has passed beyond joy and sorrow — he has become enlightened.

The Victor, the great athlete, has returned, he has returned to his country, and the fortress of his flesh has crumbled; quiet, now the fortress of his mind is crumbling too that he may pass.

All of Buddha has become a light, airy dance; every element of his body, every element of his mind rises, is liberated, becomes a dancer,

And in dancing, vanishes.

The third gate of nonexistence, Mogalana, the third gate opens.

MOGALANA Ah, I can no longer discern his face, I can no longer make out his feet, I can no longer see his hands that glittered on the ground.

SARIPOUTTA His clothes have emptied, Mogalana, don't search in vain.
Part his saffron robe, and you'll find nothing inside, for all
of Buddha has entered into nonexistence.

His voice has not merged with thunder, his breath has not
found refuge in the air, his eyes have not risen to the sun,
his ears have not become seashells; Buddha has left nothing
unliberated of his great body.

He has turned it all into spirit!

The angel of death has come and found nothing to take; the
angel of life has come and found nothing to take; all of
Buddha has been liberated from life and from death —

He has entered into nonexistence.

*(The canary warbles; all the characters stand dazed and
enchanted for a long while and listen.)*

MAGICIAN *(Takes off the yellow mask, then bows to the Old Nobleman.)*
Nobleman, Old Chiang, the performance is over, the
phantasmagoria has come to an end. With the power of
Mind, we have entered into eternity.

My brain played, leaped, danced, flashed sparks, shot out
tongues, rose, descended like fire in the middle of a
crossroad.

My mind knelt cross-legged at the crossroads where the five
shameless night-revelers meet — sight, hearing, taste, smell,
touch — and it said:

"I will make beasts, I will make men and gods, I will arm
insects, I will arm ideas, I will adorn women, I will raise
cities, I will bring Buddha;

I will bring Buddha, and I will comfort mankind."

My mind played and danced; it wants nothing any more; it
rises and says:

"I will make beasts vanish, and men and gods; I will disarm
insects, I will disarm ideas; I will make women rot, I will
sink cities, I will drive Buddha away!

My game has ended; I want nothing more; I'm tired. I blow,
and this multi-colored, holy performance vanishes.

I blow upon you, Mogalana, O restless, erudite, scheming
thought of my head; we have no more need of you," so
the mind says, and casts you off.

"I blow upon you, Brahma, Siva, Vishnu; we'll have no more

166

births or embraces; the wheel has stopped, we don't need
you anymore, go!"
The world has emptied and cleansed, both water and air have
cleansed; only this head still contaminates the abyss; my
mind breaks away like a flame from the wick of my spine.
I blow on myself and I vanish; I think that I blow on myself
and I vanish!
Nobleman, Old Chiang, warriors, peasant men and women,
my sister whores, the performance has ended, the
phantasmagoria has ended; go with my blessings — to
Nothingness!
*(Silence. Only the clarinet plays. Slowly the vision fades,
vanishes; the first set returns. The Old Man hugs his
grandson in his arms, paces back and forth triumphantly.)*
The performance is over.

OLD MAN   The performance is over; the phantasmagoria has ended!
O erudite mind, gaudy peacock, may you fare well, Hu-Ming,
for you've filled our hearts with felicity.
*(The Women who had taken Mei-Ling to the river return.
They hold extinguished candles.)*

WOMEN   She didn't speak, she didn't even open her mouth to say
farewell to the world.
She looked down at the waters, searching with longing eyes,
seeking to find her brother.
Suddenly she let out a happy cry, opened her arms and fell
in; she found him!
Ah, the river swallowed her as though she were a stone, a
bucket of rubbish; it did not know, ah, it did not realize
she was our noble lady.

OLD MAN   Why are you shouting? The performance is over, the fantasy
has ended. Why are you crying? For shame! Did you
understand nothing, then? Did the holy yellow storm burst
over your heads in vain? Didn't the silken net of Buddha
wrap itself around your entrails? Courage, friends,
approach, listen to me.
(Traces a circle on the ground with his staff.)
Here, see, in this small arena of the world, let man's virtue
shine, sisters. We cannot save ourselves from death, but we
can save ourselves from fear. Sisters, turn Necessity into

167

freedom.

Greetings, soul of man; greetings fire, that not even a river can extinguish!

(Turns to the Ancestors. Raises his grandson high above his head.)

Eh, Ancestors, listen to me for the last time: This is my grandson, there is no other. Save him, if you can.

Eh, hobgoblins, what do you want with swords and spears and great wings? Save him, that you may be saved.

O Ancestors, I have heard that you are omnipotent; this child is the only remaining seed; perform the miracle!

(The seven panoplies slide down from the wall in a heap. The Old Man stands with open mouth for several moments, then suddenly lets out a triumphant cry.)

Freedom! Freedom!

You're right, Buddha, freedom! I've escaped from the Ancestors!

(Tramples the panoplies with rage.)

PEOPLE   The clan of Chiang has been uprooted!
The world has collapsed!

OLD MAN   The road behind me has emptied. Desolate, utterly desolate is the road ahead; and I, in the middle, all alone.

O lofty, uninhabited peak, Freedom!

(Male and female slaves come up from the cellars in a fury and approach the Old Man.)

SLAVES   Our turn has come, Old Man; give us the keys! To eat, to drink, to make up for lost time!

There are no more masters and slaves; the river has arrived —
And everyone, masters and slaves, will become one!

OLD MAN   *(Laughing bitterly.)*

You blockheads! For generations you've allowed the Chiangs to eat, drink, kiss your women, sit in cool, shaded terraces in summer, and beside burning hearths in winter,

And now, you unfortunate wretches, you're remembering much too late to eat and go satiated to Hades.

SLAVES   Better late than never, Old Chiang.

OLD MAN   That's what slaves say. But noblemen say better never than

late. Here, take the keys!
(Throws them the keys.)
You are funnels, all of you! Everything enters clean and
    shining on one end and comes out filth on the other.
Koag, Old Koag, why don't you go with them? Are you
    weeping? Give me an unkind word, Koag, to ease my
    sadness now that I'm dying.

OLD KOAG   Master...

OLD MAN   Don't give me a kind word, pity me! Ah, for your sake,
    Old Koag, God should not...if He had any shame, for your
    sake, Old Koag, He should not
Have destroyed the world.
(To the Magician.)
Is the end finally approaching, Hu-Ming?

MAGICIAN   Here, *The Chronicles of Man* stop, Old Chiang. Now look
    at our wise Mandarin; he tears pages from his large
    notebook and makes paper ships to toss into the river.

OLD MAN   Let's prepare!
(Claps his hands.)
Koag, eh young, doe-eyed Koag!

BLOSSOMING   Master, he has fallen face down at Buddha's feet and prays.
CHERRY TREE

OLD MAN   Order him to bring me the paints, the perfumes, the great
    feathers, and to adorn me!
The blue Emperor is coming, the Yangtze is walking toward
    my house. Let's greet him as noblemen.
(The canary warbles as the Old Man listens ecstatically.)
I pity only you, canary, soul of man, you! What miracle is
    this? All your bones are filled with song...
Old Koag, beloved slave and master, do me one more favor,
    the last one; hang the cage high, high up on the ceiling,
    that the canary may die last.
*(A harrowing cry is heard. Blossoming Cherry Tree crumples
to the ground. Young Koag appears on the first step,
staggering, blood running down his face. He has blinded
himself. He extends a begging-bowl, murmuring in a faint
voice.)*

YOUNG KOAG	My sister...Blossoming Cherry Tree, my sister...
OLD KOAG	My child! Who blinded you, my child?
YOUNG KOAG	Where are you, my sister? Come, you liked my eyes, take them! *(Offers her the begging-bowl.)*
BLOSSOMING CHERRY TREE	My child!
YOUNG KOAG	I blinded myself and saw the light. The middle wall, the futile world, fell, and I saw the true light — the darkness!
OLD MAN	Alas! Every virtue has two heads; the one is all light, the other total darkness. Blossoming Cherry Tree, rise, courage my child; take him inside, that I may not see him. *(The tower shakes. Roar of waters, beasts growling. The people tremble. They huddle together and let out a cry.)* What is it? I seem to hear beasts growling. *(The Three Sentries enter trembling with fear.)*
FIRST SENTRY	Master, beasts from all the plains and forests have gathered in your courtyard!
SECOND SENTRY	The river drove them away, Master, and they came here, trembling, where it's high, to seek refuge.
THIRD SENTRY	Tigers, monkeys, wolves, jackals; and with them, sheep, oxen, camels...All like brothers now, trembling.
OLD MAN	May you be blessed, Yangtze! You've turned ancient enemies into brothers — tigers and sheep now understand — bless you! — that they are brothers.
WHORES	*(Dragging the men with them.)* Come! Come! We're giving good kisses away! We want nothing, nothing, they're free! Good kisses, sweet kisses, we're giving them free! Eh, musicians, strike up the music so we won't hear! *(They try to dance but their knees buckle. They crumple to the ground and begin to wail.)*
OLD MAN	Unfortunate gods, unfortunate men, unfortunate beasts... lumps of dirt!

	Hu-Ming, say a word, a simple word the people may hear to help them face death.
	To face death, Hu-Ming, without shaming themselves.
MAGICIAN	I said the word you ask for, Old Chiang; didn't you hear it?
OLD MAN	What is that word, Hu-Ming? Say it again!
MAGICIAN	Buddha!
OLD MAN	True! True! But I'm not speaking about us; Buddha is a rocky, desolate peak, too high
	Even for hawks.
	I speak of these sluggards, these half-wits, these hags, these trollops!
	Look at them wallow — some cry, others still eat and are hungry, some kiss and are kissed...and others, even more disgusting, hide their money in their bosoms...
	Hu-Ming, I loathe man, I don't want man any longer, Hu-Ming!
	Yangtze, savage monk of Buddha, sweep the earth clean! Yangtze, streetcleaner of Buddha, sweep up, cleanse the air!
	(The tower now shakes with greater vehemence, the stairs creak.)
OLD KOAG	Master, someone is climbing the stairs.
OLD MAN	It's the great nobleman, Yangtze; open the doors! Light the big lanterns!
	(Raises his grandson high.)
	We're ready; both of us, my grandson and I are ready.
	(Men and women let out a cry. Old Koag lights two huge silken lanterns with paintings of blue dragons on them to the left and right of the large door. The canary begins to sing loudly.)
	Open the doors! Stand up! Everyone erect, my friends, to welcome him,
	So he will not say — for shame! — that fear prevents us from standing on our feet.
	Eh, you lumps of earth, don't you hear, stand erect! Save man's honor!
	Musicians, strike up the music; not joyfully, not sadly, but proudly!
	You come too, Hu-Ming; come too, Old Koag, my brother;

come, grandson; let's stand at the threshold to welcome
him...
Koag, open both leaves of the doors wide!
(*Raises his eyes to the ceiling, listens to the chirping.*)
Farewell, my canary!
(*To the Mandarin.*)
You come, too, old man.

MANDARIN   No, I will not come; I've work to do, I've taken on a great
task; I've no time: I'm making paper boats out of *The
Chronicles of Man.*
(*Old Koag opens the large door wide to the frightening roar
of the rising river.*)

MAGICIAN   Nobleman, old Chiang, do you hear the roar? Do you know
who it is?

OLD MAN   (*Softly.*)
Quiet! Quiet! Don't let these wretched people hear you.
They can't endure it!

MAGICIAN   (*Softer.*)
Do you finally understand, my Nobleman, who the Yangtze
is?

OLD MAN   Yes: Buddha!
(*The Old Man walks toward the door. The waters are already
beating against the threshold, roaring. The Old Man folds
his arms and bows.*)
Welcome!
(*Curtain.*)

THE END

EXTRAORDINARY PRAISE FOR WILBUR SMITH

"Smith is at the top of his game in weaving exotic adventures."

—*Library Journal*

"Smith is a master."

—*Publishers Weekly*

"Only a handful of twentieth-century writers tantalize our senses as well as Smith. A rare author who wields a razor-sharp sword of craftsmanship."

—*Tulsa World*

"Smith paces his tale as swiftly as he can with swordplay aplenty and killing strokes that come like lightning out of a sunny blue sky."

—*Kirkus Reviews*

"Few novelists can write action scenes that all but leap off the page the way Smith can."

—*Anniston Star* (Texas)

"Each time I read a new Wilbur Smith, I say it is the best book I have ever read—until the next one."

—*Times Record News* (Wichita Falls, Texas)

"Smith is a captivating storyteller."

—*Orlando Sentinel*

"The world's leading adventure writer."

—*Daily Express* (U.K.)

"Wilbur Smith rarely misses a trick."

—*Sunday Times* (U.K.)

"Action follows action . . . mystery is piled on mystery . . . tales to delight the millions of addicts of the gutsy adventure story."

—*Sunday Express*

Also by Wilbur Smith

HUNGRY AS THE SEA

Wilbur Smith

Thomas Dunne Books
St. Martin's Griffin ✠ New York

This is a work of fiction. All of the characters, organizations, and events portrayed in this novel are either products of the author's imagination or are used fictitiously.

THOMAS DUNNE BOOKS.
An imprint of St. Martin's Press.

HUNGRY AS THE SEA. Copyright © 1978 by Wilbur Smith. All rights reserved. Printed in the United States of America. For information, address St. Martin's Press, 175 Fifth Avenue, New York, N.Y. 10010.

www.thomasdunnebooks.com
www.stmartins.com

Library of Congress Cataloging-in-Publication Data

ISBN 978-0-312-60088-4

Hungry as the Sea was originally published in Great Britain by William Heinemann Ltd. in 1978

D   10 9 8 7 6 5

This book is for my wife and the jewel of my life,
Mokhiniso, with all my love and gratitude
for the enchanted years that I have been married to her.

Nicholas Berg stepped out of the taxi on to the floodlit dock and paused to look up at the *Warlock*. At this state of the tide she rode high against the stone quay, so that even though the cranes towered above her, they did not dwarf her.

Despite the exhaustion that fogged his mind and cramped his muscles until they ached, Nicholas felt a stir of the old pride, the old sense of value achieved, as he looked at her. She looked like a warship, sleek and deadly, with the high flared bows and good lines that combined to make her safe in any seaway.

The superstructure was moulded steel and glittering armoured glass, behind which her lights burned in carnival array. The wings of her navigation bridge swept back elegantly and were covered to protect the men who must work her in the cruellest weather and most murderous seas.

Overlooking the wide stern deck was the second navigation bridge, from which a skilled seaman could operate the great winches and drums of cable, could catch and control the hawser on the hydraulically operated rising fairleads, could baby a wallowing oil rig or a mortally wounded liner in a gale or a silky calm.

Against the night sky high above it all, the twin towers replaced the squat single funnel of the old-fashioned salvage tugs—and the illusion of a man-of-war was heightened by the fire cannons on the upper platforms from which the *Warlock* could throw fifteen hundred tons of sea water an hour on to a burning vessel. From the towers themselves could be swung the boarding ladders over which men could be sent aboard a hulk, and between them was painted the small circular target that marked the miniature heliport. The whole of it, hull and upper decks, was fire-proofed so she could survive in the inferno of burning petroleum from a holed tanker or the flaming chemical from a bulk carrier.

Nicholas Berg felt a little of the despondency and spiritual exhaustion slough away, although his body still ached and his legs carried him stiffly, like those of an old man, as he started towards the gangplank.

"The hell with them all," he thought. "I built her and she is strong and good."

Although it was an hour before midnight, the crew of the *Warlock* watched him from every vantage point they could find; even the oilers had come up from the engine room when the word reached them, and now loafed unobtrusively on the stern working deck.

David Allen, the First Officer, had placed a hand at the main harbour gates with a photograph of Nicholas Berg and a five-cent piece for the telephone call box beside the gate, and the whole ship was alerted now.

David Allen stood with the Chief Engineer in the glassed wing of the main navigation bridge and they watched the solitary figure pick his way across the shadowy dock, carrying his own case.

"So that's him." David's voice was husky with awe and respect. He looked like a schoolboy under his shaggy bush of sun-bleached hair.

"He's a bloody film star." Vinny Baker, the Chief Engineer, hitched up his sagging trousers with both elbows, and his spectacles slid down the long thin nose, as he snorted. "A bloody film star," he repeated the term with utmost scorn.

"He was first to Jules Levoisin," David pointed out, and again the note of awe as he intoned that name, "and he is a tug man from way back."

"That was fifteen years ago." Vinny Baker released his elbow grip on his trousers and pushed his spectacles up on to the bridge of his nose. Immediately his trousers began their slow but inexorable slide deck-wards. "Since then he's become a bloody glamour boy—and an owner."

"Yes," David Allen agreed, and his baby face crumpled a little at the thought of those two legendary animals, master and owner, combined in one monster. A monster which was on the point of mounting his gang-way to the deck of *Warlock*.

"You'd better go down and kiss him on the soft spot," Vinny grunted comfortably, and drifted away. Two decks down was the sanctuary of his control room where neither masters nor owners could touch him. He was going there now.

David Allen was breathless and flushed when he reached the entry port. The new Master was halfway up the gangway, and he lifted his head and looked steadily at the mate as he stepped aboard.

· Though he was only a little above average, Nicholas Berg gave the impression of towering height, and the shoulders beneath the blue cashmere of his jacket were wide and powerful. He wore no hat and his hair was very dark, very thick and brushed back from a wide unlined forehead. The head was big-nosed and gaunt-boned, with a heavy jaw, blue now with new beard, and the eyes were set deep in the cages of their bony sockets, underlined with dark plum-coloured smears, as though they were bruised.

But what shocked David Allen was the man's pallor. His face was drained, as though he had been bled from the jugular. It was the pallor of mortal illness or of exhaustion close to death itself, and it was emphasized by the dark eye-sockets. This was not what David had expected of the legendary Golden Prince of Christy Marine. It was not the face he had seen so often pictured in newspapers and magazines around the world. Surprise made him mute and the man stopped and looked down at him.

"Allen?" asked Nicholas Berg quietly. His voice was low and level, without accent, but with a surprising timbre and resonance.

"Yes, sir. Welcome aboard, sir."

When Nicholas Berg smiled, the edges of sickness and exhaustion smoothed away at his brow and at the corners of his mouth. His hand was smooth and cool, but his grip was firm enough to make David blink.

"I'll show you your quarters, sir." David took the Louis Vuitton suitcase from his grip.

"I know the way," said Nick Berg. "I designed her."

He stood in the centre of the Master's day cabin, and felt the deck tilt under his feet, although the *Warlock* was fast to the stone dock, and the muscles in his thighs trembled.

"The funeral went off all right?" Nick asked.

"He was cremated, sir," David said. "That's the way he wanted it. I have made the arrangements for the ashes to be sent home to Mary. Mary is his wife, sir," he explained quickly.

"Yes," said Nick Berg. "I know. I saw her before I left London. Mac and I were shipmates once."

"He told me. He used to boast about that."

"Have you cleared all his gear?" Nick asked, and glanced around the Master's suite.

"Yes sir, we've packed it all up. There is nothing of his left in here."

"He was a good man." Nick swayed again on his feet and looked longingly at the day couch, but instead he crossed to the port and looked out on to the dock. "How did it happen?"

"My report—"

"Tell me!" said Nicholas Berg, and his voice cracked like a whip.

"The main tow-cable parted, sir. He was on the after-deck. It took his head off like a bullwhip."

Nick stood quietly for a moment, thinking about that terse description of tragedy. He had seen a tow part under stress once before. That time it had killed three men.

"All right." Nick hesitated a moment, the exhaustion had slowed and softened him so that for a moment he was on the point of explaining why he had come to take command of *Warlock* himself, rather than sending another hired man to replace Mac.

It might help to have somebody to talk to now, when he was right down on his knees, beaten and broken and tired to the very depths of his soul. He swayed again, then caught himself and forced aside the temptation. He had never whined for sympathy in his life before.

"All right," he repeated. "Please give my apologies to your officers. I have not had much sleep in the last two weeks, and the flight out from Heathrow was murder, as always. I'll meet them in the morning. Ask the cook to send a tray with my dinner."

The cook was a huge man who moved like a dancer in a snowy apron and a theatrical chef's cap. Nick Berg stared at him as he placed the tray on the table at his elbow. The cook wore his hair in a shiny carefully coiffured bob that fell to his right shoulder, but was drawn back from the left cheek to display a small diamond earring in the pierced lobe of that ear.

He lifted the cloth off the tray with a hand as hairy as that of a bull gorilla, but his voice was as lyrical as a girl's, and his eyelashes curled soft and dark on to his cheek.

"There's a lovely bowl of soup, and a *pot-au-feu*. It's one of my little special things. You will adore it," he said, and stepped back. He surveyed Nick Berg with those huge hands on his hips. "But I took one look at you as you came aboard and I just knew what you really needed." With a magician's flourish, he produced a half-bottle of Pinch Haig from the deep pocket of his apron. "Take a nip of that with your dinner, and then straight into bed with you, you poor dear."

No man had ever called Nicholas Berg "dear" before, but his tongue was too thick and slow for the retort. He stared after the cook as he disappeared with a sweep of his white apron and the twinkle of the diamond, and then he grinned weakly and shook his head, weighing the bottle in his hand.

"Damned if I don't need it," he muttered, and went to find a glass. He poured it half full, and sipped as he came back to the couch and lifted the lid of the soup pot. The steaming aroma made the little saliva glands under his tongue spurt.

The hot food and whisky in his belly taxed his last reserves, and Nicholas Berg kicked off his shoes as he staggered into his night cabin.

He awoke with the anger on him. He had not been angry in two weeks which was a measure of his despondency.

But when he shaved, the mirrored face was that of a stranger still, too pale and gaunt and set. The lines that framed his mouth were too deeply chiselled, and the early sunlight through the port caught the dark hair at his temple and he saw the frosty glitter there and leaned closer to the mirror. It was the first time he had noticed the flash of silver hair—perhaps he had never looked hard enough, or perhaps it was something new.

"Forty," he thought. "I'll be forty years old next June."

He had always believed that if a man never caught the big one before he was forty, he was doomed never to do so. So what were the rules for the man who caught the big wave before he was thirty, and rode it fast and hard and high, then lost it again before he was forty and was washed out into the trough of boiling white water? Was he doomed also? Nick stared at himself in the mirror and felt the anger in him change its form, becoming directed and functional.

He stepped into the shower, and let the needles of hot water sting his chest. Through the tiredness and disillusion, he was aware, for the first time in weeks, of the underlying strength which he had begun to doubt was still there. He felt it rising to the surface in him, and he thought again of what an extraordinary sea creature he was, how it needed only a deck under him and the smell of the sea in his throat.

He stepped from the shower and dried quickly. This was the right place to be now. This was the place to recuperate—and he realized that his decision not to replace Mac with a hired skipper had been a gut decision. He needed to be here himself.

Always he had known that if you wanted to ride the big wave, you must first be at the place where it begins to peak. It's an instinctive thing, a man just knows where that place is. Nick Berg knew deep in his being that this was the place now, and, with his rising strength, he felt the old excitement, the old "I'll show the bastards who is beaten" excitement, and he dressed swiftly and went up the Master's private companionway to the upper deck.

Immediately, the wind flew at him and flicked his dark wet hair into his face. It was force five from the south-east, and it came boiling over the great flat-topped mountain which crouched above the city and harbour. Nick looked up at it and saw the thick white cloud they called the "tablecloth" spilling off the heights, and swirling along the grey rock cliffs.

"The Cape of Storms," he murmured. Even the water in the protected dock leaped and peaked into white crests which blew away like wisps of smoke.

The tip of Africa thrust southwards into one of the most treacherous seas on all the globe. Here two oceans swept turbulently together off the rocky cliffs of Cape Point, and then roiled over the shallows of the Agulhas bank.

Here wind opposed current in eternal conflict. This was the breeding ground of the freak wave, the one that mariners called the "hundred-year wave," because statistically that was how often it should occur.

But off the Agulhas bank, it was always lurking, waiting only for the right combination of wind and current, waiting for the inphase wave sequence to send its crest rearing a hundred feet high and steep as those grey rock cliffs of Table Mountain itself.

Nick had read the accounts of seamen who had survived that wave, and, at a loss for words, they had written only of a great hole in the sea into which a ship fell helplessly. When the hole closed, the force of breaking water would bury her completely. Perhaps the *Waratah Castle* was one which had fallen into that trough. Nobody would ever know—a great ship of 9,000 tons burden, she and her crew of 211 had disappeared without trace in these seas.

Yet here was one of the busiest sea lanes on the globe, as a procession of giant tankers ploughed ponderously around that rocky Cape on their endless shuttle between the Western world and the oil Gulf of Persia. Despite their bulk, those supertankers were perhaps some of the most vulnerable vehicles yet designed by man.

Now Nick turned and looked across the wind-ripped waters of Duncan Dock at one of them. He could read her name on the stern that rose like a five-storied apartment block. She was owned by Shell Oil, 250,000 dead weight tons, and, out of ballast, she showed much of her rust-red bottom. She was in for repairs, while out in the roadstead of Table Bay, two other monsters waited patiently for their turn in the hospital dock.

So big and ponderous and vulnerable—and valuable. Nick licked his lips involuntarily—hull and cargo together, she was thirty million dollars, piled up like a mountain.

That was why he had stationed the *Warlock* here at Cape Town on the southernmost tip of Africa. He felt the strength and excitement surging upwards in him.

All right, so he had lost his wave. He was no longer cresting and racing. He was down and smothered in white water. But he could feel his head breaking the surface, and he was still on the breakline. He knew there was another big wave racing down on him. It was just beginning to peak and he knew he still had the strength to catch her, to get up high and race again.

"I did it once—I'll damned well do it again," he said aloud, and went down for breakfast.

He stepped into the saloon, and for a long moment nobody realized he was there. There was an excited buzz of comment and speculation that absorbed them all.

The Chief Engineer had an old copy of *Lloyd's List* folded at the front page and held above a plate of eggs as he read aloud. Nicholas wondered where he had found the ancient copy.

His spectacles had slid right to the end of his nose, so he had to tilt his head far backwards to see through them, and his Australian accent twanged like a guitar.

"In a joint statement issued by the new Chairman and incoming members of the Board, a tribute was paid to the fifteen years of loyal service that Mr. Nicholas Berg had given to Christy Marine."

The five officers listened avidly, ignoring their breakfasts, until David Allen glanced up at the figure in the doorway.

"Captain, sir," he shouted, and leapt to his feet, while with the other hand, he snatched the newspaper out of Vinny Baker's hands and bundled it under the table.

"Sir, may I present the officers of *Warlock*."

Shuffling, embarrassed, the younger officers shook hands hurriedly and then applied themselves silently to their congealing breakfasts with a total dedication that precluded any conversation, while Nick Berg took the Master's seat at the head of the long table in the heavy silence and David Allen sat down again on the crumpled sheets of newsprint.

The steward offered the menu to the new Captain, and returned almost immediately with a dish of stewed fruit.

"I ordered a boiled egg," said Nick mildly, and an apparition in snowy white appeared from the galley, with the chef's cap at a jaunty angle.

"The sailor's curse is constipation, Skipper. I look after my officers— that fruit is delicious and good for you. I'm doing you your eggs now, dear, but eat your fruit first." And the diamond twinkled again as he vanished.

Nick stared after him in the appalled silence.

"Fantastic cook," blurted David Allen, his fair skin flushed pinkly and the *Lloyd's List* rustled under his backside. "Could get a job on any passenger liner, could Angel."

"If he ever left the *Warlock*, half the crew would go with him," growled the Chief Engineer darkly, and hauled at his pants with elbows below the level of the table. "And I'd be one of them."

Nick Berg turned his head politely to follow the conversation.

"He's almost a doctor," David Allen went on, addressing the Chief Engineer.

"Five years at Edinburgh Medical School," agreed the Chief solemnly.

"Do you remember how he set the Second's leg? Terribly useful to have a doctor aboard."

Nick picked up his spoon, and tentatively lifted a little of the fruit to his mouth. Every officer watched him intently as he chewed. Nick took another spoonful.

"You should taste his jams, sir," David Allen addressed Nick directly at last. "Absolutely Cordon Bleu stuff."

"Thank you, gentlemen, for the advice," said Nick. The smile did not touch his mouth, but crinkled his eyes slightly. "But would somebody convey a private message to Angel that if he ever calls me 'dear' again I'll beat that ridiculous cap down about his ears."

In the relieved laughter that followed, Nick turned to David Allen and sent colour flying to his cheeks again by asking, "You seem to have finished with that old copy of the *List*, Number One. Do you mind if I glance at it again?"

Reluctantly, David lifted himself and produced the newspaper, and there was another tense silence as Nick Berg rearranged the rumpled sheets and studied the old headlines without any apparent emotion.

THE GOLDEN PRINCE OF CHRISTY MARINE DEPOSED

Nicholas hated that name. It had been old Arthur Christy's quirk to name all of his vessels with the prefix "Golden" and twelve years ago, when Nick had rocketed to head of operations at Christy Marine, some wag had stuck that label on him.

ALEXANDER TO HEAD THE
CHRISTY BOARD OF DIRECTORS

Nicholas was surprised by the force of his hatred for the man. They had fought like a pair of bulls for dominance of the herd and the tactics that Duncan Alexander had used had won. Arthur Christy had said once, "Nobody gives a damn these days whether it is moral or fair, all that counts is, will it work and can you get away with it?" For Duncan it had worked, and he had got away with it in the grandest possible style.

As Managing Director in charge of operations, Mr. Nicholas Berg helped to build Christy Marine from a small coasting and salvage company into one of the five largest owners of cargo shipping operating anywhere in the world.

After the death of Arthur Christy in 1968, Mr. Nicholas Berg succeeded him as Chairman, and continued the company's spectacular expansion.

> At present, Christy Marine has in commission eleven bulk carriers and tankers in excess of 250,000 dead weight tons, and is building the 1,000,000 ton giant ultra-tanker *Golden Dawn*. It will be the largest vessel ever launched.

There it was, stated in the baldest possible terms, the labour of a man's lifetime. Over a billion dollars of shipping, designed, financed and built almost entirely with the energy and enthusiasm and faith of Nicholas Berg.

> Mr. Nicholas Berg married Miss Chantelle Christy, the only child of Mr. Arthur Christy. However, the marriage ended in divorce in September of last year and the former Mrs. Berg has subsequently married Mr. Duncan Alexander, the new Chairman of Christy Marine.

He felt the hollow nauseous feeling in his stomach again, and in his head the vivid image of the woman. He did not want to think of her now, but could not thrust the image aside. She was bright and beautiful as a flame—and, like a flame, you could not hold her. When she went, she took everything with her, everything. He should hate her also, he really should. Everything, he thought again, the company, his life's work, and the child. When he thought of the child, he nearly succeeded in hating her, and the newsprint shook in his hand.

He became aware again that five men were watching him, and without surprise he realized that not a flicker of his emotions had shown on his face. To be a player for fifteen years in one of the world's highest games of chance, inscrutability was a minimum requirement.

> In a joint statement issued by the new Chairman and incoming members of the Board, a tribute was paid.

Duncan Alexander paid the tribute for one reason, Nick thought grimly. He wanted the 100,000 Christy Marine shares that Nick owned. Those shares were very far from a controlling interest. Chantelle had a million shares in her own name, and there were another million in the Christy Trust, but insignificant as it was, Nick's holding gave him a voice in and an entry to the company's affairs. Nick had bought and paid for every one of those shares. Nobody had given him a thing, not once in his life.

He had taken advantage of every stock option in his contract, had bartered bonus and salary for those options, and now those 100,000 shares were worth three million dollars, meagre reward for the labour which had built up a fortune of sixty million dollars for the Christy father and daughter.

It had taken Duncan Alexander almost a year to get those shares. He and Nicholas had bargained with cold loathing. They had hated each other from the first day that Duncan had walked into the Christy Building on Leadenhall Street. He had come as old Arthur Christy's latest *Wunderkind*, the financial genius fresh from his triumphs as financial controller of International Electronics, and the hatred had been instant and deep and mutual, a fierce smouldering chemical reaction between them.

In the end Duncan Alexander had won, he had won it all, except the shares, and he had bargained for those from overwhelming strength. He had bargained with patience and skill, wearing his man down over the months. Using all Christy Marine's reserves to block and frustrate Nicholas, forcing him back step by step, taxing even his strength to its limits, driving such a bargain that at the end Nicholas was forced to bow and accept a dangerous price for his shares. He had taken as full payment the subsidiary of Christy Marine, Christy Towage and Salvage, all its assets and all its debts. Nick had felt like a fighter who had been battered for fifteen rounds, and was now hanging desperately to the ropes with his legs gone, blinded by his own sweat and blood and swollen flesh; so he could not see from whence the next punch would come. But he had held on just long enough. He had got Christy Towage and Salvage—he had walked away with something that was completely and entirely his.

Nicholas Berg lowered the newspaper, and immediately his officers attacked their breakfasts ravenously and there was the clatter of cutlery.

"There is an officer missing," he said.

"It's only the Trog, sir," Dave Allen explained.

"The Trog?"

"The Radio Officer, sir. Speirs, sir. We call him the Troglodyte."

"I'd like all the officers present."

"He never comes out of his cave," Vinny Baker explained helpfully.

"All right," Nick nodded. "I will speak to him later."

They waited now, five eager young men, even Vin Baker could not completely hide his interest behind the smeared lenses of his spectacles and the tough Aussie veneer.

"I wanted to explain to you the new set-up. The Chief has kindly read to you this article, presumably for the benefit of those who were unable to do so for themselves a year ago."

Nobody said anything, but Vin Baker fiddled with his porridge spoon.

"So you are aware that I am no longer connected in any way with Christy Marine. I have now acquired Christy Towage and Salvage. It becomes a completely independent company. The name is being changed." Nicholas had resisted the vanity of calling it Berg Towage and Salvage. "It will be known as Ocean Towage and Salvage."

He had paid dearly for it, perhaps too dearly. He had given up his three million dollars' worth of Christy shares for God alone knew what. But he had been tired unto death.

"We own two vessels. The *Golden Warlock* and her sister ship which is almost ready for her sea trials, the *Golden Witch*."

He knew exactly how much the company owed on those two ships, he had agonized over the figures through long and sleepless nights. On paper the net worth of the company was around four million dollars; he had made a paper profit of a million dollars on his bargain with Duncan Alexander. But it was paper profit only; the company had debts of nearly four million more. If he missed just one month's interest payments on those debts—he dismissed the thought quickly, for on a forced sale his residue in the company would be worth nothing. He would be completely wiped out.

"The names of both ships have been changed also. They will become simply *Warlock* and *Sea Witch*. From now onwards 'Golden' is a dirty word around Ocean Salvage."

They laughed then, a release of tension, and Nick smiled with them, and lit a thin black cheroot from the crocodile-skin case while they settled down.

"I will be running this ship until *Sea Witch* is commissioned. It won't be long, and there will be promotions then."

Nick superstitiously tapped the mahogany mess table as he said it. The dockyard strike had been simmering for a long time. *Sea Witch* was still on the ways, but costing interest, and further delay would prove him mortal.

"I have got a long oil-rig tow. Bight of Australia to South America. It will give us all time to shake the ship down. You are all tug men, I don't have to tell you when the big one comes up, there will be no warning."

They stirred, and the eagerness was on them again. Even the oblique reference to prize money had roused them.

"Chief?" Nick looked across at him, and the Engineer snorted, as though the question was an insult.

"In all respects ready for sea," he said, and tried simultaneously to adjust his trousers and his spectacles.

"Number One?" Nick looked at David Allen. He had not yet become accustomed to the Mate's boyishness. He knew that he had held a master mariner's ticket for ten years, that he was over thirty years of age and that MacDonald had hand-picked him—he had to be good. Yet that fair unlined face and quick high colour under the unruly mop of blond hair made him look like an undergraduate.

"I'm waiting on some stores yet, sir," David answered quickly. "The chandlers have promised for today, but none of it is vital. I could sail in an hour, if it is necessary."

"All right." Nick stood up. "I will inspect the ship at 0900 hours. You'd best get the ladies off the ship." During the meal there had been the faint tinkle of female voices and laughter from the crew's quarters.

Nick stepped out of the saloon and Vin Baker's voice was pitched to reach him. It was a truly dreadful imitation of what the Chief believed to be a Royal Naval accent.

"0900, chaps. Jolly good show, what?"

Nick did not miss a step, and he grinned tightly to himself. It's an old Aussie custom; you needle and needle until something happens. There is no malice in it, it's just a way of getting to know your man. And once the boots and fists have stopped flying, you can be friends or enemies on a permanent basis. It was so long since he had been in elemental contact with tough physical men, straight hard men who shunned all subterfuge and sham, and he found the novelty stimulating. Perhaps that was what he really needed now, the sea and the company of real men. He felt his step quicken and the anticipation of physical confrontation lift his spirits off the bottom.

He went up the companionway to the navigation deck, taking the steps three at a time, and the doorway opposite his suite opened. From it emerged the solid grey stench of cheap Dutch cigars and a head that could have belonged to some prehistoric reptile. It too was pale grey and lined and wrinkled, the head of a sea-turtle or an iguana lizard, with the same small dark glittery eyes.

The door was that of the radio room. It had direct access to the main navigation bridge and was merely two paces from the Master's day cabin.

Despite appearances, the head was human, and Nick recalled clearly how Mac had once described his radio officer. "He is the most anti-social bastard I've ever sailed with, but he can scan eight different frequencies simultaneously, in clear and Morse, even while he is asleep. He is a mean, joyless, constipated son of a bitch—and probably the best radio man afloat."

"Captain," said the Trog, in a reedy petulant voice. Nick did not ponder the fact that the Trog recognized him instantly as the new Master. The air of command on some men is unmistakable. "Captain, I have an 'all ships signify.' "

Nick felt the heat at the base of his spine, and the electric prickle on the back of his neck. It is not sufficient merely to be on the break line when the big wave peaks, it is also necessary to recognize your wave from the hundred others that sweep by.

"Coordinates?" he snapped, as he strode down the passageway to the radio room.

"72° 16' south 32° 12' west."

Nick felt the jump in his chest and the heat mount up along his spine. The high latitudes down there in the vast and lonely wastes. There was something sinister and menacing in the mere figures. What ship could be down there?

The longitudinal coordinates fitted neatly in the chart that Nick carried in his mind, like a war chart in a military operations room. She was south and west of the Cape of Good Hope—down deep, beyond Gough and Bouvet Island, in the Weddell Sea.

He followed the Trog into the radio room. On this bright, sunny and windy morning, the room was dark and gloomy as a cave, the thick green blinds drawn across the ports; the only source of light was the glowing dials of the banked communication equipment, the most sophisticated equipment that all the wealth of Christy Marine could pack into her, a hundred thousand dollars' worth of electronic magic, but the stink of cheap cigars was overpowering.

Beyond the radio room was the operator's cabin, the bunk unmade, a tray of soiled dishes on the deck beside it.

The Trog hopped up into the swivel seat, and elbowed aside a brass shell-casing that acted as an ashtray and spilled grey flakes of ash and a couple of cold wet chewed cigar butts on to the desk.

Like a wizened gnome, the Trog tended his dials; there was a cacophony of static and electronic trash blurred with the sharp howl of Morse.

"The copy?" Nick asked, and the Trog pushed a pad at him. Nick read off quickly.

CTMZ. 0603 GMT. 72° 16' S. 32° 12' W. All ships in a position to render assistance, please signify. CTMZ.

He did not need to consult the RT Handbook to recognize that call sign "CTMZ."

With an effort of will he controlled the pressure that caught him in the chest like a giant fist. It was as though he had lived this moment before. It was too neat. He forced himself to distrust his instinct, forced himself to think with his head and not his guts.

Beyond him he heard his officers' voices on the navigation bridge, quiet voices—but charged with tension. They were up from the saloon already.

"Christ!" he thought savagely. "How do they know? So quickly?" It was as though the ship itself had come awake beneath his feet and trembled with anticipation.

The door from the bridge slid aside and David Allen stood in the opening with a copy of *Lloyd's Register* in his hands.

"CTMZ, sir, is the call sign of the *Golden Adventurer*. Twenty-two thousand tons, registered Bermuda 1975. Owners Christy Marine."

"Thank you, Number One," Nick nodded. Nicholas knew her well; he personally had ordered her construction before the collapse of the great liner traffic. Nick had planned to use her on the Europe-to-Australia run.

Her finished cost had come in at sixty-two million dollars, and she was a beautiful and graceful ship under her tall light alloy superstructure. Her accommodation was luxurious, in the same class as the *France* or the *United States*, but she had been one of Nick's few miscalculations.

When the feasibility of operation on the planned run had shown up prohibitive in the face of rising costs and diminishing trade, Nick had switched her usage. It was this type of flexible and intuitive planning and improvisation that had built Christy Marine into the Goliath she was now.

Nick had innovated the idea of adventure cruises—and changed the ship's name to *Golden Adventurer*. Now she carried rich passengers to the wild and exotic corners of the globe, from the Galapagos Islands to the Amazon, from the remote Pacific islands to the Antarctic, in search of the unusual.

She carried guest lecturers with her, experts on the environments and ecology of the areas she was to visit, and she was equipped to take her passengers ashore to study the monoliths of Easter Island or to watch the mating displays of the wandering albatross on the Falkland Islands.

She was probably one of the very few cruise liners that was still profitable, and now she stood in need of assistance.

Nicholas turned back from the Trog. "Has she been transmitting prior to this signify request?"

"She's been sending in company code since midnight. Her traffic was so heavy that I was watching her."

The green glow of the sets gave the little man a bilious cast, and made his teeth black, so that he looked like an actor from a horror movie.

"You recorded?" Nick demanded, and the Trog switched on the automatic playback of his tape monitors, recapitulating every message the distressed ship had sent or received since the previous midnight. The jumbled blocks of code poured into the room, and the paper strip printed out with the clatter of its keys.

Had Duncan Alexander changed the Christy Marine code? Nick wondered. It would be the natural procedure, completely logical to any operations man. You lose a man who has the code, you change immediately. It was that simple. Duncan had lost Nick Berg; he should change. But Duncan was not an operations man. He was a figures and paper man, he thought in numbers, not in steel and salt water.

If Duncan had changed, they would never break it. Not even with the Decca. Nick had devised the basis of the code. It was a projection that expressed the alphabet as a mathematical function based on a random six-figure master, changing the value of each letter on a progression that was impossible to monitor.

Nick hurried out of the stinking gloom of the radio room with the printout in his hands.

The navigation bridge of *Warlock* was gleaming chrome and glass, as bright and functional as a modern surgical theatre, or a futuristic kitchen layout.

The primary control console stretched the full width of the bridge, beneath the huge armored windows. The old-fashioned wheel was replaced by a single steel lever, and the remote control could be carried out on to the wings of the bridge on its long extension cable, like the remote on a television set, so that the helmsman could con the ship from any position he chose.

Illuminated digital displays informed the master instantly of every condition of his ship: speed across the bottom at bows and stern, speed through the water at bows and stern, wind direction and strength, together with all the other technical information of function and malfunction. Nick had built the ship with Christy money, and stinted not at all.

The rear of the bridge was the navigational area, and the chart-table divided it neatly with its overhead racks containing the 106 big blue volumes of the *Global Pilot* and as many other volumes of maritime publications. Below the table were the multiple drawers, wide and flat to contain the spread Admiralty charts that covered every corner of navigable water on the globe.

Against the rear bulkhead stood the battery of electronic navigational aids, like a row of fruit machines in a Vegas gambling hall.

Nick switched the big Decca Satellite Navaid into its computer mode and the display lights flashed and faded and relit in scarlet.

He fed it the six-figure control, numbers governed by the moon phase and date of dispatch. The computer digested this instantaneously, and Nick gave it the last arithmetical proportion known to him. The Decca was ready to decode and Nick gave it the block of garbled transmission—and waited for it to throw back gibberish at him. Duncan *must* have altered the code. He stared at the printout.

Christy Marine from Master of *Adventurer*. 2216 GMT. 72° 16' S. 32° 05' W. Underwater ice damage sustained midships starboard. Precautionary shutdown mains. Auxiliary generators activated during damage survey. Stand by.

So Duncan had let the code stand then. Nick groped for the croc-skin case of cheroots, and his hand was steady and firm as he held the flame to the top of the thin black tube. He felt the intense desire to shout aloud, but instead, he drew the fragrant smoke into his lungs.

"Plotted," said David Allen from behind him. Already on the spread chart of the Antarctic he had marked in the reported position. The transformation was complete, the First Officer had become a grimly competent professional. There remained no trace of the high-coloured undergraduate.

Nick glanced at the plot, saw the dotted ice line far above the *Adventurer*'s position, saw the outline of the forbidding continent of Antarctica groping for the ship with merciless fingers of ice and rock.

The Decca printed out the reply:

Master of *Adventurer* from Christy Marine. 2222 GMT. Standing by.

The next message from the recording tape was flagged nearly two hours later, but was printed out almost continuously from the Trog's recording.

Christy Marine from Master of *Adventurer*. 0005 GMT. 72° 18' S. 32° 05' W. Water contained. Restarted mains. New course CAPE TOWN direct. Speed 8 knots. Stand by.

Dave Allen worked swiftly with parallel rulers and protractor.

"While she was without power she drifted thirty-four nautical miles, south-south-east—there is a hell of a wind or big current setting down there," he said, and the other deck officers were silent and strained. Although none of them would dare crowd the Master at the Decca, yet in order of seniority they had taken up vantage points around the bridge best suited to follow the drama of a great ship in distress.

The next message ran straight out from the computer, despite the fact that it had been dispatched many hours later.

Christy Marine from Master of *Adventurer*. 0546 GMT. 72° 16' S. 32° 12' W. Explosion in flooded area. Emergency shutdown all. Water gaining. Request your clearance to issue "all ships signify." Standing by.

Master of *Adventurer* from Christy Marine. 0547 GMT. You are cleared to issue signify. Break. Break. Break. You are expressly forbidden to contract tow or salvage without reference Christy Marine. Acknowledge.

Duncan was not even putting in the old chestnut, "except in the event of danger to human life."

The reason was too apparent. Christy Marine underwrote most of its own bottoms through another of its subsidiaries, the London and European Insurance and Finance Company. The self-insurance scheme had been the brainchild of Alexander Duncan himself when first he arrived at Christy Marine. Nick Berg had opposed the scheme bitterly, and now he might live to see his reasoning being justified.

"Are we going to signify?" David Allen asked quietly.

"Radio silence," snapped Nick irritably, and began to pace the bridge, the crack of his heels muted by the cork coating on the deck.

"Is this my wave?" Nick demanded of himself, applying the old rule he had set for himself long ago, the rule of deliberate thought first, action after.

The *Golden Adventurer* was drifting in the ice-fields two thousand and more miles south of Cape Town, five days and nights of hard running for the *Warlock*. If he made the go decision, by the time he reached her, she might have effected repairs and restarted, she might be under her own command again. Again, even if she was still helpless, *Warlock* might reach her to find another salvage tug had beaten her to the scene. So now it was time to call the roll.

He stopped his pacing at the door to the radio room and spoke quietly to the Trog.

"Open the telex line and send to Bach Wackie in Bermuda quote call the roll unquote."

As he turned away, Nick was satisfied with his own forethought in installing the satellite telex system which enabled him to communicate with his agent in Bermuda, or with any other selected telex station, without his message being broadcast over the open frequencies and monitored by a competitor or any other interested party. His signals were bounced through the high stratosphere where they could not be intercepted.

While he waited, Nicholas worried. The decision to go would mean abandoning the Esso oil-rig tow. The tow fee had been a vital consideration in his cash-flow situation. Two hundred and twenty thousand sterling, without which he could not meet the quarterly interest payment due in sixty days' time—unless, unless . . . He juggled figures in his head, but the magnitude of the risk involved was growing momentarily more apparent—and the figures did not add up. He needed the Esso tow. God, how badly he needed it.

"Bach Wackie are replying," called the Trog above the chatter of the telex receiver, and Nick spun on his heel.

He had appointed Bach Wackie as the agents for Ocean Salvage because of their proven record of quick and aggressive efficiency. He glanced at his Rolex Oyster and calculated that it was about two o'clock in the morning local time in Bermuda, and yet his request for information on the disposition of all his major competitors was now being answered within minutes of receipt.

For Master *Warlock* from Bach Wackie latest reported positions. *John Ross* dry dock Durban. *Woltema Wolteraad* Esso tow Torres Straits to Alaska Shelf—

That took care of the two giant Safmarine tugs; half of the top opposition was out of the race.

Wittezee Shell exploration tow Galveston to North Sea. *Grootezee* lying Brest—

That was the two Dutchmen out of it. The names and positions of the other big salvage tugs, each of them a direct and dire threat to *Warlock*, ran swiftly from the telex and Nicholas chewed his cheroot ragged as he watched, his eyes slitted against the spiralling blue smoke, feeling the relief rise in him as each report put another of his competitors in some distant waters, far beyond range of the stricken ship.

"*La Mouette*," Nick's hands balled into fists as the name sprang on to the white paper sheet, "*La Mouette* discharged Brazgas tow Golfo San Jorge on 14th reported en route Buenos Aires."

Nick grunted like a boxer taking a low blow, and turned away from the machine. He walked out on to the open wing of the bridge and the wind tore at his hair and clothing.

La Mouette, the seagull, a fanciful name for that black squat hull, the old-fashioned high box of superstructure, the traditional single stack; Nick could see it clearly when he closed his eyes.

There was no doubt in his mind at all. Jules Levoisin was already running hard for the south, running like a hunting dog with the scent hot in its nostrils.

Jules had discharged in the southern Atlantic three days ago. He would certainly have bunkered at Comodoro. Nick knew how Jules' mind worked, he was never happy unless his bunkers were bulging.

Nick flicked the stub of his cigar away, and it was whisked far out into the harbour by the wind.

He knew that *La Mouette* had refitted and installed new engines eighteen months before. With a nostalgic twinge, he had read a snippet in *Lloyd's List*. But even nine thousand horsepower couldn't push that tubby hull at better than eighteen knots, Nick was certain of that. Yet even with *Warlock*'s superior speed, *La Mouette* was better placed by a thousand miles. There was no room for complacency. And what if *La Mouette* had set out to double Cape Horn instead of driving north up the Atlantic? If that had happened, and with Jules Levoisin's luck it might just have happened, then *La Mouette* was a long way inside him already.

Anybody else but Jules Levoisin, he thought, why did it have to be him? And oh God, why now? Why now when I am so vulnerable— emotionally, physically and financially vulnerable. Oh God, why did it come now?

He felt the false sense of cheer and well-being, with which he had buoyed himself that morning, fall away from him like a cloak, leaving him naked and sick and tired again.

"I am not ready yet," he thought; and then realized that it was probably the first time in his adult life he had ever said that to himself. He had always been ready, good and ready, for anything. But not now, not this time.

Suddenly Nicholas Berg was afraid, as he had never been before. He was empty, he realized, there was nothing in him, no strength, no confidence, no resolve. The depth of his defeat by Duncan Alexander, the despair of his rejection by the woman he loved, had broken him. He felt his fear turn to terror, knowing that his wave had come, and would sweep by him now, for he did not have the strength to ride it.

Some deep instinct warned him that it would be the last wave, there would be nothing after it. The choice was go now, or never go again. And he knew he could not go, he could not go against Jules Levoisin, he could not challenge the old master. He could not go—he could not reject the certainty of the Esso tow, he did not have the nerve now to risk all that he had left on a single throw. He had just lost a big one, he couldn't go at risk again.

The risk was too great, he was not ready for it, he did not have the strength for it.

He wanted to go to his cabin and throw himself on his bunk and sleep—and sleep. He felt his knees buckling with the great weight of his despair, and he hungered for the oblivion of sleep.

He turned back into the bridge, out of the wind. He was broken, defeated, he had given up. As he went towards the sanctuary of his day cabin, he passed the long command console and stopped involuntarily.

His officers watched him in a tense, electric silence.

His right hand went out and touched the engine telegraph, sliding the pointer from "off" to "stand by."

"Engine Room," he heard a voice speak in calm and level tones, so it could not be his own. "Start main engines," said the voice.

Seemingly from a great distance he watched the faces of his deck officers bloom with unholy joy, like old-time pirates savouring the prospect of a prize.

The strange voice went on, echoing oddly in his ears, "Number One, ask the Harbour Master for permission to clear harbour immediately— and, Pilot, course to steer for the last reported position of *Golden Adventurer*, please."

From the corner of his eye, he saw David Allen punch the Third Officer lightly but gleefully on the shoulder before he hurried to the radio telephone.

Nicholas Berg felt suddenly the urge to vomit. So he stood very still and erect at the navigation console and fought back the waves of nausea that swept over him, while his officers bustled to their seagoing stations.

"Bridge. This is the Chief Engineer," said a disembodied voice from the speaker above Nick's head. "Main engines running." A pause and then that word of special Aussie approbation. "Beauty!"—but the Chief pronounced it in three distinct syllables, "Be-yew-dy!"

W arlock's wide-flared bows were designed to cleave and push the waters open ahead of her and in those waters below latitude 40° she ran like an old bull otter, slick and wet and fast for the south.

Uninterrupted by any landmass, the cycle of great atmospheric depressions swept endlessly across those cold open seas, and the wave patterns built up into a succession of marching mountain ranges.

Warlock was taking them on her starboard shoulder, bursting through each crest in a white explosion that leapt from her bows like a torpedo strike, the water coming aboard green and clear over her high foredeck, and sweeping her from stern to stern as she twisted and broke out, dropping sheer into the valley that opened ahead of her. Her twin ferro-bronze propellers broke clear of the surface, the slamming vibration instantly controlled by the sophisticated variable-pitch gear, until she swooped forward and the propellers bit deeply again, the thrust of the twin Mirrlees diesels hurtling her towards the slope of the next swell.

Each time it seemed that she could not rise in time to meet the cliff of water that bore down on her. The water was black under the grey sunless sky. Nick had lived through typhoon and Caribbean hurricane, but had never seen water as menacing and cruel as this. It glittered like the molten slag that pours down the dump of an iron foundry and cools to the same iridescent blackness.

In the deep valleys between the crests, the wind was blanketed so they fell into an unnatural stillness, an eerie silence that only enhanced the menace of that towering slope of water.

In the trough, *Warlock* heeled and threw her head up, climbing the slope in a gut-swooping lift, that buckled the knees of the watch. As she went up, so the angle of her bridge tilted back, and that sombre cheerless sky filled the forward bridge windows with a vista of low scudding cloud.

The wind tore at the crest of the wave ahead of her, ripping it away like white cotton from the burst seams of a black mattress, splattering custard-thick spume against the armoured glass. Then *Warlock* put her sharp steel nose deeply into it. Gouging a fat wedge of racing green over her head, twisting violently at the jarring impact, dropping sideways over the crest, and breaking out to fall free and repeat the cycle again.

Nick was wedged into the canvas Master's seat in the corner of the bridge. He swayed like a camel-driver to the thrust of the sea and smoked his black cheroots quietly, his head turning every few minutes to the west, as though he expected at any moment to see the black ugly hull of *La Mouette* come up on top of the next swell. But he knew she was a thousand miles away still, racing down the far leg of the triangle which had at its apex the stricken liner.

"If she *is* running," Nick thought, and knew that there was no doubt. *La Mouette* was running as frantically as was *Warlock*—and as silently.

Jules Levoisin had taught Nick the trick of silence. He would not use his radio until he had the liner on his radar scan. Then he would come through in clear, "I will be in a position to put a line aboard you in two hours. Do you accept 'Lloyd's Open Form'?"

The Master of the distressed vessel, having believed himself abandoned without succour, would overreact to the promise of salvation, and when *La Mouette* came bustling up over the horizon, flying all her bunting and with every light blazing in as theatrical a display as Jules could put up, the relieved Master would probably leap at the offer of "Lloyd's Open Form"—a decision that would surely be regretted by the ship's owners in the cold and unemotional precincts of an arbitration court.

When Nick had supervised the design of *Warlock*, he had insisted that she look good as well as being able to perform. The master of a disabled ship was usually a man in a highly emotional state. Mere physical appearance might sway him in the choice between two salvage tugs coming up on him. *Warlock* looked magnificent; even in this cold and cheerless ocean, she looked like a warship. The trick would be to show her to the master of *Golden Adventurer* before he struck a bargain with *La Mouette*.

Nick could no longer sit inactive in his canvas seat. He judged the next towering swell and, with half a dozen quick strides, crossed the bridge deck in those fleeting moments as *Warlock* steadied in the trough. He grabbed the chrome handrail above the Decca computer.

On the keyboard he typed the function code that would set the machine in navigational mode, coordinating the transmissions she was receiving from the circling satellite stations high above the earth. From these were calculated *Warlock*'s exact position over the earth's surface, accurate to within twenty-five yards.

Nick entered the ship's position and the computer compared this with the plot that Nick had requested four hours previously. It printed out quickly the distance run and the ship's speed made good. Nick frowned angrily and swung round to watch the helmsman.

In this fiercely running cross sea, a good man could hold *Warlock* on course more efficiently than any automatic steering device. He could anticipate each trough and crest and prevent the ship paying off across the direction of the swells, and then kicking back violently as she went over, wasting critical time and distance.

Nick watched the helmsman work, judging each sea as it came

aboard, checking the ship's heading on the big repeating compass above the man's head. After ten minutes, Nick realized that there was no wastage; *Warlock* was making as good a course as was possible in these conditions.

The engine telegraph was pulled back to her maximum safe power-setting, the course was good and yet *Warlock* was not delivering those few extra knots of speed that Nick Berg had relied on when he had made the critical decision to race *La Mouette* for the prize.

Nick had relied on twenty-eight knots against the Frenchman's eighteen, and he was not getting it. Involuntarily, he glanced out to the west as *Warlock* came up on the top of the next crest. Through the streaming windows, from which the spinning wipers cleared circular areas of clean glass, Nick looked out across a wilderness of black water, forbidding and cold and devoid of other human presence.

Abruptly Nick crossed to the R/T microphone.

"Engine Room confirm we are top of the green."

"Top of the green, it is, Skipper."

The Chief's casual tones floated in above the crash of the next sea coming aboard.

"Top of the green" was the maximum safe power-setting recommended by the manufacturers for those gigantic Mirrlees diesels. It was a far higher setting than top economical power, and they were burning fuel at a prodigious rate. Nick was pushing her as high as he could without going into the "red" danger area above eighty per cent of full power, which at prolonged running might permanently damage her engines.

Nick turned away to his seat, and wedged himself into it. He groped for his cheroot case, and then checked himself, the lighter in his hand. His tongue and mouth felt furred over and dry. He had smoked without a break every waking minute since leaving Cape Town, and God knows he had slept little enough since then. He ran his tongue around his mouth with distaste before he returned the cheroot to his case, and crouched in his seat staring ahead, trying to work out why *Warlock* was running slow.

Suddenly he straightened and considered a possibility that brought a metallic green gleam of anger into Nick's eyes.

He slid out of his seat, nodded to the Third Officer who had the deck and ducked through the doorway in the back of the bridge into his day cabin. It was a ploy. He didn't want his visit below decks announced, and from his own suite he darted into the companionway.

The engine control room was as modern and gleaming as *Warlock*'s navigation bridge. It was completely enclosed with double glass to cut down the thunder of her engines. The control console was banked below the windows, and all the ship's functions were displayed in green and red digital figures.

The view beyond the windows into the main engine room was impressive, even for Nick who had designed and supervised each foot of the layout.

The two Mirrlees diesel engines filled the white-painted cavern with only walking space between, each as long as four Cadillac Eldorados parked bumper to bumper and as deep as if another four Cadillacs had been piled on top of them.

The thirty-six cylinders of each block were crowned with a moving forest of valve stems and con-rod ends, each enormous powerhouse capable of pouring out eleven thousand usable horsepower.

It was only custom that made it necessary for any visitor, including the Master, to announce his arrival in the engine room to the Chief Engineer. Ignoring custom, Nick slipped quietly through the glass sliding doors, out of the hot burned-oil stench of the engine room into the cooler and sweeter conditioned air of the control room.

Vin Baker was deep in conversation with one of his electricians, both of them kneeling before the open doors of one of the tall grey steel cabinets which housed a teeming mass of coloured cables and transistor switches. Nick had reached the control console before the Chief Engineer uncoiled his lanky body from the floor and spun round to face him.

When Nick was very angry, his lips compressed in a single thin white line, the thick dark eyebrows seemed to meet above the snapping green eyes and large slightly beaked nose.

"You pulled the override on me," he accused in a flat, passionless voice that did not betray his fury. "You're governing her out at seventy per cent of power."

"That's top of the green in my book," Vin Baker told him. "I'm not running my engines at eighty per cent in this sea. She'll shake the guts out of herself." He paused and the stern was flung up violently as *Warlock* crashed over the top of another sea. The control room shuddered with the vibration of the screws breaking out of the surface, spinning wildly in the air before they could bite again.

"Listen to her, man. You want me to pour on more of it?"

"She's built to take it."

"Nothing's built to run that hard, and live in this sea."

"I want the override out," said Nick flatly, indicating the chrome handle and pointer with which the engineer could cancel the power settings asked for by the bridge. "I don't care when you do it—just as long as it's any time within the next five seconds."

"You get out of my engine room—and go play with your toys."

"All right," Nick nodded, "I'll do it myself." And he reached for the override gear.

"You take your hands off my engines," howled Vin Baker, and picked up the iron locking handle off the deck. "You touch my engines and I'll break your teeth out of your head, you ice-cold Pommy bastard."

Even in his own anger, Nick blinked at the epithet. When he thought about the blazing passions and emotions that seethed within him, he nearly laughed aloud. *Ice-cold*, he thought, so that's how he sees me.

"You stupid Bundaberg-swilling galah," he said quietly, as he reached for the override. "I don't really care if I have to kill you first, but we are going to eighty per cent."

It was Vin Baker's turn to blink behind his smeared glasses, he had not expected to be insulted in the colloquial. He dropped the heavy steel handle to the deck. It fell with a clang.

"I don't need it," he announced, and tucked his spectacles into his back pocket and hoisted his trousers with both elbows. "It will be more fun to take you to pieces by hand."

It was only then that Nick realized how tall the engineer was. His arms were ridged with the lean wiry taut muscle of hard physical labour. His fists, as he balled them, were lumpy with scar tissue across the knuckles and the size of a pair of nine-pound hammers. He went down into a fighter's crouch, and rode the plunging deck with an easy flexing of the long powerful legs.

As Nicholas touched the chrome override handle, the first punch came from the level of Baker's knees, but it came so fast that Nick only just had time to sway away from it. It whistled up past his jaw and scraped the skin from the outside corner of his eye, but he counterpunched instinctively, swaying back and slamming it in under the armpit, feeling the blow land so solidly that his teeth jarred his own head. The

Chief's breath hissed, but he swung left-handed and a bony fist crushed the pad of muscle on the point of Nick's shoulder, bounced off and caught him high on the temple.

Even though it was a glancing blow, it felt as though a door had slammed in Nick's head, and resounding darkness closed behind his eyes. He fell forward into a clinch to ride the darkness, grabbing the lean hard body and smothering it in a bear hug as he tried to clear the singing darkness in his head.

He felt the Chief shift his weight, and was shocked at the power in that wiry frame, it took all his own strength to hold him. Suddenly and clearly he knew what was going to happen next. There were little white ridges of scar tissue half hidden by the widow's peak of flopping sandy hair on the Chief's forehead. Those scars from previous conflicts warned Nick.

Vin Baker reared back, like a cobra flaring for the strike, and then flung his head forward; it was the classic butt aimed for Nick's face and, had it landed squarely, it would have crushed in his nose and broken his teeth off level to the gums—but Nick anticipated, and dropped his own chin, tucking it down hard so that their foreheads met with a crack like a breaking oak branch.

The impact broke Nick's grip, and both of them reeled apart across the heaving deck, Vin Baker howling like a moon-sick dog and clutching his own head.

"Fight fair, you Pommy bastard!" he howled in outrage, and he came up short against the steel cabinets that lined the far side of the control room. The astonished electrician dived for cover under the control console, scattering tools across the deck.

Vin Baker lay for a moment gathering his lanky frame, and then, as *Warlock* swung hard over, rolling viciously in the cross sea, he used her momentum to hurl himself down the steeply tilting deck, dropping his head again like a battering ram to crush in Nick's ribs as he charged.

Nick turned like a cattle man working an unruly steer. He whipped one arm round Vin Baker's neck and ran with him, holding his head down and building up speed across the full length of the control room. They reached the armoured glass wall at the far end, and the top of Vin Baker's head was the point of impact with the weight of both their bodies behind it.

• • •

The Chief Engineer came round at the prick of the needle that Angel forced through the thick flap of open flesh on top of his head. He came round fighting drunkenly, but the cook held him down with one huge hairy arm.

"Easy, love." Angel pulled the needle through the torn red weeping scalp and tied the stitch.

"Where is he, where is the bastard?" slurred the Chief.

"It's all over, Chiefie," Angel told him gently. "And you are lucky he bashed you on the head—otherwise he might have hurt you." He took another stitch.

The Chief winced as Angel pulled the thread up tight and knotted it. "He tried to mess with my engines. I taught the bastard a lesson."

"You've terrified him," Angel agreed sweetly. "Now you take a swig of this and lie still. I want you in this bunk for twelve hours—and I might come and tuck you in."

"I'm going back to my engines," announced the Chief, and drained the medicine glass of brown spirit, then whistled at the bite of the fumes.

Angel left him and crossed to the telephone. He spoke quickly into it, and as the Chief lumbered off the bunk, Nick Berg stepped into the cabin, and nodded to the cook.

"Thank you, Angel."

Angel ducked out of the cabin and left them facing each other. The Chief opened his mouth to snarl at Nick.

"Jules Levoisin in *La Mouette* has probably made five hundred miles on us while you have been playing prima donna," said Nick quietly, and Vin Baker's mouth stayed open, although no sound came out of it.

"I built this ship to run fast and hard in just this kind of contest, and now you are trying to do all of us out of prize money."

Nick turned on his heel and went back up the companionway to his navigation deck. He settled into his canvas chair and fingered the big purple swelling on his forehead tenderly. His head felt as though a rope had been knotted around it and twisted up tight. He wanted to go to his cabin and take something for the pain, but he did not want to miss the call when it came.

He lit another cheroot, and it tasted like burned tarred rope. He dropped it into the sandbox and the telephone at his shoulder rang once.

"Bridge, this is the Engine Room."

"Go ahead, Chief."

"We are going to eighty per cent now."

Nick did not reply, but he felt the change in the engine vibration and the more powerful rush of the hull beneath him.

"Nobody told me *La Mouette* was running against us. No way that frog-eating bastard's going to get a line on her first," announced Vin Baker grimly, and there was a silence between them. Something more had to be said.

"I bet you a pound to a pinch of kangaroo dung," challenged the Chief, "that you don't know what a galah is, and that you've never tasted a Bundaberg rum in your life."

Nick found himself smiling, even through the blinding pain in his head.

"Be-yew-dy!" Nick said, making three syllables of it and keeping the laughter out of his voice, as he hung up the receiver.

D ave Allen's voice was apologetic. "Sorry to wake you, sir, but the *Golden Adventurer* is reporting."

"I'm coming," mumbled Nick, and swung his legs off the bunk. He had been in that black death-sleep of exhaustion, but it took him only seconds to pull back the dark curtains from his mind. It was his old training as a watch-keeping officer.

He rubbed away the last traces of sleep, feeling the rasping black stubble of his beard under his fingers as he crossed quickly to his bathroom. He spent forty seconds in bathing his face and combing his tousled hair, and regretfully decided there was no time to shave. Another rule of his was to look good in a world which so often judged a man by his appearance.

When he went out on to the navigation bridge, he knew at once that the wind had increased its velocity. He guessed it was rising force six now, and *Warlock*'s motion was more violent and abandoned. Beyond the warm, dimly lit capsule of the bridge, all those elements of cold water and vicious racing winds turned the black night to a howling tumult.

The Trog was crouched over his machines, grey and wizened and sleepless. He hardly turned his head to hand Nick the message flimsy.

"Master of *Golden Adventurer* to Christy Marine," the Decca decoded swiftly, and Nick grunted as he saw the new position report. Something had altered drastically in the liner's circumstances. "Main engines still unserviceable. Current setting easterly and increasing to eight knots, Wind rising force six from north-west. Critical ice danger to the ship. What assistance can I expect?"

There was a panicky note to that last line, and Nick saw why when he compared the liner's new position on the spread chart.

"She's going down sharply on the lee shore," David muttered as he worked quickly over the chart. "The current and wind are working together—they are driving her down on to the land."

He touched the ugly broken points of Coatsland's shoreline with the tip of one finger.

"She is eighty miles offshore now. At the rate she is drifting, it will take her only another ten hours before she goes aground."

"If she doesn't hit an iceberg first," said Nick. "From the Master's last message, it sounds as though they are into big ice."

"That's a cheerful thought," agreed David, and straightened up from the chart.

"What's our time to reach her?"

"Another forty hours, sir," David hesitated and pushed the thick white-gold lock of hair off his forehead, "if we can make good this speed—but we may have to reduce when we reach the ice."

Nick turned away to his canvas chair. He felt the need to pace back and forward, to release the pent-up forces within him. However, any movement in this heavy pounding sea was not only difficult but downright dangerous, so he groped his way to the chair and wedged himself in, staring ahead into the clamorous black night.

He thought about the terrible predicament of the liner's Captain. His ship was at deadly risk, and the lives of his crew and passengers with it.

How many lives? Nick cast his mind back and came up with the figures. The *Golden Adventurer*'s full complement of officers and crew was 235, and there was accommodation for 375 passengers, a possible total of over six hundred souls. If the ship was lost, *Warlock* would be hard put to take aboard that huge press of human life.

"Well, sir, they signed on for adventure," David Allen spoke into his thoughts as though he had heard them, "and they are getting their money's worth."

Nick glanced at him, and nodded. "Most of them will be elderly. A berth on that cruise costs a fortune, and it's usually only the oldsters who have that sort of gold. If she goes aground, we are going to lose life."

"With respect, Captain," David hesitated, and blushed again for the first time since leaving port, "if her Captain knows that assistance is on the way, it may prevent him doing something crazy."

Nick was silent. The Mate was right, of course. It was cruel to leave them in the despair of believing they were alone down there in those terrible icefields. The *Adventurer*'s Captain could make a panic decision, one that could be averted if he knew how close succour was.

"The air temperature out there is minus five degrees, and if the wind is at thirty miles an hour, that will make it a lethal chill factor. If they take to the boats in that—" David was interrupted by the Trog calling from the radio room.

"The owners are replying."

It was a long message that Christy Marine were sending to their Captain. It was filled with those same hollow assurances that a surgeon gives to a cancer patient, but one paragraph had relevance for Nick:

"All efforts being made to contact salvage tugs reported operating South Atlantic."

David Allen looked at him expectantly. It was the right humane thing to do. To tell them he was only eight hundred miles away, and closing swiftly.

Nervous energy fizzed in Nick's blood, making him restless and angry. On an impulse he left his chair and carefully crossed the heaving deck to the starboard wing of the bridge.

He slid open the door and stepped out into the gale. The shock of that icy air took his breath away and he gasped like a drowning man. He felt tears streaming from his eyes across his cheeks and the frozen spray struck into his face like steel darts.

Carefully he filled his lungs, and his nostrils flared as he smelt the ice. It was that unmistakeable dank smell, he remembered so well from the northern Arctic seas. It was like the body smell of some gigantic reptilian sea monster—and it struck the mariner's chill into his soul.

He could endure only a few seconds more of the gale, but when he stepped back into the cosy green-lit warmth of the bridge, his mind was clear, and he was thinking crisply.

"Mr. Allen, there is ice ahead."

"I have a watch on the radar, sir."

"Very good," Nick nodded, "but we'll reduce to fifty per cent of power." He hesitated, and then went on, "and maintain radio silence."

The decision was hard made, and Nick saw the accusation in David Allen's eyes before he turned away to give the orders for the reduction in power. Nick felt a sudden and uncharacteristic urge to explain the decision to him. He did not know why—perhaps he needed the Mate's understanding and sympathy. Instantly Nick saw that as a symptom of his weakness and vulnerability. He had never needed sympathy before, and he steeled himself against it now.

His decision to maintain radio silence was correct. He was dealing with two hard men. He knew he could not afford to give an inch of sea room to Jules Levoisin. He would force him to open radio contact first. He needed that advantage.

The other man with whom he had to deal was Duncan Alexander, and he was a hating man, dangerous and vindictive. He had tried once to destroy Nick—and perhaps he had already succeeded. Nick had to guard himself now, he must pick with care his moment to open negotiations with Christy Marine and the man who had displaced him at its head. Nick must be in a position of utmost strength when he did so.

Jules Levoisin must be forced to declare himself first, Nick decided. The Captain of the *Golden Adventurer* would have to be left in the agonies of doubt a little longer, and Nick consoled himself with the thought that any further drastic change in the liner's circumstances or a decision by the Master to abandon his ship and commit his company to the lifeboats would be announced on the open radio channels and would give him a chance to intervene.

Nick was about to caution the Trog to keep a particular watch on Channel 16 for *La Mouette*'s first transmission, then he checked himself. That was another thing he never did—issue unnecessary orders. The Trog's grey wrinkled head was wreathed in clouds of reeking cigar smoke but was bowed to his mass of electronic equipment, and he adjusted a dial with careful lover's fingers; his little eyes were bright and sleepless as those of an ancient sea turtle.

Nick went to his chair and settled down to wait out the few remaining hours of the short Antarctic summer night.

· · ·

The radar screen had shown strange and alien capes and headlands above the sea clutter of the storm, strange islands, anomalies which did not relate to the Admiralty charts. Between these alien masses shone myriad other smaller contacts, bright as fireflies, any one of which could have been the echo of a stricken ocean liner—but which was not.

As *Warlock* nosed cautiously down into this enchanted sea, the dawn that had never been far from the horizon flushed out, timorous as a bride, decked in colours of gold and pink that struck splendorous splinters of light off the icebergs.

The horizon ahead of them was cluttered with ice, some of the fragments were but the size of a billiard table and they bumped and scraped down the *Warlock*'s side, then swung and bobbed in her wake as she passed. There were others the size of a city block, weird and fanciful structures of honeycombed white ice, that stood as tall as *Warlock*'s upperworks as she passed.

"White ice is soft ice," Nick murmured to David Allen beside him, and then caught himself. It was an unnecessary speech, inviting familiarity, and before the Mate could answer, Nick turned quickly away to the radar-repeater and lowered his face to the eyepiece in the coned hood. For a minute he studied the images of the surrounding ice in the darkened body of the instrument, then went back to his seat and stared ahead impatiently.

Warlock was running too fast, Nick knew it; he was relying on the vigilance of his deck officers to carry her through the ice. Yet still this speed was too slow for his seething impatience.

Above their horizon rose another shoreline, a great unbroken sweep of towering cliff which caught the low sun, and glowed in emerald and amethyst, a drifting tableland of solid hard ice, forty miles across and two hundred feet high.

As they closed with that massive translucent island, so the colours that glowed through it became more hauntingly beautiful. The cliffs were rent by deep bays, and split by crevasses whose shadowy depths were dark sapphire, blue and mysterious, paling out to a thousand shades of green.

"My God, it's beautiful!" said David Allen with the reverence of a man kneeling in a cathedral.

The crests of the ice cliffs blazed in clearest ruby; to windward, the big sea piled in and crashed against those cliffs, surging up them in explosive bursts of white spray. Yet the iceberg did not dip nor swing or work, even in that murderous sea.

"Look at the lee she is making." Dave Allen pointed. "You could ride out a force twelve behind her."

On the leeward side, the waters were protected from the wind by that mountain of sheer ice. Green and docile, they lapped those mysterious blue cliffs, and *Warlock* went into the lee, passing in a ship's length from the plunging rearing action of a wild horse into the tranquillity of a mountain lake, calm, windless and unnatural.

In the calm, Angel brought trays piled with crisp brown-baked Cornish pasties and steaming mugs of thick creamy cocoa, and they ate breakfast at three in the morning, marvelling at the fine pale sunlight and the towers of incredible beauty, the younger officers shouting and laughing when a school of five black killer whales passed so close that they could see their white cheek patterns and wide grinning mouths through the icy clear waters.

The great mammals circled the ship, then ducked beneath her hull, surging up on the far side with their huge black triangular fins shearing the surface as they blew through the vents in the top of their heads. The fishy stink of their breath pervaded the bridge, and then they were gone, and *Warlock* motored calmly along in the lee of the ice, like a holiday launch of day-trippers.

Nicholas Berg did not join the spontaneous gaiety. He munched one of Angel's delicious pies full of meat and thick gravy, but he could not finish it. His stomach was too tense. He found himself resenting the high spirits of his officers. The laughter offended him, now when his whole life hung in precarious balance. He felt the temptation to quell them with a few harsh words, conscious of the power he had to plunge them into instant consternation.

Nick listened to their carefree banter and felt old enough to be their father, despite the few years' difference in their ages. He was impatient with them, irritated that they should be able to laugh like this when so much was at stake—six hundred human lives, a great ship, tens of millions of dollars, his whole future. They would probably never themselves know what it felt like to put a lifetime's work at risk on a single flip of the coin—and then suddenly, unaccountably, he envied them.

He could not understand the sensation, could not fathom why suddenly he longed to laugh with them, to share the companionship of the moment, to be free of pressure for just a little while. For fifteen years, he had not known that sort of hiatus, had never wanted it.

He stood up abruptly, and immediately the bridge was silent. Every officer concentrating on his appointed task, not one of them glancing at him as he paced once, slowly, across the wide bridge. It did not need a word to change the mood, and suddenly Nick felt guilty. It was too easy, too cheap.

Carefully Nick steeled himself, shutting out the weakness, building up his resolve and determination, bringing all his concentration to bear on the Herculean task ahead of him, and he paused at the door of the radio room. The Trog looked up from his machines, and they exchanged a single glance of understanding. Two completely dedicated men, with no time for frivolity.

Nick nodded and paced on, the strong handsome face stern and uncompromising, his step firm and measured—but when he stopped again by the side windows of the bridge and looked up at the magnificent cliff of ice, he felt the doubts surging up again within him.

How much had he sacrificed for what he had gained, how much joy and laughter had he spurned to follow the high road of challenge, how much beauty had he passed along the way without seeing it in his haste, how much love and warmth and companionship? He thought with a fierce pang of the woman who had been his wife, and who had gone now with the child who was his son. Why had they gone, and what had they left him with—after all his strivings?

Behind him, the radio crackled and hummed as the carrier beam opened Channel 16, then it pitched higher as a human voice came through clearly.

"Mayday. Mayday. Mayday. This is the *Golden Adventurer*."

Nick spun and ran to the radio room as the calm masculine voice read out the coordinates of the ship's position.

"We are in imminent danger of striking. We are preparing to abandon ship. Can any vessel render assistance? Repeat, can any vessel render assistance?"

"Good God," David Allen's voice was harsh with anxiety, "the current's got them, they're going down on Cape Alarm at nine knots—she's only fifty miles offshore and we are still two hundred and twenty miles from that position."

"Where is *La Mouette*?" growled Nick Berg. "Where the hell is she?"

"We'll have to open contact now, sir," David Allen looked up from the chart. "You cannot let them go down into the boats—not in this weather, sir. It would be murder."

"Thank you, Number One," said Nick quietly. "Your advice is always welcome." David flushed, but there was anger and not embarrassment beneath the colour. Even in the stress of the moment, Nick noted that, and adjusted his opinion of his First Officer. He had guts as well as brains.

The Mate was right, of course. There was only one thing to consider now, the conservation of human life.

Nick looked up at the top of the ice cliff and saw the low cloud tearing off it, roiling and swirling in the wind, pouring down over the edge like boiling milk frothing from the lip of a great pot.

He had to send now. *La Mouette* had won the contest of silence. Nick stared up at the cloud and composed the message he would send. He must reassure the Master, urge him to delay his decision to abandon ship and give *Warlock* the time to close the gap, perhaps even reach her before she struck on Cape Alarm.

The silence on the bridge was deepened by the absence of wind. They were all watching him now, waiting for the decision, and in that silence the carrier beam of Channel 16 hummed and throbbed.

Then suddenly a rich Gallic accent poured into the silent bridge, a full fruity voice that Nick remembered so clearly, even after all the years.

"Master of *Golden Adventurer*, this is the Master of salvage tug *La Mouette*. I am proceeding at best speed your assistance. Do you accept Lloyd's Open Form 'No cure no pay'?"

Nick kept his face from showing any emotion, but his heart barged wildly against his ribs. Jules Levoisin had broken silence.

"Plot his position report," he said quietly.

"God! She's inside us." David Allen's face was stricken as he marked *La Mouette*'s reported position on the chart. "She's a hundred miles ahead of us."

"No." Nick shook his head. "He's lying."

"Sir?"

"He's lying. He always lies." Nick lit a cheroot and when it was drawing evenly, he spoke again to his radio officer.

"Did you get a bearing?" and the Trog looked up from his radio direction-finding compass on which he was tracing *La Mouette*'s transmissions.

"I have only one coordinate, you won't get a fix—"

But Nick interrupted him, "We'll use his best course from Golfo San Jorge for a fix." He turned back to David Allen. "Plot that."

"There's a difference of over three hundred nautical miles."

"Yes." Nick nodded. "That old pirate wouldn't broadcast an accurate position to all the world. We are inside him and running five knots better, we'll put a line over *Golden Adventurer* before he's in radar contact."

"Are you going to open contact with Christy Marine now, sir?"

"No, Mr. Allen."

"But they will do a deal with *La Mouette*—unless we bid now."

"I don't think so," Nick murmured, and almost went on to say, "Duncan Alexander won't settle for Lloyd's Open Form while he is the underwriter, and his ship is free and floating. He'll fight for daily hire and bonus, and Jules Levoisin won't buy that package. He'll hold out for the big plum. They won't do a deal until the two ships are in visual contact—and by that time I'll have her in tow and I'll fight the bastard in the awards court for twenty-five per cent of her value—" But he did not say it. "Steady as she goes, Mr. Allen," was all he said, as he left the bridge.

He closed the door of his day cabin and leaned back against it, shutting his eyes tightly as he gathered himself. It had been so very close, a matter of seconds and he would have declared himself and given the advantage to *La Mouette*.

Through the door behind him, he heard David Allen's voice. "Did you see him? He didn't feel a thing—not a bloody thing. He was going to let those poor bastards go into the boats. He must piss ice-water." The voice was muffled, but the outrage in it was tempered by awe.

Nick kept his eyes shut a moment longer, then he straightened up and pushed himself away from the door. He wanted it to begin now. It was the waiting and the uncertainty which was eroding what was left of his strength.

"Please God, let me reach them in time." And he was not certain whether it was for the lives or for the salvage award that he was praying.

Captain Basil Reilly, the Master of the *Golden Adventurer*, was a tall man, with a lean and wiry frame that promised reserves of strength and endurance. His face was very darkly tanned and splotched with the dark patches of benign sun cancer. His heavy moustache was silvered like the pelt of a snow fox, and though his eyes were set in webs of finely wrinkled and pouchy skin, they were bright and calm and intelligent.

He stood on the windward wing of his navigation bridge and watched the huge black seas tumbling in to batter his helpless ship. He was taking them broadside now, and each time they struck, the hull shuddered and heeled with a sick dead motion, giving reluctantly to the swells that rose up and broke over her rails, sweeping her decks from side to side, and then cascading off her again in a tumble of white that smoked in the wind.

He adjusted the life jacket he wore, settling the rough canvas more comfortably around his shoulders as he reviewed his position once more.

Golden Adventurer had taken the ice in that eight-to-midnight watch traditionally allotted to the most junior of the navigating officers. The impact had hardly been noticeable, yet it had awoken the Master from deep sleep—just a slight check and jar that had touched some deep chord in the mariner's instinct.

The ice had been a growler, one of the most deadly of all hazards. The big bergs standing high and solid to catch the radar beams, or the eye of even the most inattentive deck watch, were easily avoided. However, the low ice lying awash, with its great bulk and weight almost completely hidden by the dark and turbulent waters, was as deadly as a predator in ambush.

The growler showed itself only in the depths of each wave trough, or in the swirl of the current around it, as though a massive sea-monster lurked there. At night, these indications would pass unnoticed by even the sharpest eyes, and below the surface, the wave action eroded the body of the growler, turning it into a horizontal blade that lay ten feet or more below the water level and reached out two or three hundred feet from the visible surface indications.

With the Third Officer on watch, and steaming at cautionary speed of a mere twelve knots, the *Golden Adventurer* had brushed against one of these monsters, and although the actual impact had gone almost unnoticed on board, the ice had opened her like the knife stroke which splits a herring for the smoking rack.

It was classic *Titanic* damage, a fourteen-foot rent through her side, twelve feet below the Plimsoll line, shearing two of her watertight compartments, one of which was her main engine-room section.

They had held the water easily until the electrical explosion, and since then, the Master had battled to keep her afloat. Slowly, step by step, fighting all the way, he had yielded to the sea. All the bilge pumps were running still, but the water was steadily gaining.

Three days ago he had brought all his passengers up from below the main deck, and he had battened down all the watertight bulkheads. The crew and passengers were accommodated now in the lounges and smoking rooms. The ship's luxury and opulence had been transformed into the crowded, unhygienic and deteriorating conditions of a city under siege.

It reminded him of the catacombs of the London underground converted to air-raid shelters during the blitz. He had been a lieutenant on shore-leave and he had passed one night there that he would remember for the rest of his life.

There was the same atmosphere on board now. The sanitary arrangements were inadequate. Fourteen toilet bowls for six hundred, many of them seasick and suffering from diarrhoea. There were no baths nor showers, and insufficient power for the heating of water in the handbasins. The emergency generators delivered barely sufficient power to work the ship, to run the pumps, to supply minimal lighting, and to keep the communicational and navigational equipment running. There was no heating in the ship and the outside air temperature had fallen to minus twenty degrees now.

The cold in the spacious public lounges was brutal. The passengers huddled in their fur coats and bulky life jackets under mounds of blankets. There were limited cooking facilities on the gas stoves usually reserved for adventure tours ashore. There was no baking or grilling, and most of the food was eaten cold and congealed from cans; only the soup and beverages steamed in the cold clammy air, like the breaths of the waiting and helpless multitude.

The desalination plants had not been in use since the ice collision and now the supply of fresh water was critical; even hot drinks were rationed.

Of the 368 paying passengers, only forty-eight were below the age of fifty, and yet the morale was extraordinary. Men and women who before the emergency could and did complain bitterly at a dress shirt not ironed to crisp perfection or a wine served a few degrees too cold, now accepted a mug of beef tea as though it were a vintage Château Margaux, and laughed and chatted animatedly in the cold, shaming with their fortitude the few that might have complained. These were an unusual sample of humanity, men and women of achievement and resilience, who had come here to this outlandish corner of the globe in search of new experience. They were mentally prepared for adventure and even danger, and seemed almost to welcome this as part of the entertainment provided by the tour.

Yet, standing on his bridge, the Master was under no illusion as to the gravity of their situation. Peering through the streaming glass, he watched a work party, led by his First Officer, toiling heroically in the bows. Four men in glistening yellow plastic suits and hoods, drenched by the icy seas, working with the slow cold-numbed movements of automatons as they struggled to stream a sea anchor and bring the ship's head up into the sea, so that she might ride more easily, and perhaps slow her precipitous rush down onto the rocky coast. Twice in the preceding days, the anchors they had rigged had been torn away by sea and wind and the ship's dead weight.

Three hours before, he had called his engineering officers up from below, where the risk to their lives had become too great to chance against the remote possibility of restoring power to his main engines. He had conceded the battle to the sea and now he was planning the final moves when he must abandon his command and attempt to remove six hundred human beings from this helpless hulk to the even greater dangers and hardships of Cape Alarm's barren and storm-rent shores.

Cape Alarm was one of those few pinnacles of barren black rock which thrust out from beneath the thick white mantle of the Antarctic cap, pounded free of ice like an anvil beneath the eternal hammering assault of storm and sea and wind.

The long straight ridge protruded almost fifty miles into the eastern extremity of the Weddell Sea, was fifty miles across at its widest point, and terminated in a pair of bull's horns which formed a small protected bay named after the polar explorer Sir Ernest Shackleton.

Shackleton Bay, with its steep purple-black beaches of round polished pebbles, was the nesting ground of a huge colony of chin-strap penguin, and for this reason was one of *Golden Adventurer*'s regular ports of call.

On each tour, the ship would anchor in the deep and calm waters of the bay, while her passengers went ashore to study and photograph the breeding birds and the extraordinary geological formations, sculptured by ice and wind into weird and grotesque shapes.

Only ten days earlier, *Golden Adventurer* had weighed anchor in Shackleton Bay and stood out into the Weddell Sea. The weather had been mild and still, with a slow oily swell and a bright clear sun. Now, before a force seven gale, in temperatures forty-five degrees colder, and borne on the wild dark sweep of the current, she was being carried back to that same black and rocky shore.

There was no doubt in Captain Reilly's mind—they were going to go aground on Cape Alarm, there was no avoiding that fate with this set of sea and wind, unless the French salvage tug reached them first.

La Mouette should have been in radar contact already, if the tug's reported position was correct, and Basil Reilly let a little frown of worry crease the brown parchment skin of his forehead and shadows were in his eyes.

"Another message from head office, sir." His Second Officer was beside him now, a young man with the shape of a teddy bear swathed in thick woolen jerseys and marine blue top coat. Basil Reilly's strict dress regulations had long ago been abandoned and their breaths steamed in the frigid air of the navigation bridge.

"Very well." Reilly glanced at the flimsy. "Send that to the tug master." The contempt was clear in his voice, his disdain for this haggling between owners and salvors, when a great ship and six hundred lives were at risk in the cold sea.

He knew what he would do if the salvage tug made contact before *Golden Adventurer* struck the waiting fangs of rock, he would override his owner's express orders and exercise his rights as Master by immediately accepting the offer of assistance under Lloyd's Open Form.

"But let him come," he murmured to himself. "Please God, let him come," and he raised his binoculars and slowly swept a long jagged horizon where the peaks of the swells seemed black and substantial as rock. He paused with a leap of his pulse when something white blinked in the field of the glasses and then, with a little sick slide, realized that it was only a random ray of sunlight catching a pinnacle of ice from one of the floating bergs.

He lowered the glasses and crossed from the windward wing of the bridge to the lee. He did not need the glasses now, Cape Alarm was black and menacing against the sow's-belly grey of the sky. Its ridges and valleys picked out with gleaming ice and banked snow, and against her steep shore, the sea creamed and leapt high in explosions of purest white.

"Sixteen miles, sir," said the First Officer, coming to stand beside him. "And the current seems to be setting a little more northerly now." They were both silent, as they balanced automatically against the violent pitch and roll of the deck.

Then the Mate spoke again with a bitter edge to his voice, "Where is that bloody frog?" And they watched the night of Antarctica begin to shroud the cruel lee shore in funereal cloaks of purple and sable, picked out with the ermine collars and cuffs of ice.

S he was very young, probably not yet twenty-five years of age, and even the layers of heavy clothing topped by a man's anorak three sizes too big could not disguise the slimness of her body, that almost coltish elegance of long fine limbs and muscle toned by youth and hard exercise.

Her head was set jauntily on the long graceful stem of her neck, like a golden sunflower, and the profuse mane of long hair was sun-bleached, streaked with silver and platinum and copper gold, twisted up carelessly into a rope almost as thick as a man's wrist and piled on top of her head. Yet loose strands floated down on to her forehead and tickled her nose so that she pursed her lips and puffed them away.

Her hands were both occupied with the heavy tray she carried, and she balanced like a skilled horsewoman against the ship's extravagant plunging as she offered it.

"Come on, Mrs. Goldberg," she wheedled. "It will warm the cockles of your tum."

"I don't think so, my dear," the white-haired woman faltered.

"Just for me, then," the girl wheedled.

"Well," the woman took one of the mugs and sipped it tentatively. "It's good," she said, and then quickly and furtively, "Samantha, has the tug come yet?"

"It will be here any minute now, and the Captain is a dashing Frenchman, just the right age for you, with a lovely tickly moustache. I'm going to introduce you first thing."

The woman was a widow in her late fifties, a little overweight and more than a little afraid, but she smiled and sat up a little straighter.

"You naughty thing," she smiled.

"Just as soon as I've finished with this," Samantha indicated the tray, "I'll come and sit with you. We'll play some klabrias, okay?" When Samantha Silver smiled, her teeth were very straight and white against the peach of her tanned cheeks and the freckles that powdered her nose like gold dust. She moved on.

They welcomed her, each of them, men and women, competing for her attention, for she was one of those rare creatures that radiate such warmth, a sort of shining innocence, like a kitten or a beautiful child, and she laughed and chided and teased them in return and left them grinning and heartened, but jealous of her going, so they followed her with their eyes. Most of them felt she belonged to them personally, and they wanted all of her time and presence, making up questions or little stories to detain her for a few extra moments.

"There was an albatross following us a little while ago, Sam."

"Yes, I saw it through the galley window—"

"It was a wandering albatross, wasn't it, Sam?"

"Oh, come on, Mr. Stewart! You know better than that. It was *Diomedea melanophris*, the black-browed albatross, but still it's good luck. All albatrosses are good luck—that's a scientifically proven fact."

Samantha had a doctorate in biology and was one of the ship's specialist guides. She was on sabbatical leave from the University of Miami where she held a research fellowship in marine ecology.

Passengers thirty years her senior treated her like a favourite daughter most of the time. However, in even the mildest crisis they became childlike in their appeal to her and in their reliance on her natural strength which they recognized and sought instinctively. She was to them a combination of beloved pet and den-mother.

While a ship's steward refilled her tray with mugs, Samantha paused at the entrance to the temporary galley they had set up in the cocktail room and looked back into the densely packed lounge.

The stink of unwashed humanity and tobacco smoke was almost a solid blue thing, but she felt a rush of affection for them. They were behaving so very well, she thought, and she was proud of them.

"Well done, team," she thought, and grinned. It was not often that she could find affection in herself for a mass of human beings. Often she had pondered how a creature so fine and noble and worthwhile as the human individual could, in its massed state, become so unattractive.

She thought briefly of the human multitudes of the crowded cities. She hated zoos and animals in cages, remembering as a little girl crying for a bear that danced endlessly against its bars, driven mad by its confinement. The concrete cages of the cities drove their captives into similar strange and bizarre behaviour. All creatures should be free to move and live and breathe, she believed, and yet man, the super-predator, who had denied that right to so many other creatures, was now destroying himself with the same single-mindedness, poisoning and imprisoning himself in an orgy that made the madness of the lemmings seem logical in comparison. It was only when she saw human beings like these in circumstances like these that she could be truly proud of them—and afraid for them.

She felt her own fear deep down, at the very periphery of her awareness, for she was a sea-creature who loved and understood the sea—and knew its monumental might. She knew what awaited them out there in the storm, and she was afraid. With a deliberate effort she lifted the slump of her shoulders, and set the smile brightly on her lips and picked up the heavy tray.

At that moment the speakers of the public-address system gave a preliminary squawk, and then filtered the Captain's cultured and measured tones into the suddenly silent ship.

"Ladies and gentlemen, this is your Captain speaking. I regret to inform you that we have not yet established radar contact with the salvage tug *La Mouette*, and that I now deem it necessary to transfer the ship's company to the lifeboats."

There was a sigh and stir in the crowded lounges, heard even above the storm. Samantha saw one of her favourite passengers reach for his wife and press her silvery-grey head to his shoulder.

"You have all practised the lifeboat drill many times and you know your teams and stations. I am sure I do not have to impress upon you the necessity to go to your stations in orderly fashion, and to obey explicitly the orders of the ship's officers."

Samantha set down her tray and crossed quickly to Mrs. Goldberg. The woman was weeping, softly and quietly, lost and bewildered, and Samantha slipped her arm around her shoulder.

"Come now," she whispered. "Don't let the others see you cry."

"Will you stay with me, Samantha?"

"Of course I will." She lifted the woman to her feet. "It will be all right—you'll see. Just think of the story you'll be able to tell your grandchildren when you get home."

Captain Reilly reviewed his preparations for leaving the ship, going over them item by item in his mind. He now knew by heart the considerable list he had compiled days previously from his own vast experience of Antarctic conditions and the sea.

The single most important consideration was that no person should be immersed, or even drenched by sea water during the transfer. Life expectation in these waters was four minutes. Even if the victim were immediately pulled from the water, it was still four minutes, unless the sodden clothing could be removed and heating provided. With this wind blowing, rising eight of the Beaufort scale at forty miles an hour and an air temperature of minus twenty degrees, the chill factor was at the extreme of stage seven, which, translated into physical terms, meant that a few minutes' exposure would numb and exhaust a man, and that mere survival was a matter of planning and precaution.

The second most important consideration was the physiological crisis of his passengers, when they left the comparative warmth and comfort and security of the ship for the shrieking cold and the violent discomfort of a life-raft afloat in an Antarctic storm.

They had been briefed, and mentally prepared as much as was possible. An officer had checked each passenger's clothing and survival equipment, they had been fed high-sugar tablets to ward off the cold, and the life-raft allocations had been carefully worked out to provide balanced complements, each with a competent crew member in command.

It was as much as he could do for them, and he turned his attention to the logistics of the transfer.

The lifeboats would go first—six of them, slung three on each side of the ship, each crewed by a navigation officer and five seamen. While the great drogue of the sea-anchor held the ship's head into the wind and the sea, they would be swung outboard on their hydraulic derricks and the winches would lower them swiftly to the surface of a sea temporarily smoothed by the oil sprayed from the pumps in the bows.

Although they were decked-in, powered, and equipped with radio, the lifeboats were not the ideal vehicles for survival in these conditions. Within hours, the men aboard them would be exhausted by the cold. For this reason, none of the passengers would be aboard them. Instead, they would go into the big inflatable life-rafts, self-righting even in the worst seas and enclosed with a double skin of insulation. Equipped with emergency rations and battery-powered locator beacons, they would ride the big black seas more easily and each provide shelter for twenty human beings, whose body warmth would keep the interior habitable, at least for the time it took to tow the rafts to land.

The motor lifeboats were merely the shepherds for the rafts. They would herd them together and then tow them in tandem to the sheltering arms of Shackleton Bay.

Even in these blustering conditions, the tow should not take more than twelve hours. Each boat would tow five rafts, and though the crews of the motor boats would have to change, brought into the canopy of the rafts and rested, there should be no insurmountable difficulties; Captain Reilly was hoping for a tow-speed of between three and four knots.

The lifeboats were packed with equipment and fuel and food sufficient to keep the shipwrecked party for a month, perhaps two on reduced rations, and once the calmer shores of the bay had been reached, the rafts would be carried ashore, the canopies reinforced with slabs of packed snow and transformed into igloo-type huts to shelter the survivors. They might be in Shackleton Bay a long time, for even when the French tug reached them, it could not take aboard six hundred persons; some would have to remain and await another rescue ship.

Captain Reilly took one more look at the land. It was very close now, and even in the gloom of the onrushing night, the peaks of ice and snow glittered like the fangs of some terrible and avaricious monster.

"All right," he nodded to his First Officer, "we will begin."

The Mate lifted the small two-way radio to his lips. "Foredeck. Bridge. You may commence laying the oil now."

From each side of the bows, the hoses threw up silver dragonfly wings of sprayed diesel oil, pumped directly from the ship's bunkers; its viscous weight resisted the wind's efforts to tear it away, and it fell in a thick coating across the surface of the sea, broken by the floodlights into the colour spectrum of the rainbow.

Immediately, the sea was soothed, the wind-riven surface flattened by the weight of oil, so the swells passed in smooth and weighty majesty beneath the ship's hull.

The two officers on the wing of the bridge could feel the sick, water-logged response of the hull. She was heavy with the water in her, no longer light and quick and alive.

"Send the boats away," said the Captain, and the mate passed the order over the radio in quiet conversational tones.

The hydraulic arms of the derricks lifted the six boats off their chocks and swung them out over the ship's side, suspended one moment high above the surface; then, as the ship fell through the trough, the oil-streaked crest raced by only feet below their keels. The officer of each lifeboat must judge the sea, and operate the winch so as to drop neatly onto the back slope of a passing swell—then instantly detach the automatic clamps and stand away from the threatening steel cliff of the ship's side.

In the floodlights, the little boats shone wetly with spray, brilliant electric yellow in colour, and decorated with garlands of ice like Christmas toys. In the small armoured-glass windows the officers' faces also glistened whitely with the strain and concentration of these terrifying moments, as each tried to judge the rushing black seas.

Suddenly the heavy nylon rope that held the cone-shaped drogue of the sea-anchor snapped with a report like a cannon shot, and the rope snaked and hissed in the air, a vicious whiplash which could have sliced a man in half.

It was like slipping the head halter from a wild stallion. *Golden Adventurer* threw up her bows, joyous to be freed of restraint. She slewed back across the scend of the sea, and was immediately pinned helplessly broadside, her starboard side into the wind, and the three yellow lifeboats still dangling.

A huge wave reared up out of the darkness. As it rushed down on the ship, one of the lifeboats sheared her cables and fell heavily to the surface, the tiny propeller churning frantically, trying to bring her round to meet the wave—but the wave caught her and dashed her back against the steel side of the ship.

She burst like a ripe melon and the guts spilled out of her; from the bridge they saw the crew swirled helplessly away into the darkness. The little locator lamps on their lifejackets burned feebly as fireflies in the darkness and then blinked out in the storm.

The forward lifeboard was swung like a door-knocker against the ship, her forward cable jammed so she dangled stern upmost, and as each wave punched into her, she was smashed against the hull. They could hear the men in her screaming, a thin pitiful sound on the wind, that went on for many minutes as the sea slowly beat the boat into a tangle of wreckage.

The third boat was also swung viciously against the hull. The releases on her clamps opened, and she dropped twenty feet into the boil and surge of water, submerging completely and then bobbing free like a yellow fishing float after the strike. Leaking and settling swiftly, she limped away into the clamorous night.

"Oh, my God," whispered Captain Reilly, and in the harsh lights of the bridge, his face was suddenly old and haggard. In a single stroke he had lost half his boats. As yet he did not mourn the men taken by the sea, that would come later—now it was the loss of the boats that appalled him, for it threatened the lives of nearly six hundred others.

"The other boats"—the First Officer's voice was ragged with shock—"the others got away safely, sir."

In the lee of the towering hull, protected from both wind and sea, the other three boats had dropped smoothly to the surface and detached swiftly. Now they circled out in the dark night, with their spotlights probing like long white fingers. One of them staggered over the wildly plunging crests to take off the crew of the stricken lifeboat, and they left the cracked hull to drift away and sink.

"Three boats," whispered the Captain, "for thirty rafts." He knew that there were insufficient shepherds for his flock—and yet he had to send them out, for even above the wind, he thought he could hear the booming artillery barrage of high surf breaking on a rocky shore. Cape Alarm was waiting hungrily for his ship. "Send the rafts away," he said quietly, and then again under his breath, "And God have mercy on us all."

• • •

Come on, Number 16," called Samantha. "Here we are, Number 16." She gathered them to her, the eighteen passengers who made up the complement of her allotted life-raft. "Here we are— all together now. No stragglers."

They were gathered at the heavy mahogany doors that opened on to the open forward deck.

"Be ready," she told them. "When we get the word, we have to move fast."

With the broadsiding seas sweeping the deck and cascading down over the lee, it would be impossible to embark from landing-nets into a raft bobbing alongside.

The rafts were being inflated on the open deck, the passengers hustled across to them and into the canopied interior between waves and then the laden rafts were lifted over the side by the clattering winches and dropped into the quieter waters afforded by the tall bulk of the ship. Immediately, one of the lifeboats picked up the tow and took each raft out to form the pitiful little convoy.

"Right!" the Third Officer burst in through the mahogany doors and held them wide. "Quickly!" he shouted. "All together."

"Let's go, gang!" sang out Samantha, and there was an awkward rush out on to the wet and slippery deck. It was only thirty paces to where the raft crouched like a monstrous yellow bullfrog, gaping its ugly dark mouth, but the wind struck like an axe and Samantha heard them cry out in dismay. Some of them faltered in the sudden merciless cold.

"Come on," Samantha shouted, pushing those ahead of her, half-supporting Mrs. Goldberg's plump body that suddenly felt as heavy and unco-operative as a full sack of wheat. "Keep going."

"Let me have her," shouted the Third Officer, and he grabbed Mrs. Goldberg's other arm. Between them they tumbled her through the entrance of the raft.

"Good on you, love," the officer grinned at Samantha briefly. His smile was attractive and warm, very masculine and likeable. His name was Ken and he was five years her senior. They would probably have become lovers fairly soon, Samantha knew, for he had pursued her furiously since she stepped aboard in New York. Although she knew she did not love him, yet he had succeeded in arousing her and she was slowly succumbing to his obvious charms and her own passionate nature. She had made the decision to have him, and had been merely savouring it up until then. Now, with a pang, she realized that the moment might never come.

"I'll help you with the others." She raised her voice above the hysterical shriek of the wind.

"Get in," he shouted back, and swung her brusquely towards the raft. She crept into the crowded interior and looked back at the brightly lit deck that glistened in the arc lamps.

Ken had started back to where one of the women had slipped and fallen. She sprawled helplessly on the wet deck, while her husband stooped over her, trying to lift her back to her feet.

Ken reached them and lifted the woman easily; the three of them were the only ones out on the open deck now, and the two men supported the woman between them, staggering against the heavy sullen roll of the waterlogged hull.

Samantha saw the wave come aboard and she shrieked a warning.

"Go back, Ken! For God's sake go back!" But he seemed not to hear her. The wave came aboard; over the windward rail like some huge black slippery sea-monster, it came with a deep silent rush.

"Ken!" she screamed, and he looked over his shoulder an instant before it reached them. Its crest was higher than his head. They could reach neither the raft, nor the shelter of the mahogany doors. She heard the clatter of the donkey-winch and the raft lifted swiftly off the deck, with a swooping tug in her guts. The operator could not let the rushing power of the wave crash into the helpless raft, throwing it against the superstructure or tearing its belly out on the ship's railing, for the frail plastic skin would rupture and it would collapse immediately.

Samantha hurled herself to the entrance and peered down. She saw the sea take the three figures in a black glittering rush. It cut them down, and swept them away. For a moment, she saw Ken clinging to the railing while the waters poured over him, burying his head in a tumbling fall of white and furious water. He disappeared and when the ship rolled sullenly back, shaking herself clear of the water, her decks were empty of any human shape.

With the next roll of the ship, the winch-operator high up in his glassed cabin swung the dangling raft outboard and lowered it swiftly and dexterously to the surface of the sea where one of the lifeboats circled anxiously, ready to take them in tow.

Samantha closed and secured the plastic door-cover, then she groped her way through the press of packed and terrified bodies until she found Mrs. Goldberg.

"Are you crying, dear?" the elderly woman quavered, clinging to her desperately.

"No," said Samantha, and placed one arm around her shoulders. "No, I'm not crying." And with her free hand, she wiped away the icy tears that streamed down her cheeks.

The Trog lifted his headset and looked at Nick through the reeking clouds of cigar smoke.

"Their radio operator has screwed down the key of his set. He's sending a single unbroken homing beam."

Nick knew what that meant—they had abandoned *Golden Adventurer*. He nodded once but remained silent. He had wedged himself into the doorway from the bridge. The restless impatience that consumed him would not allow him to sit or be still for more than a few moments at a time. He was slowly facing up to the reality of disaster. The dice had fallen against him and his gamble had been with very survival. It was absolutely certain that *Golden Adventurer* would go aground and be beaten into a total wreck by this storm. He could expect a charter from Christy Marine to assist *La Mouette* in ferrying the survivors back to Cape Town, but the fee would be a small fraction of the Esso tow fee that he had forsaken for this wild and desperate dash south.

The gamble had failed and he was a broken man. Of course, it would take months still for the effects of his folly to become apparent, but the repayments of his loans and the construction bills for the other tug still building would slowly throttle and bring him down.

"We might still reach her before she goes aground," said David Allen sturdily, and nobody else on the bridge spoke. "I mean there could be a backlash of the current close inshore which could hold her off long enough to give us a chance—" His voice trailed off as Nick looked across at him and frowned.

"We are still ten hours away from her, and for Reilly to make the decision to abandon ship, she must have been very close indeed. Reilly is a good man." Nick had personally selected him to command the *Golden*

Adventurer. "He was a destroyer captain on the North Atlantic run, the youngest in the navy, and then he was ten years with P & O. They pick only the best—" He stopped talking abruptly. He was becoming garrulous. He crossed to the radarscope and adjusted it for maximum range and illumination before looking down into the eyepiece. There was much fuzz and sea clutter, but on the extreme southern edge of the circular screen there showed the solid luminous glow of the cliffs and peaks of Cape Alarm. In good weather they were a mere five hours' steaming away, but now they had left the shelter of that giant iceberg and were staggering and plunging wildly through the angry night. She could have taken more speed, for *Warlock* was built for big seas, but always there was the deadly menace of ice, and Nick had to hold her at this cautionary speed, which meant ten hours more before they were in sight of *Golden Adventurer*—if she was still afloat.

Behind him, the Trog's voice crackled rustily with excitement. "I'm getting voice—it's only strength one, weak and intermittent. One of the lifeboats is sending on a battery-powered transmitter." He held his earphones pressed to his head with both hands as he listened.

"They are towing a batch of life-rafts with all survivors aboard to Shackleton Bay. But they've lost a life-raft," he said. "It's broken away from their towline, and they haven't got enough boats to search for it. They are asking *La Mouette* to keep a watch for it."

"Is *La Mouette* acknowledging?"

The Trog shook his head. "She's probably still out of range of this transmission."

"Very well." Nick turned back into the bridge. He had still not broken radio silence, and could feel his officers' disapproval, silent but strong. Again he felt the need for human contact, for the warmth and comfort of human conversation and friendly encouragement. He didn't yet have the strength to bear his failure alone.

He stopped beside David Allen and said, "I have been studying the Admiralty sailing directions for Cape Alarm, David," and pretended not to notice that the use of his Christian name had brought a startled look and quick colour to the mate's features. He went on evenly, "the shore is very steep-to and she is exposed to this westerly weather, but there are beaches of pebble and the glass is going up sharply again."

"Yes, sir," David nodded enthusiastically. "I have been watching it."

"Instead of hoping for a cross-current to hold her off, I suggest you offer a prayer that she goes up on one of those beaches and that the weather moderates before she is beaten to pieces. There is still a chance we can put ground tackle on her before she starts breaking up."

"I'll say ten Hail Marys, sir," grinned David. Clearly he was overwhelmed by this sudden friendliness from his silent and forbidding Captain.

"And say another ten that we hold our lead on *La Mouette*," said Nick, and smiled. It was one of the few times that David Allen had seen him smile, and he was amazed at the change it made to the stern features. They lightened with a charm and warmth and he had not before noticed the clear green of Nick Berg's eyes and how white and even were his teeth.

"Steady as she goes," said Nick. "Call me if anything changes," and he turned away to his cabin.

"Steady as she goes, it is, sir," said David Allen with a new friendliness in his voice.

The strange and marvellous lights of the aurora australis quivered and flickered in running streams of red and green fire along the horizon, and formed an incredible backdrop for the death agonies of a great ship.

Captain Reilly looked back through the small portholes of the leading lifeboat and watched her going to her fate. It seemed to him she had never been so tall and beautiful as in these terrible last moments. He had loved many ships, as if each had been a wonderful living creature, but he had loved no other ship more than *Golden Adventurer*, and he felt something of himself dying with her.

He saw her change her action. The sea was feeling the land now, the steep bank of Cape Alarm, and the ship seemed to panic at the new onslaught of wave and wind, as though she knew what fate awaited her there.

She was rolling through thirty degrees, showing the dull red streak of her belly paint as she came up short at the limit of each huge penduluming arc. There was a headland, tall black cliffs dropping sheer into the turbulent waters and it seemed that *Golden Adventurer* must go full on to them, but in the last impossible moments she slipped by, borne on the backlash of the current, avoiding the cliffs and swinging her bows on into the shallow bay beyond where she was hidden from Captain Reilly's view.

He stood for many minutes more, staring back across the leaping wave-tops and in the strange unnatural light of the heavens his face was greenish grey and heavily furrowed with the marks of grief.

Then he sighed once, very deeply, and turned away, devoting all his attention to guiding his pathetic limping little convoy to the safety of Shackleton Bay.

Almost immediately it was apparent that the fates had relented, and given them a favourable inshore current to carry them up on to the coast. The lifeboats were strung out over a distance of three miles, each of them with its string of bloated and clumsy rafts lumbering along in its wake. Captain Reilly had two-way VHF radio contact with each of them, and despite the brutal cold, they were all in good shape and making steady and unexpectedly rapid progress. Three or four hours would be sufficient, he began to hope. They had lost so much life already, and he could not be certain that there would be no further losses until he had the whole party ashore and encamped.

Perhaps the tragic run of bad luck had changed at last, he thought, and he picked up the small VHF radio. Perhaps the French tug was in range at last and he began to call her.

"*La Mouette*, do you read me? Come in, *La Mouette* . . ."

The lifeboat was low down on the water and the output of the little set was feeble in the vastness of sea and ice, yet he kept on calling.

They had accustomed themselves to the extravagant action of the disabled liner, her majestic roll and pitch, as regular as a gigantic metronome. They had adjusted to the cold of the unheated interior of the great ship, and the discomfort of her crowded and unsanitary conditions.

They had steeled themselves and tried to prepare themselves mentally for further danger and greater hardship, but not one of the survivors in life-raft Number 16 had imagined anything like this. Even Samantha, the youngest, probably physically the toughest and certainly the one most prepared by her training and her knowledge and love of the sea, had not imagined what it would be like in the raft.

It was utterly dark, not the faintest glimmer of light penetrated the insulated domed canopy, once its entrance was secured against the sea and the wind.

Samantha realized almost immediately how the darkness would crush their morale and, more dangerously, would induce disorientation and vertigo, so she ordered two of them at a time to switch on the tiny locator bulbs on their life jackets. It gave just a glimmering of light, enough to let them see each other's faces and take a little comfort in the proximity of other humans.

Then she arranged their seating, making them form a circle around the sides with all their legs pointing inwards, to give the raft better balance and to ensure that each of them had space to stretch out.

Now that Ken had gone, she had naturally taken command, and, as naturally, the others had turned to her for guidance and comfort. It was Samantha who had gone out through the opening into the brutal exposure of the night to take aboard and secure the tow rope from the lifeboat. She had come in again half-frozen, shaking in a palsy of cold, with her hands and face numbed. It had taken nearly half an hour of hard massage before feeling returned and she was certain that she had avoided frostbite.

Then the tow began, and if the movement of the light raft had been wild before, it now became a nightmare of uncoordinated movement. Each whim of sea and wind was transmitted directly to the huddling circle of survivors, and each time the raft pulled away or sheered off, the tow rope brought it up with a violent lurch and jerk. The wave crests whipped up by the wind and feeling the press of the land were up to twenty feet high, and the raft swooped over them and dropped heavily into the troughs. She did not have the lateral stability of a keel, so she spun on her axis until the tow rope jerked her up and she spun the other way. The first of them to start vomiting was Mrs. Goldberg and it spurted in a warm jet down the side of Samantha's anorak.

The canopy was almost airtight, except for the small ventilation holes near the apex of the roof, and immediately the sweetish acrid stench of vomit permeated the raft. Within minutes, half a dozen of the other survivors were vomiting also.

It was the cold, however, that frightened Samantha. The cold was the killer. It came up even through the flexible insulated double skin of the deck, and was transferred into their buttocks and legs. It came in through the plastic canopy and froze the condensation of their breaths, it even froze the vomit on their clothing and on the deck.

"Sing!" Samantha told them. "Come on, sing! Let's do 'Yankee Doodle Dandy,' first. You start, Mr. Stewart, come on. Clap your hands, clap hands with your neighbour." She hectored them relentlessly, not allowing any of them to fall into that paralytic state which is not true sleep but the trance caused by rapidly dropping body temperature. She crawled among them, prodding them awake, popping barley sugar from the emergency rations into their mouths.

"Suck and sing!" she commanded them, the sugar would combat the cold and the seasickness. "Clap your hands. Keep moving, we'll be there soon."

When they could sing no more, she told them stories—and whenever she mentioned the word "dog" they must all bark and clap their hands, or crow like the rooster, or bray like the donkey.

Samantha's throat was scratchy with singing and talking, and she was dizzy with fatigue and sick with cold, recognizing in herself the first symptoms of disinterest and lethargy, the prelude to giving up. She roused herself, struggling up into the sitting position from where she had slumped.

"I'm going to try and light the stove and get us a hot drink," she sang out brightly. Around her there was only a mild stir and somebody retched painfully.

"Who's for a mug of beef tea—" she stopped abruptly. Something had changed. It took her a long moment to realize what it was. The sound of the wind had muted and the raft was riding more easily now, it was moving into a more regular rhythm of sweep and fall, without the dreadful jerk of the tow rope snapping it back.

Frantically she crawled to the entrance of the raft, and with cold crippled fingers she tore at the fastenings.

Outside the dawn had broken into a clear cold sky of palest ethereal pinks and mauves. Although the wind had dropped to a faint whisper, the seas were still big and unruly, and the waters had changed from black to the deep bottle green of molten glass.

The tow rope had torn away at the connecting shackle, leaving only a dangling flap of plastic. Number 16 had been the last raft in the line being towed by number three, but of the convoy, Samantha could now see no sign—though she crawled out through the entrance and clung precariously to the side of the raft, scanning the wave-caps about her desperately.

There was no sign of a lifeboat, no sight even of the rocky, ice-capped shores of Cape Alarm. They had drifted away, during the night, into the vast and lonely reaches of the Weddell Sea.

Despair cramped her belly muscles, and she wanted to cry out in protest against this further cruelty of fate, but she prevented herself doing so, and stayed out in the clear and frosty air, drawing it in carefully for she knew that it could freeze her lung tissue. She searched and searched until her eyes streamed with the cold and the wind and concentration. Then at last the cold drove her back into the dark and stinking interior of the raft. She fell wearily among the supine and quiescent bodies, and pulled the hood of her anorak more tightly around her head. She knew it would not take long for them to start dying now, and somehow she did not care. Her despair was too intense, she let herself begin sinking into the morass of despondency which gripped all the others, and the cold crept up her legs and arms. She closed her eyes, and then opened them again with a huge effort.

"I'm not going to die," she told herself firmly. "I refuse to just lie down and die," and she struggled up onto her knees. It felt as though she wore a rucksack filled with lead, such was the physical weight of her despair.

She crawled to the central locker that held all their emergency rations and equipment.

The emergency locator transmitter was packed in polyurethane and her fingers were clumsy with cold and the thick mittens, but at last she brought it out. It was the size of a cigar-box, and the instructions were printed on the side of it. She did not need to read them, but switched on the set and replaced it in its slot. Now for forty-eight hours, or until the battery ran out, it would transmit a DF homing-signal on 121.5 megahertz.

It was possible, just possible, that the French tug might pick up that feeble little beam, and track it down to its source. She set it out of her mind, and devoted herself to the Herculean task of trying to heat half a mug of water on the small solid-fuel stove without scalding herself as she held the stove in her lap and balanced it against the raft's motion. While she worked, she searched for the courage and the words to tell the others of their predicament.

• • •

The *Golden Adventurer*, deserted of all human beings, her engines dead, but with her deck lights still burning, her wheel locked hard over, and the Morse key in the radio room screwed down to transmit a single unbroken pulse, drifted swiftly down on the black rock of Cape Alarm.

The rock was of so hard a type of formation that the cliffs were almost vertical, and even exposed as they were to the eternal onslaught of this mad sea, they had weathered very little. They still retained the sharp vertical edges and the glossy polished planes of cleanly fractured faults.

The sea ran in and hit the cliff without any check. The impact seemed to jar the very air, like the concussion of bursting high explosive, and the sea shot high in a white fury against the unyielding rock of the cliff, before rolling back and forming a reverse swell.

It was these returning echoes from the cliff that held *Golden Adventurer* off the cliff. The shore was so steep-to that it dropped to forty fathoms directly below the cliffs. There was no bottom on which the ship could gut herself.

The wind was blanketed by the cliff and in the eerie stillness of air, she drifted in closer and closer, rolling almost to her limits as the swells took her broadside. Once she actually touched the rock with her superstructure on one of those rolls, but then the echo-wave nudged her away. The next wave pushed her closer, and its smaller weaker offspring pushed back at her. A man could have jumped from a ledge on the cliff on to her deck as she drifted slowly, parallel to the rock.

The cliff ended in an abrupt and vertical headland, where it had calved into three tall pillars of serpentine, as graceful as the sculptured columns of a temple of Olympian Zeus.

Again, *Golden Adventurer* touched one of those pillars, she bumped it lightly with her stern. It scraped paint from her side and crushed in her rail, but then she was past.

The light bump was just sufficient to push her stern round, and she pointed her bows directly into the wide shallow bay beyond the cliffs.

Here a softer, more malleable rock-formation had been eroded by the weather, forming a wide beach of purple-black pebbles, each the size of a man's head and water-worn as round as cannon balls.

Each time the waves rushed up this stony beach, the pebbles struck against each other with a rattling roar, and the brash of rotten and mushy sea ice that filled the bay susurrated and clinked, as it rose and fell with the sea.

Now *Golden Adventurer* was clear of the cliff, she was more fully in the grip of the wind. Although the wind was dying, it still had force enough to move her steadily deeper into the bay, her bows pointed directly at the beach.

Unlike the cliff shore, the bay sloped up gently to the beach and this allowed the big waves to build up into rounded sliding humps. They did not curl and break into white water because the thick layer of brash ice weighted and flattened them, so that these swells joined with the wind to throw the ship at the beach with smoothly gathering impetus.

She took the ground with a great metallic groan of her straining plates and canted over slowly, but the moving pebble beach moulded itself quickly to her hull, giving gradually, as the waves and wind thrust her higher and higher until she was firmly aground; then, as the short night ended so the wind fell further, and in sympathy the swells moderated also and the tide drew back, letting the ship settle more heavily.

By noon of that day, *Golden Adventurer* was held firmly by the bows on the curved purple beach, canted over at an angle of 10°. Only her after end was still floating, rising and falling like a see-saw on the swell patterns which still pushed in steadily, but the plummeting air temperature was rapidly freezing the brash ice around her stern into a solid sheet.

The ship stood very tall above the glistening wet beach. Her upperworks were festooned with rime and long rapier-like stalactites of shining translucent ice hung from her scuppers and from the anchor fair-leads.

Her emergency generator was still running, and although there was no human being aboard her, her lights burned gaily and piped music played softly through her deserted public rooms.

Apart from the rent in her side, through which the sea still washed and swirled, there was no external evidence of damage, and beyond her the peaks and valleys of Cape Alarm, so wild and fierce, seemed merely to emphasize her graceful lines and to underline how rich a prize she was, a luscious ripe plum ready for the picking.

Down in her radio room, the transmitting key continued to send out an unbroken beam that could be picked up for 500 miles around.

• • •

Two hours of deathlike sleep—and then Nick Berg woke with a wild start, knowing that something of direct consequence was about to happen. But it took fully ten seconds for him to realize where he was.

He stumbled from his bunk, and he knew he had not slept long enough. His skull was stuffed with the cotton-wool of fatigue, and he swayed on his feet as he shaved in the shower, trying to steam himself awake with the scalding water.

When he went out on to the bridge, the Trog was still at his equipment. He looked up at Nick for a moment with his little rheumy pink eyes, and it was clear that he had not slept at all. Nick felt a prick of shame at his own indulgence.

"We are still inside *La Mouette*," said the Trog, and turned back to his set. "I reckon we have an edge of almost a hundred miles."

Angel appeared on the bridge, bearing a huge tray, and the saliva jetted from under Nick's tongue as he smelled it.

"I did a little special for your brekker, Skipper," said Angel. "I call it 'Eggs on Angel's Wings.' "

"I'm buying," said Nick, and turned back to the Trog with his mouth full and chewing. "What of the *Adventurer?*"

"She's still sending a DF, but her position has not altered in almost three hours."

"What do you mean?" Nick demanded, and swallowed heavily.

"No change in position."

"Then she's aground," Nick muttered, the food in his hand forgotten, and at that moment David Allen hurried on to the bridge still shrugging on his pea-jacket. His eyes were puffy and his hair was hastily wetted and combed, but spiky at the back from contact with his pillow. It had not taken him long to hear that the Captain was on the bridge. "And in one piece, if her transmitter is still sending."

"It looks like those Hail Marys worked, David." Nick flashed his rare smile and David slapped the polished teak top of the chart table.

"Touch wood, and don't dare the devil."

Nick felt his early despair slipping away with his fatigue, and he took another big mouthful and savoured it as he strode to the front windows and stared ahead.

The sea had flattened dramatically, but a weak and butter-yellow sun low on the horizon gave no warmth, and Nick glanced up at the thermometer and read the outside air temperature at minus thirty degrees.

Down here below 60° south, the weather was so unstable, caught up on the wheel of endlessly circling atmospheric depressions, that a gale could rise in minutes and drop to a flat calm almost as swiftly. Yet foul weather was the rule. For a hundred days and more each year, the wind was at galeforce or above. The photographs of Antarctica always gave a completely false impression of fine days with the sun sparkling on pristine snow fields and lovely towering icebergs. The truth was that you cannot take photographs in a blizzard or a white-out.

Nick distrusted this calm, and yet found himself praying that it would hold. He wanted to increase speed again, and was on the point of taking that chance, when the officer of the watch called a sharp alteration of course.

Ahead of them, Nick made out the sullen swirl of hidden ice below the surface, like a lurking monster, and as *Warlock* altered course to avoid it, the ice broke the surface. Black ice, striated with bands of glacial mud, ugly and deadly. Nick did not pass the order for the increase in speed.

"We should be raising Cape Alarm within the hour," David Allen gloated beside him. "If this visibility holds."

"It won't," said Nick. "We'll have fog pretty soon," and he indicated the surface of the sea, which was beginning to steam, emitting ghostly tendrils and eddies of seafret, as the difference between sea and air temperature widened.

"We'll be at the *Golden Adventurer* in four hours more." David was bubbling with renewed excitement, and he slapped the teak table again. "With your permission, sir, I'll go down and double-check the rocket-lines and tow equipment."

While the air around them thickened into a ghostly white soup, and blotted out all visibility to a few hundred yards, Nick paced the bridge like a caged lion, his hands clasped behind his back and a black unlit cheroot clamped between his teeth. He broke his pacing every time that the Trog intercepted another transmission from either Christy Marine, Jules Levoisin or Captain Reilly on his VHF radio.

At mid-morning, Reilly reported that he and his slow convoy had reached Shackleton Bay without further losses, that they were taking full advantage of the moderating weather to set up an encampment, and he ended by urging *La Mouette* to keep a watch on 121.5 megahertz to try and locate the missing life-raft that had broken away during the night. *La Mouette* did not acknowledge.

"They aren't reading on the VHF," grunted the Trog.

Nick thought briefly of the hapless souls adrift in this cold, and decided that they would probably not last out the day unless the temperature rose abruptly. Then he dismissed the thought and concentrated on the exchanges between Christy Marine and *La Mouette*.

The two parties had diametrically changed their bargaining standpoints.

While *Golden Adventurer* was adrift on the open sea, and any salvage efforts would mean that the tug should merely put a rocket-line across her, pass a messenger wire to carry the big steel hawser and then take her in tow, Jules Levoisin had pressed for Lloyd's Open Form "No cure no pay" contract.

Since the "cure" was almost certain, "pay" would follow as a matter of course. The amount of payment would be fixed by the arbitration of the committee of Lloyd's in London under the principles of international maritime law, and would be a percentage of the salved value of the vessel. The percentage decided upon by the arbitrator would depend upon the difficulties and dangers that the salvor had overcome. A clever salvor in an arbitration court could paint a picture of such daring and ingenuity that the award would be in millions of dollars.

Christy Marine had been desperately trying to avoid a "No cure no pay" contract. They had been trying to wheedle Levoisin into a daily hire and bonus contract, since this would limit the total cost of the operation, but they had been met by a Gallic acquisitiveness—right up to the moment when it became clear that *Golden Adventurer* had gone aground.

When that happened, the roles were completely reversed. Jules Levoisin, with a note of panic in his transmission, had immediately withdrawn his offer to go Lloyd's Open Form. For now the "cure" was far from certain, and the *Adventurer* might already be a total wreck, beaten to death on the rocks of Cape Alarm, in which case there would be "no pay."

Now Levoisin was desperately eager to strike a daily hire contract, including the run from South America and the ferrying of survivors back to civilization. He was offering his services at $10,000 a day, plus a bonus of 2½ percent of any salved value of the vessel. They were fair terms, for Jules Levoisin had given up the shining dream of millions and he had returned to reality.

However, Christy Marine, who had previously been offering a princely sum for daily hire, had just as rapidly withdrawn that offer.

"We will accept Lloyd's Open Form, including ferrying of survivors," they declared on Channel 16.

"Conditions on site have changed," Jules Levoisin sent back, and the Trog got another good fix on him.

"We are head-reaching on him handsomely," he announced with satisfaction, blinking his pink eyes rapidly while Nick marked the new relative positions on the chart.

The bridge of *Warlock* was once again crowded with every officer who had an excuse to be there. They were all in working rig, thick blue boiler suits and heavy sea boots, bulked up with jerseys and balaclava helmets, and they watched the plot with total fascination, arguing quietly among themselves.

David Allen came in carrying a bundle of clothing. "I've got working rig for you, sir. I borrowed it from the Chief Engineer. You are about the same size."

"Does the Chief know?" Nick asked.

"Not exactly, I just borrowed it from his cabin—"

"Well done, David," Nick chuckled. "Please put it in my day cabin." He felt himself warming more and more to the younger man.

"Captain, sir," the Trog sang out suddenly. "I'm getting another transmission. It's only strength one, and it's on 121.5 megahertz."

"Oh, shit!" David Allen paused in the entrance to the Captain's day cabin. "Oh, shit!" he repeated, and his expression was stricken. "It's that bloody missing life-raft."

"Relative bearing!" snapped Nick angrily.

"She bears 280° relative and 045° magnetic," the Trog answered instantly, and Nick felt his anger flare again.

The life-raft was somewhere out on their port beam, eighty degrees off their direct course to the *Golden Adventurer*.

The consternation on the bridge was carried in a babble of voices, that Nick silenced with a single black glance—and they stared at the plot in dismayed hush.

The position of each of the tugs was flagged with a coloured pin—

and there was another, a red flag, for the position of the *Golden Adventurer*. It was so close ahead of them now, and their lead over *La Mouette* so slender, that one of the younger officers could not remain silent.

"If we go to the raft, we'll be handing it to the bloody frog on a plate."

The words ended the restraint and they began to argue again, but in soft controlled tones. Nick Berg did not look up at them, but remained bowed over the chart, with his fist on the tabletop bunched so fiercely that the knuckles were ivory white.

"Christ, they have probably all had it by now. We'd be throwing it all away for a bunch of frozen stiffs."

"There is no telling how far off course they are, those sets have a range of a hundred miles."

"*La Mouette* will waltz away with it."

"We could pick them up later—after we put a line on *Golden Adventurer*."

Nick straightened slowly and took the cheroot out of his mouth. He looked across at David Allen and spoke levelly, without change of expression.

"Number One, will you please instruct your junior officers in the rule of the sea."

David Allen was silent for a moment, then he answered softly, "The preservation of human life at sea takes precedent over all other considerations."

"Very well, Mr. Allen," Nick nodded. "Alter 80° to port and maintain a homing course on the emergency transmission."

He turned away to his cabin. He could control his anger until he was alone, and then he turned and crashed his fist into the panel above his desk.

Out on the navigation bridge behind him nobody spoke nor moved for fully thirty seconds, then the Third Officer protested weakly.

"But we are so close!"

David Allen roused himself, and spoke angrily to the helmsman.

"New course 045° magnetic."

And as *Warlock* heeled to the change, he flung the armful of clothing bitterly on to the chart-table and went to stand beside the Trog.

"Corrections for course to intercept?" he asked.

"Bring her on to 050°," the Trog instructed, and then cackled without mirth. "First you call him an ice-water pisser—now you squeal like a baby because he answers a mayday."

And David Allen was silent as the *Warlock* turned away into the fog, every revolution of her big variable-pitch propellers carrying her directly away from her prize, and *La Mouette*'s triumphant transmissions taunted them as the Frenchman raced across the last of the open water that separated her from Cape Alarm, bargaining furiously with the owners in London.

The fog seemed so thick that it could be chopped into chunks like cheese. From the bridge it was not possible to see *Warlock*'s tall bows. Nick groped his way into it like a blind man in an unfamiliar room, and all around him the ice pressed closely.

They were in the area of huge tabular icebergs again. The echoes of the great ice islands flared green and malevolently on the radar screen and the awful smell and taste of the ice was on every breath they drew.

"Radio Officer?" Nick asked tensely, without taking his eyes from the swirling fog curtains ahead.

"Still no contact," the Trog answered, and Nick shuffled on his feet. The fog had mesmerized him, and he felt the shift of vertigo in his head. For a moment he had the illusion that his ship was listing heavily to one side, almost as though it were a space vehicle. He forcibly rejected the hallucination and stared fixedly ahead, tensing himself for the first green loom of ice through the fog.

"No contact for nearly an hour now," David muttered beside him.

"Either the battery on the DF has run down, or they have snagged ice and sunk—" volunteered the Third Officer, raising his voice just enough for Nick to hear.

"—or else their transmitter is blanketed by an iceberg," Nick finished for him, and there was silence on the bridge for another ten minutes, except for the quietly requested changes of course that kept *Warlock* zigzagging between the unseen but omnipresent icebergs.

"All right," Nick made the decision at last. "We'll have to accept that the raft has floundered and break off the search." And there was a stir of reawakening interest and enthusiasm. "Pilot, new course to *Golden Adventurer*, please, and we'll increase to fifty per cent power."

"We could still beat the frog." Again speculation and rising hope buoyed the young officers. "She could run into ice and have to reduce—"

They wished misfortune on *La Mouette* and her Captain, and even the ship beneath Nick's feet seemed to regain its lightness and vibrancy as she turned back for a last desperate run for the prize.

"All right, David," Nick spoke quietly. "One thing is certain now, we aren't going to reach the prize ahead of Levoisin. So we are going to play our ace now—" he was about to elaborate, when the Trog's voice squeaked with excitement.

"New contact, on 121.5," he cried, and the dismay on the bridge was a tangible thing.

"Christ!" said the Third Officer. "Why won't they just lie down and die!"

"The transmission was blanked by that big berg north of us," the Trog guessed. "They are close now. It won't take long."

"Just long enough to make certain we miss the prize."

The berg was so big that it formed its own weather system about it, causing eddies and currents of both air and water, enough to stir the fog.

The fog opened like a theatre curtain, and directly ahead there was a heart-stopping vista of green and blue ice, with darker strata of glacial mud banding cliffs which disappeared into the higher layers of fog above as though reaching to the very heavens. The sea had carved majestic arches of ice and deep caverns from the foot of the cliff.

"There they are!"

Nick snatched the binoculars from the canvas bin and focused on the dark specks that stood out so clearly against the backdrop of glowing ice.

"No," he grunted. Fifty emperor penguins formed a tight bunch on one of the flat floes, big black birds standing nearly as tall as a man's shoulder; even in the lens, they were deceptively humanoid.

Warlock passed them closely, and with sudden fright they dropped on to their bellies and used their stubby wings to skid themselves across the floe, and drop into the still and steaming waters below the cliff. The floe eddied and swung on the disturbance of *Warlock*'s passing.

Warlock nosed on through solid standing banks of fog and into abrupt holes of clear air where the mirages and optical illusions of Antarctica's flawed air maddened them with their inconsistencies, transforming flocks of penguins into herds of elephants or bands of waving men, and placing in their path phantom rocks and bergs which disappeared again swiftly as they approached.

The emergency transmissions from the raft faded and silenced, then beeped again loudly into the silence of the bridge, and seconds later were silent again.

"God damn them," David swore quietly and bitterly, his cheeks pink with frustration. "Where the hell are they? Why don't they put up a flare or a rocket?" And nobody answered as another white fog monster enveloped the ship, muting all sound aboard her.

"I'd like to try shaking them up with the horn, sir," he said, as *Warlock* burst once more into sparkling and blinding sunlight. Nick grunted acquiescence without lowering his binoculars.

David reached up for the red-painted foghorn handle above his head, and the deep booming blast of sound, the characteristic voice of an ocean-going salvage tug, reverberated through the fog, seeming to make it quiver with the volume of the sound. The echoes came crashing back off the ice cliffs of the bergs like the thunder of the skies.

S amantha held the solid-fuel stove in her lap using the detachable fibreglass lid of the locker as a tray. She was heating half a pint of water in the aluminium pannikin, balancing carefully against the wallowing motion of the raft.

The blue flame of the stove lit the dim cavern of plastic and radiated a feeble glow of warmth insufficient to sustain life. They were dying already.

Gavin Stewart held his wife's head against his chest, and bowed his own silver head over it. She had been dead for nearly two hours now, and her body had already cooled, the face peaceful and waxen.

Samantha could not bear to look across at them, she crouched over the stove and dropped a cube of beef into the water, stirring it slowly and blinking against the tears of penetrating cold. She felt thin watery mucus run down her nostrils and it required an effort to lift her arm and wipe it away on her sleeve. The beef tea was only a little above blood warmth, but she could not waste time and fuel on heating it further.

The metal pannikin passed slowly from mittened hand to numbed and clumsy hand. They slurped the warm liquid and passed it on reluctantly, though there were some who had neither the strength nor the interest to take it.

"Come on, Mrs. Goldberg," Samantha whispered painfully. The cold seemed to have closed her throat, and the foul air under the canopy made her head ache with grinding, throbbing pain. "You must drink—" Samantha touched the woman's face, and cut herself off. The flesh had a putty-like texture and was cooling swiftly. It took long lingering minutes for the shock to pass, then carefully Samantha pulled the hood of the old woman's parka down over her face. Nobody else seemed to have noticed. They were all too far sunk into lethargy.

"Here," whispered Samantha to the man beside her—and she pressed the pannikin into his hands, folding his stiff fingers around the metal to make certain he had hold of it. "Drink it before it cools."

The air around her seemed to tremble suddenly with a great burst of sound, like the bellow of a dying bull, or the rumble of cannon balls across the roof of the sky. For long moments, Samantha thought her mind was playing tricks with her, and only when it came again did she raise her head.

"Oh God," she whispered. "They've come. It's going to be all right. They've come to save us."

She crawled to the locker, slowly and stiffly as an old woman.

"They've come. It's all right, gang, it's going to be all right," she mumbled, and she lit the globe on her life jacket. In its pale glow, she found the packet of phosphorus flares.

"Come on now, gang. Let's hear it for Number 16." She tried to rouse them as she struggled with the fastenings of the canopy. "One more cheer," she whispered, but they were still and unresponsive, and as she fumbled her way out into the freezing fog, the tears that ran down her cheeks were not from the cold.

She looked up uncomprehendingly, it seemed that from the sky around her tumbled gigantic cascades of ice, sheer sheets of translucent menacing green ice. It took her moments to realize that the life-raft had drifted in close beneath the precipitous lee of a tabular berg. She felt tiny and inconsequential beneath that ponderous mountain of brittle glassy ice.

For what seemed an eternity, she stood, with her face lifted, staring upwards—then again the air resonated with the deep gut-shaking bellow of the siren. It filled the swirling fog-banks with solid sound that struck the cliff of ice above her and shattered into booming echoes, that bounded from wall to wall and rang through the icy caverns and crevices that split the surface of the great berg.

Samantha held aloft one of the phosphorus flares, and it required all the strength of her frozen arm to rip the igniter tab. The flare spluttered and streamed acrid white smoke, then burst into the dazzling crimson fire that denotes distress at sea. She stood like a tiny statue of liberty, holding the flare aloft in one hand and peering with streaming eyes into the sullen fog-banks.

Again the animal bellow of the siren boomed through the milky, frosted air; it was so close that it shook Samantha's body the way the wind moves the wheat on the hillside, then it went on to collide solidly with the cliff of ice that hung above her.

The working of sea and wind, and the natural erosion of changing temperatures had set tremendous forces at work within the glittering body of the berg. Those forces had found a weak point, a vertical fault line, that ran like an axe-stroke from the flattened tableland of the summit, five hundred feet down to the moulded bottom of the berg far below the surface.

The booming sound waves of *Warlock*'s horn found a sympathetic resonance with the body of the mountain that set the ice on each side of the fault vibrating in different frequencies.

Then the fault sheared, with a brittle cracking explosion of glass bursting under pressure, and the fault opened. One hundred million tons of ice began to move as it broke away from the mother berg. The block of ice that the berg calved was in itself a mountain, a slab of solid ice twice the size of Saint Paul's Cathedral—and as it swung out and twisted free, new pressures and forces came into play within it, finding smaller faults and flaws so that ice burst within ice and tore itself apart, as though dynamited with tons of high explosive.

The air itself was filled with hurtling ice, some pieces the size of a locomotive and others as small and as sharp and as deadly as steel swords; and below this plunging toppling mass, the tiny yellow plastic raft bobbed helplessly.

"There," called Nick. "On the starboard beam." The phosphorus distress flare lit the fog-banks internally with a fiery cherry red and threw grotesque patterns of light against the belly of lurking cloud. David Allen blew one last triumphant blast on the siren.

"New heading 150°," Nick told the helmsman and *Warlock* came around handily, and almost instantly burst from the enveloping bank of fog into another arena of open air.

Half a mile away, the life-raft bobbed like a fat yellow toad beneath a glassy green wall of ice. The top of the iceberg was lost in the fog high above, and the tiny human figure that stood erect on the raft and held aloft the brilliant crimson flare was an insignificant speck in this vast wilderness of fog and sea and ice.

"Prepare to pick up survivors, David," said Nick, and the mate hurried away while Nick moved to the wing of the bridge from where he could watch the rescue.

Suddenly Nick stopped and lifted his head in bewilderment. For a moment he thought it was gunfire, then the explosive crackling of sound changed to a rending shriek as of the tearing of living fibre when a giant redwood tree is falling to the axes. The volume of sound mounted into a rumbling roar, the unmistakeable roar of a mountain in avalanche.

"Good Christ!" whispered Nick, as he saw the cliff of ice begin to change shape. Slowly sagging outwards, it seemed to fold down upon itself. Faster and still faster it fell, and the hissing splinters of bursting ice formed a dense swirling cloud, while the cliff leaned further and further beyond its point of equilibrium and at last collapsed and lifted pressure waves from the green waters that raced out one behind the other, flinging *Warlock*'s bows high as she rode them and then nosed down into the troughs between.

Since Nick's oath, nobody had spoken on the bridge. They clutched for balance at the nearest support and stared in awe at that incredible display of careless might, while the water still churned and creamed with the disturbance and pieces of broken jagged ice, some the size of a country house, bobbed to the surface and revolved slowly, finding their balance as they swirled and bumped against each other.

"Closer," snapped Nick. "Get as close as you can."

Of the yellow life-raft there was no longer any sign. Jagged shards of ice had ripped open its fragile skin and the grinding, tumbling lumps had trodden it and its pitiful human cargo deep beneath the surface.

"Closer," urged Nick. If by a miracle anybody had survived that avalanche, then they had four minutes left of life, and Nick pushed *Warlock* into the still-rolling and roiling mass of broken ice—pushing it open with ice-strengthened bows.

Nick flung open the bridge doors beside him and stepped out into the freezing air of the open wing. He ignored the cold, buoyed up by new anger and frustration. He had paid the highest price to make this rescue, he had given up his chance at *Golden Adventurer* for the lives of a handful of strangers, and now, at this last moment, they had been snatched away from him. His sacrifice had been in vain, and the terrible waste of it all appalled him. Because there was no other outlet for his feelings, he let waves of anger sweep over him and he shouted at David Allen's little group on the foredeck.

"Keep your eyes open. I want those people—"

Red caught his eye, a flash of vivid red, seen through the green water, becoming brighter and more hectic as it rose to the surface.

"Both engines half astern!" he screamed. And *Warlock* stopped dead as the twin propellers changed pitch and bit into the water, pulling her up in less than her own length.

In a small open area of green water the red object broke out. Nick saw a human head in a red anorak hood, supported by the thick inflated life jacket. The head was thrown back, exposing a face as white and glistening with wetness as the deadly ice that surrounded it. The face was that of a young boy, smooth and beardless, and quite incredibly beautiful.

"Get him," Nick yelled, and at the sound of his voice the eyes in that beautiful face opened. Nick saw they were a misty green and unnaturally large in the glistening pale oval framed by the crimson hood.

David Allen was racing back, carrying life-ring and line.

"Hurry. God damn you." The boy was still alive, and Nick wanted him. He wanted him as fiercely as he had wanted anything in his life, he wanted at least this one young life in return for all he had sacrificed. He saw that the boy was watching him. "Come on, David," he shouted again.

"Here!" called David, bracing himself at the ship's rail and he threw the life-ring. He threw it with an expert round arm motion that sent it skimming forty feet to where the hooded head bobbed on the agitated water. He threw it so accurately that it hit the bobbing figure a glancing blow on the shoulder and then plopped into the water alongside, almost nudging the boy.

"Grab it," yelled Nick. "Grab hold!"

The face turned slowly, and the boy lifted a gloved hand clear of the surface, but the movement was blunderingly uncoordinated.

"There. It's right next to you," David encouraged. "Grab it, man!"

The boy had been in the water for almost two minutes already, he had lost control of his body and limbs; he made two inconclusive movements with the raised hand, one actually bumped the ring but he could not hold it and slowly the life-ring bobbed away from him.

"You bloody idiot," stormed Nick. "Grab it!" And those huge green eyes turned back to him, looking up at him with the total resignation of defeat, one stiff arm still raised—almost a farewell salute.

Nick did not realize what he was going to do until he had shrugged off his coat and kicked away his shoes; then he realized that if he stopped to think about it, he would not go.

He jumped feet first, throwing himself far out to miss the rail below him, and as the water closed over his head he experienced a terrified sense of disbelief at the cold.

It seized his chest in a vice that choked the air from his lungs, it drove needles of agony deep into his forehead, and blinded him with the pain as he rose to the surface again. The cold rushed through his light clothing, it crushed his testicles and his stomach was filled with nausea. The marrow in the bones of his legs and arms ached so that he found it difficult to force his limbs to respond, but he struck out for the floating figure.

It was only forty feet, but halfway there he was seized by a panic that he was not going to make it. He clenched his teeth and fought the icy water as though it was a mortal enemy, but it sapped away his strength with the heat of his body.

He struck the floating figure with one outflung arm before he realized he had reached him, and he clung desperately to him, peering up at *Warlock*'s deck.

David Allen had retrieved the ring by its line and he threw it again. The cold had slowed Nick down so that he could not avoid the ring and it struck him on the forehead, but he felt no pain, there was no feeling in his face or feet or hands.

The fleeting seconds counted out the life left to them as he struggled with the inert figure, slowly losing command of his own limbs as he tried to fit the ring over the boy's body. He did not accomplish it. He got the boy's head and one arm through, and he knew he could do no more.

"Pull," he screamed in rising panic, and his voice was remote and echoed strangely in his own ears.

He took a twist of line around his arm, for his fingers could no longer hold, and he clung with the remains of his strength as they dragged them in.

Jagged ice brushed and snatched at them, but he held the boy with his free arm.

"Pull," he whispered. "Oh, for God's sake, pull!" And then they were bumping against *Warlock*'s steel side, were being lifted free of the water, the twist of line smearing the wet skin from his forearm, staining his sleeve with blood that was instantly dissolved to pink by sea water. He felt no pain.

With the other arm, he hung on to the boy, holding him from slipping out of the life-ring. He did not feel the hands that grabbed at him. There was no feeling in his legs and he collapsed face forward, but David caught him before he struck the deck and they hustled him into the steaming warmth of Angel's galley, his legs dragging behind him.

"Are you okay, Skipper?" David kept demanding, and when Nick tried to reply, his jaw was locked in a frozen rictus and great shuddering spasms shook his whole body.

"Get their clothes off," grated Angel, and, with an easy swing of his heavily muscled shoulders, lifted the boy's body on to the galley table and laid it out face upwards. With a single sweep of a Solingen steel butcher's knife he split the crimson anorak from neck to crotch and stripped it away.

Nick found his voice, it was ragged and broken by the convulsions of frozen muscles.

"What the hell are you doing, David? Get your arse on deck and get this ship on course for *Golden Adventurer*," he grated, and would have added something a little more forceful, but the next convulsion caught him, and anyway David Allen had already left.

"You'll be all right." Angel did not even glance up at Nick as he worked with the knife, ripping away layer after layer of the boy's clothing. "A tough old dog like you—but I think we've got a ripe case of hypothermia here."

Two of the seamen were helping Nick out of his sodden clothing, the cloth crackled with the thin film of ice that had already formed. Nick winced with the pain of returning circulation to half-frozen hands and feet.

"Okay," he said, standing naked in the middle of the galley and scrubbing at himself with a rough towel. "I'll be all right now, return to your stations." He crossed to the kitchen range, tottering like a drunk, and welcomed the blast of heat from it, rubbing warmth into himself, still shaking and shuddering, his body mottled puce and purple with cold and his genitals shrunken and drawn up into the dense black bush at his crotch.

"Coffee's boiling. Get yourself a hot drink, Skip," Angel told him, glancing up at Nick from his work. He ran a quick appreciative glance over Nick's body, taking in the wide rangy shoulders, the dark curls of damp hair that covered his chest, and the trim lines of hard muscle that moulded his belly and waist.

"Put lots of sugar in it—it will warm you the best possible way," Angel instructed him, and returned his attention to the slim young body on the table.

Angel had put aside his camp airs, and worked with the brusque efficiency of a man who had been trained at his task.

Then suddenly he stopped and stood back for a moment. "Would you believe! No fun gun!" Angel sighed.

Nick turned just as Angel spread a thick woollen blanket over the pale naked body on the table and began to massage it vigorously.

"You better leave us girls alone together, Skipper," said Angel with a sweet smile and a twinkle of his diamond earrings, and Nick was left with the memory of a single fleeting glimpse of the stunningly lovely body of a young woman below the pale face and the thick sodden head of copper and gold hair.

Nick Berg was swaddled in a grey woollen blanket, over the boiler suit and bulk jerseys. His feet were in thick Norwegian trawlerman's socks and heavy rubber working boots. He held a china mug of almost boiling coffee in both hands, bending over it to savour the aroma of the steam. It was the third cup he had drunk in the last hour— and yet the shivering spasms still shook him every few minutes.

David Allen had moved his canvas chair across the bridge so he could watch the Trog and work the ship at the same time. Nick could see the loom of the black rock cliffs of Cape Alarm close on their port beam.

The Morse beam squealed suddenly, a long sequence of code to which every man on the bridge listened with complete attention, but it needed the Trog to say it for them.

"*La Mouette* has reached the prize." He seemed to take a perverse relish in seeing their expressions. "She's beaten us to it, lads. 12½ per cent salvage to her crew—"

"I want it word for word," snapped Nick irritably, and the Trog grinned spitefully at him before bowing over his pad.

"*La Mouette* to Christy Marine. *Golden Adventurer* is hard aground, held by ice and receding tides. Stop. Ice damage to plating appears to be below surface. Stop. Hull is flooded and open to sea. Stop. Under no circumstances will Lloyd's Open Form be acceptable. Emphasize importance of beginning salvage work immediately. Stop. Worsening weather and sea conditions. My final hire offer of $8,000 *per diem* plus 2½ per cent of salvaged value open until 1435 GMT. Standing by."

Nick lit one of his cheroots and irrelevantly decided he must conserve them in future. He had opened his last box that morning. He frowned through the blue smoke and pulled the blanket closer around his shoulders.

Jules Levoisin was playing it touch and hard now. He was dictating terms and setting ultimatums. Nick's own policy of silence was paying off. Probably by now, Jules felt completely safe that he was the only salvage tug within two thousand miles, and he was holding a big-calibre gun to Christy Marine's head.

Jules had seen the situation of the *Golden Adventurer*'s hull. If he had been certain of effecting salvage—no, even if there had been a fifty-fifty chance of a good salvage, Jules would have gone Open Form.

So Jules was not happy with his chances, and he had the shrewdest and most appraising eye in the salvage business. It was a tough one then. *Golden Adventurer* was probably held fast by the quicksand effect of beach and ice, and *La Mouette* could build up a mere nine thousand horsepower.

It would mean throwing out ground-tackle, putting power on *Adventurer*'s pumps—the problems and solutions passed in review through Nick's mind. It was going to be a tough one, but *Warlock* had twenty-two thousand rated horsepower and a dozen other high cards.

He glanced at his gold Rolex Oyster, and he saw that Jules had set a two-hour ultimatum.

"Radio Officer," he said quietly, and every man on the bridge stiffened and swayed closer, so as not to miss a word.

"Open the telex line direct to Christy Marine, London, and send quote 'Personal for Duncan Alexander from Nicholas Berg Master of

Warlock. Stop. I will be alongside *Golden Adventurer* in one hour forty minutes. Stop. I make firm offer Lloyd's Open Form Contract Salvage. Stop. Offer closes 1300 GMT.' "

The Trog looked up at him startled, and blinked his pink eyes swiftly.

"Read it back," snapped Nick, and the Trog did it in a high penetrating voice and when he finished, waited quizzically, as if expecting Nick to cancel.

"Send it," said Nick, and rose to his feet. "Mr. Allen," he turned to David, "I want you and the Chief Engineer in my day cabin right away."

The buzz of excitement and speculation began before Nick had closed the door behind him.

David knocked and followed him three minutes later, and Nick looked up from the notes he was making.

"What are they saying?" Nick asked. "That I am crazy?"

"They're just kids," shrugged David. "What do they know?"

"They know plenty, and they're right. I am crazy to go Open Form on a site unseen! But it's the craziness of a man with no other option. Sit down, David.

"When I made the decision to leave Cape Town on the chance of this job—that was when I did the crazy thing." Nick could no longer keep the steely silence. He had to say it, to talk it out. "I was throwing dice for my whole bundle. When I turned down the Esso tow, that was when I went on the line for the whole company, *Warlock* and her sister, the whole thing depended on the cash from the Esso tow—"

"I see," muttered David, and his colour was pink and high, embarrassed by this confidence from Nick Berg.

"What I am doing now is risking nothing. If I lose now, if I fail to pull *Golden Adventurer* out of there, I have lost nothing that is not already forfeit."

"We could have offered daily hire at a better rate than *La Mouette*," David suggested.

"No. Duncan Alexander is my enemy. The only way I can get the contract is to make it so attractive that he has no alternative. If he refuses my offer of Open Form, I will take him up before Lloyd's Committee and his own shareholders. I will make a rope of his own guts and hoist it around his neck. He has to go with me—whereas, if I had offered daily hire at a few thousand dollars less than *La Mouette*—" Nick broke off, reached for the box of cheroots on the corner of his desk, then arrested the gesture and swivelled in his chair at the heavy knock on the cabin door.

"Come!"

Vin Baker's overalls were pristine blue, but the bandage around his head was smeared with engine grease, and he had recovered all the bounce and swagger that Nick had banged out of him against the engine-room windows.

"Jesus!" he said. "I hear you just flipped. I hear you blew your mind and jumped overboard—and when they fished you out, you up and went Open Form on a bomber that's beating herself to death on Cape Alarm."

"I'd explain it to you," offered Nick solemnly, "only I don't know enough words of one syllable." The Chief Engineer grinned wickedly at that and Nick went on quickly, "Just believe me when I tell you that I'm playing with someone else's chips. I'm not risking anything I haven't lost already."

"That's good business," the Australian agreed handsomely, and helped himself to one of Nick's precious cheroots.

"Your share of 12½ per cent of daily hire is peanuts and apple jelly," Nick went on.

"Too right," Vin Baker agreed, and hoisted at his waistline with his elbows.

"But if we snatch *Golden Adventurer* and if we can plug her and pump her out, and if we can keep her afloat for three thousand miles, there will be a couple of big 'M's'—and that's beef and potatoes."

"You know something," Vin Baker grunted. "For a Pommy, I'm beginning to like the sound of your voice." He said it reluctantly and shook his head, as if he didn't really believe it.

"All I want from you now," Nick told him, "are your plans for getting power on to *Golden Adventurer*'s pumps and anchor-winch. If she's up on the beach, we will have to kedge her off and we won't have much time."

Kedging off was the technique of using a ship's own anchor and power winch to assist the pull of the tug in dragging off a stranding.

Vin Baker waved the cheroot airily. "Don't worry about that, I'm here." And at that moment the Trog put his head through the doorway again, this time without knocking.

"I have an urgent and personal for you, Skipper." He brandished the telex flimsy like a royal flush in spades.

Nick glanced through it once, then read it aloud:

"Master of *Warlock* from Christy Marine. Your offer Lloyd's Open Form 'No cure no pay' accepted. Stop. You are hereby appointed main salvage contractor for wreck of *Golden Adventurer*. ENDS."

Nick grinned with that rare wide irresistible flash of very white teeth. "And so, gentlemen, it looks as though we are still in business—but the devil knows for just how much longer."

Warlock rounded the headland, where the three black pillars of serpentine rock stood into a lazy green sea, across which low oily swells marched in orderly ranks to push in gently against the black cliffs.

They came round to the sudden vista of the wide, ice-choked bay. The abandoned hulk of *Golden Adventurer* was so majestic, so tall and beautiful that not even the savage mountains could belittle her. She looked like an illustration from a child's book of fairy tales, a lovely ice ship, glistening and glittering in the yellow sunlight.

"She's a beauty," whispered the Chief Engineer, and his voice captured the sorrow they all felt for a great ship in mortal distress. To every single man on the bridge of *Warlock*, a ship was a living thing for which at best they could feel love and admiration; even the dirtiest old tramp roused a grudging affection. But *Golden Adventurer* was like a lovely woman. She was something rare and special, and all of them felt it.

For Nick Berg, the bond was much more deeply felt. She was child of his inspiration, he had watched her lines take shape on the naval architect's drawingboard, he had seen her keel laid and her bare skeleton fleshed out with lovingly worked steel, and he had watched the woman who had once been his wife speak the blessing and then smash the bottle against her bows, laughing in the sunlight while the wine spurted and frothed.

She was his ship, and now, as he would never have believed possible, his destiny depended upon her.

He looked away from her at last to where *La Mouette* waited in the mouth of the bay at the edge of the ice. In contrast to the liner, she was small and squat and ugly, like a wrestler with all the weight in his shoulders. Greasy black smoke rose straight into the pale sky from her single stack, and her hull seemed to be painted the same greasy black.

Through his glasses, Nick saw the sudden bustle of activity on her bridge as *Warlock* burst into view. The headland would have blanketed *La Mouette*'s radar and, with Nick's strict radio silence, this would be the first that Jules Levoisin knew of *Warlock*'s presence. Nick could imagine the consternation on her navigation bridge, and he noted wryly that Jules Levoisin had not even gone through the motions of putting a line on to *Golden Adventurer*. He must have been completely sure of himself, of his unopposed presence. In maritime law, a line on to a prize's hull bestowed certain rights, and Jules should have made the gesture.

"Get *La Mouette* in clear," he instructed, and picked up the hand microphone as the Trog nodded to him.

"*Salut Jules, ca va?* You pot-bellied little pirate, haven't they caught and hung you yet?" Nick asked kindly in French, and there was a long disbelieving silence on Channel 16 before the fruity Gallic tones boomed from the overhead speaker.

"Admiral James Bond, I think?" and Jules chuckled, but unconvincingly. "Is that a battleship or a floating whorehouse? You always were a fancy boy, Nicholas, but what kept you so long? I expected to get a better run for my money."

"Three things you taught me, *mon brave*: the first was to take nothing for granted; the second was to keep your big yap shut tight when running for a prize; and the third was to put a line on it when you got there—you've broken your own rules, Jules."

"The line is nothing. I am arrived."

"And I, old friend, am arrived also. But the difference is that I am Christy Marine's contractor."

"*Tu rigoles!* You are joking!" Jules was shocked. "I heard nothing of this!"

"I am not joking," Nick told him. "My James Bond equipment lets me talk in private. But go ahead, call Christy Marine and ask them—and while you are doing it, move that dirty old greaser of yours out of the way. I've got work to do." Nick tossed the microphone back to the Trog. "Tape everything he sends," he instructed, and then to David Allen, "We are going to smash up that ice before it grabs too tight a hold on *Golden Adventurer*. Put your best man on the wheel."

Nick was a man transformed, no longer the brooding, moody recluse, agonizing over each decision, uncertain of himself and reacting to each check with frustrated and undirected anger.

"When he starts moving—he really burns it up," thought David Allen, as he listened to Nick on the engine-room intercom.

"I want flank power on both, Chief. We are going to break ice. Then I want you in full immersion with helmet, we are going on board her to take a peek at her engine room." He swung back to David Allen. "Number One, you can stand by to take command." The man of action glorying in the end to inactivity, he almost seemed to dance upon his feet, like a fighter at the first bell. "Tell Angel I want a hot meal for us before we go into the cold, plenty of sugar in it."

"I'll ask the steward," said David, "Angel is no good at the moment. He's playing dolls with the lass you pulled out the water. God, he'll be dressing her up and wheeling her around in a pram—"

"You tell Angel, I want food—and good food," growled Nick, and turned away to the window to study the ice that blocked the bay, "or I'll go down personally and kick his backside."

"He'd probably enjoy that," muttered David, and Nick rounded on him.

"How many times have you checked out the salvage gear since we left Cape Town?"

"Four times."

"Make it five. Do it again. I want all the diesel auxiliaries started and run up, then shut down for freezing and rigged to be swung out. I want to have power on *Adventurer* by noon tomorrow."

"Sir."

But before he could go, Nick asked, "What is the barometric reading?"

"I don't know—"

"From now until the end of this salvage, you will know, at any given moment, the exact pressure and you will inform me immediately of any variation over one millibar."

"Reading is 1018," David checked hastily.

"It's too high," said Nick. "And it's too bloody calm. Watch it. We are going to have a pressure bounce. Watch it like an eagle scout."

"Sir."

"I thought I asked you to check the gear."

The Trog called out, "Christy Marine has just called *La Mouette* and confirmed that we are the main contractor—but Levoisin has accepted daily hire to pick up a full load of survivors from Shackleton Bay and ferry them to Cape Town. Now he wants to speak to you again."

"Tell him I'm busy." Nick did not take his attention from the ice-packed bay, then he changed his mind. "No, I'll talk to him." He took the hand microphone. "Jules?"

"You don't play fair, Nicholas. You go behind the back of an old friend, a man who loves you like a brother."

"I'm a busy man. Did you truly call to tell me that?"

"I think you made a mistake, Nicholas. I think you're crazy to go Lloyd's Open on this one. That ship is stuck fast—and the weather! Did you read the met from Gough Island? You got yourself a screaming bastard there, Nicholas. You listen to an old man."

"Jules I've got twenty-two thousand horses running for me—"

"I still think you made a mistake, Nicholas. I think you're going to burn more than just your fingers."

"*Au revoir*, Jules. Come and watch me in the awards court."

"I still think that's a whorehouse, not a tug, you are sailing. You can send over a couple of blondes and a bottle of wine—"

"Goodbye, Jules."

"Good luck, *mon vieux*."

"Hey, Jules—you say 'good luck' and it's the worst possible luck. You taught me that."

"*Oui*, I know."

"Then good luck to you also, Jules." For a minute Nick looked after the departing tug. It waddled away over the oily swells, small and fat-bottomed and cheeky, for all the world like its Master—and yet there was something dejected and crestfallen about her going.

He felt a prick of affection for the little Frenchman, he had been a true and good friend as well as a teacher, and Nick felt his triumph softening to regret.

He crushed it down ruthlessly. It had been a straight, hard but fair run, and Jules had been careless. Long ago, Nick had taught himself that anybody in opposition was an enemy, to be hated and beaten, and when you had done so, you despised them. You did not feel compassion, it weakened your own resolve.

He could not quite bring himself to despise Jules Levoisin. The Frenchman would bounce back, probably snatching the next job out from under Nick's nose, and anyway he had the lucrative contract to ferry the survivors from Shackleton Bay. It would pay the costs of his long run southwards and leave some useful change over.

Nick's own dilemma was not as easily resolved. He put Jules Levoisin out of his mind, turning away before the French tug had rounded the headland and he studied the ice-choked bay before him with narrow eyes and a growing feeling of concern. Jules had been right—this was going to be a screaming bastard of a job.

The high seas that had thrown *Golden Adventurer* ashore had been made even higher by the equinoctial spring tides. Both had now abated and she was fast.

The liner's hull had swung also, so she was not aligned neatly at right angles to the beach. *Warlock* would not be able to throw a straight pull on to her. She would have to drag her sideways. Nick could see that now as he closed.

Still closer, he could see how the heavy steel hull, half filled with water, had burrowed itself into the yielding shingle. She would stick like toffee to a baby's blanket.

Then he looked at the ice, it was not only brash and pancake ice, but there were big chunks, bergie bits, from rotten and weathered icebergs, which the wind had driven into the bay, like a sheepdog with its flock.

The plunging temperatures had welded this mass of ice into a whole; like a monstrous octopus, it was wrapping thick glistening tentacles around *Adventurer*'s stern. The ice had not yet had sufficient time to become impenetrable, and *Warlock*'s bows were ice-strengthened for just such an emergency—yet Nick knew enough not to underestimate the hardness of ice. "White ice is soft ice" was the old adage, and yet here there were big lumps and hummocks of green and striated glacial ice in the mass, like fat plums in a pudding, any one of which could punch a hole through *Warlock*'s hull.

Nick grimaced at the thought of having to send Jules Levoisin a mayday.

He spoke to the helmsman quietly. "Starboard five—midships," lining *Warlock* up for a fracture-line in the ice-pack. It was vital to come in at a right angle, to take the ice fully on the stem; a glancing blow could throw the bows off line and bring the vulnerable hull in contact with razor ice.

"Stand by, engine room," he alerted them, and *Warlock* bore down on the ice at a full ten knots and Nick judged the moment of impact finely. Half a ship's length clear, he gave a crisp order.

"Both half back."

Warlock checked, going up on to the ice as she decelerated, but still with a horrid rasping roar that echoed through the ship. Her bows rose, riding up over the ice. It gave with a rending crackle, huge slabs of ice upending and tumbling together.

"Both full back."

The huge twin propellers changed their pitch smoothly into reverse thrust, and the wash boiled into the broken ice, sweeping it clear, as *Warlock* drew back into open water and Nick steadied her and lined her up again.

"Both ahead full."

Warlock charged forward, checking at the last moment, and again thick slabs of white ice broke away, and grated along the ship's side. Nick swung her stern first starboard then port, deftly using the twin screws to wash the broken ice free, then he pulled *Warlock* out and lined up again.

Butting and smashing and pivoting, *Warlock* worked her way deeper into the bay, opening a spreading web of cracks across the white sheet of ice.

David Allen was breathless, as he burst on to the bridge.

"All gear checked and ready, sir."

"Take her," said Nick. "She's broken it up now—just keep it stirred up." He wanted to add a warning that the big variable-pitch propellers were *Warlock*'s most vulnerable parts, but he had a high enough opinion now of his Mate's ability, so he went on instead, "I'm going down now to kit up."

Vin Baker was in the aft salvage hold ahead of him, he had already half finished the tray of rich food and Angel hovered over him, but, as Nick came down the steel ladder, he lifted the cover off another steaming tray.

"It's good," said Nick, although he could hardly force himself to swallow. The nerves in his stomach were bunched up too tightly. Yet food was one of the best defences against the cold.

"Samantha wants to talk to you, Skip."

"Who the hell is Samantha?"

"The girl—she wants to thank you."

"Use your head, Angel, can't you see I have other things on my mind?"

Nick was already pulling on the rubber immersion suit over a full-length woollen undersuit. He needed the assistance of a seaman to enter the opening in the chest of the suit.

He had already forgotten about the girl as they closed the chest opening of the suit with a double ring seal, and then over the watertight bootees and mittens went another full suit of polyurethane. Nick and Vin Baker looked like a pair of fat Michelin men, as their dressers helped them into the full helmets, with wraparound visors, built-in radio microphones and breathing valves.

"Okay, Chief?" Nick asked, and Vin Baker's voice squawked too loudly into his headphones.

"Clear to roll."

Nick adjusted the volume, and then shrugged into the oxygen re-breathing set. They were not going deeper than thirty feet, so Nick had decided to use oxygen rather than the bulky steel compressed-air cylinders.

"Let's go," he said, and waddled to the ladder.

The Zodiac sixteen-foot inflatable dinghy swung overboard with the four of them in it, two divers and two picked seamen to handle the boat. Vin pushed one of them aside and primed the outboard himself.

"Come on, beauty," he told it sternly, and the big Johnson Seahorse fired at the first kick. Gingerly, they began to feel their way through an open lead in the ice, with the two seamen poling away small sharp pieces that would have ripped the fabric of the Zodiac.

In Nick's radio headset, David Allen's voice spoke suddenly.

"Captain, this is the First Officer. Barometric pressure is 1021—it looks like it's going through the roof."

The pressure was bouncing, as Nick had predicted. What goes up, must come down—and the higher she goes, the lower she falls.

Jules Levoisin had warned him it was going to be a screamer.

"Did you read the last met from Gough Island?"

"They have 1005 falling, and the wind at 320° and thirty-five knots."

"Lovely," said Nick. "We've got a big blow coming." And through the visor of his helmet he looked up at the pale and beautiful sun. It was not bright enough to pain the eye, and now it wore a fine golden halo like the head of a saint in a medieval painting.

"Skipper, this is as close as we can get," Vin Baker told him, and slipped the motor into neutral. The Zodiac coasted gently into a small open pool in the ice pack, fifty yards from *Golden Adventurer*'s stern.

A solid sheet of compacted ice separated them, and Nick studied it carefully. He had not taken the chance of working *Warlock* in closer until he could get a look at the bottom here. He wanted to know what depth of water he had to manoeuvre in, and if there were hidden snags, jagged rock to rip through the *Warlock*'s hull, or flat shingle on which he could risk a bump.

He wanted to know the slope of the bottom, and if there was good holding for his ground-tackle, but most of all, he wanted to inspect the underwater damage to *Golden Adventurer*'s hull.

"Okay, Chief?" he asked, and Vin Baker grinned at him through the visor.

"Hey, I just remembered—my mommy told me not to get my feet wet. I'm going home."

Nick knew just how he felt. There was thick sheet ice between them and *Adventurer*, they had to go down and swim below it. God alone knew what currents were running under the ice, and what visibility was like down there. A man in trouble could not surface immediately, but must find his way back to open water. Nick felt a claustrophobic tightening of his belly muscles, and he worked swiftly, checking out his gear, cracking the valve on his oxygen tank to inflate the breathing bag, checking the compass and Rolex Oyster on his wrist and clipping his buddy line on to the Zodiac, a line to return along, like Theseus in the labyrinth of the Minotaur.

"Let's go," he said, and flipped backwards into the water. The cold struck through the multiple layers of rubber and cloth and polyurethane almost instantly, and Nick waited only for the Chief Engineer to break through the surface beside him in a cloud of swirling silver bubbles.

"God," Vin Baker's voice was distorted by the earphones, "it's cold enough to crack the gooseberries off a plaster saint."

Paying out the line behind him, Nick sank down into the hazy green depths, looking for bottom. It came up dimly, heavy shingle and pebble, and he checked his depth gauge—almost six fathoms—and he moved in towards the beach.

The light from the surface was filtered through thick ice, green and ghostly in the icy depths, and Nick felt unreasonable panic stirring deep in him. He tried to thrust it aside and concentrate on the job, but it flickered there, ready to burst into flame.

There was a current working under the ice, churning the sediment so that the visibility was further reduced, and they had to fin hard to make headway across the bottom, always with the hostile ceiling of sombre green ice above them, cutting them off from the real world.

Suddenly the *Golden Adventurer*'s hull loomed ahead of them, the twin propellers glinting like gigantic bronze wings in the gloom.

They moved in within arm's length of the steel hull and swam slowly along it. It was like flying along the outer wall of a tall apartment block, a sheer cliff of riveted steel plate—but the hull was moving.

The *Golden Adventurer* was hogging on the bottom, the stern dipping and swaying to the pulse of the sea, the heaving groundswell that came in under the ice; her stern bumped heavily on the pebbly bottom, like a great hammer beating time to the ocean.

Nick knew that she was settling herself in. Every hour now was making his task more difficult and he drove harder with his swim fins, pulling slightly ahead of Vin Baker. He knew exactly where to look for the damage. Reilly had reported it in minute detail to Christy Marine, but he came across it without warning.

It looked as though a monstrous axe had been swung horizontally at the hull, a clean slash, the shape of an elongated teardrop. The metal around it had been depressed, and the paint smeared away so that the steel gleamed as though it had been scoured and polished.

At its widest, the lips of the fifteen-foot rent gaped open by three feet or a little more, and it breathed like a living mouth—for the force of the groundswell pushing into the gap built up pressure within the hull, then as the swell subsided the trapped water was forcibly expelled, sucking in and out with tremendous pressure.

"It's a clean hole," Vin Baker's voice squawked harshly. "But it's too long to pump with cement."

He was right, of course, Nick had seen that at once. Liquid cement would not plug that wicked gash, and anyway, there wasn't time to use cement, not with weather coming. An idea began forming in his mind.

"I'm going to penetrate." Nick made the decision aloud, and beside him the Chief was silent for long incredulous seconds, then he covered the edge of fear in his voice with,

"Listen, cobber, every time I've ever been into an orifice shaped like that, it's always meant big trouble. Reminds me of my first wife—"

"Cover for me," Nick interrupted him. "If I'm not out in five minutes—"

"I'm coming with you," said the Chief. "I've got to take a look at her engine room. This is as good a time as any."

Nick did not argue with him.

"I'll go first," he said and tapped the Chief's shoulder. "Do what I do."

Nick hung four feet from the gash, finning to hold himself there against the current.

He watched the swirl of water rushing into the opening, and then gushing out again in a rash of silver bubbles. Then, as she began to breathe again, he darted forward.

The current caught him and he was hurled at the gap, with only time to duck his helmeted head and cover the fragile oxygen bag on his chest with both arms.

Raw steel snagged at his leg; there was no pain, but almost instantly he felt the leak of sea water into his suit. The cold stung like a razor cut, but he was through into the total darkness of the cavernous hull. He was flung into a tangle of steel piping, and he anchored himself with one arm and groped for the underwater lantern on his belt.

"You okay?" The Chief's voice boomed in his headphones.

"Fine."

Vin Baker's lantern glowed eerily in the dark waters ahead of him.

"Work fast," instructed Nick. "I've got a tear in my suit."

Each of them knew exactly what to do and where to go. Vin Baker swam first to the watertight bulkheads and checked all the seals. He was working in darkness in a totally unfamiliar engine room, but he went unerringly to the pump system, and checked the valve settings; then he rose to the surface, feeling his way up the massive blocks of the main engines.

Nick was there ahead of him. The engine room was flooded almost to the deck above and the surface was a thick stinking scum of oil and diesel, in which floated a mass of loose articles, most of them undefinable, but in the beam of his lantern Nick recognized a gumboot and a grease pot floating beside his head. The whole thick stinking soup rose and fell and agitated with the push of the current through the rent.

The lenses of their lanterns were smeared with the oily filth and threw grotesque shadows into the cavernous depths, but Nick could just make out the deck above him, and the dark opening of the vertical ventilation shaft. He wiped the filth from his visor and saw what he wanted to see and the cold was spreading up his leg. He asked brusquely, "Okay, Chief?"

"Let's get the hell out of here."

There were sickening moments of panic when Nick thought they had lost the line to the opening. It had sagged and wrapped around a steam pipe. Nick freed it and then sank down to the glimmer of light through the gash.

He judged his moment carefully, the return was more dangerous than the entry, for the raw bright metal had been driven in by the ice, like the petals of a sunflower—or the fangs in a shark's maw. He used the suck of water and shot through without a touch, turning and finning to wait for Vin Baker.

The Australian came through in the next rush of water, but Nick saw him flicked sideways by the current, and he struck the jagged opening a touching blow. There was instantly a roaring rush of escaping oxygen from his breathing bag, as the steel split it wide, and for a moment the Chief was obscured in the silver cloud of gas that was his life's breath.

"Oh God, I'm snagged," he shouted, clutching helplessly at his empty bag, plummeting sharply into the green depths at the drastic change in his buoyancy. The heavily leaded belt around his waist had been weighted to counter the flotation of the oxygen bag, and he went down like a gannet diving on a shoal of sardine.

Nick saw instantly what was about to happen. The current had him— it was dragging him down under the hull, sucking him under that hammering steel bottom, where he would be crushed against the stony beach by twenty-two thousand tons of pounding steel.

Nick went head down, finning desperately to catch the swirling body

which tumbled like a leaf in high wind. He had a fleeting glimpse of
Baker's face, contorted with terror and lack of breath, the glass visor of
his helmet already swamping with icy water as the pressure spurted
through the non-return valve. The Chief's headset microphone squealed
once and then went dead as the water shorted it out.

"Drop your belt," yelled Nick, but Baker did not respond; he had not
heard, his headset had gone and instead he fought ineffectually in the
swirling current, drawn inexorably down to brutal death.

Nick got a hand to him and threw back with all his strength on his fins
to check their downward plunge, but still they went down and Nick's
right hand was clumsy with cold and the double thickness of his mittens
as he groped for the quick-release on the Chief's belt.

He hit the rounded bottom of the great hull with his shoulder, and felt
them dragged under to where clouds of sediment blew like smoke from
the working of the keel. Locked together like a couple of waltzing
dancers, they swung around and he saw the keel, like the blade of a guil-
lotine, rise up high above them. He could not reach the Chief's release
toggle.

There were only microseconds in which to go for his one other
chance. He hit his own release and the thick belt with thirty-five pounds
of lead fell away from Nick's waist; with it went the buddy line that
would guide them back to the waiting Zodiac, for it had been clipped
into the back of the belt.

The abrupt loss of weight checked their downward plunge, and fighting with all the strength of his legs, Nick was just able to hold them clear
of the great keel as it came swinging downwards.

Within ten feet of them, steel struck stone with a force that rang in
Nick's eardrum like a bronze gong but he had an armlock on the Chief's
struggling body, and now at last his right hand found the release toggle
on the other man's belt.

He hit it, and another thirty-five pounds of lead dropped away. They
began to rise, up along the hogging steel hull, faster and faster as the
oxygen in Nick's bag expanded with the release of pressure. Now their
plight was every bit as desperate, for they were racing upwards to a roof
of solid ice with enough speed to break bone or crack a skull.

Nick emptied his lungs, exhaling on a single continuous breath, and
at the same time opened the valve to vent his bag, blowing away the precious life-giving gas in an attempt to check their rise—yet still they went

into the ice with a force that would have stunned them both, had Nick not twisted over and caught it on his shoulder and outflung arm. They were pinned there under the ice by the cork-like buoyancy of their rubber suits and the remaining gas in Nick's bag.

With mild and detached surprise Nick saw that the lower side of the ice pack was not a smooth sheet, but was worked into ridges and pinnacles, into weird flowing shapes like some abstract sculpture in pale green glass. It was only a fleeting moment that he looked at it, for beside him Baker was drowning.

His helmet was flooded with icy water and his face was empurpled and his mouth contorted into a horrible rictus; already his movements were becoming spasmodic and uncoordinated, as he struggled for breath.

Nick realized that haste would kill them both now. He had to work fast but deliberately—and he held Baker to him as he cracked the valve on his steel oxygen bottle, reinflating his chest bag.

With his right hand, he began to unscrew the breathing pipe connection into the side of Baker's helmet. It was slow, too slow. He needed touch for this delicate work.

He thought, "This could cost me my right hand," and he stripped off the thick mitten in a single angry gesture. Now he could feel—for the few seconds until the cold paralysed his fingers. The connection came free and while he worked, Nick was pumping his lungs like a bellows, hyper-ventilating, washing his blood with pure oxygen until he felt light-headed and dizzy.

One last sweet breath, and then he unscrewed his own hose connection; icy water flooded through the valve but he held his head at an angle to trap oxygen in the top of his helmet, keeping his nose and eyes clear, and he rescrewed his own hose into Baker's helmet with fingers that no longer had feeling.

He held the Chief's body close to his chest, embracing like lovers, and he cracked the last of the oxygen from his bottle. There was just sufficient pressure of gas left to expunge the water from Baker's helmet. It blew out with an explosive hiss through the valve, and Nick watched carefully with his only inches from Baker's.

The Chief was choking and coughing, gulping and gasping at the rush of cold oxygen, his eyes watery and unseeing, his spectacles blown awry and the lenses obscured by sea water, but then Nick felt his chest begin to swell and subside. Baker was breathing again, "which is more than I am doing," Nick thought grimly—and then suddenly he realized for the first time that he had lost the guide line with his weight belt.

He did not know in which direction was the shore, nor which way to swim to reach the Zodiac. He was utterly disorientated, and desperately he peered through his half-flooded visor for sight of the *Golden Adventurer's* hull to align himself. She was not there, gone in the misty green gloom—and he felt the first heave of his lungs as they demanded air. And as he denied his body the driving need to breathe, he felt the fear that had flickered deep within him flare up into true terror, swiftly becoming cold driving panic.

A suicidal urge to tear at the green ice roof of this watery tomb almost overwhelmed him. He wanted to try and rip his way through it with bare freezing hands to reach the precious air.

Then, just before panic completely obliterated his reason, he remembered the compass on his wrist. Even then his brain was sluggish, beginning to starve for oxygen, and it took precious seconds working out the reciprocal of his original bearing.

As he leaned forward to read the compass, more sea water spurted into his helmet, spiking needles of icy cold agony into the sinuses of his cheeks and forehead, making the teeth ache in his jaws, so he gasped involuntarily and immediately choked.

Still holding Baker to him, linked by the thick black umbilical cord of his oxygen hose, Nick began to swim out on the reciprocal compass heading. Immediately his lungs began to pump, convulsing in involuntary spasms, like those of childbirth, craving air, and he swam on.

With his head thrown back slightly he saw that the sheet of ice moved slowly above him; at times, when the current held them, it moved not at all, and it required all his self-control to keep finning doggedly, then the current relaxed its grip and they moved forward again, but achingly slowly.

He had time then to realize how exquisitely beautiful was the ice roof; translucent, wondrously carved and sculptured—and suddenly he remembered standing hand in hand with Chantelle beneath the arched roof of Chartres Cathedral, staring up in awe. The pain in his chest subsided, the need to breathe passed, but he did not recognize that as the sign of mortal danger, nor the images that formed before his eyes as the fantasy of a brain deprived of oxygen and slowly dying.

Chantelle's face was before him then, glowing hair soft and thick and glossy as a butterfly's wing, huge dark eyes and that wide mouth so full of the promise of delight and warmth and love.

"I loved you," he thought. "I really loved you."

And again the image changed. He saw again the incredible slippery explosive liquid burst with which his son was born, heard the first querulous cry as he dangled pink and wet and hairless from the rubber-gloved hand, and felt again the soul-consuming wonder and joy.

"A drowning man—" Nick recognized at last what was happening to him. He knew then he was dying, but the panic had passed, as the cold had passed also, and the terror. He swam on, dreamlike, into the green mists. Then he realized that his own legs were no longer moving; he lay relaxed not breathing, not feeling, and it was Baker's body that was thrusting and working against him.

Nick peered into the glass visor still only inches from his eyes, and he saw that Baker's face was set and determined. He was gulping the pure sweet oxygen and gaining strength with each breath, driving on strongly.

"You beauty," whispered Nick dreamily, and felt the water shoot into his throat, but there was no pain.

Another image formed before him, an Arrowhead-class yacht with spinnaker set, running free across a bright Mediterranean sea, and his son at the tiller, the dense tumble of curls that covered his small neat head fluttering in the wind, and the same velvety dark eyes as his mother's in the suntanned oval of his face as he laughed.

"Don't let her run by the lee, Peter," Nicholas wanted to shout to his son, but the image faded into blackness. He thought for a moment that he had passed into unconsciousness, but then he realized suddenly that it was the black rubber bottom of the Zodiac only inches from his eyes, and that the rough hands that dragged him upwards, lifting him and tearing loose the fastening of his helmet, were not part of the fantasy.

Propped against the pillowed gunwale of the Zodiac, held by the two boatmen from falling backwards, the first breaths of sub-zero air were too rich for his starved lungs, and Nick coughed and vomited weakly down the front of his suit.

· · ·

Nick came out of the shower cabinet. The cabin was thick with steam, and his body glowed dull angry red from the almost boiling water. He wrapped the towel around his waist as he stepped through into his night cabin.

Baker slouched in the armchair at the foot of his bunk. He wore fresh overalls, his hair stood up in little damp spikes around the shaven spot where Angel's catgut stitches still held the scabbed wound closed. One of the side frames of his spectacles had snapped during those desperate minutes below *Golden Adventurer*'s stern, and Baker had repaired it with black insulating tape.

He held two glasses in his left hand, and a big flat brown bottle of liquor in the other. He poured two heavy slugs into the glasses as Nick paused in the bathroom door, and the sweet, rich aroma smelled like the sugar-cane fields of northern Queensland.

Baker passed a glass to Nick, and then showed him the bottle's yellow label.

"Bundaberg rum," he announced, "the dinky die stuff, sport."

Nick recognized both the offer of liquor and the salutation as probably the highest accolade the Chief would ever give another human being.

Nick sniffed the dark honey-brown liquor and then took it in a single toss, swirled it once around his mouth, swallowed, shuddered like a spaniel shaking off water droplets, exhaled harshly and said: "It's still the finest rum in the world." Dutifully he said what was expected of him, and held out his glass.

"The Mate asked me to give you a message," said Baker as he poured another shot for each of them. "Glass hit 1035 and now it's diving like a dingo into its hole—back to 1020 already. It's going to blow—is it ever going to blow!"

They regarded each other over the rims of the glasses.

"We've wasted almost two hours, Beauty," Nick told him, and Baker blinked at the unlikely name, then grinned crookedly as he accepted it.

"How are you going to plug that hull?"

"I've got ten men at work already. We are going to fother a sail into a collision mat."

Baker blinked again, then shook his head in disbelief. "That's Hornblower stuff—"

"The *Witch of Endor*," Nick agreed. "So you can read?"

"You haven't got pressure to drive it home," Baker objected. "The trapped air from the engine room will blow it out."

"I'm going to run a wire down the ventilation shaft of the engine room and out through the gash. We'll fix the collision mat outside the hull and winch it home with the wire."

Baker stared at him for five seconds while he examined the proposition. A sail was fothered by threading the thick canvas with thousands of strands of unravelled oakum until it resembled a huge shaggy doormat. When this was placed over an aperture below a ship's waterline, the pressure of water forced it into the hole, and the water swelled the mass of fibre until it formed an almost watertight plug.

However, in *Golden Adventurer*'s case the damage was extensive and as the hull was already flooded, there was no pressure differential to drive home the plug. Nick proposed to beat that by using an internal wire to haul the plug into the gash.

"It might work." Beauty Baker was noncommittal.

Nick took the second rum at a gulp, dropped the towel and reached for his working gear laid out on the bunk.

"Let's get power on her before the blow hits us," he suggested mildly, and Baker lumbered to his feet and stuffed the Bundaberg bottle into his back pocket.

"Listen, sport," he said. "All that guff about you being a Pommy, don't take it too seriously."

"I won't," said Nick. "Actually, I was born and educated in Blighty, but my father's an American. So that makes me one also."

"Christ." Beauty hitched disgustedly at his waist with both elbows. "If there's anything worse than a bloody Pom, it's a goddamned Yank."

N ow that Nick was certain that the bottom of the bay was clean and free of underwater snags, he handled *Warlock* boldly but with a delicately skilful touch which David Allen watched with awe.

Like a fighting cock, the *Warlock* attacked the thicker ice line along the shore, smashing free huge lumps and slabs, then washing them clear with the propellers, giving herself space to work about *Golden Adventurer*'s stern.

The ominous calm of both sea and air made the work easier, although the vicious little current working below *Adventurer*'s stern complicated the transfer of the big alternator.

Nick had two Yokohama fenders slung from *Warlock*'s side, and the bloated plastic balloons cushioned the contact of steel against steel as Nick laid *Warlock* alongside the stranded liner, holding her there with delicate adjustments of power and rudder and screw pitch.

Beauty Baker and his working party, swaddled in heavy Antarctic gear, were already up on the catwalk of *Warlock*'s forward gantry, seventy feet above the bridge and overlooking *Adventurer*'s sharply canted deck.

As Nick nudged *Warlock* in, they dropped the steel boarding-ladder across the gap between the two ships and Beauty led them across in single file, like a troop of monkeys across the limb of a forest tree.

"All across," the Third Officer confirmed for Nick, and then added, "Glass has dropped again, sir. Down to 1005."

"Very well," Nick drew *Warlock* gently away from the liner's stern, and held her fifty feet off. Only then did he flick his eyes up at the sky. The midnight sun had turned into a malevolent jaundiced yellow, while the sun itself was a ball of dark satanic red above the peaks of Cape Alarm, and it seemed that the snowfields and glaciers were washed with blood.

"It's beautiful." Suddenly the girl was beside him. The top of her head was on a level with his shoulder, and in the ruddy light, her thick roped hair glowed like newly minted sovereigns in red gold. Her voice was low and a little husky with shyness, and touched a chord of response in Nick, but when she lifted her face to him he saw how young she was.

"I came to thank you," she said softly. "It's the first chance I've had."

She wore baggy, borrowed men's clothing that made her look like a little girl dressing up, and her face, free of cosmetics, had that waxy plastic glow of youth, like the polished skin of a ripe apple.

Her expression was solemn and there were traces of her recent ordeal beneath her eyes and at the corners of her mouth. Nick sensed the tension and nervousness in her.

"Angel wouldn't let me come before," she said, and suddenly she smiled. The nervousness vanished and it was the direct warm unselfconscious smile of a beautiful child that has never known rejection. Nick was shocked by the strength of his sudden physical desire for her, his body moved, clenching like a fist in his groin, and he felt his heart pound furiously in the cage of his ribs.

His shock turned to anger, for she looked but fourteen or fifteen years of age; almost she seemed as young as his own son, and he was shamed by the perversity of his attraction. Since the good bright times with Chantelle, he had not experienced such direct and instant involvement with a woman. At the thought of Chantelle, his emotions collapsed in a disordered tangle, from which only his lust and his anger emerged clearly.

He cupped the anger to him, like a match in a high wind, it gave him strength again. Strength to thrust this aside, for he knew how vulnerable he still was and how dangerous a course had opened before him, to be led by this child-woman. Suddenly he was aware that he had swayed bodily towards the girl and had been staring into her face for many long seconds, that she was meeting his gaze steadily and that something was beginning to move in her eyes like cloud shadow across the sunlit surface of a green mountain lake. Something was happening which he could not afford, could not chance—and then he realized also that the two young deck officers were watching them with undisguised curiosity, and he turned his anger on her.

"Young lady," he said. "You have an absolute genius for being in the wrong place at the wrong time." And his tone was colder and more remote than even he had intended it.

Before he turned away from her, he saw the moment of her disbelief turn to chagrin, and the green eyes misted slightly. He stood stiffly staring down the foredeck where David Allen's team was opening the forward salvage hold.

Nick's anger evaporated almost at once, to be replaced by dismay. He realized clearly that he had completely alienated the girl and he wanted to turn back to her and say something gracious that might retrieve the situation, but he could think of nothing and instead lifted the hand microphone to his lips and spoke to Baker over the VHF radio.

"How's it going, Chief?"

There were ten seconds of delay, and Nick was very conscious of the girl's presence near him.

"Their emergency generator has burned out, it will need two days' work to get it running again. We'll have to take on the alternator," Beauty told him.

"We are ready to give it to you," Nick told him, and then called David Allen on the foredeck.

"Ready, David?"

"All set."

Nick began edging *Warlock* back towards the liner's towering stern, and now at last he turned back to the girl. Unaccountably, he now wanted her approbation, so his smile was ready—but she had already gone, taking with her that special aura of brightness.

Nick's voice had a jagged edge to it as he told David Allen, "Let's do this fast and right, Number One."

Warlock nuzzled *Adventurer*'s stern, the big black Yokohama fenders gentling her touch, and on her foredeck the winch whined shrilly, the lines squealing in their blocks and from the open salvage hatch the four-ton alternator swung out. It was mounted on a sledge for easy handling. The diesel tanks were charged and the big motor primed and ready to start.

It rose swiftly, dangling from the tall gantry, and a dozen men synchronized their efforts, in those critical moments when it hung out over *Warlock*'s bows. A nasty freaky little swell lifted the tug and pushed her across, for the dangling burden was already putting a slight list on her, and it would have crashed into the steel side of the liner had not Nick thrown the screws into reverse thrust and given her a burst of power to hold her off.

The instant the swell subsided, he closed down and slid the pitch to fine forward, pressing the cushioned bows lightly back against *Adventurer*'s side.

"He's good!" David Allen watched Nicholas work. "He's better than old Mac ever was." Mackintosh, *Warlock*'s previous skipper, had been careful and experienced, but Nicholas Berg handled the ship with the flair and intuitive touch that even Mac's vast experience could never have matched.

David Allen pushed the thought aside and signalled the winchman. The huge dangling machine dropped with the control of a roosting seagull on to the liner's deck. Baker's crew leapt on it immediately, releasing the winch cable and throwing out the tackle, to drag it away on its sledge.

Warlock drew off, and when Baker's crew was ready, she went in to drop another burden, this time one of the high-speed centrifugal pumps which would augment *Golden Adventurer*'s own machinery—if Baker could get that functioning. It went up out of *Warlock*'s forward hold, followed ten minutes later by its twin.

"Both pumps secured." Baker's voice had a spark of jubilation in it, but at that moment a shadow passed over the ship, as though a vulture wheeled above on widespread pinions, and as Nick glanced up he saw the men on the foredeck lift their heads also.

It was a single cloud seeming no bigger than a man's fist, a thousand or fifteen hundred feet above them, but it had momentarily obscured the lowering sun, before scuttling on furtively down the peaks of Cape Alarm.

"There is still much to do," Nick thought, and he opened the bridge door and stepped out on to the exposed wing. There was no movement of air, and the cold seemed less intense although a glance at the glass confirmed that there were thirty degrees still of frost. No wind here, but high up it was beginning.

"Number One," Nick snapped into the microphone. "What's going on down there—do you think this is your daddy's yacht?"

And David Allen's team leapt to the task of closing down the forward hatch, and then tramped back to the double salvage holds on the long stern quarter.

"I am transferring command to the stern bridge," Nick told his deck officers and hurried back through the accommodation area to the second enclosed bridge, where every control and navigational aid was duplicated, a unique feature of salvage-tug construction where so much of the work took place on the afterdeck.

This time from the aft gantries, they lifted the loaded pallets of salvage gear on to the liner's deck, another eight tons of equipment went aboard *Golden Adventurer*. Then they pulled away and David Allen battened down again. When he came on to the bridge stamping and slapping his own shoulders, red-cheeked and gasping from the cold, Nick told him immediately.

"Take command, David, I'm going on board." Nick could not bring himself to wait out the uncertain period while Beauty Baker put power and pumps into action.

Anything mechanical was Baker's responsibility, as seamanship was strictly Nick's, but it could take many hours yet, and Nick could not remain idle that long.

From high on the forward gantry, Nick looked out across that satiny ominous sea. It was a little after midnight now and the sun was halfway down behind the mountains, a two-dimensional disc of metal heated to furious crimson. The sea was sombre purple and the icebergs were sparks of brighter cherry red. From this height he could see that the surface of the sea was crenellated, a small regular swell spreading across it like ripples across a pond, from some disturbance far out beyond the horizon.

Nick could feel the fresh movement of *Warlock*'s hull as she rode this swell, and suddenly a puff of wind hit Nick in the face like the flit of a bat's wing, and the metallic sheen of the sea was scoured by a cat's-paw of wind that scratched at the surface as it passed.

He pulled the drawstring of the hood of his anorak up more tightly under his chin and stepped out on to the open boarding-ladder, like a steeplejack, walking upright and balancing lightly seventy feet above *Warlock*'s slowly rolling foredeck.

He jumped down on to *Golden Adventurer*'s steeply canted, ice-glazed deck and saluted *Warlock*'s bridge far below in a gesture of dismissal.

I tried to warn you, dearie," said Angel gently, as she entered the steamy galley, for with a single glance he was aware of Samantha's crestfallen air. "He tore you up, didn't he?"

"What are you talking about?" She lifted her chin, and the smile was too bright and too quick. "What do you want me to do?"

"You can separate that bowl of eggs," Angel told her, and stooped again over twenty pounds of red beef, with his sleeves rolled to the elbows about his thick and hairy arms, clutching a butcher's knife in a fist like that of Rocky Marciano.

They worked in silence for five minutes, before Samantha spoke again.

"I only tried to thank him—" And again there was a grey mist in her eyes.

"He's a lower-deck pig," Angel agreed.

"He is not," Samantha came in hotly. "He's not a pig."

"Well, then, he's a selfish, heartless bastard—with jumped-up ideas."

"How *can* you say that!" Samantha's eyes flashed now. "He is not selfish—he went into the water to get me—"

Then she saw the smile on Angel's lips and the mocking quizzical expression in his eyes, and she stopped in confusion and concentrated on cracking the eggshells and slopping the contents into the mixing basin.

"He's old enough to be your father," Angel needled her, and now she was really angry; a ruddy flush under the smooth gloss of her skin made the freckles shine like gold dust.

"You talk the most awful crap, Angel."

"God, dearie, where did you learn that language?"

"Well, you're making me mad." She broke an egg with such force that it exploded down the front of her pants. "Oh, shit!" she said, and stared at him defiantly. Angel tossed her a dishcloth, she wiped herself violently and they went on working again.

"How old is he?" she demanded at last. "A hundred and fifty?"

"He's thirty-eight," Angel thought for a moment, "or thirty-nine."

"Well, smart arse," she said tartly, "the ideal age is half the man's age, plus seven."

"You aren't twenty-six, dearie," Angel said gently.

"I will be in two years' time," she told him.

"You really want him badly, hey? A fever of lust and desire?"

"That's nonsense, Angel, and you know it. I just happen to owe him a rather large debt—he saved my life—but as for wanting him, ha!" She dismissed the idea with a snort of disdain and a toss of her head.

"I'm glad," Angel nodded. "He's not a very nice person, you can see by those ferrety eyes of his—"

"He has beautiful eyes—" she flared at him, and then stopped abruptly, saw the cunning in his grin, faltered and then collapsed weakly on the bench beside him, with a cracked egg in one hand.

"Oh, Angel, you are a horrible man and I hate you. How can you make fun of me now?"

He saw how close she was to tears, and became brisk and businesslike.

"First of all, you better know something about him—" and he began to tell her, giving her a waspish biography of Nicholas Berg, embellished by a vivid imagination and a wicked sense of humour, together with a quasi-feminine love of gossip, to which Samantha listened avidly, making an occasional exclamation of surprise.

"His wife ran away with another man, she could be out of her mind, don't you think?"

"Dearie, a change is like two weeks at the seaside."

Or asking a question. "He owns this ship, actually owns it? Not just Master?"

"He owns this ship, and its sister, and the company. They used to call him the Golden Prince. He's a high flyer, dearie, didn't you recognize it?"

"I didn't—"

"Of course you did. You're too much woman not to. There is no more powerful aphrodisiac than success and power, nothing like the clink of gold to get a girl's hormones revving up, is there?"

"That's unfair, Angel. I didn't know a thing about him. I didn't know he was rich and famous. I don't give a damn for money—"

"Ho! Ho!" Angel shook his curls and the diamond studs flashed in his ears. But he saw her anger flare again. "All right, dearie, I'm teasing. But what really attracts you is his strength and air of purpose. The way other men obey, and follow and fear him. The air of command, of power and with it, success."

"I didn't—"

"Oh, be honest with yourself, love. It was not the fact he saved your life, it wasn't his beautiful eyes nor the lump in his jeans—"

"You're crude, Angel."

"You're bright and beautiful, and you just can't help yourself. You're like a nubile little gazelle, all skittish and ready, and you have just spotted the herd bull. You can't help yourself, dearie, you're just a woman."

"What am I going to do, Angel?"

"We'll make a plan, love, but one thing is certain, you're not going to trail around behind him, dressed like an escapee from a junk shop, breathing adoration and hero-worship. He's doing a job. He doesn't need to trip over you every time he turns. Play hard to get."

Samantha thought about it for a moment. "Angel, I don't want to play it that hard that I never get around to being got—if you follow me."

• • •

B eauty Baker had the work in hand, well organized and going ahead as fast as even Nick, in his overwhelming impatience, could expect.

The alternator had been manhandled through the double doors into the superstructure on B deck, and it had been secured against a steel bulkhead and lashed down.

"As soon as I have power, we'll drill the deck and bolt her down," he explained to Nick.

"Have you got the lines in?"

"I'll bypass the main junction box on C deck, and I will select from the temporary box—"

"But you've identified the foredeck winch circuit, and the pumps?"

"Jesus, sport, why don't you go sail your little boat and leave me to do my work?"

On the upper deck one of Baker's gangs was already at work with the gas welding equipment. They were opening access to the ventilation shaft of the main engine room. The gas cutter hissed viciously and red sparks showered from the steel plate of the tall dummy smokestack. The stack was merely to give the *Golden Adventurer* the traditional rakish lines, and now the welder cut the last few inches of steel plating. It fell away into the deep, dark cavern, leaving a roughly square opening six feet by six feet which gave direct access into the half-flooded engine room fifty feet below.

Despite Baker's advice, Nick took command here, directing the rigging of the winch blocks and steel wire cable that would enable a cable to be taken down into the flooded engine room and out again through that long, viciously fanged gash in the ship's side. When he looked at his Rolex Oyster again, almost an hour had passed. The sun had gone and a luminous green sky filled with the marvelous pyrotechnics of the *Aurora Australis* turned the night eerie and mysterious.

"All right, bosun, that's all we can do now. Bring your team up to the bows."

As they hurried forward along the open foredeck, the wind caught them, a single shrieking gust that had them reeling and staggering and grabbing for support; then it was past and the wind settled down to nag and whine and pry at their clothing as Nick directed the work at the two huge anchor winches; but he heard the rising sea starting to push and stir the pack-ice, making it growl and whisper menacingly.

They catted the twin sea-anchors and with two men working over *Adventurer*'s side they secured collars of heavy chain to the crown of each anchor. *Warlock* would now be able to drag those anchors out, letting them bump along the bottom, but in the opposite direction to that in which they had been designed to drag, so that the pointed flukes would not be able to dig in and hold.

Then, when the anchors were out to the full reach of their own chains, *Warlock* would drop them, the flukes would dig in and hold. This was the ground-tackle which might resist the efforts of even a force twelve wind to throw *Golden Adventurer* farther ashore.

When Baker had power on the ship, the anchor winches would be used to kedge *Golden Adventurer* off the bank. Nick placed much reliance on these enormously powerful winches to assist *Warlock*'s own engines, for even as they worked, he could feel through the soles of his feet how heavily grounded the liner was.

It was a tense and heavy labour, for they were working with enormous weights of dead-weight steel chain and shackles. The securing shackle, which held the chain collar on the anchor crown, alone weighed three hundred pounds and had to be manhandled by six men using complicated tackle.

By the time they had the work finished, the wind was rising force six, and wailing in the superstructure. The men were chilled and tired, and tempers were flashing.

Nick led them back to the shelter of the main superstructure. His boots seemed to be made of lead, and his lungs pumped for the solace of cheroot smoke, and he realized irrelevantly that he had not slept now for over fifty hours—since he had fished that disturbing little girl from the water. Quickly he pushed the thought of her aside, for it distracted him from his purpose, and, as he stepped over the door-sill into the liner's cold but wind-protected main accommodation, he reached for his cheroot-case.

Then he arrested the movement and blinked with surprise as suddenly garish light blazed throughout the shipdeck lights and internal lights, so that instantly a festival air enveloped her and from the loudspeakers on the deck above Nicholas' head wafted soft music as the broadcasting equipment switched itself in. It was the voice of Donna Summer, as limpid and ringing clear as fine-leaded crystal. The sound was utterly incongruous in this place and in these circumstances.

"Power is on!"

Nick let out a whoop and ran through to B deck. Beauty Baker was standing beside his roaring alternator and hugging himself with glee.

"Howzat, sport?" he demanded. Nick punched his shoulder.

"Right on, Beauty." He wasted a few moments and a cheroot by placing one of the precious black tubes between Baker's lips and flashing his lighter. The two of them smoked for twenty seconds in close and companionable silence.

"Okay," Nick ended it. "Pumps and winches."

"The two emergency portables are ready to start, and I'm on my way to check the ship's main pumps."

"The only thing left is to get the collision mat into place."

"That is your trick," Baker told him flatly. "You're not getting me into the water again, ever. I've even given up bathing."

"Yeah, did you notice I'm standing upwind?" Nick told him. "But somebody has got to go down again to pass the wire."

"Why don't you send Angel?" Baker grinned evilly. "Excuse me, cobber—I've got work to do." He inspected the cheroot. "After we've pulled this dog off the ground, I hope you will be able to afford decent gaspers." And he was gone into the depths of the liner, leaving Nick with the one task he had been avoiding even thinking about. Somebody had to go down into that engine room. He could call for volunteers, of course, but then it was another of his own rules never to ask another man to do what you are afraid to do yourself.

"I can leave David to lay out the ground-tackle, but I can't let anybody else put the collision mat in." He faced it now. He would have to go down again, into the cold and darkness and mortal danger of the flooded engine room.

The ground-tackle that David Allen had laid was holding *Golden Adventurer* handsomely, even in the aggravated swell which was by now pouring into the open mouth of the bay, driven on by the rising wind that was inciting it to wilder abandon.

David had justified Nick's confidence in the seamanlike manner in which he had taken the *Golden Adventurer*'s twin anchors out and dropped them a cable's length offshore, at a finely judged angle to give the best purchase and hold.

Beauty Baker had installed and test-run the two big centrifugals and he had even resuscitated two of the liner's own forward pump assemblies which had been protected by the watertight bulkhead from the sea break-in. He was ready now to throw the switch on this considerable arsenal of pumps, and he had calculated that if Nick could close that gaping rent in the hull, he would be able to pump the liner's hull dry and clean in just under four hours.

Nick was in full immersion kit again, but this time he had opted for a single-bottle Drager diving-set; he was off oxygen sets for life, he decided wryly.

Before going down, he paused on the open deck with the diving helmet under his arm. The wind must be rising seven now, he decided, for it was kicking off the tops of the waves in bursts of spray and a low scudding sky of dirty grey cloud had blotted out the rising sun and the peaks of Cape Alarm. It was a cold dark dawn, with the promise of a wilder day to follow.

Nick took one glance across at *Warlock*. David Allen was holding her nicely in position, and his own team was ready, grouped around that ugly black, freshly burned opening in *Adventurer*'s stack. He lifted the helmet on to his head, and while his helpers closed the fastenings and screwed down the hose connections, he checked the radio.

"*Warlock*, do you read me?"

Allen's voice came back immediately, acknowledging and confirming his readiness, then he went on, "The glass just went through the floor, Skipper, she's 996 and going down. Wind's force six rising seven and backing. It looks like we are fair in the dangerous quadrant of whatever is coming."

"Thank you, David," Nick replied. "You warm my heart."

He stepped forward, and they helped him into the canvas bosun's chair. Nick checked the tackle and rigging, that "once-more-for-luck" check, and then he nodded.

The interior of the engine room was no longer dark, for Baker had rigged floodlights high above in the ventilation shaft, but the water was black with engine oil, and as Nick was lowered slowly down, with legs dangling from the bosun's chair, it surged furiously back and across like some panic-stricken monster trying to break out of its steel cage. That wind-driven swell was crashing into *Golden Adventurer*'s side and boiling in through the opening, setting up its own wave action, forming its own currents and eddies which broke and leaped angrily against the steel bulkheads.

"Slower," Nick spoke into the microphone. "Stop!"

His downward progress was halted ten feet above the starboard main engine block, but the confined surge of water broke over the engine as though it were a coral reef, covering it entirely at one instant, and then sucking back and exposing it again at the next.

The rush of water could throw a man against that machinery with force enough to break every bone in his body, and Nick hung above it and studied the purchases for his blocks.

"Send down the main block," he ordered, and the huge steel block came down out of the shadows and dangled in the floodlights.

"Stop." Nick began directing the block into position. "Down two feet. Stop!"

Now waist-deep in the oily, churning water, he struggled to drive the shackle pin and secure the block to one of the main frames of the hull. Every few minutes a stronger surge would hurl the water over his head, forcing him to cling helplessly, until it relinquished its grip, and his visor cleared sufficiently to allow him to continue his task.

He had to pull out and rest after forty minutes of it. He sat as close as he could to the heat-exchangers of the running diesel engine of the alternator, taking warmth from them and drinking Angel's strong sweet Thermos coffee. He felt like a fighter between rounds, his body aching, every muscle strained and chilled by the efforts of fighting that filthy churned emulsion of sea water and oil, his flanks and ribs bruised from harsh contact with the submerged machinery. But after twenty minutes, he stood up again.

"Let's go," he said and resettled the helmet. The hiatus had given him a chance to replan the operation, thinking his way around the problems he had found down there; now the work seemed to fall more readily into place, though he had lost all sense of time alone in the infernal resounding cavern of steel and he was not sure of the hour, or the phase of the day, when at last he was ready to carry the messenger out through the gap.

"Send it down," he ordered into his headset, and the reel of light line came down, swinging and circling under the glaring floodlights to the ship's motion and throwing grotesque shadows into the far corners of the engine room.

The line was of finely plaited Dacron, with enormous strength and elasticity in relation to its thinness and lightness. One end was secured on the deck high above, and Nick threaded it into the sheave blocks carefully, so that it was free to run.

Then he clamped the reel of line on to his belt, riding it on his hip where it could be protected from snagging when he made the passage of the gap.

He realized then how close to final exhaustion he was, and he considered breaking off the work to rest again, but the heightened action of the sea into the hull warned him against further delay. An hour from now the task might be impossible, he had to go, and he reached for the reserve of strength and purpose deep inside himself, surprised to find that it was still there—for the icy chill of the water seemed to have penetrated his suit and entered his soul, dulling every sense and turning his very bones brittle and heavy.

It must be day outside, he realized, for light came through the gash of steel, pale light further obscured by the filthy muck of mixed oil and water contained in the hull.

He clung to one of the engine-room stringers, his head seven feet from the opening, breathing in the slow, even rhythm of the experienced scuba diver, feeling the ebb and flow through the hull, and trying to find some pattern in the action of the water. But it seemed entirely random, a hissing, bubbling ingestion followed by three or four irregular and weak inflows, then three vicious exhalations of such power that they would have windmilled a swimming man end over into those daggers of splayed steel. He had to choose and ride a middling-sized swell, strong enough to take him through smoothly, without the dangerous power and turbulence of those viciously large swells.

"I'm ready to go now, David," he said into his helmet. "Confirm that the work boat is standing by for the pick-up outside the hull."

"We are all ready." David Allen's voice was tense and sharp.

"Here we go," said Nick, this was his wave now. There was no point in waiting longer.

He checked the reel on his belt, ensuring that the line was free to run, and watched the gash suck in clean green water, filled with tiny bright bubbles, little diamond chips that flew past his head to warn him of the lethal speed and power of that flood.

The inflow slowed and stopped as the hull filled to capacity, building up great pressures of air and water, and then the flow reversed abruptly as the swell on the far side subsided, and trapped water began to rush out again.

Nick released his grip on the stringer and instantly the water caught him. There was no question of being able to swim in that mill-race, all he could hope for was to keep his arms at his sides and his legs straight together to give himself a smoother profile, and to steer with his fins.

The accelerating speed appalled him as he was flung head first at that murderous steel mouth, he could feel the nylon line streaming out against his leg, the reel on his belt racing as though a giant marlin had struck and hooked upon the other end.

The rush of his progress seemed to leave his guts behind him as though he rode a fairground rollercoaster, and then a flick of the current turned him, he felt himself beginning to roll—and he fought wildly for control just as he hit.

He hit with a numbing shock, so his vision starred in flashing colour and light. The shock was in his shoulders and left arm, and he thought it might have been severed by that razor steel.

Then he was swirling, end over end, completely disorientated so he did not know which direction was up. He did not know if he was still inside *Golden Adventurer*'s hull, and the nylon line was wrapping itself around his throat and chest, around the precious air tubes and cutting off his air supply like a stillborn infant strangled by its own umbilical cord.

Again he hit something, this time with the back of his head, and only the cushioning of his helmet saved his skull from cracking. He flung out his arms and found the rough irregular shape of ice above him.

Terror wrapped him again, and he screamed soundlessly into his mask, but suddenly he broke out into light and air, into the loose scum of slush and rotten ice mixed with bigger, harder chunks, one of which had hit him.

Above him towered the endless steel cliff of the liner's side and beyond that, the low bruised wind-sky, and as he struggled to disentangle himself from the coils of nylon, he realized two things. The first was that both his arms were still attached to his body, and still functioning, and the second was that *Warlock*'s work boat was only twenty feet away and butting itself busily through the brash of rotten broken ice towards him.

. . .

The collision mat looked like a five-ton Airedale terrier curled up to sleep in the bows of the work boat, just as shaggy and shapeless, and of the same wiry, furry brown colour.

Nick had shed his helmet and pulled an Arctic cloak and hood over his bare head and suited torso. He was balanced in the stern of the work boat as she plunged and rolled and porpoised in the big swells; chunks of ice crashed against her hull, knocking loose chips off her paintwork, but she was steel-hulled, wide and sea-kindly. The helmsman knew his job, working her with calm efficiency to Nick's handsignals, bringing her in close through the brash ice, under the tall sheer of *Golden Adventurer*'s stern.

The thin white nylon line was the only physical contact with the men on the liner's towering stack of decks, the messenger which would carry heavier tackle. However it was vulnerable to any jagged piece of pancake ice, or the fangs of that voracious underwater steel jaw.

Nick paid out the line through his own numbed hands, feeling for the slightest check or jerk which could mean a snag and a break-off.

With handsignals, he kept the work boat positioned so that the line ran cleanly into the pierced hull, around the sheave blocks he had placed with such heart-breaking labour in the engine room, from there up the tall ventilation shaft, out of the burned square opening in the stack and around the winch, beside which Beauty Baker was supervising the recovery of the messenger.

The gusts tore at Nick's head so that he had to crouch to shield the small two-way radio on his chest, and Baker's voice was tinny and thin in the buffeting boom of wind.

"Line running free."

"Right, we are running the wire now," Nick told him. The second line was as thick as a man's index finger, and it was of the finest Scandinavian steel cable. Nick checked the connection between nylon and steel cable himself, the nylon messenger was strong enough to carry the weight of steel, but the connection was the weakest point.

He nodded to the crew, and they let it go over the side; the white nylon disappeared into the cold green water and now the black steel cable ran out slowly from the revolving drum.

Nick felt the check as the connection hit the sheave block in the engine room. He felt his heart jump. If it caught now, they would lose it all; no man could penetrate that hull again, the sea was now too vicious.

They would lose the tackle, and they would lose *Golden Adventurer*; she would break up in the seas that were coming.

"Please God, let it run," Nick whispered in the boom and burst of sea wind. The drum halted, made a half turn and jammed. Somewhere down there, the cable had snagged and Nick signalled to the helmsman to take the work boat in closer, to change the angle of the line into the hull.

He could almost feel the strain along his nerves as the winch took up the pull, and he could imagine the fibres of the nylon messenger stretching and creaking.

"Let it run! Let it run!" prayed Nick, and then suddenly he saw the drum begin to revolve again, the cable feeding out smoothly, and streaming down into the sea.

Nick felt light-headed, almost dizzy with relief, as he heard Baker's voice over the VHF, strident with triumph.

"Wire secured."

"Stand by," Nick told him. "We are connecting the two-inch wire now."

Again, the whole laborious, touchy, nerve-scouring process as the massive two-inch steel cable was drawn out by its thinner, weaker forerunner—and it was a further forty vital minutes, with the wind and sea rising every moment, before Baker shouted, "Main cable secured, we are ready to haul!"

"Negative," Nick told him urgently. "Take the strain and hold." If the collision mat in the bows hooked and held on the work boat's gunwale, Baker would pull the bows under and swamp her.

Nick signalled to his crew and the five of them shambled up into the bows, bulky and clumsy in their electric-yellow oilskins and work boots. With handsignals, Nick positioned them around the shaggy head-high pile of the collision mat before he signalled to the helmsman to throw the gear in reverse and pull back from *Golden Adventurer*'s side.

The mass of unravelled oakum quivered and shook as the two-inch cable came up taut and they struggled to heave the whole untidy mass overboard.

There was nearly five tons of it and the weight would have been impossible to handle were it not for the reverse pull of the work boat against the cable. Slowly, they heaved the mat forward and outward, and the work boat took on a dangerous list under the transfer of weight. She was down at the bows and canting at an angle of twenty degrees, the diesel motor screaming angrily and her single propeller threshing frantically, trying to pull her out from under her cumbersome burden.

The mat slid forward another foot, and snagged on the gunwale, sea water slopped inboard, ankle-deep around their rubber boots as they strained and heaved at the reluctant mass of coarse fibre.

Some instinct of danger made Nick look up and out to sea. *Warlock* was lying a quarter of a mile farther out in the bay, at the edge of the ice, and beyond her, Nick saw the rearing shape of a big wave alter the line of the horizon. It was merely a forerunner of the truly big waves that the storm was running before her, like hounds before the hunter, but it was big enough to make *Warlock* throw up her stern sharply, and even then the sea creamed over the tug's bows and streamed from her scuppers.

It would hit the exposed and hampered work boat in twenty-five seconds, it would hit her broadside while her bows were held down and anchored by mat and cable. When she swamped, the five men who made up her crew would die within minutes, pulled down by their bulky clothing, frozen by the icy green water.

"Beauty," Nick's voice was a scream in the microphone, "heave all—pull, damn you, pull."

Almost instantly the cable began to run, drawn in by the powerful winch on *Golden Adventurer*'s deck; the strain pulled the work boat down sharply and water cascaded over her gunwale.

Nick seized one of the oaken oars and thrust it under the mat at the point where it was snagged, and using it as a lever he threw all his weight upon it.

"Lend a hand," he yelled at the man beside him, and he strained until he felt his vision darkening and the fibres of his back muscles creaking and popping.

The work boat was swamping, they were almost knee-deep now and the wave raced down on them. It came with a great silent rush of irresistible power, lifting the mass of broken ice and tossing it carelessly aside without a check.

Suddenly, the snag cleared and the whole lumpy massive weight of oakum slid overboard. The work boat bounded away, relieved of her intolerable burden, and Nick windmilled frantically with both arms to get the helmsman to bring her bows round to the wave.

They went up the wave with a gut-swooping rush that threw them down on to the floorboards of the half-flooded work boat, and then crashed over the crest.

Behind them the wave slogged into *Golden Adventurer*'s stern, and shot up it with an explosion of white and furious water that turned to white driven spray in the wind.

The helmsman already had the work boat pushing heavily through the pack-ice, back towards the waiting *Warlock*.

"Stop," Nick signalled him. "Back up."

Already he was struggling out of his hood and oilskins, as he staggered back to the stern.

He shouted in the helmsman's face, "I'm going down to check," and he saw the disbelieving, almost pleading, expression on the man's face. He wanted to get out of there now, back to the safety of *Warlock*, but relentlessly Nick resettled the diving helmet and connected his air hose.

The collision mat was floating hard against *Golden Adventurer*'s side, buoyant with trapped air among the mass of wiry fibre.

Nick positioned himself beneath it, twenty feet from the maelstrom created by the gashed steel.

It took him only a few seconds to ensure that the cable was free, and he blessed Beauty Baker silently for stopping the winch immediately it had pulled the mat free of the work boat. Now he could direct the final task.

"She's looking good," he told Baker. "But take her up slowly, fifty feet a minute on the winch."

"Fifty feet, it is," Baker confirmed.

And slowly the bobbing mat was drawn down below the surface.

"Good, keep it at that."

It was like pressing a field-dressing into an open bleeding wound. The outside pressure of water drove it deep into the gash, while from the inside the two-inch cable plugged it deeper into place. The wound was staunched almost instantly and Nick finned down, and swam carefully over it.

The deadly suck and blow of high pressure through the gap was killed now, and he detected only the lightest movement of water around the edges of the mat; but the oakum fibres would swell now they were submerged and, within hours, the plug would be watertight.

"It's done," said Nick into his microphone. "Hold a twenty-ton pull on the cable—and you can start your pumps and suck the bitch clean."

It was a measure of his stress and relief and fatigue that Nick called
that beautiful ship a bitch, and he regretted the word as soon as it was
spoken.

Nick craved sleep, every nerve, every muscle shrieked for
surcease, and in his bathroom mirror his eyes were inflamed, angry with salt and wind and cold; the smears of exhaustion that
underlined them were as lurid as the fresh bruises and abrasions that
covered his shoulders and thighs and ribs.

His hands shook in a mild palsy with the need for rest and his legs
could hardly carry him as he forced himself back to *Warlock*'s navigation
bridge.

"Congratulations, sir," said David Allen, and his admiration was
transparent.

"How's the glass, David?" Nick asked, trying to keep the weariness
from showing.

"994 and dropping, sir."

Nick looked across the *Golden Adventurer*. Below that dingy low sky,
she stood like a pier, unmoved by the big swells that marched on her in
endless ranks, and she shrugged aside each burst of spray, hard aground
and heavy with the water in her womb. However, that water was being
flung from her, in solid white sheets.

Baker's big centrifugals were running at full power, and from both
her port and starboard quarters the water poured. It looked as though the
floodgates had been opened on a concrete dam, so powerful was the rush
of expelled water.

The oil and diesel mixed with that discharge formed a sullen, iridescent slick around her, sullying the ice and the pebble beach on which she
lay. The wind caught the jets from the pump outlets and tore them away
in glistening plumes, like great ostrich feathers of spray.

"Chief," Nick called the ship. "What's your discharge rate?"

"We are moving nigh on five hundred thousand gallons an hour."

"Call me as soon as she alters her trim," he said, and then glanced up
at the pointer of the anemometer above the control panel. The wind force
was riding eight now, but he had to blink his stinging swollen eyes to
read the scale.

"David," he said, and he could hear the hoarseness in his voice, the flat dead tone. "It will be four hours before she will be light enough to make an attempt to haul her off, but I want you to put the main towing cable on board her and make fast, so we will be ready when she is."

"Sir."

"Use a rocket-line," said Nick, and then stood dumbly, trying to think of the other orders he must give, but his brain was blank.

"Are you all right, sir?" David asked with quick concern, and immediately Nick felt the prick of annoyance. He had never wanted sympathy in his life, and he found his voice again. But he stopped the sharp words that came so quickly to his lips.

"You know what to do, David. I won't give you any other advice." He turned like a drunkard towards his quarters. "Call me when you've done it, or if Baker reports alteration of trim—or if anything else changes, anything, anything at all, you understand."

He made it to the cabin before his knees buckled and he dropped his terry robe as he toppled backwards on to his bunk.

At 60° south latitude, there runs the only sea lane that circumnavigates the entire globe, unbroken by any land mass. This wide girdle of open water runs south of Cape Horn and Australasia and the Cape of Good Hope, and it has the fearsome reputation of breeding the wildest weather on earth. It is the meeting-ground of two vast air masses, the cold slumping Antarctic air, and the warmer, more buoyant airs of the subtropics. These are flung together by the centrifugal forces generated by the earth as it revolves on its own axis, and their movement is further complicated by the enormous torque of the Coriolis force. As they strike each other, the opposing air masses split into smaller fragments that retain their individual characteristics. They begin to revolve upon themselves, gigantic whirlpools of tortured air, and as they advance, so they gain in strength and power and velocity.

The high-pressure system which had brought that ominously calm and silken weather to Cape Alarm, had bounced the pressure right up to 1035 millibars, while the great depression which pursued it so closely and swiftly had a centre pressure as low as 985 millibars. Such a sharp contrast meant that the winds along the pressure gradient were ferocious.

The depression itself was almost fifteen hundred miles across its circumference, and it reached up to the high troposphere, thirty thousand feet above the level of the sea. The mighty winds it contained reached right off the maximum of the Beaufort scale of force twelve, gusting 120 miles an hour and more. They roared unfettered upon a terrible sea, unchecked by the bulwark of any land mass, nothing in their path, but the sudden jagged barrier of Cape Alarm.

While Nicholas Berg slept the deathlike sleep of utter exhaustion, and Beauty Baker tended his machines, driving them to their limits in an effort to pump *Golden Adventurer* free of her burden of salt water, the storm rushed down upon them.

W hen her knock was unanswered, Samantha stood uncertainly, balancing the heavy tray against the *Warlock*'s extravagant action as she rode the rising swells at the entrance to the bay.

Her uncertainty lasted not more than three seconds, for she was a lady given to swift decisions. She tried the door-latch and when it turned, she pushed it open slowly enough to warn anybody on the far side, and stepped into the Captain's day cabin.

"He ordered food," she justified her intrusion, and closed the door behind her, glancing swiftly around the empty cabin. It had been furnished in the high style of the old White Star liners. Real rosewood panelling and the couch and chairs were in rich brown calf hide, polished and buttoned, while the deck was carpeted in thick shaggy wool, the colour of tropical forest leaves.

Samantha placed the tray on the table that ran below the starboard portholes, and she called softly. There was no reply, and she stepped to the open doorway into the night cabin.

A white terry robe lay in a heap in the centre of the deck, and she thought for one disturbing moment that the body on the bed was naked, but then she saw he wore a thin pair of white silk boxer shorts.

"Captain Berg," she called again, but softly enough not to disturb him, and with a completely feminine gesture picked up the robe from the floor, folded it and dropped it over a chair, moving forward at the same time until she stood beside his bunk.

She felt a quick flare of concern when she saw the bruises which stood out so vividly on the smooth pale skin, and concern turned to dismay when she realized how he lay like a dead man, his legs trailing over the edge of the bunk and his body twisted awkwardly, one arm thrown back over his shoulder and his head lolling from side to side as *Warlock* rolled.

She reached out quickly and touched his cheek, experiencing a lift of real relief as she felt the warmth of his flesh and saw his eyelids quiver at her touch.

Gently she lifted his legs and he rolled easily on to his side, exposing the sickening abrasion that wrapped itself angrily across back and shoulder. She touched it with a light exploring fingertip and knew that it needed attention, but she sensed that rest was what he needed more.

She stood back and for long seconds gave herself over to the pleasure of looking at him. His body was fined down, he carried no fat on his belly or flanks; clearly she could see the rack of his ribs below the skin, and the muscles of his arms and legs were smooth but well defined, a body that had been cared for and honed by hard exercise. Yet there was a certain denseness to it, that thickening of shoulder and neck, and the distinctive hair patterns of the mature man.

It might not have the grace and delicacy of the boys she had known, yet it was more powerful than that of even the strongest of the young men who had until then filled her world. She thought of one of them whom she had believed she loved. They had spent two months in Tahiti together on the same field expedition. She had surfed with him, danced and drunk wine, worked and slept sixty consecutive days and nights with him; in the same period they had become engaged to marry, and had argued, and parted, with surprisingly little regret on her part—but he had had the most beautifully tanned and sculptured body she had ever known. Now, looking at the sleeping figure on the bunk, she knew that even he would not have been able to match this man in physical determination and strength.

Angel had been right. It was the power that attracted her so strongly. The powerful, rangy body with the dark coarse hair covering his chest and exploding in flak bursts in his armpits—this, together with the power of his presence.

She had never known a man like this, he filled her with a sense of awe. It was not only the legend that surrounded him, nor the formidable list of his accomplishments that Angel had recounted for her, nor yet was it only the physical strength which he had just demonstrated while the entire crew of *Warlock*, she among them, had watched and listened avidly over the VHF relay. She leaned over him again, and she saw that even in repose, his jawline was hard and uncompromising, and the little creases and lines and marks that life had chiselled into his face, around the eyes at the corners of the mouth, heightened the effect of power and determination, the face of a man who dictated his own terms to life.

She wanted him. Angel was right, oh God, how she wanted him! They said there was no love at first sight—they had to be mad.

She turned away and unfolded the eiderdown from the foot of the bunk, spreading it over him, and then once again she stooped and gently lifted the fall of thick dark hair from his forehead, smoothing it back with a maternally protective gesture.

Although he had slept on while she lifted and covered him, strangely this lightest of touches brought him to the edge of consciousness and he sighed and twisted, then whispered hoarsely, "Chantelle, is that you?"

Samantha recoiled at the bitter sharp pang of jealousy with which another woman's name stabbed her. She turned away and left him, but in the day cabin she paused again beside his desk.

There were a few small personal items thrown carelessly on the leather-bound blotter—a gold money clip holding a mixed sheath of currency notes, five pounds sterling, fifty US dollars, Deutschmarks and francs, a gold Rolex Oyster perpetual watch, a gold Dunhill lighter with a single white diamond set in it, and a billfold of the smoothest finest calf leather. They described clearly the man who owned them and, feeling like a thief, she picked up the billfold and opened it.

There were a dozen cards in their little plastic envelopes, American Express, Diners, Bank American, Carte Blanche, Hertz No. 1, Pan Am VIP and the rest. But opposite them was a colour photograph. Three people: a man, Nicholas in a cable-stitch jersey, his face bronzed, his hair windruffled; a small boy in a yachting jacket with a mop of curly hair and solemn eyes above a smiling mouth—and a woman. She was probably one of the most beautiful women Samantha had ever seen, and she closed the billfold, replaced it carefully, and quietly left the cabin.

• • •

D avid Allen called the Captain's suite for three minutes without an answer, slapping his open palm on the mahogany chart table with impatience and staring through the navigation windows at the spectacle of a world gone mad.

For almost two hours, the wind had blown steadily from the northwest at a little over thirty knots, and although the big lumpy seas still tumbled into the mouth of the bay, *Warlock* had ridden them easily, even connected, as she was, to *Golden Adventurer* by the main tow-cable.

David had put a messenger over the liner's stern, firing the nylon line from a rocket gun, and Baker's men had retrieved the line and winched across first the carrier wire and then the main cable itself.

Warlock had let the main cable be drawn out of her by *Adventurer*'s winches, slowly revolving off the great winch drums in the compartment under the tug's stern deck, out through the cable ports below the after navigation bridge where David stood controlling each inch of run and play with light touches on the controls.

A good man could work that massive cable like a fly-fisherman playing a big salmon in the turbulent water of a mountain torrent, letting it slip against the clutchplates, or run free, or recover slack, bringing it up hard and fast under a pull of five hundred tons—or, in dire emergency, he could hit the shear button, and snip through the flexible steel fibre, instantaneously relinquishing the tow, possibly saving the tug itself from being pulled under or being rushed by the vessel it was towing.

It had taken an hour of delicate work, but now the tow was in place, a double yoke made fast to *Golden Adventurer*'s main deck bollards, one on her starboard and one on her port stern quarters.

The yoke was Y-shaped, drooping over the high stern to join at the white nylon spring, three times the thickness of a man's thigh and with the elasticity to absorb sudden shock which might have snapped rigid steel cable. From the yoke connection, the single main cable looped back to the tug.

David Allen was lying back a thousand yards from the shore, holding enough strain on the tow-cable to prevent it from sagging to touch and possibly snag on the unknown bottom. He was holding his station with gentle play on the pitch and power of the twin screws, and checking his exact position against the electronic dials which gave him his speed across the ground in both directions, accurate to within a foot a minute.

It was all nicely under control, and every time he glanced up at the liner, the discharge of water still boiled from her pump outlets.

Half an hour previously, he had been unable to contain his impatience, for he knew with a seaman's deep instinct what was coming down upon them out of the dangerous quadrant of the wind. He had called Baker to ask how the work on the liner was progressing. It had been a mistake.

"You've got nothing better to do than call me out of the engine room to ask about my piles, and the FA Cup final? I'll tell you when I'm ready, believe me, sonny, I'll call you. If you are bored, go down and give Angel a kiss, but for God's sake, leave me alone."

Beauty Baker was working with two of his men in that filthy, freezing steel box deep down in the liner's stern that housed the emergency steering-gear. The rudder was right across at full port lock. Unless he could get power on the steering machinery, she would be almost unmanageable, once she was under tow, especially if she was pulled off stern first. It was vital that the big ship was responding to her helm when *Warlock* tried to haul her off.

Baker cursed and cajoled the greasy machinery, knocking loose a flap of thick white skin from his knuckles when a spanner slipped, but working on grimly without even bothering to lift the injury to his mouth to suck away the welling blood. He let it drop on to the spanner and thicken into a sticky jelly, swearing softly but viciously as he concentrated all his skills on the obdurate steel mass of the steering gear. He knew every bit as well as the First Officer what was coming down upon them.

The wind had dropped to a gentle force four, a moderate steady breeze that blew for twenty minutes, just long enough for the crests of the waves to stop breaking over on themselves. Then slowly, it veered north—and without any further warning, it was upon them.

It came roaring like a ravening beast, lifting the surface of the sea away in white sheets of spray that looked as though red-hot steel had been quenched in it. It laid *Warlock* right over, so that her port rail went under and she was flung up so harshly on her main cable that her stern was pulled down sharply, water pouring in through her stern scuppers.

It took David by surprise, so that she payed off dangerously before he could slam open the port throttle and throw the starboard screw into full reverse thrust. As she came up, he hit the call to the Captain's suite, watching with rising disbelief as the mad world dissolved around him.

Nick heard the call from far away, it only just penetrated to his fatigue-drugged brain, and he tried to respond, but it felt as though his body was crushed under an enormous weight and that his brain was slow and sluggish as a hibernating reptile.

The buzzer insisted, a tinny, nagging whine and he tried to force his eyes open, but they would not respond. Then dimly, but deeply, he felt the wild anguished action of his ship and the tumult that he believed at first was in his own ears, but was the violent uproar of the storm about the tug's superstructure.

He forced himself up on one elbow, and his body ached in every joint. He still could not open his eyes but he groped for the handset.

"Captain to the after bridge!" He could hear something in David Allen's voice that forced him to his feet.

When Nick staggered on to the after navigation bridge, the First Officer turned gratefully to him.

"Thank God you've come, sir."

The wind had taken the surface off the sea, had stripped it away, tearing each wave to a shrieking fog of white spray and mingling it with the sleet and snow that drove horizontally across the bay.

Nick glanced once at the dial of the wind anemometer, and then discounted the reading. The needle was stuck at the top of the scale. It made no sense, a wind speed of 120 miles an hour was too much to accept, the instrument had been damaged by the initial gusts of this wind, and he refused to believe it; to do so now would be to admit disaster, for nobody could salvage an ocean-going liner in wind velocities right off the Beaufort scale.

Warlock stood on her tail, like a performing dolphin begging for a meal, as the cable brought her up short and the bridge deck became a vertical cliff down which Nick was hurled. He crashed into the control panel and clung for purchase to the foul-weather rail.

"We'll have to shear the cable and stand out to sea." David Allen's voice was pitched too high and too loud, even for the tumult of the wind and the storm.

There were men on board *Golden Adventurer*; Baker and sixteen others, Nick thought swiftly, and even her twin anchors could not be trusted to hold in this.

Nick clung to the rail and peered out into the storm. Frozen spray and sleet and impacted snow drove on the wind, coming in with the force of buckshot fired at point-blank range, cracking into the armoured glass of the bridge and building up in thick clots and lumps that defeated the efforts of the spinning "clear vision" panels.

He looked across a thousand yards and the hull of the liner was just visible, a denser area in the howling, swirling, white wilderness.

"Baker?" he asked into the hand microphone. "What is your position?"

"The wind's got her, she's slewing. The starboard anchor is dragging." And then, while Nick thought swiftly, "You'll not be able to take us off in this." It was a flat statement, an acceptance of the fact that the destinies of Baker and his sixteen men were inexorably linked to that of the doomed ship.

"No," Nick agreed. "We won't be able to get you off." To approach the stricken ship was certain disaster for all of them.

"Shear the cable and stand off," Baker advised. "We'll try to get ashore as she breaks up." Then, with a hangman's chuckle, he went on, "Just don't forget to come and fetch us when the weather moderates—that is if there is anybody to fetch."

Abruptly Nick's anger came to the surface through the layers of fatigue, anger at the knowledge that all he had risked and suffered was now to be in vain, that he was to lose *Golden Adventurer*, and probably with her sixteen men, one of whom had become a friend.

"Are you ready to heave on the anchor winches?" he asked. "We are going to pull the bitch off."

"Jesus!" said Baker. "She's still half flooded—"

"We will have a lash at it, cobber," said Nick quietly.

"The steering-gear is locked, you won't be able to control her. You'll lose *Warlock* as well as—" but Nicholas cut Baker short.

"Listen, you stupid Queensland sheep-shagger, get on to those winches." As he said it, *Golden Adventurer* disappeared, her bulk blotted out completely by the solid, white curtains of the blizzard.

"Engine room," Nick spoke crisply to the Second Engineer. "Disengage the override, and give me direct control of both power and pitch."

"Control transferred to bridge, sir," the Engineer confirmed, and Nick touched the shining stainless-steel levers with fingers as sensitive as those of a concert pianist. *Warlock*'s response was instantaneous. She pivoted, shrugging aside a green slithering burst of water which came in over her shoulder and thundered down the side of her superstructure.

"Anchor winches manned." Beauty Baker's tone was almost casual.

"Stand by," said Nick, and felt his way through that white inferno. It was impossible to maintain visual reference, the entire world was white and swirling, even the surface of the sea was gone in torn streamers of white; the very pull of gravity, that should have defined even a simple up or down, was confused by the violent pitch and roll of the deck.

Nick felt his exhausted brain begin to lurch dizzily in the first attacks of vertigo. Swiftly he switched his attention to the big compass and the heading indicator.

"David," he said, "take the wheel." He wanted somebody swift and bright at the helm now.

Warlock plunged suddenly, so viciously that Nick's bruised ribs were brought in brutal contact with the edge of the control console. He grunted involuntarily with the pain. *Warlock* was feeling her cable, she had come up hard.

"Starboard ten," said Nick to David, bringing her bows up into that hideous wind.

"Chief," he spoke into the microphone, his voice still ragged with the pain in his chest. "Haul starboard winch, full power."

"Full power starboard."

Nick slid pitch control to fully fine, and then slowly nudged open the throttles, bringing in twenty-two thousand horsepower.

Held by her tail, driven by the great wind, and tortured by the sea, lashed by her own enormous propellers, *Warlock* went berserk. She corkscrewed and porpoised to her very limits, every frame in her hull shook with the vibration of her screws as her propellers burst out of the surface and spun wildly in the air.

Nick had to clench his jaws as the vibration threatened to crack his teeth, and when he glanced across at the forward and lateral speed-indicators, he saw that David Allen's face was icy white and set like that of a corpse.

Warlock was slewing down on the wind, describing a slow left-hand circle at the limit of the cable as the engine torque and the wind took her around.

"Starboard twenty," Nick snapped, correcting the turn, and despite the rigour of his features, David Allen's response was instantaneous.

"Twenty degrees of starboard wheel on, sir."

Nick saw the lateral drift stop on the ground speed-indicator, and then with a wild lurch of elation he saw the forward speed-indicator flicked into green. Its electronic digital read out, changing swiftly—they were moving forward at 150 feet a minute.

"We are moving her," Nick cried aloud, and he snatched up the microphone.

"Full power both winches."

"Both full and holding," answered Baker immediately.

And Nick glanced back at the forward speed across the ground, 150, 110, 75 feet a minute, *Warlock*'s forward impetus slowed, and Nick realized with a slide of dismay that it was merely the elasticity of the nylon spring that had given them that reading. The spring was stretching out to its limit.

For two or three seconds, the dial recorded a zero rate of speed. *Warlock* was standing still, the cable drawn out to the full limit of her strength, then abruptly the dial flicked into vivid red; they were going backwards, as the nylon spring exerted pressures beyond that of the twin diesels and the big bronze screws—*Warlock* was being dragged back towards that dreadful shore.

For another five minutes, Nick kept both clenched fists on the control levers, pressing them with all his strength to the limit of their travel, sending the great engines shrieking, driving the needles up around the dials, deep into the red "never exceed" sectors.

He felt tears of anger and frustration scalding his swollen eyelids, and the ship shuddered and shook and screamed under him, her torment transmitted through the soles of his feet and the palms of his hands.

Warlock was held down by cable and power, so she could not rise to meet the seas that came out of the roaring whiteness. They tumbled aboard her, piling up on each other, so she burrowed deeper and more dangerously.

"For God's sake, sir," David Allen was no longer able to contain himself. His eyes looked huge in his bone-white face. "You'll drive her clean under."

"Baker," Nick ignored his Mate, "are you gaining?"

"No recovery either winch," Beauty told him. "She is not moving."

Nick pulled back the stainless steel levers, the needles sank swiftly back around their dials, and *Warlock* reacted gratefully, shaking herself free of the piled waters.

"You'll have to shear the tow." Baker's disembodied voice was muted by the clamour of the storm. "We'll take our chances, sport."

Beside him, David Allen reached for the red-painted steel box that housed the shear button. It was protected by the box from accidental usage; David Allen opened the box and looked expectantly, almost pleadingly, at Nick.

"Belay that!" Nick snarled at him, and then to Baker, "I'm shortening tow. Be ready to haul again, when I am in position."

David Allen stared at him, his right hand still on the open lid of the red box.

"Close that bloody thing," Nick said, and turned to the main cable controls. He moved the green lever to reverse, and felt the vibration in the deck as below him in the main cable room the big drums began to revolve, drawing the thick ice-encrusted cable up over *Warlock*'s stern.

Fighting every inch of the way like a wild horse on a head halter, *Warlock* was drawn in cautiously by her own winches, and the officers watched in mounting horror as out of the white terror of the blizzard emerged the mountainous ice-covered bulk of *Golden Adventurer*.

She was so close that the main cable no longer dipped below the surface of the sea, but ran directly from the liner's stern to the tug's massive fairleads on her stern quarter.

"Now we can see what we are doing," Nick told them grimly. He could see now that much of *Warlock*'s power had been wasted by not exerting a pull on exactly the same plane as *Golden Adventurer*'s keel. He had been disoriented in the white-out of the blizzard, and had allowed *Warlock* to pull at an angle. It would not happen now.

"Chief," he said. "Pull, pull all, pull until she bursts her guts!" And again he slid the throttle handles fully home.

Warlock flung up against the elastic yoke, and Nick saw the water spurt from the woven fibres and turn instantly to ice crystals as it was whipped away on the shrieking wind.

"She's not moving, sir," David cried beside him.

"No recovery either winch," Baker confirmed almost immediately. "She's solid!"

"Too much water still in her," said David, and Nick turned on him as though to strike him to the deck.

"Give me the wheel," he said, his voice cracking with his anger and frustration.

With both engines boiling the sea to white foam, and roaring like dying bulls, Nick swung the wheel to full port lock.

Wildly *Warlock* dug her shoulder in, water pouring on board her as she rolled, instantly Nick spun the wheel to full starboard lock and she lurched against the tow, throwing an extra ton of pressure on to it.

Even above the storm, they heard *Golden Adventurer* groan, the steel of her hull protesting at the weight of water in her and the intolerable pressure of the anchor winches and *Warlock*'s tow cable.

The groan became a crackling hiss as the pebble bottom gave and moved under her.

"Christ, she's coming!" shrieked Baker, and Nick swung her to full port lock again, swinging *Warlock* into a deep trough between waves, then a solid ridge of steaming water buried her, and Nick was not certain she could survive that press of furious sea. It came green and slick over the superstructure and she shuddered wearily, gone slow and unwieldy. Then she lifted her bows and, like a spaniel, shook herself free, becoming again quick and light.

"Pull, my darling, pull," Nick pleaded with her.

With a slow reluctant rumble, *Golden Adventurer*'s hull began to slide over the holding, clinging bottom.

"Both winches recovering," Baker howled gleefully, and *Warlock*'s ground speed-indicator flicked into the green, its little angular figures changing in twinkling electronic progression as *Warlock* gathered way.

They all saw *Golden Adventurer*'s stern swinging to meet the next great ridge of water as it burst around her. She was floating, and for moments Nick was paralysed by the wonder of seeing that great and beautiful ship come to life again, become a living, vital sea creature as she took the seas and rose to meet them.

"We've done it, Christ, we've done it!" howled Baker, but it was too soon for self-congratulation. As *Golden Adventurer* came free of the ground and gathered sternway under *Warlock*'s tow, so her rudder bit and swung her tall stern across the wind.

She swung, exposing the enormous windage of her starboard side to the full force of the storm. It was like setting a mainsail, and the wind took her down swiftly on the rocky headland with its sentinel columns that guarded the entrance to the bay.

Nick's first instinct was to try and hold her off, to oppose the force of the wind directly, and he flung *Warlock* into the task, relying on her great diesels and the two anchors to keep the liner from going ashore again—but the wind toyed with them, it ripped the anchors out of the pebble bottom and *Warlock* was drawn stern first through the water, straight down on the jagged rock of the headland.

"Chief, get those anchors up," Nick snapped into the microphone. "They'll never hold in this."

Twenty years earlier, bathing off a lonely beach in the Seychelles, Nick had been caught out of his depth by one of those killer currents that flow around the headlands of oceanic islands, and it had sped him out into the open sea so that within minutes the silhouette of the land was low and indistinct on his watery horizon. He had fought that current, swimming directly against it, and it had nearly killed him. Only in the last stages of exhaustion had he begun to think, and instead of battling it, he had ridden the current, angling slowly across it, using its impetus rather than opposing it.

The lesson he had learned that day was well remembered, and as he watched Baker bring *Golden Adventurer*'s dripping anchors out of the wild water he was driving *Warlock* hard, bringing her around on her cable so the wind was no longer in her teeth, but over her stern quarter.

Now the wind and *Warlock*'s screws were no longer opposed, but *Warlock* was pulling two points off the wind, as fine a course as Nick could judge barely to clear the most seaward of the rocky sentinels; now the liner's locked rudder was holding her steady into the wind—but opposing *Warlock*'s attempt to angle her away from the land.

It was a problem of simple vectors of force, that Nick tried to work out in his head and prove in physical terms, as he delicately judged the angle of his tow and the direction of the wind, balancing them against the tremendous leverage of the liner's locked rudder, the rudder which was dragging her suicidally down upon the land.

Grimly, he stared ahead to where the black rock cliffs were still hidden in the white nothingness. They were invisible, but their presence was recorded on the cluttered screen of the radar repeater. With both wind and engines driving them, their speed was too high, and if *Golden Adventurer* went on to the cliffs like this, her hull would shatter like a watermelon hurled against a brick wall.

It was another five minutes before Nick was absolutely certain they would not make it. They were only two miles off the cliffs now, he glanced again at the radar screen, and they would have to drag *Golden*

Adventurer at least half a mile across the wind to clear the land. They were just not going to make it.

Helplessly, Nick stood and peered into the storm, waiting for the first glimpse of black rock through the swirling eddies of snow and frozen spray, and he had never felt more tired and unmanned in his entire life as he moved to the shear button, ready to cut *Golden Adventurer* loose and let her go to her doom.

His officers were silent and tense around him, while under his feet *Warlock* shuddered and buffeted wildly, driven to her mortal limits by the sea and her own engines, but still the land sucked at them.

"Look!" David Allen shouted suddenly, and Nick spun to the urgency in his voice.

For a moment he did not understand what was happening. He knew only that the shape of *Golden Adventurer*'s stern was altered subtly.

"The rudder," shouted David Allen again. And Nick saw it revolving slowly on its stock as the ship lifted on another big sea.

Almost immediately, he felt *Warlock* making offing from under that lee shore, and he swung her up another point into the wind, *Golden Adventurer* answering her tow with a more docile air, and still the rudder revolved slowly.

"I've got power on the emergency steering gear now," said Baker.

"Rudder amidships," Nick ordered.

"Amidships it is," Baker repeated, and now he was pulling her out stern first, almost at right angles across the wind.

Through the white inferno appeared the dim snow-blurred outline of the rock sentinels, and the sea broke upon them like the thunder of the heavens.

"God, they are close," whispered David Allen. So close that they could feel the backlash of the gale as it rebounded from the tall rock walls, moderating the tremendous force that was bearing them down— moderating just enough to allow them to slide past the three hungry rocks, and before them lay three thousand miles of wild and tumultuous water, all of it open sea room.

"We made it. This time we really made it," said Baker, as though he did not believe it was true, and Nick pulled back the throttle controls taking the intolerable strain off her engines before they tore themselves to pieces.

"Anchors and all," Nick replied. It was a point of honour to retrieve even the anchors. They had taken her off clean and intact—anchors and all.

"Chief," he said, "instead of sitting there hugging yourself, how about pumping her full of Tannerax?" The anti-corrosive chemical would save her engines and much of her vital equipment from further sea-water damage, adding enormously to her salvaged value.

"You just never let up, do you?" Baker answered accusingly.

"Don't you believe it," said Nick. He felt stupid and frivolous with exhaustion and triumph. Even the storm that still roared about them seemed to have lost its murderous intensity. "Right now I'm going down to my bunk to sleep for twelve hours—and I'll kill anybody who tries to wake me."

He hung the handmike on its bracket and put his hand on David Allen's shoulder. He squeezed once, and said:

"You did well—you all did very well. Now take her, Number One, and look after her."

Then he stumbled from the bridge.

It was eight days before they saw the land again. They rode out the storm in the open sea, eight days of unrelenting tension and heart-breaking labour.

The first task was to move the two-cable to *Golden Adventurer*'s bows. In that sea, the transfer took almost 24 hours, and three abortive attempts before they had her head-on to the wind. Now she rode more easily, and *Warlock* had merely to hang on like a drogue, using full power only when one of the big icebergs came within dangerous range, and it was necessary to draw her off.

However, the tension was always there and Nick spent most of those days on the bridge, watchful and worried, nagged by the fear that the plug in the gashed hull would not hold. Baker used timbers from the ship's store to shore up the temporary patch, but he could not put steel in place while *Golden Adventurer* plunged and rolled in the heavy seas, and Nick could not go aboard to check and supervise the work.

Slowly, the great wheel of low pressure revolved over them, the winds changed direction, backing steadily into the west, as the epicentre marched on down the sea lane towards Australasia—and at last it had passed.

Now *Warlock* could work up towing speed. Even in those towering glassy swells of black water that the storm had left them as a legacy, she was able to make four knots.

Then one clear and windy morning under a cold yellow sun, she brought *Golden Adventurer* into the sheltered waters of Shackleton Bay. It was like a diminutive guide-dog leading a blinded colossus.

As the two ships came up into the still waters under the sheltering arm of the bay, the survivors came down from their encampment to the water's edge, lining the steep black pebble beach, and their cheers and shouts of welcome and relief carried thinly on the wind to the officers on *Warlock*'s bridge.

Even before the liner's twin anchors splashed into the clear green water, Captain Reilly's boat was puttering out to *Warlock*, and when he came aboard, his eyes were haunted by the hardship and difficulties of these last days, by the disaster of a lot command and the lives that had been ended with it. But when he shook hands with Nick, his grasp was firm.

"My thanks and congratulations, sir!"

He had known Nicholas Berg as Chairman of Christy Marine, and, as no other, he was aware of the magnitude of this most recent accomplishment. His respect was apparent.

"It's good to see you again," Nick told him. "Naturally you have access to my ship's communications to report to your owners."

Immediately he turned back to the task of manoeuvring *Warlock* alongside, so that steel plate could be swung up from her salvage holds to the liner's deck; it was another hour before Captain Reilly emerged from the radio room.

"Can I offer you a drink, Captain?" Nick led him to his day cabin, and began with tact to deal with the hundred details which had to be settled between them. It was a delicate situation, for Reilly was no longer Master of his own ship. Command had passed to Nicholas as salvage master.

"The accommodation aboard *Golden Adventurer* is still quite serviceable, and, I imagine, a great deal warmer and more comfortable than that occupied by your passengers at present—" Nick made it easier for him while never for a moment letting him lose sight of his command position, and Reilly responded gratefully.

Within half an hour, they had made all the necessary arrangements to transfer the survivors aboard the liner. Levoisin on *La Mouette* had been able to take only one hundred and twenty supernumeraries on board his little tug. The oldest and weakest of them had gone and Christy Marine was negotiating for a charter from Cape Town to Shackleton Bay to take off the rest of them. Now that charter was unnecessary, but the cost of it would form part of Nick's claim for salvage award.

"I won't take up more of your time." Reilly drained his glass and stood. "You have much to do."

There were another four days and nights of hard work. Nick went aboard *Golden Adventurer* and saw the cavernous engine room lit by the eye-scorching blue glare of the electric welding flames, as Baker placed his steel over the wound and welded it into place. Even then, neither he nor Nick was satisfied until the new patches had been shored and stiffened with baulks of heavy timber. There was a hard passage through the roaring forties ahead of them, and until they had *Golden Adventurer* safely moored in Cape Town docks, the salvage was incomplete.

They sat side by side among the greasy machinery and the stink of the anti-corrosives, and drank steaming Thermos coffee laced with Bundaberg rum.

"We get this beauty into Duncan Docks—and you are going to be a rich man," Nick said.

"I've been rich before. With me it never lasts long—and it's always a relief when I've spent the stuff." Beauty gargled the rum and coffee appreciatively, before he went on, shrewdly. "So you don't have to worry about losing the best goddamned engineer afloat."

Nick laughed with delight. Baker had read him accurately. He did not want to lose this man.

Nick left him and went to see to the trim of the liner, studying her carefully and using the experience of the last days to determine her best points of tow, before giving his orders to David Allen to raise her slightly by the head.

Then there was the transfer from the liner's bunkers of sufficient bunker oil to top up *Warlock*'s own tanks against the long tow ahead, and Bach Wackie in Bermuda kept the telex clattering with relays from underwriters and Lloyd's, with the first tentative advances from Christy Marine; already Duncan Alexander was trying out the angles, manoeuvring for a liberal settlement of Nick's claims, without, as he put it, the expense of the arbitration court.

"Tell him I'm going to roast him," Nick answered with grim relish. "Remind him that as Chairman of Christy Marine I advised against underwriting our own bottoms—and now I'm going to rub his nose in it."

The days and nights blurred together, the illusion made complete by the imbalance of time down here in the high latitudes, so that Nick could often believe neither his senses nor his watch when he had been working eighteen hours straight and yet the sun still burned, and his watch told him it was three o'clock in the morning.

Then again, it did not seem part of reality when his senior officers, gathered around the mahogany table in his day cabin, reported that the work was completed—the repairs and preparation, the loading of fuel, the embarkation of passengers and the hundred other details had all been attended to, and *Warlock* was ready to drag her massive charge out into the unpredictable sea, thousands of miles to the southernmost tip of Africa.

Nick passed the cheroot-box around the circle and while the blue smoke clouded the cabin, he allowed them all a few minutes to luxuriate in the feeling of work done, and done well.

"We'll rest the ship's company for twenty-four hours," he announced in a rush of generosity. "And take in tow at 0800 hours Monday. I'm hoping for a two speed of six knots—twenty-one days to Cape Town, gentlemen."

When they rose to leave, David Allen lingered self-consciously. "The wardroom is arranging a little Christmas celebration tonight, sir, and we would like you to be our guest."

The wardroom was the junior officers' club from which, traditionally, the Master was excluded. He could enter the small panelled cabin only as an invited guest, but there was no doubt at all about the genuine warmth of the welcome they gave him. Even the Trog was there. They stood and applauded him when he entered, and it was clear that most of them had made an early start on the gin. David Allen made a speech which he read haltingly from a scrap of paper which he tried to conceal in the palm of one hand. It was a speech full of hyperbole, clichés and superlatives, and he was clearly mightily relieved once it was over.

Then Angel brought in a cake he had baked for the occasion. It was iced in the shape of *Golden Adventurer*, a minor work of art, with the figures "12½%" picked out in gold on its hull, and they applauded him. That 12½ per cent had significance to set them all grinning and exclaiming.

Then they called on Nick to speak, and his style was relaxed and easy. He had them hooting with glee within minutes—a mere mention of the prize money that would be due to them once they brought *Golden Adventurer* into Cape Town had them in ecstasy.

The girl was wedged into a corner, almost swallowed in the knot of young officers who found it necessary to press as closely around her as was possible without actually smothering her.

She laughed with a clear unaffected exuberance, her voice ringing high above the growl of masculine mirth, so that Nick found it difficult not to keep looking across at her.

She wore a dress of green clinging material, and Nick wondered where it had come from, until he remembered that *Golden Adventurer*'s passenger accommodation was intact and that earlier that morning, he had noticed the girl standing beside David Allen in the stern of the work boat as it returned from the liner, with a large suitcase at her feet. She had been to fetch her gear and she probably should have stayed aboard the liner. Nick was pleased she had not.

Nick finished his little speech, having mentioned every one of his officers by name and given to each the praise they deserved, and David Allen pressed another large whisky into his one hand and an inelegant wedge of cake into the other, and then left hurriedly to join the tight circle around the girl. It opened reluctantly, yielding to his seniority and Nick found himself almost deserted.

He watched with indulgence the open competition for her attention. She was shorter than any of them, so Nick saw only the top of that magnificent mane of sun-streaked hair, hair the colour of precious metal that shone as she nodded and tilted her head, catching the overhead lights.

Beauty Baker was on one side of her, dressed in a ready-made suit of shiny imitation sharkskin that made a startling contrast to his plaid shirt and acid-yellow tie; the trousers of the suit needed hoisting every few minutes and his spectacles glittered lustfully as he hung over the girl.

David Allen was close on her other side, blushing pinkly every time she turned to speak to him, plying her with cake and liquor—and Nick found his indulgence turning to irritation.

He was irritated by the presence of a tongue-tied fourth officer who had clearly been delegated to entertain him, and was completely awed by the responsibility. He was irritated by the antics of his senior officers. They were behaving like a troupe of performing seals in their competition for the girl's attention.

For a few moments, the tight circle around her opened, and Nick was left with a few vivid impressions. The green of her dress matched exactly the brilliant sparkling green of her eyes. Her teeth were very white, and her tongue as pink as a cat's when she laughed. She was not the child he had imagined from their earlier encounters; with colour touched to her lips and pearls at her throat, he realized she was in her twenties, early twenties perhaps, but a full woman, nevertheless.

She looked across the wardroom and their eyes met. The laughter stilled on her lips, and she returned his gaze. It was a solemn enigmatic gaze, and he found himself once again regretting his previous rudeness to her. He dropped his gaze from hers and saw now that under the clinging green material, her body was slim and beautifully formed, with a lithe athletic grace. He remembered vividly that one nude glimpse he had been given.

Although the green dress was high-necked, he saw that her breasts were large and pointed, and that they were not trussed by any undergarments; the young shapely flesh was as strikingly arresting as if it had been naked.

It made him angry to see her body displayed in this manner. It did not matter that every young girl in the streets of New York or London went so uncorseted, here it made him angry to see her do the same, and he looked back into her eyes. Something charged there, a challenge perhaps, his own anger reflected? He was not sure. She tilted her head slightly, now it was an invitation—or was it? He had known and handled easily so many, many women. Yet this one left him with a feeling of uncertainty, perhaps it was merely her youth, or was it some special quality she possessed? Nicholas Berg was uncertain and he did not relish the feeling.

David Allen hurried to her with another offering, and cut off the gaze that passed between them, and Nick found himself staring at the Chief

Officer's slim, boyish back, and listening to the girl's laughter again, sweet and high. But somehow it seemed to be directed tauntingly at Nick, and he said to the young officer beside him,

"Please ask Mr. Allen for a moment of his time." Patently relieved the officer went to fetch him.

"Thank you for your hospitality, David," said Nick, when he came.

"You aren't going yet, sir?" Nick took a small sadistic pleasure in the Mate's obvious dismay.

H e sat at the desk in his day cabin and tried to concentrate. It was the first opportunity he had had to consider the paperwork that awaited him. The muted sounds of revelry from the deck below distracted him, and he found himself listening for the sounds of her laughter while he should have been composing his submissions to his London attorneys, which would be taken to the arbitrators of Lloyd's, a document and record of vital importance, the whole basis of his claim against *Golden Adventurer*'s underwriters. And yet he could not concentrate.

He swung his chair away from the desk and began to pace the thick, sound-deadening carpet, stopping once to listen again as he heard the girl's voice calling gaily, the words unintelligible, but the tone unmistakable. They were dancing, or playing some raucous game which consisted of a great deal of bumping and thumping and shrieks of laughter.

He began to pace again, and suddenly Nick realized he was lonely. The thought stopped him dead again. He was lonely, and completely alone. It was a disturbing realization, especially for a man who had travelled much of life's journey as a loner. Before it had never troubled him, but now he felt desperately the need for somebody to share his triumph. Triumph it was, of course. Against the most improbable odds, he had snatched spectacular victory, and he crossed slowly to the cabin portholes and looked across the darkened bay to where *Golden Adventurer* lay at anchor, all her lights burning, a gay and festive air about her.

He had been knocked off his perch at the top of the tree, deprived of a life's work, a wife and a son—yet it had taken him only a few short months to clamber back to the top.

With this simple operation, he had transformed Ocean Salvage from a dangerously insecure venture, a tottering cash-starved, problem-hounded long chance, into something of real value. He was off and running again now, with a place to go and the means of getting there. Then why did it suddenly seem of so little worth? He toyed with the idea of returning to the revelry in the wardroom, and grimaced as he imagined the dismay of his officers at the Master's inhibiting intrusion.

He turned away from the porthole and poured whisky into a glass, lit a cheroot and dropped into the chair. The whisky tasted like toothpaste and the cheroot was bitter. He left the glass on his desk and stubbed the cheroot before he went through on to the navigation bridge.

The night lights were so dim after his brightly lit cabin that he did not notice Graham, the Third Officer, until his eyes adjusted to the ruby glow.

"Good evening, Mr. Graham." He moved to the chart-table and checked the log. Graham was hovering anxiously, and Nick searched for something to say.

"Missing the party?" he asked at last.

"Sir."

It was not a promising conversational opening, and despite his loneliness of a few minutes previously, Nick suddenly wanted to be alone again.

"I will stand the rest of your watch. Go off and enjoy yourself."

The Third Officer gawped at him.

"You've got three seconds before I change my mind."

"That's jolly decent of you, sir," called Graham over his shoulder as he fled.

The party in the wardroom had by now degenerated into open competition for Samantha's attention and approbation.

David Allen, wearing a lampshade on his head and, for some unaccountable reason, with his right hand thrust into his jacket in a Napoleonic gesture, was standing on the wardroom bar counter and declaiming Henry's speech before Agincourt, glossing over the passages which he had forgotten with a "dum-de-dum." However, when Tim Graham entered, he became immediately the First Officer. He removed the lampshade and inquired frostily,

"Mr. Graham, am I correct in believing that you are officer of the watch? Your station at this moment is on the bridge—"

"The old man came and offered to stand my watch," said Tim Graham.

"Good Lord!" David replaced his lampshade, and poured a large gin for his Third Officer. "The old bastard must have come over all soft suddenly."

Beauty Baker, who was hanging off the wall like a gibbon ape, dropped to his feet and drew himself up with rather unsteady dignity, hitched his trousers and announced ominously,

"If anybody calls the old bastard a bastard, I will personally kick his teeth down his throat." He swept the wardroom with an eye that was belligerent and truculent, until it alighted on Samantha. Immediately it softened. "That one doesn't count, Sammy!" he said.

"Of course not," Samantha agreed. "You can start again."

Beauty returned to the starting point of the obstacle course, fortified himself with a draught of rum, pushed up his spectacles with a thumb and spat on his palms.

"One to get ready, two to get steady—and three to be off," sang out Samantha, and clicked the stopwatch. Beauty Baker swung dizzily from the roof, clawing his way around the wardroom without touching the deck, cheered on by the entire company.

"Eight point six seconds!" Samantha clicked the watch, as he ended up on the bar counter, the finishing post. "A new world record."

"A drink for the new world champion."

"I'm next, time me, Sammy!"

They were like schoolboys. "Hey, watch me, Sammy!" But after another ten minutes, she handed the stopwatch to Tim Graham, who as a late arrival was still sober.

"I'll be back," she lied, picked up a plate with a large untouched hunk of Angel's cake upon it and was gone before any of them realized it was happening.

Nick Berg was working over the chart-table, so intently that he was not aware of her for many seconds. In the dramatic lighting of the single overhead lamp, the strength of his features was emphasized. She saw the hard line of his jawbone, the heavy brow and the alert, widely spaced set of his eyes. His nose was large and slightly hooked, like that of a plains Indian or a desert Bedouin, and there were lines at the corners of his mouth and around his eyes that were picked out in dark shadow. In his complete absorption with the charts and *Admiralty Pilot*, he had relaxed his mouth from its usual severe line. She saw now that the lips were full without being fleshy, and there was a certain sensitivity and voluptuousness there that she had not noticed before.

She stood quietly, enchanted with him, until he looked up suddenly, catching the rapt expression upon her face.

She tried not to appear flustered, but even in her own ears her voice was breathless.

"I'm sorry to disturb you. I brought some cake for Timmy Graham."

"I sent him below to join the party."

"Oh, I didn't notice him. I thought he was here."

She made no move to leave, holding the plate in one hand, and they were silent a moment longer.

"I don't suppose I could interest you in a slice? It's going begging."

"Share it," he suggested, and she came to the chart-table.

"I owe you an apology," he said, and was immediately aware of the harshness in his own voice. He hated to apologize, and she sensed it.

"I picked a bad moment," she said, and broke off a piece of the cake. "But this seems a better time. Thank you again, and I'm sorry for all the trouble I caused. I understand now that it nearly cost you the *Golden Adventurer*."

They both turned to look out of the big armoured glass windows to where she lay.

"She is beautiful, isn't she?" said Nick, and his voice had lost its edge.

"Yes, she's beautiful," Samantha agreed, and suddenly they were very close in the intimate ruddy glow of the night lights.

He began to talk, stiffly and self-consciously at first, but she drew him on, and with secret joy, she sensed him warming and relaxing. Only then did she begin to put her own ideas forward.

Nick was surprised and a little disconcerted at the depth of her view, and at her easy coherent expression of ideas, for he was still very much aware of her youth. He had expected the giddiness and the giggle, the shallowness and uninformed self-interest of immaturity, but it was not there, and suddenly the difference in their ages was of no importance.

They were very close in the night, touching only with their minds, but becoming each minute so much more closely involved in their ideas that time had no significance.

They spoke about the sea, for they were both creatures of that element and as they discovered this, so their mutual delight in each other grew.

From below came the faint unmelodious strains of Beauty Baker leading the ship's officers in a chorus of:

> *"—The working class can kiss my arse*
> *I've got my 12½ per cent at last!"*

And at another stage in the evening, a very worried Tim Graham appeared on the bridge and blurted out,

"Captain, sir, Doctor Silver is missing. She's not in her cabin and we have searched—" He saw her then, sitting in the Captain's chair and his worry turned to consternation. "Oh, I see. We didn't know—I mean we didn't expect—I'm sorry, sir. Excuse me, sir. Goodnight, sir." And again he fled the bridge.

"Doctor?" Nick asked.

"I'm afraid so," she smiled, and then went on to talk about the university, explaining her research project, and the other work she had in mind. Nicholas listened silently, for like all highly competitive and successful men, he respected achievement and ambition.

The chasm that he imagined existed between them shrank rapidly, so that it was an intrusion when the eight-to-twelve watch ended, and the relief brought other human presence to the bridge, shattering the fragile mood they had created around themselves, and denying them further excuse for remaining together.

"Goodnight, Captain Berg," she said.

"Goodnight, Doctor Silver," he answered reluctantly. Until that night, he had not even known her name, and there was so much more he wanted to know now, but she was gone from the bridge. As he entered his own suite, Nick's earlier loneliness returned, but with even more poignancy.

During the long day of getting *Golden Adventurer* under tow, the hours of trim and accommodation to the sea, until she was following meekly settling down to the long journey ahead, Nick thought of the girl at unlikely moments; but when he changed his usual routine and dined in

the saloon rather than his own cabin, she was surrounded by a solidly attentive phalanx of young men and, with a small shock of self-honesty,
Nick realized that he was actually jealous of them. Twice during the
meal, he had to suppress the sharp jibes that came to his lips, and would
have plunged the unfortunate recipient into uncomprehending confusion.

Nick ate no dessert and took coffee alone in his day cabin. He might
have relished Beauty Baker's company, but the Australian was aboard
Golden Adventurer, working on her main engines. Then, despite the tensions and endeavours of the day, his bunk had no attractions for him. He
glanced at the clock on the panelled bulkhead above his desk and saw
that it was a few minutes after eight o'clock.

On impulse he went through to the navigation bridge, and Tim Graham leapt guiltily to his feet. He had been sitting in the Master's chair, a
liberty which deserved at the least a sharp reprimand, but Nick pretended
not to notice and made a slow round of the bridge, checking every detail
from the cable tensions of the tow and power settings of *Warlock*'s engines, to the riding lights on both ships and the last log entry.

"Mr. Graham," he said, and the young officer stiffened to attention
like the victim before a firing squad, "I will stand this watch—you may
go and get some dinner."

The Third Officer was so thunderstruck that he needed a large gin before he could bring himself to tell the wardroom of his good fortune.

Samantha did not look up from the board but moved a bishop flaunt-
ingly across the front of David Allen's queen, and when David pounced
on it with a gurgle of glee, she unleashed her rook from the rear file and
said, "Mate in three, David."

"One more, Sam, give me my revenge," pleaded David, but she shook
her head and slipped out of the wardroom.

Nicholas became aware of the waft of her perfume. It was an inex-
pensive but exuberant fragrance—"Babe," that was it, the one advertised
by Hemingway's granddaughter. It suited Samantha perfectly. He turned
to her, and it was only then that he was honest enough to admit to himself
that he had relieved his Third Officer with the express intention of luring
the girl up to the bridge.

"There are whales ahead," he told her, and smiled one of those rare,
irresistible smiles that she had come to treasure. "I hoped you might
come up."

"Where? Where are they?" she asked with unfeigned excitement, and then they both saw the spout, a golden feather of spray in the low night sunlight two miles ahead.

"*Balaenoptera musculus!*" she exclaimed.

"I'll take your word for it, Doctor Silver, but to me it's still a blue whale." Nick was still smiling, and she looked abashed for a moment.

"Sorry, I wasn't trying to dazzle you with science." Then she looked back at the humpy, uninviting cold sea as the whale blew again, a far and ethereal column of lonely spray.

"One," she said, "only one." And the excitement in her voice cooled. "There are so few of them left now—that might be the last one we will ever see."

"So few that they cannot find each other in the vastness of the ocean to breed." Nick's smile was gone also, and again they talked of the sea, of their own involvement with it, their mutual concern at what man had done to it, and what he was still doing to it.

"When the Marxist government of Mozambique took over from the Portuguese colonists, it allowed the Soviets to send in dredgers—not trawlers, but dredgers—and they dredged the weed beds of Delagoa Bay. They actually *dredged* the breeding grounds of the Mozambique prawn. They took out a thousand tons of prawn, and destroyed the grounds for ever—and they drove an entire species into extinction in six short months." Her outrage was in her voice as she told it.

"Two months ago the Australians arrested a Japanese trawler in their territorial waters. She had in her freezers the meat of 120,000 giant clams that her crew had torn from the barrier reef with crowbars. The clam population of a single coral reef would not exceed 20,000. That means they had denuded six oceanic reefs in one expedition—and they fined the Captain a thousand pounds."

"It was the Japanese who perfected the 'long line,'" Nick agreed, "the endless floating line, armed with specially designed hooks, and laid across the lanes of migration of the big pelagic surface-feeding fish, the tuna and the marlin. They wipe out the shoals as they advance—wipe them out to the last fish."

"You cannot reduce any animal population beyond a certain point." Samantha seemed much older as she turned her face up to Nick. "Look what they did to the whales."

Together they turned back to the windows, gazing out in hope of another glimpse of that gentle monster, doomed now to extinction, one last look at another creature that would disappear from the seas.

"The Japanese and the Russians again," said Nick. "They would not sign the whaling treaty until there were not enough blues left in the seas to make their killing an economic proposition. Then they signed it. When there were two or three thousand blue whales left in all the oceans, that is when they signed."

"Now they will hunt the fin and the sei and the minke to extinction."

As they stood side by side staring into the bizarre sun-lit night, searching vainly for that spark of life in the watery wilderness, without thinking Nick lifted his arm; he would have placed it around her shoulders, the age-old protective attitude of man to his woman, but he caught himself at the last moment before he actually touched her. She had felt his movement and tensed for it, swaying slightly towards him in anticipation, but he stepped away, letting his arm fall and stooped over the radarscope. She only realized then how much she had wanted him to touch her, but for the rest of that evening he stayed within the physical limits which he seemed to have set for himself.

The next evening she declined the wardroom's importunate invitations, and after dinner waited in her own cabin, the door an inch ajar so she heard Tim Graham leave the bridge, clattering down the companionway with exuberance, relieved once more of his watch. The moment he entered the wardroom, Samantha slipped from her cabin and ran lightly up to the bridge.

She was with him only minutes after he had assumed the watch and Nick was amused by the strength of his pleasure. They grinned at each other like schoolchildren in a successful piece of mischief.

Before the light went, they passed close by one of the big tabular bergs, and she pointed out the line of filth that marked the white ice like the ring around a bathtub that had been used by a chimney sweep.

"Paraffin wax," she said, "and undissolved hydrocarbons."

"No," he said, "that's only glacial striation."

"It's crude oil," she answered him. "I've sampled it. It was one of the reasons I took the guide job on *Golden Adventurer*, I wanted first-hand knowledge of these seas."

"But we are two thousand miles south of the tanker lanes."

"The beach at Shackleton Bay is thick with wax balls and crude droplets. We found oil-soaked penguins on Cape Alarm, dead and dying.

They hit an oil slick within fifty miles of that isolated shore."

"I can hardly believe—" Nick started, but she cut across him.

"That's just it!" she said. "Nobody wants to believe it. Just walk on by, as though it's another mugging victim lying on the sidewalk."

"You're right," Nick admitted grudgingly. "Very few people really care."

"A few dead penguins, a few little black tar balls sticking to your feet on the beach. It doesn't seem much to shout about, but it's what we cannot see that should terrify us. Those millions of tons of poisonous hydrocarbons that dissolve into the sea, that kill slowly and insidiously, but surely. That's what should really terrify us, Nicholas!"

She had used his given name for the first time, and they were both acutely aware of it. They were silent again, staring intently at the big iceberg as it passed slowly. The sun had touched it with ethereal pinks and dreaming amethyst, but that dark line of poisonous filth was still there.

"The world has to use fossil fuels, and we sailors have to transport them," he said at last.

"But not at such appalling risks, not with an eye only to the profits. Not in the same greedy thoughtless grabbing petty way as man wiped out the whale, not at the cost of turning the sea into a stinking festering cesspool."

"There are unscrupulous owners—" he agreed, and she cut across him angrily.

"Sailing under flags of convenience, without control, ships built to dangerous standards, equipped with a single boiler—" she reeled out the charges and he was silent.

"Then they waived the winter load-line for tankers rounding the Cape of Good Hope in the southern winter, to enable them to carry that extra fifty thousand tons of crude. The Agulhas Bank, the most dangerous winter sea in the world, and they send overloaded tankers into it."

"That was criminal," he agreed.

"Yet you were Chairman of Christy Marine, you had a representative on the Board of Control."

She saw that she had made a mistake. His expression was suddenly ferocious. His anger seemed to crackle like electricity in the ruby gloom of the bridge. She felt an unaccountable flutter of real fear. She had forgotten what kind of man he was.

But he turned away and made a slow circuit of the bridge, elaborately checking each of the gauges and instruments, and then he paused at the far wing and lit a cheroot. She ached to offer some token of reconciliation, but instinctively she knew not to do so. He was not the kind of man who respected compromise or retreat.

He came back to her at last, and the glow of the cheroot lit his features so that she could see the anger had passed.

"Christy Marine seems like another existence to me now," he said softly, and she could sense the deep pain of unhealed wounds. "Forgive me, your reference to it took me off balance. I did not realize that you know of my past history."

"Everybody on board knows."

"Of course," he nodded, and drew deeply on the cheroot before he spoke again. "When I ran Christy Marine, I insisted on the highest standards of safety and seamanship for every one of our vessels. We opposed the Cape winter-line decision, and none of my tankers loaded to their summer-line on the Good Hope passage. None of my tankers made do with only one boiler, the design and engineering of every Christy Marine vessel was of the same standard as that ship there," he pointed back at *Golden Adventurer*, "or this one here," and he stamped once on the deck.

"Even the *Golden Dawn*?" she asked softly, braving his anger again—but he merely nodded.

"*Golden Dawn*," he repeated softly. "It sounds such an absurdly presumptuous name, doesn't it? But I really thought of her as that, when I conceived her. The first million-ton tanker, with every refinement and safety feature that man has so far tested and proved. From inert gas scrubbers to independently articulated main tanks, not one boiler but four, just like one of the old White Star liners—she was really to be the golden dawn of crude oil transportation.

"However, I am no longer Chairman of Christy Marine, and I am no longer in control of *Golden Dawn*, neither her design nor her construction." His voice was hollow, and in the dim light his eyes seemed shrunken into their cavities like those of a skull. "Nor yet am I in control of her operation."

It was all turning out so badly; she did not want to argue with him, nor make him unhappy. However, she had stirred memories and regrets within him, and she wished vainly that she had not disturbed him so. Her instinct warned her she should leave him now.

"Goodnight, Doctor Silver," he nodded non-committally at her sudden plea of tiredness.

"My name is Sam," she told him, wishing that she could comfort him in some way, any way, "or Samantha, if you prefer it."

"I do prefer it," he said, without smiling. "Goodnight, Samantha."

She was angry with both herself and him, angry that the good feeling between them had been destroyed, so she flashed at him:

"You really are old-fashioned, aren't you?" and hurried from the bridge.

The following evening she almost did not go up to him, for she was ashamed of those parting words, for having pointed up their age difference so offensively. She knew he was sufficiently aware of their differences, without being reminded. She had done herself harm, and she did not want to face him again.

While she was in the shower of the guest cabin, she heard Tim Graham come clattering down the stairs on the other side of the thin bulkhead. She knew that Nicholas had relieved him.

"I'm not going up," she told herself firmly, and took her time drying and talcuming and brushing out her hair before she clambered naked and still pink from the hot water into her bunk.

She read for half an hour, a western that Beauty Baker had lent her, and it required all her concentration to follow the print, for her mind kept trying to wander. At last she gave an exclamation of self-disgust, threw back the blankets and began dressing.

His relief and pleasure, when she appeared beside him, were transparent, and his smile was a princely welcome for her. She was suddenly very glad she had come, and this night she effortlessly steered past all the pitfalls.

She asked him to explain how the Lloyd's Open Form contract worked, and she followed his explanations swiftly.

"If they take into consideration the danger and difficulties involved in the salvage," she mused, "you should be able to claim an enormous award."

"I'm going to ask for twenty per cent of the hull value—"

"What is the hull value of *Golden Adventurer*?"

And he told her. She was silent a moment as she checked his mental arithmetic.

"That's six million dollars," she whispered in awe.

"Give or take a few cents," he agreed.

"But there isn't that much money in the world!" She turned and stared back at the liner.

"Duncan Alexander is going to agree with you." Nick smiled a little grimly.

"But," she shook her head, "what would anybody do with that much money?"

"I'm asking for six—but I won't get it. I'll walk away with three or four million."

"Still, that's too much. Nobody could spend that much, not if they tried for a lifetime."

"It's spent already. It will just about enable me to pay off my loans, launch my other tug, and to keep Ocean Salvage going for another few months."

"You owe three or four million dollars?" She stared at him now in open wonder. "I'd never sleep, not one minute would I be able to sleep—"

"Money isn't for spending," he explained. "There is a limit to the amount of food you can eat, or clothes you can wear. Money is a game, the biggest most exciting game in town."

She listened attentively to it all, happy because tonight he was gay and excited with grand designs and further plans, and because he shared them with her.

"What we will do is this, we'll come down here with both tugs and catch an iceberg."

She laughed. "Oh, come on!"

"I'm not joking," he assured her, but laughing also. "We'll put tow-lines on a big berg. It may take a week to build up tow speed, but once we get it moving nothing will stop it. We will guide it up into the middle forties, catch the roaring forties and, just like the old wool clippers on the Australian passage, we will run our eastings down." He moved to the chart-table, selected a large-scale chart of the Indian Ocean and beckoned her to join him.

"You're serious." She stopped laughing, and stared at him again. "You really are serious, aren't you?"

He nodded, still smiling, and traced it out with his finger. "Then we'll swing northwards, up into the Western Australian current, letting the flow carry us north in a great circle, until we hit the easterly monsoon and the north equatorial current." He described the circle, but she watched his face. They stood very close, but still not touching and she felt herself stirred by the timbre of his voice, as though to the touch of fingers. "We will cross the Indian Ocean to the east coast of Africa with the current pushing all the way, just in time to catch the south-westerly monsoon drift—right into the Persian Gulf." He straightened up and smiled again.

"A hundred billion tons of fresh water delivered right into the driest and richest corner of the globe."

"But—but—" she shook her head, "it would melt!"

"From a helicopter we spray it with a reflective polyurethane skin to lessen the effect of the sun, and we moor it in a shallow specially prepared dock where it will cool its own surrounds. Sure, it will melt, but not for a year or two and then we'll just go out and catch another one and bring it in, like roping wild horses."

"How would you handle it?" she objected. "It's too big."

"My two tugs hustle forty-four thousand horses—we could pull in Everest, if we wanted."

"Yes, but once you get it to the Persian Gulf?"

"We cut it into manageable hunks with a laser lance, and lift the hunks into a melting dam with an overhead crane."

She thought about it. "It could work," she admitted.

"It will work," he told her. "I've sold the idea to the Saudis already. They are already building the dock and the dams. We'll give them water at one hundredth the cost of using nuclear condensers on sea water, and without the risk of radioactive contamination."

She was absorbed with his vision, and he with hers. As they talked deep into the long watches of the night, they drew closer in spirit only.

Although each of them treasured those shared hours, somehow neither could bridge the narrow chasm between friendliness and real intimacy. She was instinctively aware of his reserves, that he was a man who had considered life and established his code by which to live it. She guessed that he did nothing unless it was deeply felt, and that a casual physical relationship would offer no attraction to him; she knew of the turmoil to which his life had so recently been reduced, and that he was pulling himself out of that by main strength, but that he was now wary of further hurt. There was time, she told herself, plenty of time—but *Warlock* bore steadily north by north-east, dragging her crippled ward up through the roaring forties; those notorious winds treated her kindly and she made good the six knots that Nick had hoped for.

On board *Warlock*, the attitude of the officers towards Samantha Sil-

ver changed from fawning adulation to wistful respect. Every one of
them knew of the nightly ritual of the eight-to-midnight watch.

"Bloody cradle-snatcher," groused Tim Graham.

"Mr. Graham, it is fortunate I did not hear that remark," David Allen
warned him with glacial coldness—but they all resented Nicholas Berg,
it was unfair competition, yet they kept a new respectful distance from
the girl, not one of them daring to challenge the herd bull.

T he time that Samantha had looked upon as endless was running
out now, and she closed her mind to it. Even when David Allen
showed her the fuzzy luminescence of the African continent on
the extreme range of the radar screen, she pretended to herself that it
would go on like this—if not for ever, at least until something special
happened.

During the long voyage up from Shackleton Bay, Samantha had
streamed a very fine-meshed net from *Warlock*'s stern, collecting an incredible variety of krill and plankton and other microscopic marine life.
Angel had grudgingly given her a small corner of his scullery in return
for her services as honorary assistant under-chef and unpaid waitress,
and she spent many absorbed hours there each day, identifying and pre-
serving her specimens.

She was working there when the helicopter came out to *Warlock*. She
looked up at the buffeting of the machine's rotors as they changed into
fine pitch for the landing on *Warlock*'s heli-deck, and she was tempted to
go up like every idle and curious hand on board, but she was in the middle of staining a slide, and somehow she resented the encroachment on
this little island of her happiness. She worked on, but now her pleasure
was spoiled, and she cocked her head when she heard the roar of the rotors as the helicopter rose from the deck again and she was left with a
sense of foreboding.

Angel came in from the deck, wiping his hands on his apron and he
paused in the doorway.

"You didn't tell me he was going, dearie."

"What do you mean?" Samantha looked up at him, startled.

"Your boyfriend, darling. Socks and toothbrush and all." Angel
watched her shrewdly. "Don't tell me he didn't even kiss you goodbye."

She dropped the glass slide into the stainless steel sink and it snapped in half. She was panting as she gripped the rail of the upper deck and stared after the cumbersome yellow machine.

It flew low across the green wind-chopped sea, hump-backed and nose low, still close enough to read the operating company's name "COURT" emblazoned on its fuselage, but it dwindled swiftly towards the far blue line of mountains.

Nick Berg sat in the jump seat between the two pilots of the big S. 58T Sikorsky and looked ahead towards the flat silhouette of Table Mountain. It was overlaid by a thick mattress of snowy cloud, at the south-easterly wind swirled across its summit.

From their altitude of a mere thousand feet, there were still five big tankers in sight, ploughing stolidly through the green sea on their endless odyssey, seeming to be alien to their element, not designed to live in harmony with it, but to oppose every movement of the waters. Even in this low sea, they wore thick garlands of white at their stubby rounded bows, and Nick watched one of them dip suddenly and take spray as high as her foremast. In any sort of blow, she would be like a pier with pylons set on solid ground. The seas would break right over her. It was not the way a ship should be, and now he twisted in his seat and looked back.

Far behind them, *Warlock* was still visible. Even at this distance, and despite the fact that she was dwarfed by her charge, her lines pleased the seaman in him. She looked good, but that backward glance invoked a pang of regret that he had been so stubbornly trying to ignore—and he had a vivid image of green eyes and hair of platinum and gold.

His regret was spiced by the persistent notion that he had been cowardly. He had left *Warlock* without being able to bring himself to say goodbye to the girl, and he knew why he had done so. He would not take the chance of making a fool of himself. He grimaced with distaste as he remembered her exact words, "You really are old-fashioned, aren't you?"

There was something vaguely repulsive in a middle-aged man lusting after young flesh—and he supposed he must now look upon himself as middle-aged. In six months he would be forty years of age, and he did not really expect to live to eighty. So he was in the middle of the road.

He had always scorned those grey, lined, balding, unattractive little men with big cigars, sitting in expensive restaurants with pretty young girls beside them, the young thing pretending to hang on every pearl-like word, while her eyes focused beyond his shoulder—on some younger man.

But still, it had been cowardice. She had become a friend during those weeks, and she could hardly have been aware of the emotions that she had aroused in him during those long dark hours on *Warlock*'s bridge. She was not to blame for his unruly passions, in no way had she encouraged him to believe that he was more than just an older man, not even a father figure, but just someone with whom to pass an otherwise empty hour. She had been as friendly and cheerful to everyone else on board *Warlock*, from the Mate to the cook.

He really had owed her the common courtesy of a handshake and an assurance of the pleasure he had taken from her company, but he had not been certain he could restrict it to that.

He winced again as he imagined her horror as he blurted out some sort of declaration, some proposal to prolong their relationship or alter its structure into something more intimate, her disenchantment when she realized that behind the façade of the mature and cultured man, he was just as grimy an old lecher as the furtive drooling browsers in the porno-shops of Times Square.

"Let it go," he had decided. No matter that he was probably in better physical shape now than he had been at twenty-five, to Dr. Samantha Silver he was an old man—and he had a frightening vision of an episode from his own youth.

A woman, a friend of his mother's, had trapped the nineteen-year-old Nicholas alone one rainy day in the old beach house at Martha's Vineyard. He remembered his own revulsion at the sagging white flesh, the wrinkles, the lines of stria across her belly and breasts, and the *oldness* of her. She would then have been a woman of forty, the same age as he was now, and he had done her the service she required out of some obligation of pity, but afterwards he had scrubbed his teeth until the gums bled and he had stood under the shower for almost an hour.

It was one of the cruel deceits of life that a person aged from the outside inwards. He had thought of himself in the fullness of his physical and mental powers, especially now after bringing in *Golden Adventurer*. He was ready for them to lead on the dragons and he would tear out their jugulars with his bare hands—then she had called him an old-fashioned thing, and he had realized that the sexual fantasy which was slowly becoming an obsession must be associated with the male menopause, a sorry symptom of the ageing process of which he had not been conscious until then. He grinned wryly at the thought.

The girl would probably hardly notice that he had left the ship, at the worst might be a little piqued by his lack of manners, but in a week would have forgotten his name. As for himself, there was enough, and more than enough to fill the days ahead, so that the image of a slim young body and that precious mane of silver and gold would fade until it became the fairy tale it really was.

Resolutely he turned in the jump seat and looked ahead. Always look ahead, there are never regrets in that direction.

They clattered in over False Bay, crossing the narrow isthmus of the Cape Peninsula under the bulk of the cloud-capped mountain, from the Indian Ocean to the Atlantic in under ten minutes.

He saw the gathering, like vultures at the lion kill, as the Sikorsky lowered to her roost on the helipad within the main harbour area of Table Bay.

As Nick jumped down, ducking instinctively under the still-turning rotors, they surged forward, ignoring the efforts of the Courtline dispatcher to keep the pad clear; they were led by a big red-faced man with a scorched-looking bald head and the furry arms of a tame bear.

"Larry Fry, Mr. Berg," he growled. "You remember me?"

"Hello, Larry." He was the local manager for Bach Wackie & Co., Nick's agents.

"I thought you might say a few words to the Press." But the journalists swarmed around Nick now, demanding, importuning, jostling each other, their minions firing flash bulbs.

Nick felt his irritation flare, and he needed a deep breath and a conscious effort to control his anger.

"All right, lads and ladies." He held up both hands, and grinned that special boyish grin. They were doing a tough job, he reminded himself. It couldn't be easy to be forced daily into the company of rich and successful men, grabbing for tidbits, and being grossly underpaid for your efforts with the long-term expectation of ulcers and cirrhosis of the liver.

"Play the game with me and I'll play it with you," he promised, and thought for a moment how it would be if they *didn't* want to speak with him, how it would be if they didn't know who he was, and didn't care.

"Where have you booked me?" he asked Larry Fry now, and turned back to them. "In two hours' time I'll be in my suite at the Mount Nelson Hotel. You're invited, and there'll be whisky."

They laughed and tried a few more half-hearted questions, but they had accepted the compromise—at least they had got the pictures.

As they went up the palm-lined drive to the gracious old hotel, built in the days when space included five acres of carefully groomed gardens, Nick felt the stir of memory, but he suppressed that and listened intently to the list of appointments and matters of urgency from which Larry Fry read. The change in the big man's attitude was dramatic. When Nick had first arrived to take command of *Warlock*, Larry Fry had given him ten minutes of his time and sent a deputy to complete the business.

Then Nick had been touched by the mark of the beast, a man on his way down, with as much appeal as a leper. Larry Fry had accorded him the minimum courtesy due the master of a small vessel, but now he was treating him like visiting royalty, limousine and fawning attention.

"We have chartered a 707 from South African Airways to fly *Golden Adventurer*'s passengers to London, and they will take scheduled commercial flights to their separate destinations from there."

"What about berthing for *Golden Adventurer*?"

"The Harbour Master is sending out an inspector to check the hull before he lets her enter harbour."

"You have made the arrangements?" Nick asked sharply. He had not completed the salvage until the liner was officially handed over to the company commissioned to undertake the repairs.

"Court are flying him out now," Larry Fry assured him. "We'll have a decision before nightfall."

"Have the underwriters appointed a contractor for the repairs?"

"They've called for tenders."

The hotel manager himself met Nicholas under the entrance portico.

"Good to see you again, Mr. Berg." He waived the registration procedures. "We can do that when Mr. Berg has settled in." And then he assured Nick, "We have given you the same suite."

Nick would have protested, but already they were ushering him into the sitting room. If it had been a room lacking completely in character or taste, the memories might not have been so poignant. However, unlike one of those soulless plastic and vinyl coops built by the big chains and so often offered to travellers under the misnomer of "inns," this room was furnished with antique furniture, oil-paintings and flowers. The memories were as fresh as those flowers, but not as pleasing.

The telephone was ringing as they entered, and Larry Fry seized it immediately, while Nick stood in the centre of the room. It had been two years since last he stood here, but it seemed as many days, so clear was the memory.

"The Harbour Master has given permission for *Golden Adventurer* to enter harbour." Larry Fry grinned triumphantly at Nick, and gave him the thumbs-up signal.

Nick nodded, the news was an anti-climax after the draining endeavours of the last weeks. Nick walked through to the bedroom. The wallpaper was a quietly tasteful floral design with matching curtains.

From the four-poster bed, Nick remembered, you could look out over the lawns. He remembered Chantelle sitting under that canopy, with a gossamer-sheer bed-robe over her creamy shoulders, eating thin strips of marmaladed toast and then delicately and carefully licking each slim tapered finger with a pink pointed tongue.

Nicholas had come out to negotiate the transportation of South African coal from Richards Bay, and iron ore from Saldanha Bay to Japan. He had insisted that Chantelle accompany him. Perhaps he had the premonition of imminent loss, but he had overridden her objections.

"But Africa is such a primitive place, Nicky, they have things that bite."

And she had in the end gone with him. He had been rewarded with four days of rare happiness. The last four days ever, for though he did not then even suspect it, he was already sharing her bed and body with Duncan Alexander. He had never tired in thirteen years of that lovely smooth creamy body; rather, he had delighted in its slow luscious ripening into full womanhood, believing without question that it belonged to him.

Chantelle was one of those unusual women who grew more beautiful with time; it had always been one of his pleasures to watch her enter a room filled with other internationally acclaimed beauties, and see them pale beside his wife. And suddenly, for no good reason, he imagined Samantha Silver beside Chantelle—the girl's coltish grace would be transmuted to gawkiness beside Chantelle's poise, her manner as gauche as a schoolgirl's beside Chantelle's mature control, a warm lovable little bunny beside the sleekly beautiful mink—

"Mr. Berg, London." Larry Fry called from the sitting room interrupting him, and with relief Nick picked up the telephone. "Just keep going forward," he reminded himself, and before he spoke, he thought again of the two women, and wondered suddenly how much that thick rich golden mane of Samantha's hair would pale beside Chantelle's lustrous sable, and just how much of the mother-of-pearl glow would fade from that young, clear skin—

"Berg," he said abruptly into the telephone.

"Mr. Berg, good morning. Will you speak to Mr. Duncan Alexander of Christy Marine?"

Nick was silent for five full seconds. He needed that long to adjust to the name, but Duncan Alexander was the natural extension of his previous thoughts. In the silence he heard the banging of doors and rising clamour of voices, as the journalists converged on the liquor cabinet next door.

"Mr. Berg, are you there?"

"Yes," he said, and his voice was steady and cool. "Put him on."

"Nicholas, my dear fellow." The voice was glossy as satin, slow as honey, Eton and King's College, a hundred thousand pound accent, impossible to imitate, not quite foppish nor indolent, razor steel in a scabbard of velvet encrusted with golden filigree and precious stones—and Nicholas had seen the steel bared. "It seems that it is impossible to hold a good man down."

"But you tried, young Duncan," Nick answered lightly. "Don't feel bad about it, indeed you tried."

"Come, Nicholas. Life is too short for recriminations. This is a new deck of cards, we start equal again." Duncan chuckled softly. "At least be gracious enough to accept my congratulations."

"Accepted," Nicholas agreed. "Now what do we talk about?"

"Is *Golden Adventurer* in dock yet?"

"She has been cleared to enter. She'll be tied up within twenty-four hours—and you'd better have your cheque book ready."

"I hoped that we might avoid going up before the Committee. There has been too much bitterness already. Let's try and keep it in the family, Nicholas."

"The family?"

"Christy Marine is the family—you, Chantelle, old Arthur Christy—and Peter."

It was the very dirtiest form of fighting, and Nick found suddenly that he was shaking like a man in fever and that his fist around the receiver was white with the force of his grip. It was the mention of his son that had affected him so.

"I'm not in that family any more."

"In a way you will always be part of it. It is as much your achievement as any man's, and your son—"

Nick cut across him brusquely, his voice gravelly.

"You and Chantelle made me a stranger. Now treat me like one."

"Nicholas—"

"Ocean Salvage as main contractor for the recovery of *Golden Adventurer* is open to an offer."

"Nicholas—"

"Make an offer."

"As bluntly as that?"

"I'm waiting."

"Well now. My Board has considered the whole operation in depth, and I am empowered to make you an outright settlement of three-quarters of a million dollars."

Nick's tone did not alter. "We have been set down for a hearing at Lloyd's on the 27th of next month."

"Nicholas, the offer is negotiable within reasonable limits—"

"You are speaking a foreign language," Nick cut him off. "We are so far apart that we are wasting each other's time."

"Nicholas, I know how you feel about Christy Marine, you know the company is underwriting its own—"

"Now you are really wasting my time."

"Nicholas, it's not a third party, it's not some big insurance consortium, it's Christy Marine—"

He used his name again, though it scalded his tongue.

"Duncan, you're breaking my heart. I'll see you on the 27th of next month, at the arbitration court." He dropped the receiver on to its bracket, and moved across to the mirror, swiftly combing his hair and composing his features, startled to see how hard and bleak his expression was, and how fierce his eyes.

However, when he went through to the lounge of the suite, he was relaxed and urbane and smiling.

"All right, ladies and gentlemen. I'm all yours," and one of the ladies of the press, blonde, pretty and not yet thirty but with eyes as old as life itself, took another sip of her whisky as she studied him, then murmured huskily, "I wouldn't mind at all, duckie."

G olden Adventurer stood tall and very beautiful against the wharf of Cape Town harbour, waiting her turn to go into the dry dock.

Globe Engineering, the contractors who had been appointed to repair her, had signed for her and legally taken over responsibility from Warlock's First Officer. But David Allen still felt an immense proprietary pride in her.

From Warlock's navigation bridge, he could look across the main harbour basin and see the tall, snowy superstructure glistening in the bright hot summer sunshine, towering as high as the giraffe-necked steel wharf cranes; and in gloating self-indulgence, David dwelt on a picture of the liner, wreathed in snow, half obscured by driving sleet and sea fume, staggering in the mountainous black seas off Antarctica. It gave him a solid feeling of achievement, and he thrust his hands deeply into his pockets and whistled softly to himself, smiling and watching the liner.

The Trog thrust his wrinkled head from the radio room.

"There's a call for you on the landline," he said, and David picked up the handset.

"David?"

"Yessir." He drew himself to his full height as he recognized Nicholas Berg's voice.

"Are you ready for sea?"

David gulped, then glanced at the bulkhead clock. "We discharged tow an hour and ten minutes ago."

"Yes, I know. How soon?"

David was tempted to lie, estimate short, and then fake it for the extra time he needed. Instinct warned him against lying deliberately to Nicholas Berg.

"Twelve hours," he said.

"It's an oil-rig tow, Rio to the North Sea, a semi-submersible rig."

"Yessir," David adjusted quickly, thank God he had not yet let any of his crew ashore. He had arranged for bunkering at 1300 hours. He could make it. "When are you coming aboard, sir?"

"I'm not," said Nick. "You're the new Master. I'm leaving for London on the five o'clock flight. I won't even get down to shout at you. She's all yours, David."

"Thank you, sir," David stuttered, feeling himself flush hot scarlet.

"Bach Wackie will telex you full details of the tow at sea, and you and I will work out your own contract later. But I want you running at top economic power for Rio by dawn tomorrow."

"Yessir."

"I've watched you carefully, David." Nick's voice changed, becoming personal, warmer. "You're a damn good tug-man. Just keep telling yourself that."

"Thank you, Mr. Berg."

S amantha had spent half the afternoon helping with the arrangements for taking off the remaining passengers from *Golden Adventurer* and embarking them in the waiting fleet of tourist buses which would distribute them to hotels throughout the city while they waited for the London charter flight.

It had been a sad occasion, farewell to many who had become friends, and remembering those who had not come back from Cape Alarm with them—Ken, who might have been her lover, and the crew of raft Number 16 who had been her special charges.

Once the final bus had left, with the occupants waving for the last time to Samantha, "Take care, honey!" "You come and visit with us now, you hear?" she was as lonely and forlorn as the silent ship. She stood for a long time staring up the liner's high side, examining the damage where sea and ice had battered her—then she turned and picked her way dejectedly along the edge of the basin, ignoring the occasional whistle or ribald invitation from the fishermen and crew members of the freighters on their moorings.

Warlock seemed as welcoming as home, rakish and gallant, wearing her new scars with high panache, already thrusting and impatient at the restraint of her mooring lines. And then Samantha remembered that

Nicholas Berg was no longer aboard her, and her spirits sagged again.

"God," Tim Graham met her at the gangplank. "I'm glad you got back. I didn't know what to do with your gear."

"What do you mean?" Samantha demanded. "Are you throwing me off the ship?"

"Unless you want to come with us to Rio." He thought about that for a moment, and then he grinned, "Hey, that's not a bad idea, how about it, old girl? Rio in Carnival time, you and me—"

"Don't get carried away, Timothy," she warned him. "Why Rio?"

"The Captain—"

"Captain Berg?"

"No, David Allen, he's the new skipper," and she lost interest.

"When are you sailing?"

"Midnight."

"I'd best go pack up." She left him on the quarterdeck, and Angel pounced on her as she passed the galley.

"Where have you been?" He was in a flutter, all wrists and tossing hair, "I've been beside myself, darling."

"What is it, Angel?"

"It's probably too late already."

"What is it?" She caught his urgency. "Tell me."

"He's still in town."

"Who?" But she knew, they spoke of only one person in these emotional terms.

"Don't be dense, luv. Your crumpet." She hated it when he referred to Nick like that, but now she let him go on. "But he won't be very much longer. His plane leaves at five o'clock, he is making the local flight to Johannesburg, and connecting there for London."

She stared at him.

"Well what are you waiting for?" Angel keened. "It's almost four o'clock now, and it will take you at least half an hour to reach the airport."

She did not move. "But, Angel," she almost wrung her hands in anguish, "but what do I do when I get there?"

Angel shook his head and twinkled his diamonds in exasperation. "Sweet merciful heavens, duckie." Then he sighed. "When I was a boy I had two guinea pigs, and they also refused to get it on. I think they were retarded, or something. I tried everything, even hormones, but neither of them survived the shots. Alas, their love was never consummated—"

"Be serious, Angel."

"You could hold him down while I give him a hormone shot—"

"I hate you, Angel." She had to laugh, even in her anxiety.

"Dearie, every night for the past month you have tried to set him on fire with your dulcet silvery voice—and we haven't even passed 'GO' and collected our first $200—"

"I know, Angel. I know."

"It seems to me, sweetie, that it's time now to cut out the jawing and to ignite him with that magic little tinderbox of yours."

"You mean right there in the departure lounge of the airport?" She clapped her hands with delight, then struck a lascivious pose. "I'm Sam—fly me!"

"Hop, poppet there is a taxi on the wharf—he's been waiting an hour, with his meter running."

There is no first-class lounge in Cape Town's DF Malan Airport, so Nicholas sat in the snake-pit, amongst the distraught mothers and their whining, sticky offspring, the harassed tourists loaded like camels with souvenirs and the florid-faced commercial travellers, but he was alone in a multitude; with unconscious deference they allowed him a little circle of privacy and he used the Louis Vuitton briefcase on his knee as a desk.

It occurred to him suddenly how dramatically the balance had swung in the last mere forty days, since he had recognized his wave peaking, but had almost not been able to find the strength for it.

A shadow passed across his eyes, and the little creased crow's foot appeared between them as he remembered the physical and emotional effort that it had taken to make the "Go" decision on *Golden Adventurer*, and he shivered slightly in fear of what might have happened if he had not gone. He would have missed his wave, and there would never have been another.

With a small firm movement of his head, he pushed that memory of fear behind him. He had caught his wave, and he was riding high and fast. Now it seemed that the fates were intent on smothering him with largesse: the oil-rig for *Warlock*, Rio to the Bravo Sierra field off

Norway—then a back-to-back tow from the North Sea through Suez to the new South Australian field, would keep *Warlock* fully employed for the next six months. That was not all, the threatening dockyard strike at Construction Navale Atlantique had been smoothed over and the delivery date for the new tug had come forward by two months. At midnight the night before, a telephone call from Bach Wackie had awakened him to let him know Kuwait and Qatar were now also studying the iceberg-to-water project with a view to commissioning similar schemes; he would have to build himself another two vessels if they decided to go.

"All I need now is to hear that I have won the football pools," he thought, and turned his head, started and caught his breath with a hiss, as though he had been punched in the ribs.

She stood by the automatic doors, and the wind had caught her hair and torn it loose from its thick twisted knot so that fine gold tendrils floated down on to her cheeks—cheeks that were flushed as though she had run fast, and her chest heaved so that she held one hand upon it, fingers spread like a star between those fine pointed breasts. She was poised like a forest animal that has scented the leopard, fearful, tremulous, but not yet certain in which direction to run. Her agitation was so apparent that he thrust aside his briefcase and stood up.

She saw him instantly, and her face lit with an expression of such unutterable joy, that he was halted in his intention of going towards her, while she in contrast wheeled and started to run towards him.

She collided with a portly, sweating tourist, nearly flooring him and shaking loose a rain of carved native curios and anonymous packets which clattered to the floor around him like ripe fruit.

He snarled angrily, then his expression changed as he looked at her. "Sorry!" She stooped swiftly, picked up a packet, thrust it into his arms, hit him with her smile, and left him beaming bemusedly after her.

However, now she was more restrained, her precipitous rush calmed to that long-legged, thrusting, hip-swinging walk of hers, and the smile was a little uncertain as she pushed vainly at the loose streamers of golden hair, trying to tuck them up into the twisted rope on top of her head.

"I thought I'd missed you." She stopped a little in front of him.

"Is something wrong?" he asked quickly, still alarmed by her behaviour.

"Oh no," she assured him hurriedly. "Not any more," and suddenly she was awkward and coltish again. "I thought," her voice hushed, "it was just that I thought I'd missed you." And her eyes slid away from him. "You didn't say goodbye—"

"I thought it was better that way." And now her eyes flew back to his face, sparkling with green fire.

"Why?" she demanded, and he had no answer to give her.

"I didn't want to—" How could he say it to her, without making the kind of statement that would embarrass them both?

Above them, the public address system squawked into life.

"South African Airways announces the departure of their Airbus flight 235 to Johannesburg. Will passengers please board at Gate Number Two."

She had run out of time. "I'm Sam—Fly Me! Please!" she thought, and felt the urge to giggle, but instead she said:

"Nicholas, tomorrow you'll be in London—in mid-winter."

"It's a sobering thought," he agreed, and for the first time smiled; his smile closed like a fist around her heart and her legs felt suddenly weak.

"Tomorrow or at least the day after, I'll be riding the long sea at Cape St. Francis," she said. They had spoken of that, on those enchanted nights. He had told her how he had first ridden the surf at Waikiki Beach long ago before the sport had become a craze, and it had been part of their shared experience, part of their love of the sea, drawing them closer together.

"I hope the surf's up for you," he said. Cape St. Francis was three hundred and fifty miles north of Cape Town, simply another beach and headland in a shoreline that stretched in unbroken splendour for six thousand miles, and yet it was unique in all the world. The young and the young-at-heart came in almost religious pilgrimage to ride the long sea at Cape St. Francis. They came from Hawaii and California, from Tahiti and Queensland, for there was no other wave quite like it.

At the departure gate, the shuffling queue was shortening, and Nick stooped to pick up his briefcase, but she reached out and laid her hand on his biceps, and he froze.

It was the first time she had deliberately touched him, and the shock of it spread through his body like ripples on a quiet lake. All the emotions and passions which he had so strenuously denied came tumbling back upon him, and it seemed that their strength had grown a hundred-fold while under restraint. He ached for her, with a deep, yearning, wanting ache.

"Come with me, Nicholas," she whispered, and his own throat closed so he could not answer. He stared at her, and already the ground hostesses at the gate were peering around irritably for their missing passenger.

She had to convince him and she shook his arm urgently, startled at the hardness of the muscle under her fingers.

"Nicholas, I really want," she began, intending to finish, "you to," but her tongue played a Freudian trick on her, and she said, "I really want you."

"Oh God," she thought, as she heard herself say it, "I sound like a whore," and in panic she corrected herself.

"I really want you to," and she flushed, the blood came up from her neck, dark under the peach of her tan so the freckles glowed on her skin like flakes of gold-dust.

"Which one is it?" he asked, and then smiled again.

"There isn't time to argue." She stamped her foot, feigning impatience, hiding her confusion, then added, "Damn you!" for no good reason.

"Who is arguing?" he asked quietly, and suddenly, like magic, she was in his arms, trying to burrow herself deeper and deeper into his embrace, trying to draw all the man smell of him into her lungs, amazed at the softness and warmth of his mouth and the hard rasp of new beard on his chin and cheek, making little soft mewing sounds of comfort deep in her throat as she clung to him.

"Passenger Berg. Will passenger Berg please report to the departure gate," chanted the public address.

"They're calling me," Nicholas murmured.

"They can go right to the back of the queue," she mumbled into his lips.

Sunlight was made for Samantha. She wore it like a cloak that had been woven especially for her. She wore it in her hair, sparkling like jewellery, she used it to paint her face and body in lustrous shades of burnt honey and polished amber, she wore it glowing in golden freckles on her cheeks and nose.

She moved in sunlight with wondrous grace, barefooted in the white sand, so that her hips and buttocks roistered brazenly under the thin green stuff of her bikini.

She sprawled in the sunlight like a sleeping cat, offering her face and her naked belly to it, so he felt that if he laid his hands against her throat he would feel her purr deep inside her chest.

She ran in the sunlight, light as a gull in flight, along the hard wet sand at the water's edge, and he ran beside her, tirelessly, mile after mile, the two of them alone in a world of green sea and sun and tall pale hot skies. The beach curved away in both directions to the limit of the eye, smooth and white as the snows of Antarctica, devoid of human life or the scars of man's petty endeavours, and she laughed beside him in the sunlight, holding his hand as they ran together.

They found a deep, clear rock pool in a far and secret place. The sunlight off the water dappled her body, exploding silently upon it like the reflections of light from a gigantic diamond, as she cast aside the two green wisps of her bikini, let down the thick rope of her hair and stepped into the pool, turning, knee-deep, to look back at him. Her hair hung almost to her waist, springing and thick and trying to curl in the salt and wind, it cloaked her shoulders and her breasts peeped through the thick curtains of it. Her breasts, untouched by the sun, were rich as cream and tipped in rose, so big and full and exuberant that he wondered that he had ever thought her a child; they bounced and swung as she moved, and she pulled back her shoulders and laughed at him shamelessly when she saw the direction of his eyes.

She turned back to the pool and her buttocks were white with the pinkish sheen of a deep-sea pearl, round and tight and deeply divided, and, as she bent forward to dive, a tiny twist of copper gold curls peeped briefly and coyly from the wedge where the deep cleft split into her tanned smooth thighs.

Through the cool water, her body was warm as bread fresh from the oven, cold and heat together, and when he told her this, she entwined her arms around his neck.

"I'm Sam the baked Alaska, eat me!" she laughed, and the droplets clung to her eyelashes like diamond chips in the sunlight.

Even in the presence of others, they walked alone; for them, nobody else really existed. Among those who had come from all over the world to ride the long sea at Cape St. Francis were many who knew Samantha, from Florida and California, from Australia and Hawaii, where her field trips and her preoccupation with the sea and the life of the sea had taken her.

"Hey, Sam!" they shouted, dropping their boards in the sand and running to her, tall muscular men, burned dark as chestnuts in the sun. She smiled at them vaguely, holding Nicholas' hand a little tighter, and replied to their chatter absentmindedly, drifting away at the first opportunity.

"Who was that?"

"It's terrible, but I can't remember—I'm not even sure where I met him or when." And it was true, she could concentrate on nothing but Nicholas, and the others sensed it swiftly and left them alone.

Nicholas had not been in the sun for over a year, his body was the colour of old ivory, in sharp contrast to the thick dark body hair which covered his chest and belly. At the end of that first day in the sun, the ivory colour had turned to a dull angry red.

"You'll suffer," she told him, but the next morning his body and limbs had gone the colour of mahogany and she drew back the sheets and marvelled at it, touching him exploringly with the tip of her fingers.

"I'm lucky, I've got a hide like a buffalo," he told her.

Each day he turned darker, until he was the weathered bronze of an American Indian, and his high cheekbones heightened the resemblance.

"You must have Indian blood," she told him, tracing his nose with her fingertip.

"I only know two generations back," he smiled at her. "I've always been terrified to look further than that."

She sat over him, cross-legged in the big bed and touched him, exploring him with her hands, touching his lips and the lobes of his ears, smoothing the thick dark curve of his eyebrows, the little black mole on his cheek, and exclaiming at each new discovery.

She touched him when they walked, reaching for his hand, pressing her hip against him when they stood, on the beach sitting between his spread knees and leaning back against his chest, her head tucked into his shoulder—it was as if she needed constant physical assurance of his presence.

When they sat astride their boards, waiting far out beyond the three-mile reef for the set of the wave, she reached across to touch his shoulder, balancing the board under her like a skilled horsewoman, the two of them close and spiritually isolated from the loose assembly of thirty or forty surf-riders strung out along the line of the long set.

This far out, the shore was a low dark green rind, above the shaded green and limpid blues of the water. In the blue distance, the mountains were blue on the blue of the sky and above them, the thunderheads piled dazzling silver, tall and arrogant enough to dwarf the very earth.

"This must be the most beautiful land in the world," she said, moving her board so that her knee lay against his thigh.

"Because you are here," he told her.

Under them, the green water breathed like a living thing, rising and falling, the swells long and glassy, sliding away towards the land.

Growing impatient, one of the inexperienced riders would move to catch a bad swell, kneeling on the board and paddling with both hands, coming up unsteadily on to his feet and then toppling and falling as the water left him, and the taunts and friendly catcalls of his peers greeted him as he surfaced, grinning sheepishly, and crawled back on to his board.

Then the ripple of excitement, and a voice calling, "A three set!" the boards quickly rearranging themselves, sculled by cupped bare hands, spacing out for running room, the riders peering back eagerly over their dark burned shoulders, laughing and kidding each other as the wave set bumped up on the horizon, still four miles out at sea, but big enough so that they could count the individual swells that made up the set.

Running at fifty miles an hour, the swells took nearly five minutes, from the moment when they were sighted, to reach the line, and during that time Samantha had a little ritual of preparation. First, she hoisted the bottom of her bikini which had usually slipped down to expose a pair of dimples and a little of the deep cleft of her buttocks, then she tightened her top hamper, pulling open the brassière of her costume and cupping each breast in turn, settling it firmly in its sheath of thin green cloth, grinning at Nick as she did it.

"You're not supposed to watch."

"I know, it's bad for my heart."

Then she plucked out a pair of hairpins and held them in her mouth as she twisted the wrist-thick plait of hair tighter until it hung down between her shoulder blades and pinned back the wisps over her ears.

"All set?" he called, and she nodded and answered,

"Ride three?"

The third wave in the set was traditionally the big one, and they let the first one swing them high and drop them again into its trough. Half the other riders were up and away, only their heads still visible above the peak of the wave, the land obscured by the moving wall of water.

The second wave came through, bigger, more powerful, but swooping up and over the crest and most of the other riders went on it, two or three tumbling on the steep front of water, losing their boards, dragged under as the ankle lines came up taut.

"Here we go!" exulted Samantha, and three came rustling, green and peaking, and in the transparent wall of water four big bottle-nosed porpoises were framed, in perfect motion, racing in the wave, pumping their flat delta-shaped tails and grinning that fixed porpoise grin of delight.

"Oh look!" sang Samantha. "Just look at them, Nicholas!"

Then the wave was upon them and they sculled frantically, weight high on the board, the heart-stopping moment when it seemed the water would sweep away and leave them, then suddenly the boards coming alive under them and starting to run, tipping steeply forward, with the hiss of the waxed fibreglass through the water.

Then they were both up and laughing in the sunlight, dancing the intricate steps that balanced and controlled the boards, lifted high on the crest, so they could see the sweep of the beach three miles ahead, and the ranks of other riders on the twin waves that had gone before them.

One of the porpoises frolicked with them on the racing crest, ducking under the flying boards, turning on its side to grin up at Samantha, so she stooped and stretched out a hand to touch him, lost her balance, and almost fell while the porpoise grinned at her mischievously and flipped away to rise fin up on her far side.

Now, out on their right hand, the wave was feeling the reef and starting to curl over on itself, the crest arching forwards, holding that lovely shape for long moments, then slowly collapsing.

"Go left," Nick called urgently to her, and they kicked the boards around and danced up on to the stubby prows, bending at the knees to ride the hurtling craft, their speed rocketing as they cut across the green face of the wave, but behind them the arching wave spread rapidly towards them, faster than they could run before it.

Now at their left shoulders, the water formed a steep vertical wall, and, glancing at it, Samantha found the porpoise swimming head-high beside her, his great tail pumping powerfully, and she was afraid, for the majesty and strength of that wave belittled her.

"Nicholas!" she screamed, and the wave fanned out over her head, arcing across the sky, cutting out the sunlight, and now they flew down a long, perfectly rounded tunnel of roaring water. The sides were smooth as blown glass, and the light was green and luminous and weird as though they sped through a deep submarine cavern, only ahead of them was the perfect round opening at the mouth of the tunnel—while behind her, close behind her, the tunnel was collapsing in a furious thunder of murderous white water; and she was as terrified and as exultant as she had ever been in her life.

He yelled at her, "We must beat the curl," and his voice was far away and almost lost in the roar of water, but obediently she went forward on her board until all her bare toes were curled over the leading edge.

For long moments they held their own, then slowly they began to gain, and at last they shot out through the open mouth of the tunnel into the sunlight again, and she laughed wildly, still high on the exultation of fresh terror.

Then they were past the reef and the wave firmed up, leaving the white water like lace on the surface far behind.

"Let's go right!" Samantha sang out to stay within the good structure of the wave, and they turned and went back, swinging across the steep face. The splatter of flung water sparkled on her belly and thighs, and the plait of her hair stood out behind her head like the tail of an angry lioness, her arms were extended and her hands held open, unconsciously making the delicate finger gestures of a Balinese temple dancer as she balanced; and miraculously the porpoise swam, fin up, beside her, following like a trained dog.

Then at last, the wave felt the beach and ran berserk, tumbling wildly upon itself, booming angrily, and churning the sand like gruel, and they kicked out of the wave, falling back over the crest and dropping into the sea beside the bobbing boards, laughing and panting at each other with the excitement and terror and the joy of it.

Samantha was a sea-creature with a huge appetite for the fruits of the sea, cracking open the crayfish legs in her fingers and sucking the white sticks of flesh into her mouth with a noisy sensuality, while her lips were polished with butter sauce, not taking her eyes from his face as she ate.

Samantha in the candlelight gulping those huge Knysna oysters, and then slurping the juice out of the shells.

"You're talking with your mouth full."

"It's just that I've still got so much to tell you," she explained.

Samantha was laughter, laughter in fifty different tones and intensities, from the sleepy morning chortle when she awoke and found him beside her, to the wild laughter yelled from the crest of a racing wave.

Samantha was loving. With a face of thundering innocence and the virginal, guileless green eyes of a child, she combined hands and a mouth whose wiles and wicked cunning left Nick stunned and disbelieving.

"The reason I ran away without a word was that I did not want to have your ravishment and violation on my conscience," he shook his head at her disbelievingly.

"I wrote my Ph.D. thesis in those subjects," she told him blithely, using her forefinger to twist spit-curls in his sweat-dampened chest hairs. "And what's more, buster, that was just the introductory offer—now we sign you up for a full course of treatment."

Her delight in his body was endless, she must touch and examine every inch of it, exclaiming and revelling in it without a trace of self-consciousness, holding his hand in her lap and bending her head studiously over it, tracing the lines of his palm with her fingernail.

"You are going to meet a beautiful wanton blonde, give her fifteen babies and live to be a hundred and fifty."

She touched the little chiselled lines around his eyes and at the corners of his mouth with the tip of her tongue, leaving cool damp smears of saliva on his skin.

"I always wanted a real craggy man all for myself."

Then, when her examination became more intimate and clinical and he demurred, she told him severely, "Hold still, this is a private thing between me and himself."

Then a little later.

"Oh wow! He's real poison!"

"Poison?" he demanded, his manhood denigrated.

"Poison," she sighed. "Because he just slays me!"

In fairness, she offered herself for his touch and scrutiny, guiding his hands, displaying herself eagerly.

"Look, touch, it's yours—all yours," wanting his approval, not able to give him sufficient to satisfy her own need to give. "Do you like it, Nicholas? Is this good for you? Is there anything else you want, Nicholas, anything at all that I can give you?"

And when he told her how beautiful she was, when he told her how much he wanted her, when he touched and marvelled over the gifts she brought to him, she glowed and stretched and purred like a great golden cat so that when he learned that the zodiacal sign of her birthday was Leo, he was not at all surprised.

Samantha was loving in the early slippery grey-pearl light of dawn, soft sleepy loving, with small gasps and murmurs and chuckles of deep contentment.

Samantha was loving in the sunlight, spread like a beautiful starfish in the fierce reflected sunlight of the sculptured dunes. The sand coated her body like crystals of sugar, and their cries rose together, high and ecstatic as those of the curious seagulls that floated above them on motionless white wings.

Samantha was loving in the green cool water, their two heads bobbing beyond the first line of breakers, his toes only just touching the sandy bottom and she twined about him like sea kelp about a submerged rock, clutching both their swimsuits in one hand and gurgling merrily.

"What's good enough for a lady blue whale is good enough for Samantha Silver! Thar blows Moby Dick!"

And Samantha was loving in the night, with her hair brushed out carefully and spread over him, lustrous and fragrant, a canopy of gold in the lamplight, and she kneeling astride him in almost religious awe, like a temple maid making the sacrifice.

But more than anything else, Samantha was vibrant, bursting life—and youth eternal.

Through her, Nicholas recaptured those emotions which he had believed long atrophied by cynicism and the pragmatism of living. He shared her childlike delight in the small wonders of nature, the flight of a gull, the presence of the porpoise, the discovery of the perfect translucent fan of papery nautilus shell washed up on the white sand with the rare tentacled creature still alive within the convoluted interior.

He shared her outrage when even those remote and lonely beaches were invaded by an oil slick, tank washings from a VLCC out on the Agulhas current, and the filthy clinging globules of spilled crude oil stuck to the soles of their feet, smeared the rocks and smothered the carcasses of the jackass penguins they found at the water's edge.

Samantha was life itself, just to touch the warmth of her and to drink the sound of her laughter was to be rejuvenated. To walk beside her was to feel vital and strong.

Strong enough for the long days in the sea and sun, strong enough to dance to the loud wild music half the night, and then strong enough to lift her when she faltered and carry her down to their bungalow above the beach, she in his arms like a sleepy child, her skin tingling with the memory of the sun, her muscles aching deliciously with fatigue, and her belly crammed with rich food.

"Oh Nicholas, Nicholas—I'm so happy I want to cry."

Then Larry Fry arrived; he arrived on a cloud of indignation, red-faced and accusing as a cuckolded husband.

"Two weeks," he blared. "London and Bermuda and St. Nazaire have been driving me mad for two weeks!" And he brandished a sheath of telex flimsies that looked like the galley proofs for the *Encyclopaedia Britannica*.

"Nobody knew what had happened to you. You just disappeared." He ordered a large gin and tonic from the white-jacketed bartender and sank wearily on to the stool beside Nick. "You nearly cost me my job, Mr. Berg, and that's the truth. You'd have thought I'd bumped you off personally and dumped your body in the bay. I had to hire a private detective to check every hotel register in the country." He took a long, soothing draught of the gin.

At that moment, Samantha drifted into the cocktail lounge. She wore a loose, floating dress the same green as her eyes, and a respectful hush fell on the pre-luncheon drinkers as they watched her cross the room. Larry Fry forgot his indignation and gaped at her, his bald scorched head growing shining under a thin film of perspiration.

"Godstrewth," he muttered. "I'd rather feel that, than feel sick." And then his admiration turned to consternation when she came directly to Nicholas, laid her hand on his shoulder and in full view of the entire room kissed him lingeringly on the mouth.

There was a soft collective sigh from the watchers and Larry Fry knocked over his gin.

W e must go now, today," Samantha decided. "We mustn't stay even another hour, Nicholas, or we will spoil it. It was perfect, but now we must go."

Nicholas understood. Like him she had the compulsion to keep moving forward. Within the hour, he had chartered a twin-engined Beechcraft Baron. It picked them up at the little earth strip near the hotel and put them down at Johannesburg's Jan Smuts Airport an hour before the departure of the UTA flight for Paris.

"I always rode in the back of the bus before," said Samantha, as she looked around the first-class cabin appraisingly. "Is it true that up this end you can eat and drink as much as you like, for free?"

"Yes." Then Nick added hastily, "But you don't have to take that as a personal challenge." Nicholas had come to stand in awe of Samantha's appetites.

They stayed overnight at the Georges V in Paris and caught the mid-morning TAT flight down to Nantes, the nearest airfield to the shipyards at St. Nazaire, and Jules Levoisin was there to meet them at the Château Bougon field.

"Nicholas!" he shouted joyfully, and stood on tiptoe to buss both his cheeks, enveloping him in a fragrant cloud of eau de Cologne and pomade. "You are a pirate, Nicholas, you stole that ship from under my nose. I hate you." He held Nicholas at arm's length. "I warned you not to take the job, didn't I?"

"You did, Jules, you did."

"So why do you make a fool of me?" he demanded, and twirled his moustaches. He was wearing expensive cashmere and an Yves St. Laurent necktie; ashore, Jules was always the dandy.

"Jules, I am going to buy lunch for you at La Rôtisserie," Nicholas promised.

"I forgive you," said Jules, it was one of his favourite eating-places—but at that moment Jules became aware that Nicholas was not travelling alone.

He stood back, took one long look at Samantha and it seemed that tri-colours unfurled around him and brass bands burst into the opening bars of "La Marseillaise." For if dalliance was the national sport, Jules Lev-oisin considered himself veteran champion of all France.

He bowed over her hand, and tickled the back of it with his still-black moustache. Then he told Nicholas, "She is too good for you, *mon petit*, I am going to take her away from you."

"The same way you did *Golden Adventurer?*" Nick asked innocently.

Jules had his ancient Citroën in the car park. It was lovingly waxed and fitted with shiny gewgaws and dangling mascots. He handed Saman-tha into the front seat as though it was a Rolls Camargue.

"He's beautiful," she whispered, as he scampered around to the dri-ver's door.

Jules could not devote attention to both the road ahead and to Saman-tha, so he concentrated solely upon her, without deviating from the Cit-roën's top speed, only occasionally turning to shout, "*Cochon!*" at another driver or jerk his fist at them with the second finger pointed stiffly upwards in ribald salutation.

"Jules' great-grandfather charged with the Emperor's cavalry at Qua-tre Bras," Nick explained. "He is a man without fear."

"You will enjoy La Rôtisserie," Jules told Samantha. "I can only af-ford to eat there when I find somebody rich who wishes a favour of me."

"How do you know I want a favour?" Nick asked from the back seat, clinging to the door-handle.

"Three telegrams, a telephone call from Bermuda—another from Jo-hannesburg," Jules chuckled fruitily and winked at Samantha. "You think I believe Nicholas Berg wants to discuss old times? You think I be-lieve he feels so deeply for his old friend, who taught him everything he knows? A man who treated him like a son, and whom he blatantly robbed—" Jules sped across the Loire bridge and plunged into that tan-gled web of narrow one-way streets and teeming traffic which is Nantes; a way opened for him miraculously.

In the Place Briand, he handed Samantha gallantly from the Citroën, and in the restaurant he puffed out his cheeks and made little anxious clucking and tut-tutting noises, as Nicholas discussed the wine list with the *sommelier*—but he nodded reluctant approval when they settled on a Chablis Moutonne and a Chambertin-Clos-de-Bèze, then he applied himself with equal gusto to the food, the wine and Samantha.

"You can tell a woman who is made for life and love, by the way she eats," and when Samantha made wide lascivious eyes at him over her trout, Nicholas expected him to crow like a cockerel.

Only when the cognac was in front of them, and both he and Nick had lit cheroots, did he demand abruptly:

"So, now, Nicholas, I am in a good mood. Ask me."

"I need a Master for my new tug," said Nick, and Jules veiled his face behind a thick blue curtain of cigar smoke.

They fenced like masters of épée all the way from Nantes to St. Nazaire.

"Those ships you build, Nicholas, are not tugs. They are fancy toys, floating bordellos—all those gimmicks and gadgets—"

"Those gimmicks and gadgets enabled me to deal with Christy Marine while you still hadn't realized that I was within a thousand miles." Jules blew out his cheeks and muttered to himself.

"Twenty-two thousand horsepower, *c'est ridicule!* They are overpowered—"

"I needed every single one of those horses when I pulled *Golden Adventurer* off Cape Alarm."

"Nicholas, do not keep reminding me of that shameful episode." He turned to Samantha. "I am hungry, *ma petite*, and in the next village there is a *pâtisserie*," he sighed and kissed his bunched fingers, "you will adore the pastry."

"Try me," she invited, and Jules had found a soulmate.

"Those fancy propellers—variable pitch—ouf!" Jules spoke through a mouthful of pastry, and there was whipped cream on his moustache.

"I can make twenty-five knots and then slam *Warlock* into reverse thrust and stop her within her own length."

Jules changed pace, and attacked from a new direction.

"You'll never find full employment for two big expensive ships like that."

"I'm going to need four, not two," Nick contradicted him. "We are going to catch icebergs," and Jules forgot to chew, as he listened intently for the next ten minutes. "One of the beauties of the iceberg scheme is that all my ships will be operating right on the tanker lanes, the busiest shipping lanes in all the oceans—"

"Nicholas," Jules shook his head in admiration, "you move too fast for me. I am an old man, old-fashioned—"

"You're not old," Samantha told him firmly. "You're only just in your prime." And Jules threw up both hands theatrically.

"Now you have a pretty girl heaping flattery on my bowed grey head," he looked at Nicholas; "is no trick too deceitful for you?"

It was snowing the next morning, a slow sparse sprinkling from a grey woollen sky, when they drove into St. Nazaire from the little seaside resort of La Baule twenty-five kilometers up the Atlantic coast.

Jules had a small flat in one of the apartment blocks. It was a convenient arrangement, for *La Mouette*, his command, was owned by a Breton company and St. Nazaire was her home port. It was a mere twenty-minute drive before they made out the elegant arch of the suspension bridge which crosses the estuarine mouth of the Loire river at St. Nazaire.

Jules drove through the narrow streets of that area of the docks just below the bridge which comprises the sprawling shipbuilding yard of Construction Navale Atlantique, one of the three largest shipbuilding companies in Europe.

The slipways for the larger vessels, the bulk carriers and naval craft, faced directly on to the wide smooth reach of the river; but the ways for the small vessels backed on to the inner harbour.

So Jules parked the Citroën at the security gates nearest the inner harbour, and they walked through to where Charles Gras was waiting for them in his offices overlooking the inner basin.

"Nicholas, it is good to see you again." Gras was one of Atlantique's top engineers, a tall stooped man with a pale face and lank black hair that fell to his eyebrows, but he had the sharp foxy Parisian features and quick bright eyes that belied the morose unsmiling manner.

He and Nicholas had known each other many years, and they used the familiar "tu" form of address.

Charles Gras changed to heavily accented English when he was introduced to Samantha, and back to French when he asked Nicholas,

"If I know you, you will want to go directly to see your ship now, *n'est-ce pas?*"

Sea Witch stood high on her ways, and although she was an identical twin to *Warlock*, she seemed almost twice her size with her underwater hull exposed. Despite the fact that the superstructure was incomplete and she was painted in the drab oxide red of marine primer, yet it was impossible to disguise the symmetrically functional beauty of her lines.

Jules puffed, and muttered "*Bordello*" and made remarks about "Admiral Berg and his battleship," but he could not hide the gleam in his eye as he strutted about the incomplete navigation bridge, or listened intently as Charles Gras explained the electronic equipment and the other refinements that made the ship so fast, efficient and manoeuvrable.

Nick realized that the two experts should be left alone now to convince each other; it was clear that although this was their first meeting the two of them had established an immediate rapport.

"Come." Nick quietly took Samantha's arm and they stepped carefully around the scaffolding and loose equipment, picking their way through groups of workmen to the upper deck.

The snow had stopped, but a razor of a wind snickered in from the Atlantic. They found a sheltered corner, and Samantha pressed close to Nick, snuggling into the circle of his arm.

High on her ways, *Sea Witch* gave them a sweeping view, through the forest of construction cranes, over the roofs of the warehouses and offices to the river slipways where the keels of the truly big hulls were laid down.

"You spoke about *Golden Dawn*," Nick said. "There she is."

It took some moments for Samantha to realize she was looking at a ship.

"My God," she breathed. "It's so big."

"They don't come bigger," he agreed.

The structure of steel was almost a mile and a half long, three city blocks, and the hull was as tall as a five-storey building, while the navigation tower was another 100 feet higher than that.

Samantha shook her head. "It's beyond belief. It looks like—like a city! It's terrifying to think of that thing afloat."

"That is only the main hull, the tank pods have been constructed in Japan. The last I heard is that they are under tow direct to the Persian Gulf."

Nick stared solemnly across the ship, blinking his eyes against the stinging wind.

"I must have been out of my mind," he whispered, "to dream up a monster like that." But there was a touch of defiant pride in his tone.

"It's so big—beyond imagination," she encouraged him to talk about it. "How big is it?"

"It's not a single vessel," he explained. "No harbour in the world could take a ship that size, it could not even approach the continental United States, for that matter, there is just not enough water to float it."

"Yes?" She loved to listen to him expound his vision, she loved to hear the force and power of his convictions.

"What you're seeing is the carrying platform, the accommodation and the main power source." He held her closer. "On to that, we attach the four tank pods, each one of them capable of carrying a quarter of a million tons of crude oil, each tank almost as large as the biggest ship afloat."

He was still explaining the concept while they sat at lunch, and Charles Gras and Jules Levoisin listened as avidly as she did.

"A single rigid hull of those dimensions would crack and break up in heavy seas," he took the cruet set and used it to demonstrate, "but the four individual pods have been designed so that they can move independently of each other. This gives them the ability to ride and absorb the movement of heavy seas. It is the most important principle of ship construction, a hull must ride the water—not try to oppose it."

Across the table, Charles Gras nodded lugubrious agreement.

"The tank pods hive on to the main hull, and are carried upon it like remora on the body of a shark, not using their own propulsion systems, but relying on the multiple boilers and quadruple screws of the main hull to carry them across the oceans." He pushed the cruet set around the table and they all watched it with fascination. "Then, when it reaches the continental shelf opposite the shore discharge site, the main hull anchors, forty or fifty, even a hundred miles offshore, detaches one or two or all of its pod tanks, and they make those last few miles under their own propulsion. In protected water and in chosen weather conditions, their propulsion systems will handle them safely. Then the empty pod ballasts itself and returns to hook on to the main hull."

As he spoke, Nicholas detached the salt cellar from the cruet and docked it against Samantha's plate. The two Frenchmen were silent, staring at the silver salt cellar, but Samantha watched Nick's face. It was burned dark by the sun now, lean and handsome, and he seemed charged and vital, like a thoroughbred horse in the peak of training, and she was proud of him, proud of the force of his personality that made other men listen when he spoke, proud of the imagination and the courage it took to conceive and then put into operation a project of this magnitude. Even though it were no longer his—yet his had been the vision.

Now Nicholas was talking again. "Civilization is addicted to liquid fossil fuels. Without them, it would be forced into a withdrawal trauma too horrible to contemplate. If then we have to use crude, let's pipe it out of the earth, transport and ship it with all possible precautions to protect ourselves from its side effects—"

"Nicholas," Charles Gras interrupted him abruptly. "When last did you inspect the drawings of *Golden Dawn?*"

Nick paused, taken in full stride and a little off balance. He frowned as he cast back, "I walked out of Christy Marine just over a year ago." And the darkness of those days settled upon him, making his eyes bleak.

"A year ago we had not even been awarded the contract for the construction of *Golden Dawn.*" Charles Gras twisted the stem of his wineglass between his fingers, and thrust out his bottom lip. "The ship you have just described to us is very different from the ship we are building out there."

"In what way, Charles?" Nick's concern was immediate, a father hearing of radical surgery upon his firstborn.

"The concept is the same. The mother vessel and the four tank pods, but—" Charles shrugged, that eloquent Gallic gesture, "it would be easier to show it to you. Immediately after lunch."

"*D'accord,*" Jules Levoisin nodded. "But on the condition that it does not interfere with the further enjoyment of this fine meal." He nudged Nicholas. "If you eat with a scowl on your face, *mon vieux*, you will grow yourself ulcers like a bunch of Loire grapes."

Standing beneath the bulk of *Golden Dawn*, she seemed to reach up into that low grey snow-sky, like a mighty alp of steel. The men working on the giddy heights of her scaffolding were small as insects, and quite unbelievably, as Samantha stared up at them, a little torn streamer of wet grey cloud, coming up the Loire basin from the sea, blew over the ship, obscuring the top of her navigation bridge for a few moments.

"She reaches up to the clouds," said Nick beside her, and the pride was in his voice as he turned back to Charles Gras. "She looks good?" It was a question, not a statement. "She looks like the ship I planned—"

"Come, Nicholas."

The little party picked its way through the chaos of the yard. The squeal of power cranes and the rumble of heavy steel transporters, the electric hissing crackle of the huge automatic running welders combined with the roaring gunfire barrage of the riveters into a cacophony that numbed the senses. The scaffolding and hoist systems formed an almost impenetrable forest about the mountainous hull, and steel and concrete were glistening wet and rimmed with thin clear ice.

It was a long walk through the crowded yard, almost twenty minutes merely to round the tanker's stern—and suddenly Nicholas stopped so abruptly that Samantha collided with him and might have fallen on the icy concrete, but he caught her arm and held her as he stared up at the bulbous stern.

It formed a great overhanging roof like that of a medieval cathedral, so that Nick's head was flung back, and the grip on her arm tightened so fiercely that she protested. He seemed not to hear, but went on staring upwards.

"Yes," Charles Gras nodded, and the lank black hair flopped against his forehead. "That is one difference from the ship you designed."

The propeller was in lustrous ferro-bronze, six-bladed, each shaped with the beauty and symmetry of a butterfly's wing, but so enormous as to make the comparison laughable. It was so big that not even the bulk of *Golden Dawn*'s own hull could dwarf it, each separate blade was longer and broader than the full wingspan of a jumbo-jet airliner, a gargantuan sculpture in gleaming metal.

"One!" whispered Nick. "One only."

"Yes," Charles Gras agreed. "Not four—but one propeller only. Also, Nicholas, it is fixed pitch."

They were all silent as they rode up in the cage of the hoist. The hoist ran up the outside of the hull to the level of the main deck, and though the wind searched for them remorselessly through the open mesh of the cage, it was not the cold that kept them silent.

The engine compartment was an echoing cavern, harshly lit by the overhead floodlights, and they stood high on one of the overhead steel catwalks looking down fifty feet on to the boiler and condensers of the main engine.

Nick stared down for almost five minutes. He asked no questions, made no judgements, but at last he turned to Charles Gras and nodded once curtly.

"All right. I've seen enough," he said, and the engineer led them to the elevator station. Again they rode upwards. It was like being in a modern office block—the polished chrome and wood panelling of the elevator, the carpeted passageways high in the navigation tower along which Charles Gras led them to the Master's suite and unlocked the carved mahogany doorway with a key from his watch chain.

Jules Levoisin looked slowly about the suite and shook his head wonderingly. "Ah, this is the way to live," he breathed. "Nicholas, I absolutely insist that the Master's quarters of *Sea Witch* be decorated like this."

Nick did not smile, but crossed to the view windows that looked forward along the tanker's main deck to her round, blunt, unlovely prow a mile and a quarter away. He stood with his hands clasped behind his back, legs apart, chin thrust out angrily and nobody else spoke while Charles Gras opened the elaborate bar and poured cognac into the crystal brandy balloons. He carried a glass to Nick who turned away from the window.

"Thank you, Charles. I need something to warm the chill in my guts." Nick sipped the cognac and rolled it on his tongue as he looked slowly around the opulent cabin.

It occupied almost half the width of the navigation bridge, and was large enough to house a diplomatic reception. Duncan Alexander had picked a good decorator to do the job, and without the view from the window it might have been an elegant Fifth Avenue New York apartment, or one of those penthouses high on the cliffs above Monte Carlo, overlooking the harbour.

Slowly Nick crossed the thick green carpet, woven with the house device, the entwined letters C and M for Christy Marine, and he stopped before the Degas in its place of honour above the marble fireplace.

He remembered Chantelle's bubbling joy at the purchase of that painting. It was one of Degas' ballet pieces, soft, almost luminous light on the limbs of the dancers, and, remembering the unfailing delight that Chantelle had taken in it during the years, he was amazed that she had allowed it to be used on board one of the company ships, and that it was left here virtually unguarded and vulnerable. That painting was worth a quarter of a million pounds.

He leaned closer to it, and only then did he realize how clever a copy of the original it was. He shook his head in dismissal.

"The owners were advised that the sea air may damage the original,"

Charles Gras shrugged, and spread his hands deprecatingly, "and not many people would know the difference."

That was typical of Duncan Alexander, Nicholas thought savagely. It could only be his idea, the sharp accountant's brain. The conviction that it was possible to fool all of the people all of the time.

Everybody knew that Chantelle owned that work, therefore nobody would doubt its authenticity. That's the way Duncan Alexander would reason it. It could not be Chantelle's idea. She had never been one to accept anything that was sham or dross; it was a measure of the power that he exerted over her, for her to go along with this cheap little fraud.

Nicholas indicated the forgery with his glass and spoke directly to Charles Gras.

"This is a cheat," he spoke quietly, his anger contained and controlled, "but it is harmless." Now he turned away from it and, with a wider gesture that embraced the whole ship, went on, "But this other cheat, this enormous fraud," he paused to control the metallic edge that had entered his tone, going on quietly again, "this is a vicious, murderous gamble he is taking. He has bastardized the entire concept of the scheme. One propeller instead of four—it cannot manoeuvre a hull of these dimensions with safety in any hazardous situation, it cannot deliver sufficient thrust to avoid collision, to fight her off a lee shore, to handle heavy seas." Nick stopped, and his voice dropped even lower, yet somehow it was more compelling. "This ship cannot, by all moral and natural laws, he operated on a single boiler. My design called for eight separate boilers and condensers, the standard set for the old White Star and Cunard Lines. But Duncan Alexander has installed a single boiler system. There is no back-up, no fail-safe—a few gallons of sea water in the system could disable this monster."

Nicholas stopped suddenly as a new thought struck him. "Charles," his voice sharper still, "the pod tanks, the design of the pod tanks. He hasn't altered that, has he? He hasn't cut the corners there? Tell me, old friend, they are still self-propelled, are they not?"

Charles Gras brought the Courvoisier bottle to where Nicholas stood, and when Nick would have refused the addition to his glass, Charles told him sorrowfully, "Come, Nicholas, you will need it for what I have to tell you now."

As he poured, he said, "The pod tankers, their design has been altered also." He drew a breath to tell it with a rush. "They no longer have their own propulsion units. They are now only dumb barges that must be docked and undocked from the main hull and manoeuvred only by attendant tugs."

Nicholas stared at him, his lips blanched to thin white lines. "No. I do not believe it. Not even Duncan—"

"Duncan Alexander has saved forty-two million dollars by redesigning *Golden Dawn* and equipping her with only a single boiler and propeller." Charles Gras shrugged again. "And forty-two million dollars is a lot of money."

There was a pale gleam of wintry sunlight that flickered through the low grey cloud and lit the fields not far from the River Thames with that incredibly vivid shade of English green.

Samantha and Nicholas stood in a thin line of miserably cold parents and watched the pile of struggling boys across the field in their coloured jerseys; the light blue and black of Eton, the black and white of St. Paul's, were so muddied as to be barely distinguishable.

"What are they doing?" Samantha demanded, holding the collar of her coat around her ears.

"It's called a scrum," Nick told her. "That's how they decide which team gets the ball."

"Wow. There must be an easier way."

There was a flurry of sudden movement and the slippery egg-shaped ball flew back in a lazy curve that was snapped up by a boy in the Etonian colours. He started to run.

"It's Peter, isn't it?" cried Samantha.

"Go it, Peter boy!" Nick roared, and the child ran with the ball clutched to his chest and his head thrown back. He ran strongly with the reaching coordinated stride of an older boy, swerving round a knot of his opponents, leaving them floundering in the churned mud, and angling across the lush thick grass towards the white-painted goal line, trying to reach the corner before a taller, more powerfully built lad who was pounding across the field to intercept him.

Samantha began to leap up and down on the same spot, shrieking wildly, completely uncertain of what was happening, but wild with excitement that infected Nicholas.

The two runners converged at an angle which would bring them to the white line at the same moment, at a point directly in front of where Nick and Samantha stood.

Nick saw the contortion of his son's face, and realized that this was a total effort. He felt a physical constriction of his own chest as he watched the boy drive himself to his utmost limits, the sinews standing out in his throat, his lips drawn back in a frozen rictus of endeavour that exposed the teeth clenched in his jaw.

From infancy, Peter Berg had brought to any task that faced him the same complete focus of all his capabilities. Like his grandfather, old Arthur Christy, and his own father, he would be one of life's winners. Nick knew this instinctively, as he watched him run. He had inherited the intelligence, the comeliness and the charisma, but he bolstered all that with this unquenchable desire to succeed in all he did. The single-minded determination to focus all his talents on the immediate project. Nick felt the pressure in his chest swell. The boy was all right, more than all right, and pride threatened to choke him.

Sheer force of will had driven Peter Berg a pace ahead of his bigger, longer-legged adversary, and now he leaned forward with the ball held in both hands, arms fully extended, reaching for the line to make the touch-down.

He was ten feet from where Nick stood, a mere instant from success, but he was unbalanced, and the St. Paul's boy dived at him, crashing into the side of his chest, the impact jarring and brutal, hurling Peter out of the field of play with the ball spinning from his hands and bouncing away loosely, while Peter smashed into the earth on both knees, then rolled forward head over heels, and sprawled face down on the soggy turf.

"It's a touchdown!" Samantha was still leaping up and down.

"No," said Nick. "No, it isn't."

Peter Berg dragged himself upright. His cheek was streaked with chocolate mud and both his knees were running blood, the skin smeared open by the coarse grass.

He did not glance down at his injuries, and he shrugged away the St. Paul boy's patronizing hand, holding himself erect against the pain as he limped back on to the field. He did not look at his father, and the moisture that filled his eyes and threatened to flood over the thick dark lashes were not tears of pain, but of humiliation and failure. With an overwhelming feeling of kinship, Nick knew that for his son those feelings were harder to bear than any physical agony.

When the game ended he came to Nicholas, all bloodied and mud-smeared, and shook hands solemnly.

"I am so glad you came, sir," he said. "I wish you could have watched us win."

Nick wanted to say: "It doesn't matter, Peter, it's only a game." But he did not. To Peter Berg, it mattered very deeply, so Nicholas nodded agreement and then he introduced Samantha.

Again Peter shook hands solemnly and startled her by calling her, "M'am." But when she told him, "Hi, Pete. A great game, you deserved to slam them," he smiled, that sudden dazzling irresistible flash that reminded her so of Nicholas that she felt her heart squeezed. Then when the boy hurried away to shower and change, she took Nick's arm.

"He's a beautiful boy, but does he always call you 'sir'?"

"I haven't seen him in three months. It takes us both a little while to relax."

"Three months is a long time—"

"It's all tied up by the lawyers. Access and visiting rights—what's good for the child, not what's good for the parents. Today was a special concession from Chantelle, but I still have to deliver him to her at five o'clock. Not five past five, five o'clock."

They went to the Cockpit teashop and Peter startled Samantha again by pulling out her chair and seating her formally. While they waited for the best muffins in Britain to be brought to the table, Nicholas and Peter engaged each other in conversation that was stiff with self-consciousness.

"Your mother sent me a copy of your report, Peter. I cannot tell you how delighted I was."

"I had hoped to do better, sir. There are still three others ahead of me."

And Samantha ached for them. Peter Berg was twelve years of age. She wished he could just throw his arms around Nicholas' neck and say, "Daddy, I love you," for the love was transparent, even through the veneer of public-school manners. It shone behind the thick dark lashes that fringed the boy's golden brown eyes, and glowed on the cheeks still as creamy and smooth as a girl's.

She wanted desperately to help them both, and on inspiration she launched into an account of *Warlock*'s salvage of *Golden Adventurer*, a tale with emphasis on the derring-do of *Warlock*'s Master, not forgetting his rescue of Samantha Silver from the icy seas of Antarctica.

Peter's eyes grew enormous as he listened, never leaving her face except to demand of Nicholas, "Is that true, Dad?" And when the story was told, he was silent for a long moment before announcing, "I'm going to be a tug captain when I'm big."

Then he showed Samantha how to spread strawberry jam on her muffins in the correct way, and chewing together heartily with cream on their lips the two of them became fast friends, and Nicholas joined their chatter more easily, smiling his thanks to Samantha and reaching under the table to squeeze her hand.

He had to end it at last. "Listen, Peter, if we are to make Lynwood by five—" and the boy sobered instantly.

"Dad, couldn't you telephone Mother? She might just let me spend the weekend in London with you."

"I already tried that." Nick shook his head. "It didn't work," and Peter stood up, his feeling choked by an expression of stoic resignation.

From the back of Nick's Mercedes 450 Coupé the boy leaned forward into the space between the two bucket seats, and the three of them were very close in the snug interior of the speeding car, their laughter that of old friends.

It was almost dark when Nicholas turned in through Lynwood's stone gateway, and he glanced at the luminous dial of his Rolex. "We'll just make it."

The drive climbed the hill in a series of broad, even curves through the carefully tended woods, and the three-storied Georgian country house on the crest was ablaze with light in every window.

Nick never came here without that strange hollow feeling in the bottom of his stomach. Once this had been his home, every room, every acre of the grounds had its memories, and now, as he parked under the white columned portico, they came crowding back.

"I have finished the model Spitfire you sent me for Christmas, Dad." Peter was playing desperately for time now. "Won't you come up and see it?"

"I don't think so—" Nicholas began, and Peter blurted out before he could finish,

"It's all right, Uncle Duncan won't be here. He always comes down

late from London on Friday nights, and his Rolls isn't in the garage yet."
Then, in a tone that tore at Nick like thorns, "Please . . . I won't see you
again until Easter."

"Go," said Samantha. "I'll wait here." And Peter turned on her, "You
come too, Sam, please."

Samantha felt herself infected by that fatal curiosity, the desire to see,
to know more of Nick's past life; she knew he was going to demur further, but she forestalled him, slipping quickly out of the Mercedes.

"Okay, Pete, let's go."

Nick must follow them up the broad steps to the double oaken doors,
and he felt himself carried along on a tide of events over which he had no
control. It was a sensation that he never relished.

In the entrance hall Samantha looked around her quickly, feeling herself overcome by awe. It was so grand, there was no other word to describe the house. The stairwell reached up the full height of the three
storeys, and the broad staircase was in white marble with a marble
balustrade, while on each side of the hall, glass doors opened on to long
reception rooms. But she did not have a chance to look further, for Peter
seized her hand and raced her up the staircase, while Nick followed them
up to Peter's room at a more sedate pace.

The Spitfire had place of honour on the shelf above Peter's bed. He
brought it down proudly, and they examined it with suitable expressions
of admiration. Peter responded to their praise like a flower to the sun.

When at last they descended the staircase, the sadness and restraint of
parting was on them all, but they were stopped in the centre of the hall by
the voice from the drawing-room door on the left.

"Peter, darling." A woman stood in the open doorway, and she was
even more beautiful than the photograph that Samantha had seen of her.

Dutifully Peter crossed to her. "Good evening, Mother."

She stooped over him, cupping his face in her hands, and she kissed
him tenderly, then she straightened, holding his hand so he was ranged at
her side, a subtle drawing of boundaries.

"Nicholas," she tilted her head, "you look marvellous—so brown and
fit."

Chantelle Alexander was only a few inches taller than her son, but she
seemed to fill and light the huge house with a shimmering presence, the
way a single beautiful bird can light a dim forest.

Her hair was dark and soft and glowing, and her skin and the huge dark sloe eyes were a legacy from the beautiful Persian noblewoman that old Arthur Christy had married for her fortune, and come to love with an obsessive passion.

She was dainty. Her tiny, narrow feet peeped from below the long, dark green silk skirt, and the exquisite little hand that held Peter's was emphasized by a single deep throbbing green emerald the size of a ripe acorn.

Now she turned her head on the long graceful neck, and her eyes took the slightly oriental slant of a modern-day Nefertiti as she looked at Samantha.

For seconds only, the two women studied each other, and Samantha's chin came up firmly as she looked into those deep dark gazelle eyes, touched with all the mystery and intrigue of the East. They understood each other instantly. It was an intuitive flash, like a discharge of static electricity, then Chantelle smiled, and when she smiled the impossible happened—she became more beautiful than before.

"May I present Dr. Silver?" Nick began, but Peter tugged at his mother's hand.

"I asked Sam to see my model. She's a marine biologist, and she's a professor at Miami University—"

"Not yet, Pete," Samantha corrected him, "but give me time."

"Good evening, Dr. Silver. It seems you have made a conquest." Chantelle let the statement hang ambiguously as she turned back to Nick. "I was waiting for you, Nicholas, and I'm so glad to have a chance to speak to you." She glanced again at Samantha. "I do hope you will excuse us for a few minutes, Dr. Silver. It is a matter of some urgency. Peter will be delighted to entertain you. As a biologist, you will find his guinea pigs of interest, I'm sure."

The commands were given so graciously, by a lady in such control of her situation, that Peter went to take Samantha's hand and lead her away.

It was one of the customs of Lynwood that all serious discussion took place in the study. Chantelle led the way, and went immediately to the false-fronted bookcase that concealed the liquor cabinet, and commenced the ritual of preparing a drink for Nicholas. He wanted to stop her. It was something from long ago, recalling too much that was painful, but instead, he watched the delicate but precise movements of her hands pouring exactly the correct measure of Chivas Royal Salute into the crystal glass, adding the soda and the single cube of ice.

"What a pretty young girl, Nicholas."

He said nothing. On the ornate Louis Quatorze desk was a silver-framed photograph of Duncan Alexander and Chantelle together, and he looked away and moved to the fireplace, standing with his back to the blaze as he had done on a thousand other evenings.

Chantelle brought the glass to him, and stood close, looking up at him—and her fragrance touched a deep nostalgic chord. He had first bought *Calèche* for her on a spring morning in Paris; with an effort he forced the memory aside.

"What did you want to speak to me about, is it Peter?"

"No. Peter is doing as well as we can hope for, in the circumstances. He still resents Duncan—but—" she shrugged, and moved away. He had almost forgotten how narrow was her waist, he would still be able to span it with both hands.

"It's hard to explain, but it's Christy Marine, Nicholas. I desperately need the advice of someone I can trust."

"You can trust me?" he asked.

"Isn't it strange? I would still trust you with my life." She came back to him, standing disconcertingly close, enveloping him with her scent and heady beauty. He sipped at the whisky to distract himself.

"Even though I have no right to ask you, Nicholas, still I know you won't refuse me, will you?"

She wove spells, he could feel the mesh falling like gossamer around him.

"I always was a sucker, wasn't I?"

Now she touched his arm. "No, Nicholas, please don't be bitter." She held his gaze directly.

"How can I help you?" Her touch on his arm disturbed him, and, sensing this, she increased the pressure of her fingers for a moment, then lifted her hand and glanced at the slim white gold Piaget on her wrist.

"Duncan will be home soon—and what I have to tell you is long and complicated. Can we meet in London early next week?"

"Chantelle," he began.

"Nicky, please." *Nicky*, she was the only one who ever called him that. It was too familiar, too intimate.

"When?"

"You are meeting Duncan on Tuesday morning to discuss the arbitration of *Golden Adventurer*."

"Yes."

"Will you call me at Eaton Square when you finish? I'll wait by the telephone."

"Chantelle—"

"Nicky, I have nobody else to turn to."

He had never been able to refuse her—which was part of the reason he had lost her, he thought wryly.

T here was no engine noise, just the low rush of air past the body of the Mercedes.

"Damn these seats, they weren't made for lovers," Samantha said.

"We'll be home in an hour."

"I don't know if I can wait that long," Samantha whispered huskily. "I want to be closer to you."

And they were silent again, until they slowed for the weekend traffic through Hammersmith.

"Peter is a knockout. If only I were ten years old, I'd cash in my dolls."

"My guess is he would swop his Spitfire."

"How much longer?"

"Another half-hour."

"Nicholas, I feel threatened," her voice had a sudden panicky edge to it. "I have this terrible foreboding—"

"That's nonsense."

"It's been too good—for too long."

J ames Teacher was the head of Salmon, Peters and Teacher, the lawyers that Nick had retained for Ocean Salvage. He was a man with a formidable reputation in the City, a leading expert on maritime law—and a tough bargainer. He was florid and bald, and so short that his feet did not touch the floorboards of the Bentley when he sat on the back seat.

He and Nick had discussed in detail where this preliminary meeting with Christy Marine should be held, and at last they had agreed to go to the mountain, but James Teacher had insisted on arriving in his chocolate-coloured Bentley, rather than a cab.

"Smoked salmon, Mr. Berg, not fish and chips—that's what we are after."

Christy House was one of those conservative smoke-stained stone buildings fronted on to Leadenhall Street, the centre of Britain's shipping industry. Almost directly opposite was Trafalgar House, and a hundred yards farther was Lloyd's of London. The doorman crossed the pavement to open Nicholas' door.

"Good to see you again, Mr. Berg sir."

"Hello, Alfred. You taking good care of the shop?"

"Indeed, sir."

The following cab, containing James Teacher's two juniors and their bulky briefcases, pulled up behind the Bentley and they assembled on the pavement like a party of raiding Vikings before the gates of a medieval city. The three lawyers settled their bowler hats firmly and then moved forward determinedly in spearhead formation.

In the lobby, the doorman passed them on to a senior clerk who was waiting by the desk.

"Good morning, Mr. Berg. You are looking very well, sir."

They rode up at a sedate pace in the elevator with its antique steel concertina doors. Nicholas had never brought himself to exchange them for those swift modern boxes. And the clerk ushered them out on to the top-floor landing.

"Will you follow me, please, gentlemen?"

There was an antechamber that opened on to the board room, a large room, panelled and hung with a single portrait of old Arthur Christy on the entrance wall—fighting jaw and a sharp black eyes under beetling white eyebrows. A log fire burned in the open grate, and there was sherry and Madeira in crystal decanters on the central table—another one of the old man's little traditions—that both James Teacher and Nick refused curtly.

They waited quietly, standing facing the door into the Chairman's suite. They waited for exactly four minutes before the door was thrown open and Duncan Alexander stepped through it.

His eyes flicked across the room and settled instantly on Nick, locking with his, like the horns of two great bull buffalo, and the room was very still.

The lawyers around Nick seemed to shrink back and the men behind

Duncan Alexander waited, not yet following him into the antechamber, but all of them watched and waited avidly; this meeting would be the gossip of the City for weeks to come. It was a classic confrontation, and they wanted to miss not a moment of it.

Duncan Alexander was a strikingly good-looking man, very tall, two inches taller than Nick, but slim as a dancer, and he carried his body with a dancer's control. His face also was narrow, with the long lantern jaw of a young Lincoln, already chiselled by life around the eyes and at the corners of the mouth.

His hair was very dense and a metallic blond; though he wore it fashionably long over the ears, yet it was so carefully groomed that each gleaming wave seemed to have been sculptured.

His skin was smooth and tanned darker than his hair, sunlamp or skiing at Chantelle's lodge at Gstaad perhaps, and now when he smiled his teeth were dazzlingly white, perfect large teeth in the wide friendly mouth—but the eyes did not smile though they crinkled at the corners. Duncan Alexander watched from behind the handsome face like a sniper in ambush.

"Nicholas," he said, without moving forward or offering a hand.

"Duncan," said Nick quietly, not answering the smile, and Duncan Alexander adjusted the hang of his lapel. His clothes were beautifully cut, and the cloth was the finest, softest wool, but there were foppish little touches: the hacking slits in the tails of the jacket, the double-flapped pockets, and the waistcoat in plum-coloured velvet. Now he touched the buttons with his fingertips, another little distracting gesture, the only evidence of any discomfort.

Nicholas stared at him steadily, trying to measure him dispassionately, and now for the first time he began to see how it might have happened. There was a sense of excitement about the man, a wicked air of danger, the fascination of the leopard—or some other powerful predator. Nick could understand the almost irresistible attraction he had for women, especially for a spoiled and bored lady, a matron of thirteen years who believed there was still excitement and adventure in life that she was missing. Duncan had done his cobra dance, and Chantelle had watched like a mesmerized bird of paradise—until she had toppled from the branch—or that's how Nicholas liked to think it had happened. He was wiser now, much wiser and more cynical.

"Before we begin," Nick knew that anger was seething to his still surface, must soon bubble through unless he could give it release, "I should like five minutes in private."

"Of course." Duncan inclined his head, and there was a hurried scampering as his minions cleared the doorway into the Chairman's suite. "Come through."

Duncan stood aside, and Nick walked through. The offices had been completely redecorated, and Nick blinked with surprise, white carpets and furniture in chrome and perspex, stark abstract geometrical art in solid primary colours on the walls; the ceiling had been lowered by an eggcrate design in chrome steel and free-swivelling studio spotlights gave selected light patterns on wall and ceiling. It was no improvement, Nick decided.

"I was in St. Nazaire last week." Nicholas turned in the centre of the wide snowy floor and faced Duncan Alexander as he closed the door.

"Yes, I know."

"I went over *Golden Dawn*."

Duncan Alexander snapped open a gold cigarette case and offered it to Nick, then when he shook his head in refusal, selected one himself. They were a special blend, custom-made for him by Benson and Hedges.

"Charles Gras exceeded his authority," Duncan nodded. "Visitors are not allowed on *Golden Dawn*."

"I am not surprised you are ashamed of that death-trap you are building."

"But you do surprise me, Nicholas." Duncan showed his teeth again. "It was your design."

"You know it was not. You took the idea, and bastardized it. Duncan, you cannot send that," Nick sought the word, "monster on to the open sea. Not with one propulsion unit, and a single screw. The risk is too appalling."

"I tell you this for no good reason, except perhaps that this was once your office," Duncan made a gesture that embraced the room, "and because it amuses me to point out to you the faults in your original planning. The concept was sound, but you soured the cream by adding those preposterous, shall we call them Bergean, touches. Five separate propulsion units, and a forest of boilers. It wasn't viable, Nicholas."

"It was good, the figures were right."

"The whole tanker market has changed since you left Christy Marine. I had to rework it."

"You should have dropped the whole concept if the cost-structure changed."

"Oh no, Nicholas, I restructured. My way, even in these hard times, I will recover capital in a year, and with a five-year life on the hull there is two hundred million dollars' profit in it."

"I was going to build a ship that would last for thirty years," Nick told him. "Something of which we could be proud—"

"Pride is an expensive commodity. We aren't building dynasties any more, we are in the game of selling tanker space." Duncan's tone was patronizing, that impeccable accent drawn out, emphasizing the difference in their backgrounds. "I'm aiming at a five-year life, two hundred million profit, and then we sell the hull to the Greeks or Japs. It's a one-time thing."

"You always were a smash-and-grab artist," Nick agreed. "But it isn't like dealing in commodities. Ships aren't wheat and bacon, and the oceans aren't the orderly market floors."

"I disagree, I'm afraid. The principles are the same—one buys, one sells."

"Ships are living things, the ocean is a battleground of all the elements."

"Come, Nicholas, you don't really believe that romantic nonsense." Duncan drew a gold Hunter from his waist pocket, and snapped open the lid to read the dial, another of his affectations which irritated Nicholas. "Those are very expensive gentlemen waiting next door."

"You will be risking human life, the men who sail her."

"Seamen are well paid—"

"You will be taking a monstrous risk with the life of the oceans. Wherever she goes *Golden Dawn* will be a potential—"

"For God's sake, Nicholas, two hundred million dollars is worth some kind of risk."

"All right," Nick nodded. "Let's forget the environment, and the human life, and consider the important aspects—the money."

Duncan sighed, and wagged that fine head, smiling as at a recalcitrant child.

"I have considered the money—in detail."

"You will not get an A1 rating at Lloyd's. You will not get insurance on that hull—unless you underwrite yourself, the same way you did with

Golden Adventurer, and if you think that's wise, just wait until I've finished with my salvage claim."

Duncan Alexander's smile twisted slowly, and blood darkened his cheeks under the snow-tan. "I do not need a Lloyd's rating, though I am sure I could get one if I wanted it. I have arranged continental and oriental underwriters. She will be fully insured."

"Against pollution claims, also? If you burst that bag of crude on the continental shelf of America, or Europe, they'll hit you for half a billion dollars. Nobody would underwrite that."

"*Golden Dawn* is registered in Venezuela, and she has no sister ships for the authorities to seize, like they did with the *Torrey Canyon*. To whom will they address the pollution bill? A defunct South American Company? No, Nicholas, Christy Marine will not be paying any pollution bills."

"I cannot believe it, even of you." Nick stared at him. "You are cold-bloodedly talking about the possibility—no, the probability—of dumping a million tons of crude oil into the sea."

"Your moral indignation is touching. It really is. However, Nicholas, may I remind you that this is family and house business—and you are no longer either family or house."

"I fought you every time you cut a corner," Nick reminded him. "I tried to teach you that cheap is always expensive in the long run."

"You taught me?" For the first time Duncan taunted him openly. "What could you ever teach me about ships or money," and he rolled his tongue gloating around the next words, "or women?"

Nick made the first movement of lunging at him, but he caught himself, and forced himself to unclench his fists at his sides. The blood sang in his ears.

"I'm going to fight you," he said quietly. "I'm going to fight you from here to the maritime conference, and beyond." He made the decision in that moment, he hadn't realized he was going to do it until then.

"A maritime conference has never taken less than five years to reach a decision restricting one of its members. By that time *Golden Dawn* will belong to some Japanese, Hong-Kong-based company—and Christy Marine will have banked two hundred million."

"I'll have the oil ports closed to you—"

"By whom? Oil-thirsty governments, with lobbies of the big oil companies?" Duncan laughed lightly, he had replaced the urbane mask. "You

really are out of your depth again. We have bumped heads a dozen times
before, Nicholas—and I'm still on my feet. I'm not about to fold up to
your fine threats now."

After that, there was no hope that the meeting in the panelled
boardroom would lead to conciliation. The atmosphere crackled
and smouldered with the antagonism of the two leading characters, so that they seemed to be the only persons on the stage.

They sat opposite each other, separated by the glossy surface of the
rosewood table top, and their gazes seldom disengaged. They leaned forward in their chairs, and when they smiled at each other, it was like the
silent snarl of two old dog wolves circling with hackles erect.

It took an enormous effort of self-control for Nicholas to force back
his anger far enough to be able to think clearly, and to allow his intuition
to pick up the gut-impressions, the subtle hints of the thinking and planning that were taking place across the table behind Duncan Alexander's
handsome mask of a face.

It was half an hour before he was convinced that something other
than personal rivalry and antagonism was motivating the man before
him. His counter-offer was too low to have any hope of being accepted,
so low that it became clear that he did not want to settle. Duncan Alexander wanted to go to arbitration—and yet there was nothing he could gain
by that. It must be obvious to everyone at the table, beyond any doubt
whatsoever, that Nicholas' claim was worth four million dollars.
Nicholas would have settled for four, even in his anger he would have
gone for four—risking that an arbitration board might have awarded six,
and knowing the delay and costs of going to litigation might amount to
another million. He would have settled.

Duncan Alexander was offering two and a half. It was a frivolous offer.
Duncan was going through the motions only. There was no serious attempt
at finding a settlement. He didn't want to come to terms, and it seemed to
Nicholas that by refusing to settle he was gaining nothing, and risking a
great deal. He was a big enough boy to know that you never, but never, go
to litigation if there is another way out. It was a rule that Nicholas had
graven on his heart in letters of fire. Litigation makes only lawyers fat.

Why was Duncan baulking, what was he to gain by this obstruction?

Nicholas crushed down the temptation to stand up and walk out of the room with an exclamation of disgust. Instead, he lit another cheroot and leaned forward again, staring into Duncan Alexander's steely grey eyes, trying to fathom him, needling, probing for the soft rotten spot—and thinking hard.

What had Duncan Alexander to gain from not settling now? Why did he not try with a low, but realistic offer—what was he to gain?

Then quite suddenly he knew what it was. Chantelle's enigmatic appeal for help and advice flashed back to him, and he knew what it was. Duncan Alexander wanted time. It was as simple as that. Duncan Alexander needed time.

"All right." Satisfied at last, Nicholas leaned back in the deep leather-padded chair, and veiled his eyes. "We are still a hundred miles apart. There will be only one meeting-ground. That's in the upper room at Lloyd's. It's set down for the 27th. Are we at least agreed on that date?"

"Of course." Duncan leaned back also and Nicholas saw the shift of his eyes, the little jump of nerves in the point of his clenched jaws, the tightening of the long pianist's fingers that lay before him on the leather-bound blotter. "Of course," Duncan repeated, and began to stand up, a gesture of dismissal. He lied beautifully; had Nicholas not known he would lie, he might have missed the little tell-tale signs.

In the ancient lift, James Teacher was jubilant, rubbing his little fat hands together. "We'll give him a go!" Nicholas glanced at him sourly. Win, lose or draw, James Teacher would still draw his fee, and Duncan Alexander's refusal to settle had quadrupled that fee. There was something almost obscene about the little lawyer's exultation.

"They are going to duck," Nick said grimly, and James Teacher sobered slightly.

"Before noon tomorrow, Christy Marine will have lodged for postponement of hearing," Nick prophesied. "You'll have to use *Warlock* with full power on both to pull them before the arbitration board."

"Yes, you're right," James Teacher nodded. "They had me puzzled, I sensed something—"

"I'm not paying you to be puzzled," Nick's voice was low and hard. "I'm paying you to out-guess and out-jump them. I want them at the hearing on the 27th, get them there, Mr. Teacher." He did not have to voice the threat, and in a moment, the exultation on James Teacher's rotund features had changed to apprehension and deep concern.

• • •

T he drawing-room in Eaton Square was decorated in cream and pale gold, cleverly designed as a frame for the single exquisite work of art which it contained, the original of the group of Degas ballet-dancers whose copy hung in *Golden Dawn*'s stateroom. It was the room's centrepiece; cunningly lit by a hidden spotlight, it glowed like a precious jewel. Even the flowers on the ivory grand piano were cream and white roses and carnations, whose pale ethereal blossoms put the painting into stronger contrast.

The only other flash of brightness was worn by Chantelle. She had the oriental knack of carrying vivid colour without it seeming gaudy. She wore a flaming Pucci that could not pale her beauty, and as she rose from the huge shaggy white sofa and came to Nicholas, he felt the soft warm melting sensation in his stomach spreading slowly through his body like a draught of some powerful aphrodisiac. He knew he would never be immune to her.

"Dear Nicky, I knew I could rely upon you." She took his hand and looked up at him, and still holding his hand she led him to the sofa, and then she settled beside him, like a bright, lovely bird alighting. She drew her legs up under her, her calves and ankles flashed like carved and polished ivory before she tucked the brilliant skirt around them, and lifted the Wedgwood porcelain teapot.

"Orange pekoe," she smiled at him. "No lemon and no sugar."

He had to smile back at her. "You never forget," and he took the cup.

"I told you that you looked well," she said, slowly and unselfconsciously studying him. "And you really do, Nicholas. When you came down to Lynwood for Peter's birthday in June I was so worried about you. You looked terribly ill and tired—but now," she tilted her head critically, "you look absolutely marvellous."

Now he should tell her that she was beautiful as ever, he thought grimly, and then they would start talking about Peter and their old mutual friends.

"What did you want to talk to me about?" he asked quietly, and there was a passing shadow of hurt in her dark eyes.

"Nicholas, you can be so remote, so—" she hesitated, seeking the correct word, "so detached."

"Recently someone called me an ice-cold Pommy bastard," he agreed, but she shook her head.

"No. I know you are not, but if only—"

"The three most dangerous and inflammatory phrases in the English language," he stopped her. "They are 'you always' and 'you never' and 'if only.' Chantelle, I came here to help you with a problem. Let's discuss that—only."

She stood up quickly, and he knew her well enough to recognize the fury in the snapping dark eyes and the quick dancing steps that carried her to the mantelpiece, and she stood looking up at the Degas with her small fists clenched at her sides.

"Are you sleeping with that child?" she asked, and now the fury was raw in her voice.

Nicholas stood up from the sofa.

"Goodbye, Chantelle."

She turned and flew to him, taking his arm.

"Oh, Nicholas, that was unforgivable, I don't know what possessed me. Please don't go." And when he tried to dislodge her hand, "I beg you, for the first time ever, I beg you, Nicholas. Please don't go."

He was still stiff with anger when he sank back on the sofa, and they were silent for nearly a minute while she regained her composure.

"This is all going so terribly badly. I didn't want this to happen."

"All right, let's get on to safer ground."

"Nicholas," she started, "you and Daddy created Christy Marine. If anything, it was more yours than his. The great days were the last ten years when you were Chairman, all the tremendous achievements of those years—"

He made a gesture of denial and impatience, but she went on softly.

"Too much of your life is locked up in Christy Marine, you are still deeply involved, Nicholas."

"There are only two things I am involved with now," he told her harshly. "Ocean Salvage and Nicholas Berg."

"We both know that is not true," she whispered. "You are a special type of man." She sighed. "It took me so long to recognize that. I thought all men were like you. I believed strength and nobility of mind were common goods on the market—" she shrugged. "Some people learn the hard way," and she smiled, but it was an uncertain, twisted little smile.

He said nothing for a moment, thinking of all that was revealed by those words, then he replied,

"If you believe that, then tell me what is worrying you."

"Nicholas, something is terribly wrong with Christy Marine. There is something happening there that I don't understand."

"Tell me."

She turned her head away for a moment, and then looked back at him. Her eyes seemed to change shape and colour, growing darker and sadder. "It is so difficult not to be disloyal, so difficult to find expression for vague doubts and fears," she stopped and bit her lower lip softly. "Nicholas, I have transferred my shares in Christy Marine to Duncan as my nominee, with voting rights."

Nicholas felt the shock of it jump down his nerves and string them tight. He shifted restlessly on the sofa and stared at her, and she nodded.

"I know it was madness. The madness of those crazy days a year ago. I would have given him anything he asked for."

He felt the premonition that she had not yet told him all and he waited while she rose and went to the window, looked out guiltily and then turned back to him.

"May I get you a drink?"

He glanced at his Rolex. "The sun is over the yardarm, what about Duncan?"

"These days he is never home before eight or nine." She went to the decanter on the silver tray and poured the whisky with her back to him, and now her voice was so low that he barely caught the words.

"A year ago I resigned as executrix of the Trust."

He did not answer, it was what he had been waiting for, he had known there was something else. The Trust that old Arthur Christy had set up was the backbone and sinews of Christy Marine. One million voting shares administered by three executors: a banker, a lawyer and a member of the Christy family.

Chantelle turned and brought the drink to him.

"Did you hear what I said?" she asked, and he nodded and sipped the drink before he asked,

"The other executors? Pickstone of Lloyd's and Rollo still?"

She shook her head and again bit her lip.

"No, it's not Lloyd's any more, it's Cyril Forbes."

"Who is he?" Nick demanded.

"He is the head of London and European."

"But that's Duncan's own bank," Nick protested.

"It's still a registered bank."

"And Rollo?"

"Rollo had a heart attack six months ago. He resigned, and Duncan put in another younger man. You don't know him."

"My God, three men and each of them is Duncan Alexander—he has had a free hand with Christy Marine for over a year, Chantelle, there is no check on him."

"I know," she whispered. "It was a madness. I just cannot explain it."

"It's the oldest madness in the world." Nick pitied her then; for the first time, he realized and accepted that she had been under a compulsion, driven by forces over which she had no control, and he pitied her.

"I am so afraid, Nicholas. I'm afraid to find out what I have done. Deep down I know there is something terribly wrong, but I'm afraid of the truth."

"All right, tell me everything."

"There isn't anything else."

"If you lie to me, I cannot help you," he pointed out gently.

"I have tried to follow the new structuring of the company, it's all so complicated, Nicholas. London and European is the new holding company, and—and—" her voice trailed off. "It just goes round and round in circles, and I cannot pry too deep or ask too many questions."

"Why not?" he demanded.

"You don't know Duncan."

"I am beginning to," he answered her grimly. "But, Chantelle, you have every right to ask and get answers."

"Let me get you another drink." She jumped up lightly.

"I haven't finished this one."

"The ice has melted, I know you don't like that." She took the glass and emptied the diluted spirit, refilled it and brought it back to him.

"All right," he said. "What else?"

Suddenly she was weeping. Smiling at him wistfully and weeping. There was no sobbing or sniffing, the tears merely welled up slowly as oil or blood from the huge dark eyes, broke from the thick, arched lashes and rolled softly down her cheeks. Yet she still smiled.

"The madness is over, Nicholas. It didn't last very long—but it was a holocaust while it did."

"He comes home at nine o'clock now," Nicholas said.

"Yes, he comes home at nine o'clock."

He took the linen handkerchief from his inner pocket and handed it to her.

"Thank you."

She dabbed away the tears, still smiling softly.

"What must I do, Nicholas?"

"Call in a team of auditors," he began, but she shook her head and cut him short.

"You don't know Duncan," she repeated.

"There is nothing he could do."

"He could do anything," she contradicted him. "He is capable of anything. I am afraid, Nicholas, terribly afraid, not only for myself, but for Peter also."

Nicholas sat erect then.

"Peter. Do you mean you are afraid of something physical?"

"I don't know, Nicholas. I'm so confused and alone. You are the only person in the world I can trust."

He could no longer remain seated. He stood up and began to pace about the room, frowning heavily, looking down at the glass in his hand and swirling the ice so that it tinkled softly.

"All right," he said at last. "I will do what I can. The first thing is to find out just how much substance there is to your fears."

"How will you do that?"

"It's best you don't know, yet."

He drained his glass and she stood up, quick with alarm.

"You aren't going, are you?"

"There is nothing else to discuss now. I will contact you when or if I learn anything."

"I'll see you down."

In the hall she dismissed the uniformed West Indian maid with a shake of her head, and fetched Nicholas' topcoat from the closet herself.

"Shall I send for the car? You'll not get a cab at five o'clock."

"I'll walk," he said.

"Nicholas, I cannot tell you how grateful I am. I had forgotten how safe and secure it is to be with you." Now she was standing very close to him, her head lifted, and her lips were soft and glossy and ripe, her eyes still flooded and bright. He knew he should leave immediately. "I know it's going to be all right now."

She placed one of those dainty ivory hands on his lapel, adjusting it unnecessarily with that proprietary feminine gesture, and she moistened her lips.

"We are all fools, Nicholas, every one of us. We all complicate our lives—when it's so easy to be happy."

"The trick is to recognize happiness when you stumble on it, I suppose."

"I'm sorry, Nicholas. That's the first time I've ever apologized to you. It's a day of many first times, isn't it? But I am truly sorry for everything I have ever done to hurt you. I wish with all my heart that it were possible to wipe it all out and begin again."

"Unfortunately, it doesn't work that way." With a major effort of will he broke the spell, and stepped back. In another moment he would have stooped to those soft red lips.

"I'll call you if I learn anything," he said, as he buttoned the top of his coat and opened the front door.

Nicholas stepped out furiously with the cold striking colour into his cheeks, but her presence kept pace with him and his blood raced not from physical exertion alone.

He knew then, beyond all doubt, that he was not a man who could switch love on and off at will.

"You old-fashioned thing." Samantha's words came back to him clearly—and she was right, of course. He was cursed by a constancy of loyalty and emotion that restricted his freedom of action. He was breaking one of his own rules now, he was no longer moving ahead. He was circling back.

He had loved Chantelle Christy to the limits of his soul, and had devoted almost half of his life to Christy Marine. He realized then that those things could never change, not for him, not for Nicholas Berg, prisoner of his own conscience.

Suddenly he found himself opposite the Kensington Natural History Museum in the Cromwell Road, and swiftly he crossed to the main gates—but it was a quarter to six and they were closed already. Samantha would not have been in the public rooms anyway, but in those labyrinthine vaults below the great stone building. In a few short days,

she had made half a dozen cronies among the museum staff. He felt a
stab of jealousy, that she was with other human beings, revelling in their
companionship, delighting in the pleasures of the mind—had probably
forgotten he existed.

Then suddenly the unfairness of it occurred to him, how his emotions
of a minute previously had been stirring and boiling with the memories
of another woman. Only then did he realize that it was possible to be in
love with two different people, in two entirely different ways, at exactly
the same time.

Troubled, torn by conflicting loves, conflicting loyalties, he turned
away from the barred iron gates of the museum.

Nicholas' apartment was on the fifth floor of one of those reno-
vated and redecorated buildings in Queen's Gate.

It looked as though a party of gypsies were passing through.
He had not hung the paintings, nor had he arranged his books on the
shelves. The paintings were stacked against the wall in the hallway, and
his books were pyramided at unlikely spots around the lounge floor, the
carpet still rolled and pushed aside, two chairs facing the television set,
and another two drawn up to the dining-room table.

It was an eating and sleeping place, sustaining the bare minima of existence; in two years he had probably slept here on sixty nights, few of them
consecutive. It was impersonal, it contained no memories, no warmth.

He poured a whisky and carried it through into the bedroom, slipping
the knot of his tie and shrugging out of his jacket. Here it was different,
for evidence of Samantha's presence was everywhere. Though she had
remade the bed that morning before leaving, still she had left a pair of
shoes abandoned at the foot of it, a booby trap to break the ankles of the
unwary; her simple jewellery was strewn on the bedside table, together
with a book, Noel Mostert's *Supership*, opened face down and in dire
danger of a broken spine; the cupboard door was open and his suits had
been bunched up in one corner to give hanging space to her slacks and
dresses; two very erotic and transparent pairs of panties hung over the
bath to dry; her talcum powder still dusted the tiled floor and her special
fragrance pervaded the entire apartment.

He missed her with a physical ache in the chest, so that when the front door banged and she arrived like a high wind, shouting for him, "Nicholas, it's me!" as though it could possibly have been anyone else, her hair tangled and wild with the wind and high colour under the golden tan of her cheeks, he almost ran to her and seized her with a suppressed violence.

"Wow," she whispered huskily. "Who is a hungry baby, then?" And they tumbled on to the bed clinging to each other with a need that was almost desperation.

Afterwards they did not turn the light on in the room that had gone dark except for the dim light of the street lamps filtered by the curtains and reflected off the ceiling.

"What was that all about?" she asked, then snuggled against his chest, "Not that I'm complaining, mind you."

"I've had a hell of a day. I needed you, badly."

"You saw Duncan Alexander?"

"I saw Duncan."

"Did you settle?"

"No. There was never really any chance."

"I'm hungry," she said. "Your loving always makes me hungry."

So he put on his pants and went down to the Italian restaurant at the corner for pizzas. They ate them in bed with a white Chianti from whisky tumblers, and when she was finished, she sighed and said:

"Nicholas, I have to go home."

"You can't go," he protested instantly.

"I have work to do—also."

"But," he felt a physical nausea at the thought of losing her, "but you can't go before the hearing."

"Why not?"

"It would be the worst possible luck, you are my fortune."

"A sort of good-luck charm?" She pulled a face. "Is that all I'm good for?"

"You are good for many things. May I demonstrate one of them?"

"Oh, yes please."

An hour later Nick went for more pizzas.

"You have to stay until the 27th," he said with his mouth full.

"Darling Nicholas, I just don't know—"

"You can ring them, tell them your aunt died, that you are getting married."

"Even if I were getting married, it wouldn't lessen the importance of my work. I think you know that is something I will never give up."

"Yes, I do know, but it's only a couple of days more."

"All right, I'll call Tom Parker tomorrow." Then she grinned at him. "Don't look like that. I'll be just across the Atlantic, we'll be virtually next-door neighbours."

"Call him now. It's lunchtime in Florida."

She spoke for twenty minutes, wheedling and charming, while the blood-curdling transatlantic rumblings on the receiver slowly muted to reluctant and resigned mutterings.

"You're going to get me into trouble one of these days, Nicholas Berg," she told him primly as she hung up.

"Now *there* is a happy thought," Nick agreed, and she hit him with her pillow.

The telephone rang at two minutes past nine the next morning. They were in the bath together and Nicholas swore and went through naked and steaming and dripping suds.

"Mr. Berg?" James Teacher's voice was sharp and businesslike. "You were right, Christy Marine petitioned for postponement of hearing late yesterday afternoon."

"How long?" Nicholas snapped.

"Ninety days."

"The bastard," grunted Nick. "What grounds?"

"They want time to prepare their submission."

"Block them," Nick instructed.

"I have a meeting with the Secretary at eleven. I'm going to ask for an immediate preliminary hearing to set down and confirm the return date."

"Get him before the arbitrators," said Nick.

"We'll get him."

Samantha welcomed him back to the tub by drawing her knees up under her chin. Her hair was piled on top of her head, but damp wisps hung down her neck and on to her cheeks. She looked pink and dewy as a little girl.

"Careful where you put your toes, sir," she cautioned him, and he felt the tension along his nerves easing. She had that effect on him.

"I'll buy you lunch at Les A if you can tear yourself away from your microscope and fishy-smelling specimens for an hour or two."

"Les Ambassadeurs? I've heard about it! For lunch there I'd walk across London on freshly amputated stumps."

"That won't be necessary, but you will have to charm a tribe of wild desert Sheikhs. I understand they are very sympathetic towards blondes."

"Are you going to sell me into a harem—sounds fun, I've always fancied myself in baggy, transparent bloomers."

"You, I'm not selling—icebergs, I am. I'll pick you up at the front gate of the museum at one o'clock sharp."

She went with laughter and a great clatter and banging of doors and Nicholas settled at the telephone.

"I'd like to speak to Sir Richard personally, it's Nicholas Berg." Sir Richard was at Lloyd's, an old and good friend.

Then he called and spoke to Charles Gras.

There were no new delays or threats to *Sea Witch*'s completion date.

"I am sorry for any trouble you had with Alexander."

"*Ça ne fait rien*, Nicholas. Good luck at the hearing. I will be watching the *Lloyd's List*." Nicholas felt a sense of relief. Charles Gras had risked his career to show him *Golden Dawn*. It could have been serious.

Then Nick spoke for nearly half an hour to Bernard Wackie of Bach Wackie in Bermuda. *Warlock* had reported on the telex two hours previously; she was making good passage with her oil-rig tow, would drop off at Bravo II on schedule and pick up her next tow as soon as she had anchored.

"David Allen is a good youngster," Bernard told Nick. "But you have got Levoisin for *Sea Witch*?"

"Jules is playing the prima donna, he has not said yes, but he'll come."

"You'll have a good team, then. What's the latest date for *Sea Witch*?"

"End March."

"The sooner the better, I've got contacts to keep both tugs running hard until the iceberg project matures."

"I'm having lunch with the Sheikhs today."

"I know. There's a lot of interest. I've got a good feeling. There is something big brewing, but they are a cagey bunch. The inscrutable smile on the face of the sphinx—when do we see you?"

"I'll come across just as soon as I've got Duncan Alexander into the arbitration court—end of the month, hopefully."

"We've got a lot to talk about, Nicholas."

Nick hesitated for the time it took to smoke the first cheroot of the day before he called Monte Carlo—for the call would cost him at least fifty thousand dollars, probably closer to seventy-five. The best is always the cheapest, he reminded himself, picked up the receiver and spoke to a secretary in Monte Carlo, giving his name.

While he waited for the connection he thought how his life was complicating itself once more. Very soon Bach Wackie would not be enough, there would have to be a London branch of Ocean Salvage, offices, secretaries, files, accounts, and then a New York branch, a branch in Saudi, the whole cycle again. He thought suddenly of Samantha, uncluttered and simple happiness, life without its wearisome trappings—then the connection was made and he heard the thin, high, almost feminine voice.

"Mr. Berg—Claud Lazarus." No other greeting, no expressions of pleasure at the renewal of contact. Nick imagined him sitting at his desk in the suite high above the harbour, like a human foetus—preserved in spirits, bottled on the museum shelf. The huge bald, domed head, the soft, putty-coloured rudimentary features, the nose hardly large enough to support the thick spectacles. The eyes distorted and startled by the lens, changing shape like those of a fish in an aquarium as the light moved. The body underdeveloped, as that of a foetus, narrow shoulders, seemingly tapering away to the bowed question mark of a body.

"Mr. Lazarus. Are you in a position to undertake an indepth study for me?" It was the euphemism for financial and industrial espionage; Claud Lazarus' network was not limited by frontiers or continents; it spanned the globe with delicately probing tentacles.

"Of course," he piped softly.

"I want the financial structuring, the lines of control and management, the names of the nominees and their principals, the location and inter-relationship of all the elements of the Christy Marine Group and London European Insurance and Banking Co. Group, with particular reference to any changes in structure during the previous fourteen months. Do you have that?"

"This is being recorded, Mr. Berg."

"Of course. Further, I want the country of registration, the insurers and underwriters of all bottoms traceable to their holdings."

"Please continue."

"I want an accurate estimate of the reserves of London and European Insurance in relations to their potential liability."

"Continue."

"I am particularly interested in the vessel *Golden Dawn* presently building at the yards of Construction Navale Atlantique at St. Nazaire. I want to know if she has been chartered or has contracted with any oil company for carriage of crude and, if so, on what routes and at what rates."

"Yes?" Lazarus squeaked softly.

"Time is of the essence—and, as always, so is discretion."

"You need not have mentioned that, Mr. Berg."

"My contact, when you are ready to pass information, is Back Wackie in Bermuda."

"I will keep you informed of progress."

"Thank you, Mr. Lazarus."

"Good day, Mr. Berg."

It was refreshing not to have to pretend to be the bosom comrade of somebody who supplied essentials but nonetheless revolted him, Nick thought, and comforting to know he had the best man in the world for the job.

He looked at his watch. It was lunchtime, and he felt the quick lift of his spirits at the thought of being with Samantha.

L ime Street is a narrow alleyway, with tall buildings down each side of it, which opens off Leadenhall Street. A few yards from the junction, on the left-hand side as you leave the street of shipping, is the covered entrance to Lloyd's of London.

Nicholas stepped out of James Teacher's Bentley and took Samantha on his arm. He paused a moment, with a feeling of certain reverence.

As a seaman, the history of this remarkable institution touched him intimately. Not that the building itself was particularly old or venerable. Nothing now remained of the original coffee house, except some of the traditions: the caller who intoned the brokers' names like the offertory in the temple of some exotic religion, the stalls in which the underwriters conducted their business and the name and uniform of the institution's servants, the "waiters" with brass buttons and red collar tabs.

Rather it was the tradition of concern that was enshrined here, the concern for ships and for all men who went down to the sea in those ships and did their business in great waters.

Perhaps later, Nicholas would find time to take Samantha through the Nelson rooms and show her the displays of memorabilia associated with the greatest of Britain's sailors, the plate and letters and awards. Certainly he would have her as lunch guest in the big dining room, at the table set aside specifically for visiting sea captains.

But now there were more important considerations to demand all his attention. He had come to hear the verdict given on his future—within a few hours he would know just how high and how fast the wave of his fortune had carried him.

"Come," he said to Samantha, and led her up the short flight of steps into the lobby, where there was a waiter alerted to receive them.

"We will be using the Committee Room today, sir."

The earlier submissions by both parties had been heard in one of the smaller offices, leading off the high gallery above the vast floor of the exchange with its rows of underwriters' stalls. However, due to the extraordinary nature of this action, the Committee of Lloyd's had made a unique decision—to have their arbitrators give their findings and make their award in surroundings more in keeping with the importance of the occasion.

They rode up in silence, all of them too tense to make the effort of smalltalk and the waiter led them down the wide corridor, past the Chairman's suite of offices and through the double doors into the grandeur of the room designed by Adam for Bowood House, the country home of the Marquess of Lansdowne. It had been taken to pieces, panel by panel, floor, ceiling, fireplace and plaster mouldings, transported to London and re-erected in its entirety with such care and attention that when Lord Lansdowne inspected it, he found that the floorboards squeaked in exactly the same places as they had before.

At the long table, under the massive glittering pyramids of the three chandeliers, the two arbitrators were already seated. Both of them were master mariners, selected for their deep knowledge and experience of the sea, and their faces were toughened and leathery from the effects of sea and salt water. They talked quietly together, without acknowledging in any way the rows of quietly attentive faces in the rows of chairs facing them—until the minute hand of the antique clock on the Adam fireplace touched its zenith. Then the President of the Court looked across at the waiter who obediently closed the double doors and stood to attention before them.

This Arbitration Court has been set up under the Committee of Lloyd's and empowered to receive evidence in the matter between the Christy Marine Steamship Co. Ltd. and the Ocean Salvage and Towage Co. Ltd. This Court finds common ground in the following areas:

"Firstly, a contract of salvage under Lloyd's Open Form 'No cure no pay' for the recovery of the passenger liner *Golden Adventurer*, a ship of 22,000 tons gross burden and registered at Southampton, exists between the parties.

"Secondly, that the Master of the *Golden Adventurer* while steaming on a south-westerly heading during the night of December 16th at or near 72° 16' south and 32° 12' west—"

The President let no dramatics intrude on his assembly of the facts. He recounted it all in the driest possible terms, succeeding in making *Golden Adventurer*'s plight and the desperate endeavours of her rescuers sound boring. Indeed, his colleague seemed to descend into a condition of coma at the telling of it. His eyes slowly closed, and his head sagged gently sideways, his lips vibrating slightly at each breath—a volume not quite sufficient to make it a snore.

It took nearly an hour, with the occasional consultation of the ship's logbooks and a loose volume of handwritten and typed notes, before the President was satisfied that he had recounted all the facts, and now he rocked back in his chair and hooked his thumbs into his waistcoat. His expression became decisive, and while he surveyed the crowded room, his colleague stirred, opened his eyes, took out a white linen handkerchief and blew two sharp blasts, one for each nostril, like the herald angel sounding the crack of doom.

There was a stir of reawakened interest, they all recognized the moment of decision, and for the first time Duncan Alexander and Nicholas Berg looked directly at each other over the heads of the lawyers and company men. Neither of them changed expression, no smile nor scowl, but something implacable and clearly understood passed between them.

They did not unlock their gaze, until the President began to speak again.

"Taking into consideration the foregoing, this Court is of the firm opinion that a fair and good salvage of the vessel was effected by the salvors, and that therefore, they are entitled to salvage awards commensurate with the services rendered to the owners and underwriters."

Nicholas felt Samantha's fingers groping for his. He took her hand, and it was slim and cold and dry; he interlocked their fingers and laid their hands upon his upper thigh.

"This Court, in arriving at the value of the salvor's services, has taken into consideration, firstly, the situation and conditions existing on the site of operations. We have heard evidence that much of the work was carried out in extreme weather conditions. Temperatures of thirty degrees below freezing, wind forces exceeding twelve on the Beaufort scale, and extreme icing.

"We have also considered that the vessel *Golden Adventurer* was no longer under command. That she had been abandoned by her passengers, her crew and her Master. She was aground on a remote and hostile coast.

"We have further noted that the salvors undertook a voyage of many thousands of miles, without any guarantee of recompense, but merely in order to be in a position to offer assistance, should that have become necessary."

Nicholas glanced across the aisle at Duncan Alexander. He sat at ease, as though he were in his box at Ascot. His suit was of sombre gunmetal grey, but on him it seemed flamboyant and the I Zingari tie as rakish as any of Cardin's fantasies.

Duncan turned that fine leonine head and looked directly at Nicholas again. This time Nicholas saw the deep angry glow in his eyes as when a vagrant breeze fans the coals of an open fire. Then Duncan turned his face back towards the President, and he balanced his thrusting square chin on the clenched, carefully manicured fingers of his right fist.

"Furthermore, we have taken into consideration the transportation of the survivors from the site of the striking, to the nearest port of succour, Cape Town in the Republic of South Africa."

The President was summing up strongly in favour of Ocean Salvage. It was a dangerous sign; so often a judge about to deliver an unfavourable decision prefaced it by building a strong case for the loser and then tearing it down again.

Nicholas steeled himself; anything below three million dollars would not be sufficient to keep Ocean Salvage alive. That was the barest minimum he needed to keep *Warlock* afloat, and to put *Sea Witch* on the water for the first time. He felt the spasm of his stomach muscles as he contemplated his commitments—even with three million he would be at the mercy of the Sheikhs, unable to manoeuvre, a slave to any conditions they wished to set. He would not be off his knees even.

Nicholas squeezed Samantha's hand for luck, and she pressed her shoulder against his.

Four million dollars would give him a fighting chance, a slim margin of choice—but he would still be fighting hard, pressed on all sides. Yet he would have settled for four million, if Duncan Alexander had made the offer. Perhaps Duncan had been wise after all, perhaps he might yet see Nicholas broken at a single stroke.

"Three." Nicholas held the figure in his head. "Let it be three, at least let it be three."

"This Court has considered the written reports of the Globe Engineering Co., the contractors charged with the repairing and refurbishing of *Golden Adventurer*, together with those of two independent marine engineering experts commissioned separately by the owners and the salvors to report on the condition of the vessel. We have also had the benefit of a survey carried out by a senior inspector of Lloyd's of London. From all of this, it seems apparent that the vessel sustained remarkably light damage. There was no loss of equipment, the salvors recovering even the main anchors and chains—"

Strange how that impressed a salvage court. "We took her off, anchors and all," Nick thought, with a stir of pride.

"Prompt anti-corrosion precautions by the salvors resulted in minimal damage to the main engines and ancillary equipment—"

It went on and on. Why cannot he come to it now? I cannot wait much longer, Nicholas thought.

"This Court has heard expert opinion and readily accepts that the residual value of the *Golden Adventurer*'s hull, as delivered to the contractors in Cape Town can be fairly set at twenty-six million US dollars or fifteen million, three hundred thousand pounds sterling, and in consideration of the foregoing, we are further of the firm opinion that the salvors are entitled to an award of twenty per cent of the residual hull value—"

For long cold seconds Nicholas doubted his hearing, and then he felt the flush of exultation burning on his cheeks.

"In addition, it was necessary to compute the value of the passage provided to the survivors of the vessel—"

It was six—six million dollars! He was clear and running free as a wild albatross sweeping across the oceans on wide pinions.

Nicholas turned his head and looked at Duncan Alexander, and he smiled. He had never felt so strong and vital and alive in his life before. He felt like a giant, immortal, and at his side was the vibrant young body pressing to him, endowing him with eternal youth.

Across the aisle, Duncan Alexander tossed his head, a gesture of dismissal and turned to speak briefly with his counsel who sat beside him. He did not look at Nicholas, however, and there was a waxen cast to his skin now as though it had a fine sheen of perspiration laid upon it, and the blood had drained away beneath the tan.

A nyway, another few days and you'd probably have started to find me a boring dolly-bird, or one of us would have had a heart attack." Samantha smiled at him, a pathetic, lopsided little grin, nothing like her usual brilliant golden flashing smile. "I like to quit while I'm still ahead."

They sat close on the couch in the Pan Am Clipper Lounge at Heathrow.

Nicholas was shocked by the extent of his own desolation. It felt as though he were about to be deprived of the vital force of life itself, he felt the youth and strength draining away as he looked at her and knew that in a few minutes she would be gone.

"Samantha," he said. "Stay here with me."

"Nicholas," she whispered huskily, "I have to go, my darling. It's not for very long but I have to go."

"Why?" he demanded.

"Because it's my life."

"Make me your life."

She touched his cheek, as she countered his offer.

"I have a better idea, give up *Warlock* and *Sea Witch*—forget your icebergs and come with me."

"You know I cannot do that."

"No," she agreed, "you could not, and I would not want you to. But, Nicholas, my love, no more can I give up my life."

"All right, then, marry me," he said.

"Why, Nicholas?"

"So I don't lose my lucky charm, so that you'd damn well have to do what I tell you."

And she laughed delightedly and snuggled against his chest. "It doesn't work like that any more, my fine Victorian gentleman. There is only one good reason for marrying, Nicholas, and that's to have babies. Do you want to give me a baby?"

"What a splendid idea."

"So that I can warm the bottles and wash the nappies while you go off to the ends of the oceans—and we'll have lunch together once a month?" She shook her head. "We might have a baby together one day—but not now, there is still too much to do, there is still too much life to live."

"Damn it." He shook his head. "I don't like to let you run around loose. Next thing you'll take off with some twenty-five-year-old oaf, bulging with muscles and—"

"You have given me a taste for vintage wine," she laughed in denial. "Come as soon as you can, Nicholas. As soon as you have done your work here, come to Florida and I'll show you my life."

The hostess crossed the lounge towards them, a pretty smiling girl in the neat blue Pan Am uniform.

"Dr. Silver? They are calling Flight 432 now."

They stood and looked at each other, awkward as strangers.

"Come soon," she said, and then she stood on tiptoe and placed her arms around his shoulders. "Come as soon as you can."

Nicholas had protested vigorously as soon as James Teacher advanced the proposition. "I don't want to speak to him, Mr. Teacher. The only thing I want from Duncan Alexander is his cheque for six million dollars, preferably guaranteed by a reputable bank—and I want it before the 10th of next month."

The lawyer had wheedled and jollied Nicholas along. "Think of the pleasure of watching his face—indulge yourself, Mr. Berg, gloat on him a little."

"I will obtain no pleasure by watching his face, offhand I can think of a thousand faces I'd rather watch." But in the end Nicholas had agreed, stipulating only that this time the meeting should be at a place of Nicholas' choice, an unsubtle reminder of whose hand now held the whip.

James Teacher's rooms were in one of those picturesque, stone buildings in the Inns of Court covered with ivy, surrounded by small velvety lawns, bisected with paved walkways that connected the numerous blocks, the entire complex reeking of history and tradition and totally devoid of modern comforts. Its austerity was calculated to instil confidence in the clients.

Teacher's rooms were on the third floor. There was no elevator and the stairs were narrow, steep and dangerous. Duncan Alexander arrived slightly out of breath and flushed under his tan. Teacher's clerk surveyed him discouragingly from his cubicle.

"Mr. who?" he asked, cupping his hand to one ear. The clerk was a man as old, grey and picturesque as the building. He even affected a black alpaca suit, shiny and greenish with age, together with a butterfly collar and a black string tie like that last worn by Neville Chamberlain as he promised peace in our time.

"Mr. who?" and Duncan Alexander flushed deeper. He was not accustomed to having to repeat his name.

"Do you have an appointment, Mr. Arbuthnot?" the clerk enquired frostily, and laboriously consulted his diary before at last waving Duncan Alexander through into the spartan waiting room.

Nicholas kept him there exactly eight minutes, twice as long as he himself had waited in the board room of Christy Marine, and he stood by the small electric fire in the fireplace, not answering Duncan's brilliant smile as he entered.

James Teacher sat at his desk under the windows, out of the direct line of confrontation, like the umpire at Wimbledon, and Duncan Alexander barely glanced at him.

"Congratulations, Nicholas," Duncan shook that magnificent head and the smile faded to a rueful grin. "You turned one up for the books, you truly did."

"Thank you, Duncan. However, I must warn you that today I have an impossible schedule to meet, I can give you only ten minutes." Nicholas glanced at his watch. "Fortunately I can imagine only one thing that you and I have to discuss. The tenth of next month, either a transfer to the Bermuda account of Ocean Salvage, or a guaranteed draft by registered airmail to Bach Wackie."

Duncan held up his hand in mock protest. "Come now, Nicholas—the salvage money will be there, on the due date set by the Court."

"That's fine," Nicholas told him, still smiling. "I have no taste for another brawl in the debtors' court."

"I wanted to remind you of something that old Arthur Christy once said—"

"Ah, of course, our mutual father-in-law." Nicholas said softly, and Duncan pretended not to hear; instead he went on unruffled.

"He said, with Berg and Alexander I have put together one of the finest teams in the world of shipping."

"The old man was getting senile towards the end." Nicholas had still not smiled.

"He was right, of course. We just never got into step. My God, Nicholas, can you imagine if we had been working together, instead of against each other? You the best salt and steel man in the business, and I—"

"I'm touched, Duncan, deeply touched by this new and gratifying esteem in which I find myself held."

"You rubbed my nose in it, Nicholas. Just as you said you would. And I'm the kind of man who learns by his mistakes, turning disaster to triumph is a trick of mine."

"Play your trick now," Nicholas invited. "Let's see you turn six million dollars into a flock of butterflies."

"Six million dollars and Ocean Salvage would buy you back into Christy Marine. We'd be on equal terms."

The surprise did not show on Nicholas' face, not a flicker of an eyelid, not even a tightening of the lips, but his mind raced to get ahead of the man.

"Together we would be unstoppable. We would build Christy Marine into a giant that controlled the oceans, we'd diversify out into ocean oil exploration, chemical containers." The man had immense presence and charm, he was almost—but not quite—irresistible, his enthusiasm brimming and overflowing, his fire flaring and spreading to light the dingy room, and Nicholas studied him carefully, learning more about him every second.

"Good God, Nicholas, you are the type of man who can conceive of a venture like the *Golden Dawn* or salvage a giant liner in a sub-zero gale, and I am the man who can put together a billion dollars on a wink and whistle. Nothing could stand before us, there would be no frontiers we could not cross." He paused now and returned Nicholas' scrutiny as boldly, studying the effect of his words. Nicholas lit the cheroot he was holding, but his eyes watched shrewdly through the fine blue veil of smoke.

"I understand what you are thinking," Duncan went on, his voice dropping confidentially. "I know that you are stretched out, I know that you need those six big Ms to keep Ocean Salvage floating. Christy Marine will guarantee Ocean Salvage outstandings, that's a minor detail. The important thing is us together, like old Arthur Christy saw it, Berg and Alexander."

Nicholas took the cheroot from his mouth and inspected the tip briefly before he looked back at him.

"Tell me, Duncan," he asked mildly, "in this great sharing you envisage, do we put our women into the kitty also?"

Duncan's mouth tightened, and the flesh wrinkled at the corners of his eyes.

"Nicholas," he began, but Nicholas silenced him with a gesture.

"You said that I need that six million badly, and you were right. I need three million of it for Ocean Salvage and the other three to stop you running that monster you have built. Even if I don't get it, I will still use it to stop you. I'll slap a garnishee order on you by ten minutes past nine on the morning of the eleventh. I told you I would fight you and *Golden Dawn*. The warning still stands."

"You are being petty," Duncan said. "I never expected to see you join the lunatic fringe."

"There are many things you do not know about me, Duncan. But, by God, you are going to learn—the hard way."

Chantelle had chosen San Lorenzo in Beauchamp Place when Nicholas had refused to go again to Eaton Square. He had learned that it was dangerous to be alone with her, but San Lorenzo was also a bad choice of meeting-ground.

It carried too many memories from the golden days. It had been a family ritual, Sunday lunch whenever they were in town. Chantelle, Peter and Nicholas laughing together at the corner table. Mara had given them the corner table again.

"Will you have the *osso bucco*?" Chantelle asked, peeping at him over the top of her menu.

Nicholas always had the *osso bucco*, and Peter always had the *lasagne*, it was part of the ritual.

"I'm going to have a sole." Nicholas turned to the waiter who was hovering solicitously. "And we'll drink the house white." Always the wine had been a Sancerre; Nicholas was deliberately downgrading the occasion by ordering the carafe.

"It's good." Chantelle sipped it and then set the glass aside. "I spoke to Peter last night, he is in the san with flu, but he will be up today, and he sent you his love."

"Thank you," he spoke stiffly, stilted by the curious glances from some of the other tables where they had been recognized. The scandal would fly around London like the plague.

"I want to take Peter to Bermuda with me for part of the Easter holidays," Nicholas told her.

"I shall miss him—he's such a delight."

Nicholas waited for the main course to be served before he asked bluntly, "What did you want to speak to me about?"

Chantelle leaned towards him, and her perfume was light and subtle and evocative.

"Did you find out anything, Nicholas?"

"No," he thought to himself. "That's not what she wants." It was the Persian in her blood, the love of secrecy, the intrigue. There was something else here.

"I have learned nothing," he said. "If I had, I would have called you." His eyes bored into hers, green and hard and searching. "That is not what you wanted," he told her flatly.

She smiled and dropped her eyes from his. "No," she admitted, "it wasn't."

She had surprising breasts, they seemed small, but really they were too big for her dainty body. It was only their perfect proportions and the springy elasticity of the creamy flesh that created the illusion. She wore a flimsy silk blouse with a low lacy front, which exposed the deep cleft between them. Nicholas knew them so well, and he found himself staring at them now.

She looked up suddenly and caught his eyes, and the huge eyes slanted with a sly heart-stopping sexuality. Her lips pouted softly and she moistened them with the tip of her tongue.

Nick felt himself sway in his seat, it was a tell-tale mannerism of hers. That set of lips and movement of tongue were the heralds of her arousal, and instantly he felt the response of his own body, too powerful to deny, although he tried desperately.

"What was it?" He did not hear the husk in his voice, but she did and recognized it as readily as he had the flicker of her tongue. She reached across the table and took his wrist, and she felt the leap of his pulse under her fingers.

"Duncan wants you to come back into Christy Marine," she said. "And so do I."

"Duncan sent you to me." And when she nodded, he asked, "Why does he want me back? God knows what pains the two of you took to get rid of me." And he gently pulled his wrist from her fingers and dropped both hands into his lap.

"I don't know why Duncan wants it. He says that he needs your expertise." She shrugged, and her breasts moved under the silk. He felt the tense ache of his groin, it confused his thinking. "It isn't the true reason, I'm sure of that. But he wants you."

"Did he ask you to tell me that?"

"Of course not." She fiddled with the stem of her glass; her fingers were long and perfectly tapered, the painted nails set upon them with the brilliance of butterflies' wings. "It was to come from me alone."

"Why do you think he wants me?"

"There are two possibilities that I can imagine." She surprised him sometimes with her almost masculine appraisal. That was what made her lapse so amazing; as he listened to her now, Nicholas wondered again how she could ever have let control of Christy Marine pass to Duncan Alexander—then he remembered what a wild and passionate creature she could be. "The first possibility is that Christy Marine owes you six million dollars, and he has thought up some scheme to avoid having to pay you out."

"Yes," Nicholas nodded. "And the other possibility?"

"There are strange and exciting rumours in the City about you and

Ocean Salvage—they say that you are on the brink of something big. Something in Saudi Arabia. Perhaps Duncan wants a share of that."

Nicholas blinked. The iceberg project was something between the Sheikhs and himself, then he remembered that others knew. Bernard Wackie in Bermuda, Samantha Silver, James Teacher—there had been a leak somewhere then.

"And you? What are your reasons?"

"I have two reasons, Nicholas," she answered. "I want control back from Duncan. I want the voting rights in my shares, and I want my rightful place on the Trust. I didn't know what I was doing, it was madness when I made Duncan my nominee. I want it back now, and I want you to get it for me."

Nicholas smiled, a bitter wintry smile. "You're hiring yourself a gunman, just the way they do in the Western serials. Duncan and I alone on the deserted street, spurs clinking." The smile turned to a chuckle, but he was thinking hard, watching her—was she lying? It was almost impossible to tell, she was so mysterious and unfathomable. Then he saw tears well in the depths of those huge eyes, and he stopped laughing. Were the tears genuine, or all part of the intrigue?

"You said you had two reasons." And now his voice was gentler. She did not answer immediately, but he could see her agitation, the rapid rise and fall of those lovely breasts under the silk, then she caught her breath with a little hiss of decision and she spoke so softly that he barely caught the words.

"I want you back. That's the other reason, Nicholas." And he stared at her while she went on. "It was all part of the madness. I didn't realize what I was doing. But the madness is over now. Sweet merciful God, you'll never know how much I've missed you. You'll never know how I've suffered." She stopped and fluttered one small hand. "I'll make it up to you, Nicholas, I swear it to you. But Peter and I need you, we both need you desperately."

He could not answer for a moment, she had taken him by surprise and he felt his whole life shaken again and the separate parts of it tumbled like dice from the cup of chance.

"There is no road back, Chantelle. We can only go forward."

"I always get what I want, Nicholas, you know that," she warned him.

"Not this time, Chantelle." He shook his head, but he knew her words would wear away at him.

• • • •

D uncan Alexander slumped on the luxurious calf-hide seat of the Rolls, and he spoke into the telephone extension that connected him directly with his office in Leadenhall Street.

"Were you able to reach Kurt Streicher?" he asked.

"I'm sorry, Mr. Alexander. His office was unable to contact him. He is in Africa on a hunting safari. They did not know when to expect him back in Geneva."

"Thank you, Myrtle." Duncan's smile was completely lacking in humour. Streicher was suddenly one of the world's most industrious sportsmen—last week he had been skiing and was out of contact, this week he was in Africa slaughtering elephant, perhaps next week he would be chasing polar bears in the Arctic. And by then, it would be too late, of course.

Streicher was not alone. Since the salvage award on *Golden Adventurer*, so many of his financial contacts had become elusive, veritable will-o'-the-wisps skipping ahead of him with their chequebooks firmly buttoned into their pockets.

"I shall not be back at the office again today," he told his secretary. "Please have my pending tray sent round to Eaton Square. I will work on it tonight, and do you think you could get in an hour earlier tomorrow morning?"

"Of course, Mr. Alexander."

He replaced the handset and glanced out of the window. The Rolls was passing Regent's Park, heading in the direction of St. John's Wood; three times in the last six months he had taken this route, and suddenly Duncan felt that hot scalding lump deep under his ribs. He straightened up in his seat but the pain persisted, and he sighed and opened the rosewood liquor cabinet, spilled a spoonful of the powder into a glass and topped it with soda water.

He considered the turbid draught with distaste, then drank it at a gulp. It left an aftertaste of peppermint on his tongue, but the relief was almost immediate. He felt the acid burn subside, and he belched softly.

He did not need a doctor to tell him that it was a duodenal ulcer, probably a whole bunch of them—or was that the correct collective noun, a tribe of ulcers, a convocation? He smiled again, and carefully combed his brazen waves of hair, watching himself in the mirror.

The strain did not show on his face, he was sure of that. The façade was intact, devoid of cracks. He had always had the strength, the courage to ride with his decisions. This had been a hard ride, however, the hardest of his life.

He closed his eyes briefly, and saw *Golden Dawn* standing on her ways. Like a mountain. The vision gave him strength, he felt it rising deep within him, welling up to fill his soul.

They thought of him only as a money man, a paper man. There was no salt in his blood nor steel in his guts—that was what they said of him in the City. When he had ousted Berg from Christy Marine, they had shied off, watching him shrewdly, standing aside and waiting for him to show his guts, forcing him to live upon the fat of Christy Marine, devouring himself like a camel in the desert, running him thin.

"The bastards," he thought, but it was without rancour. They had done merely what he would have done, they had played by the hard rules which Duncan knew and respected, and by those same rules, once he had shown his guts to be of steel, they would ply him with largesse. This was the testing time. It was so close now, two months still to live through— yet those sixty days seemed as daunting as the hard year through which he had lived already.

The stranding of *Golden Adventurer* had been a disaster. Her hull value had formed part of the collateral on which he had borrowed; the cash she generated with her luxury cruises was budgeted carefully to carry him through the dangerous times before *Golden Dawn* was launched. Now all that had altered drastically. The flow of cash had been switched off, and he had to find six million in real hard money—and find it before the 10th of the month. Today was the 6th, and time was running through his fingers like quicksilver.

If only he had been able to stall Berg. He felt a corrosive welling up of hatred again; if only he had been able to stall him. The bogus offer of partnership might have held him just long enough, but Berg had brushed it aside contemptuously. Duncan had been forced to scurry about in undignified haste, trying to pull together the money. Kurt Streicher was not the only one suddenly unavailable, it was strange how they could smell it on a man, he had the same gift of detecting vulnerability or weakness in others so he understood how it worked. It was almost as though the silver blotches showed on his hands and face and he walked the city pavements chanting the old leper's cry, "Unclean. Beware. Unclean."

With so much at stake, it was a piddling amount, six million for two months, the insignificance of it was an insult, and he felt the tension in his belly muscles again and the rising hot acid sting of his digestive juices. He forced himself to relax, glancing again from the window to find that the Rolls was turning into the cul-de-sac of yellow-face brick apartments piled upon each other like hen-coops, angular and unimaginatively lower middle class.

He squared his shoulders and watched himself in the mirror, practising the smile. It was only six million, and for only two months, he reminded himself, as the Rolls slid to a halt before one of the anonymous buildings.

Duncan nodded to his chauffeur as he held the door open and handed Duncan the pigskin briefcase.

"Thank you, Edward. I should not be very long."

Duncan took the case and he crossed the pavement with the long, confident stride of an athlete, his shoulders thrown back, wearing his topcoat like an opera cloak, the sleeves empty and the tails swirling about his legs, and even in the grey overcast of a March afternoon, his head shone like a beacon fire.

The man who opened the door to him seemed only half Duncan's height, despite the tall black Homburg hat that he wore squarely over his ears.

"Mr. Alexander, shalom, shalom." His beard was so dense and bushy black that it covered the starched white collar and white tie, regulation dress of the strict Hasidic Jew. "Even though you come to me last, you still bring honour on my house," and his eyes twinkled, a mischievous sparkling black under thick brows.

"That is because you have a heart of stone and blood like iced water," said Duncan, and the man laughed delightedly, as though he had been paid the highest compliment.

"Come," he said, taking Duncan's arm. "Come in, let us drink a little tea together and let us talk." He led Duncan down the narrow corridor, and halfway they collided with two boys wearing yarmulke on their curly heads coming at speed in the opposite direction.

"Ruffians," cried the man, stooping to embrace them briefly and then send them on their way with a fond slap on their backsides. Still beaming and shaking the ringlets that dangled out from under the black Homburg, he ushered Duncan into a small crowded bedroom that had been converted to an office. A tall old-fashioned pigeon-holed desk filled one wall and against the other stood an overstuffed horsehair sofa on which were piled ledgers and box files.

The man swept the books aside, making room for Duncan. "Be seated," he ordered, and stood aside while a jolly little woman his size brought in the teatray.

"I saw the award court's arbitration on *Golden Adventurer* in *Lloyd's List*," the Jew said when they were alone. "Nicholas Berg is an amazing man, a hard act to follow—I think that is the expression." He pondered, watching the sudden bloom of anger on Duncan's cheeks and the murderous expression in the pale eyes.

Duncan controlled his anger with an effort, but each time that somebody spoke that way of Nicholas Berg, he found it more difficult. There was always the comparison, the snide remarks, and Duncan wanted to stand up and leave this cluttered little room and the veiled taunts, but he knew he could not afford to, nor could he speak just yet for his anger was very close to the surface. They sat in silence for what seemed a long time.

"How much?" The man broke the silence at last, and Duncan could not bring himself to name the figure for it was too closely related to the subject that had just infuriated him.

"It is not a large amount, and for a short period—sixty days only."

"How much?"

"Six million," Duncan said. "Dollars."

"Six million is not an impossibly large amount of money, when you have it—but it is a great fortune when you do not." The man tugged at the thick black bush of his beard. "And sixty days can be an eternity."

"I have a charter for *Golden Dawn*," Duncan said softly. "A ten-year charter." He slipped the nine-carat gold catches on the slim, finely grained pigskin briefcase and brought out a batch of xeroxed sheets. "As you see, it is signed by both parties already."

"Ten years?" asked the man, watching the papers in Duncan's hand.

"Ten years, at ten cents a hundred ton miles and a guaranteed minimum annual of 75,000 miles."

The hand on the man's thick black beard stilled. "*Golden Dawn* has a burden of a million tons—that will gross a minimum of seventy-five million dollars a year." With an effort he managed to disguise his awe, and the hand resumed its gentle tugging at the beard. "Who is the charterer?" The thick eyebrows formed two thick black question marks.

"Orient Amex," said Duncan, and handed him the Xeroxed papers.

"The El Barras field." The man's eyebrows stayed up as he read swiftly. "You are a brave man, Mr. Alexander. But I never once doubted that." He read on in silence for another minute, shaking his head slowly so that the ringlets danced on his cheeks. "The El Barras field." He folded the papers and looked up at Duncan. "I think Christy Marine may have found a worthy successor to Nicholas Berg—perhaps the shoes are even a little small, maybe they will begin to pinch your toes soon, Mr. Alexander." He squirmed down in his chair thinking furiously, and Duncan watched him, hiding his trepidation behind a remotely amused half-smile.

"What about the environmentalists, Mr. Alexander? The new American administration, this man Carter is very conscious of environmental dangers."

"The lunatic fringe," said Duncan. "There is too much invested already. Orient Amex have nearly a billion in the new cadmium cracking plants at Galveston, and three of the other oil giants are in it. Let them fuss, we'll still carry in the new cad-rich crudes."

Duncan spoke with the force of complete conviction. "There is too much at stake, the potential profits are too large and the opposition is too weak. The whole world is sick of the doom-merchants, the woolly-headed sentimentalists," he dismissed them with a short abrupt gesture. "Man has already adjusted to a little oil on the beaches, a little smoke in the air, a few less fish in the sea or birds in the sky, and he will go on adjusting."

The man nodded, listening avidly. "Yes," he nodded. "You are a brave man. The world needs men like you."

"The important thing is a cadmium catalyst cracking system which breaks down the high carbon atoms of crude and gives back a 90 per cent yield in low carbon instead of the 40 per cent we hope for now. 90 per cent yield, double-double profits, double efficiency—"

"—and double danger." The man smiled behind his beard.

"There is danger in taking a bath. You might slip and crack your skull, and we haven't invested a billion dollars in bathing."

"Cadmium in concentrations of 100 parts to the million is more poisonous than cyanide or arsenic; the cad-rich crudes of the El Barras field are concentrated 2,000 parts to the million."

"That's what makes them so valuable," Duncan nodded. "To enrich crude artificially with cadmium would make the whole cracking process hopelessly uneconomic. We've turned what appeared to be a hopelessly contaminated oilfield into one of the most brilliant advances in oil refining."

"I hope you have not underestimated the resistance to the transportation of—"

Duncan cut him short. "There will be no publicity. The loading and unloading of the crude will be conducted with the utmost discretion, and the world will not know the difference. Just another ultra-tanker moving across the oceans with nothing to suggest that she is carrying cadrich."

"But, just suppose the news did leak?"

Duncan shrugged. "The world is conditioned to accept anything, from DDT to Concorde, nobody really cares any more. Come hell and high water, we'll carry the El Barras oil. Nobody is strong enough to stop us."

Duncan gathered his papers and went on softly, "I need six million dollars for sixty days—and I need it by noon tomorrow."

"You are a brave man," the man repeated softly. "But you are finely stretched out. Already my brothers and I have made a considerable investment in your courage. To be blunt, Mr. Alexander, Christy Marine has exhausted its collateral. Even *Golden Dawn* is pawned down to her last rivet—and the charter for Orient Amex does not change that."

Duncan took another sheaf of papers, bound in a brown folder, and the man lifted an eyebrow in question.

"My personal assets," Duncan explained, and the man skimmed swiftly through the typed lists.

"Paper values, Mr. Alexander. Actual values are 50 per cent of those you list, and that is not six million dollars of collateral." He handed the folder back to Duncan. "They will do for a start, but we'll need more than that."

"What more is there?"

"Share options, stock options in Christy Marine. If we are to share risk, then we must have a share of the winnings."

"Do you want my soul also?" Duncan demanded harshly, and the man laughed.

"We'll take a slice of that as well," he agreed amiably.

* * *

It was two hours later that Duncan sank wearily into the leather-work of the Rolls. The muscles in his thighs trembled as though he had run a long way and there was a nerve in the corner of his eye that jumped as though a cricket was trapped beneath the skin. He had made the gamble, everything—Christy Marine, his personal fortune, his very soul. It was all at risk now.

"Eaton Square, sir?" the chauffeur asked.

"No," Duncan told him. He knew what he needed now to smooth away the grinding, destroying tension that wracked his body, but he needed it quickly without fuss and, like the peppermint-tasting powder, like a medicine.

"The Senator Club in Frith Street," he told the chauffeur.

Duncan lay face down on the massage table in the small green-curtained cubicle. He was naked, except for the towel, and his body was smooth and lean. The girl worked up his spine with strong skilled fingers, finding the little knots of tension in the sleek muscle and unravelling them.

"Do you want the soft massage, sir?" she asked.

"Yes," he said and rolled on to his back. She lifted away the towel from around his waist. She was a pretty blonde girl in a short green tunic with the golden laurel leaf club insignia on the pocket, and her manner was brisk and businesslike.

"Do you want any extras, sir?" Her tone was neutral, and she began to unbutton the green tunic automatically.

"No," Duncan said. "No extras," and closed his eyes, surrendering himself completely to the touch of her expert fingers.

He thought of Chantelle, feeling the sneaking guilt of the moment, but it was so seldom these days that he had the energy for her smouldering, demanding Persian passions. He did not have the strength for her, he was drained and weary, and all he wanted was the release, swift and simple. In two months' time it would be different, he would have the strength and energy to pick the world up in his bare hands and shake it like a toy.

His mind was separated from his body, and odd disconnected images flitted across the red darkness of his closed eyelids. He thought again how long it had been since last he and Chantelle had made love together, and he wondered what the world would say if they knew of it.

"Nicholas Berg left a big empty place in his bed also," they would say.

"The hell with them," Duncan thought, but without the energy for real anger.

"The hell with all of them." And he gave himself up to the explosion of light that burst against his eyelids and the dark, but too fleeting, peace that followed it.

Nicholas lay back in the rather tatty old brown leather armchair which was one of James Teacher's concessions to creature comfort and he stared at the cheap hunting prints on the faded wallpaper through a thin fug of cheroot smoke. Teacher could have afforded a decent Gauguin or a Turner, but such vulgar display was frowned on in the Inns of Court. It might lead prospective clients to ponder the amount of the fees that they were to be charged.

James Teacher replaced the telephone and stood up behind his desk. It did not make much difference to his height.

"Well, I think we have covered all the entrances to the warren," he announced cheerfully, and he began to tick off the items on his fingers. "The sheriff of the South African supreme court will serve notice of attachment on the hull of *Golden Adventurer* at noon local time tomorrow. Our French correspondent will do the same on *Golden Dawn*—" He spoke for three minutes more, and, listening to him, Nicholas reluctantly admitted to himself that he earned the greater proportion of his enormous fees.

"Well, there it is, Mr. Berg. If your hunch is correct—"

"It's not a hunch, Mr. Teacher. It's a certainty. Duncan Alexander has his backside pinched in the doorway. He's been rushing round the City like a demented man looking for money. My God, he even tried to stall me with that incredible offer of a partnership. No, Mr. Teacher, it's not a hunch. Christy Marine is going to default."

"I cannot understand that. Six millions is peanuts," said James Teacher. "At least it's peanuts to a company like Christy Marine, one of the healthiest shipping owners."

"It was, a year ago," Nicholas agreed grimly. "But since then, Alexander has had a clear run, no checks, it's not a public company, he administers the shares in the Trust." He drew on his cheroot. "I'm going to use this to force a full investigation of the company's affairs. I'm going to have Alexander under the microscope and we'll have a close look at all his pimples and warts."

Teacher chuckled and picked up the telephone at the first ring. "Teacher," he chuckled, and then laughed out loud, nodding, "Yes," and "Yes!" again. He hung up and turned to Nicholas, his face bright red with mirth, fat and round as the setting sun.

"I have a disappointment for you, Mr. Berg." He guffawed. "An hour ago a transfer was made to the credit of Ocean Salvage in Bermuda by Christy Marine."

"How much?"

"Every penny, Mr. Berg. In full and final payment. Six million and some odd dollars in the legal currency of the United States of America."

Nicholas stared at him, uncertain as to which of his emotions prevailed—relief at having the money, or disappointment at being prevented from tearing Duncan Alexander to shreds.

"He's a high roller and very fast on his feet," said Teacher. "It wouldn't pay to underestimate a man like Duncan Alexander."

"No, it would not," Nicholas agreed quietly, knowing that he had done so more than once and each time it had cost him dearly.

"I wonder if your clerk could find out from British Airways when the next flight leaves for Bermuda?"

"You are leaving so soon? Will it be in order to mark my brief and send it direct to Bach Wackie in Bermuda?" Teacher asked delicately.

B ernard Wackie was waiting in person for Nicholas beyond the customs barrier. He was tall and lean and alert, burned dark as a stick of chew tobacco by the sun, and dressed in open-neck shirt and cotton trousers.

"Nicholas, it's good to see you." His handshake was hard and dry and cool. He was under sixty and over forty; it was impossible to get nearer to his age. "I'm taking you directly to the office, there is too much to discuss. I don't want to waste time." And he took Nicholas' arm and hurried him through burning sunlight into the shivery cold of the Rolls's airconditioning.

The car was too big for the island's narrow winding roads. Here ownership of automobiles was restricted to one per family unit, but Bernard made the most of his rights.

He was one of those men whose combination of energy and brilliance made it impossible for him to live in England and to subject himself to the punitive taxes of envy.

"It's hard to be a winner, in a society dedicated to the glorification of the losers," he had told Nicholas, and had moved his whole operation to this taxless haven.

To a lesser man it would have been suicide, but Bernard had taken over the top floor of the Bank of Bermuda building, with a magnificent view across Hamilton Harbour, and had fitted it out with a marine operations room and a communications system the equal of NATO Command.

From it, he offered a service so efficient, so personally involved, so orientated to every single facet of ship ownership and operation, that not only had his old clients followed him, but others had come flocking.

"No taxes, Nicholas," he smiled. "And look at the view." The picturesque buildings of Hamilton town were painted in candy colours, strawberries and limes, plum and lemon—and across the bay the cedar trees stood tall in the sunlight, and the yachts from the pink-painted clubhouse spread multicoloured sails across green waters. "It's better than London in winter, isn't it?"

"The same temperature," said Nicholas, and glanced up at the air-conditioning.

"I'm a hot-blooded man," Bernard explained, and when his tall nubile secretary entered to his ring, bearing the Ocean Salvage files like a high priestess carrying the sacrament, Bernard fell into an awed silence, concentrating all his attention on her pneumatic bosoms; they bounced and strained against the laws of gravity as though filled with helium.

She flashed a dazzling, painted smile at Nicholas as she placed the files on Bernard's desk, and then she left with her perfectly rounded buttocks under the tightly tailored skirt, swinging and dancing to a distant music. "She can type too," Bernard assured Nick with a sigh, and shook his head as if to clear it. He opened the top file.

"Right," he began. "The deposit from Christy Marine—"

The money had come in, and only just in time. The next instalment on *Sea Witch* was already forty-eight hours overdue and Atlantique were becoming highly agitated.

"Son of a gun," said Bernard. "You would not think six million was an easy sum of money to get rid of, would you?"

"You don't even have to try," Nick agreed. "It just spends itself." Then with a scowl, "What's this?"

"They've invoked the escalation clause again, another 3 + 106 per cent." *Sea Witch*'s builders had included a clause that related the contract price to the index cost of steel and the Union labour rates. They had avoided the threatened dockyard strike by capitulating to Union demands, and now the figures came back to Nicholas. They were big fat ugly figures. The clause was a festering canker to Nicholas, draining his strength and money.

They worked on through the afternoon, paying, paying and paying. Bunkers and the other running costs of *Warlock*, interest and capital re-payments on the debts of Ocean Salvage, lawyers' fees, agents' fees, the six million whittled away. One of the few payments that gave Nicholas any pleasure was the 12½ per cent salvage money to the crew of *Warlock*. David Allen's share was almost thirty thousand dollars; Beauty Baker another twenty-five thousand—Nick included a note with that cheque, "Have a Bundaberg on me!"

"Is that all the payments?" Nicholas asked at last.

"Isn't it enough?"

"It's enough." Nick felt groggy with jetlag and from juggling with fig-ures. "What's next?"

"Good news, next." Bernard picked up the second file. "I think I've squared Esso. They hate you, they have threatened never to use your tugs again, but they are not going to sue." Nicholas had breached contract when he deserted the Esso tow and ran south for *Golden Adventurer*; the breach of contract suit had been hanging since then. It was a relief to have it aside. Bernard Wackie was worth every penny of his hire.

"Okay. Next?"

It went on for another six unbroken hours, piled on top of the jetlag that Nicholas had accumulated across the Atlantic.

"You okay?" Bernard asked at last. Nicholas nodded, though his eyes felt like hard-boiled eggs, and his chin was dark and raspy with beard.

"You want something to eat?" Bernard asked, and then Nick shook his head and realized that it was dark outside. "Drink? You'll need one for what comes next."

"Scotch," Nicholas agreed, and the secretary brought the tray through, and poured the drinks in another respectful hush.

"That will be all, Mr. Wackie?"

"For now, honey." Bernard watched her go, and then saluted Nicholas with his glass.

"I give you the Golden Prince!" And when Nicholas scowled, he went on swiftly, "No, Nicholas, I'm not shafting you. It's for real. You've done it again. The sheikhs are fixing to make you an offer. They want to buy you out, clean, take over the whole show, liabilities, everything. Of course, they'll want you to run it for them—two years, while you train one of their own men. A hell of a salary," he went on crisply, and Nicholas stared at him.

"How much?"

"Two hundred grand, plus 2½ per cent profits."

"Not the salary," Nicholas told him. "How much are they offering for the company?"

"They are Arabs. The first offer is just to stir the pot a little."

"How much?" Nicholas asked impatiently.

"The sum of five was delicately mentioned."

"What do you think they'll go to?"

"Seven, seven and half—eight, perhaps."

Through the fuzz of fatigue, far off like a lantern in the window on a winter's night, Nicholas saw the vision of a new life, a life such as Samantha had shown him. A life uncluttered, uncomplicated, shorn of all but joy and purpose.

"Eight million dollars clear?" Nicholas' voice was husky, and he tried to wipe away the fatigue from his stinging eyelids with thumb and forefinger.

"Maybe only seven," Bernard demurred, "but I'd try for eight."

"I'll have another drink," Nicholas said.

"That's a splendid idea," Bernard agreed, and rang for his secretary with an anticipatory sparkle in his eyes.

Samantha wore her hair in twin braids down her back, and hacked-off denim pants which left her long brown legs bare and exposed a pale sliver of tight round buttock at each step as she walked away. She had sandals on her feet and sunglasses pushed up on top of her head.

"I thought you were never coming," she challenged Nick as he stepped through the barrier at Miami International. He dropped his bag and fielded her rush against his chest. She clung to him and he had forgotten the clean, sun-drenched smell of her hair.

She was trembling with a suppressed eagerness like a puppy, and it was only when a small quivering sob shook her shoulders that he realized she was weeping.

"Hey now!" He lifted her chin, and her eyes were flooded. She snuffled once loudly.

"What's the trouble, little one?"

"I'm just so happy," Samantha told him, and Nicholas deeply envied the ability to live so near the surface. To be able to cry with joy seemed to him at that moment to be the supreme human accomplishment. He kissed her and she tasted salty with tears. With surprise he felt a choke deep in his own throat.

The jaded airport crowds had to open and trickle around the two of them like water around a rock, and they were oblivious to it all.

Even when they came out of the building into the Florida sunlight, she had both arms around his waist, hampering his stride, as she led him to her vehicle.

"Good God!" exclaimed Nicholas, and he shied when he saw it. It was a Chevy van, but its paintwork had been restyled. "What's that?"

"It's a masterpiece," she laughed. "Isn't it?" It was rainbowed, in layers of vibrant colour and panels of fantastic landscapes and seascapes.

"You did that?" Nick asked, and he took his dark glasses from his breast pocket, and inspected the seagulls and palm trees and flowers through them.

"It's not that bad," she protested. "I was bored and depressed without you. I needed something to brighten my life."

One of the panels depicted the translucent green of a curling wave, and on the face of the wave a pair of human figures on Hawaii boards and a graceful dolphin shape flew in formation together. Nick leaned closer and barely recognized the male figure as himself; each detail of the features had been rendered with loving attention, and he came out of it looking like something between Clark Gable and Superman—only a little more glamorous.

"From memory," she said proudly.

"It's tremendous," he told her. "But I've got bigger biceps, and I'm more beautiful."

Despite the wild choice of colour and the romantic style, he realized she had real talent.

"You don't expect me to ride in that—what if one of my creditors saw me!"

"Get your mind out of its stiff collar and blue suit, mister. You have just signed on for the voyage to Never-Never land by way of the moon."

Before she started the engine she looked at him seriously out of those great shining green eyes.

"How long, Nicholas?" she asked. "How long have we got together this time?"

"Ten days," he told her. "Sorry, but I must be back in London by the 25th. There is a big one coming up, *the* big one. I'll tell you about it."

"No." She covered her ears with both hands. "I don't want to hear about it, not yet."

She drove the Chevy with careless unforced skill, very fast and efficiently, acknowledging the homage of other male drivers with a grin and a shake of her braids.

When she slipped off Highway 95 and parked in the lot of a supermarket, Nicholas raised an eyebrow.

"Food," she explained, and then with a lascivious roll of her eyes, "I reckon to get mighty hungry later."

She chose steaks, a bag full of groceries and a jug of California Riesling, and would not let him pay. "In this town, you are my guest."

Then she paid the toll and took the Rickenbacker causeway across the water to Virginia Key.

"That's the marine division of the University of Miami and that's my lab at the top of the jetty, just beyond that white fishing boat—see it?"

The low buildings were crowded into a corner of the island, between the seaquarium and the wharves and jetties of the University's own little harbour.

"We aren't stopping," Nicholas observed.

"Are you kidding?" she laughed at him. "I don't need a controlled scientific environment for the experiment I am about to conduct."

And with no diminution of speed, the Chevy flew across the long bridge between Virginia Key and Key Biscayne, and three miles on she turned off sharply left on a narrow dirt track that twisted through a lush tropical maritime forest of banyan and palmetto and palm, and ended at a clapboard shack just above the water.

"I live close to the shop," Samantha explained, as she clattered up on to the screened porch, her arms full of groceries.

"This is yours?" Nicholas asked. He could just make out the tops of big blocks of condominiums on each side; they were incompletely screened by the palms.

"Pa left it to me. He bought it the year I was born," Samantha explained proudly. "My ground stretches from there to there."

A few hundred yards, but Nicholas realized the value of it. Everybody in the world wants to live on the water, and those condominiums were pressing in closely.

"It must be worth a million."

"There is no price on it," she said firmly. "That's what I tell those awful sweaty little men with their big cigars. Pa left it to me and it's not for sale."

She had the door open now, bumping it with her denim-clad backside.

"Don't just stand there, Nicholas," she implored him. "We've only got ten days."

He followed her into the kitchen as she dumped her load into the sink, and whirled back to him.

"Welcome to my house, Nicholas," and then as she slid her arms around his waist, jerked his shirt tails out of his belt and slid her hands up his bare back, "You'll never know just how welcome. Come, let me show you around—this is the living room."

It had spartan furniture, with Indian rugs and pottery, and Samantha's chopped-off denims were discarded in the centre of the floor along with Nicholas' shirt.

"And this—surprise! surprise!—is the bedroom." She dragged him by one hand, and under the short tee-shirt her bottom reminded him of a chipmunk with its cheeks stuffed with nuts, chewing vigorously.

The tiny bedroom overlooked the beach. The sea breeze fluffed out the curtains and the sound of the low surf breathed like a sleeping giant, a deep regular hiss and sigh that filled the air around them.

The bed was too big for the room, all ornate antique brass, with a cloudy soft mattress and an old-fashioned patchwork quilt in a hundred coloured and patterned squares.

"I don't think I could have lived another day without you," she said, and unwound the thick plaits of her hair. "You came like the cavalry, in the very nick of time."

He reached up and took the golden tresses of hair, winding them thickly around his wrist, twining them in his fingers, and he pulled her gently down beside him.

Suddenly Nick's life was uncluttered and simple again. Suddenly he was young and utterly carefree again. The petty strivings, the subterfuge, the lies and the cheating did not exist in this little universe that encompassed a tiny wooden shack on the edge of the ocean, and a huge brass bed that clanged and rattled and banged and squeaked with the wholesale, the completely abandoned happiness that was the special miracle called Samantha Silver.

Samantha's laboratory was a square room, built on piles over the water, and the soft hum of the electric pumps blended with the slap of the wavelets below and the burble and blurp of the tanks.

"This is my kingdom," she told him. "And these are my subjects."

There were almost a hundred tanks, like the small glass-sided aquaria for goldfish, and suspended over each of them was a complicated arrangement of coils and bottles and electric wiring.

Nick sauntered across to the nearest of the tanks and peered into it. It contained a single large salt-water clam; the animal was feeding with the double shells agape, the pink soft flesh and frilly gills rippling and undulating in the gentle flow of pumped and filtered sea water. To each half of the shell, thin copper wires were attached with blobs of polyurethane cement.

Samantha came to stand beside him, touching, and he asked her, "What's happening?"

She touched a switch and immediately the cylindrical scroll above the tank began to revolve slowly and a stylus, after a few preliminary jerks and quivers, began to trace out a regular pattern on the paper scroll, a trough and double peak, the second a fraction lower than the first, and then the trough again.

She said, "He's wired and bugged."

"You're a member of the CIA," he accused.

And she laughed. "His heartbeat. I'm passing an electric impulse through the heart—the heart is only a millimetre across—but each spasm changes the resistance and moves the stylus." She studied the curve for a moment. "This fellow is one very healthy cheerful *Spisula solidissima*."

"Is that his name?" Nick asked. "I thought he was a clam."

"One of fifteen thousand bivalves who use that common generic," she corrected.

"I had to pick an egghead," said Nicholas ruefully. "But what's so interesting about his heart?"

"It's the closest and cheapest thing to a pollution metre that we have discovered so far—or rather," she corrected herself without false modesty, "that I have discovered."

She took his hand and led him down the long rows of tanks. "They are sensitive, incredibly sensitive to any contamination of their environment, and the heartbeat will register almost immediately any foreign element or chemical, organic or otherwise, in such low concentrate that it would take a highly trained specialist with a spectroscope to detect otherwise."

Nicholas felt his mild attention changing and growing into real interest as Samantha began to prepare samples of common pollutants on the single bench against the forewall of the cluttered little laboratory.

"Here," she held up one test tube, "aromatic carbons, the more poisonous elements of crude petroleum—and here," she indicated the next tube, "mercury in a concentration of 100 parts to the million. Did you see the photographs of the human vegetables and the Japanese children with the flesh falling off their bones at Kiojo? That was mercury. Lovely stuff." She picked up another tube. "PCB, a by-product of the electrical industry, the Hudson River is thick with it. And these, tetrahydrofurane, cyclohexane, methylbenzene—all industrial by-products but don't let the fancy names throw you. One day they will come back to haunt us, in newspaper headlines, as THF or CMB—one day there will be other human cabbages and babies born without arms or legs." She touched the other tubes. "Arsenic, old-fashioned Agatha Christie vintage poison. And then here is the real living and breathing bastard daddy of them all—this is cadmium; as a sulphide so it's easily absorbed. In 100 parts to the million it's as lethal as a neutron bomb."

While he watched, she carried the tray of tubes across to the tanks and set the ECG monitors running. Each began to record the normal double-peaked heartbeat of a healthy clam.

"Now," she said, "watch this."

Under controlled conditions, she began to drip the weak poisoned solutions into the reticulated water systems, a different solution to each of the tanks.

"These concentrations are so low that the animals will not even be aware of trauma, they will continue to feed and breed without any but long-term indications of systemic poisoning."

Samantha was a different person, a cool quick-thinking professional. Even the white dust-coat that she had slipped over her tee-shirt altered her image and she had aged twenty years in poise and authority as she passed back and forth along the row of tanks.

"There," she said, with grim satisfaction as the stylus on one recording drum made a slightly double beat at its peak and then just detectably flattened the second peak. "Typical aromatic carbon reaction."

The distorted heartbeat was repeated endlessly on the slowly turning drum, and she passed on to the next tank.

"See the pulse in the trough, see the fractional speeding up of the heart spasm? That's cadmium in ten parts to the million, at 100 parts it will kill all sea life, at five hundred it will kill man slowly, at seven hundred parts in air or solution it will kill him very quickly indeed."

Nicholas' interest became total fascination, as he helped Samantha record the experiments and control the flow and concentration in the tanks. Slowly they increased the dosage of each substance and the moving stylus dispassionately recorded the increasing distress and the final convulsions and spasmodic throes that preceded death.

Nicholas voiced the tickle of horror and revulsion he felt at watching the process of degeneration.

"It's macabre."

"Yes." She stood back from the tanks. "Death always is. But these organisms have such rudimentary nervous systems that they don't experience pain as we know it." She shuddered slightly herself and went on. "But imagine an entire ocean poisoned like one of these tanks, imagine the incredible agonies of tens of millions of seabirds, of the mammals, seals and porpoises and whales. Then think of what would happen to man himself—" Samantha shrugged off her white dust-coat.

"Now I'm hungry," she announced, and then looking up at the fibreglass panels in the roof, "No wonder! It's dark already!"

While they cleaned and tidied the laboratory, and made a last check of the pumps and running equipment, Samantha told him, "In five hours we have tested over a hundred and fifty samples of contaminated water and got accurate indications of nearly fifty dangerous substances—at a probable cost of fifty cents a sample." She switched out the lights. "To do the same with a gas spectroscope would have cost almost ten thousand dollars and taken a highly specialized team two weeks of hard work."

"It's a hell of a trick," Nicholas told her. "You're a clever lady—I'm impressed, I really am."

At the psychedelic Chevy van she stopped him, and in the light of the street lamp, she looked up at him guiltily.

"Do you mind if I show you off, Nicholas?"

"What does that mean?" he asked suspiciously.

"The gang are eating shrimps tonight. Then they'll sleep over on the boat and have the first shot at fish tagging tomorrow—but we don't have to go. We could just get some more steaks and another jug of wine." But he could see she really wanted to go.

She was fifty-five foot, an old purse-seiner with the ungainly wheel-house forward looking like a sentry box or an old-fashioned pit la-trine. Even with her coat of new paint, she had an old-fashioned look.

She was tied up at the end of the University jetty, and as they walked out to her, so they could hear the voices and the laughter coming up from below decks.

"*Tricky Dicky*," Nicholas read her name on the high ugly rounded stern.

"But we love her," Samantha said, and led him across the narrow, rickety gangplank. "She belongs to the University. She's only one of our four research vessels. The others are all fancy modern ships, two-hundred-footers, but the *Dicky* is our boat for short field trips to the Gulf or down the Keys, and she's also the faculty clubhouse."

The main cabin was monastically furnished, bare planking and hard benches, a single long table, but it was as crowded as a fashionable dis-cotheque, packed solid with sunburned young people, girls and boys all in faded jeans and tee-shirts, impossible to judge sexes by clothing or by the length of their sun-tortured and wind-tangled hair.

The air was thick with the rich smell of broiling Gulf shrimps and molten butter, and there were gallon jugs of California wine on the table.

"Hey!" Samantha shouted above the uproar of voices raised in heated dispute and jovial repartee. "This is Nicholas."

A comparative silence descended on the gathering, and they looked him over with the curious veiled group hostility of any tribe for an interloper, an intruder in a closed and carefully guarded group. Nick returned the scrutiny calmly, met each pair of eyes, while realizing that despite the affected informality of their dress and some of the wildly unkempt hairstyles and the impressive profusion of beards, they were an élite group. There was not a face that was not intelligent, not a pair of eyes that was not alert and quick, and there was that special feeling of pride and self-confidence in all of them.

At the head of the table sat a big impressive figure, the oldest man in the cabin, perhaps Nick's age or a little older, for there were silver strands in his beard and his face was lined and beaten by sun and wind and time.

"Hi, Nick," he boomed. "I won't pretend we've never heard of you. Sam has given us all cauliflower ears—"

"You cut that out, Tom Parker," Samantha stopped him sharply, and there was a ripple of laughter, a relaxation of tension and a casual round of greetings.

"Hi, Nick, I'm Sally-Anne." A pretty girl with china-blue eyes behind wire-framed spectacles put a heavy tumbler of wine into his hand.

"We are short of glasses, guess you and Sam will have to share."

She slid up along the bench and gave them a few inches of space and Samantha perched on Nicholas' lap. The wine was a rough fighting red, and it galloped, booted and spurred across his palate but Samantha sipped her share with the same relish as if it had been a '53 Château Lafitte, and she nuzzled Nicholas' ear and whispered:

"Tom is prof of the Biology Department. He's a honey. After you— he's my most favourite man in the world."

A woman came through from the galley, carrying a huge platter piled high with bright pink shrimps and a bowl of molten butter. There was a roar of applause for her as she placed the dishes in the centre of the table, and they fell upon the food with unashamed gusto.

The woman was tall with dark hair in braids and a strong capable face, lean and supple in tight breeches, but she was older than the other women and she paused beside Tom Parker and draped one arm across his shoulders in a comfortable gesture of long-established affection.

"That's Antoinette, his wife." The woman heard her name and smiled across at them, and with dark gentle eyes she studied Nicholas and then nodded and made the continental "O" of thumb and forefinger at Samantha, before slipping back into the galley.

The food did not inhibit the talk, the lively contentious flow of discussion that swung swiftly from banter to deadly seriousness and back again, bright, trained, informed minds clicking and cannoning off each other with the crispness of ivory billiard balls, while at the same time buttery fingers ripped the whiskered heads off the shrimps, delving for the crescent of sweet white flesh, then leaving greasy fingerprints on the wine tumblers.

As each of them spoke, Samantha whispered their names and credentials. "Hank Petersen, he's doing a Ph.D. on the bluefin tuna—spawning and a trace of its migratory routes. He's the one running the tagging tomorrow.

"That's Michelle Rand, she's on loan from UCLA, and she's porpoises and whales."

Then suddenly they were all discussing indignantly a rogue tanker captain who the week before had scrubbed his tanks in the middle of the Florida straits and left a thirty-mile slick down the Gulf Stream. He had done it under cover of night, and changed course as soon as he was into the Atlantic proper.

"We fingerprinted him," Tom Parker spoke like an angry bear, "we had him made, dead in the cross-hairs." Nick knew he was talking of the finger-printing of oil residues, the breakdown of samples of the slick under gas spectroscopy which could match them exactly to the samples taken by the Coast Guard from the offender's tanks. The identification was good enough to bear up in an international court of law. "But the trick is getting the son-of-a-bitch into court." Tom Parker went on. "He was fifty miles outside our territorial waters by the time the Coast Guard got to him, and he's registered in Liberia."

"We tried to cover cases like that in the set of proposals I put up to the last maritime conference."

Nick joined the conversation for the first time. He told them of the difficulties of legislating on an international scale, of policing and bringing to justice the blatant transgressors; then he listed for them what had been done so far, what was in process and finally what he believed should still be done to protect the seas.

He spoke quietly, succinctly, and Samantha noticed again, with a swell of pride, how all the men listened when Nicholas Berg talked. The moment he paused, they came at him from every direction, using their bright young minds like scalpels, tearing into him with sharp lancing questions. He answered them in the same fashion, sharp and hard, armed with total knowledge of his subject, and he saw the shift in the group attitude, the blooming of respect, the subtle opening of ranks to admit him, for he had spoken the correct passwords and they recognized him as one of their own number, as one of the élite.

At the head of the table, Tom Parker sat and listened, nodding and frowning, sitting in judgement with his arm around Antoinette's slim waist and she stood beside him and played idly with a curl of thick wiry hair on the top of his head.

Tom Parker found fish forty miles offshore where the Gulf Stream was setting blue and warm and fast into the north. The birds were working, falling on folded wings down the backdrop of cumulonimbus storm clouds that bruised the horizon. The birds were bright, white pinpoints of light as they fell, and they struck the dark blue water with tiny explosions of white spray, and went deep. Seconds later they popped to the surface, stretching their necks to force down another morsel into their distended crops, before launching into flight again, climbing in steep circles against the sky to join the hunt again. There were hundreds of them and they swirled and fell like snowflakes.

"Anchovy," grunted Tom Parker, and they could see the agitated surface of the water under the bird flock where the frenzied bait-fish churned. "Could be bonito working under them."

"No," said Nick. "They are blues."

"You sure?" Tom grinned a challenge.

"The way they are bunching and holding the bait-fish, it's tuna," Nick repeated.

"Five bucks?" Tom asked, as he swung the wheel over, and *Tricky Dicky*'s big diesel engine boomed as she went on to the top of her speed.

"You're on," Nick grinned back at him, and at that moment, they both saw a fish jump clear. It was a brilliant shimmering torpedo, as long as a man's arm. It went six feet into the air, turned in flight and hit the water again with a smack they heard clearly above the diesel.

"Blues," said Nick flatly. "Shoal blues—they'll go twenty pounds each."

"Five bucks," Tom grunted with disgust. "Son of a gun, I don't think I can afford you, man," and he delivered a playful punch to the shoulder which rattled Nick's teeth, then he turned to the open window of the wheelhouse and bellowed out on to the deck, "Okay, kids, they are blues."

There was a scramble and chatter of excitement as they rushed for lines and tagging poles. It was Hank's show: he was the bluefin tunny expert; he knew as much about their sex habits, their migratory routes and food chains as any man living, but when it came to catching them, Nick observed drily, he could probably do a better job as a blacksmith.

Tom Parker was no fisherman either. He ran down the shoal, charging *Tricky Dicky* through the centre of it, scattering birds and fish in panic— but by sheer chance one of the gang in the stern hooked in, and after a great deal of heaving and huffing and shouted encouragement from his peers, dragged a single luckless baby bluefin tuna over the rail. It skittered and jumped around the deck, its tail hammering against the planking, pursued by a shrieking band of scientists who slid and slipped in the fish slime, knocked each other down and finally cornered the fish against the rail. The first three attempts to affix the plastic tag were unsuccessful, Hank's lunges with the dart pole becoming wilder as his frustration mounted. He almost succeeded in tagging Samantha's raised backside as she knelt on the deck trying to cradle the fish in both arms.

"You do this often?" Nicholas asked mildly.

"First time with this gang," Tom Parker admitted sheepishly. "Thought you'd never guess."

By now the triumphant band was solicitously returning the fish to the sea, the barbed dart of the plastic tag embedded dangerously near its vitals; and if that didn't eventually kill it, the rough handling probably would. It had pounded its head on the deck so heavily that blood oozed from the gill covers. It floated away, belly up on the stream, oblivious of Samantha's anguished cries of:

"Swim, fish, get in there and swim!"

"Mind if we try it my way?" Nick asked, and Tom relinquished command without a struggle.

Nicholas picked the four strongest and best co-ordinated of the young men, and gave them a quick demonstration and lecture on how to handle the heavy handlines with the Japanese feather lures, showing them how to throw the bait, and the recovery with an underhand flick that recoiled the line between the feet. Then he gave each a station along the starboard rail, with the second member of each team ready with a tagging pole and Hank Petersen on the roof of the wheelhouse to record the fish taken and the numbers of the tags.

They found another shoal within the hour and Nicholas circled up on it, closing steadily at good trolling speed, helping the feeding tuna bunch the shoal of frenzied anchovy on the surface, until he could lock *Tricky Dicky*'s wheel hard down starboard and leave her to describe her own sedate circles around the shoal. Then he hurried out on to the deck.

The trapped and surrounded fish thrashed the surface until it boiled like a porridge of molten, flashing silver; through it drove the fast dark torpedoes of the hungry tuna.

Within minutes Nick had his four fishermen working to the steady rhythm of throwing the lures into the frothing water, almost instantly striking back on the line as a tuna snatched the feathers, and then swinging hand over head, recovering and coiling line fast with minimum effort, swinging the fish out and up with both hands and then catching its streamlined body under the left armpit like a quarterback picking up a long pass, clamping it there firmly, although the cold, firm, silver bullet shape juddered and quivered and the tail beat in a blur of movement. Then he taught them to slip the hook from the jaw, careful not to damage the vulnerable gills, holding the fish firmly but gently while the assistant pressed the barbed dart into the thick muscle at the back of the dorsal fin. When the fish was dropped back over the side, there were so few aftereffects that it almost immediately began feeding again on the packed masses of tiny anchovies.

Each plastic tag was numbered and imprinted with a request in five languages to mail it back to the University of Miami with details of the date and place of capture, providing a valuable trace of the movements of the shoals in their annual circumnavigation of the globe. From their spawning grounds somewhere in the Caribbean they worked the Gulf Stream north and east across the Atlantic, then south down and around the Cape of Good Hope with an occasional foray down the length of the Mediterranean Sea—although now the dangerous pollution of that land-locked water was changing their habits. From Good Hope east again south of Australia to take a gigantic swing up and around the Pacific, running the gauntlet of the Japanese long-liners and the California tunny men before ducking down under the terrible icy seas of the Horn and back to their spawning grounds in the Caribbean.

As the *Dicky* ran home in the sunset, they sat up on the wheelhouse drinking beer and talking. Nicholas studied them casually and saw that they possessed so many of the qualities he valued in his fellow humans; they were intelligent and motivated, they were dedicated and free of that particular avarice that mars so many others.

Tom Parker crumpled the empty beer can in a huge fist as easily as if it had been a paper packet, fished two more from the pack beside him and tossed one across to Nick. The gesture seemed to have some special significance and Nicholas saluted him with the can before he drank.

Samantha was snuggled down in luxurious weariness against his shoulder, and the sunset was a magnificence of purple and hot molten crimson. Nicholas thought idly how pleasant it would be to spend the rest of his life doing things like this with people like these.

Tom Parker's office had shelves to the ceiling, and they were sagging with hundreds of bottled specimens and rows of scientific papers and publications.

He sat well back in his swivel chair with ankles crossed neatly in the centre of the cluttered desk.

"I ran a check on you, Nicholas. Damned nerve, wasn't it? You have my apology."

"Was it an interesting exercise?" Nicholas asked mildly.

"It wasn't difficult. You have left a trail behind you like a—" Tom sought for a comparison, "like a grizzly bear through a honey farm. Son of a gun, Nicholas, that's a hell of a track record you've got yourself."

"I've kept busy," Nicholas admitted.

"Beer?" Tom crossed to the refrigerator in the corner that was labelled "Zoological Specimens. DO NOT OPEN."

"It's too early for me."

"Never too early," said Tom and pulled the tag on a dewy can of

Miller and then picked up Nicholas' statement. "Yes, you have kept busy. Strange, isn't it, that around some men things just happen." Nicholas did not reply, and Tom went on. "We need a man around here who can *do*. It's all right thinking it out, then you need the catalyst to transform thought and intention into action." Tom sucked at the can and then licked the froth off his moustache. "I know what you have done. I've heard you speak, I've seen you move, and those things count. But most important of all, I know you care. I've been watching you carefully, Nick, and you really care, down deep in your guts, the way we do."

"It sounds as though you're offering me a job, Tom."

"I'm not going to horse around, Nick, I *am* offering you a job." He waved a huge paw, like a bunch of broiled pork sausages. "Hell, I know you're a busy man, but I'd like to romance you into an associate professorship. We'd want a little of your time when it came to hassling and negotiating up in Washington, we'd call for you when we needed real muscle to put our case, when we need the right contacts, somebody with a big reputation to open doors, when we need a man who knows the practical side of the oceans and the men that use them and abuse them.

"We need a man who is a hard-headed businessman, who knows the economics of sea trade, who has built and run tankers, who knows that human need is of paramount importance, but who can balance the human need for protein and fossil fuels against the greater danger of turning the oceans into watery deserts." Tom lubricated his throat with beer, watching shrewdly for some reaction from Nicholas, and when he received no encouragement, he went on more persuasively. "We are specialists, perhaps we have the specialist's narrow view; God knows, they think of us as sentimentalists, the lunatic fringe of doomsayers, long-haired intellectual hippies. What we need is a man with real clout in the establishment—shit, Nicholas, if you walked into a Congressional committee they'd really jerk out of their geriatric trance and switch on their hearing-aids." Nicholas was silent still and Tom was becoming desperate. "What can we offer in return? I know you aren't short of cash, and it would be a lousy 12,000 a year, but an associate professorship is a nice title. We start out holding hands with that. Then we might start going steady, a full professorship—chair of applied oceanology, or some juicy title like that which we'd think up. I don't know what else we can offer you, Nick, except perhaps the warm good feeling in your guts when you're doing a tough job that has to be done." He stopped again, running out of words, and he wagged his big shaggy head sadly.

"You aren't interested, are you?" he asked.

Nick stirred himself. "When do I start?" he asked, and as Tom's face split into a great beaming grin, Nick held out his hand. "I think I'll take that beer now."

The water was cool enough to be invigorating. Nick and Samantha swam so far out that the land was almost lost in the lowering gloom of dusk, and then they turned and swam back side by side. The beach was deserted; in their mood, the lights of the nearest condominiums were no more intrusive than the stars, the faint sound of music and laughter no more intrusive than the cry of gulls.

It was the right time to tell her, and he did it in detail beginning with the offer by the Sheikhs to buy out Ocean Salvage and Towage.

"Will you sell?" she asked quietly. "You won't, will you?"

"For seven million dollars clear?" he asked. "Do you know how much money that is?"

"I can't count that far," she admitted. "But what would you do if you sold? I cannot imagine you playing bowls or golf for the rest of your life."

"Part of the deal is that I run Ocean Salvage for them for two years, and then I've been offered a part-time assignment which will fill any spare time I've got left over."

"What is it?"

"Associate Professor at Miami University."

She stopped dead and dragged him around to face her.

"You're having me on!" she accused.

"That's a start only," he admitted. "In two years or so, when I've finished with Ocean Salvage, there may be a full chair of applied oceanology."

"It's not true!" she said, and took him by the arms, shaking him with surprising strength.

"Tom wants me to ramrod the applied aspects of the environmental research. I'll troubleshoot with legislators and the maritime conference, a sort of hired gun for the Greenpeacers—"

"Oh, Nicholas, Nicholas!"

"Sweet Christ!" he accused. "You're crying again."

"I just can't help it." She was in his arms still wet and cold and gritty with beach sand. She clung to him, quivering with joy. "Do you know what this means, Nicholas? You don't, do you? You just don't realize what this means."

"Tell me," he invited. "What does it mean?"

"What it means is that, in future, we can do everything together, not just munch food and go boom in bed—but everything, work and play and, and *live* together like a man and woman should!" She sounded stunned and frightened by the magnitude of the vision.

"The prospect daunts me not at all," he murmured gently, and lifted her chin.

They washed off the salt and the sand, crowding together into the thick, perfumed steam of the shower cubicle and afterwards they lay together on the patchwork quilt in the darkness with the sound of the sea as background music to the plans and dreams they wove together.

Every time they both descended to the very frontiers of sleep, one of them would think of something vitally important and prod the other awake to say it.

"I've got to be in London on Tuesday."

"Don't spoil it all, now," she murmured sleepily.

"And then we're launching *Sea Witch* on the 7th April."

"I'm not listening," she whispered. "I've got my fingers in my ears."

"Will you launch her—I mean break the bottle of bubbly and bless her?"

"I've just taken my fingers out again."

"Jules would love it."

"Nicholas, I cannot spend my life commuting across the Atlantic, not even for you. I've got work to do."

"Peter will be there, I'll work that as a bribe."

"That's unfair pressure," she protested.

"Will you come?"

"You know I will, you sexy bastard. I wouldn't miss it for all the world." She moved across the quilt and found his ear with her lips. "I am honoured."

"Both of you are sea witches," Nick told her.

"And you are my warlock."

"Sea witch and warlock," he chuckled. "Together we will work miracles."

"Look, I know it's terribly forward of me, but seeing that we are both wide awake, and it's only two o'clock in the morning, I would be super ultra-grateful if you could work one of your little miracles for me right now."

"It will be a great pleasure," Nick told her.

Nicholas was early, he saw as he came out of the American Consulate and glanced at his Rolex, so he moderated his pace across the Place de la Concorde, despite the gentle misty rain that settled in minute droplets on the shoulders of his trench coat.

Lazarus was at the rendezvous ahead of him, standing under one of the statues in the corner of the square closest to the French naval headquarters.

He was heavily muffled against the cold, dressed all in sombre blue with a long cashmere scarf wound around his throat and a dark blue hat pulled down so low as to conceal the pale smooth bulge of his forehead.

"Let's find a warm place," Nick suggested, without greeting the little man.

"No," said Lazarus, looking up at him through the thick distorting lenses of his spectacles. "Let us walk." And he led the way through the underpass on to the promenade above the embankment of the Seine, and set off in the direction of the Petit Palais.

In the middle of such an inclement afternoon they were the only strollers, and they walked in silence three or four hundred yards while Lazarus satisfied himself absolutely of this, and while he adjusted his mincing little steps to Nick's stride. It was like taking Toulouse-Lautrec for a stroll, Nick smiled to himself. Even when Lazarus began speaking, he kept glancing back over his shoulder, and once when two bearded Algerian students in combat jackets overtook them, he let them get well ahead before he went on.

"You know there will be nothing in writing?" he piped.

"I have a recorder in my pocket," Nick assured him.

"Very well, you are entitled to that."

"Thank you," murmured Nick dryly.

Lazarus paused, it was almost as though a new reel was being fitted into the computer, and when he began talking again, his voice had a different timbre, a monotonous, almost electronic tone, as though he was indeed an automaton.

First, there was a recital of share movements in the thirty-three companies which make up the Christy Marine complex, every movement in the previous eighteen months.

The little man reeled them off steadily, as though he were actually reading from the share registers of the companies. He must have had access, Nicholas realized, to achieve such accuracy. He had the date, the number of the shares, the transferor and transferee, even the transfer of shares in Ocean Salvage and Towage to Nicholas himself, and the reciprocal transfer of Christy Marine stock was faithfully detailed, confirming the accuracy of Lazarus' other information. It was all an impressive exhibition of total knowledge and total recall, but much too complicated for Nicholas to make any sense of it. He would have to study it carefully. All that he would hazard was that somebody was putting up a smokescreen.

Lazarus stopped on the corner of the Champs Elysées and the rue de la Boétie. Nicholas glanced down at him and saw his shapeless blob of a nose was an unhealthy purplish pink in the cold, and that his breathing had coarsened and laboured with the exertion of walking. Nick realized suddenly that the little man was probably asthmatic, and as if to confirm this, he took a little silver and turquoise pill-box from his pocket and slipped a single pink capsule into his mouth before leading Nicholas into the foyer of a movie house and buying two tickets.

It was a porno movie, a French version of *Deep Throat* entitled *Gorge Profonde*. The print was scratched and the French dubbing was out of synchronization. The cinema was almost empty, so they found two seats in isolation at the rear of the stalls.

Lazarus stared unblinkingly at the screen, as he began the second part of his report. This was a detailed breakdown of cash movements within the Christy Marine Group, and Nick was again amazed at the man's penetration.

He drew a verbal picture of the assemblage of enormous sums of money, marshalled and channelled into orderly flows by a master tactician. The genius of Duncan Alexander was as clearly identifiable as that flourishing signature with the flamboyant "A" and "X" which Nicholas had seen him dash off with studied panache. Then suddenly the cashflow was not so steady and untroubled, there were eddies and breaks, little gaps and inconsistencies that nagged at Nicholas like the false chimes of a broken clock. Lazarus finished this section of his report with a brief summation of the Group's cash and credit position as at a date four days previously and Nicholas realized that the doubts were justified. Duncan had run the Group out along a knife-edge.

Nicholas sat hunched down in the threadbare velvet seat, both hands thrust into the pockets of his trench coat, watching the incredible feats of Miss Lovelace on the screen, without really seeing them, while beside him Lazarus took an aerosol can from his pocket, screwed a nozzle on to it and noisily sprayed a fine mist down his own throat. It seemed to relieve him almost immediately.

"Insurance and marine underwriting of vessels owned by the Christy Marine Group of companies." He began again with names and figures and dates, and Nicholas picked up the trend. Duncan was using his own captive company, London and European Insurance and Banking, to lead the risk on all his vessels, and then he was reinsuring in the marketplace, spreading part of the risk, but carrying a whacking deductible himself, the principle of self-insurance that Nicholas had opposed so vigorously, and which had rebounded so seriously upon Duncan's head with the salvage of *Golden Adventurer*.

The last of the vessels in Lazarus' recital was *Golden Dawn*, and Nicholas shifted restlessly in his seat at the mention of the name, and almost immediately he realized that something strange was taking place.

"Christy Marine did not apply for a Lloyd's survey of this vessel." Nicholas knew that already. "But she has been rated first class by the continental surveyors." It was a much easier rating to obtain, and consequently less acceptable than the prestigious A1 at Lloyd's.

Lazarus went on, lowering his voice slightly as another patron entered the almost deserted cinema and took a seat two rows in front of them.

"And insurance has been effected outside Lloyd's." The risk was led by London and European Insurance. Again, Duncan was self-insuring, Nicholas noted grimly, but not all of it. "And further lines were written by—" Lazarus listed the other companies which carried a part of the risk, with whom Duncan had reinsured. But it was all too thin, too nebulous. Again, only careful study of the figures would enable Nicholas to analyse what Duncan was doing, how much was real insurance and how much was bluff to convince his financiers that the risk was truly covered, and their investment protected.

Some of the names of the reinsurers were familiar; they had been on the list of transferees who had taken stock positions in Christy Marine.

"Is Duncan buying insurance with capital?" Nicholas pondered. Was he buying at desperate prices? He must have cover, of course. Without insurance the finance houses, the banks and institutions which had loaned the money to Christy Marine to build the monstrous tanker, would dig in against Duncan. His own shareholders would raise such hell—No, Duncan Alexander had to have cover, even if it was paper only, without substance, a mere incestuous circle, a snake eating itself tail first.

Oh, but the trail was so cleverly confused, so carefully swept and tied up, only Nicholas' intimate knowledge of Christy Marine made him suspicious, and it might take a team of investigators years to unravel the tortured tapestry of deceit. In the first instant, it had occurred to Nicholas that the easiest way to stop Duncan Alexander was to leak his freshly gleaned suspicions to Duncan's major creditors, to those who had financed the building of *Golden Dawn*. But immediately he realized that this was not enough. There were no hard facts, it was all inference and innuendo. By the time the facts could be exhumed and laid out in all their putrefaction for autopsy, *Golden Dawn* would be on the high seas, carrying a million tons of crude. Duncan might have won sufficient time to make his profit and sell out to some completely uncontrollable Greek or Chinaman, as he had boasted he would do. It would not be so simple to stop Duncan Alexander; it was folly to have believed that for one moment. Even if his creditors were made aware of the flimsy insurance cover over *Golden Dawn*, were they too deeply in already? Would they not then accept the risks, spreading them where they could, and simply twist the financial rope a little tighter around Duncan's throat? No, it was not the way to stop him. Duncan had to be forced to remodify the giant tanker's hull, forced to make her an acceptable moral risk, forced to accept the standard Nicholas had originally stipulated for the vessel.

Lazarus had finished the insurance portion of his report and he stood up abruptly, just as Miss Lovelace was about to attempt the impossible. With relief, Nick followed him down the aisle and into the chill of a Parisian evening, and they breathed the fumes that the teeming city exhaled as Lazarus led him back eastwards through the VIIIᵉ Arrondissement with those little dancing steps, while he recited the details of the charters of all Christy Marine's vessels, the charterer, the rates, the dates of expiry of contract; and Nicholas recognized most of them, contracts that he himself had negotiated, or those that had been renewed on expiry with minor alterations to the terms. He was relying on the recorder in his pocket, listening only with the surface layer of his mind, pondering all he had heard so far from this extraordinary little man—so that when it came he almost did not realize what he was hearing.

"On 10th January Christy Marine entered a contract of carriage with Orient Amex. The tenure is ten years. The vessel to be employed is the *Golden Dawn*. The rate is 10 cents US per hundred ton miles with a minimum annual guaranteed usage of 75,000 nautical miles."

Nicholas registered the trigger word *Golden Dawn* and then he assimilated it all. The price, ten cents per hundred ton miles, that was wrong, high, much too high, ridiculously high in this depressed market. Then the name, Orient Amex—what was there about it that jarred his memory?

He stopped dead, and a following pedestrian bumped him. Nicholas shouldered him aside thoughtlessly and stood thinking, ransacking his mind for buried items of information. Lazarus had stopped also and was waiting patiently, and now Nicholas laid a hand on the little man's shoulder.

"I need a drink."

He drew him into a brasserie which was thick with steam from the coffee machine and the smoke of Caporal and Disque Bleu, and sat him at a tiny table by the window overlooking the sidewalk.

Primly, Lazarus asked for a Vittel water and sipped it with an air of virtue, while Nicholas poured soda into his whisky.

"Orient Amex," Nicholas asked, as soon as the waiter had left. "Tell me about it."

"That is outside my original terms of reference," Lazarus demurred delicately.

"Charge me for it," Nicholas invited, and Lazarus paused as the computer reels clicked in his mind, then he began to speak.

"Orient Amex is an American-registered company, with an issued capital of twenty-five million shares at a par value of ten dollars—" Lazarus recited the dry statistics. "The company is presently undertaking substantial dry-land exploration in Western Australia and Ethiopia, and offshore exploration within the territorial waters of Norway and Chile. It has erected a refinery at Galveston in Texas to operate under the new atomic catalyst-cracking process, first employed at its pilot plant on the same site. The plant is projected for initial operation in June this year, and full production in five years."

It was all vaguely familiar to Nicholas, the names, the process of cracking the low-value high-carbon molecules, breaking up the carbon atoms and reassembling them in volatile low-carbon molecules of high value.

"The company operates producing wells in Texas, and in the Santa Barbara offshore field, in Southern Nigeria, and has proven crude reserves in the El Barras field of Kuwait, which will be utilized by the new cracking plant in Galveston."

"Good God," Nicholas stared at him. "The El Barras field—but it's cadmium-contaminated, it's been condemned by—"

"The El Barras field is a high cadmium field, naturally enriched with the catalyst necessary for the new process."

"What are the cadmium elements?" Nicholas demanded.

"The western area of the El Barras field has sampled at 2,000 parts per million, and the north and eastern anticline have sampled as high as 42,000 parts per million." Lazarus recited the figures pedantically. "The American and Nigerian crudes will be blended with the El Barras crudes during the revolutionary cracking process. It is projected that the yield of low-carbon volatiles will be increased from 40 per cent to 85 per cent by this process, making it five to eight times more profitable, and extending the life of the world's known reserves of crude petroleum by between ten and fifteen years."

As he listened, Nicholas had a vivid mental image of the stylus in Samantha's laboratory recording the death throes of a cadmium-poisoned clam. Lazarus was talking on dispassionately. "During the cracking process, the cadmium sulphide will be reduced to its pure metallic, non-toxic form, and will be a valuable by-product, reducing the costs of refining."

Nicholas shook his head in disbelief, and he spoke aloud. "Duncan is going to do it. Across two oceans, a million tons at a time, in that vulnerable jerry-built monster of his, Duncan is going to do what no other shipowner has ever dared to do—he's going to carry the cad-rich crudes of El Barras!"

• • • •

From the balcony windows of his suite in the Ritz, Nicholas could look out across the Place Vendôme at the column in the centre of the square with its spiral bas-relief made from the Russian and Austrian guns and commemorating the little Corsican's feats of arms against those two nations. While he studied the column and waited for his connection, he did a quick calculation and realized that it would be three o'clock in the morning on the eastern seaboard of North America. At least he would find her at home. Then he smiled to himself. If she wasn't at home, he'd want to know the reason why.

The telephone rang and he picked it up without turning away from the window.

There was a confused mumbling and Nicholas asked, "Who is this?"

"It's Sam Silver—what's the time? Who is it? Good God, it's three o'clock. What do you want?"

"Tell that other guy to put his pants on and go home."

"Nicholas!" There was a joyous squeal, followed immediately by a crash and clatter that made Nicholas wince and lift the receiver well away from his ear.

"Oh damn it to hell, I've knocked the table over. Nicholas, are you there? Speak to me, for God's sake!"

"I love you."

"Say that again, please. Where are you?"

"Paris. I love you."

"Oh," her tone drooped miserably. "You sound so close. I thought—" Then she rallied gamely. "I love you too—how's himself?"

"On the dole."

"Who is she?"

"Dole is unemployment insurance—welfare—" He sought the American equivalent. "I mean he is temporarily unemployed."

"Great. Keep him that way. Did I tell you I love you, I forget?"

"Wake up. Shake yourself. I've got something to tell you."

"I'm awake—well, almost anyway."

"Samantha, what would happen if somebody dumped a million tons of 40,000 parts concentration of cadmium sulphide in an emulsion of aromatic Arabian crude into the Gulf Stream, say thirty nautical miles off Key West?"

"That's a freaky question, Nicholas. For three in the morning, that's a bomber."

"What would happen?" he insisted.

"The crude would act as a transporting medium," she was struggling to project a scenario through her sleepiness, "it would spread out on the surface to a thickness of a quarter of an inch or so, so you'd end up with a slick of a few thousand miles long and four or five hundred wide, and it would keep going."

"What would be the results?"

"It would wipe out most of the marine life on the Bahamas and on the eastern seaboard of the States, no, correct that—it would wipe out all marine life, that includes the spawning grounds of the tuna, the freshwater eels and the sperm whale, and it would contaminate—" she was coming fully awake now, and a stirring horror altered her tone. "You're macabre, Nicholas, what a sick thing to think about, especially at three in the morning."

"Human life?" he asked.

"Yes, there would be heavy loss," she said. "As sulphide, it would be readily absorbed and in that concentration it would be poisonous on contact, fishermen, vacationers, anybody who walked on a contaminated beach." She was truly beginning to realize the enormity of it. "A large part of the population of the cities on the east coast—Nicholas, it could amount to hundreds of thousands of human beings, and if it was carried beyond America on the Gulf Stream, the Newfoundland Banks, Iceland, the North Sea, it would poison the cod fisheries, it would kill everything, man, fish, bird and animal. Then the tail of the Gulf Stream twists around the British Isles and the north continent of Europe—but why are you asking me this, what kind of crazy guessing game is this, Nicholas?"

"Christy Marine has signed a ten-year contract to carry one million ton loads of crude from the El Barras field on the South Arabian Gulf to the Orient Amex refinery in Galveston. The El Barras crude has a cadmium sulphide constituent of between 2,000 and 40,000 parts per million."

Now there was trembling outrage in her voice as she whispered, "A million tons! That's some sort of genocide, Nicholas, there has probably never been a more deadly cargo in the history of seafaring."

"In a few weeks' time *Golden Dawn* will run down her ways at St. Nazaire—and when she does, the seeds of catastrophe will be sown upon the oceans."

"Her route from the Arabian Gulf takes her around Good Hope."

"One of the most dangerous seas in the world, the home of the hundred-year wave," Nicholas agreed.

"Then across the southern Atlantic—"

"—and into the bottleneck of the Gulf Stream between Key West and Cuba, into the Devil's Triangle, the breeding ground of the hurricanes—"

"You can't let them do it, Nicholas," she said quietly. "You just have to stop them."

"It won't be easy, but I'll be working hard on it this side, there are a dozen tricks I am going to try, but you have to take over on your side," he told her. "Samantha, you go get Tom Parker. Get him out of bed, if necessary. He has to hit Washington with the news, hit all the media—television, radio and the press. A confrontation with Orient Amex, challenge them to make a statement."

Samantha picked up the line he was taking. "We'll get the Greenpeacers to picket the Orient Amex refinery in Galveston, the one which will process the cadmium crudes. We'll have every environmental agency in the country at work—we'll raise a stink like that of a million corpses," she promised.

"Fine," he said. "You do all that, but don't forget to get your chubby little backside across here for the launching of Sea Witch."

"Chubby obese, or chubby nice?" she demanded.

"Chubby beautiful," he grinned. "And I'll have room service ready to send up the food, in a front-end loader."

Nicholas sat over the telephone for the rest of the day, having his meals brought up to the suite, while he worked systematically down the long list of names he had drawn up with the help of the tape recording of Lazarus' report.

The list began with all those who it seemed had loaned capital to Christy Marine for the construction of Golden Dawn, and then went on to those who had written lines of insurance on the hull, and on the pollution cover for the tanker.

Nicholas dared not be too specific in the summation he gave to each of them, he did not want to give Duncan Alexander an opportunity to throw out a smokescreen of libel actions against him. But in each case, Nicholas spoke to the top men, mostly men he knew well enough to use their Christian names, and he said just enough to show that he knew the exact amount of their involvement with Christy Marine, to suggest they re-examine the whole project, especially with regard to *Golden Dawn*'s underwriting and to her contract of carriage with Orient Amex.

In the quiet intervals between each telephone call, or while a name was tracked down by a secretary, Nicholas sat over the Place Vendôme and carefully re-examined himself and his reasons for what he was doing.

It is so very easy for a man to attribute to himself the most noble motives. The sea had given Nicholas a wonderful life, and had rewarded him in wealth, reputation and achievement. Now it was time to repay part of that debt, to use some of that wealth to protect and guard the oceans, the way a prudent farmer cherishes his soil. It was a fine thought, but when he looked below its shining surface, he saw the shape and movement of less savoury creatures, like the shadows of shark and barracuda in the depths.

There was pride. *Golden Dawn* had been his creation, the culmination of a lifetime's work, it was going to be the laurel crown on his career. But it had been taken from him, and bastardized—and when it failed, when the whole marvellous concept collapsed in disaster and misery, Nicholas Berg's name would still be on it. The world would remember then that the whole grandiose design had originated with him.

There was pride, and then there was hatred. Duncan Alexander had taken his woman and child. Duncan Alexander had wrested his very life from him. Duncan Alexander was the enemy, and by Nicholas' rules, he must be fought with the same single-mindedness, with the same ruthlessness, as he did everything in his life.

Nicholas poured himself another cup of coffee and lit a cheroot; brooding alone in the magnificence of his suite, he asked himself the question:

"If it had been another man in another ship who was going to transport the El Barras crudes—would I have opposed him so bitterly?"

The question needed no formal reply. Duncan Alexander was the enemy.

Nicholas picked up the telephone, and placed the call he had been delaying. He did not need to look in the red calf-bound notebook for the number of the house in Eaton Square.

"Mrs. Chantelle Alexander, please."

"I am sorry, sir. Mrs. Alexander is at Cap Ferrat."

"Of course," he muttered. "Thank you."

"Do you want the number?"

"That's all right, I have it." He had lost track of time. He dialled
again, this time down to the Mediterranean coast.

"This is the residence of Mrs. Alexander. Her son Peter Berg speaking."

Nicholas felt the rush of emotion through his blood, so that it burned
his cheeks and stung his eyes.

"Hello, my boy." Even in his own ears his voice sounded stilted, perhaps pompous.

"Father," undisguised delight. "Dad, how are you—sir? Did you get
my letters?"

"No, I didn't, where did you send them?"

"The flat—in Queen's Gate."

"I haven't been back there for," Nicholas thought, "for nearly a
month."

"I got your cards, Dad, the one from Bermuda and the one from
Florida. I just wrote to tell you—" and there was a recital of schoolboy
triumphs and disasters.

"That's tremendous, Peter. I'm really proud."

Nicholas imagined the face of his son as he listened, and his heart
was squeezed—by guilt, that he could do so little, could give him so little of his time, squeezed by longing for what he had lost. For it was only
at times such as these that he could admit how much he missed his son.

"That's great, Peter—" The boy was trying to tell it all at the same
time, gabbling out the news he had stored so carefully, flitting from subject to subject, as one thing reminded him of another. Then, of course,
the inevitable question:

"When can I come to you, Dad?"

"I'll have to arrange that with your mother, Peter. But it will be soon.
I promise you that." Let's get away from that, Nick thought, desperately.
"How is *Apache*? Have you raced her yet these holidays?"

"Oh yes, Mother let me have a new set of Terylene sails, in red and
yellow. I raced her yesterday." *Apache* had not actually been placed first
in the event, but Nicholas gained the impression that the blame lay not
with her skipper but rather on the vagaries of the wind, the unsporting

behaviour of the other competitors who bumped when they had the weather gauge, and finally the starter who had wanted to disqualify *Apache* for beating the gun. "But," Peter went on, "I'm racing again on Saturday morning—"

"Peter, where is your mother?"

"She's down at the boathouse."

"Can you put this call through there? I must speak to her, Peter."

"Of course." The disappointment in the child's voice was almost completely disguised. "Hey, Dad. You promised, didn't you? It will be soon?"

"I promised."

"Cheerio, sir."

There was a clicking and humming on the line and then suddenly her voice, with its marvellous timbre and serenity.

"*C'est Chantelle Alexander qui parle.*"

"*C'est Nicholas ici.*"

"Oh, my dear. How good to hear your voice. How are you?"

"Are you alone?"

"No, I have friends lunching with me. The Contessa is here with his new boyfriend, a matador no less!"

The "Contessa" was an outrageously camp and wealthy homosexual who danced at Chantelle's court. Nicholas could imagine the scene on the wide paved terrace, screened from the cliffs above by the sighing pines and the rococo pink boathouse with its turrets and rusty-coloured tiles. There would be gay and brilliant company under the colourful umbrellas.

"Pierre and Mimi sailed across from Cannes for the day." Pierre was the son of the largest manufacturer of civil and military jet aircraft in Europe. "And Robert—"

Below the terrace was the private jetty and small beautifully equipped yacht basin. Her visitors would have moored their craft there, the bare masts nodding lazily against the sky and the small Mediterranean-blue wavelets lapping the stone jetty. Nicholas could hear the laughter and the tinkle of glasses in the background, and he cut short the recital of the guest list.

"Is Duncan there?"

"No, he's still in London—he won't be out until next week."

"I have news. Can you get up to Paris?"

"It's impossible, Nicky." Strange how the pet name did not jar from her. "I must be at Monte Carlo tomorrow, I'm helping Grace with the Spring Charity—"

"It's important, Chantelle."

"Then there's Peter. I don't like to leave him. Can't you come here? There is a direct flight at nine tomorrow. I'll get rid of the house guests so we can talk in private."

He thought quickly, then, "All right, will you book me a suite at the Negresco?"

"Don't be silly, Nicky. We've thirteen perfectly good bedrooms here—we are both civilized people and Peter would love to see you, you know that."

The Côte d'Azur was revelling in a freakish burst of early spring weather when Nicholas came down the boarding ladder at Nice Airport, and Peter was waiting for him at the boundary fence, hopping up and down and waving both hands above his head like a semaphore signaller. But when Nicholas came through the gate he regained his composure and shook hands formally.

"It's jolly good to see you, Dad."

"I swear you've grown six inches," said Nicholas, and on impulse stooped and hugged the child. For a moment they clung to each other, and it was Peter who pulled away first. Both of them were embarrassed by that display of affection for a moment, then quite deliberately Nicholas placed his hand on Peter's shoulder and squeezed.

"Where is the car?"

He kept his hand on the child's shoulder as they crossed the airport foyer, and as Peter became more accustomed to this unusual gesture of affection, so he pressed closer to his father, and seemed to swell with pride.

Characteristically, Nicholas wondered what had changed about him that made it easier for him to act naturally towards those he loved. The answer was obvious, it was Samantha Silver who had taught him to let go.

"Let go, Nicholas." He could almost hear her voice now.

The chauffeur was new, a silent unobtrusive man, and there were only the two of them in the back seat of the Rolls on the drive back through Nice, and along the coast road.

"Mother has gone across to the Palace. She won't be back until dinner time."

"Yes, she told me. We've got the day to ourselves," Nicholas grinned, as the chauffeur turned in through the electric gates and white columns that guarded the entrance to the estate. "What are we going to do?"

They swam and they played tennis and took Peter's Arrowhead-class yacht *Apache* on a long reach up the coast as far as Menton and then raced back, gull-winged and spinnaker set on the wind with the spray kicking up over the bows and flicking into their faces. They laughed a lot and they talked even more, and while Nicholas changed for dinner, he found himself caught up in the almost postcoital melancholy of too much happiness—happiness that was transitory and soon must end. He tried to push the sadness aside, but it persisted as he dressed in a white silk rollneck and double-breasted blazer and went down to the terrace room.

Peter was there before him, early as a child on Christmas morning, his hair still wet and slicked down from the shower and his face glowing pinkly from the sun and happiness.

"Can I pour you a drink, Dad?" he asked eagerly, already hovering over the silver drinks tray.

"Leave a little in the bottle," Nicholas cautioned him, not wanting to deny him the pleasure of performing this grown-up service, but with a healthy respect for the elephantine tots that Peter dispensed in a sense of misplaced generosity.

He tasted the drink cautiously, gasped, and added more soda. "That's fine," he said, Peter looked proud, and at that moment Chantelle came down the wide staircase into the room.

Nicholas found it impossible not to stare. Was it possible she had grown more lovely since their last meeting, or had she merely taken special pains this evening?

She was dressed in ivory silk, woven gossamer fine, so it floated about her body as she moved, and as she crossed the last ruddy glow of the dying day that came in from the French windows of the terrace, the light struck through the sheer material and put the dainty line of her legs into momentary silhouette. Closer to him, he saw the silk was embroidered with the same thread, ivory on ivory, a marvellous understatement of elegance, and under it the shadowy outline of her breasts, those fine shapely breasts that he remembered so well, and the faint dusky rose suggestion of her nipples. He looked away quickly and she smiled.

"Nicky," she said, "I'm so sorry to have left you alone."

"Peter and I have had a high old time," he said.

She had emphasized the shape and size of her eyes, and the planes of the bone structure of her cheeks and jawline, with a subtlety that made it appear she wore no make-up, and her hair had a springing electrical fire to it, a rich glowing sable cloud about the small head. The honeyed ivory of her skin had tanned to the velvety texture of a cream-coloured rose petal across her bare shoulders and arms.

He had forgotten how relaxed and gracious she could be, and this magnificent building filled with its treasures standing in its pine forest high above the darkening ocean and the fairy lights of the coast was her natural setting. She filled the huge room with a special glow and gaiety, and she and Peter shared an impish sense of fun that had them all laughing at the old well-remembered jokes.

Nicholas could not sustain his resentment, could not bring himself to dwell on her betrayal in this environment, so the laughter was easy and the warmth uncontrived. When they went through to the small informal dining room, they sat at the table as they had done so often before; they seemed to be transported back in time to those happy almost forgotten years.

There were moments which might have jarred, but Chantelle's instinct was so certain that she could skirt delicately around these. She treated Nicholas as an honoured guest, not as the master of the house; instead she made Peter the host. "Peter darling, will you carve for us?" and the boy's pride and importance was almost overwhelming, although the bird looked as though it had been caught in a combine harvester by the time he had finished with it. Chantelle served food and wine, a chicken stuffed in Creole style and a petit Chablis, that had no special associations from the past; and the choice of music was Peter's. "Music to develop ulcers by," as Nicholas remarked aside, to Chantelle.

Peter fought a valiant rearguard action to delay the passage of time, but finally resigned himself when Nicholas told him, "I'll come and see you up to bed."

He waited while Peter cleaned his teeth with an impressive vigour that might have continued beyond midnight if Nicholas had not protested mildly. When at last he was installed between the sheets, Nicholas stooped over him and the boy wrapped both arms around his neck with a quiet desperation.

"I'm so happy," he whispered against Nicholas' neck and when they kissed he crushed Nicholas' lips painfully with his mouth—then, "Wouldn't it be fabulous if we could be like this always?" he asked. "If you didn't have to go away again, Dad?"

Chantelle had changed the wild music to the muted haunting melodies of Liszt, and as he came back into the room she was pouring cognac into a thin crystal balloon.

"Did he settle down?" she asked, and then answered herself immediately. "He's exhausted, although he doesn't know it."

She brought him the cognac and then turned away and went out through the doors on to the terrace. He followed her out, and they stood at the stone balustrade side by side. The air was clear but chill.

"It's beautiful," she said. The moon paved a wide silver path across the surface of the sea. "I always thought that the highway to my dreams."

"Duncan," he said. "Let's talk about Duncan Alexander," and she shivered slightly, folding her arms across her breasts and grasping her own naked shoulders.

"What do you want to know?"

"In what terms did you give him control of your shares?"

"As an agent, my personal agent."

"With full discretion?"

She nodded, and he asked next, "Did you have an escape clause? In what circumstances can you reclaim control?"

"The dissolution of marriage," she said, and then shook her head. "But I think I knew that no court would uphold the agreement if I wanted to change it. It's too Victorian. Anytime I want to I could simply apply to have the appointment of Duncan as my agent set aside."

"Yes, I think you're right," Nicholas agreed. "But it might take a year or more, unless you could prove malafides, unless you could prove he deliberately betrayed the trust of agency."

"Can I prove that, Nicky?" She turned to him now, lifting her face to him. "Has he betrayed that trust?"

"I don't know yet," Nicholas told her cautiously, and she cut in.

"I've made a terrible fool of myself, haven't I?" He kept silent, and she went on tremulously, "I know there is no way I can apologize to you for—for what I did. There is no way that I can make it up to you, but believe me, Nicholas—please believe me when I tell you, I have never regretted anything so much in all my life."

"It's past, Chantelle. It's over. There is no profit in looking back."

"I don't think there is another man in the world who would do what you are doing now, who would repay deceit and betrayal with help and comfort. I just wanted to say that."

She was standing very close to him now, and in the cool night he could feel the warmth of her flesh across the inches that separated them, and her perfume had a subtly altered fragrance on that creamy skin. She always wore perfume so well, the same way she wore her clothes.

"It's getting cold," he said brusquely, took her elbow and steered her back into the light, out of that dangerous intimacy. "We still have a great deal to discuss."

He paced the thick forest-green carpet, quickly establishing a beat as regular as that of a sentry, ten paces from the glass doors, passing in front of where she sat in the centre of the wide velvet couch, turning just before he reached the headless marble statue of a Greek athlete from antiquity that guarded the double oaken doors into the lobby, and then back in front of her again. As he paced, he told her in carefully prepared sequence all that he had learned from Lazarus.

She sat like a bird on the point of flight, turning her head to watch him, those huge dark eyes seeming to swell larger as she listened.

It was not necessary to explain it to her in layman's language, she was Arthur Christy's daughter, she understood when he told her how he suspected that Duncan Alexander had been forced to self-insure the hull of *Golden Dawn* and how he had used Christy stock to buy reinsurance, stock that he had probably already pledged to finance construction of the vessel.

Nicholas reconstructed the whole inverted pyramid of Duncan Alexander's machinations for her to examine, and almost immediately she saw how vulnerable, how unstable it was.

"Are you certain of all this?" she whispered, and her face was drained of all its lustrous rose tints.

He shook his head. "I've reconstructed the Tyrannosaurus from a jawbone," he admitted frankly. "The shape of it might be a little different, but one thing I am certain of is that it's a big and dangerous beast."

"Duncan could destroy Christy Marine," she whispered again. "Completely!" She looked around slowly, at the house—at the room and its treasures, the symbols of her life. "He has risked everything that is mine, and Peter's."

Nicholas did not reply, but he stopped in front of her and watched her carefully as she absorbed the enormity of it all.

He saw outrage turn slowly to confusion, to fear and finally to terror. He had never seen her even afraid before—but now, faced with the prospect of being stripped naked of the armour which had always protected her, she was like a lost animal, he could even see that flutter of her heart under the pale swelling flesh of her bosom, and she shivered again.

"Could he lose everything, Nicholas? He couldn't, could he?" She wanted assurance, but he could not give it to her, all he could give her was pity. Pity was the one emotion, probably the only one she had never aroused in him, not once in all the years he had known her.

"What can I do, Nicholas?" she pleaded. "Please help me. Oh God, what must I do?"

"You can stop Duncan launching *Golden Dawn*—until the hull and propulsion has been modified, until it has been properly surveyed and underwritten—and until you have taken full control of Christy Marine out of his hands again." And his voice was gentle, filled with his compassion as he told her.

"That's enough for one day, Chantelle. If we go on now, we will begin chasing our tails. Tonight you know what could happen, tomorrow we will discuss how we can prevent it. Have you a Valium?"

She shook her head. "I've never used drugs to hide from things." It was true, he knew, that she had never lacked courage. "How much longer can you stay?"

"I have a seat on the eleven o'clock plane. I have to be back in London by tomorrow night—we'll have time tomorrow morning."

The guest suite opened on to the second-floor balcony which ran along the entire front of the building overlooking the sea and the private harbour. The five main bedrooms all opened on to this balcony, an arrangement from fifty years previously when internal security against kidnapping and forcible entry had been of no importance.

Nicholas determined to speak to Chantelle about that in the morning. Peter was an obvious target for extortion, and he felt the goose bumps of

horror rise on his arms as he imagined his son in the hands of those de-
generate monsters who were everywhere allowed to strike and destroy
with impunity. There was a price to pay these days for being rich and
successful. The smell of it attracted the hyenas and vultures. Peter must
be better protected, he decided.

In the sitting-room, there was a well-stocked liquor cabinet concealed
behind mirrors, nothing so obvious and resoundingly middle-class as a
private bar. The daily papers, in English, French and German were set
out on the television table, *France-Soir, The Times, Allgemeine Zeitung*,
with even an airmail version of *The New York Times*.

Nicholas flipped open *The Times* and glanced quickly at the closing
prices. Christy Marine common stock was at £5.32p, up 15p on yesterday's prices. The market had not sniffed corruption—yet.

He pulled off his silk rollneck, and even though he had bathed three
hours previously, the tension had left his skin feeling itchy and unclean.
The bathroom had been lavishly redecorated in green onyx panels and the
fittings were eighteen-carat gold, in the shape of dolphins. Steaming water gushed from their gaping mouths at a touch. It could have been vulgar,
but Chantelle's unerring touch steered it into Persian opulence instead.

He showered, turning the setting high so that the stinging needles of
water scalded away his fatigue and the feeling of being unclean. There
were half a dozen thick white terry towelling robes in the glass-fronted
warming cupboard, and he selected one and went through into the bedroom, belting it around his naked waist. In his briefcase there was a draft
of the agreement of sale of Ocean Salvage and Towage to the Sheikhs.
James Teacher and his gang of bright young lawyers had read it, and
made a thick sheaf of notes. Nicholas must study these before tomorrow
evening when he met them in London.

He took the papers from his case and carried them through into the
sitting room, glancing at the top page before dropping them carelessly on
to the low coffee table while he went to pour himself a small whisky,
heavily diluted. He brought the drink back with him and sprawled into
the deep leather armchair, picked up the papers and began to work.

He became aware of her perfume first, and felt his blood quicken uncontrollably at the fragrance, and the papers rustled in his hand.

Slowly he lifted his head. She had come in utter silence on small bare
feet. She had removed all her jewellery and had let down her hair brushing it out on to her shoulders.

It made her seem younger, more vulnerable, and the gown she wore was cuffed and collared in fine soft lace. She moved slowly towards his chair, timorous and for once uncertain, the eyes huge and dark and haunted, and when he rose from the armchair, she stopped and one hand went to her throat.

"Nicholas," she whispered, "I'm so afraid, and so alone." She moved a step closer, and saw his eyes shift, his lips harden, and she stopped instantly.

"Please," she pleaded softly, "don't send me away, Nicky. Not tonight, not yet. I'm afraid to be alone—please."

He knew then that this had been going to happen, he had hidden the certainty of it from himself all that evening, but now it was upon him, and he could do nothing to avoid it. It was as though he had lost the will to resist, as though he stood mesmerized, his resolve softening and melting like wax in the candle flame of her beauty, of the passions which she commanded so skilfully, and his thoughts lost coherence, began to tumble and swirl like storm surf breaking on rock.

She recognized the exact instant when it happened to him, and she came forward silently, with small gliding footsteps, not making the mistake of speaking again and pressed her face to his bare chest framed in the collar of his robe. The thick curling hair was springing over hard flat muscle, and she flared her nostrils at the clean virile animal smell of his skin.

He was still resisting, standing stiffly with his hands hanging at his sides. Oh, she knew him so well. The terrible conflict he must suffer before he could be made to act against that iron code of his own. Oh, she knew him, knew that he was as sexual and physical an animal as she was herself, that he was the only man who had ever been able to match her appetites. She knew the defences he had erected about himself, the fortressing of his passions, the controls and repressions, but she knew so well how to subvert these elaborate defences, she knew exactly what to do and what to say, how to move and touch. As she began now, she found the deliberate act of breaking down his resistance excited her so swiftly that it was pain almost, agony almost, and it required all her own control not to advance too swiftly for him, to control the shaking of her legs and the pumping of her lungs, to play still the hurt and bewildered and frightened child, using his kindness, the sense of chivalry which would not allow him to send her away, in such obvious distress.

Oh God, how her body churned, her stomach cramped with the strength of her wanting, her breasts felt swollen and so sensitive that the contact of silk and lace was almost too painfully abrasive to bear.

"Oh, Nicky, please—just for a moment. Just once, hold me. Please, I cannot go on alone. Just for a moment, please."

She felt him lift his hands, felt the fingers on her shoulders, and the terrible pain of wanting was too much to bear, she could not control it—she cried out, it was a soft little whimper, but the force of it shook her body, and immediately she felt his reaction. Her timing had been immaculate, her natural womanly cunning had guided her. His fingers on her shoulders had been gentle and kindly, but now they hooked cruelly into her flesh.

His back arched involuntarily, his breath drummed from his chest under her ear, a single agonized exhalation like that of a boxer taking a heavy body punch. She felt his every muscle become taut, and she knew again the frightening power, the delirious giddy power she could still wield. Then, at last, joyously, almost fearfully, she experienced the great lordly lift and thrust of his loins—as though the whole world had moved and shifted about her.

She cried out again, fiercely, for now she could slip the hounds she had held so short upon the leash, she could let them run and hunt again. They had been too long denied, but now there was no longer need for care and restraint.

She knew exactly how to hunt him beyond the frontiers of reason, to course him like a flying stag, and his fingers tangled frantically in the foaming lace at her throat as he tried to free her tight swollen breasts. She cried out a third time, and with a single movement jerked open the fastening at his waist, exposing the full hard lean length of his body, and her hands were as frantic as his.

"Oh, sweet God, you're so hard and strong—oh sweet God, I've missed you so."

There was time later for all the refinements and nuances of love, but now her need was too cruel and demanding to be denied another moment. It had to happen this instant before she died of the lack.

Nicholas rose slowly towards the surface of sleep, aware of a brooding sense of regret. Just before he reached consciousness, a dream image formed in his sleep-starved brain, he relived a moment from the distant past. A fragment of time, recaptured so vividly as to seem whole and perfect. Long ago he had picked a deep-sea trumpet shell at five fathoms from the oceanic wall of the coral reef beyond the Anse Baudoin lagoon of Praslin Island. It was the size of a ripe coconut and once again he found himself holding the shell in both cupped hands, gazing into the narrow oval opening, around which the weed-furred and barnacle-encrusted exterior changed dramatically, flaring into the pouting lips and exposing the inner mother-of-pearl surfaces that were slippery to the touch, a glossy satin sheen, pale translucent pink, folded and convoluted upon themselves, shading darker into fleshy crimsons and wine purples as the passage narrowed and sank away into the mysterious lustrous depths of the shell.

Then abruptly, the dream image changed in his mind. The projected opening in the trumpet shell expanded, articulating on jaw-hinges and he was gaping into the deep and terrible maw of some great predatory sea-creature, lined with multiple rows of serrated triangular teeth—shark-like, terrifying, so he cried out in half-sleep, startling himself awake, and he rolled quickly on to his side and raised himself on one elbow. Her perfume still lingered on his skin, mingled with the smell of his own sweat, but the bed beside him was empty, though warm and redolent with the memory of her body.

Across the room, the early sun struck a long sliver of light through a narrow chink in the curtains. It looked like a blade, a golden blade. It reminded him instantly of Samantha Silver. He saw her again wearing sunlight like a cloak, barefoot in the sand—and it seemed that the blade of sunlight was being driven up slowly under his ribs.

He swung his feet off the wide bed and padded softly across to the gold and onyx bathroom. There was a dull ache of sleeplessness and remorse behind his eyes and as he ran hot water from the dolphin's mouth into the basin, he looked at himself in the mirror although the steam slowly clouded the image of his own face. There were dark smears below his eyes and his features were gaunt, harsh angles of bone beneath drawn skin.

"You bastard," he whispered at the shadowy face in the mirror. "You bloody bastard."

They were waiting breakfast for him, in the sunlight on the terrace under the gaily coloured umbrellas. Peter had preserved the mood of the previous evening, and he ran laughing to meet Nicholas.

"Dad, hey Dad." He seized Nicholas' hand and led him to the table.

Chantelle wore a long loose housegown, and her hair was down on her shoulders, so soft that it stirred like spun silk in even that whisper of breeze. It was calculated, Chantelle did nothing by chance; the intimately elegant attire and the lose fall of her hair set the mood of domesticity—and Nicholas found himself resisting it fiercely.

Peter sensed his father's change of mood with an intuitive understanding beyond his years, and his dismay was a palpable thing, the hurt and reproach in his eyes as he looked at Nicholas; and then the chatter died on his lips and he bent his head studiously over his plate and ate in silence.

Nicholas deliberately refused the festival array of food, took only a cup of coffee, and lit a cheroot, without asking Chantelle's permission, knowing how she would resent that. He waited in silence and as soon as Peter had eaten he said:

"I'd like to speak to your mother, Peter."

The boy stood up obediently.

"Will I see you before you leave, sir?"

"Yes." Nicholas felt his heart wrung again. "Of course."

"We could sail again?"

"I'm sorry, my boy. We won't have time. Not today."

"Very well, sir." Peter walked to the end of the terrace, very erect and dignified, then suddenly he began to run, taking the steps down two at a time, and he fled into the pine forest beyond the boathouse as though pursued, feet flying and arms pumping wildly.

"He needs you, Nicky," said Chantelle softly.

"You should have thought about that two years ago."

She poured fresh coffee into his cup. "Both of us have been stupid—all right, worse than that. We've been wicked. I have had my Duncan, and you have had that American child."

"Don't make me angry now," he warned her softly. "You've done enough for one day."

"It's as simple as this, Nicholas. I love you, I have always loved you—God, since I was a gawky schoolgirl." She had never been that, but Nicholas let it pass. "Since I saw you that first day on the bridge of old *Golden Eagle*, the dashing ship's captain—"

"Chantelle. All we have to discuss is *Golden Dawn* and Christy Marine."

"No, Nicholas. We were born for each other. Daddy saw that immediately, we both knew it at the same time—it was only a madness, a crazy whim that made me doubt it for a moment."

"Stop it, Chantelle."

"Duncan was a stupid mistake. But it's unimportant—"

"No, it's not unimportant. It changed everything. It can never be the same again, besides—"

"Besides, what? Nicky, what were you going to say?"

"Besides, I am building myself another life now. With another very different person."

"Oh God, Nicky, you aren't serious?" She laughed then, genuine amusement, clapping her hands delightedly. "My dear, she's young enough to be your daughter. It's the forty syndrome, the Lolita complex." Then she saw his real anger, and she was quick, retrieving the situation neatly, aware that she had carried it too far.

"I'm sorry, Nicky. I should never have said that." She paused, and then went on. "I will say she's a pretty little thing, and I'm sure she's sweet—Peter liked her." She damned Samantha with light condescension, and then dismissed her as though she were merely a childlike prank of Nicholas', a light and passing folly of no real significance.

"I understand, Nicholas, truly I do. However, when you are ready, as you will be soon, then Peter and I and Christy Marine are waiting for you still. This is your world, Nicholas." She made a gesture which embraced it all. "This is your world; you will never really leave it."

"You are wrong, Chantelle."

"No." She shook her head. "I am very seldom wrong, and on this I cannot be wrong. Last night proved that, it is still there—every bit of it. But let's discuss the other thing now, *Golden Dawn* and Christy Marine."

Chantelle Alexander lifted her face to the sky and watched the big silver bird fly. It climbed nose high, glinting in the sunlight, twin trails of dark unconsumed fuel spinning out behind it as the engines howled under the full thrust. With the wind in this quarter, the extended centreline of the main Nice runway brought it out over Cap Ferrat.

Beside Chantelle, only an inch or two shorter than she was, Peter stood and watched it also and she took his arm, tucking her small dainty hand into the crook of his elbow.

"He stayed such a short time," Peter said, and overhead the big airbus turned steeply on to its crosswind leg.

"We will have him with us again soon," Chantelle promised, and then she went on. "Where were you, Peter? We hunted all over when it was time for Daddy to go."

"I was in the forest," he said evasively. He had heard them calling, but Peter was hidden in the secret place, the smuggler's cleft in the yellow rock of the cliff; he would have killed himself rather than let Nicholas Berg see him weeping.

"Wouldn't it be lovely if it was like the old times again?" Chantelle asked softly, and the boy stirred beside her, but unable to take his gaze from the aircraft. "Just the three of us again?"

"Without Uncle Duncan?" he asked incredulously, and high above them the aircraft, with a last twinkle of sunlight, drove deeply into the banks of cumulus cloud that buttressed the northern sky. Peter turned at last to face her.

"Without Uncle Duncan?" he demanded again. "But that's impossible."

"Not if you help me, darling." She took his face in her cupped hands. "You will help me, won't you?" she asked, and he nodded once, a sharply incisive gesture of assent; she leaned forward and kissed him tenderly on the forehead.

"That's my man," she whispered.

M r. Alexander is not available. May I take a message?"

"This is Mrs. Alexander. Tell my husband that it's urgent."

"Oh, I'm terribly sorry, Mrs. Alexander." The secretary's voice changed instantly, cool caution becoming effusive servility. "I didn't recognize your voice. The line is dreadful. Mr. Alexander will speak to you directly."

Chantelle waited, staring impatiently from the study windows. The weather had changed in the middle of the morning with the cold front sweeping down off the mountains, and now icy wind and rain battered at the windows.

"Chantelle, my dear," said the rich glossy voice that had once so dazzled her. "Is this my call to you?"

"It's mine, Duncan. I must speak to you urgently."

"Good," he agreed with her. "I wanted to speak to you also. Things are happening swiftly here. It's necessary for you to come up to St. Nazaire next Tuesday, instead of my joining you at Cap Ferrat."

"Duncan—"

But he went on over her protest, his voice as full of self-confidence, as ebullient as she had not heard it in over a year.

"I have been able to save almost four weeks on *Golden Dawn*."

"Duncan, listen to me."

"We will be able to launch on Tuesday. It will be a makeshift ceremony, I'm afraid, at such short notice." He was inordinately proud of his own achievement. It annoyed her to hear him. "What I have arranged is that the pod tanks will be delivered direct to the Gulf from the Japanese yards. They are towing them in their ballast with four American tugs. I will launch the hull here, with workmen still aboard her, and they will finish her off at sea during the passage around Good Hope, in time for her to take on her tanks and cargo at El Barras. We'll save nearly seven and a half million—"

"Duncan!" Chantelle cried again, and this time something in her tone stopped him.

"What is it?"

"This can't wait until Tuesday, I want to see you right away."

"That's impossible," he laughed, lightly, confidently. "It's only five days."

"Five days is too long."

"Tell me now," he invited. "What is it?"

"All right," she said deliberately, and the vicious streak of Persian cruelty was in her voice. "I'll tell you. I want a divorce, Duncan, and I want control of my shares in Christy Marine again."

There was a long, hissing crackling silence on the line, and she waited, the way the cat waits for the first movement of the crippled mouse.

"This is very sudden." His voice had changed completely, it was bleak and flat, lacking any timbre or resonance.

"We both know it is not," she contradicted him.

"You have no grounds." There was a thin edge of fear now. "Divorce isn't quite as easy as that, Chantelle."

"How is this for grounds, Duncan?" she asked, and there was a spiteful sting in her voice now. "If you aren't here by noon tomorrow, then my auditors will be in Leadenhall Street and there will be an urgent order before the courts—"

She did not have to go on, he spoke across her and there was a note of panic in his voice. She had never heard it before. He said, "You are right. We do have to talk right away." Then he was silent again, collecting himself, and his voice was once more calm and careful when he went on, "I can charter a Falcon and be at Nice before midday. Will that do?"

"I'll have the car meet you," she said, and broke the connection with one finger. She held the bar down for a second, then lifted her finger.

"I want to place an international call," she said in her fluent rippling French when the operator answered. "I do not know the number, but it is person to person. Doctor Samantha Silver at the University of Miami."

"There is a delay of more than two hours, madame."

"*J'attendrai*," she said, and replaced the receiver.

The Bank of the East is in Curzon Street, almost opposite the White Elephant Club. It has a narrow frontage of bronze and marble and glass, and Nicholas had been there, with his lawyers, since ten o'clock that morning. He was learning at first hand the leisurely age-old ritual of oriental bargaining.

He was selling Ocean Salvage, plus two years of his future labour— and even for seven million dollars he was beginning to wonder if it was worth it—and it was not a certain seven million either. The words tripped lightly, the figures seemed to have no substance in this setting. The only constant was the figure of the Prince himself, seated on the low couch, in a Savile Row suit but with the fine white cotton and gold-corded headdress framing his dark handsome features with theatrical dash.

Beyond him moved a shadowy, ever-changing background of unctuous whispering figures. Every time that Nicholas believed that a point had been definitely agreed, another rose-pink or acid-yellow Rolls-Royce with Arabic script numberplates would deposit three or four more dark-featured Arabs at the front doors and they would hurry through to kiss the Prince on his forehead, on the bridge of his nose and on the back of his hand, and the hushed discussion would begin all over again with the newcomers picking up at the point they had been an hour previously.

James Teacher showed no impatience, and he smiled and nodded and went through the ritual like an Arab born, sipping the little thimbles of treacly coffee and watching patiently for the interminable whisperings to be translated into English before making a measured counter proposal.

"We are doing fine, Mr. Berg," he assured Nicholas quietly. "A few more days."

Nicholas had a headache from the strong coffee and the Turkish tobacco smoke, and he found it difficult to concentrate. He kept worrying about Samantha. For four days he had tried to contact her. He had to get out for a while and he excused himself to the Prince, and went down to the Enquiries Desk in the Bank's entrance hall and the girl told him,

"I'm sorry, sir, there is no reply to either of those numbers."

"There must be," Nicholas told her. One number was Samantha's shack at Key Biscayne and the other was her private number in her laboratory.

She shook her head. "I've tried every hour."

"Can you send a cable for me?"

"Of course, sir."

She gave him a pad of forms and he wrote out the message.

"Please phone me urgently, reverse charges to—" he gave the number of the Queen's Gate flat and James Teacher's rooms, then he thought with the pen poised, trying to find the words to express his concern, but there were none.

"I love you," he wrote. "I really do."

S ince Nicholas' midnight call to tell her of the carriage of cad-rich crude petroleum, Samantha Silver had been caught up in a kaleidoscope whirl of time and events.

After a series of meetings with the leaders of Green-peace, and other conservation bodies in an effort to publicize and oppose this new threat to the oceans, she and Tom Parker had flown to Washington and met with a deputy director of the Environmental Protection Agency and with two

young senators who spearheaded the conservation lobby—but their efforts to go further had been frustrated by the granite walls of big oil interest. Even usually cooperative sources had been wary of condemning
or speaking out against Orient Amex's new carbon-cracking technology.
As one thirty-year-old Democrat senator had pointed out, "It's tough to
try and take a shot at something that's going to increase the fossil fuel
yield by fifty per cent."

"That's not what we are shooting at," Samantha had flared, bitter with
fatigue and frustration. "It's this irresponsible method of carrying the
cad-rich through sensitive and highly vulnerable seaways we are trying
to prevent." But when she presented the scenario she had worked out,
picturing the effects on the North Atlantic deluged with a million tons of
toxic crude, she saw the disbelief in the man's eyes and the condescend-
ing smile of the sane for the slightly demented.

"Oh God, why is common sense the hardest thing in the world to
sell?" she had lamented.

She and Tom had gone on to meet the leaders of Greenpeace in the
north, and in the west, and they had given advice and promises of support. The Californian Chapter counselled physical intervention as a last
resort, as some of their members had successfully interposed small craft
between the Russian whalers and the breeding minkes they were hunting
in the Californian Gulf.

In Galveston, they met the young Texans who would picket the Orient
Amex refinery as soon as they were certain the ultra-tanker had entered
the Gulf of Mexico.

However, none of their efforts were successful in provoking confrontation with Orient Amex. The big oil company simply ignored invitations to debate the charges on radio or television, and stonewalled
questions from the media. It's hard to stir up interest in a one-sided argument, Samantha found.

They managed one local Texas television show, but without controversy to give it zip, the producer cut Samantha's time down to forty-five
seconds, and then tried to date her for dinner.

The energy crisis, oil tankers and oil pollution were joyless subjects.
Nobody had ever heard of cadmium pollution, the Cape of Good Hope
was half a world away, a million tons was a meaningless figure, impossible to visualize, and it was all rather a bore.

The media let it drop flat on its face.

"We're just going to have to smoke those fat cats at Orient Amex out into the open," Tom Parker growled angrily, "and kick their arses blue for them. The only way we are going to do that is through Greenpeace."

They had landed back at Miami International, exhausted and disappointed, but not yet despondent. "Like the man said," Samantha muttered grimly, as she threaded her gaudy van back into the city traffic flow, "we have only just begun to fight."

She had only a few hours to clean herself up and stretch out on the patchwork quilt before she had to dress again and race back to the airport. The Australian had already passed through customs and was looking lost and dejected in the terminal lobby.

"Hi, I'm Sam Silver." She pushed away fatigue, and hoisted that brilliant golden smile like a flag.

His name was Mr. Dennis O'Connor and he was the top man in his field, doing fascinating and important work on the reef populations of Eastern Australian waters, and he had come a long way to talk to her and see her experiments.

"I didn't expect you to be so young." She had signed her correspondence "Doctor Silver" and he gave the standard reaction to her. Samantha was just tired and angry enough not to take it.

"And I'm a woman. You didn't expect that either," she agreed. "It's a crying bastard, isn't it? But then, I bet some of your best friends are young females."

He was a dinky-die Aussie, and he loved it. He burst into an appreciative grin, and as they shook hands, he said, "You are not going to believe this, but I like you just the way you are."

He was tall and lean, sunburned and just a little grizzled at the temples, and within minutes they were friends, and the respect with which he viewed her work confirmed that.

The Australian had brought with him, in an oxygenated container, five thousand live specimens of *E. digitalis*, the common Australian water snail, for inclusion in Samantha's experimentation. He had selected these animals for their abundance and their importance in the ecology of the Australian inshore waters, and the two of them were soon so absorbed in the application of Samantha's techniques to this new creature that when her assistant stuck her head through and yelled, "Hey, Sam, there's a call for you," she shouted back, "Take a message. If they're lucky I'll call them back."

"It's international, person to person!" and Samantha's pulse raced; instantly forgotten was the host of spiral-coned sea snails.

"Nicholas!" she shouted happily, spilled half a pint of sea water down the Australian's trouser leg and ran wildly to the small cubicle at the end of the laboratory.

She was breathless with excitement as she snatched up the receiver and she pressed one hand against her heart to stop it thumping.

"Is that Doctor Silver?"

"Yes! It's me." Then correcting her grammar, "It is she!"

"Go ahead, please," said the operator, and there was a click and pulse on the line as it came alive.

"Nicholas!" she exulted. "Darling Nicholas, is that you?"

"No." The voice was very clear and serene, as though the speaker stood beside her, and it was familiar, disconcertingly so, and for no good reason Samantha felt her heart shrink with dread.

"This is Chantelle Alexander, Peter's mother. We have met briefly."

"Yes." Samantha's voice was now small, and still breathless.

"I thought it would be kind to tell you in person, before you hear from other sources—that Nicholas and I have decided to remarry."

Samantha sat down jerkily on the office stool.

"Are you there?" Chantelle asked after a moment.

"I don't believe you," whispered Samantha.

"I'm sorry," Chantelle told her gently. "But there is Peter, you see, and we have rediscovered each other—discovered that we had never stopped loving each other."

"Nicholas wouldn't—" her voice broke, and she could not go on.

"You must understand and forgive him, my dear," Chantelle explained. "After our divorce he was hurt and lonely. I'm sure he did not mean to take advantage of you."

"But, but—we were supposed to, we were going to—"

"I know. Please believe me, this has not been easy for any of us. For all our sakes—"

"We had planned a whole life together." Samantha shook her head wildly, and a thick skein of golden hair came loose and flopped into her face, she pushed it back with a combing gesture. "I don't believe it, why didn't Nicholas tell me himself? I won't believe it until he tells me."

Chantelle's voice was compassionate, gentle. "I so wanted not to make it ugly for you, my child, but now what can I do but tell you that

Nicholas spent last night in my house, in my bed, in my arms, where he truly belongs."

It was almost miraculous, a physical thing, but sitting hunched on the hard round stool Samantha Silver felt her youth fall away from her, sloughed off like a glittering reptilian skin. She was left with the sensation of timelessness, possessed of all the suffering and sorrow of every woman who had lived before. She felt very old and wise and sad, and she lifted her fingers and touched her own cheek, mildly surprised to feel that the skin was not dried and withered like that of some ancient crone.

"I have already made the arrangements for a divorce from my present husband, and Nicholas will resume his position at the head of Christy Marine."

It was true, Samantha knew then that it was true. There was no question, no doubt, and slowly she replaced the receiver of the telephone, and sat staring blankly at the bare wall of the cubicle. She did not cry, she felt as though she would never cry, nor laugh, again in her life.

C hantelle Alexander studied her husband carefully, trying to stand outside herself, and to see him dispassionately. She found it easier now that the giddy insanity had burned away.

He was a handsome man, tall and lean, with those carefully groomed metallic waves of coppery hair. Even the wrist that he shot from the crisp white cuff of his sleeve was covered with those fine gleaming hairs. She knew so well that even his lean chest was covered with thick golden curls, crisp and curly as fresh lettuce leaves. She had never been attracted by smooth hairless men.

"May I smoke?" he asked, and she inclined her head. His voice had also attracted her from the first, deep and resonant, but with those high-bred accents, the gentle softening of the vowel sounds, the lazy drawling of consonants. The voice and the patrician manner were things that she had been trained to appreciate—and yet, under the mannered cultivated exterior was the flash of exciting wickedness, that showed in the wolfish white gleam of smile, and the sharp glittering grey steel of his gaze.

He lit the custom-made cigarette with the gold lighter she had given him—her very first gift, the night they had become lovers. Even now, the memory of it was piquant, and for a moment she felt the soft melting warmth in her lower belly and she stirred restlessly in her chair. There had been reason, and good reason for that madness, and even now it was over, she would never regret it.

It had been a period in her life which she had not been able to deny herself. The grand sweeping illicit passion, the last flush of her youth, the final careless autumn that preceded middle age. Another ordinary woman might have had to content herself with sweaty sordid gropings and grapplings in anonymous hotel bedrooms, but not Chantelle Christy. Her world was shaped by her own whims and desires, and, as she had told Nicholas, whatever she desired was hers to take. Long ago, her father had taught her that there were special rules for Chantelle Christy, and the rules were those she made herself.

It had been marvellous, she shivered slightly at the lingering sensuality of those early days, but now it was over. During the past months she had been carefully comparing the two men. Her decision had not been lightly made.

She had watched Nicholas retrieve his life from the gulf of disaster. On his own, stripped naked of all but that invisible indefinable mantle of strength and determination, he had fought his way back out of the gulf. Strength and power had always moved her, but she had over the years grown accustomed to Nicholas. Familiarity had staled their relationship for her. But now her interlude with Duncan had freshened her view of him, and he had for her all the novel appeal of a new lover—yet with the proven values and qualities of long intimate acquaintance. Duncan Alexander was finished; Nicholas Berg was the future.

But, no, she would never regret this interlude in her life. It had been a time of rejuvenation. She would not even regret Nicholas' involvement with the pretty American child. Later, it would add a certain perverse spice to their own sexuality, she thought, and felt the shiver run down her thighs and the soft secret stirring of her flesh, like the opening of a petalled rosebud. Duncan had taught her many things, bizarre little tricks of arousal, made more poignant by being forbidden and wicked. Unfortunately Duncan relied almost entirely on the tricks, and not all of them had worked for her—the corners of her mouth turned down with distaste as she remembered; perhaps it was just that which had begun the curdling process.

No, Duncan Alexander had not been able to match her raw, elemental sexuality and soaring abandon. Only one man had ever been able to do that. Duncan had served a purpose, but now it was over. It might have dragged on a little longer, but Duncan Alexander had endangered Christy Marine. Never had she thought of that possibility; Christy Marine was a fact of her life, as vast and immutable as the heavens, but now the foundations of heaven were being shaken. His sexual attraction had staled. She might have forgiven him that, but not the other.

She became aware of Duncan's discomfort. He twisted sideways in his chair, crossing and uncrossing his long legs, and he rolled the cigarette between his fingers, studying the rising spiral of blue smoke to avoid the level, expressionless gaze of her dark fathomless eyes. She had been staring at him, but seeing the other man. Now, with an effort, she focused her attention on him.

"Thank you for coming so promptly," she said.

"It did seem rather urgent." He smiled for the first time, glossy and urbane—but with fear down there in the cool grey eyes, and his tension was betrayed by the clenched sinew in the point of his jaw.

Looking closely, as she had not done for many months, she saw how he was fined down. The long tapered fingers were bony, and never still. There were new harder lines to his mouth, and a frown to the set of his eyes. The skin at the corners cracked like oil paint into hundreds of fine wrinkles that the deep brown snow-tan hid from a casual glance. Now he returned her scrutiny directly.

"From what you told me yesterday—"

She lifted her hand to stop him. "That can wait. I merely wanted to impress you with the seriousness of what is happening. What is really of prime importance now is what you have done with control of my shares and those of the Trust."

His hands went very still. "What does that mean?"

"I want auditors, my appointed auditors, sent in—"

He shrugged. "All this will take time, Chantelle, and I'm not certain that I'm ready to relinquish control." He was very cool, very casual now and the fear was gone.

She felt a stir of relief, perhaps the horror story that Nicholas had told her was untrue, perhaps the danger was imaginary only. Christy Marine was so big, so invulnerable.

"Not just at the moment, anyway. You'd have to prove to me that doing so was in the best interest of the company and of the Trust."

"I don't have to prove anything, to anyone," she said flatly.

"This time you do. You have appointed me—"

"No court of law would uphold that agreement."

"Perhaps not, Chantelle, but do you want to drag all this through the courts—at a time like this?"

"I'm not afraid, Duncan." She stood up quickly, light on her feet as a dancer, the lovely legs in loose black silk trousers, soft flat shoes making her seem still smaller, a slim gold chain emphasizing the narrowness of the tiny waist. "You know I'm afraid of nothing." She stood over him, and pointed the accuser's finger. The nails tipped in scarlet, the colour of fresh arterial blood. "You should be the one to fear."

"And precisely what is it you are accusing me of?"

And she told him, reeling off swiftly the lists of guarantees made by the Trust, the transfer of shares and the issues of new shares and guarantees within the Christy Marine group of subsidiaries, she listed the known layering of underwriting cover on *Golden Dawn* that Nicholas had unearthed.

"When my auditors have finished, Duncan darling, not only will the courts return control of Christy Marine to me, but they will probably sentence you to five years of hard labour. They take this sort of thing rather seriously, you know."

He smiled. He actually smiled! She felt her fury seething to the surface and the set of her eyes altered, colour tinted the smooth pale olive of her cheeks.

"You dare to grin at me," she hissed. "I will break you for that."

"No," he shook his head. "No, you won't."

"Are you denying—" she snapped, but he cut her off with a raised hand, and a shake of that handsome arrogant head.

"I am denying nothing, my love. On the contrary, I am going to admit it—and more, much more." He flicked the cigarette away, and it hissed sharply in the lapping blue wavelets of the yacht basin. While she stared at him, struck speechless, he let the silence play out like a skilled actor as he selected and lit another cigarette from the gold case.

"For some weeks now I have been fully aware that somebody was prying very deeply into my affairs and those of the company." He blew a long blue feather of cigarette smoke, and cocked one eyebrow at her, a cynical mocking gesture which increased her fury, but left her feeling suddenly afraid and uncertain. "It didn't take long to establish that the trace was coming from a little man in Monte Carlo who makes a living at financial and industrial espionage. Lazarus is good, excellent, the very best. I have used him myself, in fact it was I who introduced him to Nicholas Berg." He chuckled then, shaking his head indulgently. "The silly things we do sometimes. The connection was immediate. Berg and Lazarus. I have run my own check on what they have come up with and I estimate that even Lazarus could not have uncovered more than twenty-five per cent of the answers." He leaned forward and suddenly his voice snapped with a new authority. "You see, Chantelle dear, I am probably one of the best in the world myself. They could never have traced it all."

"You are not denying then—" She heard the faltering tone in her own voice, and hated herself for it. He brushed her aside contemptuously.

"Be quiet, you silly little woman, and listen to me. I am going to tell you just how deeply you are in—I am going to explain to you, in terms that even you can understand, why you will not send in your auditors, why you will not fire me, and why you will do exactly what I tell you to do."

He paused and stared into her eyes, a direct trial of strength which she could not meet. She was confused and uncertain, for once not in control of her own destiny. She dropped her eyes, and he nodded with satisfaction.

"Very well. Now listen. I have put it all—everything that is Christy Marine—it is all riding on *Golden Dawn*."

Chantelle felt the earth turn giddily under her feet and the sudden roaring rush of blood in her ears. She stepped back and the stone parapet caught the back of her knees. She sat down heavily.

"What are you talking about?" she whispered. And he told her, in substantial detail, from the beginning, how it had worked out. From the laying of *Golden Dawn*'s keel in the times of vast tanker tonnage demand. "My calculations were based on demand for tanker space two years ago, and on construction costs of that time."

The energy crisis and collapse in demand for tankers had come with the vicious rise in inflation, bloating the costs of construction of *Golden Dawn* by more than double. Duncan had countered by altering the design of the gigantic tanker. He had reduced the four propulsion units to one, he had cut down the steel structuring of the hull reinforcement by twenty per cent, he had done away with elaborate safety functions and fail-safe systems designed by Nicholas Berg, and he had cut it too fine. He had forfeited the Al Lloyd's rating, the mark of approval from the inspectors of that venerable body; without the insurance backing of that huge underwriting market, he had been forced to look elsewhere to find the cover to satisfy his financiers. The premiums had been crippling. He had to pledge Christy Marine stock, the Trust stock. Then the spiralling cost of production had overtaken him again and he needed money and more money. He had taken it where he could find it, at rates of interest that were demanded, and used more Christy stock as collateral.

Then the insurance cover had been insufficient to cover the huge increase in the cost of the ultra-tanker's hull.

"When luck runs out—" Duncan shrugged eloquently, and went on. "I had to pledge more Christy stock, all of it. It's all at risk, Chantelle, every single piece of paper, even the shares we retrieved from your Nicholas—and even that wasn't enough. I have had to write cover through front companies, cover that is worthless. Then," Duncan smiled again, relaxed and unruffled, almost as though he was enjoying himself, "then, there was that awful fiasco when *Golden Adventurer* went up on the ice, and I had to find six million dollars to pay the salvage award. That was the last of it, I went out for everything then, all of it. The Trust, the whole of Christy Marine."

"I'll break you," she whispered. "I'll smash you. I swear before God—"

"You don't understand, do you?" He shook his head sorrowfully, as though at an obtuse child. "You cannot break me, without breaking Christy Marine and yourself. You are in it, Chantelle, much much deeper than I am. You have everything, every penny, this house, that emerald on your finger, the future of your brat—all of it is riding on *Golden Dawn*."

"No." She closed her eyes very tightly, and there was no colour in her cheeks now.

"Yes. I'm afraid it's yes," he contradicted. "I didn't plan it that way. I saw a profit of 200 millions in it, but we have been caught up in circumstances, I'm afraid."

They were both silent, and Chantelle swayed slightly as the full enormity of it overwhelmed her.

"If you whistle up your hounds now, if you call in your axemen, there will be plenty for them to work on," he laughed again, "buckets of dung for us all to wallow in. And my backers will line up to cancel out. *Golden Dawn* will never run down her ways—she is not fully covered, as I explained to you. It all hangs on a single thread, Chantelle. If the launching of *Golden Dawn* is delayed now, delayed by a month—no, by a week even, it will all come tumbling down."

"I'm going to be sick," she whispered thickly.

"No, you are not." He stood up and crossed quickly to her. Coldly he slapped her face, two hard open-handed back and forth blows, that snapped her head from side to side, leaving the livid marks of his fingers on her pale cheeks. It was the first time ever that a man had struck her, but she could not find the indignation to protest. She merely stared at him.

"Pull yourself together," he snarled at her, and gripped her shoulders fiercely, shaking her as he went on. "Listen to me. I have told you the worst that can happen. Now, I will tell you the best. If we stand together now, if you obey me implicitly, without question, I will pull off one of the greatest financial coups of the century for you. All it needs is one successful voyage by *Golden Dawn* and we are home free—a single voyage, a few short weeks, and I will have doubled your fortune." She was staring at him, sickened and shaken to the core of her existence. "I have signed an agreement of charter with Orient Amex, that will pull us out from under a single voyage, and the day *Golden Dawn* anchors in Galveston roads and sends in her tank pods to discharge, I will have a dozen buyers for her." He stepped back, and straightened the lapels of his jacket. "Men are going to remember my name. In future when they talk of tankers, they are going to talk of Duncan Alexander."

"I hate you," she said softly. "I truly hate you."

"That is not important." He waved it away. "When it is over, I can afford to walk away—and you can afford to let me go. But not a moment before."

"How much will you make from this, if it succeeds?" she asked, and she was recovering, her voice firmer.

"A great deal. A very great deal of money—but my real reward will be in reputation and achievement. After this, I will be a man who can write his own ticket."

"For once, you will be able to stand comparison with Nicholas Berg. Is that it?" She saw she had scored immediately, and she pressed harder, trying to wound and destroy. "But you and I both know it is not true. *Golden Dawn* was Nicholas' inspiration and he would not have had to descend to the cheat and sham—"

"My dear Chantelle—"

"You will never be, could never be the man Nicholas is."

"Damn you." Suddenly he was shaking with anger, and she was screaming at him.

"You're a cheat and a liar. For all your airs, you're still a cheap little barrow-boy at heart. You're small and shoddy—"

"I've beaten Nicholas Berg every time I've met him."

"No, you haven't, Duncan. It was I who beat him for you—"

"I took you."

"For a while," she sneered. "Just for a short fling, Duncan dear. But when he wanted me he took me right back again."

"What do you mean by that?" he demanded.

"The night before last, Nicholas was here, and he loved me in a way you never could. I'm going back to him, and I'll tell the world why."

"You bitch."

"He is so strong, Duncan. Strong where you are weak."

"And you are a whore." He half turned away, and then paused. "Just be at St. Nazaire on Tuesday." But she could see he was hurt, at last she had cut through the carapace and touched raw quick nerves.

"He loved me four times in one night, Duncan. Magnificent, soaring love. Did you ever do that?"

"I want you at St. Nazaire, smiling at the creditors on Tuesday."

"Even if you succeed with *Golden Dawn*, within six months Nicholas will have your job."

"But until then you'll do exactly what I say." Duncan braced himself, a visible effort, and began to walk away.

"You are going to be the loser, Duncan Alexander," she screamed after him, her voice cracking shrilly with frustration and outrage. "I will see to that—I swear it to you."

He subdued the urge to run, and crossed the terrace, holding himself carefully erect, and the storm of her hatred and frustration burst around him.

"Go into the streets where you belong, into the gutter where I found you," she screamed, and he went up the stone staircase and out of her sight. Now he could hurry, but he found his legs were trembling underneath him, his breath was ragged and broken, and there was a tight knot of anger and jealousy turning his guts into a ball.

"The bastard," he spoke aloud. "That bastard Berg."

. . .

Tom? Tom Parker?"
"That's right, who is this, please?" His voice was so clear and strong, although the Atlantic Ocean separated them.

"It's Nicholas, Nicholas Berg."

"Nick, how are you?" the big voice boomed with genuine pleasure. "God, I'm glad you called. I've been trying to reach you. I've got good news. The best."

Nicholas felt a quick lift of relief.

"Samantha?"

"No, damn it," Tom laughed. "It's the job. Your job. It went up before the Board of Governors of the University yesterday. I had to sell it to them hard—I'll tell you that for free—but they okayed it. You're on, Nick, isn't that great?"

"It's terrific, Tom."

"You're on the Biology faculty as an associate. It's the thin end of the wedge, Nicholas. We'll have you a chair by the end of next year, you wait and see."

"I'm delighted."

"Christ, you don't sound it," Tom roared. "What's bugging you, boy?"

"Tom, what the hell has happened to Samantha?"

And Nicholas sensed the mood change, the silence lasted a beat too long, and then Tom's tone was guileless.

"She went off on a field trip—down the Keys, didn't she tell you?"

"Down the Keys?" Nicholas' voice rose with his anger and frustration. "Damn it, Tom. She was supposed to be here in France. She promised to come over for the launching of my new vessel. I've been trying to get in touch with her for a week now."

"She left Sunday," said Tom.

"What is she playing at?"

"That's a question she might want to ask you sometime."

"What does that mean, Tom?"

"Well, before she took off, she came up here and had a good weep with Antoinette—you know, my wife. She plays den mother for every hysterical female within fifty miles, she does."

Now it was Nicholas' turn to be silent, while the coldness settled on his chest, the coldness of formless dread.

"What was the trouble?"

"Good God, Nick, you don't expect me to follow the intimate details of the love life—"

"Can I speak to Antoinette?"

"She isn't here, Nick. She went up to Orlando for a meeting. She won't be back until the weekend."

The silence again.

"All that heavy breathing is costing you a fortune, Nicholas. You're paying for this call."

"I don't know what got into Sam." But he did. Nicholas knew—and the guilt was strong upon him.

"Listen, Nick. A word to the wise. Get your ass across here, boy. Just as soon as you can. That girl needs talking to, badly. That is, if you care about it."

"I care about it," Nicholas said quickly. "But hell, I am launching a tug in two days' time. I've got sea trials, and a meeting in London."

Tom's voice had an air of finality. "A man's got to do what he's got to do."

"Tom, I'll be across there as soon as I possibly can."

"I believe it."

"If you see her, tell her that for me, will you?"

"I'll tell her."

"Thanks, Tom."

"The governors will want to meet you, Nicholas. Come as soon as you can."

"It's a promise."

Nicholas cradled the receiver, and stood staring out of the windows of the site office. The view across the inner harbour was completely blocked by the towering hull of his tug. She stood tall on her ways. Her hull already wore its final coat of glistening white and the wide flaring bows bore the name *Sea Witch* and below that the port of registration, "Bermuda."

She was beautiful, magnificent, but now Nicholas did not even see her. He was overwhelmed by a sense of imminent loss, the cold premonition of onrushing disaster. Until that moment when he faced the prospect of losing her, he had not truly known how large a part that lovely golden girl had come to play in his existence, and in his plans for the future.

There was no way that Samantha could have learned of that single night of weakness, the betrayal that still left Nicholas sickened with guilt—there must be something else that had come between them. He bunched his right fist and slammed it against the sill of the window. The skin on his knuckles smeared, but he did not feel the pain, only the bitter frustration of being tied down here in St. Nazaire, weighed down by his responsibilities, when he should have been free to follow the jack-o'-lantern of happiness.

The loudspeaker above his head gave a preliminary squawk, and then crackled out the message, "Monsieur Berg. Will Monsieur attend upon the bridge?"

It was a welcome distraction, and Nicholas hurried out into the spring sunshine. Looking upwards, he could see Jules Levoisin on the wing of the bridge, his portly figure foreshortened against the open sky, like a small pugnacious rooster. He stood facing the electronics engineer who was responsible for the installation of *Sea Witch*'s communications system, and Jules' cries of "Sacré bleu" and "Merde" and "Imbécile" carried clearly above the cacophony of shipyard noises.

Nicholas started to run as he saw the engineer's arms begin to wave and his strident Gallic cries blended with those of *Sea Witch*'s new Master. It was only the third time that Jules Levoisin had become hysterical that day, however it was not yet noon. As the hour of launching came steadily closer, so the little Frenchman's nerves played him tricks. He was behaving like a prima ballerina awaiting the opening curtain. Unless Nicholas reached the bridge within the next few minutes, he would need either a new Master or a new electronics engineer.

Ten minutes later, Nicholas had a cheroot in each of their mouths. The atmosphere was still tense but no longer explosive, and gently Nick took the engineer by the elbow, placed his other arm around Jules Levoisin's shoulders and led them both back into the wheelhouse.

The bridge installation was complete, and Jules Levoisin was accepting delivery of the special equipment from the contractors, a negotiation every bit as traumatic as the Treaty of Versailles.

"I myself authorized the modification of the MK IV transponder," Nicholas explained patiently. "We had trouble with the same unit on *Warlock*. I should have told you, Jules."

"You should have," agreed the little Master huffily.

"But you were perceptive to notice the change from the specification," Nicholas soothed him, and Jules puffed out his chest a little and rolled the cheroot in his mouth.

"I may be an old dog, but I know all the new tricks." He removed the cheroot and smugly blew a perfect smoke ring.

When Nicholas at last left them chatting amiably over the massed array of sophisticated equipment that lined the navigation area at the back of the bridge, they were paging him from the site office.

"What is it?" he asked, as he came in through the door.

"It's a lady," the foreman indicated the telephone lying on the littered desk below the window.

"Samantha," Nick thought, and snatched up the receiver.

"Nicky." He felt the shock of quick guilt at the voice.

"Chantelle, where are you?"

"In La Baule." The fashionable resort town just up the Atlantic coast was a better setting for Chantelle Alexander than the grubby port with its sprawling dockyards. "Staying at the Castille. God, it's too awful. I'd forgotten how awful it was."

They had stayed there together, once long ago, in a different life it seemed now.

"But the restaurant is still quite cute, Nicholas. Have lunch with me. I must speak to you."

"I can't leave here." He would not walk into the trap again.

"It's important. I must see you." He could hear that husky tone in her voice, imagine clearly the sensuous droop of the eyelids over those bold Persian eyes. "For an hour, only an hour. You can spare that." Despite himself, he felt the pull of temptation, the dull ache of it at the base of his belly—and he was angry at her for the power she could still exert over him.

"If it's important, then come here," he said brusquely, and she sighed at his intransigence.

"All right, Nicholas. How will I find you?"

The Rolls was parked opposite the dockyard gates and Nicholas crossed the road and stepped through the door that the chauffeur held open for him.

Chantelle lifted her face to him. Her hair was cloudy dark and shot with light like a bolt of silk, her lips the colour of ripe fruit, moist and slightly parted. He ignored the invitation and touched her cheek with his lips before settling into the corner opposite her.

She made a little moue, and slanted her eyes at him in amusement. "How chaste we are, Nicky."

Nicholas touched the button on the control console and the glass soundproof partition slid up noiselessly between them and the chauffeur.

"Did you send in the auditors?" he asked.

"You look tired, darling, and harassed."

"Have you blown the whistle on Duncan?" he avoided the distraction. "The work on *Golden Dawn* is still going ahead. The arc lights were burning over her all night and the talk in the yards is that she is being launched at noon tomorrow, almost a month ahead of schedule. What happened, Chantelle?"

"There is a little bistro at Mindin, it's just across the bridge—"

"Damn it, Chantelle. I haven't time to fool around."

But the Rolls was already gliding swiftly through the narrow streets of the port, between the high warehouse buildings.

"It will take five minutes, and the Lobster Armoricaine is the local speciality—not to be confused with Lobster Américaine. They do it in a cream sauce, it's superb," she chatted archly, and the Rolls turned out on to the quay. Across the narrow waters of the inner harbour humped the ugly camouflaged mounds of the Nazi submarine pens, armoured concrete so thick as to resist the bombs of the RAF and the efforts of all demolition experts over the years since then.

"Peter asked me to give you his love. He has got his junior team colours. I'm so proud."

Nicholas thrust his hands deep into his jacket pockets and slumped down resignedly against the soft leather seat.

"I am delighted to hear it," he said.

And they were silent then until the chauffeur checked the Rolls at the toll barrier to pay before accelerating out on to the ramp of the St. Nazaire bridge. The great span of the bridge rose in a regal curve, three hundred feet above the waters of the Loire river. The river was almost three miles wide here, and from the highest point of the bridge there was an aerial view over the dockyards of the town.

There were half a dozen vessels building along the banks of the broad muddy river, a mighty forest of steel scaffolding, tall gantries and half-assembled hulls, but all of it insignificant under the mountainous bulk of

Golden Dawn. Without her pod tanks, she had an incomplete gutted appearance, as though the Eiffel Tower had toppled over and somebody had built a modernistic apartment block at one end. It seemed impossible that such a structure was capable of floating. God, she was ugly, Nick thought.

"They are still working on her," he said. One of the gantries was moving ponderously along the length of the ship like an arthritic dinosaur, and at fifty paces the brilliant blue electric fires of the welding torches flickered; while upon the grotesquely riven hull crawled human figures reduced to ant-like insignificance by the sheer size of the vessel.

"They are still working," he repeated it as an accusation.

"Nicholas, nothing in this life is simple—"

"Did you spell it out for Duncan?"

"—except for people like you."

"You didn't confront Duncan, did you?" he accused her bitterly.

"It's easy for you to be strong. It's one of the things that first attracted me."

And Nicholas almost laughed aloud. It was ludicrous to talk of strength, after his many displays of weakness with this very woman.

"Did you call Duncan's cards?" he insisted, but she put him off with a smile.

"Let's wait until we have a glass of wine—"

"Now," he snapped. "Tell me right now. Chantelle, I haven't time for games."

"Yes, I spoke to him," she nodded. "I called him down to Cap Ferrat, and I accused him—of what you suspected."

"He denied it? If he denies it, I now have further proof—"

"No, Nicholas. He didn't deny a thing. He told me that I knew only the half of it." Her voice rose sharply, and suddenly it all spilled out in a torrent of tortured words. Her composure was eroded swiftly away as she relived the enormity of her predicament. "He's gambled with my fortune, Nicholas. He's risked the family share of Christy Marine, the Trust shares, my shares, it's all at risk. And he gloated as he told me, he truly gloried in his betrayal."

"We've got him now." Nicholas had straightened slowly in his seat as he listened. His voice was grimly satisfied and he nodded. "That's it. We will stop the *Golden Dawn*, like that—" he hammered his bunched fist into the palm of the other hand with a sharp crack. "We will get an urgent order before the courts."

Nicholas stopped suddenly and stared at her. Chantelle was shaking her head slowly from side to side. Her eyes slowly filled, making them huge and glistening, a single tear spilled over the lid and clung in the thick dark lashes like a drop of morning dew.

The Rolls had stopped now outside the tiny bistro. It was on the river front, with a view across the water to the dockyards. To the west the river debouched into the open sea and in the east the beautiful arch of the bridge across the pale blue spring sky.

The chauffeur held open the door and Chantelle was gone with her swift birdlike grace, leaving Nicholas no choice but to follow her.

The proprietor came through from his kitchen and fussed over Chantelle, seating her at the window and lingering to discuss the menu.

"Oh, let's drink the Muscadet, Nicholas." She had always had the most amazing powers of recovery, and now the tears were gone and she was brittle and gay and beautiful, smiling at him over the rim of her glass. The sunlight through the leaded window panes danced in the cool golden wine and rippled on the smoky dark fall of her hair.

"Here's to us, Nicholas darling. We are the last of the great." It was a toast from long ago, from the other life, and it irritated him now but he drank it silently and then set down the glass.

"Chantelle, when and how are you going to stop Duncan?"

"Don't spoil the meal, darling."

"In about thirty seconds I'm going to start becoming very angry."

She studied him for a moment, and saw that it was true. "All right then," she agreed reluctantly.

"When are you going to stop him?"

"I'm not, darling."

He stared at her. "What did you say?" he asked quietly.

"I'm going to do everything in my power to help him launch and sail the *Golden Dawn*."

"You don't understand, Chantelle. You're talking about risking a million tons of the most deadly poison—"

"Don't be silly, Nicky. Keep that heroic talk for the newspapers. I don't care if Duncan dumps a million tons of cadmium in the water supply of Greater London, just as long as he pulls the Trust and me out of the fire."

"There is still time to make the modifications to *Golden Dawn*."

"No, there isn't. You don't understand, darling. Duncan has put us so deeply into it that a delay of a few days even would bring us down. He has stripped the cupboard bare, Nicky. There is no money for modifications, no time for anything, except to get *Golden Dawn* under way."

"There is always a way and a means."

"Yes, and the way is to fill *Golden Dawn*'s pod tanks with crude."

"He's frightened you by—"

"Yes," she agreed. "I am frightened. I have never been so frightened in my life, Nicky. I could lose everything—I am terrified. I could lose it all." She shivered with the horror of it. "I would kill myself if that happened."

"I am still going to stop Duncan."

"No, Nicky. Please leave it, for my sake—for Peter's sake. It's Peter's inheritance that we are talking about. Let *Golden Dawn* make one voyage, just one voyage—and I will be safe."

"It's the risk to an ocean, to God alone knows how many human lives, we are talking about."

"Don't shout, Nicky. People are looking."

"Let them look. I'm going to stop that monster."

"No, Nicholas. Without me, you cannot do a thing."

"You best believe it."

"Darling, I promise you, after her first voyage we will sell *Golden Dawn*. We'll be safe then, and I can rid myself of Duncan. It will be you and I again, Nicky. A few short weeks, that's all."

It took all his self-control to prevent his anger showing. He clenched his fists on the starched white tablecloth, but his voice was cool and even.

"Just one more question, Chantelle. When did you telephone Samantha Silver?"

She looked puzzled for a moment as though she was trying to put a face to a name. "Samantha, oh, your little friend. Why should I want to telephone her?" And then her expression changed. "Oh, Nicky, you don't really believe I'd do that? You don't really believe I would tell anybody about it, about that wonderful—" Now she was stricken, again those huge eyes brimmed and she reached across and stroked the fine black hairs on the back of Nicholas' big square hand. "You don't think that of me! I'm not that much of a bitch. I don't have to cheat to get the things I want. I don't have to inflict unnecessary hurt on people."

"No," Nicholas agreed quietly. "You'd not murder more than a mil-

lion or poison more than a single ocean at a time, would you?" He
pushed back his chair.

"Sit down, Nicky. Eat your lobster."

"Suddenly I'm not hungry." He stripped two one-hundred-franc notes
from his money clip and dropped them beside his plate.

"I forbid you to leave," she hissed angrily. "You are humiliating me,
Nicholas."

"I'll send your car back," he said, and walked out into the sunlight. He
found with surprise that he was trembling, and that his jaws were
clenched so tightly that his teeth ached.

T
he wind turned during the night, and the morning was cold with
drifts of low, grey, fast-flying cloud that threatened rain. Nicholas
pulled up his collar against the wind and the tails of his coat
flogged about his legs, for he was exposed on the highest point of the
arched bridge of St. Nazaire.

Thousands of others had braved the wind, and the guardrail was lined
two and three deep, all the way across the curve of the northern span.
The traffic had backed up and half a dozen gendarmes were trying to get
it moving again; their whistles shrilled plaintively. Faintly the sound of a
band floated up to them, rising and falling in volume as the wind caught
it, and even with the naked eye Nicholas could make out the wreaths of
gaily coloured bunting which fluttered on the high cumbersome stern
tower of *Golden Dawn*.

He glanced at his wristwatch, and saw it was a few minutes before
noon. A helicopter clattered noisily under the grey belly of cloud, and
hovered about the yards of Construction Navale Atlantique on the gleaming silver coin of its rotor.

Nicholas lifted the binoculars and the eyepieces were painfully cold
against his skin. Through the lens, he could almost make out individual
features among the small gathering on the rostrum under the tanker's
stern.

The platform was decorated with a tricolour and a Union Jack, and as
he watched the band fell silent and lowered their instruments.

"Speech time," Nicholas murmured, and now he could make out

Duncan Alexander, his bared head catching one of the fleeting rays of sun, a glimmer of coppery gold as he looked up at the towering stern of *Golden Dawn*.

His bulk almost obscured the tiny feminine figure beside him. Chantelle wore that particular shade of malachite green which she so dearly loved. There was confused activity around Chantelle, half a dozen gentlemen assisting in the ceremony she had performed so very often. Chantelle had broken the champagne on almost all of Christy Marine's fleet; the first time had been when she was Arthur Christy's fourteen-year-old darling—it was another of the company's many traditions.

Nicholas blinked, believing for an instant that his eyes had tricked him, for it seemed that the very earth had changed its shape and was moving.

Then he saw that the great hull of *Golden Dawn* had begun to slide forward. The band burst into the "Marseillaise," the heroic strains watered down by wind and distance, while *Golden Dawn* gathered momentum.

It was an incredible, even a stirring sight, and despite himself, Nicholas felt the goosebumps rise upon his forearms and the hair lift on the back of his neck. He was a sailor, and he was watching the birthing of the mightiest vessel ever built.

She was grotesque, monstrous, but she was part of him. No matter that others had bastardized and perverted his grand design—still the original design was his and he found himself gripping the binoculars with hands that shook.

He watched the massive wooden-wedged arresters kick out from under that great sliding mass of steel as they served to control her stern-first rush down the ways. Steel cable whipped and snaked upon itself like the Medusa's hair, and *Golden Dawn*'s stern struck the water.

The brown muddy water of the estuary opened before her, cleaved by the irresistible rush and weight, and the hull drove deep; opening white-capped rollers that spread out across the channel and broke upon the shores with a dull roar that carried clearly to where Nicholas stood.

The crowd that lined the bridge was cheering wildly. Beside him, a mother held her infant up to watch, both of them screaming with glee.

While *Golden Dawn*'s bows were still on the dockyard's ways her stern was thrusting irresistibly a mile out into the river; forced down by the raised bows it must now be almost touching the muddy bottom for the wave was breaking around her stern quarters.

God, she was huge! Nicholas shook his head in wonder. If only he had been able to build her the right way, what a ship she would have been. What a magnificent concept!

Now her bows left the end of the slips, and the waters burst about her, seething and leaping into swirling vortices.

Her stern started to rise, gathering speed as her own buoyancy caught her, and she burst out like a great whale rising to blow. The waters spilled from her, creaming and cascading through the steelwork of her open decks, boiling madly in the cavernous openings that would hold the pod tanks when she was fully loaded.

Now she came up short on the hundreds of retaining cables that prevented her from driving clear across the river and throwing herself ashore on the far bank.

She fought against this restraint, as though having felt the water she was now eager to run. She rolled and dipped and swung with a ponderous majesty that kept the crowds along the bridge cheering wildly. Then slowly she settled and floated quietly, seeming to fill the Loire river from bank to bank and to reach as high as the soaring spans of the bridge itself.

The four attendant harbour tugs moved in quickly to assist the ship to turn its prodigious length and to line up for the roads and the open sea.

They butted and backed, working as a highly skilled team, and slowly they coaxed *Golden Dawn* around. Her sideways motion left a mile-wide sweep of disturbed water across the estuary. Then suddenly there was a tremendous boil under her counter, and Nicholas saw the bronze flash of her single screw sweeping slowly through the brown water. Faster and still faster it turned, and despite himself Nicholas thrilled to see her come alive. A ripple formed under her bows, and almost imperceptibly she began to creep forward, overcoming the vast inertia of her weight, gathering steerage way, under command at last.

The harbour tugs fell back respectfully, and as the mighty bows lined up with the open sea she drove forward determinedly.

Silver spouts of steam from the sirens of the tugs shot high, and moments later, the booming bellow of their salute crashed against the skies.

The crowds had dispersed and Nicholas stood alone in the wind on the high bridge and watched the structured steel towers of *Golden Dawn*'s hull blending with the grey and misted horizon. He watched her turn, coming around on to her great circle course that would carry her six thousand miles southward to Good Hope, and even at this distance he sensed her change in mood as she steadied and her single screw began to push her up to top economic speed.

Nicholas checked his watch and murmured the age-old Master's command that commenced every voyage.

"Full away at 1700 hours," he said, and turned to trudge back along the bridge to where he had left the hired Renault.

It was after six o'clock and the site office was empty by the time Nicholas got back to *Sea Witch*. He threw himself into a chair and lit a cheroot while he thumbed quickly through his address book. He found what he wanted, dialled the direct London code, and then the number.

"Good afternoon. This is the *Sunday Times*. May I help you?"

"Is Mr. Herbstein available?" Nicholas asked.

"Hold on, please."

While he waited, Nicholas checked his address book for his next most likely contact, should the journalist be climbing the Himalayas or visiting a guerrilla training camp in Central Africa, either of which were highly likely—but within seconds he heard his voice.

"Denis," he said. "This is Nicholas Berg. How are you? I've got a hell of a story for you."

Nicholas tried to bear the indignity of it with stoicism, but the thick coating of pancake make-up seemed to clog the pores of his skin and he moved restlessly in the make-up chair.

"Please keep still, sir," the make-up girl snapped irritably; there was a line of unfortunates awaiting her ministrations along the bench at the back of the narrow room. One of them was Duncan Alexander and he caught Nicholas' eye in the mirror and raised an eyebrow in a mocking salute.

In the chair beside him, the anchorman of *The Today and Tomorrow Show* lolled graciously; he was tall and elegant with dyed and permanently waved hair, a carnation in his buttonhole, a high camp manner and an ostentatiously liberal image.

"I've given you the first slot. If it gets interesting, I'll run you four minutes forty seconds, otherwise I'll cut it off at two."

Denis Herbstein's Sunday article had been done with high professionalism, especially bearing in mind the very short time he had to put it together. It had included interviews with representatives of Lloyd's of London, the oil companies, environmental experts both in America and England, and even with the United States Coast Guard.

"Try to make it tight and hard," advised the anchorman. "Let's not pussyfoot around." He wanted sensation, not too many facts or figures, good gory horror stuff—or a satisfying punch-up. The *Sunday Times* article had flushed them out at Orient Amex and Christy Marine; they had not been able to ignore the challenge for there was a question tabled for Thursday by a Labour member in the Commons, and ominous stirrings in the ranks of the American Coast Guard service.

There had been enough fuss to excite the interest of *The Today and Tomorrow Show*. They had invited the parties to meet their accuser, and both Christy Marine and Orient Amex had fielded their first teams. Duncan Alexander with all his charisma had come to speak for Christy Marine, and Orient Amex had selected one of their directors who looked like Gary Cooper. With his craggy honest face and the silver hairs at his temples he looked like the kind of man you wanted flying your airliner or looking after your money.

The make-up girl dusted Nicholas' face with powder.

"I'm going to invite you to speak first. Tell us about this stuff—what is it, cadmium?" the interviewer checked his script.

Nicholas nodded, he could not speak for he was suffering the ultimate indignity. The girl was painting his lips.

The television studio was the size of an aircraft hangar, the concrete floor strewn with thick black cables and the roof lost in the gloomy heights, but they had created the illusion of intimacy in the small shell of the stage around which the big mobile cameras cluttered like mechanical crabs around the carcass of a dead fish.

The egg-shaped chairs made it impossible either to loll or to sit upright, and the merciless white glare of the arc lamps fried the thick layer of greasy make-up on Nicholas' skin. It was small consolation that across the table Duncan looked like a Japanese Kabuki dancer in make-up too white for his coppery hair.

An assistant director in a sweatshirt and jeans clipped the small microphone into Nicholas' lapel and whispered,

"Give them hell, ducky."

Somebody else in the darkness beyond the lights was intoning solemnly, "Four, three, two, one—you're on!" and the red light lit on the middle camera.

"Welcome to *The Today and Tomorrow Show*," the anchorman's voice was suddenly warm and intimate and mellifluous. "Last week in the French shipbuilding port of St. Nazaire, the largest ship in the world was launched—" In a dozen sentences he sketched out the facts, while on the repeating screens beyond the cameras Nicholas saw that they were running newsreel footage of *Golden Dawn*'s launching. He remembered the helicopter hovering over the dockyard, and he was so fascinated by the aerial views of the enormous vessel taking to the water that when the cameras switched suddenly to him, he was taken by surprise and saw himself start on the little screen as the interviewer began introducing him, swiftly running a thumbnail portrait and then going on:

"Mr. Berg has some very definite views on this ship."

"In her present design and construction, she is not safe to carry even regular crude petroleum oil," Nicholas said. "However, she will be employed in the carriage of crude oil that has been contaminated by cadmium sulphide in such concentrations as to make it one of the more toxic substances in nature."

"Your first statement, Mr. Berg, does anyone else share your doubts as to the safety of her design?"

"She does not carry the Al rating by the marine inspectors of Lloyd's of London," said Nicholas.

"Now can you tell us about the cargo she will carry—the so-called cad-rich crudes?"

Nicholas knew he had perhaps fifteen seconds to draw a verbal picture of the Atlantic Ocean turned into a sterile poisoned desert; it was too short a time, and twice Duncan Alexander interjected, skilfully breaking up the logic of Nicholas' presentation and before he had finished, the anchorman glanced at his watch and cut him short.

"Thank you, Mr. Berg. Now Mr. Kemp is a director of the oil company."

"My company, Orient Amex, last year allocated the sum of two million U.S. dollars as grants to assist in the scientific study of world environmental problems. I can tell you folks, right now, that we at Orient Amex are very conscious of the problems of modern technology—" He was projecting the oil-company image, the benefactors of all humanity.

"Your company's profit last year, after taxation, was four hundred and twenty-five million dollars," Nicholas cut in clearly. "That makes point four seven per cent on environmental research—all of it tax deductible. Congratulations, Mr. Kemp."

The oil man looked pained and went on: "Now we at Orient Amex," plugging the company name again neatly, "are working towards a better quality of life for all peoples. But we do realize that it is impossible to put back the clock a hundred years. We cannot allow ourselves to be blinded by the romantic wishful thinking of *amateur* environmentalists, the weekend scientists and the doomcriers who—"

"Cry *Torrey Canyon*," Nicholas suggested helpfully, and the oil man suppressed a shudder and went on quickly.

"—who would have us discontinue such research as the revolutionary cadmium cracking process, which could extend the world's utilization of fossil fuels by a staggering forty per cent and give the world's oil reserves an extended life of twenty years or more."

Again the anchorman glanced at his watch, cut the oil man off in midflow and switched his attention to Duncan Alexander.

"Mr. Alexander, your so-called ultra-tanker will carry the cad-rich crudes. How would you reply to Mr. Berg?"

Duncan smiled, a deep secret smile. "When Mr. Berg had my job as head of Christy Marine, the *Golden Dawn* was the best idea in the world. Since he was fired, it's suddenly the worst."

They laughed, even one of the cameramen out beyond the lights guffawed uncontrollably, and Nicholas felt the hot red rush of his anger.

"Is the *Golden Dawn* rated A1 at Lloyd's?" asked the anchorman.

"Christy Marine has not applied for a Lloyd's listing—we arranged our insurance in other markets."

Even through his anger Nicholas had to concede how good he was. He had a mind like quicksilver.

"How safe is your ship, Mr. Alexander?"

Now Duncan turned his head and looked directly across the table at Nicholas.

"I believe she is as safe as the world's leading marine architects and naval engineers can make her." He paused, and there was a malevolent gleam in his eyes now, "So safe, that I have decided to end this ridiculous controversy by a display of my personal confidence."

"What form will this show of faith take, Mr. Alexander?" The anchorman sensed the sensational line for which he had been groping and he leaned forward eagerly.

"On *Golden Dawn*'s maiden voyage, when she returns from the Persian Gulf fully laden with the El Barras crudes, I and my family, my wife and my stepson, will travel aboard her for the final six thousand miles of her voyage—from Cape Town on the Cape of Good Hope to Galveston in the Gulf of Mexico." As Nicholas gaped at him wordlessly, he went on evenly, "That's how convinced I am that *Golden Dawn* is capable of performing her task in perfect safety."

"Thank you." The anchorman recognized a good exit line, when he heard one. "Thank you, Mr. Alexander. You've convinced me—and I am sure you have convinced many of our viewers. We are now crossing to Washington via satellite where—"

The moment the red "in use" light flickered out on the television camera, Nicholas was on his feet and facing Duncan Alexander. His anger was fanned by the realization that Duncan had easily grandstanded him with that adroit display of showmanship, and by the stabbing anxiety at the threat to take Peter aboard *Golden Dawn* on her hazardous maiden voyage.

"You're not taking Peter on that death trap of yours," he snapped.

"That's his mother's decision," said Duncan evenly. "As the daughter of Arthur Christy, she's decided to give the company her full support," he emphasized the word "full."

"I won't let either of you endanger my son's life for a wild public-relations stunt."

"I'm sure you will try to prevent it," Duncan nodded and smiled, "and I'm sure your efforts will be as ineffectual as your attempts to stop *Golden Dawn*." He deliberately turned his back on Nicholas and spoke to the oil man. "I do think that went off rather well," he said, "don't you?"

• • •

James Teacher gave a graphic demonstration of why he could charge the highest fees in London and still have his desk piled high with important briefs. He had Nicholas' urgent application before a Judge-in-Chambers within seventy-two hours, petitioning for a writ to restrain Chantelle Alexander from allowing the son of their former marriage, one Peter Nicholas Berg, aged twelve years, to accompany her on an intended voyage from Cape Town in the Republic of South Africa to Galveston in the state of Texas aboard the bulk crude-carrier *Golden Dawn*, and/or to prevent the said Chantelle Alexander from allowing the child to undertake any other voyage aboard the said vessel.

The Judge heard the petition during a recess in the criminal trial of a young post-office worker standing accused of multiple rape. The Judge's oak-panelled book-lined chambers were overcrowded by the two parties, their lawyers, the judge's registrar and the considerable bulk of the judge himself.

Still in his wig and robes from the public court, the judge read swiftly through the written submission of both sides, listened attentively to James Teacher's short address and the rebuttal by his opposite number, before turning sternly to Chantelle.

"Mrs. Alexander." The stern expression wavered slightly as he looked upon the devastating beauty which sat demurely before him. "Do you love your son?"

"More than anything else in this life." Chantelle looked at him steadily out of those vast dark eyes.

"And you are happy to take him on this journey with you?"

"I am the daughter of a sailor. If there was danger I would understand it. I am happy to go myself and take my son with me."

The judge nodded, looked down at the papers on his desk for a moment.

"As I understand the circumstances, Mr. Teacher, it is common ground that the mother has custody?"

"That is so, my lord. But the father is the child's guardian."

"I'm fully aware of that, thank you," he snapped acidly. He paused again before resuming in the measured tones of judgement, "We are concerned here exclusively with the welfare and safety of the child. It has been shown that the proposed journey will be made during the holidays and that no loss of schooling will result. On the other hand, I do not believe that the petitioner has shown that reasonable doubts exist about the safety of the vessel on which the voyage will be made. It seems to be a modern and sophisticated ship. To grant the petition would, in my view, be placing unreasonable restraint on the child's mother." He swivelled in his chair to face Nicholas and James Teacher. "I regret, therefore, that I see insufficient grounds to accede to your petition."

In the back seat of James Teacher's Bentley, the little lawyer murmured apologetically. "He was right, of course, Nicholas. I would have done the same in his place. These domestic squabbles are always—"

Nicholas was not listening. "What would happen if I picked up Peter and took him to Bermuda or the States?"

"Abduct him!" James Teacher's voice shot up an octave, and he caught Nicholas' arm with genuine alarm. "I beg of you, dismiss the thought. They would have the police waiting for you—God!" Now he wriggled miserably in his seat. "I can't bear to think of what might happen. Apart from getting you sent to gaol, your former wife might even get an order restraining you from seeing your boy again. She could get guardianship away from you. If you did that, you could lose the child, Nicholas. Don't do it. Please don't do it!"

Now he patted Nicholas' arm ingratiatingly. "You'd be playing right into their hands." And then with relief he switched his attention to the briefcase on his lap.

"Can we read through the latest draft of the agreement of sale again?" he asked. "We haven't got much time, you know." Then, without waiting for a reply, he began on the preamble to the agreement which would transfer all the assets and liabilities of Ocean Salvage and Towage to the Directors of the Bank of the East, as nominees for parties unnamed.

Nicholas slumped in the far corner of the seat, and stared thoughtfully out of the window as the Bentley crawled in the traffic stream out of the Strand, around Trafalgar Square with its wheeling clouds of pigeons and milling throngs of tourists, swung into the Mall and accelerated down the long straight towards the Palace.

"I want you to stall them," Nicholas said suddenly, and Teacher broke off in the middle of a sentence and stared at him distractedly.

"I beg your pardon?"

"I want you to find a way to stall the Sheikhs."

"Good God, man." James Teacher was utterly astounded. "It's taken me nearly a month—four hard weeks to get them ripe to sign," his voice choked a little at the memory of the long hours of negotiation. "I've written every line of the agreement in my own blood."

"I need to have control of my tugs. I need to be free to act—"

"Nicholas, we are talking about seven million dollars."

"We are talking about my son," said Nicholas quietly. "Can you stall them?"

"Yes, of course I can, if that's what you truly want." Wearily James Teacher closed the file on his lap. "How long?"

"Six weeks—long enough for *Golden Dawn* to finish her maiden voyage, one way or the other."

"You realize that this may blow the whole deal, don't you?"

"Yes, I realize that."

"And you realize also that there isn't another buyer?"

"Yes."

They were silent then, until the Bentley pulled up before the Bank building in Curzon Street, and they stepped out on to the pavement.

"Are you absolutely certain?" Teacher asked softly.

"Just do it," Nicholas replied, and the doorman held the bronze and glass doors open for them.

B ermuda asserted its calming influence over Nicholas the moment he stepped out of the aircraft into its comfortable warmth and clean, glittering sunlight. Bernard Wackie's gorgeous burnt-honey-coloured secretary was there to welcome him. She wore a thin cotton dress the colour of freshly cut pineapple and a flashing white smile.

"Mr. Wackie's waiting for you at the Bank, sir."

"Are you out of your mind, Nicholas?" Bernard greeted him. "Jimmy Teacher tells me you blew the Arabs out of the window. Tell me it's not true, please tell me it's not true."

"Oh, come on, Bernard," Nicholas shook his head and patted him consolingly on the shoulder, "your commission would only have been a lousy point seven million, anyway."

"Then you did it!" Bernard wailed, and tried to pull his hand out of Nicholas' grip. "You screwed it all up."

"The Sheikhs have been screwing us up for over a month, Bernie baby. I just gave them a belt of the same medicine, and do you know what? They loved it. The Prince sat up and showed real interest for the first time. For the first time we were speaking the same language. They'll still be around six weeks from now."

"But why? I don't understand. Just explain to me why you did it."

"Let's go into the plot, and I'll explain it to you."

In the plot Nicholas stood over the perspex map of the oceans of the globe, and studied it carefully for fully five minutes without speaking.

"That's *Sea Witch*'s latest position. She's making good passage?"

The green plastic disc that bore the tug's number was set in mid-Atlantic.

"She reported two hours ago." Bernie nodded, and then said with professional interest, "How did her sea trials go off?"

"There were the usual wrinkles to iron out, that's what kept me in St. Nazaire so long. But we got them straight—and Jules has fallen in love with her."

"He's still the best skipper in the game."

But already Nicholas' attention had switched halfway across the world.

"*Warlock*'s still in Mauritius," his voice snapped like a whip.

"I had to fly out a new armature for the main generator. It was just bad luck that she broke down in that Godforsaken part of the world."

"When will she be ready for sea?"

"Allen promises noon tomorrow. Do you want to telex him for an update on that?"

"Later." Nicholas wet the tip of a cheroot carefully, without taking his eyes off the plot, calculating distances and currents and speeds.

"*Golden Dawn*?" he asked, and lit the cheroot while he listened to Bernard's reply.

"Her pod tanks arrived under tow at the new Orient Amex depot on El Barras three weeks ago." Bernie picked up the pointer and touched the upper bight of the deep Persian Gulf. "They took on their full cargoes of crude and lay inshore to await *Golden Dawn*'s arrival."

For a moment, Nicholas contemplated the task of towing those four gigantic pod tanks from Japan to the Gulf, and then he discarded the thought and listened to Bernard.

"*Golden Dawn* arrived last Thursday and, according to my agent at El Barras, she coupled up with her pod tanks and made her turn around within three hours." Bernard slid the tip of the pointer southwards down the eastern coast of the African continent. "I have had no report of her since then, but if she makes good her twenty-two knots, then she'll be somewhere off the coast of Mozambique, or Maputo as they call it now, and she should double the Cape within the next few days. I will have a report on her then. She'll be taking on mail as she passes Cape Town."

"And passengers," said Nicholas grimly; he knew that Peter and Chantelle were in Cape Town already. He had telephoned the boy the night before and Peter had been wildly elated at the prospect of the voyage on the ultra-tanker.

"It's going to be tremendous fun, Dad," his voice cracking with the onset of both excitement and puberty. "We'll be flying out to the ship in a helicopter."

Bernard Wackie changed the subject, now picking up a sheaf of telex flimsies and thumbing swiftly through them.

"Right, I've confirmed the standby contract for *Sea Witch*." Nicholas nodded, the contract was for Jules Levoisin and the new tug to stand by three offshore working rigs, standard exploration rigs, that were drilling in the Florida Bay, that elbow of shallow water formed by the sweep of the Florida Keys and the low swampy morass of the Everglades. "It's ridiculous to use a twenty-two-thousand-horsepower ocean-going tug as an oil-rig standby," Bernard lowered the file, and could no longer contain his irritation. "Jules is going to go bananas sitting around playing nursemaid. You are going to have a mutiny on your hands—and you'll be losing money. The daily hire won't cover your direct costs."

"She will be sitting exactly where I want her," said Nicholas, and switched his attention back to the tiny dot of an island in the middle of the Indian Ocean. "Now *Warlock*."

"Right. *Warlock*." Bernie picked up another file. "I have tendered for a deep-sea tow."

"Cancel it," said Nicholas. "Just as soon as Allen has repaired his generator, I want him running top of the green for Cape Town."

"For Cape Town—top of the green?" Bernard stared at him. "Christ, Nicholas. What for?"

"He won't be able to catch *Golden Dawn* before she rounds the Cape, but I want him to follow her."

"Nicholas, you're out of your mind—do you know what that would cost?"

"If *Golden Dawn* gets into trouble he'll be only a day or two behind her. Tell Allen he is to shadow her all the way into Galveston roads."

"Nicholas, you're letting this whole thing get out of all proportion. It's become an obsession with you, for God's sake!"

"With her superior speed, *Warlock* should be up with her before she enters the—"

"Listen to me, Nicholas. Let's think this all out carefully. What are the chances of *Golden Dawn* suffering structural failure or crippling breakdown on her maiden voyage—a hundred to one against it? It's that high?"

"That's about right." Nicholas agreed. "A hundred to one."

"What is it going to cost to hold one ocean-going salvage tug on standby, at a lousy 1,500 dollars a day—and then to send another halfway around the world at top of the green?" Bernard clasped his brow theatrically. "It's going to cost you a quarter of a million dollars, if you take into consideration the loss of earnings on both vessels—that's the very least it's going to cost you. Don't you have respect for money any longer?"

"Now you understand why I had to stall the Sheikhs," Nicholas smiled calmly. "I couldn't shoot their money on a hundred-to-one chance—but it's not their money yet. Its mine. *Sea Witch* and *Warlock* aren't their tugs, they are mine. Peter isn't their son, he's mine."

"You're serious," said Bernard incredulously. "I do believe you are serious."

"Right," Nicholas agreed. "Damned right, I am. Now get a telex off to David Allen and ask him for his estimated time of arrival in Cape Town."

S amantha Silver had one towel wrapped around her head like a turban. Her hair was still wet from the luxurious shampooing it had just received. She wore the other towel tucked under her armpits, making a short sarong of it. She still glowed all over from the steaming tub and she smelled of soap and talcum powder.

After a long field trip, it took two or three of these soakings and scrubbings to get the salt and the smell of the mangroves out of her pores, and the Everglades mud from under her nails.

She poured the batter into the pan, the oil spitting and crackling with the heat and she sang out, "How many waffles can you eat?"

He came through from the bathroom, a wet towel wrapped around his waist, and he stood in the doorway and grinned at her. "How many have you got?" he asked. She had still not accustomed her ear to the Australian twang.

He was burned and brown as she was, and his hair was bleached at the ends, hanging now, wet from the shower, into his face.

They had worked well together, and she had learned much from him. The drift into intimacy had been gradual, but inevitable. In her hurt, she had turned to him for comfort, and also in deliberate spite of Nicholas. But now, if she turned her head away, she would not really be able to remember his features clearly. It took an effort to remember his name— Dennis, of course, Doctor Dennis O'Connor.

She was detached from it all, as though a sheet of armoured glass separated her from the real world. She went through the motions of working and playing, of eating and sleeping, of laughing and loving, but it was all a sham.

Dennis was watching her from the doorway now, with that slightly puzzled expression, the helpless look of a person who watches another one drowning and is powerless to give aid.

Samantha turned away quickly. "Ready in two minutes," she said, and he turned back into the bedroom to finish dressing.

She flipped the waffles on to a plate and poured a fresh batch of batter.

Beside her, the telephone rang and she sucked her fingers clean and picked it up with her free hand.

"Sam Silver," she said.

"Thank God. I've been going out of my mind. What happened to you, darling?"

Her knees went rubbery under her, and she had to sit down quickly on one of the stools.

"Samantha, can you hear me?"

She opened her mouth, but no sound came out.

"Tell me what's happening—" She could see his face before her, clearly, each detail of it so vividly remembered, the clear green eyes below the heavy brow, the line of cheekbone and jaw, and the sound of his voice made her shiver.

"Samantha."

"How is your wife, Nicholas?" she asked softly—and he broke off. She held the receiver to her ear with both hands, and the silence lasted only a few beats of her heart, but it was long enough. Once or twice, in moments of weakness during the last two weeks, she had tried to convince herself that it was not true. That it had all been the viciousness of a lying woman. Now she knew beyond any question that her instinct had been correct. His silence was the admission, and she waited for the lie that she knew would come next.

"Would it help to tell you I love you?" he asked softly, and she could not answer. Even in her distress, she felt the rush of relief. He had not lied. At that moment it was the most important thing in her life. He had not lied. She felt it begin to tear painfully, deep in her chest. Her shoulders shook spasmodically.

"I'm coming to get you," he said into the silence.

"I won't be here," she whispered, but she felt it welling up into her throat, uncontrollably. She had not wept before, she had kept it all safely bottled away—but now, the first sob burst from her, and with both hands she slammed the telephone back on to its cradle.

She stood there still, shaking wildly, and the tears poured down her cheeks and dripped from her chin.

Dennis came into the kitchen behind her, tucking his shirt into the top of his trousers, his hair shiny and wet with the straight lines of the comb through it.

"Who was that?" he asked cheerfully, and then stopped aghast.

"What is it, love?" He started forward again, "Come on now."

"Don't touch me, please," she whispered huskily, and he stopped again uncertainly. "We are fresh out of milk," she said without turning. "Will you take the van down to the shopping centre?"

By the time Dennis returned, she was dressed and she had rinsed her face and tied a scarf around her head like a gypsy. They chewed cold, unappetizing waffles in silence, until she spoke.

"Dennis, we've got to talk—"

"No," he smiled at her. "It's all right, Sam. You don't have to say it. I should have moved on days ago, anyway."

"Thanks," she said.

"It was Nicholas, wasn't it?"

She regretted having told him now, but at the time it had been vitally necessary to speak to somebody.

She nodded, and his voice had a sting to it as he went on.

"I'd like to bust that bastard in the mouth."

"We levelled the score, didn't we?" She smiled, but it was an unconvincing smile, and she didn't try to hold it.

"Sam, I want you to know that for me it was not just another quick shack job."

"I know that." Impulsively she reached out and squeezed his hand. "And thanks for understanding—but is it okay if we don't talk about it any more?"

P eter Berg had twisted round in his safety straps, so that he could press his face to the round perspex window in the fuselage of the big Sikorsky helicopter.

The night was completely, utterly black.

Across the cabin, the Flight Engineer stood in the open doorway, the wind ripping at his bright orange overalls, fluttering them around his body, and he turned and grinned across at the boy, then he made a wind-milling gesture with his hand and stabbed downwards with his thumb. It was impossible to speak in the clattering, rushing roar of wind and engine and rotor.

The helicopter banked gently and Peter gasped with excitement as the ship came into view.

She was burning all her lights; tier upon tier, the brilliantly lit floors of her stern quarters rose above the altitude at which the Sikorsky was hovering, and, seeming to reach ahead to the black horizon, the tank deck was outlined with rows of hooded lamps, like the street lamps of a deserted city.

She was so huge that she looked like a city. There seemed to be no end to her, stretched to the horizon and towering into the sky.

The helicopter sank in a controlled sweep towards the white circular target on the heliport, guided down by the engineer in the open doorway. Skilfully the pilot matched his descent to the forward motion of the ultra-tanker, twenty-two knots at top economical—Peter had swotted the figures avidly—and the deck moved with grudging majesty to the scend of the tall Cape rollers pushing in unchecked from across the length of the Atlantic Ocean.

The pilot hovered, judging his approach against the brisk north-westerly crosswind, and from fifty feet Peter could see that the decks were almost level with the surface of the sea, pressed down deeply by the weight of her cargo. Every few seconds, one of the rollers that raced down her length would flip aboard and spread like spilled milk, white and frothy in the deck lights, before cascading back over the side.

Made arrogant and unyielding by her vast bulk, the *Golden Dawn* did not woo the ocean, as other ships do. Instead, her great blunt bows crushed the swells, churning them under or shouldering them contemptuously aside.

Peter had been around boats since before he could walk. He too was a sea-creature. But though his eye was keen, it was as yet unschooled, so he did not notice the working of the long wide deck.

Sitting beside Peter on the bench seat, Duncan Alexander knew to look for the movement in the hull. He watched the hull twisting and hogging, but so slightly, so barely perceptibly, that Duncan blinked it away, and looked again. From bows to stern she was a mile and a half long, and in essence she was merely four steel pods held together by an elaborate flexible steel scaffolding and driven forward by the mighty propulsion unit in the stern. There was small independent movement of each of the tank pods, so the deck twisted as she rolled, and flexed like a longbow as she took the swells under her. The crest of these swells were a quarter of a mile apart. At any one time, there were four separate wave patterns beneath *Golden Dawn*'s hull, with the peaks thrusting up and the troughs allowing the tremendous dead weight of her cargo to push downwards; the elastic steel groaned and gave to meet these shearing forces.

No hull is ever completely rigid, and elasticity had been part of the ultra-tanker's original design, but those designs had been altered. Duncan Alexander had saved almost two thousand tons of steel, by reducing the stiffening of the central pillar that docked the four pods together, and he had dispensed with the double skins of the pods themselves. He had honed *Golden Dawn* down to the limits at which his own architects had baulked; then he had hired Japanese architects to rework the designs. They had expressed themselves satisfied that the hull was safe, but had also respectfully pointed out that nobody had ever carried a million tons of crude petroleum in a single cargo before.

The helicopter sank the last few feet and bumped gently on to the insulated green deck, with its thick coat of plasticized paint which prevented the striking of spark. Even a grain of sand trodden between leather sole and bare steel could ignite an explosive air and petroleum gas mixture.

The ship's party swarmed forward, doubled under the swirling rotor. The luggage in its net beneath the fuselage was dragged away and strong hands swung Peter down on to the deck. He stood blinking in the glare of deck lamps and wrinkling his nose to the characteristic tanker stench. It is a smell that pervades everything aboard one of these ships: the food, the furniture, the crew's clothing—even their hair and skin.

It is the thin, acrid chemical stench of under-rich fumes vented off from the tanks. Oxygen and petroleum gas are only explosive in a mixture within narrow limits: too much oxygen makes the blend under-rich and too much petroleum gas makes it over-rich, either of which mixtures are non-explosive, non-combustible.

Chantelle Alexander was handed down next from the cabin of the helicopter, bringing an instant flash of elegance to the starkly lit scene of bleak steel and ugly functional machinery. She wore a catsuit of dark green with a bright Jean Patou scarf on her head. Two ship's officers closed in solicitously on each side of her and led her quickly away towards the towering stern quarters, out of the rude and blustering wind and the helicopter engine roar.

Duncan Alexander followed her down to the deck and shook hands quickly with the First Officer.

"Captain Randle's compliments, sir. He is unable to leave the bridge while the ship is in the inshore channel."

"I understand." Duncan flashed that marvellous smile. The great ship drew almost twenty fathoms fully laden and she had come in very close, as close as was prudent to the mountainous coastline of Good Hope with its notorious currents and wild winds. However, Chantelle Christy must not be exposed to the ear-numbing discomfort of the helicopter flight for a moment longer than was necessary, and so *Golden Dawn* had come in through the inner channel, perilously close to the guardian rocks of Robben Island that stood in the open mouth of Table Bay.

Even before the helicopter rose and circled away towards the distant glow of Cape Town city under its dark square mountain, the tanker's great blunt bows were swinging away towards the west, and Duncan imagined the relief of Captain Randle as he gave the order to make the offing into the open Atlantic with the oceanic depths under his cumbersome ship.

Duncan smiled again and reached for Peter Berg's hand.

"Come on, my boy."

"I'm all right, sir."

Skilfully Peter avoided the hand and the smile, containing his wild excitement so that he walked ahead like a man, without the skipping energy of a little boy. Duncan Alexander felt the customary flare of annoyance. No, more than that—bare anger at this further rejection by Berg's puppy. They went in single file along the steel catwalk with the child leading. He had never been able to get close to the boy and he had tried hard in the beginning. Now Duncan stopped his anger with the satisfying memory of how neatly he had used the child to slap Berg in the face, and draw the fangs of his opposition.

Berg would be worrying too much about his brat to have time for anything else. He followed Chantelle and the child into the gleaming chrome and plastic corridors of the stern quarters. It was difficult to think of decks and bulkheads rather than floors and walls in here. It was too much like a modern apartment block, even the elevator which bore them swiftly and silently five storeys up to the navigation bridge helped to dispel the feelings of being shipborne.

On the bridge itself, they were so high above the sea as to be divorced from it. The deck lights had been extinguished once the helicopter had gone, and the darkness of the night, silenced by the thick double-glazed windows, heightened the peace and isolation. The riding lights in the bows seemed remote as the very stars, and the gentle lulling movement of the immense hull was only just noticeable.

The Master was a man of Duncan Alexander's own choosing. The command of the flagship of Christy Marine should have gone to Basil Reilly, the senior captain of the fleet. However, Reilly was Berg's man, and Duncan had used the foundering of *Golden Adventurer* to force premature retirement on the old sailor.

Randle was young for the responsibility—just a little over thirty years of age—but his training and his credentials were impeccable, and he was an honours graduate of the tanker school in France. Here top men received realistic training in the specialized handling of these freakish giants in cunningly constructed lakes and scale-model harbours, working thirty-foot models of the bulk carriers that had all the handling characteristics of the real ships.

Since Duncan had given him the command, he had been a staunch ally, and he had stoutly defended the design and construction of his ship when the reporters, whipped up by Nicholas Berg, had questioned him. He was loyal, which weighed heavily, tipping the balance for Duncan against his youth and inexperience.

He hurried to meet his important visitors as they stepped out of the elevator into his spacious, gleaming modern bridge, a short stocky figure with a bull neck and the thrusting heavy jaw of great determination or great stubbornness. His greeting had just the right mixture of warmth and servility, and Duncan noted approvingly that he treated even the boy with careful respect. Randle was bright enough to realize that one day the child would be head of Christy Marine. Duncan liked a man who could think so clearly and so far ahead, but Randle was not quite prepared for Peter Berg.

"Can I see your engine room, Captain?"

"You mean right now?"

"Yes." For Peter the question was superfluous. "If you don't mind, sir," he added quickly. Today was for doing things and tomorrow was lost in the mists of the future. Right now, would be just fine.

"Well now," the Captain realized the request was deadly serious, and that this lad could not be put off very easily, "we go on automatic during the night. There's nobody down there now—and it wouldn't be fair to wake the engineer, would it? It's been a hard day."

"I suppose not." Bitterly disappointed, but amenable to convincing argument, Peter nodded.

"But I am certain the Chief would be delighted to have you as his guest directly after breakfast."

The Chief Engineer was a Scot with three sons of his own in Glasgow, the youngest of them almost exactly Peter's age. He was more than delighted. Within twenty-four hours, Peter was the ship's favourite, with his own blue company-issue overalls altered to fit him and his name embroidered across the back by the lascar steward, "PETER BERG." He wore his bright yellow plastic hard hat at the same jaunty angle as the Chief did, and carried a wad of cotton waste in his back pocket to wipe his greasy hands after helping one of the stokers clean the fuel filters—the messiest job on board, and the greatest fun.

Although the engine control room with its rough camaraderie, endless supplies of sandwiches and cocoa and satisfying grease and oil that made a man look like a professional, was Peter's favourite station, yet he stood other watches.

Every morning he joined the First Officer on his inspection. Starting in the bows, they worked their way back, checking each of the pod tanks, every valve, and every one of the heavy hydraulic docking clamps that held the pod tanks attached to the main frames of the hull. Most important of all they checked the gauges on each compartment which gave the precise indication of the gas mixtures contained in the air spaces under the main deck of the crude tanks.

Golden Dawn operated on the "inert" system to keep the trapped fumes in an over-rich and safe condition. The exhaust fumes of the ship's engine were caught, passed through filters and scrubbers to remove the corrosive sulphur elements and then, as almost pure carbon dioxide and carbon monoxide, they were forced into the air spaces of the petroleum tanks. The evaporating fumes of the volatile elements of the crude mingled with the exhaust fumes to form an over-rich, oxygen-poor, and unexplosive gas.

However, a leak through one of the hundreds of valves and connections would allow air into the tanks, and the checks to detect this were elaborate, ranging from an unceasing electronic monitoring of each tank to the daily physical inspection, in which Peter now assisted.

Peter usually left the First Officer's party when it returned to the stern quarters, he might then pass the time of day with the two-man crew in the central pump room.

From here the tanks were monitored and controlled, loaded and off-floaded, the flow of inert gas balanced, and the crude petroleum could be pushed through the giant centrifugal pumps and transferred from tank to tank to make alterations to the ship's trim, during partial discharge, or when one or more tanks were detached and taken inshore for discharge.

In the pump room was kept a display that always fascinated Peter. It was the sample cupboard with its rows of screw-topped bottles, each containing samples of the cargo taken during loading. As all four of *Golden Dawn's* tanks had been filled at the same offshore loading point and all with crude from the same field, each of the bottles bore the identical label.

EL BARRAS CRUDE
BUNKERS "C"
HIGH CADMIUM

Peter liked to take one of the bottles and hold it to the light. Somehow he had always expected the crude oil to be treacly and tar-like, but it was thin as human blood and when he shook the bottle, it coated the glass and the light through it was dark red, again like congealing blood.

"Some of the crudes are black, some yellow and the Nigerians are green," the pump foreman told him. "This is the first red that I've seen."

"I suppose it's the cadmium in it," Peter told him.

"Guess it is," the foreman agreed seriously; all on board had very soon learned not to talk down to Peter Berg. He expected to be treated on equal terms.

By this time it was mid-morning and Peter had worked up enough appetite to visit the galley, where he was greeted like visiting royalty. Within days, Peter knew his way unerringly through the labyrinthine and usually deserted passageways. It was characteristic of these great crude-carriers that you might wander through them for hours without meeting another human being. With their huge bulk and their tiny crews, the only place where there was always human presence was the navigation bridge on the top floor of the stern quarters.

The bridge was always one of Peter's obligatory stops.

"Good morning, Tug," the officer of the watch would greet him. Peter had been christened with his nickname when he had announced at the breakfast table on his first morning:

"Tankers are great, but I'm going to be a tug captain, like my dad."

On the bridge the ship might be taken out of automatic to allow Peter to spell the helmsman for a while, or he would assist the junior deck officers while they made a sun shot as an exercise to check against the satellite navigational Decca; then, after socializing with Captain Randle for a while, it was time to report to his true station in the engine.

"We were waiting on you, Tug," growled the Chief. "Get your overalls on, man, we're going down the propeller shaft tunnel."

The only unpleasant period of the day was when Peter's mother insisted that he scrub off the top layers of grease and fuel oil, dress in his number ones, and act as an unpaid steward during the cocktail hour in the elaborate lounge of the owner's suite.

It was the only time that Chantelle Alexander fraternized with the ship's officers and it was a painfully stilted hour, with Peter one of the major sufferers—but the rest of the time he was successful in avoiding the clinging restrictive rulings of his mother and the fiercely hated but silently resented presence of Duncan Alexander, his stepfather.

Still, he was instinctively aware of the new and disturbing tensions between his mother and Duncan Alexander. In the night he heard the raised voices from the master cabin, and he strained to catch the words. Once, when he had heard the cries of his mother's distress, he had left his bunk and gone barefooted to knock on the cabin door. Duncan Alexander had opened it to him. He was in a silk dressing gown and his handsome features were swollen and flushed with anger.

"Go back to bed."

"I want to see my mother," Peter had told him quietly.

"You need a damned good hiding," Duncan had flared. "Now do as you are told."

"I want to see my mother." Peter had stood his ground, standing very straight in his pyjamas with both his tone and expression neutral, and Chantelle had come to him in her nightdress and knelt to embrace him.

"It's all right, darling. It's perfectly all right." But she had been weeping. After that there had been no more loud voices in the night.

However, except for an hour in the afternoon, when the swimming pool was placed out of bounds to officers and crew, while Chantelle swam and sunbathed, she spent the rest of the time in the owner's suite, eating all her meals there, withdrawn and silent, sitting at the panoramic windows of her cabin, coming to life only for an hour in the evenings while she played the owner's wife to the ship's officers.

Duncan Alexander, on the other hand, was like a caged animal. He paced the open decks, composing long messages which were sent off regularly over the telex in company code to Christy Marine in Leadenhall Street.

Then he would stand out on the open wing of *Golden Dawn*'s bridge, staring fixedly ahead at the northern horizon, awaiting the reply to his last telex, chafing openly at having to conduct the company's business at such long remove, and goaded by the devils of doubt and impatience and fear.

Often it seemed as though he were trying to forge the mighty hull on-wards, faster and faster into the north, by the sheer power of his will.

In the north-western corner of the Caribbean basin, there is an area of shallow warm water, hemmed in on one side by the island chain of the Great Antilles, the bulwark of Cuba and Hispaniola, while in the west the sweep of the Yucatan peninsula runs south through Panama into the great land-mass of South America—shallow, warm, trapped water and saturated tropical air, enclosed by land masses which can heat very rapidly in the high hot sun of the tropics. However, all of it is gently cooled and moderated by the benign influence of the north-easterly trade winds— winds so unvarying in strength and direction that over the centuries, seafaring men have placed their lives and their fortunes at risk upon their balmy wings, gambling on the constancy of that vast moving body of mild air.

But the wind does fail; for no apparent reason and without previous warning, it dies away, often merely for an hour or two, but occasionally—very occasionally—for days or weeks at a time.

Far to the south and east of this devil's spawning ground, the *Golden Dawn* ploughed massively on through the sweltering air and silken calm of the doldrums, northwards across the equator, changing course every few hours to maintain the great circle track that would carry her well clear of that glittering shield of islands that the Caribbean carries, like an armoured knight, on its shoulder.

The treacherous channels and passages through the islands were not for a vessel of *Golden Dawn*'s immense bulk, deep draught and limited manoeuvrability. She was to go high above the Tropic of Cancer, and just south of the island of Bermuda she would make her westings and enter the wider and safer waters of the Florida Straits above Grand Bahamas. On this course, she would be constricted by narrow and shallow seaways for only a few hundred miles before she was out into the open waters of the Gulf of Mexico again.

But while she ran on northwards, out of the area of equatorial calm, she should have come out at last into the sweet cool airs of the trades, but she did not. Day after day, the calm persisted, and stifling still air pressed down on the ship. It did not in any way slow or affect her passage, but her Master remarked to Duncan Alexander:

"Another corker today, by the looks of it."

When he received no reply from his brooding, silent Chairman, he retired discreetly, leaving Duncan alone on the open wing of the bridge, with only the breeze of the ship's passage ruffling his thick coppery hair.

However, the calm was not merely local. It extended westwards in a wide, hot belt across the thousand islands and the basin of shallow sea they enclosed.

The calm lay heavily on the oily waters, and the sun beat down on the enclosing land masses. Every hour the air heated and sucked up the evaporating waters; a fat bubble like a swelling blister began to rise, the first movement of air in many days. It was not a big bubble, only a hundred miles across, but as it rose, the rotation of the earth's surface began to twist the rising air, spinning it like a top, so that the satellite cameras, hundreds of miles above, recorded a creamy little spiral wisp like the decorative-icing flower on a wedding cake.

The cameras relayed the picture through many channels, until at last it reached the desk of the senior forecaster of the hurricane watch at the meteorological headquarters at Miami in southern Florida.

"Looks like a ripe one," he grunted to his assistant, recognizing that all the favourable conditions for the formation of a revolving tropical storm were present. "We'll ask air force for a fly-through."

At forty-five thousand feet the pilot of the US Air Force B52 saw the rising dome of the storm from two hundred miles away. It had grown enormously in only six hours.

As the warm saturated air was forced upwards, so the icy cold of the upper troposphere condensed the water vapour into thick, puffed-up silver clouds. They boiled upwards, roiling and swirling upon themselves. Already the dome of cloud and ferociously turbulent air was higher than the aircraft.

Under it, a partial vacuum was formed, and the surrounding surface air tried to move in to fill it. But it was compelled into an anticlockwise track around the centre by the mysterious forces of the earth's rotation. Compelled to travel the long route, the velocity of the air mass accelerated ferociously, and the entire system became more unstable, more dangerous by the hour, turning faster, perpetuating itself by creating greater wind velocities and steeper pressure gradients.

The cloud at the top of the enormous rising dome reached an altitude where the temperature was thirty degrees below freezing and the droplets of rain turned to crystals of ice and were smeared away by upper-level jet-streams. Long, beautiful patterns of cirrus against the high blue sky were blown hundreds of miles ahead of the storm to serve as its heralds.

The US Air Force B52 hit the first clear-air turbulence one hundred and fifty miles from the storm's centre. It was as though an invisible predator had seized the fuselage and shaken it until the wings were almost torn from their roots, and in one surge, the aircraft was flung five thousand feet straight upwards.

"Very severe turbulence," the pilot reported. "We have vertical wind speeds of three hundred miles an hour plus."

The senior forecaster in Miami picked up the telephone and called the computer programmer on the floor above him. "Ask Charlie for a hurricane code name."

And a minute later the programmer called him back. "Charlie says to call the bitch 'Lorna.'"

Six hundred miles south-west of Miami the storm began to move forward, slowly at first but every hour gathering power, spiralling upon itself at unbelievable velocities, its high dome swelling upwards now through fifty thousand feet and still climbing. The centre of the storm opened like a flower, the calm eye extended upwards in a vertical tunnel with smooth walls of solid cloud rising to the very summit of the dome, now sixty thousand feet above the surface of the wind-tortured sea.

The entire mass began to move faster, back towards the east, in a directly contrary direction to the usual track of the gentle trade winds. Spinning and roaring upon itself, devouring everything in its path, the she-devil called Lorna launched itself across the Caribbean Sea.

Nicholas Berg turned his head to look down upon the impressive skyline of Miami Beach. The rampart of tall, elegant hotel buildings followed the curve of the beach into the north, and behind it lay the ugly sprawled tangle of urban development and snarled highways.

The Eastern Airlines direct flight from Bermuda turned on to its base leg and then on to the final approach, losing height over the beach and Biscayne Bay.

Nicholas felt uncomfortable, the nagging of guilt and uncertainty. His guilt was of two kinds. He felt guilty that he had deserted his post at the moment when he was likely to be desperately needed.

Ocean Salvage's two vessels were out there somewhere in the Atlantic, *Warlock* running hard up the length of the Atlantic in a desperate attempt to catch up with *Golden Dawn*, while Jules Levoisin in *Sea Witch* was now approaching the eastern seaboard of America where he would refuel before going on to his assignment as standby tug on the exploration field in the Gulf of Mexico. At any moment, the Master of either vessel might urgently need to have his instructions.

Then there was *Golden Dawn*. She had rounded the Cape of Good Hope almost three weeks ago. Since then, even Bernard Wackie had been unable to fix her position. She had not been reported by other craft, and any communications she had made with Christy Main must have been by satellite telex, for she had maintained strict silence on the radio channels. However, she must rapidly be nearing the most critical part of her voyage when she turned west and began her approach to the continental shelf of North America and the passage of the islands into the Gulf. Peter Berg was on board that monster, and Nicholas felt the chill of guilt. His place was at the centre, in the control room of Bach Wackie on the top floor of the Bank of Bermuda building in Hamilton town. His post was there where he could assess changing conditions and issue instant commands to coordinate his salvage tugs.

Now he had deserted his post, and even though he had made arrangements to maintain contact with Bernard Wackie, still it would take him hours, perhaps even days, to get back to where he was needed, if there was an emergency.

But then there was Samantha. His instincts warned him that every day, every hour he delayed in going to her would reduce his chances of having her again.

There was more guilt there, the guilt of betrayal. It was no help to tell himself that he had made no marriage vows to Samantha Silver, that his night of weakness with Chantelle had been forced upon him in circumstances almost impossible to resist, that any other man in his position would have done the same, and that in the end the episode had been a catharsis and a release that had left him free for ever of Chantelle.

To Samantha, it had been betrayal, and he knew that much was destroyed by it. He felt terrible aching guilt, not for the act—sexual intercourse without love is fleeting and insignificant—but for the betrayal and for the damage he had wrought.

Now he was uncertain, uncertain as to just how much he had destroyed, how much was left for him to build upon. All that he was certain of was that he needed her, more than he had needed anything in his life. She was still the promise of eternal youth and of the new life towards which he was groping so uncertainly. If love was needing, then he loved Samantha Silver with something close to desperation.

She had told him she would not be there when he came. He had to hope now that she had lied. He felt physically sick at the thought that she meant it.

He had only a single Louis Vuitton overnight valise as cabin luggage so he passed swiftly through customs, and as he went into the telephone booths, he checked his watch. It was after six o'clock; she'd be home by now.

He had dialled the first four digits of her number before he checked himself.

"What the hell am I phoning for?" he asked himself grimly. "To tell her I'm here, so she can have a flying start when she runs for the bushes?"

There is nothing so doomed as a timid lover. He dropped the receiver back on its cradle, and went for the Hertz desk at the terminal doors.

"What's the smallest you've got?" he asked.

"A Cougar," the pretty blonde in the yellow uniform told him. In America, "small" is a relative term. He was just lucky she hadn't offered him a Sherman tank.

The brightly painted Chevy van was in the lean-to shelter under the spread branches of the ficus tree, and he parked the Cougar's nose almost touching its tailgate. There was no way she could escape now, unless she went out through the far wall of the shed. Knowing her, that was always a possibility, he grinned mirthlessly.

He knocked once on the screen door of the kitchen and went straight in. There was a coffee pot beside the range, and he touched it as he passed. It was still warm.

He went through into the living room, and called:

"Samantha!"

The bedroom door was ajar. He pushed it open. There was a suit of denims, and some pale transparent wisps of underwear thrown carelessly over the patchwork quilt.

The shack was deserted. He went down the steps of the front stoop and straight on to the beach. The tide had swept the sand smooth, and her prints were the only ones. She had dropped her towel above the high-water mark but he had to shade his eyes against the ruddy glare of the lowering sun before he could make out her bobbing head—five hundred yards out.

He sat down beside her towel in the fluffy dry sand and lit a cheroot.

He waited, while the sun settled in a wild, fiery flood of light, and he lost the shape of her head against the darkening sea. She was half a mile out now, but he felt no urgency, and the darkness was almost complete when she rose suddenly, waist-deep from the edge of the gentle surf, waded ashore and came up the beach, twisting the rope of her hair over her one shoulder to wring the water from it.

Nicholas felt his heart flop over and he flicked the cheroot away and stood up. She halted abruptly, like a startled forest animal, and stood completely still, staring uncertainly at the tall, dark figure before her. She was so young and slim and smooth and beautiful.

"What do you want?" she faltered.

"You," he said.

"Why? Are you starting a harem?" Her voice hardened and she straightened; he could not see the expression of her eyes, but her shoulders took on a stubborn set.

He stepped forward and she was rigid in his arms and her lips hard and tightly unresponsive under his.

"Sam, there are things I'll never be able to explain. I don't even understand them myself, but what I do know very clearly is that I love you, that without you my life is going to be flat and plain goddamned miserable—"

There was no relaxation of the rigid muscles. Her hands were still held stiffly at her sides and her body felt cold and wet and unyielding.

"Samantha, I wish I were perfect—I'm not. But all I am sure of is that I can't make it without you."

"I couldn't take it again. I couldn't live through this again," she said tightly.

"I need you. I am certain of that," he insisted.

"You'd better be, you son of a bitch. You cheat on me one time more and you won't have anything left to cheat with—I'll take it off clean, at the roots." Then she was clinging to him. "Oh God, Nicholas, how I hated you, and how I missed you—and how long you took to come back," and her lips were soft and tasted of the sea.

He picked her up and carried her up through the soft sand. He didn't trust himself to speak. It would be so easy to say the wrong thing now.

N icholas, I've been sitting here waiting for your call." Bernard Wackie's voice was sharp and alert, the tension barely contained. "How soon can you get yourself back here?"

"What is it?"

"It is starting to pop. I've got to hand it to you, baby, you've got a nose for it. You smelled this coming."

"Come on, Bernie!" Nicholas snapped.

"This call is going through three open exchanges," Bernie told him. "You want chapter and verse, or did nobody ever tell you that it's a tough game you are in? There is a lot of competition cluttering up the scene. The cheese-heads have one lying handy." Probably *Wittezee* or one of the other big Dutch tugs, Nicholas thought swiftly. "They could be streaming a towing wire within a couple of days. And the Yanks are pretty hot numbers. McCormick has one stationed in the Hudson River."

"All right," Nick cut through the relish with which Bernie was detailing the threat of hovering competition.

"There is a direct flight at seven tomorrow morning—if I can't make that, I'll connect with the British Airways flight from Nassau at noon tomorrow. Meet me," Nick ordered.

"You shouldn't have gone running off," said Bernard Wackie, showing amazing hindsight. Before he could deliver any more pearls of wisdom, Nicholas hung up on him.

Samantha was sitting up in the centre of the bed. She was stark naked, but she hugged her knees to her chest with both arms, and under the gorgeous tangle of her hair her face was desolate as that of a lost child and her green eyes haunted.

"You're going again," she said softly. "You only just came, and now you're going again. Oh God, Nicholas, loving you is the toughest job I've ever had in my life. I don't think I have got the muscle for it."

He reached for her quickly and she clung to him, pressing her face into the thick pad of coarse dark hair that covered his chest.

"I have to go—I think it's *Golden Dawn*," he said, and she listened quietly while he told it to her. Only when he finished speaking did she begin to ask the questions which kept them talking quietly, locked in each other's arms in the old brass bed, until long after midnight.

She insisted on cooking his breakfast for him, even though it was still dark outside and she was more than half asleep, hanging on to the range for support and turning up the early morning radio show so that the music might shake her awake.

"Good morning, early birds, this is WWOK with another lovely day ahead of you. A predicted 85° at Fort Lauderdale and the coast, and 80° inland with a 10 per cent chance of rain. We've got a report on Hurricane Lorna for you also. She's dipping away south, towards the lesser Antilles—so we can all relax, folks—relax and listen to Elton John."

"I love Elton John," Samantha said sleepily. "Don't you?"

"Who is he?" Nicholas asked.

"There! I knew right away we had a lot in common." She blinked at him owlishly. "Did you kiss me good morning? I forget."

"Come here," he instructed. "You're not going to forget this one."

Then, a few minutes later, "Nicholas, you'll miss your plane."

"Not if I cut breakfast."

"It would have been a grotty breakfast anyway." She was coming awake fast now.

She gave him the last kiss through the open window of the Cougar. "You've got an hour—you'll just about make it."

He started the engine and still she held on to the sill.

"Nicholas, one day we will be together—I mean all the time, like we planned? You and me doing our own thing, our own way? We will, won't we?"

"It's a promise."

"Hurry back," she said, and he gunned the Cougar up the sandy driveway without looking back.

• • •

There were eight of them crowded into Tom Parker's office. Although there was only seating for three, the others found perches against the tiered shelves with their rows of biological specimens in bottles of formaldehyde or on the piles of reference books and white papers that were stacked against the walls.

Samantha sat on the corner of Tom's desk, swinging her long denim-clad legs, and answered the questions that were fired at her.

"How do you know she will take the passage of the Florida Straits?"

"It's an educated guess. She's just too big and clumsy to thread the needle of the islands." Samantha's replies were quick. "Nicholas is betting on it."

"I'll go along with that then," Tom grunted.

"The Straits are a hundred miles wide—"

"I know what you're going to say," Samantha smiled, and turned to one of the other girls. "Sally-Anne will answer that one."

"You all know my brother is in the Coast Guard—all traffic through the Straits reports to Fort Lauderdale," she explained. "And the coast-guard aircraft patrol out as far as Grand Bahama."

"We'll have a fix on her immediately she enters the Straits—we've got the whole US Coast Guard rooting for us."

They argued and discussed for ten minutes more, before Tom Parker slapped an open palm on the desk in front of him and they subsided reluctantly into silence.

"Okay," he said. "Do I understand the proposal to be that this Chapter of Greenpeace intercepts the tanker carrying cad-rich crudes before it enters American territorial waters and attempts to delay or divert the ship?"

"That's exactly it," Samantha nodded, and looked about her for support. They were all nodding and murmuring in agreement.

"What are we trying to achieve? Do we truly believe that we will be able to hold up the delivery of toxic crudes to the refinery at Galveston? Let's define our objectives," Tom insisted.

"In order for evil men to triumph it is necessary only that good men do nothing. We are doing something."

"Bullshit, Sam," Tom growled. "Let's cut down on the rhetoric—it's one of the things that does us more harm than good. You talk like a nut and you discredit yourself before you have begun."

"All right," Samantha grinned. "We are publicizing the dangers, and our opposition to them."

"Okay," Tom nodded. "That's better. What are our other objectives?"

They discussed that for twenty minutes more, and then Tom Parker took over again.

"Fine, now how do we get out there in the Straits to confront this vessel—do we put on our waterwings and swim?"

Even Samantha looked sheepish now. She glanced around for support, but the others were studying their fingernails or gazing with sudden fascination out of the windows.

"Well," Samantha began, and then hesitated. "We thought—"

"Go on," Tom encouraged her. "Of course, you weren't thinking of using University property, were you? There is actually a law in this country against taking other people's ships—it's called piracy."

"As a matter of fact—" Samantha gave a helpless shrug.

"And as a senior and highly respected member of the faculty, you would not expect me to be party to a criminal act."

They were all silent, watching Samantha, for she was their leader, but for once she was at a loss.

"On the other hand, if a party of graduate researchers put in a requisition, through the proper channels, I would be quite happy to authorize an extended field expedition across the Straits to Grand Bahama on board the *Dicky*."

"Tom, you're a darling," said Samantha.

"That's a hell of a way to speak to your Professor," said Tom, and scowled happily at her.

T hey came in on the British Airways flight from Heathrow yesterday afternoon. Three of them; here is a list of the names," Bernard Wackie slid a notepad across the desk, and Nicholas glanced at it quickly.

"Charles Gras—I know him, he's Chief Engineer at Construction Navale Atlantique," Nicholas explained.

"Right," Bernard nodded. "He gave his occupation and employer to Immigration."

"Isn't that privileged information?"

Bernard grinned. "I keep my ear to the ground," and then he was deadly serious again. "All right, so these three engineers have a small suitcase each and a crate in the hold that weighs three hundred and fifty kilos, and it's marked 'Industrial Machinery.' "

"Don't stop now," Nicholas encouraged him.

"And there is an S61N Sikorsky helicopter sitting waiting for them on the tarmac. The helicopter has been chartered direct from London by Christy Marine of Leadenhall Street. The three engineers and the case of machinery are shuttled aboard the Sikorsky so fast that it looks like a conjuring trick, and she takes off and egg-beats for the south."

"Did the Sikorsky pilot file a flight-plan?"

"Sure did. Servicing shipping, course 196° magnetic. ETA to be reported."

"What's the range of the 61N—500 nautical miles?"

"Not bad," Bernard conceded. "533 for the standard, but this model has long-range tanks. She's good for 750. But that's one way, not the return journey. The helicopter hasn't returned to Bermuda yet."

"She could refuel aboard—or, if they aren't carrying avgas, she could stay on until final destination," Nicholas said. "What else have you got?"

"You want more?" Bernard looked aghast. "Doesn't anything ever satisfy you?"

"Did you monitor the communications between Bermuda Control, the chopper, and the ship she was servicing?"

"Nix," Bernard shook his head. "There was a box-up." He looked shamefaced. "It happens to the best of us."

"Spare me the details. Can you get information from Bermuda Control of the time the chopper closed her flight-plan?"

"Jesus, Nicholas, you know better than that. It's an offence to listen in on the aviation frequencies, let alone ask them."

Nicholas jumped up, and crossed swiftly to the perspex plot. He brooded over it, leaning on clenched fists, his expression smouldering as he studied the large-scale map.

"What does all this mean to you, Nicholas?" Bernard came to stand beside him.

"It means that a vessel at sea, belonging to the Christy Marine fleet, has requested its head office to send machinery spares and specialist personnel by the fastest possible means, without regard to expense. Have you figured the air freight on a package of 350 kilos?"

Nicholas straightened up and groped for the crocodile-skin cheroot case.

"It means that the vessel is broken down or in imminent danger of breakdown somewhere in an area south-west of Bermuda, within an arc of four hundred and fifty miles—probably much closer, otherwise she would have requested service from the Bahamas, and it's highly unlikely they would have operated the chopper at extreme range."

"Right," Bernard agreed. Nicholas lit his cheroot and they were both silent a moment.

"A hell of a small needle in a bloody big haystack," said Bernard.

"You let me worry about that," Nicholas murmured, still without taking his eyes from the plot.

"That's what you are paid for," Bernard agreed amiably. "it's *Golden Dawn*, isn't it?"

"Has Christy Marine got any other vessels in the area?"

"Not as far as I know."

"Then that was a bloody stupid question."

"Take it easy, Nicholas."

"I'm sorry." Nicholas touched his arm. "My boy's on that pig." He took a deep draw on the cheroot, held it a moment, and then slowly exhaled. His voice was calm and businesslike, as he went on:

"What's our weather?"

"Wind at 060° and 15 knots. Cloud three eighths stratocumulus at four thousand feet. Long-range projection, no change."

"Steady trade winds again," Nicholas nodded. "Thank God for all small mercies."

"There is a hurricane warning out, as you know, but on its present position and track, it will blow itself out to sea a thousand miles south of Grand Bahama."

"Good," Nicholas nodded again. "Please ask both *Warlock* and *Sea Witch* to report their positions, course, speed and fuel conditions."

Bernard had the two telex flimsies for him within twenty minutes.

"*Warlock* has made a good run of it," Nicholas murmured, as the position of the tug was marked on the plot.

"She crossed the equator three days ago," said Bernard.

"And *Sea Witch* will reach Charleston late tomorrow," Nicholas observed. "Are any of the opposition inside us?"

Bernard shook his head. "McCormick has one in New York and *Wittezee* is halfway back to Rotterdam."

"We are in good shape," Nicholas decided, as he balanced the triangles of relative speeds and distances between the vessels.

"Is there another chopper available on the island to get me out to *Warlock*?"

"No," Bernard shook his head. "The 61N is the only one based on Bermuda."

"Can you arrange bunkering for *Warlock*, I mean immediate bunkering—here in Hamilton?"

"We can have her tanks filled an hour after she comes in."

Nicholas paused and then made the decision. "Please telex David Allen on *Warlock*, TO MASTER WARLOCK FROM BERG IMMEDIATE AND URGENT NEW SPEED TOP OF THE GREEN NEW COURSE HAMILTON HARBOUR BERMUDA ISLAND DIRECT REPORT EXPECTED TIME OF ARRIVAL ENDS."

"You're going to run, then?" Bernard asked. "You are going to run with both your ships?"

"Yes," Nicholas nodded. "I'm running with everything I've got."

G*olden Dawn* wallowed with the dead heavy weight of one million tons of crude oil. Her motion was that of a waterlogged hulk. Broadside to the set of the swells, her tank decks were almost awash. The low seas broke against her starboard rail and the occasional crest flopped over and spread like pretty patches of white lace-work over the green plastic-coated decks.

She had been drifting powerlessly for four days now.

The main bearing of the single propeller shaft had begun to run hot forty-eight hours after crossing the equator, and the Chief Engineer had asked for shutdown to inspect the bearing and effect any repairs. Duncan Alexander had forbidden any shutdown, overriding the good judgement of both his Master and Chief Engineer, and had only grudgingly agreed to a reduction in the ship's speed.

He ordered the Chief Engineer to trace any fault and to effect what repairs he could, while under reduced power.

Within four hours, the Chief had traced the damaged and leaking gland in the pump that force-lubricated the bearing, but even the running under reduced power setting had done significant damage to the main bearing, and now there was noticeable vibration, jarring even *Golden Dawn*'s massive hull.

"I have to get the pump stripped down or we'll burn her clear out," the Chief faced up to Duncan Alexander at last. "Then you'll *have* to shut down and not just a couple of hours either. It will take two days to fit new bearing shells at sea." The Chief was pale and his lips trembled, for he knew of this man's reputation. The engineer knew that he discarded those who crossed him, and he had the reputation of a special vindictiveness to hound a man until he was broken. The Chief was afraid, but his concern for the ship was just strong enough.

Duncan Alexander changed direction. "What was the cause of the pump failure in the first place? Why wasn't it noticed earlier? It looks like a case of negligence to me."

Stung at last, the Chief blurted out, "If there had been a back-up pump on this ship, we could have switched to secondary system and done proper maintenance."

Duncan Alexander flushed and turned away. The modifications he had personally ordered to *Golden Dawn*'s design had excluded most of the duplicated back-up systems; anything that kept down the cost of construction had been ordered.

"How long do you need?" He stopped in the centre of the owner's stateroom and glared at his engineer.

"Four hours," the Scot replied promptly.

"You've got exactly four hours," he said grimly. "If you haven't finished by then you will live to regret it. I swear that to you."

While the engineer stopped his engines, stripped, repaired and reassembled the lubrication pump, Duncan was on the bridge with the Master.

"We've lost time, too much time," he said. "I want that made up."

"It will mean pushing over best economic speed," Captain Randle warned carefully.

"Captain Randle, the value of our cargo is 85 dollars a ton. We have on board one million tons. I want the time made up." Duncan brushed his objection aside. "We have a deadline to meet in Galveston roads. This ship, this whole concept of carrying crude is on trial, Captain. I don't have to keep reminding you of that. The hell with the costs, I want to meet the deadline."

"Yes, Mr. Alexander," Randle nodded. "We'll make up the time."

Three and a half hours later, the Chief Engineer came up to the bridge.

"Well?" Duncan turned on him fiercely as he stepped out of the elevator.

"The pump is repaired, but—"

"What is it, man?"

"I've got a feeling. We ran her too long. I've got a nasty feeling about that bearing. It wouldn't be clever to run her over 50 per cent of power, not until it's been taken down and inspected—"

"I'm ordering revolutions for 25 knots," Randle told him uneasily.

"I wouldn't do that, man," the Chief shook his head rather mournfully.

"Your station is in the engine room," Duncan dismissed him brusquely, nodded to Randle to order resumption of sailing, and went out to his customary place on the open wing of the bridge. He looked back over the high round stern as the white turbulence of the great propeller boiled out from under the counter and then settled in a long slick wake that soon reached back to the horizon. Duncan stood out in the wind until after dark, and when he went below, Chantelle was waiting for him. She stood up from the long couch under the forward windows of the stateroom.

"We are under way again."

"Yes," he said. "It's going to be all right."

The engine control was switched to automatic at nine o'clock local time that night. The engine room personnel went up to dinner, and to bed, all except the Chief Engineer. He lingered for another two hours shaking his head and mumbling bitterly over the massive bearing assembly in the long, narrow shaft tunnel. Every few minutes, he laid his hand on the massive casting, feeling for the heat and vibration that would warn of structural damage.

At eleven o'clock, he spat on the steadily revolving propeller shaft. It was thick as an oak trunk and polished brilliant silver in the stark white lights of the tunnel. He pushed himself up stiffly from his crouch beside the bearing.

In the control room, he checked again that all the ship's systems were

on automatic, and that all circuits were functioning and repeating on the
big control board, then he stepped into the elevator and went up.

Thirty-five minutes later, one of the tiny transistors in the board blew
with a pop like a champagne cork and a puff of grey smoke. There was
nobody in the control room to hear or see it. The system was not duplicated, there was no back-up to switch itself in automatically, so that
when the temperature of the bearing began to rise again, there was no
impulse carried to the alarm system, no automatic shutdown of power.

The massive shaft spun on while the overheated bearing closed its
grip upon the area of rough metal, damaged by the previous prolonged
running. A fine sliver of metal lifted from the polished surface of the
spinning shaft, and curled like a silver hairspring, was caught up and
smeared into the bearing. The whole assembly began to glow a sullen
cherry red and then the oxide paint that was daubed on the outer surfaces
of the bearing began to blister and blacken. Still the tremendous power
of the engine forced the shaft around.

What oil was still being fed between the glowing surfaces of the spinning shaft and the shells of the bearing turned instantly thin as water in
the heat, then reached its flash-point and burst into flame and ran in little
fiery rivulets down the heavy casting of the main bearing, flashing the
blistered paintwork alight. The shaft tunnel filled with thick billows of
stinking chemical-tainted smoke, and only then did the fire sensors come
to life and their alarms repeated on the navigation bridge and in the quarters of Master, First Officer and Chief Engineer.

But the great engine was still pounding along at 70 per cent of power,
and the shaft still turned in the disintegrating bearing, smearing heat-
softened metal, buckling and distorting under unbearable strains.

The Chief Engineer was the first to reach the central console in the
engine control room, and without orders from the bridge he began emergency shutdown of all systems.

It was another hour before the team under the direction of the First
Officer had the fire in the shaft tunnel under control. They used carbon
dioxide gas to smother the burning paint and oil, for cold water on the
heated metal would have aggravated the damage done by heat distortion
and buckling.

The metal of the main bearing casting was still so hot when the Chief
Engineer began opening it up, that it scorched the thick leather and as-
bestos gloves worn by his team.

The bearing shells had disintegrated, and the shaft itself was brutally scored and pitted. If there was distortion, the Chief knew it would not be detected by eye. However, even a buckling of one ten thousandth of an inch would be critical.

He cursed softly as he worked, making the obscenities sound like a lullaby; he cursed the manufacturers of the lubricating pump, the men who had installed and tested it, the damaged gland and the lack of a back-up system, but mostly he cursed the stubbornness and intractability of the Chairman of Christy Marine whose ill-advised judgement had turned this functionally beautiful machinery into blackened, smoking twisted metal.

It was mid-morning by the time the Chief had the spare bearing shells brought up from stores and unpacked from their wood shavings in the wooden cases; but it was only when they came to fit them that they realized that the cases had been incorrectly stencilled. The half-shells that they contained were obsolete non-metric types, and they were five millimetres undersized for *Golden Dawn*'s shaft; that tiny variation in size made them utterly useless.

It was only then that Duncan Alexander's steely urbane control began to crack; he raged about the bridge for twenty minutes, making no effort to think his way out of the predicament, but abusing Randle and his engineer in wild and extravagant terms. His rage had a paralysing effect on all *Golden Dawn*'s officers and they stood white-faced and silently guilty.

Peter Berg had sensed the excitement and slipped up unobtrusively to watch. He was fascinated by his step-father's rage. He had never seen a display like it before, and at one stage he hoped that Duncan Alexander's eyeballs might actually burst like overripe grapes; he held his breath in anticipation, and felt cheated when it did not happen.

At last, Duncan stopped and ran both hands through his thick waving hair; two spikes of hair stood up like devil's horns. He was still panting, but he had recovered partial control.

"Now sir, what do you propose?" he demanded of Randle, and in the silence Peter Berg piped up.

"You could have new shells sent from Bermuda—it's only three hundred miles away. We checked it this morning."

"How did you get in here?" Duncan swung round. "Get back to your mother."

Peter scampered, appalled at his own indiscretion, and only when he left the bridge did the Chief speak.

"We could have spares flown out from London to Bermuda—"

"There must be a boat—" Randle cut in swiftly.

"Or an aircraft to drop it to us—"

"Or a helicopter—"

"Get Christy Main on the telex," snapped Duncan Alexander fiercely.

I t was good to have a deck under his feet again, Nicholas exulted. He felt himself coming fully alive again.

"I'm a sea-creature," he grinned to himself. "And I keep forgetting it."

He looked back to the low silhouette of the Bermuda islands, the receding arms of Hamilton Harbour and the flecking of the multicoloured buildings amongst the cedar trees, and then returned his attention to the spread charts on the navigation table before him.

Warlock was still at cautionary speed. Even though the channel was wide and clearly buoyed, yet the coral reef on each hand was sharp and hungry, and David Allen's full attention was on the business of conning *Warlock* out into the open sea. But as they passed the 100 fathom line, he gave the order to his deck officer,

"Full away at 0900 hours, pilot," and hurried across to join Nicholas.

"I didn't have much of a chance to welcome you on board, sir."

"Thank you, David. It's good to be back." Nicholas looked up and smiled at him. "Will you bring her round on to 240° magnetic and increase to 80 per cent power?"

Quickly David repeated his order to the helm and then shifted from one foot to the other, beginning to flush under the salt-water tan.

"Mr. Berg, my officers are driving me mad. They've been plaguing me since we left Cape Town—are we running on a job—or is this a pleasure cruise?"

Nicholas laughed aloud then. He felt the excitement of the hunt, a good hot scent in the nostrils, and the prospect of a fat prize. Now he had *Warlock* under him, his concern for Peter's safety had abated. Whatever happened now, he could get there very fast. No, he felt good, very good.

"We're hunting, David," he told him. "Nothing certain yet—" he paused, and then relented, "Get Beauty Baker up to my cabin, tell Angel to send up a big pot of coffee and a mess of sandwiches—I missed breakfast—and while we are eating, I'll fill both of you in."

Beauty Baker accepted one of Nicholas' cheroots.

"Still smoking cheap," he observed, and sniffed at the four-dollar cheroot sourly, but there was a twinkle of pleasure behind the smeared lenses of his spectacles. Then, unable to contain himself, he actually grinned.

"Skipper tells me we are hunting, is that right?"

"This is the picture—" Nicholas began to spell it out to them in detail, and while he talked, he thought with comfortable self-indulgence, "I must be getting old and soft—I didn't always talk so much."

Both men listened in silence, and only when he finished did the two of them begin bombarding him with the perceptive penetrating questions he had expected.

"Sounds like a generator armature," Beauty Baker guessed, as he puzzled the contents of the wooden case that had been flown out to *Golden Dawn*. I cannot believe that *Golden Dawn* doesn't carry a full set of mechanical spares."

While Baker was fully preoccupied with the mechanics of the situation, David Allen concentrated on the problems of seamanship. "What was the range of the helicopter? Has it returned to base yet? With her draught, she must be heading for the Florida Straits. Our best bet would be to shape a course for Matanilla Reef at the mouth of the Straits."

There was a peremptory knock on the door of the guest cabin, and the Trog stuck his grey wrinkled tortoise head through. He glanced at Nicholas, but did not greet him. "Captain, Miami is broadcasting a new hurricane alert. 'Lorna' has kicked northwards, they're predicting a track of north north-west and a speed over the ground of twenty knots."

He closed the door and they stared at each other in silence for a moment.

Nicholas spoke at last.

"It is never one single mistake that causes disaster," he said. "It is always a series of contributory errors, most of them of small consequence in themselves—but when taken with a little bad luck—" he was silent for a moment and then, softly, "Hurricane Lorna could just be that bit of bad luck."

He stood up and took one turn around the small guest cabin, feeling caged and wishing for the space of the Master's suite which was now David Allen's. He turned back to Beauty Baker and David Allen, and suddenly he realized that they were hoping for disaster. They were like two old sea wolves with the scent of the prey in their nostrils. He felt his anger rising coldly against them, they were wishing disaster on his son.

"Just one thing I didn't tell you," he said. "My son is on *Golden Dawn*."

The immense revolving storm that was code-named Lorna was nearing full development. Her crest was reared high above the freezing levels so she wore a splendid mane of frosted white ice particles that streamed out three hundred miles ahead of her on the jet stream of the upper troposphere.

From one side to the other, she now measured one hundred and fifty miles across, and the power unleashed within her was of unmeasurable savagery.

The winds that blew around her centre tore the surface off the sea and bore it aloft at speeds in excess of one hundred and fifty miles an hour, generating precipitation that was as far beyond rain as death is beyond life. Water filled the dense cloud-banks so that there was no clear line between sea and air.

It seemed now that madness fed upon madness, and like a blinded and berserk monster, she blundered across the confined waters of the Caribbean, ripping the trees and buildings, even the very earth from the tiny islands which stood in her path.

But there were still forces controlling what seemed uncontrollable, dictating what seemed to be random, for, as she spun upon a spinning globe, the storm showed the primary trait of gyroscopic inertia, a rigidity in space that was constant as long as no outside force was applied.

Obeying this natural law, the entire system moved steadily eastwards at constant speed and altitude above the surface of the earth, until her northern edge touched the landmass of the long ridge of land that forms the greater Antilles.

Immediately another gyroscopic law came into force, the law of precession. When a deflecting force is applied to the rim of a spinning gyro, the gyro moves not away from, but *directly towards* that force.

Hurricane Lorna felt the land and, like a maddened bull at the flirt of the matador's cape, she turned and charged towards it, crossing the narrow high strips of Haiti in an orgy of destruction and terror until she burst out of the narrow channel of the Windward Passage into the open beyond.

Yet still she kept on spinning and moving. Now, barely three hundred miles ahead of her, across those shallow reefs and banks prophetically named "Hurricane Flats" after the thousands of other such storms that had followed the same route during the memory of man, lay the deeper waters of the Florida Straits and the mainland of the continental United States of America.

At twenty miles an hour, the whole incredible heaven-high mass of crazed wind and churning clouds trundled north-westwards.

D uncan Alexander stood under the bogus Degas ballet dancers in the owner's stateroom. He balanced easily on the balls of his feet and his hands were clasped lightly behind his back, but his brow was heavily furrowed with worry and his eyes darkly underscored with plum-coloured swollen bags of sleeplessness.

Seated on the long couch and on the imitation Louis Quatorze chairs flanking the fireplace, were the senior officers of *Golden Dawn*—her Captain, Mate and Chief Engineer, and in the leather-studded wing-backed chair across the wide cabin sat Charles Gras, the engineer from Atlantique. It seemed as though he had chosen his seat to keep himself aloof from the owner and officers of the crippled ultra-tanker.

He spoke now in heavily accented English, falling back on the occasional French word which Duncan translated quickly. The four men listened to him with complete attention, never taking their eyes from the sharp, pale Parisian features and the foxy bright eyes.

"My men will have completed the reassembly of the main bearing by noon today. To the best of my ability, I have examined and tested the main shaft. I can find no evidence of structural damage, but I must emphasize that this does not mean that no damage exists. At the very best, the repairs must be considered to be temporary." He paused and they waited, while he turned deliberately to Captain Randle. "I must urge you to seek proper repair in the nearest port open to you, and to proceed there at the lowest speed which will enable you efficiently to work the ship."

Randle twisted uncomfortably in his seat, and glanced across at Duncan. The Frenchman saw the exchange and a little steel came into his voice.

"If there is structural distortion in the main shaft, operation at speeds higher than this may result in permanent and irreversible damage and complete breakdown. I must make this point most forcibly."

Duncan intervened smoothly. "We are fully burdened and drawing twenty fathoms of water. There are no safe harbours on the eastern seaboard of America, that is even supposing that we could get permission to enter territorial waters with engine trouble. The Americans aren't likely to welcome us. Our nearest safe anchorage is Galveston roads, on the Texas coast of the Gulf of Mexico—and then only after the tugs have taken off our pod tanks outside the 100-fathom line."

The tanker's First Officer was a young man, probably not over thirty years of age, but he had so far conducted himself impeccably in the emergencies the ship had encountered. He had a firm jaw and a clear level eye, and he had been the first into the smoke-filled shaft tunnel.

"With respect, sir," and they all turned their heads towards him, "Miami has broadcast a revised hurricane alert that includes the Straits and southern Florida. We would be on a reciprocal course to the hurricane track, a directly converging course."

"Even at fifteen knots, we would be through the Straits and into the Gulf with twenty-four hours to spare," Duncan stated, and looked to Randle for confirmation.

"At the present speed of the storm's advance—yes," Randle qualified carefully. "But conditions may change—"

The Mate persisted. "Again, with respect, sir. Our nearest safe anchorage is the lee of Bermuda Island—"

"Do you have any idea of the value of this cargo?" Duncan's voice rasped. "No, you do not. Well, I will inform you. It is $85,000,000. The interest on that amount is in the region of $25,000 a day." His voice rose an octave, again that wild note to it. "Bermuda does not have the facilities to effect major repairs—"

The door from the private accommodation opened silently and Chantelle Alexander stepped into the stateroom. She wore no jewellery, a plain pearl silk blouse and a simple dark woollen skirt, but her skin had been gilded by the sun and she had lightly touched her dark eyes with a make-up that emphasized their size and shape. Her beauty silenced them all and she was fully aware of it as she crossed to stand beside Duncan.

"It is necessary that this ship and her cargo proceed directly to Galveston," she said softly.

"Chantelle—" Duncan began, and she silenced him with a brusque gesture of one hand.

"There is no question about the destination and the route that is to be taken."

Charles Gras looked to Captain Randle, waiting for him to assert the authority vested in him by law. But when the young Captain remained silent, the Frenchman smiled sardonically and shrugged a world-weary dismissal of further interest. "Then I must ask that arrangements be made for my two assistants and myself to leave this ship immediately we have completed the temporary repairs." Again Gras emphasized the word "temporary."

Duncan nodded. "If we resume our sailing when you anticipate, and even taking into consideration the low fuel condition of the helicopter, we will be within easy range of the east coast of Florida by dawn tomorrow."

Chantelle had not taken her eyes from the *Golden Dawn*'s officers during this exchange, and now she went on in the same quiet voice.

"I am quite prepared to accept the resignation of any of the officers of this ship who wish to join that flight."

Duncan opened his mouth to make some protest at her assumption of his authority, but she turned to him with a small lift of the chin, and something in her expression and the set of her head upon her shoulders reminded him forcibly of old Arthur Christy. There was the same toughness and resilience there, the same granite determination; strange that he had not noticed it before.

"Perhaps I have never looked before," he thought. Chantelle recognized the moment of his capitulation, and calmly she turned back to face *Golden Dawn*'s officers.

One by one, they dropped their eyes from hers; Randle was the first to stand up.

"If you will excuse me, Mrs. Alexander, I must make preparations to get under way again."

Charles Gras paused and looked back at her, and he smiled again, as only a Frenchman smiles at a pretty woman.

"*Magnifique!*" he murmured, and lifted one hand in a graceful salute of admiration before he stepped out of the stateroom.

When Chantelle and Duncan were alone together, she turned to him slowly, and she let the contempt show in her expression.

"Any time you feel you have not got the guts for it, let me know, will you?"

"Chantelle—"

"You have got us into this, me and Christy Marine. Now you'll get us out of it, even if it kills you." Her lips compressed into a thinner line and her eyes slitted vindictively. "And it would be nice if it did," she said softly.

The pilot of the Beechcraft Baron pulled back the throttles to 22" of boost on both engines, and slid the propellers into fully fine pitch, simultaneously beginning a gentle descending turn towards the extraordinary-looking vessel that came up swiftly out of the low early morning haze that spilled over from the islands.

The same haze had blotted the low silhouette of the Florida coast from the western horizon, and even the pale green water and shaded reefs of little Bahamas Bank were washed pale by the haze, and partially obscured by the intermittent layer of stratocumulus cloud at four thousand feet.

The Baron pilot selected 20° of flap to give the aircraft a nosedown attitude which would afford a better forward vision, and continued his descent down through the cloud. It burst in a brief grey puff across the windshield before they were out into sunlight again.

"What do you make of her?" he asked his co-pilot.

"She's a big baby," the co-pilot tried to steady his binoculars. "Can't read her name."

The enormously wide low bows were pushing up a fat sparkling pillow of churning water, and the green decks seemed to reach back almost to the limits of visibility before rising sheer into the stern quarters.

"Son of a gun," the pilot shook his head. "She looks like the vehicle-assembly building on Cape Kennedy."

"She does too," agreed his co-pilot. The same square unlovely bulk of that enormous structure was repeated in smaller scale by the navigation bridge of the big ship. "I'll give her a call on 16." The co-pilot lowered his binoculars and thumbed the microphone as he lifted it to his lips.

"Southbound bulk carrier, this is Coast Guard November Charlie One Fife Niner overhead. Do you read me?"

There was the expected delay; even in confined and heavily trafficked waters, these big bastards kept a sloppy watch and the spotter fumed silently.

"Coast Guard One Fife Niner, this is *Golden Dawn*. Reading you fife by fife. Going up to 22."

Two hundred miles away the Trog knocked over the shell-casing, spilling damp and stinking cigar butts over the deck, in his haste to change frequency to channel 22 as the operator on board *Golden Dawn* had stipulated, at the same time switching on both the tape recorder and the radio direction-finder equipment.

High up in *Warlock*'s fire-control tower, the big metal ring of the direction-finding aerial turned slowly, lining up on the transmissions that boomed so clearly across the ether, repeating the relative bearing on the dial of the instrument on the Trog's cluttered bench.

"Good morning to you, *Golden Dawn*," the lilting Southern twang of the coastguard navigator came back. "I would be mightily obliged for your port of registry and your cargo manifest."

"This ship is registered Venezuela." The Trog dexterously made the fine tuning, scribbled the bearing on his pad, ripped off the page and darted into *Warlock*'s navigation bridge.

"*Golden Dawn* is sending in clear," he squeaked with an expression of malicious glee.

"Call the Captain," snapped the deck officer, and then as an after-thought, "and ask Mr. Berg to come to the bridge."

The conversation between coastguard and ultra-tanker was still go-ing on when Nicholas burst into the radio room, belting his dressing gown.

"Thank you for your courtesy, sir," the coastguard navigator was using extravagant Southern gallantry, fully aware that *Golden Dawn* was outside United States territorial waters, and officially beyond his government's jurisdiction. "I would appreciate your port of final destination."

"We are en route to Galveston for full discharge of cargo."

"Thank you again, sir. And are you apprised of the hurricane alert in force at this time?"

"Affirmative."

From *Warlock*'s bridge, David Allen appeared in the doorway, his face set and flushed.

"She must be under way again," he said, his disappointment so plain that it angered Nicholas yet again. "She is into the channel already."

"I'd be obliged if you would immediately put this ship on a course to enter the Straits and close with her as soon as is possible," Nicholas snapped, and David Allen blinked at him once then disappeared on to his bridge, calling for the change in course and increase in speed as he went.

Over the loudspeaker, the coastguard was being politely persistent.

"Are you further apprised, sir, of the update on that hurricane alert predicting storm passage of the main navigable channel at 1200 hours local time tomorrow?"

"Affirmative." *Golden Dawn*'s replies had become curt.

"May I further trouble you, sir, in view of your sensitive cargo and the special weather conditions, for your expected time of arrival abeam of the Dry Tortugas Bank marine beacon and when you anticipate clearing the channel and shaping a northerly course away from the predicted hurricane track?"

"Standby." There was a brief hum of static while the operator consulted the deck officer and then the *Golden Dawn* came back, "Our ETA Dry Tortugas Bank beacon is 0130 tomorrow."

There was a long pause now as the coastguard consulted his headquarters ashore on one of the closed frequencies, and then:

"I am requested respectfully, but officially, to bring to your attention that very heavy weather is expected ahead of the storm centre and that your present ETA Dry Tortugas Bank leaves you very fine margins of safety, sir."

"Thank you, coastguard One Fife Niner. Your transmission will be entered in the ship's log. This is *Golden Dawn* over and out."

The coastguard's frustration was evident. Clearly he would have loved to order the tanker to reverse her course. "We will be following your progress with interest, *Golden Dawn*. Bon voyage, this is coastguard One Fife Niner over and out."

C harles Gras held his blue beret on with one hand, while with the other he lugged his suitcase. He ran doubled up, instinctively avoiding the ear-numbing clatter of the helicopter's rotor.

He threw his suitcase through the open fuselage door and then hesitated, turned and scampered back to where the ship's Chief Engineer stood at the edge of the white-painted helipad target on *Golden Dawn*'s tank deck.

Charles grabbed the Engineer's upper arm and leaned close to shout in his ear.

"Remember, my friend, treat her like a baby, like a tender virgin—if you have to increase speed, do so gently—very gently." The Engineer nodded, his sparse sandy hair fluttering in the down draught.

"Good luck," shouted the Frenchman. "*Bonne chance!*" He slapped the man's shoulder. "I hope you don't need it!"

He darted back and scrambled up into the fuselage of the Sikorsky, and his face appeared in one of the portholes. He waved once, and then the big ungainly machine rose slowly into the air, hovered for a moment and then banked away low over the water, setting off in its characteristic nose-down attitude for the mainland, still hidden by haze and distance.

D r. Samantha Silver, dressed in thigh-high rubber waders and with her sleeves rolled up above the elbows, staggered under the weight of two ten-gallon plastic buckets of clams as she climbed the back steps of the laboratory building.

"Sam!" down the length of the long passageway, Sally-Anne screamed at her. "We were going to leave without you!"

"What is it?" Sam dumped the buckets with relief, slopping salt water down the steps.

"Johnny called—the anti-pollution patrol bespoke *Golden Dawn* an hour ago. She's in the Straits. She was abeam Matanilla reef when they spotted her and she will be abeam of Biscayne Key before we can get out there, if we don't leave now."

"I'm coming." Sam hefted her heavy buckets, and broke into a rubber-kneed trot. "I'll meet you down on the wharf—did you call the TV studio?"

"There's a camera team on the way," Sally-Anne yelled back as she ran for the front doors. "Hurry, Sam—fast as you like!"

Samantha dumped the clams into one of her tanks, switched on the oxygen and as soon as it began to bubble to the surface, she turned and raced from the laboratory and out of the front doors.

G*olden Dawn*'s deck officer stopped beside the radar-scope, glanced down at it idly, then stooped with more attention and took a bearing on the little glowing pinpoint of green light that showed up clearly inside the ten-mile circle of the sweep.

He grunted, straightened, and walked quickly to the front of the bridge. Slowly, he scanned the green wind-chopped sea ahead of the tanker's ponderous bows.

"Fishing boat," he said to the helmsman. "But they are under way." He had seen the tiny flash of a bow wave. "And they are right in the main navigational channel—they must have seen us by now, they are making a turn to pass us to starboard." He dropped the binoculars and let them dangle against his chest. "Oh thank you." He took the cup of cocoa from the steward, and sipped it with relish as he turned away to the chart-table.

One of the tanker's junior officers came out of the radio room at the back of the bridge.

"Still no score," he said, "and only injury time left now," and they fell into a concerned discussion of the World Cup soccer match being played under floodlights at Wembley Stadium on the other side of the Atlantic.

"If it's a draw then it means that France is in the—"

There was an excited shout from the radio room, and the junior officer ran to the door and then turned back with an excited grin. "England has scored!"

The deck officer chuckled happily. "That will wrap it up." Then with a start of guilt he turned back to his duties, and had another start, this time of surprise, when he glanced into the radarscope.

"What the hell are they playing at!" he exclaimed irritably, and hurried forward to scan the sea ahead.

The fishing boat had continued its turn and was now bows on.

"Damn them. We'll give them a buzz." He reached up for the handle of the foghorn and blew three long blasts that echoed out mournfully across the shallow greenish water of the Straits. There was a general movement among the officers to get a better view ahead through the forward bridge windows.

"They must be half asleep out there." The deck officer thought quickly about calling the Captain to the bridge. If it came to manoeuvring the ship in these confined waters, he flinched from the responsibility. Even at this reduced speed, it would take *Golden Dawn* half an hour and seven nautical miles to come to a stop; a turn in either direction would swing through a wide arc of many miles before the ship was able to make a 90° change of course—God, then there was the effect of the wind against the enormously exposed area of the towering stern quarters, and the full bore of the Gulf Stream driving out of the narrows of the Straits. The problems of manoeuvring the vessel struck a chill of panic into the officer—and the fishing boat was on collision course, the range closing swiftly under the combined speeds of both vessels. He reached for the call button of the intercom that connected the bridge directly to the Captain's quarters on the deck below, but at that moment Captain Randle came bounding up the private staircase from his day cabin.

"What is it?" he demanded. "What was that blast on the horn?"

"Small vessel holding on to collision course, sir." The officer's relief was evident, and Randle seized the handle of the foghorn and hung on to it.

"God, what's wrong with them?"

"The deck is crowded," exclaimed one of the officers without lowering his binoculars. "Looks as though they have a movie-camera team on the top deck."

Randle judged the closing range anxiously; already the small fishing vessel was too close for the *Golden Dawn* to stop in time.

"Thank God," somebody exclaimed. "They are turning away."

"They are streaming some sort of banner. Can anybody read that?"

"They are heaving-to," the deck officer yelled suddenly. "They are heaving-to right under our bows."

• • •

amantha Silver had not expected the tanker to be so big. From directly ahead, her bows seemed to fill the horizon from one side to the other, and the bow wave she threw up ahead of her creamed and curved like the set of the long wave at Cape St. Francis when the surf was up.

Beyond the bows, the massive tower of her navigation bridge stood so tall that it looked like the skyline of The Miami Beach, one of those massive hotel buildings seen from close inshore.

It made her feel distinctly uneasy to be directly under that on-rushing steel avalanche.

"Do you think they have seen us?" Sally-Anne asked beside her, and when Samantha heard her own unease echoed by the pretty girl beside her, it steeled her.

"Of course they have," she announced stoutly so that everyone in the small wheelhouse could hear her. "That's why they blew their siren. We'll turn aside at the last minute."

"They aren't slowing down," Hank Petersen, the helmsman, pointed out huskily, and Samantha wished that Tom Parker had been on board with them. However, Tom was up in Washington again, and they had taken the *Dicky* to sea with a scratch crew, and without Tom Parker's written authorization. "What do you want to do, Sam?" And they all looked at her.

"I know a thing that size can't stop, but at least we're going to make them slow down.

"Are the TV boys getting some stuff?" Samantha asked, to delay the moment of decision. "Go up, Sally-Anne, and check them." Then to the others, "You-all get the banner ready. We'll let them get a good look at that."

"Listen, Sam." Hank Petersen's tanned intelligent face was strained. He was a tunny expert, and was not accustomed to handling the vessel except in calm and uncluttered waters. "I don't like this, we're getting much too close. That thing could churn us right under, and not even notice the bump. I want to turn away now." His voice was almost drowned by the sudden sky-crashing blast of the tanker's foghorns.

"Son of a gun, Sam, I don't like playing chicken-chicken with somebody that size."

"Don't worry, we'll get out of their way at the last moment. All right!" Samantha decided. "Turn 90° to port, Hank. Let's show them the signs. I'm going to help them on deck."

The wind tore at the thin white canvas banner as they tried to run it out along the side of the deckhouse, and the little vessel was rolling uncomfortably while the TV producer was shouting confused stage directions at them from the top of the wheelhouse.

Bitterly Samantha wished there was somebody to take command, somebody like Nicholas Berg—and the banner tried to wrap itself around her head.

The *Dicky* was coming around fast now, and Samantha shot a glance at the oncoming tanker and felt the shock of it strike in the pit of her stomach like the blow of a fist. It was huge, and very close—much too close, even she realized that.

At last she managed to get a turn of the thin line that secured the banner around the stern rail—but the light canvas had twisted so that only one word of the slogan was readable. "POISONER," it accused in scarlet, crudely painted letters followed by a grinning skull and crossed bones.

Samantha dived across the deck and struggled with the flapping canvas; above her head the producer was shouting excitedly; two of the others were trying to help her; Sally-Anne was screaming "Go back! Go back!" and waving both arms at the great tanker. "You poison our oceans!"

Everything was becoming confused and out of control. The *Dicky* swung ahead into the wind and pitched steeply, the person next to her lost his footing and knocked painfully into Samantha, and at that moment she felt the change of the engine beat.

Tricky Dicky's diesel had been bellowing furiously as Hank opened the throttle to its stop, using full power to bring the little vessel around from under the menace of those steel bows.

The smoking splutter of the exhaust pipe that rose vertically up the side of the deckhouse had made all speech difficult—but now it died away, and suddenly there was only the sound of the wind.

Even their own raised voices were silenced, and they froze, staring out at *Golden Dawn* as she bore down on them without the slightest check in her majestic approach.

Samantha was the first one to recover, then she ran across the plunging deck to the wheelhouse.

Hank Petersen was down on his knees beside the bulkhead, struggling ineffectually with the conduit that housed the controls to the engine room on the deck below.

"Why have you stopped?" Samantha yelled at him, and he looked up at her as though he were mortally wounded.

"It's the throttle linkage," he said. "It's snapped again."

"Can't you fix it?" and the question was a mockery. A mile away, *Golden Dawn* came down on them—silent, menacing, unstoppable.

For ten seconds Randle stood rigid, both hands gripping the foul weather rail below the sill of the bridge windows.

His face was set, pale and finely drawn, as he watched the stern of the wallowing fishing boat for the renewed churning of its prop.

He knew that he could not turn nor stop his ship in time to avoid collision, unless the small vessel got under way immediately, and took evasive action by going out to starboard under full power.

"Damn them to hell," he thought bitterly, they were in gross default. He had all the law and the custom of the sea behind him; a collision would cause very little damage to *Golden Dawn*, perhaps she would lose a little paint, at most a slightly buckled plate in the reinforced bows—and they had asked for it.

He had no doubts about the object of this crazy, irresponsible seamanship. There had been controversy before the *Golden Dawn* sailed. He had read the objections and seen the nutcase environmentalists on television. The scarlet-painted banner with the ridiculously melodramatic Jolly Roger made it clear that this was a boatload of nutters who were attempting to prevent *Golden Dawn* from entering American waters.

He felt his anger boiling up fiercely. These people always made him furious. If they had their way, there would be no tanker trade, and now they were deliberately threatening him, placing him in a position which might prejudice his own career. He already had the task of taking his ship through the Straits ahead of the hurricane. Every moment was vital—and now there was this.

He would be happy to maintain course and speed, and to run them down. They were flaunting themselves, challenging him to do it—and, by God, they deserved it.

However, he was a seaman, with a seaman's deep concern for human life at sea. It would go against all his instincts not to make an effort to avoid collision, no matter how futile that effort would be. Then beside him one of his officers triggered him.

"There are women on board her—look at that! Those are women!"

That was enough. Without waiting for confirmation, Randle snapped at the helmsman beside him.

"Full port rudder!"

And with two swift paces he had reached the engine room telegraph. It rang shrilly as he pulled back the chromed handle to "Full Astern."

Almost immediately, the changed beat came up through the soles of his feet, as the great engine seven decks below the bridge thundered suddenly under all emergency power, and the direction of the spinning main propellor shaft was abruptly reversed.

Randle spun back to face ahead. For almost five minutes, the bows held steady on the horizon without making any answer to the full application of the rudder. The inertia of a million tons of crude oil, the immense drag of the hull through water and the press of wind and current held her on course, and although the single ferro-bronze propeller bit deeply into the green waters, there was not the slightest diminution of the tanker's speed.

Randle kept his hand on the engine telegraph, pulling back on the silver handle with all his strength, as though this might arrest the great ship's forward way through the water.

"Turn!" he whispered to the ship, and he stared at the fishing boat that still lay, rolling wildly, directly in _Golden Dawn_'s path. He noticed irrelevantly that the tiny human figures along the rear rail were waving frantically, and that the banner with its scarlet denunciation had torn loose at one end and was now whipping and twisting like a Tibetan prayer flag over the heads of the crew.

"Turn," Randle whispered, and he saw the first response of the hull; the angle between the bows and the fishing boat altered, it was a noticeable change, but slowly accelerating and a quick glance at the control console showed a small check in the ship's forward speed.

"Turn, damn it, turn." Randle held the engine telegraph locked at full astern, and felt the sudden influence of the Gulf Stream current on the ship as she began to come across the direction of flow.

Ahead, the fishing boat was almost about to disappear from sight behind _Golden Dawn_'s high blunt bows.

He had been holding the ship at full astern for almost seven minutes now, and suddenly Randle felt a change in *Golden Dawn*, something he had never experienced before.

There was a harsh, tearing, pounding vibration coming up through the deck. He realized just how severe that vibration must be, when *Golden Dawn*'s monumental hull began to shake violently—but he could not release his grip on the engine telegraph, not with that helpless vessel lying in his track.

Then suddenly, miraculously, all vibration in the deck under his feet ceased altogether. There was only the calm press of the hull through the water, no longer the feel of the engine's thrust, a sensation much more alarming to a mariner than the vibration which had preceded it, and simultaneously, a fiery rash of red warning lights bloomed on the ship's main control console, and the strident screech of the full emergency audio-alarm deafened them all.

Only then did Captain Randle push the engine telegraph to "stop." He stood staring ahead as the tiny fishing boat disappeared from view, hidden by the angle from the navigation bridge which was a mile behind the bows.

One of the officers reached across and hit the cut-out on the audio-alarm. In the sudden silence every officer stood frozen, waiting for the impact of collision.

G olden Dawn's Chief Engineer paced slowly along the engine-room control console, never taking his eyes from the electronic displays which monitored all the ship's mechanical and electrical functions.

When he reached the alarm aboard, he stopped and frowned at it angrily. The failure of the single transistor, a few dollars' worth of equipment, had been the cause of such brutal damage to his beloved machinery. He leaned across and pressed the "test" button, checking out each alarm circuit, yet, while he was doing it, recognizing the fact that it was too late. He was nursing the ship along, with God alone knew what undiscovered damage to engine and main shaft only kept in check by this reduced power setting—but there was a hurricane down there below the southern horizon, and the Chief could only guess at what emergency his machinery might have to meet in the next few days.

It made him nervous and edgy to think about it. He searched in his back pocket, found a sticky mint humbug, carefully picked off the little pieces of lint and fluff before tucking it into his cheek like a squirrel with a nut, sucking noisily upon it as he resumed his restless prowling up and down the control console.

His on-duty stokers and the oilers watched him surreptitiously. When the old man was in a mood, it was best not to attract attention.

"Dickson!" the Chief said suddenly. "Get your lid on. We are going down the shaft tunnel again."

The oiler sighed, exchanged a resigned glance with one of his mates and clapped his hard-hat on his head. He and the Chief had been down the tunnel an hour previously. It was an uncomfortable, noisy and dirty journey.

The oiler closed the watertight doors into the shaft tunnel behind them, screwing down the clamps firmly under the Chief's frosty scrutiny, and then both men stopped in the confined headroom and started off along the brightly-lit, pale grey painted tunnel.

The spinning shaft in its deep bed generated a high-pitched whine that seemed to resonate in the steel box of the tunnel, as though it was the body of a violin. Surprisingly, the noise was more pronounced at this low speed setting. It seemed to bore into the teeth at the back of the oiler's jaw like a dentist's drill.

The Chief did not seem to be affected. He paused beside the main bearing for almost ten minutes, testing it with the palm of his hand, feeling for heat or vibration. His expression was morose, and he worried the mint humbug in his cheek and shook his head with foreboding before going on up the tunnel.

When he reached the main gland, he squatted down suddenly and peered at it closely. With a deliberate flexing of his jaw he crushed the remains of the humbug between his teeth, and his eyes narrowed thoughtfully.

There was a thin trickle of seawater oozing through the gland and running down into the bilges. The Chief touched it with his finger. Something had shifted, some balance was disturbed, the seal of the gland was no longer watertight—such a small sign, a few gallons of seawater, could be the first warning of major structural damage.

The Chief shuffled around, still hunched down beside the shaft bed, and he lowered his face until it was only inches from the spinning steel main shaft. He closed one eye, and cocked his head, trying once again to decide if the faint blurring of the shaft's outline was real or merely his over-active imagination, whether what he was seeing was distortion or his own fears.

Suddenly, startlingly, the shaft slammed into stillness. The deceleration was so abrupt that the Chief could actually see the torque transferred into the shaft bed, and the metal walls creaked and popped with the strain.

He rocked back on to his heels, and almost instantly the shaft began to spin again, but this time in reverse thrust. The whine built up swiftly into a rising shriek. They were pulling emergency power from the bridge, and it was madness, suicidal madness.

The Chief seized the oiler by the shoulder and shouted into his ear, "Get back to control—find out what the hell they are doing on the bridge."

The oiler scrambled away down the tunnel; it would take him ten minutes to negotiate the long narrow passage, open the watertight doors and reach the control room and as long again to return.

The Chief considered going after him, but somehow he could not leave the shaft now. He lowered his head again, and now he could clearly see the flickering outline of the shaft. It wasn't imagination at all, there was a little ghost of movement. He clamped his hands over his ears to cut out the painful shriek of the spinning metal, but there was a new note to it, the squeal of bare metal on metal and before his eyes he saw the ghost outline along the edge of the shaft growing, the flutter of machinery out of balance, and the metal deck under his feet began to quiver.

"God! They are going to blow the whole thing!" he shouted, and jumped up from his crouch. Now the deck was juddering and shaking under his feet. He started back along the shaft, but the entire tunnel was agitating so violently that he had to grab the metal bulkhead to steady himself, and he reeled drunkenly, thrown about like a captive insect in a cruel child's box.

Ahead of him, he saw the huge metal casting of the main bearing twisting and shaking, and the vibration chattered his teeth in his clenched jaw and drove up his spine like a jackhammer.

Disbelievingly he saw the huge silver shaft beginning to rise and buckle in its bed, the bearing tearing loose from its mountings.

"Shut down!" he screamed. "For God's sake, shut down!" but his voice was lost in the shriek and scream of tortured metal and machinery that was tearing itself to pieces in a suicidal frenzy.

The main bearing exploded, and the shaft slammed it into the bulkhead, tearing steel plate like paper.

The shaft itself began to snake and whip. The Chief cowered back, pressing his back to the bulkhead and covering his ears to protect them from the unbearable volume of noise.

A sliver of heated steel flew from the bearing and struck him in the face, laying open his upper lip to the bone, crushing his nose and snapping off his front teeth at the level of his gums.

He toppled forward, and the whipping, kicking shaft seized him like a mindless predator and tore his body to pieces, pounding him and crushing him in the shaft bed and splattering him against the pale metal walls.

The main shaft snapped like a rotten twig at the point where it had been heated and weakened. The unbalanced weight of the revolving propeller ripped the stump out through the after seal, as though it were a tooth plucked from a rotting jaw.

The sea rushed in through the opening, flooding the tunnel instantly until it slammed into the watertight doors—and the huge glistening bronze propeller, with the stump of the main shaft still attached, the whole unit weighing one hundred and fifty tons, plummeted downwards through four hundred fathoms to embed itself deeply in the soft mud of the sea bottom.

Freed of the intolerable goad of her damaged shaft, *Golden Dawn* was suddenly silent and her decks still and steady as she trundled on, slowly losing way as the water dragged at her hull.

Samantha had one awful moment of sickening guilt. She saw clearly that she was responsible for the deadly danger into which she had led these people, and she stared out over the boat's side at the *Golden Dawn*.

The tanker was coming on without any check in her speed; perhaps she had turned a few degrees, for her bows were no longer pointed directly at them, but her speed was constant.

She was achingly aware of her inexperience, of her helplessness in this alien situation. She tried to think, to force herself out of this frozen despondency.

"Life jackets!" she thought, and yelled to Sally-Anne out on the deck, "The life jackets are in the lockers behind the wheelhouse."

Their faces turned to her, suddenly stricken. Up to this moment it had all been a glorious romp, the old fun-game of challenging the money-grabbers, prodding the establishment, but now suddenly it was mortal danger.

"Move!" Samantha shrieked at them, and there was a rush back along the deck.

"Think!" Samantha shook her head, as though to clear it. "Think!" she urged herself fiercely. She could hear the tanker now, the silken rustling sound of the water under its hull, the sough of the bow wave curling upon itself.

The *Dicky*'s throttle linkage had broken before, when they had been off Key West a year ago. It had broken between the bridge and the engine, and Samantha had watched Tom Parker fiddling with the engine, holding the lantern for him to see in the gloomy confines of the smelly little engine room. She had not been certain how he did it, but she remembered that he had controlled the revolutions of the engine by hand—something on the side of the engine block, below the big bowl of the air filter.

Samantha turned and dived down the vertical ladder into the engine room. The diesel was running, burbling away quietly at idling speed, not generating sufficient power to move the little vessel through the water.

She tripped and sprawled on the greasy deck, and pulled herself up, crying out with pain as her hand touched the red-hot manifold of the engine exhaust.

On the far side of the engine block, she groped desperately under the air filter, pushing and tugging at anything her fingers touched. She found a coil spring, and dropped to her knees to examine it.

She tried not to think of the huge steel hull bearing down on them, of being down in this tiny box that stank of diesel and exhaust fumes and old bilges. She tried not to think of not having a life jacket, or that the tanker could tramp the little vessel deep down under the surface and crush her like a matchbox.

Instead, she traced the little coil spring to where it was pinned into a flat upright lever. Desperately she pushed the lever against the tension of the spring—and instantly the diesel engine bellowed deafeningly in her ears, startling her so that she flinched and lost the lever. The diesel's beat died away into the bumbling idle and she wasted seconds while she found the lever again and pushed it hard against its stops once more. The engine roared, and she felt the ship picking up speed under her. She began to pray incoherently.

She could not hear the words in the engine noise, and she was not sure she was making sense, but she held the throttle open, and kept on praying.

She did not hear the screams from the deck above her. She did not know how close the *Golden Dawn* was; she did not know if Hank Petersen was still in the wheelhouse conning the little vessel out of the path of the onrushing tanker—but she held the throttle open and prayed.

The impact, when it came, was shattering, the crash and crackle of timbers breaking, the rending lurch and the roll of the deck giving to the tearing force of it.

Samantha was hurled against the hot steel of the engine, her forehead striking with such a force that her vision starred into blinding white light; she dropped backwards, her body loose and relaxed, darkness ringing in her ears, and lay huddled on the deck.

She did not know how long she was unconscious, but it could not have been for more than a few seconds; the spray of icy cold water on her face roused her and she pulled herself up on to her knees.

In the glare of the single bare electric globe in the deck above her, Samantha saw the spurts of water jets through the starting planking of the bulkhead beside her.

Her shirt and denim pants were soaked, salt water half blinded her, and her head felt as though the skull were cracked and someone was forcing the sharp end of a bradawl between her eyes.

Dimly she was aware that the diesel engine was idling noisily, and that the deck was sloshing with water as the boat rolled wildly in some powerful turbulence. She wondered if the whole vessel had been trodden under the tanker.

Then she realized it must be the wake of the giant hull which was throwing them about so mercilessly, but they were still afloat.

She began to crawl down the plunging deck. She knew where the bilge pump was, that was one thing Tom had taught all of them—and she crawled on grimly towards it.

• • •

Hank Petersen ducked out of the wheelhouse, flapping his arms wildly as he struggled into the life jacket. He was not certain of the best action to take, whether to jump over the side and begin swimming away from the tanker's slightly angled course, or to stay on board and take his chances with the collision which was now only seconds away.

Around him, the others were in the grip of the same indecision; they were huddled silently at the rail staring up at the mountain of smooth rounded steel that seemed to blot out half the sky. Only the TV cameraman on the wheelhouse roof, a true fanatic oblivious of all danger, kept his camera running. His exclamations of delight and the burr of the camera motor blended with the rushing sibilance of *Golden Dawn*'s bow wave. It was fifteen feet high, that wave, and it sounded like wild fire in dry grass.

Suddenly the exhaust of the diesel engine above Hank's head bellowed harshly, and then subsided into a soft burbling idle again. He looked up at it uncomprehendingly, now it roared again, fiercely, and the deck lurched beneath him. From the stern he heard the boil of water driven by the propeller, and the *Dicky* shrugged off her lethargy and lifted her bows to the short steep swell of the Gulf Stream.

A moment longer Hank stood frozen, and then he dived back into the wheelhouse and spun the spokes of the wheel through his fingers, sheering off sharply, but still staring out through the side glass.

The *Golden Dawn*'s bows filled his whole vision now, but the smaller vessel was scooting frantically out to one side, and the tanker's bows were swinging majestically in the opposite direction.

A few seconds more and they would be clear, but the bow wave caught them and Hank was flung across the wheelhouse. He felt something break in his chest, and heard the snap of bone as he hit, then immediately afterwards there was the crackling rending tearing impact as the two hulls came together and he was thrown back the other way, sprawling wildly across the deck.

He tried to claw himself upright, but the little fishing boat was pitching and cavorting with such abandon that he was thrown flat again. There was another tearing impact as the vessel was dragged down the tanker's side, and then flung free to roll her rails under and bob like a cork in the mill race of the huge ship's wake.

Now, at last, he was able to pull himself to his feet, and doubled over, clutching his injured ribs. He peered dazedly through the wheelhouse glass.

Half a mile away, the tanker was lazily turning up into the wind, and there was no propeller wash from under her counter. Hank staggered to the doorway, and looked out. The deck was still awash, but the water they had taken on was pouring out through the scuppers. The railing was smashed, most of it dangling overboard and the planking was splintered and torn, the ripped timber as white as bone in the sunlight.

Behind him, Samantha came crawling up the ladder from the engine room. There was a purple swelling in the centre of her forehead, she was soaking wet and her hands were filthy with black grease. He saw a livid red burn across the back of one hand as she lifted it to brush tumbled blonde hair out of her face.

"Are you all right, Sam?"

"Water's pouring in," she said. "I don't know how long the pump can hold it."

"Did you fix the motor?" he asked.

Samantha nodded. "I held the throttle open," she said, and then with feeling, "but I'll be damned to hell if I'll do it again. Somebody else can go down there, I've had my turn."

"Show me how," Hank said, "and you can take the wheel. The sooner we get back to Key Biscayne, the happier I'll be."

Samantha peered across at the receding bulk of *Golden Dawn*.

"My God!" she shook her head with wonder. "My God! We were lucky!"

> *"Mackerel skies and mares' tails,*
> *Make tall ships carry short sails."*

Nicholas Berg recited the old sailor's doggerel to himself, shading his eyes with one hand as he looked upwards.

The cloud was beautiful as fine lacework; very high against the tall blue of the heavens it spread swiftly in those long filmy scrolls. Nicholas could see the patterns developing and expanding as he watched, and that was a measure of the speed with which the high winds were blowing. The cloud was at least thirty thousand feet high, and below it the air was clear and crisp—only out on the western horizon the billowing silver and the blue thunder-heads were rising, generated by the landmass of Florida whose low silhouette was still below their horizon.

They had been in the main current of the Gulf Stream for six hours now. It was easy to recognize this characteristic scend of the sea, the short steep swells marching close together, the particular brilliance of these waters that had been first warmed in the shallow tropical basin of the Caribbean, the increased bulk flooding through into the Gulf of Mexico and there heated further, swelling in volume until they formed a hillock of water which at last rushed out through this narrow drainhole of the Florida Straits, swinging north and east in a wide benevolent wash, tempering the climate of all countries whose shores it touched and warming the fishing grounds of the North Atlantic.

In the middle of this stream, somewhere directly ahead of *Warlock*'s thrusting bows, the *Golden Dawn* was struggling southwards, directly opposed to the current which would clip eighty miles a day off her speed, and driving directly into the face of one of the most evil and dangerous storms that nature could summon.

Nicholas found himself brooding again on the mentality of anybody who would do that; again he glanced upwards at the harbingers of the storm, those delicate wisps of lacy cloud.

Nicholas had sailed through a hurricane once, twenty years ago, as a junior officer on one of Christy Marine's small grain carriers, and he shuddered now at the memory of it.

Duncan Alexander was a desperate man even to contemplate that risk, a man gambling everything on one fall of the dice. Nicholas could understand the forces that drove him, for he had been driven himself— but he hated him now for the chances he was taking. Duncan Alexander was risking Nicholas' son, and he was risking the life of an ocean and of the millions of people whose existence was tied to that ocean. Duncan Alexander was gambling with stakes that were not his to place at hazard.

Nicholas wanted one thing only now, and that was to get alongside *Golden Dawn* and take off his son. He would do that, even if it meant boarding her like a buccaneer. In the Master's suite, there was a locked and sealed arms cupboard with two riot guns, automatic 12-gauge shotguns and six Walther PK.38 pistols. *Warlock* had been equipped for every possible emergency in any ocean of the world, and those emergencies could include piracy or mutiny aboard a vessel under salvage. Now Nicholas was fully prepared to take an armed party on board *Golden Dawn*, and to take his chances in any court of law afterwards.

Warlock was racing into the chop of the Gulf Stream and scattering the spray like startled white doves, but she was running too slowly for Nicholas and he turned away impatiently and strode into the navigation bridge.

David Allen looked up at him, a small frown of preoccupation marring the smooth boyish features.

"Wind is moderating and veering westerly," he said, and Nicholas remembered another line of doggerel:

> *"When the wind moves against the sun*
> *Trust her not for back she'll run."*

He did not recite it, however, he merely nodded and said:

"We are running into the extreme influence of Lorna. The wind will back again as we move closer to the centre."

Nicholas went on to the radio room and the Trog looked up at him. It was not necessary for Nicholas to ask, the Trog shook his head. Since that long exchange with the coastguard patrol early that morning, *Golden Dawn* had kept her silence.

Nicholas crossed to the radarscope and studied the circular field for a few minutes; this usually busy seaway was peculiarly empty. There were some small craft crossing the main channel, probably fishing boats or pleasure craft scuttling for protection from the coming storm. All across the islands and on the mainland of Florida the elaborate precautions against the hurricane assault would be coming into force. Since the highway had been laid down on the spur of little islands that formed the Florida Keys, more than three hundred thousand people had crowded in there, in the process transforming those wild lovely islands into the Taj Mahal of ticky-tacky. If the hurricane struck there, the loss of life and property would be enormous. It was probably the most vulnerable spot on a long exposed coastline. For a few minutes, Nicholas tried to imagine the chaos that would result if a million tons of toxic crude oil was driven ashore on a littoral already ravaged by hurricane winds. It baulked his imagination, and he left the radar and moved to the front of the bridge. He stood staring down the narrow throat of water at a horizon that concealed all the terrors and desperate alarms that his imagination could conjure up.

The door to the radio shack was open and the bridge was quiet, so that they all heard it clearly; they could even catch the hiss of breath as the speaker paused between each sentence, and the urgency of his tone was not covered by the slight distortion of the VHF carrier beam.

"Mayday! Mayday! Mayday! This is the bulk oil carrier *Golden Dawn*. Our position is 79° 50' West 25° 43' North."

Before Nicholas reached the chart-table, he knew she was still a hundred miles ahead of them, and, as he pored over the table, he saw his estimate confirmed.

"We have lost our propeller with main shaft failure and we are drifting out of control."

Nicholas' head flinched as though he had been hit in the face. He could imagine no more dangerous condition and position for a ship of that size—and Peter was on board.

"This is *Golden Dawn* calling the United States Coast Guard service or any ship in a position to afford assistance—"

Nicholas reached the radio shack with three long strides, and the Trog handed him the microphone and nodded.

"*Golden Dawn*, this is the salvage tug *Warlock*. I will be in a position to render assistance within four hours—"

Damn the rule of silence, Peter was on board her.

"—Tell Alexander I am offering Lloyd's Open Form and I want immediate acceptance."

He dropped the microphone and stormed back on to the bridge, his voice clipped and harsh as he caught David Allen's arm.

"Interception course and push her through the gate," he ordered grimly. "Tell Beauty Baker to open all the taps." He dropped David's arm and spun back to the radio room.

"Telex Levoisin on *Sea Witch*. I want him to give me a time to reach *Golden Dawn* at his best possible speed," and he wondered briefly if even the two tugs would be able to control the crippled and powerless *Golden Dawn* in the winds of a hurricane.

.   .   .

Jules replied almost immediately. He had bunkered at Charleston, and cleared harbour six hours previously. He was running hard now and he gave a time to *Golden Dawn*'s position for noon the next day, which was also the forecast time of passage of the Straits for Hurricane Lorna, according to the meteorological up-date they had got from Miami two hours before, Nicholas thought as he read the telex and turned to David Allen.

"David, there is no precedent for this that I know of—but with my son on board *Golden Dawn* I just have to assume command of this ship, on a temporary basis, of course."

"I'd be honoured to act as your First Officer again, sir," David told him quietly, and Nicholas could see he meant it.

"If there is a good salvage, the Master's share will still be yours," Nicholas promised him, and thanked him with a touch on the arm. "Would you check out the preparations to put a line aboard the tanker?"

David turned to leave the bridge, but Nicholas stopped him. "By the time we get there, we will have the kind of wind you have only dreamed about in your worst nightmares—just keep that in mind."

"Telex," screeched the Trog. "*Golden Dawn* is replying to our offer."

Nicholas strode across to the radio room, and read the first few lines of message as it printed out.

OFFER CONTRACT OF DAILY HIRE FOR TOWAGE THIS VESSEL FROM
PRESENT POSITION TO GALVESTON ROADS

"The bastard," Nicholas snarled. "He's playing his fancy games with me, in the teeth of a hurricane and with my boy aboard." Furiously he punched his fist into the palm of his other hand. "Right!" he snapped. "We'll play just as rough! Get me the Director of the US Coast Guard at the Fort Lauderdale Headquarters—get him on the emergency coast-guard frequency and I will talk to him in clear."

The Trog's face lit with malicious glee and he made the contact.

"Colonel Ramsden," Nicholas said. "This is the Master of *Warlock*. I'm the only salvage vessel that can reach *Golden Dawn* before passage of Lorna, and I'm probably the only tug on the eastern seaboard of America with 22,000 horsepower. Unless the *Golden Dawn*'s Master accepts Lloyd's Open Form within the next sixty minutes, I shall be obliged to see to the safety of my vessel and crew by running for the nearest anchorage—and you're going to have a million tons of highly toxic crude oil drifting out of control into your territorial waters, in hurricane conditions."

The Coast Guard Director had a deep measured voice, and the calm tones of a man upon whom the mantle of authority was a familiar garment.

"Stand by, *Warlock*, I am going to contact *Golden Dawn* direct on Channel 16."

Nicholas signalled the Trog to turn up the volume on Channel 16 and they listened to Ramsden speaking directly to Duncan Alexander.

"In the event your vessel enters United States territorial waters without control or without an attendant tug capable of exerting that control, I shall be obliged under the powers vested in me to seize your vessel and take such steps to prevent pollution of our waters as I see fit. I have to warn you that those steps may include destruction of your cargo."

Ten minutes later the Trog copied a telex from Duncan Alexander personal to Nicholas Berg accepting Lloyd's Open Form and requesting him to exercise all dispatch in taking *Golden Dawn* in tow.

"I estimate we will be drifting over the 100-fathom line and entering US territorial waters within two hours," the message ended.

While Nicholas read it, standing out on the protected wing of *Warlock*'s bridge, the wind suddenly fluttered the paper in his hand and flattened his cotton shirt against his chest. He looked up quickly and saw the wind was backing violently into the east, and beginning to claw the tops of the Gulf Stream swells. The setting sun was bleeding copiously across the high veils of cirrus cloud which now covered the sky from horizon to horizon.

There was nothing more that Nicholas could do now. *Warlock* was running as hard as she could, and all her crew were quietly going about their preparations to pass a wire and take on tow. All he could do was wait, but that was always the hardest part.

Darkness came swiftly but with the last of the light, Nicholas could just make out a dark and mountainous shape beginning to hump up above the southern horizon like an impatient monster. He stared at it with awful fascination, until mercifully the night hid Lorna's dreadful face.

. . .

The wind chopped the Gulf Stream up into quick confused seas, and it did not blow steadily, but flogged them with squally gusts and rain that crackled against the bridge windows with startling suddenness.

The night was utterly black, there were no stars, no source of light whatsoever, and *Warlock* lurched and heeled to the patternless seas.

"Barometer's rising sharply," David Allen called suddenly. "It's jumped three millibars—back to 1005."

"The trough," said Nicholas grimly. It was a classic hurricane formation, that narrow girdle of higher pressure that demarcated the outer fringe of the great revolving spiral of tormented air. "We are going into it now."

And as he spoke the darkness lifted, the heavens began to burn like a bed of hot coals, and the sea shone with a sullen ruddy luminosity as though the doors of a furnace had been thrown wide.

Nobody spoke on *Warlock*'s bridge, they lifted their faces with the same awed expressions as worshippers in a lofty cathedral and they looked up at the skies.

Low cloud raced above them, cloud that glowed and shone with that terrible ominous flare. Slowly the light faded and changed, turning a paler sickly greenish hue, like the shine on putrid meat. Nicholas spoke first.

"The Devil's Beacon," he said, and he wanted to rationalize it to break the superstitious mood that gripped them all. It was merely the rays of the sun below the western horizon catching the cloud peaks of the storm and reflected downwards through the weak cloud cover of the trough—but somehow he could not find the right words to denigrate that phenomenon that was part of the mariner's lore, the malignant beacon that leads a doomed ship on to its fate.

The weird light faded slowly away leaving the night even darker and more foreboding than it had been before.

"David," Nicholas thought quickly of something to distract his officers, "have we got a radar contact yet?" and the new Mate roused himself with a visible effort and crossed to the radarscope.

"The range is very confused," he said, his voice still subdued, and Nicholas joined him at the screen.

The sweeping arm lit a swirling mass of sea clutter, and the strange ghost echoes thrown up by electrical discharges within the approaching storm. The outline of the Florida mainland and of the nearest islands of the Grand Bahamas bank were firm and immediately recognizable. They reminded Nicholas yet again of how little sea-room there was in which to manoeuvre his tugs and their monstrous prize.

Then, in the trash of false echo and sea clutter, his trained eye picked out a harder echo on the extreme limits of the set's range. He watched it carefully for half a dozen revolutions of the radar's sweep, and each time it was constant and clearer.

"Radar contact," he said. "Tell *Golden Dawn* we are in contact, range sixty-five nautical miles. Tell them we will take on tow before midnight." And then, under his breath, the old sailor's qualifications, "God willing and weather permitting."

T he lights on *Warlock*'s bridge had been rheostatted down to a dull rose glow to protect the night vision of her officers, and the four of them stared out to where they knew the tanker lay.

Her image on the radar was bright and firm, lying within the two mile ring of the screen, but from the bridge she was invisible.

In the two hours since first contact, the barometer had gone through its brief peak as the trough passed, and then fallen steeply.

From 1005 it had crashed to 900 and was still plummeting, and the weather coming in from the east was blustering and squalling. The wind mourned about them on a forever rising note, and torrential rain obscured all vision outside an arc of a few hundred yards. Even *Warlock*'s twin searchlights, set seventy feet above the main deck on the summit of the fire-control gantry, could not pierce those solid white curtains of rain.

Nicholas groped like a blind man through the rain fog, using pitch and power to close carefully with *Golden Dawn*, giving his orders to the helm in a cool impersonal tone which belied the pale set of his features and the alert brightness of his eyes as he reached the swirling bank of rain.

Abruptly another squall struck *Warlock*. With a demented shriek, it heeled the big tug sharply and shredded the curtains of rain, ripping them open so that for a moment Nicholas saw *Golden Dawn*.

She was exactly where he had expected her to be, but the wind had caught the tanker's high navigation bridge like the mainsail of a tall ship, and she was going swiftly astern.

All her deck and port lights were burning, and she carried the twin red riding lights at her stubby masthead that identified a vessel drifting out of control. The following sea, driven on by the rising wind, piled on to her tank decks, smothering them with white foam and spray, so that the ship looked like a submerged coral reef.

"Half ahead both," Nicholas told the helmsman. "Steer for her starboard side."

He closed quickly with the tanker, staying in visual contact now; even when the rain mists closed down again, they could make out the ghostly shape of her and the glow of her riding lights.

David Allen was looking at him expectantly and Nicholas asked, "What bottom?" without taking his eyes from the stricken ship.

"One hundred sixteen fathoms and shelving fast." They were being blown quickly out of the main channel, on to the shallow ledge of the Florida littoral.

"I'm going to tow her out stern first," said Nicholas, and immediately David saw the wisdom of it. Nobody would be able to get up into her bows to secure a towline, the seas were breaking over them and sweeping them with ten and fifteen feet of green water.

"I'll go aft—" David began, but Nicholas stopped him.

"No, David. I want you here—because I'm going on board *Golden Dawn*."

"Sir," David wanted to tell him that it was dangerous to delay passing the towing cable—with that lee shore waiting.

"This will be our last chance to get passengers off her before the full hurricane hits us," said Nicholas, and David saw that it was futile to protest. Nicholas Berg was going to fetch his son.

From the height of *Golden Dawn*'s towering navigation bridge, they could look directly down on to the main deck of the tug as she came alongside.

Peter Berg stood beside his mother, almost as tall as she was. He wore a full life-jacket and a corduroy cap pulled down over his ears.

"It will be all right," he comforted Chantelle. "Dad is here. It will be just fine now." And he took her hand protectively.

Warlock staggered and reeled in the grip of wind as she came up into the tanker's lee, rain blew over her like dense white smoke and every few minutes she put her nose down and threw a thick green slice of sea water back along her decks.

In comparison to the tug's wild action, *Golden Dawn* wallowed heavily, held down by the oppressive weight of a million tons of crude oil, and the seas beat upon her with increasing fury, as if affronted by her indifference. *Warlock* edged in closer and still closer.

Duncan Alexander came through from the communications room at the rear of the bridge. He balanced easily against *Golden Dawn*'s ponderous motion but his face was swollen and flushed with anger.

"Berg is coming on board," he burst out. "He's wasting valuable time. I warned him that we must get out into deeper water."

Peter Berg interrupted suddenly and pointed down at *Warlock*.

"Look!" he cried.

Until that moment, the night and the storm had hidden the small huddle of human shapes in the tug's high forward tower. They wore wet, glistening oilskins and their life jackets gave them a swollen pregnant look. They were lowering the boarding gantry into the horizontal position.

"There is Dad!" Peter shouted. "That's him in front."

At the extremity of her roll, *Warlock*'s boarding gantry touched the railing of the tanker's quarterdeck, ten feet above the swamped tank deck—and the leading figure on the tug's upperworks ran out lightly along the gantry, balanced for a moment high above the roaring, racing green water and then leapt across five feet of open space, caught a hand hold and then pulled himself over *Golden Dawn*'s rail.

Immediately the tug sheered off and fell in fifty yards off the tanker's starboard side, half hidden in the rain mists, but holding her station steadily, despite all the wind's and the sea's spiteful efforts to separate the two vessels.

The whole manoeuvre had been performed with an expertise which made it seem almost casual.

"Dad's carried a line across," Peter said proudly, and Chantelle, looking down, saw that a delicate white nylon thread was being hove in by two seamen on the tanker's quarter deck, while from the tug's fire-control tower a canvas bosun's chair was being winched across.

The elevator doors slid open with a whine and Nicholas Berg strode on to the tanker's bridge. His oilskins still ran with rainwater that splattered on to the deck at his feet.

"Dad!" Peter ran to meet him and Nicholas stooped and embraced him fiercely before straightening; with one arm still about his son's shoulders, he confronted Chantelle and Duncan Alexander.

"I hope both of you are satisfied now," he said quietly, "but I for one don't rate our chances of saving this ship very highly, so I'm taking off everybody who is not needed on board to handle her."

"Your tug," burst out Duncan, "you've got 22,000 horsepower, and can—"

"There is a hurricane on its way," said Nicholas coldly, and he shot a glance at the roaring night. "This is just the overture." He turned back to Randle. "How many men do you want to keep on board?"

Randle thought for a moment. "Myself, a helmsman, and five seamen to handle the towlines and work the ship." He paused and then went on, "And the pump-room personnel to control the cargo."

"You will act as helmsman, I will control the pump room, and I'll need only three seamen. Get me volunteers," Nicholas decided. "Send everybody else off."

"Sir," Randle began to protest.

"May I remind you, Captain, that I am salvage master, my authority now supersedes yours." Nicholas did not wait for his reply. "Chantelle," he picked her out, "take Peter down to the quarterdeck. You'll go across first."

"Listen here, Berg," Duncan could no longer contain himself, "I insist you pass the towing cable, this ship is in danger."

"Get down there with them," Nicholas snapped. "I'll decide the procedures."

"Do as he says, darling," Chantelle smiled up at her husband vindictively. "You've lost. Nicholas is the only winner now."

"Shut up, damn you," Duncan hissed at her.

"Get down to the afterdeck," Nicholas' voice cracked like breaking ice.

"I'm staying on board this ship," said Duncan abruptly. "It's my responsibility. I said I'd see it out and by God I will. I am going to be here to make sure you do your job, Berg."

Nicholas checked himself, studied him for a long moment, and then smiled mirthlessly.

"Nobody ever called you a coward," he nodded reluctantly. "Other things—but not a coward. Stay if you will, we might need an extra hand." Then to Peter, "Come, my boy." And he led him towards the elevator.

• • •

At the quarterdeck rail, Nicholas hugged the boy, holding him in his arms, their cheeks pressed tightly together, and drawing out the moment while the wind cannoned and thrummed about their heads.

"I love you, Dad."

"And I love you, Peter, more than I can ever tell you—but you must go now."

He broke the embrace and lifted the child into the deep canvas bucket of the bosun's chair, stepped back and windmilled his right arm. Immediately, the winch party in *Warlock*'s upperworks swung him swiftly out into the gap between the two ships and the nylon cable seemed as fragile and insubstantial as a spider's thread.

As the two ships rolled and dipped, so the line tightened and sagged, one moment dropping the white canvas bucket almost to the water level where the hungry waves snatched at it with cold green fangs, and the next, pulling the line up so tightly that it hummed with tension, threatening to snap and drop the child back into the sea, but at last it reached the tug and four pairs of strong hands lifted the boy clear. For one moment, he waved back at Nicholas and then he was hustled away, and the empty bosun's chair was coming back.

Only then did Nicholas become aware that Chantelle was clinging to his arm and he looked down into her face. Her eyelashes were dewed and stuck together with the flying raindrops. Her face ran with wetness and she seemed very small and childlike under the bulky oilskins and life jacket. She was as beautiful as she had ever been but her eyes were huge and darkly troubled.

"Nicholas, I've always needed you," she husked. "But never as I need you now."

Her existence was being blown away on the wind, and she was afraid.

"You and this ship are all I have left."

"No, only the ship," he said brusquely, and he was amazed that the spell was broken. That soft area of his soul which she had been able to touch so unerringly was now armoured against her. With a sudden surge of relief, he realized he was free of her, for ever. It was over; here in the storm, he was free at last.

She sensed it—for the fear in her eyes changed to real terror.

"Nicholas, you cannot desert me now. Oh Nicholas, what will become of me without you and Christy Marine?"

"I don't know," he told her quietly, and caught the bosun's chair as it came in over *Golden Dawn*'s rail. He lifted her as easily as he had lifted his son and placed her in the canvas bucket.

"And to tell you the truth, Chantelle, I don't really care," he said, and stepping back, he windmilled his right arm. The chair swooped out across the narrow water, swinging like a pendulum in the wind. Chantelle shouted something at him but Nicholas had turned away, and was already going aft in a lurching run to where the three volunteers were waiting.

He saw at a glance that they were big, powerful, competent-looking men.

Quickly Nicholas checked their equipment, from the thick leather gauntlets to the bolt cutters and jemmy bars for handling heavy cable.

"You'll do," he said. "We will use the bosun's tackle to bring across a message from the tug—just as soon as the last man leaves this ship."

W orking with men to whom the task was unfamiliar, and in rapidly deteriorating conditions of sea and weather, it took almost another hour before they had the main cable across from *Warlock* secured by its thick nylon spring to the tanker's stern bollards— yet the time had passed so swiftly for Nicholas that when he stood back and glanced at his watch, he was shocked. Before this wind they must have been going down very fast on the land. He staggered into the tanker's stern quarters, and left a trail of sea water down the passageway to the elevators.

On the bridge, Captain Randle was standing grim-faced at the helm, and Duncan Alexander snapped accusingly at him.

"You've cut it damned fine." A single glance at the digital printout of the depth gauge on the tanker's control console bore him out. They had thirty-eight fathoms of water under them now, and the *Golden Dawn*'s swollen belly sagged down twenty fathoms below the surface. They were going down very swiftly before the easterly gale winds. It was damned fine, Nicholas had to agree, but he showed no alarm or agitation as he crossed to Randle's side and unhooked the hand microphone.

"David," he asked quietly, "are you ready to haul us off?"

"Ready, sir," David Allen's voice came from the speaker above his head.

"I'm going to give you full port rudder to help your turn across the wind," said Nicholas, and then nodded to Randle. "Full port rudder."

"Forty degrees of port rudder on," Randle reported.

They felt the tiny shock as the tow-cable came up taut, and carefully *Warlock* began the delicate task of turning the huge ship across the rising gusting wind and then dragging her out tail first into the deeper water of the channel where she would have her best chance of riding out the hurricane.

I t was clear now that *Golden Dawn* lay directly in the track of Lorna, and the storm unleashed its true nature upon them. Out there upon the sane and rational world, the sun was rising, but here there was no dawn, for there was no horizon and no sky. There was only madness and wind and water, and all three elements were so intermingled as to form one substance.

An hour—which seemed like a lifetime—ago, the wind had ripped away the anemometer and the weather-recording equipment on top of the navigation bridge, so Nicholas had no way of judging the wind's strength and direction.

Out beyond the bridge windows, the wind took the top off the sea; it took it off in thick sheets of salt water and lifted them over the navigation bridge in a shrieking white curtain that cut off visibility at the glass of the windows. The tank deck had disappeared in the racing white emulsion of wind and water, even the railing of the bridge wings six feet from the windows was invisible.

The entire superstructure groaned and popped and whimpered under the assault of the wind, the pressed aluminium bulkheads bulging and distorting, the very deck flexing and juddering at the solid weight of the storm.

Through the saturated, racing, swirling air, a leaden and ominous grey light filtered, and every few minutes the electrical impulses generated within the sixty-thousand-foot-high mountain of racing, spinning air released themselves in shattering cannonades of thunder and sudden brilliance of eye-searing white lightning.

There was no visual contact with *Warlock*. The massive electrical disturbance of the storm and the clutter of high seas and almost solid cloud and turbulence had reduced the radar range to a few miles, and even then it was unreliable. Radio contact with the tug was drowned with buzzing squealing static. It was possible to understand only odd disconnected words from David Allen.

Nicholas was powerless, caged in the groaning, vibrating box of the navigation bridge, blinded and deafened by the unleashed powers of the heavens. There was nothing any of them could do.

Randle had locked the ultra-tanker's helm amidships, and now he stood with Duncan and the three seamen by the chart-table, all of them clinging to it for support, all their faces pale and set as though carved from chalk.

Only Nicholas moved restlessly about the bridge; from the stern windows where he peered down vainly, trying to get a glimpse of either the tow-cable and its spring, or of the tug's looming shape through the racing white storm, then he came forward carefully, using the foul-weather rail to steady himself against the huge ship's wild and unpredictable motion, and he stood before the control console, studying the display of lights that monitored the pod tanks and the ship's navigational and mechanical functions.

None of the petroleum tanks had lost any crude oil and in all of them the nature of the inert gas was constant. There had been no ingress of air to them; they were all still intact then. One of the reasons that Nicholas had taken the tanker in tow stern first was so that the navigation tower might break the worst of wind and sea, and the fragile bloated tanks would receive some protection from it.

Yet desperately he wished for a momentary sight of the tank deck, merely to reassure himself. There could be malfunction in the pump control instruments, the storm could have clawed one of the pod tanks open, and even now *Golden Dawn* could be bleeding her poison into the sea. But there was no view of the tank decks through the storm, and Nick stooped to the radarscope. The screen glowed and danced and flickered with ghost images and trash—he wasn't too certain if even *Warlock*'s image was constant, the range seemed to be opening, as though the towline had parted. He straightened up and stood balanced on the balls of his feet, reassuring himself by the feel of the deck that *Golden Dawn* was still under tow. He could feel by the way she resisted the wind and the sea that the tow was still good.

Yet there was no means of telling their position. The satellite navigational system was completely blanketed, the radio waves were distorted and diverted by tens of thousands of feet of electrical storm, and the same forces were blanketing the marine radio beacons on the American mainland.

The only indication was the ship's electronic log which gave Nicholas the speed of the ship's hull through the water and the speed across the sea bottom, and the depth finder which recorded the water under her keel.

For the first two hours of the tow, *Warlock* had been able to pull the ship back towards the main channel at three and a half knots, and slowly the water had become deeper until they had 150 fathoms under them.

Then as the wind velocity increased, the windage of *Golden Dawn*'s superstructure had acted as a vast mainsail and the storm had taken control. Now, despite all the power in *Warlock*'s big twin propellers, both tug and tanker were being pushed once more back towards the 100-fathom line and the American mainland.

"Where is *Sea Witch?*" Nicholas wondered, as he stared helplessly at the gauges. They were going towards the shore at a little over two knots, and the bottom was shelving steeply. *Sea Witch* might be the ace that took the trick, if she could reach them through these murderous seas and savage winds, and if she could find them in this wilderness of mad air and water.

Again, Nicholas groped his way to the communications room, and still clinging to the bulkhead with one hand he thumbed the microphone.

"*Sea Witch. Sea Witch.* This is *Warlock.* Calling *Sea Witch.*"

He listened then, trying to tune out the snarl and crackle of static, crouching over the set. Faintly he thought he heard a human voice, a scratchy whisper through the interference and he called again and listened, and called again. There was the voice again, but so indistinct he could not make out a single word.

Above his head, there was a tearing screech of rending metal. Nicholas dropped the microphone and staggered through on to the bridge. There was another deafening banging and hammering and all of them stood staring up at the metal roof of the bridge. It sagged and shook, there was one more crash and then with a scraping, dragging rush, a confused tangle of metal and wire and cable tumbled over the forward edge of the bridge and flapped and swung wildly in the wind.

It took a moment for Nicholas to realize what it was.

"The radar antennae!" he shouted. He recognized the elongated dish of the aerial, dangling on a thick coil of cable, then the wind tore that loose also, and the entire mass of equipment flapped away like a giant bat and was instantly lost in the teeming white curtains of the storm.

With two quick paces, he reached the radarscope, and one glance was enough. The screen was black and dead. They had lost their eyes now, and, unbelievably, the sound of the storm was rising again.

It boomed against the square box of the bridge, and the men within it cowered from its fury.

Then abruptly, Duncan was screaming something at Nicholas, and pointing up at the master display of the control console. Nicholas, still hanging on to the radarscope, roused himself with an effort and looked up at the display. The speed across the ground had changed drastically. It was now almost eight knots, and the depth was ninety-two fathoms.

Nicholas felt icy despair clutch and squeeze his guts. The ship was moving differently under him, he could feel her now in mortal distress; that same gust which had torn away the radar mast had done other damage.

He knew what that damage was, and the thought of it made him want to vomit, but he had to be sure. He had to be absolutely certain, and he began to hand himself along the foul-weather rail towards the elevator doors.

Across the bridge the others were watching him intently, but even from twenty feet it was impossible to make himself heard above the clamorous assault of the storm.

One of the seamen seemed suddenly to guess his intention. He left the chart-table and groped his way along the bulkhead towards Nicholas.

"Good man!" Nicholas grabbed his arm to steady him, and they fell forward into the elevator as *Golden Dawn* began another of those ponderous wallowing rolls and the deck fell out from under their feet.

The ride down in the elevator car slammed them back and forth across the little coffin-like box, and even here in the depths of the ship they had to shout to hear each other.

"The tow cable," Nicholas yelled in the man's ear. "Check the tow cable."

From the elevator they went carefully aft along the central passageway, and when they reached the double storm doors, Nicholas tried to push the inner door open, but the pressure of the wind held it closed.

"Help me," he shouted at the seaman, and they threw their combined weight against it. The instant that they forced the jamb open a crack, the vacuum of pressure was released and the wind took the three-inch mahogany doors and ripped them effortlessly from their hinges, and whisked them away, as though they were a pair of playing cards—and Nicholas and the seaman were exposed in the open doorway.

The wind flung itself upon them, and hurled them to the deck, smothering them in the icy deluge of water that ripped at their faces as abrasively as ground glass.

Nicholas rolled down the deck and crashed into the stern rail with such jarring force that he thought his lungs had been crushed, and the wind pinned him there, and blinded and smothered him with salt water.

He lay there helpless as a newborn infant, and near him he heard the seaman screaming thinly. The sound steeled him, and Nicholas slowly dragged himself to his knees, desperately clutching at the rail to resist the wind.

Still the man screamed and Nicholas began to creep forward on his hands and knees. It was impossible to stand in that wind and he could move only with support from the rail.

Six feet ahead of him, the extreme limit of his vision, the railing had been torn away, a long section of it dangling over the ship's side, and to this was clinging the seaman. His weight driven by the wind must have hit the rail with sufficient force to tear it loose, and now he was hanging on with one arm hooked through the railing and the other arm twisted from a shattered shoulder and waving a crazy salute as the wind whipped it about. When he looked up at Nicholas his mouth had been smashed in. It looked as though he had half chewed a mouthful of blackcurrants, and the jagged stumps of his broken front teeth were bright red with the juice.

On his belly, Nicholas reached for him, and as he did so, the wind came again, unbelievably it was stronger still, and it took the damaged railing with the man still upon it and tore it bodily away. They disappeared instantly in the blinding white-out of the storm, and Nicholas felt himself hurled forward towards the edge. He clung with all his strength to the remaining section of the rail, and felt it buckle and begin to give.

On his knees still he clawed himself away from that fatal beckoning gap, towards the stern, and the wind struck him full in the face, blinding and choking him. Sightlessly, he dragged himself on until one out-stretched arm struck the cold cast iron of the port stern bollard, and he flung both arms about it like a lover, choking and retching from the salt water that the wind had forced through his nose and mouth and down his throat.

Still blind, he felt for the woven steel of *Warlock*'s main tow-wire. He found it and he could not span it with his fist—but he felt the quick lift of his hopes.

The cable was still secured. He had catted and prevented it with a dozen nylon strops, and it was still holding. He crawled forward, drag-ging himself along the tow-cable, and immediately he realized that his relief had been premature. There was no tension in the cable and when he reached the edge of the deck it dangled straight down. It was not stretched out into the whiteness, to where he had hoped *Warlock* was still holding them like a great sea anchor.

He knew then that what he had dreaded had happened. The storm had been too powerful; it had snapped the steel cable like a thread of cotton, and *Golden Dawn* was loose, without control, and this wild and savage wind was blowing her down swiftly on to the land.

Nicholas felt suddenly exhausted to his bones. He lay flat on the deck, closed his eyes and clung weakly to the severed cable. The wind wanted to hurl him over the side; it ballooned his oilskins and ripped at his face. It would be so easy to open his fingers and to let go—and it took all his resolve to resist the impulse.

Slowly, as painfully as a crippled insect, he dragged himself back through the open, shattered doorway into the central passageway of the stern quarters—but still the wind followed him. It roared down the pas-sageway, driving in torrents of rain and salt water that flooded the deck and forced Nicholas to cling for support like a drunkard.

After the open storm, the car of the elevator seemed silent and tran-quil as the inner sanctum of a cathedral. He looked at himself in the wall mirror, and saw that his eyes were scoured red and painful-looking by salt and wind, and his cheeks and lips looked raw and bruised, as though the skin had been rasped away. He touched his face and there was no feeling in his nose nor in his lips.

The elevator doors slid open and he reeled out on to the navigation bridge. The group of men at the chart-table seemed not to have moved, but their heads turned to him.

Nicholas reached the table and clung to it. They were silent, watching his face.

"I lost a man," he said, and his voice was hoarse and roughened by salt and weariness. "He went overboard. The wind got him."

Still none of them moved nor spoke, and Nicholas coughed, his lungs ached from the water he had breathed. When the spasm passed, he went on.

"The tow-cable has parted. We are loose—and *Warlock* will never be able to re-establish tow. Not in this."

All their heads turned now to the forward bridge windows, to that impenetrable racing whiteness beyond the glass, that was lit internally with its glowing bursts of lightning.

Nicholas broke the spell that held them all. He reached up to the signal locker above the chart-table and brought down a cardboard packet of distress flares. He broke open the seals and spilled the flares on to the table. They looked like sticks of dynamite, cylinders of heavily varnished waterproof paper. The flares could be lit, and would spurt out crimson flames, even if immersed in water, once the self-igniter tab at one end was pulled.

Nicholas stuffed half a dozen of the flares into the inner pockets of his oilskins.

"Listen," he had to shout, even though they were only feet away. "We are going to be aground within two hours. This ship is going to start breaking up immediately we strike."

He paused and studied their faces; Duncan was the only one who did not seem to understand. He had picked up a handful of the signal flares from the table and he was looking inquiringly at Nicholas.

"I will give you the word; as soon as we reach the twenty-fathom line and she touches bottom, you will go over the side. We will try and get a raft away. There is a chance you could be carried ashore."

He paused again, and he could see that Randle and his two seamen realized clearly just how remote that chance was.

"I will give you twenty minutes to get clear. By then, the pod tanks will have begun breaking up—" He didn't want this to sound melodramatic and searched for some way to make it sound less theatrical, but could think of none. "Once the first tank ruptures, I will ignite the escaping crude with a signal flare."

"Christ!" Randle mouthed the blasphemy, and the storm censored it on his lips. Then he raised his voice. "A million tons of crude. It will fire-ball, man."

"Better than a million-ton slick down the Gulf Stream," Nicholas told him wearily.

"None of us will have a chance. A million tons. It will go up like an atom bomb." Randle was white-faced and shaking now. "You can't do it!"

"Think of a better way," said Nicholas and left the table to stagger across to the radio room. They watched him go, and then Duncan looked down at the signal flares in his hand for a moment before thrusting them into the pocket of his jacket.

In the radio room, Nicholas called quietly into the microphone. "Come in, *Sea Witch—Sea Witch*, this is *Golden Dawn*." And only the static howled in reply.

"*Warlock*. Come in, *Warlock*. This is *Golden Dawn*."

Something else went in the wind, they heard it tear loose, and the whole superstructure shook and trembled. The ship was beginning to break up; it had not been designed to withstand winds like this.

Through the open radio room door, Nicholas could see the control console display. There were seventy-one fathoms of water under the ship, and the wind was punching her, flogging her on towards the shore.

"Come in, *Sea Witch*," Nicholas called with quiet desperation. "This is *Golden Dawn*. Do you read me?"

The wind charged the ship, crashing into it like a monster, and she groaned and reeled from the blow.

"Come in, *Warlock*."

Randle lurched across to the forward windows, and clinging to the rail he bowed over the gauges that monitored the condition of the ship's cargo, checking for tank damage.

"At least he is still thinking." Nicholas watched him, and above the Captain's head, the sounding showed sixty-eight fathoms.

Randle straightened slowly, began to turn, and the wind struck again.

Nicholas felt the blow in his stomach. It was a solid thing, like a mountain in avalanche, a defeaning boom of sound and the forward bridge window above the control console broke inwards.

It burst in a glittering explosion of glass shards that engulfed the fig-ure of Captain Randle standing directly before it. In a fleeting moment of horror, Nicholas saw his head half severed from his shoulders by a guil-

lotine of flying glass, then he crumpled to the deck and instantly the
bright pulsing hose of his blood was diluted to spreading pale pink in the
torrent of wind and blown water that poured in through the opening, and
smothered the navigation bridge.

Charts and books were ripped from their shelves and fluttered like
trapped birds as the wind blustered and swirled in the confines of glass
and steel.

Nicholas reached the Captain's body, protecting his own face with an
arm crooked across it, but there was nothing he could do for him. He left
Randle lying on the deck and shouted to the others.

"Keep clear of the windows."

He gathered them in the rear of the bridge, against the bulkhead
where stood the Decca and navigational systems. The four of them kept
close together, as though they gained comfort from the close proximity
of other humans, but the wind did not relent.

It poured in through the shattered window and raged about the bridge,
tearing at their clothing and filling the air with a fine mist of water, flooding the deck ankle deep so that it sloshed and ran as the tanker rolled almost to her beam ends.

Randle's limp and sodden body slid back and forth in the wash and
roll, until Nicholas left the dubious security of the after bulkhead, half-
lifted the corpse under the arms, and dragged it into the radio room and
wedged it into the radio operator's bunk. Swift blood stained the crisply
ironed sheets, and Nicholas threw a fold of the blanket over Randle and
staggered back into the bridge.

Still the wind rose, and now Nicholas felt himself numbed by the
force and persistence of it.

Some loose material, perhaps a sheet of aluminium from the superstructure, or a length of piping ripped from the tank deck below, smashed
into the tip of the bridge like a cannon ball and then flipped away into the
storm, leaving a jagged rent which the wind exploited, tearing and worrying at it, enlarging the opening, so that the plating flapped and hammered and a solid deluge of rain poured in through it.

Nicholas realized that the ship's superstructure was beginning to go;
like a gigantic vulture, soon the wind would begin stripping the carcass
down to its bones.

He knew he should get the survivors down nearer the water line, so
that when they were forced to commit themselves to the sea, they could

do so quickly. But his brain was numbed by the tumult, and he stood stolidly. It needed all his remaining strength merely to brace himself against the tearing wind and the ship's anguished motion.

In the days of sail, the crew would tie themselves to the main mast, when they reached this stage of despair.

Dully, he registered that the depth of water under the ship was now only fifty-seven fathoms, and the barometer was reading 955 millibars. Nicholas had never heard of a reading that low; surely it could not go lower, they must be almost at the centre of the revolving hurricane.

With an effort, he lifted his arm and read the time. It was still only ten o'clock in the morning, they had been in the hurricane for only two and a half hours.

A great burning light struck through the torn roof, a light that blinded them with its intensity, and Nicholas threw up his hands to protect his eyes. He could not understand what was happening. He thought his hearing had gone, for suddenly the terrible tumult of the wind was muted, fading away.

Then he understood. "The eye," he croaked, "we are into the eye," and his voice resounded strangely in his own ears. He stumbled to the front of the bridge.

Although the *Golden Dawn* still rolled ponderously, describing an arc of almost forty degrees from side to side, she was free of the unbearable weight of the wind and brilliant sunshine poured down upon her. It beamed down like the dazzling arc lamps of a stage set, out of the throat of a dark funnel of dense racing swirling cloud.

The cloud lay to the very surface of the sea, and encompassed the full sweep of the horizon in an unbroken wall. Only directly overhead was it open, and the sky was an angry unnatural purple, set with the glaring, merciless eye of the sun.

The sea was still wild and confused, leaping into peaks and troughs and covered with a thick frothy mattress of spindrift, whipped into a custard by the wild winds. But already the sea was subsiding in the total calm of the eye and *Golden Dawn* was rolling less viciously.

Nicholas turned his head stiffly to watch the receding wall of racing cloud. How long would it take for the eye to pass over them, he wondered.

Not very long, he was sure of that, half an hour perhaps—an hour at the most—and then the storm would be on them again, with its renewed fury every bit as sudden as its passing. But this time, the wind would come from exactly the opposite direction as they crossed the hub and went into the far side of the revolving wall of cloud.

Nicholas jerked his eyes away from that racing, heaven-high bank of cloud, and looked down on to the tank deck. He saw at a single glance that *Golden Dawn* had already sustained mortal damage. The forward port pod tank was half torn from its hydraulic coupling, holding only by the bows and lying at almost twenty degrees from the line of the other three tanks. The entire tank deck was twisted like the limb of an arthritic giant. It rolled and pitched out of sequence with the rest of the hull.

Golden Dawn's back was broken. It had broken where Duncan had weakened the hull to save steel. Only the buoyancy of the crude petroleum in her four tanks was holding her together now. Nicholas expected to see the dark, glistening ooze of slick leaking from her; he could not believe that not one of the four tanks had ruptured, and he glanced at the electronic cargo monitor. Loads and gas contents of all tanks were still normal. They had been freakishly lucky so far, but when they went into the far side of the hurricane he knew that *Golden Dawn*'s weakened spine would give completely, and when that happened it must pinch and tear the thin skins of the pod tanks.

He made a decision then, forcing his mind to work, not certain how good a decision it was but determined to act on it.

"Duncan," he called to him across the swamped and battered bridge. "I'm sending you and the others off on one of the life-rafts. This will be your only chance to launch one. I'll stay on board to fire the cargo when the storm hits again."

"The storm has passed," suddenly Duncan was screaming at him like a madman. "The ship is safe now. You're going to destroy my ship— you're deliberately trying to break me." He was lunging across the heaving bridge. "It's deliberate. You know I've won now. You are going to destroy this ship. It's the only way you can stop me now." He swung a clumsy round arm blow. Nicholas ducked under it and caught Duncan around the chest.

"Listen to me," he shouted, trying to calm him. "This is only the eye—"

"You'd do anything to stop me. You swore you would stop me—"

"Help me," Nicholas called to the two seamen, and they grabbed Duncan's arms. He bucked and fought like a madman, screaming wildly at Nicholas, his face contorted and swollen with rage, sodden hair flopping into his eyes. "You'd do anything to destroy me, to destroy my ship—"

"Take him down to the raft deck," Nicholas ordered the two seamen. He knew he could not reason with Duncan now, and he turned away and stiffened suddenly.

"Wait!" he stopped them leaving the bridge.

Nicholas felt the terrible burden of weariness and despair slip from his shoulders, felt new strength rippling through his body, recharging his courage and his resolution—for a mile away, from behind that receding wall of dreadful grey cloud, *Sea Witch* burst abruptly into the sunlight, tearing bravely along with the water bursting over her bows and flying back as high as her bridgework, running without regard to the hazard of sea and storm.

"Jules," Nicholas whispered.

Jules was driving her like only a tugman can drive a ship, racing to beat the far wall of the storm.

Nicholas felt his throat constricting and suddenly the scalding tears of relief and thankfulness half-blinded him—for a mile out on *Sea Witch*'s port side, and barely a cable-length astern of her, *Warlock* came crashing out of the storm bank, running every bit as hard as her sister ship.

"David," Nicholas spoke aloud. "You too, David."

He realized only then that they must have been in radar contact with him through those wild tempestuous hours of storm passage, hovering there, holding station on *Golden Dawn*'s crippled bulk and waiting for their first opportunity.

Above the wail and crackle of static from the overhead loudspeaker boomed Jules Levoisin's voice. He was close enough and in the clear eye the interference allowed a readable radio contact.

"*Golden Dawn*, this is *Sea Witch*. Come in, *Golden Dawn*."

Nicholas reached the radio bench and snatched up the microphone.

"Jules." He did not waste a moment in greeting or congratulations. "We are going to take the tanks off her, and let the hull go. Do you understand?"

"I understand to take off the tanks," Jules responded immediately.

Nicholas' brain was crisp and clear again. He could see just how it must be done. "*Warlock* takes off the port tanks first—in tandem."

In tandem, the two tanks would be strung like beads on a string, they had been designed to tow that way.

"Then you will take off the starboard side—"

"You must save the hull." Duncan still fought the two seamen who held him. "Goddamn you, Berg. I'll not let you destroy me."

Nicholas ignored his ravings until he had finished giving his orders to the two tug masters. Then he dropped the microphone and grabbed Duncan by the shoulders. Nicholas seemed to be possessed suddenly by supernatural strength, and he shook him as though he were a child. He shook him so his head snapped back and forth and his teeth rattled in his head.

"You bloody idiot," he shouted in Duncan's face. "Don't you understand the storm will resume again in minutes?"

He jerked Duncan's body out of the grip of the two seamen and dragged him bodily to the windows overlooking the tank deck.

"Can't you see this monster you have built is finished, finished! There is no propeller, her back is broken, the superstructure will go minutes after the wind hits again."

He dragged Duncan round to face him, their eyes were inches apart.

"It's over, Duncan. We will be lucky to get away with our lives. We'll be luckier still to save the cargo."

"But don't you understand—we've got to save the hull—without it—" Duncan started to struggle, he was a powerful man, and quickly he was rousing himself, within minutes he would be dangerous—and there was no time, already *Warlock* was swinging up into her position on *Golden Dawn*'s port beam for tank transfer.

"I'll not let you take off—" Duncan wrenched himself out of Nicholas' grip, there was a mad fanatic light in his eyes.

Nicholas swivelled; coming up on to his toes and swinging from the shoulders he aimed for the point of Duncan's jaw, just below the ear and the thick sodden wedge of Duncan's red-gold sideburns. But Duncan rolled his head with the punch, and the blow glanced off his temple, and *Golden Dawn* rolled back the other way as Nicholas was unbalanced.

He fell back against the control console, and Duncan drove at him, two running paces like a quarterback taking a field goal, and he kicked right-legged for Nicholas' lower body.

"I'll kill you, Berg," he screamed, and Nicholas had only time to roll sideways and lift his leg, scissoring it to protect his crotch. Duncan's kick caught him in the upper thigh. An explosion of white pain shot up into his belly and numbed his leg to the thigh, but he used the control console and his good leg to launch himself into a counter-punch, hooking with his right again, under the ribs—and the wind went out of Duncan's lungs with a whoosh as he doubled. Nicholas transferred his weight smoothly and swung his left fist up into Duncan's face. It sounded like a watermelon dropped on a concrete floor, and Duncan was hurled backwards against the bulkhead, pinned there for a moment by the ship's roll. Nicholas followed him, hobbling painfully on the injured leg, and he hit him twice more. Left and right, short, hard, hissing blows that cracked his skull backwards against the bulkhead, and brought quick bright rosettes of blood from his lips and nostrils.

As his legs buckled, Nicholas caught him by the throat with his left hand and held him upright, searching his eyes for further resistance, ready to hit again, but there was no fight left in him.

Nicholas let him go, and went to the signal locker. He snatched three of the small walkie-talkie radios from the radio shelves and handed one to each of the two seamen.

"You know the pod tank undocking procedures for a tandem tow?" he asked.

"We've practised it," one of them replied.

"Let's go," said Nicholas.

I t was a job that was scheduled for a dozen men, and there were three of them. Duncan was of no use to them, and Nicholas left him in the pump control room on the lowest deck of *Golden Dawn*'s stern quarter, after he had closed down the inert gas pumps, sealed the gas vents, and armed the hydraulic releases of the pod tanks for undocking.

They worked sometimes neck-deep in the bursts of green, frothing water that poured over the ultra-tanker's foredeck. They took on board and secured *Warlock*'s main cable, unlocked the hydraulic clamps that held the forward pod tank attached to the hull and, as David Allen eased it clear of the crippled hull, they turned and lumbered back along the twisted and wind-torn catwalk, handicapped by the heavy seaboots and oilskins and the confused seas that still swamped the tank-deck every few minutes.

On the after tank, the whole laborious energy-sapping procedure had to be repeated, but here it was complicated by the chain coupling which connected the two half-mile-long pod tanks. Over the walkie-talkie Nicholas had to co-ordinate the efforts of his seamen to those of David Allen at the helm of *Warlock*.

When at last *Warlock* threw on power to both of her big propellers and sheered away from the wallowing hull, she had both port pod tanks in tow. They floated just level with the surface of the sea, offering no windage for the hurricane winds that would soon be upon them again.

Hanging on to the rail of the raised catwalk Nicholas watched for two precious minutes with an appraising professional eye. It was an incredible sight, two great shiny black whales, their backs showing only in the troughs, and the gallant little ship leading them away. They followed meekly, and Nicholas' anxiety was lessened. He was not confident, not even satisfied, for there was still a hurricane to navigate—but there was hope now.

"*Sea Witch*," he spoke into the small portable radio. "Are you ready to take on tow?"

Jules Levoisin fired the rocket-line across personally. Nicholas recognized his portly but nimble figure high in the fire-control tower, and the rocket left a thin trail of snaking white smoke high against the backdrop of racing, grey hurricane clouds. Arching high over the tanker's tank-deck, the thin nylon rocket-line fell over the catwalk ten feet from where Nicholas stood.

They worked with a kind of restrained frenzy, and Jules Levoisin brought the big graceful tug in so close beside them that glancing up Nicholas could see the flash of a gold filling in Jules' white smile of encouragement. It was only a glance that Nicholas allowed himself, and then he raised his face and looked at the storm.

The wall of cloud was slippery and smooth and grey, like the body of a gigantic slug, and at its foot trailed a glistening white slimy line where the winds frothed the surface of the sea. It was very close now, ten miles, no more, and above them the sun had gone, cut out by the spiralling vortex of leaden cloud. Yet still that open narrow funnel of clear calm air reached right up to a dark and ominous sky.

There was no hydraulic pressure on the clamps of the starboard forward pod tank. Somewhere in the twisted damaged hull the hydraulic line must have sheared. Nicholas and one of the seamen had to work the emergency release, pumping it open slowly and laboriously by hand.

Still it would not release, the hull was distorted, the clamp jaws out of alignment.

"Pull," Nicholas commanded Jules in desperation. "Pull all together." The storm front was five miles away, and already he could hear the deadly whisper of the wind, and a cold puff touched Nicholas' uplifted face.

The sea boiled under *Sea Witch*'s counter, spewing out in a swift white wake as Jules brought in both engines. The tow-cable came up hard and straight; for half a minute nothing gave, nothing moved—except the wall of racing grey cloud bearing down upon them.

Then, with a resounding metallic clang, the clamps slipped and the tank slid ponderously out of its dock in *Golden Dawn*'s hull—and as it came free, so the hull, held together until that moment by the tanks' bulk and buoyancy, began to collapse.

The catwalk on which Nicholas stood began to twist and tilt so that he had to grab for a handhold, and he stood frozen in horrified fascination as he watched *Golden Dawn* begin the final break-up.

The whole tank deck, now only a gutted skeleton, began to bend at its weakened centre, began to hinge like an enormous pair of nutcrackers—and caught between the jaws of the nutcracker was the starboard after pod tank. It was a nut the size of Chartres Cathedral, with a soft liquid centre, and a shell as thin as the span of a man's hand.

Nicholas broke into a lurching, blundering run down the twisting, tilting catwalk, calling urgently into the radio as he went.

"Shear!" he shouted to the seamen almost half a mile away across that undulating plane of tortured steel. "Shear the tandem tow!"

For the two starboard pod tanks were linked by the heavy chain of the tandem, and the forward tank was linked to *Sea Witch* by the main tow-cable. So *Sea Witch* and the doomed *Golden Dawn* were coupled inexorably, unless they could cut the two tanks apart and let *Sea Witch* escape with the forward tank which she had just undocked.

The shear control was in the control box halfway back along the tank deck, and at that moment the nearest seaman was two hundred yards from it.

Nicholas could see him staggering wildly back along the twisting, juddering catwalk. Clearly he realized the danger, but his haste was fatal, for as he jumped from the catwalk, the deck opened under him, gaping open like the jaws of a steel monster and the seaman fell through, waist deep, into the opening between two moving plates, then as he squirmed feebly, the next lurch of the ship's hull closed the plates, sliding them across each other like the blades of a pair of scissors.

The man shrieked once and a wave burst over the deck, smothering his mutilated body in cold, green water. When it poured back over the ship's side there was no sign of the man. The deck was washed glisteningly clean.

Nicholas reached the same point in the deck, judged the gaping and closing movement of the steel plate and the next rush of sea coming on board, before he leapt across the deadly gap.

He reached the control box, and slid back the hatch, pressing himself into the tiny steel cubicle as he unlocked the red lid that housed the shear button. He hit the button with the heel of his hand.

The four heavy chains of the tandem tow lay between the electrodes of the shear mechanism. With a gross surge of power from the ship's generators and a flash of blue electric flame, the thick steel links sheared as cleanly as cheese under the cutting wire—and, half a mile away, *Sea Witch* felt the release and pounded ahead under the full thrust of her propellers, taking with her the forward starboard tank still held on main tow.

Nicholas paused in the opening of the control cubicle, hanging on to the sill for support and he stared down at the single remaining tank, still caught inextricably in the tangled moving forest of *Golden Dawn*'s twisting, contorting hull. It was as though an invisible giant had taken the Eiffel Tower at each end and was bending it across his knee.

Suddenly there was a sharp chemical stink in the air, and Nicholas gagged on it. The stink of crude petroleum oil gushing from the ruptured tank.

"Nicholas! Nicholas!" The radio set slung over his shoulder squawked, and he lifted it to his lips without taking his eyes from the *Golden Dawn*'s terrible death throes.

"Go ahead, Jules."

"Nicholas, I am turning to pick you up."

"You can't turn, not with that tow."

"I will put my bows against the starboard quarterdeck rail, directly under the forward wing of the bridge. Be ready to jump aboard."

"Jules, you are out of your head!"

"I have been that way for fifty years," Jules agreed amiably. "Be ready."

"Jules, drop your tow first," Nicholas pleaded. It would be almost impossible to manoeuvre the *Sea Witch* with that monstrous dead weight hanging on her tail. "Drop tow. We can pick up again later."

"You teach your grandfather to break eggs," Jules blithely mangled the old saying, giving it a sinister twist.

"Listen, Jules, the No. 4 tank has ruptured. I want you to shut down for fire. Do you understand? Full fire shut down. Once I am aboard, we will put a rocket into her and burn off cargo."

"I hear you, Nicholas, but I wish I had not."

Nicholas left the control cubicle, jumped the gaping, chewing gap in the decking and scrambled up the steel ladder on to the central catwalk.

Glancing over his shoulder, he could see the endlessly slippery grey wall of racing cloud and wind; its menace was overpowering, so that for a moment he faltered before forcing himself into running back along the catwalk towards the tanker's stern tower half a mile ahead.

The single remaining seaman was on the catwalk a hundred yards ahead of him, pounding determinedly back towards the pick-up point. He also had heard Jules Levoisin's last transmission.

A quarter of a mile across the roiling, leaping waters, Jules Levoisin was bringing *Sea Witch* around. At another time Nicholas would have been impressed by the consummate skill with which the little Frenchman was handling his ship and its burdensome tow, but now there was time and energy for one thing only.

The air stank. The heavy fumes of crude oil burned Nicholas' pumping lungs, and constricted his throat. He coughed and gasped as he ran, the taste and reek of it coated his tongue and seared his nostrils.

Below the catwalk, the bloated pod-tank was punctured in a hundred places by the steel lances of the disintegrating hull, pinched and torn by moving steel girders, and the dark red oil spurted and dribbled and oozed from it like the poisonous blood from the carcass of a mortally wounded dragon.

Nicholas reached the stern tower, barged in through the storm doors to the lowest deck and reached the pump control room.

Duncan Alexander turned to him, as he entered, his face swollen and bruised where Nicholas had beaten him.

"We are abandoning now," said Nicholas. "*Sea Witch* is taking us off."

"I hated you from that very first day," Duncan was very calm, very controlled, his voice even, deep and cultured. "Did you know that?"

"There's no time for that now." Nicholas grabbed his arm, and Duncan followed him readily into the passageway.

"That's what the game is all about, isn't it, Nicholas, power and wealth and women—that's the game we played."

Nicholas was barely listening. They were out on to the quarterdeck, standing at its starboard rail, below the bridge, the pick-up point that Jules had stipulated. *Sea Witch* was turning in, only five hundred yards out, and Nicholas had time now to watch Jules handle his ship.

He was running out the heavy tow cable on free spool, deliberately letting a long bight of it form between the tug and its enormous whalelike burden, and he was using the slack in the cable to cut in towards *Golden Dawn*'s battered, sagging hulk. He would be alongside for the pick-up in less than a minute.

"That was the game we played, you and I," Duncan was still talking calmly. "Power and wealth and women—"

Below them *Golden Dawn* poured her substance into the sea in a slick, stinking flood. The waves, battering against her side, churned the oil to a thick filthy emulsion, and it was spreading away across the surface, bleeding its deadly poison into the Gulf Stream to broadcast it to the entire ocean.

"I won," Duncan went on reasonably. "I won it all, every time—" He was groping in his pockets, but Nicholas hardly heard him, was not watching him. "—until now."

Duncan took one of the self-igniting signal flares from his pocket and held it against his chest with both hands, slipping his index finger through the metal ring of the igniter tab.

"And yet I win this one also, Nicholas," he said. "Game, set and match." And he pulled the tab on the flare with a sharp jerk, and stepped back, holding it aloft.

It spluttered once and then burst into brilliant sparkling red flame, white phosphorescent smoke billowing from it.

Now at last Nicholas turned to face him, and for a moment he was too appalled to move. Then he lunged for Duncan's raised hand that held the burning flare, but Duncan was too fast for him to reach it.

He whirled and threw the flame in a high spluttering arc, out over the leaking, stinking tank-deck.

It struck the steel tank and bounced once, and then rolled down the canted oil-coated plating.

Nicholas stood paralysed at the rail staring down at it. He expected a violent explosion, but nothing happened; the flare rolled innocently across the deck, burning with its pretty red twinkling light.

"It's not burning," Duncan cried. "Why doesn't it burn?"

Of course, the gas was only explosive in a confined space, and it needed spark. Out here in the open air the oil had a very high flashpoint; it must be heated to release its volatiles.

The flare caught in the scuppers and fizzled in a black pool of crude, and only then the crude caught. It caught with a red, slow, sulky flame that spread quickly but not explosively over the entire deck, and instantly, thick billows of dark smoke rose in a dense choking cloud.

Below where Nicholas stood, the *Sea Witch* thrust her bows in and touched them against the tanker's side. The seaman beside Nicholas jumped and landed neatly on the tug's bows, then raced back along *Sea Witch*'s deck.

"Nicholas," Jules' voice thundered over the loud hailer. "Jump, Nicholas."

Nicholas spun back to the rail, and poised himself to jump.

Duncan caught him from behind, whipping one arm around his throat, and pulling him backwards away from the rail.

"No," Duncan shouted. "You're staying, my friend. You are not going anywhere. You are staying here with me."

A greasy wave of black choking smoke engulfed them, and Jules' magnified voice roared in Nicholas' ears.

"Nicholas, I cannot hold her here. Jump, quickly, jump!"

Duncan had him off-balance, dragging him backwards, away from the ship's side, and suddenly Nicholas knew what he must do.

Instead of resisting Duncan's arm, he hurled himself backwards and they crashed together into the superstructure—but Duncan bore the combined weight of both their bodies.

His armlock around the throat relaxed slightly and Nicholas drove his elbow into Duncan's side below the ribs, then wrenched his body forward from the waist, reached between his own braced legs and caught

Duncan's ankles. He straightened up again, dragging Duncan off his feet and the same instant dropped backwards with his full weight on to the deck.

Duncan gasped and his arm fell away, as Nicholas bounced to his feet again, choking in the greasy billows of smoke, and he reached the ship's side.

Below him, the gap between *Sea Witch*'s bows and the tanker's side was rapidly widening and the thrust of the sea and the drag of the tug pulled them apart.

Nicholas vaulted on to the rail, poised for an instant and then jumped. He struck the deck and his teeth cracked together with the impact; his injured leg gave under him and he rolled once, then he was up on his hands and knees.

He looked up at *Golden Dawn*. She was completely enveloped now in the boiling column of black smoke. As the flames heated the leaking crude, so it burned more readily. The bank of smoke was shot through now with the satanic crimson of high, hot flame.

As *Sea Witch* sheered desperately away, the first rush of the storm hit them, and for a moment it smeared the smoke away, exposing the tanker's high quarterdeck.

Duncan Alexander stood at the rail above the roaring holocaust of the tank-deck. He stood with his arms extended, and he was burning; his clothing burned fiercely and his hair was a bright torch of flame. He stood like a ritual cross, outlined in fire, and then slowly he seemed to shrivel and he toppled forward over the rail into the bubbling, spurting, burning cargo of the monstrous ship that he had built—and the black smoke closed over him like a funeral cloak.

A s the crude oil escaping from the pierced pod tank fed the flames, so the heat built up swiftly, still sufficient to consume only the volatile aromatic spirits which constituted less than half the bulk of the cargo.

The heavy carbon elements, not yet hot enough to burn, boiled off in that solid black column of smoke, and as the returning winds of the hurricane raced over the *Golden Dawn* once more, so that filthy pall was mixed with air and lifted into the cloud bank of the storm, rising first a thousand, then ten, then twenty thousand feet above the surface of the ocean.

And still *Golden Dawn* burned, and the temperatures of the gas and oil mixture trapped in her hull rocketed steeply. Steel glowed red, then brilliant white, ran like molten wax, and then like water—and suddenly the flashpoint of heavy carbon smoke in a mixture of air and water vapour was reached in the womb of this mighty furnace.

Golden Dawn and her entire cargo turned into a fireball.

The steel and glass and metal of her hull disappeared in an instantaneous explosive combustion that released temperatures like those upon the surface of the sun. Her cargo, a quarter of a million tons of it, burned in an instant, releasing a white blooming rose of pure heat so fierce that it shot up into the upper stratosphere and consumed the billowing pall of its own hydrocarbon gas and smoke.

The very air burst into flame, the surface of the sea flamed in that white fireball of heat and even the clouds of smoke burned as the oxygen and hydrocarbon they contained exploded.

Once an entire city had been subjected to this phenomenon of fireball, when stone and earth and air had exploded, and five thousand German citizens of the city of Cologne had been vaporized, and that vapour burned in the heat of its own release.

But this fireball was spawned by a quarter of a million tons of volatile liquids.

C an't you get us further away?" Nicholas shouted above the thunder of the hurricane. His mouth was only inches from Jules Levoisin's ear.

They were standing side by side, hanging from the overhead railing that gave purchase on this wildly pitching deck.

"If I open the taps I will part the tow wire," Jules shouted back.

Sea Witch was alternately standing on her nose and then her tail. There was no forward view from the bridge, only green washes of sea water and banks of spray.

The full force of the hurricane was on them once more, and a glance at the radarscope showed the glowing image of *Golden Dawn*'s crippled and bleeding hull only half a mile astern.

Suddenly the glass of the windows was obscured by an impenetrable blackness, and the light in *Sea Witch*'s navigation bridge was reduced to only the glow of her fire-lights and the electronic instruments of her control console.

Jules Levoisin turned his face to Nicholas, his plump features haunted by green shadows in the gloom.

"Smoke bank," Nicholas shouted an explanation. There was no reek of the filthy hydrocarbon in the bridge, for *Sea Witch* was shut down for fire drill, all her ports and ventilators sealed, her internal air-conditioning on a closed circuit, the air being scrubbed and recharged with oxygen by the big Carrier unit above the main engine room. "We are directly downwind of the *Golden Dawn.*"

A fiercer rush of the hurricane winds laid *Sea Witch* over on her side, the lee rail deep under the racing green sea, and held her there, unable to rise against the careless might of the storm for many minutes. Her crew hung desperately from any hand hold, the irksome burden of her tow helping to drag her down farther; the propellers found no grip in the air, and her engines screamed in anguish.

But *Sea Witch* had been built to live in any sea, and the moment the wind hesitated, she fought off the water that had come aboard and began to swing back.

"Where is *Warlock?*" Jules bellowed anxiously. The danger of collision preyed upon him constantly, two ships and their elephantine tows manoeuvring closely in confined hurricane waters was nightmare on top of nightmare.

"Ten miles east of us." Nicholas picked the other tug's image out of the trash on the radarscope. "They had a start, ahead of the wind—"

He would have gone on, but the boiling bank of hydrocarbon smoke that surrounded *Sea Witch* turned to fierce white light, a light that blinded every man on the bridge as though a photograph flashlight had been fired in his face.

"Fireball!" Nicholas shouted, and, completely blinded, reached for the remote controls of the water cannons seventy feet above the bridge on *Sea Witch*'s fire-control tower.

Minutes before, he had aligned the four water cannons, training them down at their maximum angle of depression, so now as he locked down the multiple triggers, *Sea Witch* deluged herself in a pounding cascade of sea water.

Sea Witch was caught in a furnace of burning air, and despite the torrents of water she spewed over herself, her paintwork was burned away in instantaneous combustion so fierce that it consumed its own smoke, and almost instantly the bare scorched metal of her exposed upperworks began to glow with heat.

The heat was so savage that it struck through the insulated hull, through the double glazing of the two-inch armoured glass of her bridge windows, scorching and frizzling away Nicholas' eyelashes and blistering his lips as he lifted his face to it.

The glass of the bridge windows wavered and swam as they began to melt—and then abruptly there was no more oxygen. The fireball had extinguished itself, consumed everything in its twenty seconds of life, everything from sea level to thirty thousand feet above it, a brief and devastating orgasm of destruction.

It left a vacuum, a weak spot in the earth's thin skin of air; it formed another low pressure system smaller, but much more intense, and more hungry to be filled than the eye of Hurricane Lorna itself.

It literally tore the guts out of that great revolving storm, setting up counter winds and a vortex within the established system that ripped it apart.

New gales blew from every point about the fireball's vacuum, swiftly beginning their own dervish spirals and twenty miles short of the mainland of Florida, hurricane Lorna checked her mindless, blundering charge, fell in upon herself and disintegrated into fifty different willy-nilly squalls and whirlpools of air that collided and split again, slowly degenerating into nothingness.

On a morning in April in Galveston roads, the salvage tug *Sea Witch* dropped off tow to four smaller harbour tugs who would take the *Golden Dawn* No. 3 pod tank up the narrows to the Orient Amex discharge installation below Houston.

Her sister ship *Warlock*, Captain David Allen commanding, had dropped off his tandem tow of No. 1 and No. 2 pod tanks to the same tugs forty-eight hours previously.

Between the two ships, they had made good salvage under Lloyd's Open Form of three-quarters of a million tons of crude petroleum valued at $85.50 US a ton. To the prize would be added the value of the three tanks themselves—not less than sixty-five million dollars all told, Nicholas calculated, and he owned both ships and the full share of the salvage award. He had not sold to the Sheikhs yet, though for every day of the tow from the Florida Straits to Texas, there had been frantic telex messages from James Teacher in London. The Sheikhs were desperate to sign now, but Nicholas would let them wait a little longer.

Nicholas stood on the open wing of Sea Witch's bridge and watched the four smaller harbour tugs bustling importantly about their ungainly charge.

He lifted the cheroot to his lips carefully, for they were still blistered from the heat of the fireball—and he pondered the question of how much he had achieved, apart from spectacular riches.

He had reduced the spill from a million to a quarter of a million tons of cad-rich crude, and he had burned it in a fireball. Nevertheless, there had been losses, toxins had been lifted high above the fireball. They had spread and settled across Florida as far as Tampa and Tallahassee, poisoning the pastures and killing thousands of head of domestic stock. But the American authorities had been quick to extend the hurricane emergency procedures. There had been no loss of human life. He had achieved that much.

Now he had delivered the salvaged pod tanks to Orient Amex. The new cracking process would benefit all mankind, and nothing that Nicholas could do would prevent men from carrying the cad-rich crudes of El Barras across the oceans. But would they do so in the same blindly irresponsible manner that Duncan Alexander had attempted?

He knew then with utter certainty that it was his appointed life's work from now on, to try and ensure that they did not. He knew how he was to embark upon that work. He had the wealth that was necessary, and Tom Parker had given him the other instruments to do the job.

He knew, with equal certainty, who would be his companion in that life's work—and standing on the fire-scorched deck of the gallant little vessel he had a vivid image of a golden girl who walked forever beside him in sunlight and in laughter.

"Samantha."

He said her name aloud just once, and suddenly he was very eager to begin.

Turn the page for a sneak peek at
Wilbur Smith's new novel

THOSE IN PERIL

Available May 2011

Copyright © 2011 by Wilbur Smith

The Khamseen had been blowing for five days now. The dust clouds rolled towards them across the brooding expanse of the desert. Hector Cross wore a striped keffiyeh wrapped around his neck and desert goggles over his eyes. His short dark beard protected most of his face, but the areas of exposed skin felt as though they had been scoured raw by the stinging grains of sand. Even above the growl of the wind he picked out the throbbing beat of the approaching helicopter. He was aware without looking at them that none of the men around him had heard it as yet. He would have been mortified if he had not been the first. Though he was ten years older than most of them, as their leader he had to be the sharpest and the quickest. Then Uthmann Waddah stirred slightly and glanced at him. Hector's nod of acknowledgement was barely perceptible. Uthmann was one of his most trusted operatives. Their friendship went back many years, to the day Uthmann had pulled Hector out of a burning vehicle under sniper fire in a Baghdad street. Even then Hector had been suspicious of the fact that he was a Sunni Muslim, but in time Uthmann had proved himself worthy. Now he was indispensable. Among his other virtues he had coached Hector until his spoken Arabic was almost perfect. It would take a skilled interrogator to discern that Hector was not a native-born speaker.

By some trick of the sunlight high above, the monstrously distorted shadow of the helicopter was thrown against the cloud banks like a magic lantern show, so that when the big Russian MIL-26 painted in the crimson and white colours of Bannock Oil broke through into the clear it seemed insignificant in comparison. It wasn't until it was three hundred feet above the landing pad that it was visible. In view of the importance of the single passenger, Hector had radioed the pilot while he was still on the ground at Sidi el Razig, the company base on the coast where the oil pipeline terminated, and ordered him not to fly in these conditions. The woman had countermanded his order, and Hector was not accustomed to being gainsaid.

Although they had not yet met, the relationship between Hector and the woman was a delicate one. Strictly speaking he was not her employee. He was the sole owner of 'Cross Bow Security Limited'. However, the company was contracted to Bannock Oil to guard its installations and its personnel. Old Henry Bannock had hand-picked Hector from amongst the many security firms eager to provide him with their services.

The helicopter settled delicately on the landing pad, and as the door in the fuselage slid open, Hector strode forward to meet the woman for the first time. She appeared in the doorway, and paused there looking about her. Hector was reminded of a leopard balancing on the high bough of a Marula tree surveying its prey before it sprang. Though he thought that he knew her well enough by repute, in the flesh she was charged with such power and grace that it took him by surprise. As part of his research he had studied hundreds of photographs of her, read reams of script and watched hours of video footage. The earlier images of her were on the Centre Court of Wimbledon being beaten in a hard fought quarter-final match by Navratilova, or three years later accepting the trophy for the women's singles at the Australian Open in Sydney. Then a year later came her marriage to Henry Bannock, the head of Bannock Oil, a flamboyant billionaire tycoon thirty-one years her senior. After that came images of her and her husband chatting and laughing with heads of state, or with film stars and other show business personalities, shooting pheasant at Sandringham as the guests of Her Majesty and Prince Philip or holidaying in the Carribean on their yacht the *Amorous Dolphin*. Then there were clips of her sitting beside her husband on the podium at the annual general meeting of the company; other clips of her fencing skilfully with Larry King on his talk show. Much later she was wearing widow's weeds and holding the hand of her lovely young daughter as they watched Henry Bannock's sarcophagus being installed in the mausoleum on his ranch in the Colorado mountains.

After that her battle with the shareholders and banks and her particularly venomous stepson was gleefully chronicled by business media around the world. When at last she succeeded in wresting the rights that she had inherited from Henry out of the grasping fingers of her stepson and she took her husband's place at the head of the board of Bannock Oil, the price of Bannock shares plummeted steeply. The investors evaporated, the bank loans dried up. Nobody wanted to bet on a some-time tennis player cum society glamour girl turned oil baroness. But they had not taken into account her innate business acumen or the years of her tutelage under Henry Bannock which were worth a hundred MBA degrees. Like the crowds at the Roman circus her detractors and critics waited in grisly anticipation for her to be devoured by the lions. Then to the chagrin of all she brought in the Zara Number Eight.

Forbes magazine blazoned the image of Hazel in white tennis kit, holding a racquet in her right hand, on its front cover. The headline read: 'Hazel Bannock aces the opposition. The richest oil strike for the last sixty years. She takes on the mantel of her husband, Henry the Great.' The main article began:

In the bleak hinterland of a godforsaken and impoverished little Emirate named Abu Zara lies an oil concession once owned by Shell. The field had been pumped dry and abandoned in the period directly after WWII. For almost sixty years it had lain forgotten. That was until Mrs Hazel Bannock came on the scene. She picked up the concession for a few paltry millions of dollars and the pundits nudged each other and smirked. Ignoring the protests of her advisors she spent many millions more in sinking a rotary cone drill into a tiny subterranean anomaly at the northern extremity of the field; an anomaly which with the primitive exploration techniques of sixty years previously had been reckoned to be an ancillary of the main reservoir. The geologists of that time had agreed that any oil contained in this area had long ago drained into the main reservoir and been pumped to the surface leaving the entire field dry and worthless.

However when Mrs Bannock's drill pierced the impervious salt dome of the diapir, a vast subterranean chamber in which the oil deposits had been trapped, the gas overpressure roared up through the drill hole with such force that it ejected almost 8 kilometres of steel drill string like toothpaste from the tube, and the hole blew out. High

grade crude oil spurted hundreds of feet into the air. At last it became
evident that the old Zara Nos. 1 to 7 fields which had been abandoned
by Shell were only a fraction of the total reserves. The new reservoir
lay at a depth of 21,866 feet and held estimated reserves of 5 billion
barrels of sweet and light crude.

As the helicopter touched down the flight engineer dropped the landing
ladder and dismounted, then reached up to his illustrious passenger. She
ignored his proffered hand and jumped the four feet to the ground, landing as lightly as the leopard that she so much resembled. She wore a
sleekly tailored khaki safari suit with suede desert boots and a bright
Hermès scarf at her throat. The thick golden hair, which was her trade-
mark, was unfettered and it rippled in the Khamseen. How old was she,
Hector wondered? Nobody seemed to know for sure. She looked thirtyish,
but she had to be forty at the very least. Briefly she took the hand that Hector proffered, her grip honed by hundreds of hours on the tennis court.

'Welcome to your Zara No. 8, ma'am,' he said. She spared him only a
glance. Her eyes were a shade of blue that reminded him of sunlight ra-
diating through the walls of an ice cave in a high mountain crevasse. She
was far more comely than he had been led to believe by her photographs.

'Major Cross.' She acknowledged him coolly. Once again she surprised him by the fact that she knew his name, then he recalled that she
had the reputation of leaving nothing to chance. She must have re-
searched every one of the dozens of her senior employees that she was
likely to meet on this first visit to her new oilfield.

If that's the case, she should have known that I don't use my military
rank any longer, he thought, then it occurred to him that she probably did
know and she was deliberately riling him. He suppressed the grim smile
that rose to his lips.

For some reason she doesn't like me and she makes no effort to hide
the fact, he thought. *This lady is built like one of her oil drills, all steel*
and diamonds. But she had already turned away from him to meet the
three men who tumbled out of the big sand-coloured Hummvee that
braked to a halt beside her and formed an obsequious welcoming line,
grinning and wriggling like puppies. She shook hands with Bert Simpson, her general manager.

'I am sorry it took me so long to visit you, Mr Simpson, however I
have been rather tied up at the office.' She gave him a quick, brilliant

smile, but did not wait for his reply. She moved on and in rapid succession greeted her chief engineer and senior geologist.

'Thank you, gentlemen. Now let us get out of this nasty wind. We will have time to become better acquainted later.' Her voice was soft, almost lilting, but the inflexion was sharp and clearly Southern African. Hector knew that she had been born in Cape Town and had only taken up US citizenship after she married Henry Bannock. Bert Simpson opened the passenger door of the Hummvee and she slipped into the seat. By the time Bert had taken his place at the wheel, Hector was in an escort position in the second Hummvee close behind him. A third Hummvee was in the lead. All the vehicles had the logo of a medieval crossbow painted on the doors. Uthmann was in the first, and he led the little convoy out onto the service track which ran alongside the great silver python of the pipeline that carried the precious muck a hundred miles down to the waiting tankers. As they drove on the oil rigs appeared out of the yellow haze on each side, rank upon rank like the skeletons of a lost legion of warriors. Before they reached the dried-out wadi Uthmann turned off the track and they climbed a ridge of gaunt rock, sooty black as though scorched by fire. The main building complex was perched on the highest point.

Two Cross Bow sentries in battle fatigues swung the gates open and the three Hummvees raced through. Immediately the vehicle carrying Hazel Bannock peeled off from the formation and crossed the interior compound to stop before the heavy doors that led into the air-conditioned luxury of the executive suites. Hazel was whisked through them by Bert Simpson and half a dozen uniformed servants. The doors closed ponderously. It seemed to Hector that something was lacking once she had gone—even the Khamseen wind howled with less fury—and as he paused at the doorway to Cross Bow headquarters and looked up at the sky he saw that the dust clouds were indeed breaking up and subsiding on themselves.

In his private quarters he removed the goggles and unwound the keffiyeh from his throat. Then he washed the grime from his face and hands, squirted soothing drops into his bloodshot eyes and examined his face in the wall mirror. The short stubble of dark beard gave him a piratical air. The skin above it was darkly tanned by the desert sun, except for the silver scar above his right eye where years ago a bayonet thrust had exposed the bone of his skull. His nose was large and imperial. His eyes were a cool and steady green. His teeth were very white like those of predator.

'It is the only face you are ever going to get, Hector my lad. But that doesn't mean you have to love it,' he murmured then he answered himself, 'But, thank the Lord for all those ladies of less fastidious tastes out there.' He laughed softly and went through into the situation room. The hum of the men's conversation died away as he entered. Hector stood on the dais and looked them over. These ten were his squad leaders. Each of them commanded a stick of ten men, and he felt a small prickle of pride. They were the tried and true, hardened warriors who had learned their trade in the Congo and Afghanistan, in Pakistan and Iraq and in other bloody fields around the wicked old world. It had taken a long time for him to assemble them, and they were a totally reprehensible bunch of reprobates and hardened killers, and he loved them like his brothers.

'Where are the scratches and teeth bites, boss? Don't tell us you got away from her scot free,' one of them called. Hector smiled tolerantly and gave them a minute to deliver their heavy humour and to settle down. Then he held up his hand.

'Gentlemen, and I use the term loosely, gentlemen, we have in our care a lady who will attract the ardent attention of every thug from Khinshasa to Baghdad, from Kabul to Mogadishu. If anything nasty befalls her I will personally cut the balls off the man who let it happen. I give you my solemn oath on that.' They knew this was not an idle threat. The laughter subsided and they dropped their eyes as he stared at them expressionlessly for a few seconds after silence had fallen. At last he picked up the pointer from the desk in front of him and turned to the huge aerial blow-up of the concession on the wall behind him and began his final briefing. He delegated their duties to them and reinforced his previous orders. He did not want any carelessness on this job. Half an hour later he turned back to face them.

'Questions?' There were none and he dismissed them with the curt order, 'When in doubt shoot first and make damned sure you don't miss.' He took the helicopter and had Hans Lategan, the pilot, fly him along the pipeline as far as the terminal on the shore of the Gulf. They flew at very low level. Hector was in the front seat beside Hans, searching the track for any sign of unexplained activity; alien human footprints or wheel tracks made by any vehicle other than his own GM patrol trucks or the engineering teams servicing the pipeline. All his Cross Bow operatives wore boots with a distinctive arrowhead tread on the soles so even from this height Hector could tell friendly tracks from those of a potential thug.

During Hector's tenure as head of security there had already been three vicious sabotage attempts on the Bannock Oil installations in Abu Zara. No terrorist group had as yet claimed responsibility for these acts, probably because none of the attacks had succeeded.

The Emir of Abu Zara, Prince Farid al Mazra, was a staunch ally of Bannock Oil. The oil royalties that accrued to him from the company amounted to hundreds of millions of dollars a year. Hector had forged a strong alliance with the head of the Abu Zara police force, Prince Mohammed who was a brother-in-law of the Emir. Prince Mohammed's intelligence was strong and three years previously he had alerted Hector to an impending seaborne attack. Hector and Ronnie Wells, his area commander at the terminal, had been able to intercept the raiders at sea with the Bannock patrol boat, which was an ex-Israeli motor torpedo boat, with a good turn of speed and twin 50 calibre Browning machine guns mounted in the bows. There were eight terrorists on board the attacking dhow, together with several hundred pounds of Semtex plastic explosive. Ronnie Wells was a former Royal Marine sergeant-major, a seaman of vast experience and an expert handler of small attack craft. He came out of the darkness astern of the dhow, and took the crew by complete surprise. When Hector called on them to surrender over the loud-hailer they replied with a fusillade of automatic fire. The first burst from the Brownings touched off the cargo of Semtex in the hold of the dhow. All eight terrorists on board had simultaneously departed for the Gardens of Paradise, leaving behind them very little trace of their previous existence on this earth. The Emir and Prince Mohammed had been delighted with the outcome. They ensured that the international media were given not even a sniff of the incident. Abu Zara was proud of its reputation as a stable, progressive and peace-loving country.

Hector landed at the terminal at Sidi el Razig and spent a few hours with Ronnie Wells. As always Ronnie had everything shipshape, renewing Hector's faith in him. After their meeting they walked out together to where Hans was waiting in the helicopter. Ronnie glanced obliquely at him, and Hector knew exactly what was worrying him. In three months' time Ronnie would be sixty-five. His children had long ago lost interest in him and he had no home outside Cross Bow, except possibly the Royal Hospital, Chelsea if they would accept him as a pensioner. His contract with Cross Bow would come up for renewal a few weeks before his birthday.

'Oh, by the way, Ronnie,' Hector said, 'I have got your new contract on my desk. I should have brought it with me for you to sign.'

'Thanks, Hector.' Ronnie grinned, his bald head glowing. 'But you do know I will be sixty-five in October?'

'You old bastard!' Hector grinned back at him. 'Here I have been thinking you were twenty-five for the last ten years.' He swung up into the helicopter and they flew back just above the sandy surface of the track alongside the pipeline. The Khamseen wind had swept the surface like an industrious house maid so that even the tracks of the desert bustards and oryx were clearly printed on it. Twice they landed for Hector to examine any sign that was less self-evident and might have been made by unwelcome strangers. These proved innocuous. They had been made by wandering Bedouin probably searching for lost camels.

They landed again for the last time at the site where three years previously an ambush had been laid by six persons unknown who had infiltrated the concession from the south. They had covered sixty miles on foot through the desert to reach the pipeline. When they arrived the intruders made the unfortunate choice of attacking the patrol truck in which Hector was riding in the front seat. Hector spotted something suspicious halfway up the dune that ran beside the track as they drove along it.

'Stop!' he yelled at his driver, and he scrambled onto the roof of the truck. He stared up at the object that had caught his attention. It moved again, a tiny slithering movement like a crawling red snake. That movement was what had first caught his attention. But there were no red snakes in this desert. One end of the snake protruded from the sand and the other end disappeared under the scrawny hanging branches of a thornbush. He studied it carefully. The bush was sufficiently dense to hide a man lying behind it. The red object was like nothing in nature that he knew of. Then it twitched again and he made up his mind. He mounted his assault rifle to his shoulder and fired a three-shot burst into the thornbush. The man who had been lying behind it leaped to his feet. He was turbanned and cloaked with his AK-47 slung over his shoulder and a small black box in his hands, from which dangled the thin red insulated cable.

'Bomb!' Hector screamed. 'Heads down!' The man on the dune detonated the bomb, and with a thunderous explosion the track 150 metres ahead of the truck erupted in a towering column of dust and fire. The shock wave almost knocked Hector off the roof of the truck, but he braced himself and kept his balance.

The bomber was almost at the top of the dune, running like a desert gazelle. Hector was still unsighted by the blast, and his first burst churned up the sand around the Arab's feet, but he kept running. Hector caught his breath and steadied himself. He saw his next burst catch the Arab across his back, dust flying from his robe as the bullets struck. The man pirouetted like a ballet dancer and went down. Then Hector saw his five companions leap up out of cover amongst the scrub. They crossed the skyline and disappeared before he could take them under fire.

Hector swept a glance along the face of the dune. It extended for three or four miles both forward and aft of their present position. Along its whole length it was too steep and soft for the truck to climb. It would have to be a foot chase, he decided.

'Phase Two!' Hector shouted at his men, 'Hot pursuit! Go! Go! Go!' He leapt from the truck and led the four of them up the dune face at a run. When they reached the top the five insurgents were still in a loose group running across the flat salt-pan almost half a mile away. They had established that lead while Hector and his stick where forced to struggle up the face of the dune. Looking after them, Hector smiled grimly.

'Big mistake, my beauties! You should have bomb-shelled, each of you should have taken a different direction! Now we have you nicely grouped.' Hector knew with absolute certainty that in a straight chase there was no Arab born who could run away from these men of his.

'Come along, boys. Don't dawdle. We have to bag these bastards before sundown.' It took four hours; 'these bastards' were just a wee bit tougher than Hector had reckoned. But then they made their final mistake. They stood to fight it out. They picked a likely depression, a natural strong point with a clear field of fire in all directions, and went to ground. Hector looked up at the sun. It was twenty degrees above the horizon. They had to finish this thing quickly. While his men kept the terrorists' heads down, Hector wriggled forward to where he could have a better view of the field of play. Immediately he saw that they could not take the Arab position head-on. He would lose most if not all of his men. For ten minutes more he studied the terrain, and then with a soldier's eye he picked out the weak spot. Running past the rear of the Arab position was a very shallow fold of ground; too shallow to deserve the name of wadi or donga but it might conceal a man crawling on his belly. He squinted his eyes against the low sun and judged that the fold crossed forty paces behind the enemy's redoubt. He nodded with satisfaction and wriggled back to where his men lay.

'I am going to get around behind them and toss in a grenade. Charge as soon as it blows.' Hector had to take a wide detour around the enemy to keep out of their sight, and once he was into the donga he could only move very slowly so as not to raise the dust and warn them of his approach. His men made the Arabs keep their heads well down, shooting at any movement above the rim of the depression. However, by the time Hector reached the nearest point to the depression there was probably only another ten minutes of shooting light before the sun went down below the horizon. He rolled onto his knees and with his teeth pulled the pin on the grenade he was holding in his right hand. Then he sprang upright and judged the distance. It was at extreme range. Forty or maybe fifty metres to lob the heavy fragmentation grenade. He put his shoulder and all his strength behind the throw and sent it up on a high looping trajectory. Though it was a good throw, one of his very best, it struck the rim of the redoubt and for an instant seemed as if it would stick there. But then it rolled forward and dropped in amongst the crouching Arabs. Hector heard the screams as they realized what it was. He leapt to his feet and drew his pistol as he raced forward. The grenade exploded just before he reached the redoubt. He paused on the edge and looked down on the carnage. Four of the thugs had been torn into bloody rags. The last one had been partially shielded by the bodies of his comrades. Nonetheless shrapnel had ripped through his chest into his lungs.

He was coughing up gouts of frothing blood and struggling to catch his last breath as Hector stood over him. He looked up and to Hector's astonishment recognized him. The man spoke through bubbling blood and his voice was faint and slurred, but Hector understood what he was saying.

'My name is Anwar. Remember it, Cross, you pig of the great pig. The debt has not been settled. The Blood Feud continues. Others will come.'

Now, three years later Hector stood on the same spot, and once again puzzled over those words. He could still make no sense of them. Who was the dying man? How had he known Hector? At last he shook his head, then turned and walked back to where the helicopter stood with its rotors turning idly. He climbed aboard and they flew on. The day melted away swiftly in the desert heat and when they got back to the compound at No. 8 there was only an hour before sunset. Hector took advantage of what remained of the light to go out to the range and fire a hundred rounds each from both his Beretta M9 9 mm pistol and his SC 70/90 automatic assault rifle. All his men where expected to fire at least 500 rounds a week and turn in their targets to the armourer. Hector regularly checked all of them. His men were all deadly shots, but he did not want any complacency or sloppiness to creep in. They were good but they had to stay that way.

When he got back to the compound from the range the sun had gone and in the brief desert twilight the night came swiftly. He went to the well-equipped gym and ran for an hour on a treadmill and finished with half an hour of weights. He took a steaming hot shower in his private quarters and changed his dusty camouflage fatigues for a freshly washed and ironed pair, and at last went down to the mess. Bert Simpson and the other senior executives were at the private bar. They all looked tired and drawn.

'Join us for a drink?' Bert offered.

'Decent of you,' Hector told him and he nodded to the barman who poured him a double tot of the Oban 18-year-old single malt. Hector saluted Bert with the glass and they both drank.

'So, how is our lady boss?' Hector asked.

Bert rolled his eyes. 'You don't want to know.'

'Try me.'

'She is not human.'

'She looked more than just a touch human to me,' Hector commented.

'It's an illusion, old boy. Done with bloody mirrors or something. I will say no more. You can find out for yourself.'

'What does that mean?' Hector demanded.

'You are taking her for a run, matey.'

'When?'

'First thing in the morning, day after tomorrow. Meet 0530 hours sharp at the main gates. Ten miles, she stipulated. I would hazard a guess that the pace she sets will be somewhat faster than a stroll. Don't let her lose you.'